The Face of the Third Reich

THE FACE
OF THE
THIRD REICH

Portraits of the Nazi Leadership

JOACHIM C. FEST

Translated from the German by Michael Bullock

 PANTHEON BOOKS, NEW YORK

Library of Congress Catalog Card Number: 66-10412
ISBN: 0-394-73407-6

Manufactured in the United States of America

9876543

To my father

Contents

Contents

A forest takes a century to grow; it burns down in a night.

Georges Sorel

No nation will let its fingers be burnt twice. The trick of the Pied Piper of Hamelin catches people only once.

Adolf Hitler

Foreword

The tree on which the owl of Minerva sits has many branches. The portraits in this book have, from a strictly scholarly viewpoint, a rather profane origin. They are taken from a series of broadcasts on recent German history which I wrote for RIAS, the radio station in the American sector of Berlin. The broadcasts were in response to the need mentioned by many listeners for an investigation into the psychological background of the National Socialist regime and the National Socialist individual, a field hitherto largely neglected by historians.

As soon as I began work, I realised that to concentrate exclusively on the personal profiles of the leading figures of the Third Reich – the emotional make-up that had shaped their political careers, their motives, and so on – would be unnecessarily and indeed undesirably restrictive. Consequently I have attempted to fill in each individual portrait with the appropriate background. This means, for example, that in dealing with Ribbentrop I have also analysed a number of important features of National Socialist foreign policy; Bormann provided the cue for considering the government structure of Hitler's Reich as a whole; Himmler prompted a discussion of the essence and aims of the SS state; and Goebbels gave me the opportunity to study the maxims, assumptions and style of National Socialist propaganda. In this way, each portrait looks beyond individual characteristics to the significance of each man within an overall portrait of the Third Reich. Only the section on Hitler attempts at the same time to give an account of the events of the twenty-five years that form the common historical background – though even here the emphasis is on biography. Although this method of presentation inevitably gives the account an appearance of following a system, it is in no sense a rigidly systematic study of the National Socialist regime. Its aim is more modest. Just as portraits, following the rules of portraiture, confine themselves to the essential lines, and for the rest exercise the art of omission, so I have deliberately focused attention on what seem to me the most important facets of the idea and the reality of the Third Reich.

At the same time, I have taken care to include, as far as possible, all the essential features of this whole apparatus of power, so that the reader should be left with more than merely a composite picture made up of the chosen figures. So, in addition to individuals, I have also described the behaviour of certain groups, in so far as they were not adequately represented by any single figure: for example, the generals; the so-called intellectuals; and women, whose role was so essential to the rise of Hitler and hence of the whole National Socialist movement. Just as in certain areas it is individuals who constitute typical features of the 'face of the Third Reich', so in others social groups contribute to its total physiognomy.

At this point certain reservations must be made. The aim of this book is the description and analysis of psychological structures; the vulnerability to the totalitarian ideology, as demonstrated by the National Socialist example. Leading figures in the government apparatus of the Third Reich who might have had a claim to our interest within a comprehensive treatment of the problem but whose personalities cast no new light on that problem are not dealt with here. One example is Robert Ley, leader of the Labour Front. The significance of the 'socialist' element within the National Socialist ideology – the regime's success with unemployment – which is still noted with respect today – its social and economic policies, would have called for a special chapter in any comprehensive study. But Ley, as well as being feeble, eccentric and coarse, and in the final reckoning insignificant, was easily omitted because his personality differed very little from that of a number of others among Hitler's followers. Much the same applies to Julius Streicher, Fritz Sauckel and Wilhelm Frick, and – though for different reasons – to Hindenburg. Even today, an almost incomprehensible importance is still attached to Hindenburg, a classic example of the unpredictable way myths grow around very ordinary individuals of no lasting historical significance. He too, the 'grey-haired Field Marshal of the Great War', forms part of the face of the Third Reich, alongside the 'Unknown Soldier' of that same war.

Beyond these individuals and groups, I might have supplemented the group portrait with a study of the behaviour of the political parties, the civil service, the legal profession, the churches, and finally the industrialists. Yet it is precisely this last group that provides a perfect example of the grounds on which I omitted consideration of certain other individuals and groups. No doubt the support that Hitler received from this quarter was crucial, but what smoothed his path was not so much the millions that came into his funds (especially from heavy industry) as the lack of political sense and judgment on the part of millions of dissatisfied, embittered individuals, terrified of social levelling, who, under the pressures of the times, surrendered themselves ever more feverishly to the redeemer cult that was systematically developed around the person of the 'Führer'. The failure of such groups as industry, the civil service and the political parties reflected the failure of the whole population. To single out the misguided behaviour of individual groups would, at least within the context of this book, simply encourage the existing tendency to put the blame on others, and further blunt awareness of the guilt unquestionably shared by the whole German nation for what happened in those years.

Finally, the use of the term 'Third Reich' in the title and throughout the text may be criticised, since it is not, strictly speaking, exact. The National Socialist regime, after the 'Proclamation of the Third Reich' in 1933, in pursuance of its explosive urge to expansion, came to be described as the 'Greater German Reich' and, at its peak, in its leaders' extravagant plans for world domination, as the 'Greater Germanic Reich'. The term 'Third Reich' was intended not merely to indicate a numerical sequence, but even more to express the hopes and longings appropriate to the idea of the millennium, the chiliastic undertone that echoed on in the later terms. Even though perverted in a curiously ambivalent way and subordinated to a monstrous and smothering demand for power, it was nonetheless always the 'Third Reich' which inspired the regime's drive for achievement and its crimes, as well as the misdirected enthusiasm of its supporters and, at times, of almost the whole nation.

It is the purpose of this book to contribute towards an explanation of modern man's vulnerability to totalitarianism. Recent history, which inspired this inquiry and determines its limits, also explains why it is restricted to a single nation. The impression may be gained from many passages that we are dealing with a collection of typically German failures to meet the demands of history and politics. But we have here perhaps merely one specific complex of causes. Elsewhere different preconditions might lead to the same or similar totalitarian phenomena. The question then arises whether the universal precondition for man's self-renunciation, which is not something fostered only by totalitarian regimes but is joyfully embraced by millions of people of their own free will, is not his lack of intellectual and moral direction, his personal weakness, his blind hunger for the apparent certainties of a universal philosophy. If this is so, then any particular nation's historical, social, and psychological structure will merely determine the greater or lesser force and the specific shape of the totalitarian urge. This raises the further question how – and whether – the totalitarian impulse can be withstood.

This question, however, lies outside the scope of this book. Indeed, it is one that must be answered not so much by books as by men themselves.

J.C.F.

PART ONE

Adolf Hitler's Path from Men's Hostel to Reich Chancellery

I The Incubation Period

I believe that it was the will of God to send a boy from here into the Reich, to make him great, to raise him up to be the Führer of the nation.
Adolf Hitler, 1938, in Linz

He alone knows Hitler the Führer who knows Hitler the boy.
Franz Jetzinger

The rise of Adolf Hitler, the 'poor devil' from Braunau and inmate of a Vienna men's hostel, to the position of ruler of Germany and a sizeable part of the globe is one of the most astounding and disquieting careers in history. It was made possible by a unique coincidence of individual and historical circumstances, by the mysterious way in which the age complemented the man and the man the age. The curiously fragmented, neurotic character of the post-1918 era brought about by the collapse of a traditional order, the difficulties of adapting to new forms of state, the loss of economic and social status by broad sections of the population, and, connected with this, the widespread fear of life, the exhaustion in the face of a time that was out of joint together with an increasing mass flight into irrationality, the mindless readiness to renounce reason, and an ever more uninhibited susceptibility to myth: all this could by itself have led to crisis and distress, but, without the person of Hitler, never to those extremes, reversals of established order, mass hysteria and barbaric explosions which actually resulted. For a long time he seemed to bear within himself all the nation's psychological and social depression; eventually, he was widely regarded as the saviour who promised to give a new and happy turn to German history, which had gone so tragically awry. During the final phase of the Republic, when he flew about Germany from one meeting to another on his famous tours, he would on occasion order the plane to circle a few times over the rallying place. The illuminated airplane in the night sky, the masses of people waiting patiently in the darkness, despairing, discouraged, and yet awaiting this moment, this man who came down to them like a god to take up his dominion: in this picture the power and the myth of Hitler are to be seen at their most vivid. What we call National Socialism is inconceivable without his person. Any definition of this movement, this ideology, this phenomenon, which did not contain the name of Hitler would miss the point. In the story of the movement's rise, as in the period of its triumph down to its catastrophically delayed end, he was all in one:

3

organiser of the party, creator of its ideology, tactician of its campaign for power, rhetorical mover of the masses, dominant focal point, operative centre, and, by virtue of the charisma which he alone possessed, the ultimate and underived authority: leader, saviour, redeemer. It was to him that the masses looked in their hunger for faith, their longing for self-surrender, and their aversion from responsibility. When Hans Frank stated in retrospect 'It was Hitler's regime, Hitler's policy, Hitler's rule of force, Hitler's victory, and Hitler's defeat – nothing else,'[1] these words contained, apart from the obvious desire for an apologia, the true secret and the inner mechanism of National Socialism. 'Then came the great thrill of happiness,' says a contemporary account of a meeting with Hitler, to which there are countless parallels. 'I looked into his eyes, he looked into mine, and I was left with only one wish – to be at home and alone with the great, overwhelming experience.'[2]

What emerges in the emotional fervour of such confessions is more than the effects of a propaganda that systematically elevated Hitler to supernatural heights. Before any attempt at a description of 'demonic' or 'magical' characteristics, it should be pointed out that in addition to everything else Hitler was the National Socialist *par excellence*, not only the Führer but also the protagonist of the movement. In none of his followers can the individual features of the National Socialist 'nature' be observed in such intensified and typical form. His life story gives expression to all this movement's basic psychological, social and ideological drives. The disgruntlement, resentment and protest that were to be seen distorted and often one-sidedly accentuated in his colleagues and sympathisers combined in him in model proportions. Rather than the qualities which raised him from the masses, it was those qualities he shared with them and of which he was a representative example that laid the foundations for his success. He was the incarnation of the average, 'the man who lent the masses his voice and through whom the masses spoke'.[3] In him the masses encountered themselves. The story of his rise from men's hostel to Reich Chancellery is the story of the projection of an individual failure onto a whole nation. He was ahead of the nation in so far as he had long ago found the formulae for overcoming the personal distresses, humiliations and disappointments that littered his early path, formulae that he later presented to the nation.

The pathological factors which Hitler the individual shared with the postwar society that brought him to the top may be observed from many different points of view. There was the overvaluation of the individual and of society that had met with such sudden disillusionment, the seething desires of restless millions and their inability to meet the demands of responsible and independent existence, the embittering experience of proletarianisation that went hand in hand with a search for objects of blame and hate, the erroneous attitudes and maniac emotions which made any realistic approach to life impossible and created that distorted image of man in which both Hitler and his age saw themselves. The analysis of Hitler's personality will repeatedly bring to light elements characteristic of the period of his rise, and vice versa.

An account of his life must go back to the time before his birth. The indulgence normally accorded to a man's origins is out of place in the case of Adolf Hitler, who made documentary proof of Aryan ancestry a matter of life and death for millions of people but himself possessed no such document. He did not know who his grandfather was. Intensive research into his origins, accounts of which have been distorted by propagandist legends and which are in any case confused and murky, has failed so far to produce a clear picture. National Socialist versions skimmed over the facts and emphasised, for example, that the population of the so-called Waldviertel, from which Hitler came, had been 'tribally German since the Migration of the Peoples', or more generally, that Hitler had 'absorbed the power-ful forces of this German granite landscape into his blood through his father'.[4]

On June 7, 1837, in the house of a small farmer named Trummelschlager in Strones, the maid Maria Anna Schicklgruber, aged forty-one and single, gave birth to a son. The father was and remains unknown, and the most various and daring guesses have been made. There is some evidence to support the account given by Hans Frank during his Nuremberg statement, and it has never been entirely disproved. According to this, Hitler received in 1930 a letter from the son of a half brother, possibly an attempt at blackmail, which darkly hinted at 'very definite facts concerning our family history'. Frank was instructed to inquire into the matter confidentially and concluded:

Hitler's father was the illegitimate child of a cook named Schickelgruber from Leonding, near Linz, employed in a household at Graz. This cook Schickelgruber, the grandmother of Adolf Hitler, was working for a Jewish family named Frankenberger when she gave birth to her child [this should read 'when she became pregnant']. At that time – this happened in the 1830s – Frankenberger paid Schickelgruber on behalf of his son, then about nineteen, a paternity allowance from the time of her child's birth up to his fourteenth year. There was also a correspondence between these Frankenbergers and Hitler's grandmother, the general trend of which was the unexpressed common knowl-edge of the correspondents that Schickelgruber's child had been conceived in circum-stances which rendered the Frankenbergers liable to pay a paternity allowance.[5]

Maria Anna Schicklgruber's son came at an early age into the care of the peasant Johann Nepomuk Hiedler, subsequently the mother's brother-in-law. Up to his fortieth year he was called Alois Schicklgruber, then, evidently on the initiative of his 'foster father' and with the help of a mistake by the pastor of Döllersheim, who kept the register of births and deaths, he changed his name. From January 1877 onwards Alois Schicklgruber called himself Alois Hitler, No one can say what effect it had on his son when he learned these facts just as he was setting out to conquer power in Germany; but there is some reason to suppose that the sombre aggression he had always felt towards his father now became open hate. In May 1938, only a few weeks after the German occupation of Austria, he had the village of Döllersheim and its environs turned into an army training area. His father's birthplace and his grandmother's burial place were obliterated by the tanks of the Wehrmacht.[6]

Alois Schicklgruber-Hitler learned the shoemaker's trade and then entered the Austrian revenue office. His intelligence and ambition took him to the highest grade in the Imperial and Royal Customs Authority open to a man with his educational qualifications. He was evidently austere and conscientious. He married three times and – contrary to his son's transparent later slanders – was reasonably prosperous. In his third marriage there was born to him on April 20, 1889, in Braunau on the Inn, a son, who was christened Adolf.

Records of Adolf Hitler's childhood and youth are meagre. There are self-created legends embellished, as people began to idolise the Führer, with moving details intended to give an impression of the early maturity associated with genius. According to these he was always a victorious leader on the village common and continually produced for his playmates carefully thought-out plans for adventurous exploration or other exploits. His ostensible enthusiasm for the military life, his extraordinary empathy which, in his own words, 'enabled him to understand and grasp the meaning of history', as well as his enthusiastic nationalism, foreshadowed his future career, and the fable of the poor orphan boy forced to go abroad and earn his living at the age of seventeen added an effective touch of sentimentality. That this was fiction has since been almost completely proved.[7] On the contrary, Adolf Hitler was evidently an alert pupil of average gifts whose abilities were thwarted by lack of self-discipline from an early age and a tendency towards an easygoing, irregular way of life. His primary schools found him a good pupil, but twice during his five years at a *Realschule* (secondary school) he was held back for a year and once he had to sit an examination a second time. Almost all his reports rate his industriousness as 'uneven', and in mathematics, natural history, French and even German his work is considered 'unsatisfactory'. The report of September 1905 rates his history, in which he was supposed to have been ahead of the whole class, as only 'satisfactory'; in gymnastics alone is he rated 'excellent'; on the whole this report was so unsatisfactory that he left the school. Hitler later explained this as a stubborn reaction to his father's attempt to force him into the career of a civil servant; but by the time he left school his father had been dead for two years and his ailing mother opposed the obstinate and short-tempered boy with nothing more than an unconcealed anxiety about his future.

Adolf Hitler wanted to be an artist. There is reason to suppose that his choice of the profession was determined not least by vague notions of the unfettered bohemian life in the mind of a provincial middle-class boy; it certainly sprang also from a wish to avoid the demands of a practical training. In any case, the sixteen-year-old did not at first take any serious step towards realising the ambition to which he claimed such passionate devotion. Nevertheless his mother began gradually to give way. Soon after her husband's death she had sold the house in Leonding and moved into an apartment in Linz. Here her son now sat about, occupied only with amateurish painting exercises; aimless, clumsy designs for sumptuous villas and public buildings. For a time he took piano lessons, until he grew tired of them and gave them up. He visited cafés, the theatre and the opera. It was the life half of a man of private means, half of a good-for-nothing, and he was able to lead it thanks to his mother's pension as a widow. He refused to take up any definite work, a 'bread-and-butter job', as he contemptuously described it. Even at this time his great love was the music of Richard Wagner, which had an extraordinary power over him. Increasingly, and according to his boyhood friend August Kubizek, with a positively maniac eagerness, he allowed himself to be transported by this music into the unreal world which he finally erected beside and above real life, whose demands he evaded with a mixture of laziness and supreme contempt. Kubizek has described Hitler's ecstatic reaction after they had attended a performance of Wagner's opera *Rienzi*, which concerns Cola di Rienzo, the medieval rebel and tribune of the people. 'Like a damned-up flood bursting through the embankments, the words came rushing out of him. In grandiose, stirring images he painted for me his future and the future of his people.' When Kubizek later reminded Hitler of this scene, in 1939 in Bayreuth, Hitler is supposed to have replied portentously, 'At that hour it all began!'[8]

Filled with faith in his special vocation, Hitler went in 1907, now in his nineteenth year, to Vienna to enrol in the painting class at the Academy of Fine Arts; but he failed the entrance examination and was rejected. Soon afterwards his mother died. 'Even today,' he wrote later, looking back in self-pity on his years in Vienna, 'the mention of that city arouses only gloomy thoughts in my mind. Five years of poverty in that town of Phaecians. Five years in which, first as a casual labourer and then as a humble painter, I had to earn my daily bread. And a meagre morsel indeed it was, not even enough to still my constant hunger. That hunger was the faithful guardian which never left me but took part in everything I did.'[9]

But even this was untrue. A precise calculation of his income has shown that with the inheritance from his father, his mother's estate, an orphan's pension gained by false pretences, and later with support from an aunt, he had an average monthly income of almost 100 kronen (about \$140 or £50).[10] He again tried and failed to enter the Academy of Fine Arts; after showing his work, he was not even allowed to take the examination. But he did not give up the aimless life to which he had meanwhile become accustomed. Kubizek, who, as a music student, for a time shared with him the room at the back of the house at 29 Stumpergasse, has given a vivid description of this phase of Hitler's development. Even then Hitler used not to get up till about midday; he would go for a stroll in Schönbrunn Park, then sit up late at night over grandiose and senseless projects in which practical incompetence fought with impatient self-inflation. He planned to rebuild the Hofburg, whose tiled roof he did not like; he designed concert halls, theatres, museums and castles. Side by side with attacks on the civil service, the educational system or landlords, he developed projects for social reform or fantasies about a new popular drink. Without any musical knowledge he set about writing an opera, 'Wieland the Smith,' once planned by Richard Wagner. He tried his hand as a dramatist, drawing his material from the Teutonic sagas; meanwhile his postcards bristled with spelling mistakes.[11] He carried nothing through to the end. He had an extraordinary unstable temperament; feverish euphoria alternated abruptly with depression, when he would be at odds with the whole world, complaining about 'traps skilfully laid by the world around him for the sole purpose of hindering his rise'.[12]

By 1909 the savings left him by his parents had evidently all been used up, and, still incapable of leading a regular life, Hitler now began to go downhill. That summer he spent chiefly on park benches in the town; then he took refuge in a charity ward at Meidling. His subsequent claim to have worked as a labourer on building sites, which he even associated with his political awakening, has been proved false.[13] A tramp by the name of Reinhold Hanisch whom he got to know in the Meidling charity ward recalls that he wore at this time a frock coat reaching below his knees, given to him by another inmate with whom he was on friendly terms, a Hungarian Jew named Neumann. Hanisch adds: 'From under a greasy black derby hat, his hair hung long over his coat collar and a thick ruff of fluffy beard encircled his chin.'[14]

Hanisch found Hitler lazy and moody. Whereas Hanisch did casual labour, Hitler tried to supplement his twenty-four-kronen orphan's pension, which he was still getting on the pretext of being an art student, by begging, when he did not simply drift. Hanisch's efforts to persuade him to join him in the search for work were mostly unsuccessful. 'Over and over again,' he recalls, 'there were days when he simply refused to work. He would hang around night shelters, living on the bread and soup he got there, and discussing politics, often getting into heated arguments.' One day Hanisch asked him what trade he had learned. Hitler replied that he was a painter. 'Thinking that he was a house decorator, I said it would surely be easy to make money at this trade. He was offended and said he was not that sort of painter, but an academician and an artist.' It was Hanisch's bright idea that they should team up. They moved into the Brigittenau hostel for men, and Hitler sat in the reading room copying postcards, which Hanisch, disguised as a blind man or a consumptive, hawked around the low taverns on the outskirts in the evenings, sharing the profits.[15]

In the hierarchy of the dregs of society, Hitler's move from the charity ward to the men's hostel was a step up. He probably owed it to the help of his Aunt Johanna, who had once lived with his parents. But here too he was for the most part surrounded by the shiftless and homeless. Among the social flotsam washed up in the city's wards and hostels of the multination state were impoverished Hungarian nobles, bankrupt traders, down-and-outs from the dual monarchy's Italian provinces, petty clerks and moneylenders, gone-to-seed artists and so-called *Handelees*, Jews from the eastern regions of the Empire trying laboriously to rise in the world as old-clothes men, hosiers or pedlars. This pathological, evil-smelling world of envy, spite and egotism, where everyone was on edge for a chance to scramble upwards and only ruthlessness guaranteed escape, became for the next few years Hitler's home and formative background. Here his idea of mankind and his picture of society were moulded; here he received his first political impressions and asked his first political questions, to which he responded with the growing resentment, the hate and impotence of the outcast. He found here the reverse of the world of dreams and fantasies he had erected as a shelter for his frustrated hopes as an artist; he found it equally unreal and removed from the normal life which was becoming more and more closed to him.

Kubizek already noted with dismay the element of frenzy in his friend's make-up, the sudden unrestrained attacks of rage, the wild outbursts, the capacity for hatred. Hitler's growing lack of human contact, his inability to communicate, turned his conflicts inwards, where they renewed and intensified his aggressions. These in turn merely increased his isolation. Right up to the end, even when he was parading in triumph before hundreds of thousands of people, there remained a curious element of solitude in his life. From time to time he tried to involve the inmates of the men's hostel in heated political argument, but no one agreed with him and for the most part they merely jeered. For days on end he would sit about, at the mercy of his inner tensions, sullenly brooding on the injustice of things. With a typical mixture of self-pity and self-obsession, he judged his environment from the viewpoint not of a down-at-heel painter, but of a forcibly suppressed genius.

The living conditions and experiences of almost six years spent in Vienna left their mark on Hitler's character. He himself declared later:

During those years a view of life and a definite outlook on the world took shape in my mind. These became the granite basis of my conduct at that time. Since then I have extended that foundation only very little, and I have changed nothing in it. On the contrary.[16]

In fact, his view of the world was not the product of his own thinking, though he tried hard later to deny that there had been any intellectual influences at work on him, in an effort to add to the picture of himself as a natural leader, that of a totally original thinker who derived his ideology from direct communication with the spirit. On the other hand, he writes of his Vienna years: 'I read a great deal and I pondered deeply over what I read.' In so far as this claim referred to his supposed study of Marxism, he himself contradicted it when in another passage of his profession of faith, *Mein Kampf*, he stated that a lecture by Gottfried Feder introduced him for the first time in his life to certain economic problems.[17] Equally revealing is his account of his conversion to anti-Semitism. To begin with, he wrote, looking back on his past, he sought 'as always in such cases' to resolve his growing doubts 'by reading books. For the first time in my life I bought myself some anti-Semitic pamphlets for a few *heller*.' This equating of 'books' with 'pamphlets' casts further doubt on his claims; he is probably referring to widely distributed gutter pamphlets sold through Viennese tobacconists by the founder of so-called 'Ariosophy', who used the name Jörg Lanz von Liebenfels. Under the title *Ostara. Briefbücherei der blonden Mannesrechtler* (Newsletters of the Blond Fighters for the Rights of Men), these pamphlets won wide support for the doctrine of the struggle of the ace-men or heroes against the inferior races, the ape-men or satyrs, which was advanced with an affectation of wisdom as abstruse as malicious.[18]

The rest of what Hitler put forward as his philosophy was the sum of the clichés current in Vienna at the turn of the century. Konrad Heiden has pointed out that anti-socialism and anti-Semitism were 'fashionable among the ruling classes and good form in the middle-class circles to which Hitler aspired' or to which, with the stubborn pride of the proletarianised petty bourgeois, he still felt he belonged.[19] A similar philosophy marked the Pan-German Party of Georg Ritter von Schönerer, where it had a nationalistic, pan-German side reflected in propaganda for the incorporation into the Reich of areas of the Austro-Hungarian monarchy where there were people of German ancestry. The man who made the most lasting impression on Hitler was clearly the Mayor of Vienna, Karl Lueger, the 'idol of old men and concierges, of women and chaplains,' whom Hitler himself described as the 'mightiest German burgomaster of all time'.[20] Hitler admired this knowledgeable and adroit demagogue, who with consummate skill combined the prevailing social, anti-Jewish and Christian convictions and emotions with his political ambitions and showed a rare mastery of the art of influencing the masses. The only personal touch which Hitler added to this drab and arbitrary conglomeration of secondhand ideas was a primitive Darwinism that matched his own experiences in the men's hostel. As he later declared:

The idea of struggle is as old as life itself, for life is only preserved because other living things perish through struggle. In this struggle, the stronger, the more able, win, while the less able, the weak, lose. Struggle is the father of all things. It is not by the principles of humanity that man lives or is able to preserve himself above the animal world, but solely by means of the most brutal struggle.[21]

What he was putting forward in these and countless similar declarations was nothing more than the outlook of the men's hostel, the philosophy of the outcast, the intellectual refuse from a world whose inhabitants know that there are too many of them and that therefore they must rise out of it or be trapped like spiders in a pot. This hackneyed philosophy can be traced continuously in Hitler's opinions from the Vienna years onward, whether he was writing admiringly of his model Karl Lueger, the Mayor, that he 'was very careful not to take men as something better than they were in reality', or assuring those around him that 'it pays to be cunning', or celebrating brutality as a creative principle, or boasting that he had 'no bourgeois scruples'.[22] Always the vulgar Machiavellianism of the men's hostel, the school of baseness, was to be seen in such ideas; its corrupting influence had permeated his thought over a period of years. By interpreting men exclusively in the light of that twisted experience and seeing in their motives nothing but hate, ruthlessness, corruption, greed, lust for power, cruelty, or fear, he imagined, with provincial complacency, that he had come close to ultimate knowledge, whereas actually he was merely revealing his own desperate and depraved personality.

His feeling of superiority, which was necessary to him after he had failed in every personal challenge he had met, was founded not only on an arrogant contempt for mankind but also on the racial-biological twist which, clearly following in the footsteps of Lanz von Liebenfels, he gave to his vulgarised

Darwinian ideas. On the coincidence of belonging to one particular race, the failure could build up the self-importance his inflated ego demanded ever more urgently because of the abysmal depths of his own being. The Aryan – this was soon to become the firm core of his anti-Semitism – was 'the highest image and likeness of the Lord', and just as he had been the source of all the great achievements of culture and civilisation in the past, so under the creative plan of providence he was destined in the future too for the loftiest position, for mastery. Meanwhile the Jew, as the principle of destruction and evil, with the hate and vengefulness characteristic of the inferior, increasingly opposed the Aryan in order to subjugate the world by the means peculiar to him: planned corruption, deliberate pollution of the pure Aryan blood, and the systematic poisoning of public life. 'Was there any shady undertaking,' Hitler demanded later, 'any form of foulness, especially in cultural life, in which at least one Jew did not participate? On putting the probing knife to that kind of abscess one immediately discovered, like the maggot in a putrescent body, a little Jew who was often blinded by the sudden light.'[23] The press, art, prostitution, land speculation, syphilis, capitalism as well as Marxism, but also pacifism, the idea of world citizenship and liberalism, were the camouflages adopted at different times to conceal a world conspiracy, and behind all of them stood the figure of the Eternal Jew. The last obstacle to the Jew's plans was the German nation with its high proportion of Aryan blood; if that champion was vanquished in the mighty conflict, the victory of mongrel man, the end of civilisation and the disruption of the plan of creation were at hand; a stop must be put to this threat. 'In standing guard against the Jew I am defending the handiwork of the Lord.'[24]

It is not difficult to trace in the endless variations of this ideology the influence both of 'Ariosophy' and of the young Hitler's personal humiliations and failures. Moreover, in his description of the 'anti-man' we come again and again upon unmistakable projections of Hitler's own character: the Jews' alleged obsession with revenge, their feelings of inferiority, their lust to subjugate and destroy, represent the transference onto his enemy of compulsive character traits which Hitler sensed within himself. At the same time we must seek for some experience that impelled such a 'flight into hate' by this son of liberal parents, who on his own admission could not remember 'even having heard the word [Jew] at home during my father's lifetime',[25] and who had been on friendly terms with a Jew during his first years in Vienna. August Kubizek has pointed out that at an early stage Hitler quarrelled with everyone and felt hatred wherever he looked. Possibly, therefore, his anti-Semitism was merely the concentration of his hitherto unfocused hate, which at last found in the Jew an object to which to attach itself and so become aware of itself. On the other hand, Hitler's anti-Semitism has been attributed to the sexual envy of the unsatisfied, lonely, shut-in inmate of the men's hostel, and there is convincing evidence of this. There is his nervously clumsy, repressed attitude towards women from an early age. This is seen in the story of the relationship, which never went further than looks, with 'Stefanie', the romantic idol of his youth, and also in the alternating moods of

11

revulsion and hysterical adoration that later marked his approach to women. There is even stronger evidence in the very style and content of Hitler's writings.[26] The pages of *Mein Kampf* devoted to anti-Semitism give off a stench of naked obscenity, half concealed by that affectation of 'erudite moral philosophy in which pornographic works are accustomed to wrap themselves.'[27]

This Judaising of our spiritual life and mammonising of our natural instinct for pro-creation will sooner or later work havoc with our whole posterity.

The adulteration of the blood and racial deterioration conditioned thereby are the only causes that account for the decline of ancient civilisations; for it is never by wars that nations are ruined, but by the loss of their powers of resistance, which are exclusively a characteristic of pure racial blood.

The black-haired Jewish youth lies in wait for hours on end, satanically glaring at and spying on the unsuspecting girl whom he plans to seduce, adulterating her blood and removing her from her own people. The Jew uses every possible means to undermine the racial foundations of a subjugated people. In his systematic efforts to ruin girls and women he strives to break down the last barriers of discrimination between him and other people. The Jews were responsible for bringing Negroes into the Rhineland, with the ultimate idea of bastardising the white race which they hate and thus lowering its cultural and political level so that the Jew might dominate.

With the anguished monotony of the insane, he returns again and again to these obscene fantasies, patently tormented for pages on end by the forbidden images of his overheated and unaired imagination. For him, 'woman and sex have re-mained within the domain of sinful feverish fantasies. His central political concept is a hackneyed rationalisation of this obsessional idea: an insane world in which history, politics and the "life struggle of the peoples" are pictured solely in terms of coupling, fornication, pollution of the blood, selective breeding, hybridisation, generation in the primeval slime which will improve or mar the race, violation, rape, and harassment of the woman – world history as an orgy of rut, in which dissolute and devilish submen lie in wait for the golden-haired female.'[28]

A similar example of the squalidly feverish was offered by Hitler later as his reason for finally leaving Vienna, after years of brooding inactivity, eccentric daydreams, and continual flight into extravagant fantasy: 'The gigantic city seemed to me the incarnation of mongrel depravity.'[29] He spoke too of his longing 'to be among those who lived and worked in that land from which the movement would be launched, the object of which would be the fulfilment of what my heart always longed for, namely, the union of the country in which I was born with one common fatherland, the German Empire.' In actual fact, his military papers, which have now come to light, and which he strove for in vain immediately after the invasion of Austria, leave no doubt that he was guilty of avoiding compulsory military service. He not only gave his nationality as 'state-less' at the Munich police station, but also made a false statement about the date he left Vienna. He did not leave the city in spring 1912, but in May 1913. When the authorities finally tracked him down, he wrote a long, tearful letter to the 'Linz Municipal Council Dept. II.' This not merely reveals that his knowledge of

German language and spelling was still inadequate, but also indicates in its description of his living conditions that his life continued to run on the same chaotic lines as in Vienna.[30] He squandered much of his time in cafés, where he greedily and morosely devoured huge quantities of cakes, buried himself behind the newspapers provided for customers, and launched into angry monologues about Jewry, social democracy or nationalism in front of anyone who happened to be there, before relapsing into his brooding twilight. His aversion for all regular work remained insuperable. He earned an uncertain income by the occasional sale of sketches, posters, or small watercolours of Munich subjects. 'Thus my income is only very modest,' he wrote to the Linz Municipal Council, 'just large enough to keep my head above water. I enclose as proof my income tax certificate.'[31] He was still vaguely inclined towards a career as an architect, 'on a smaller or a larger scale as destiny would allot to me'. Josef Greiner, an acquaintance from his Vienna days, asked him at this period what his plans for the future were, and received the reply that there was bound to be a war and then it wouldn't matter whether he had learned a trade or not.[32]

He was right. A snapshot has been preserved showing Hitler on August 1, 1914, among the enthusiastic crowd in the Odeonplatz, Munich, during the proclamation of a state of war. His face is clearly discernible with the parted lips, and the excited eyes that at last have an aim and see a future. 'For me,' he wrote later, 'these hours came as a deliverance from the distress that had weighed upon me during the days of my youth. I am not ashamed to acknowledge today that I was carried away by the enthusiasm of the moment and that I sank down upon my knees and thanked Heaven from the fullness of my heart for the favour of having been permitted to live at such a time.'[33] For this war promised an end to his loneliness, despondency and mistakes. At last he could flee from the misery of his aimless hate, his misunderstood and damned-up emotions, his exaltations, into the security of a great community. For the first time in his life he had work to do, could feel solidarity with others, could identify himself with the strength and prestige of a powerful institution. For the first time Adolf Hitler, twenty-five years old, without a trade, for years the inmate of a men's hostel and a copier of postcards, knew where he belonged. The war was his second great formative experience, his positive one. He himself asserted with the telltale arrogance of the dropout: 'The war caused me to think deeply on all things human. Four years of war give a man more than thirty years at a university in the way of education in the problems of life.'[34]

His four years as a regimental staff runner set the course of his life. The sixth chapter of *Mein Kampf* makes a revealing comparison between the shortcomings of German propaganda and the success of Allied propaganda. It shows that beyond an anti-Semitic interpretation of the war as a conspiracy by the universal enemy against the German Reich, which had meanwhile become a rooted conviction, Hitler saw it exclusively as a struggle between two propaganda techniques. Now he began to fit together the elements of the theories which, according to his companions' accounts and his own self-portrait, he had already hit upon through his *Rienzi* experience, the emergence of Lueger, Social Democratic agitation, and not least his own experiments as a poster artist. His conception of political events hardened into a formula: only the ignorant populace, always referred to in a tone of contempt, took part in the actual fighting for ideas; it was really the methods by which these ideas were propagated that held the key to power or impotence. Here in embryo was what was later to become the 'secret doctrine' of his inner circle, the cynical prescription for success which led to his rise – but also later to his fall.

No doubt the reserved, inhibited lance corporal of the List Regiment was far from possessing the certainty with which he was later to apply this knowledge; but it already gave him a feeling of inner superiority and for the first time something more than the sullenly rebellious conviction that he knew better than other people. His comrades, listening to his excited outbursts, smiled at the bombastic insistence with which he held himself personally responsible for the progress of the war. He made no friends; he was the odd man out, the 'dreamer', as they reported almost unanimously. He often sat in a corner 'with his helmet on his head, lost in thought, and none of us was able to coax him out of his apathy'.[35] He was certainly brave, was twice wounded, and was decorated with the Iron Cross First and Second Class. And yet he never rose above corporal. His then regimental adjutant has stated that all his superiors agreed that this doubtless courageous but extremely odd individual could not be made a sergeant. He would never command respect.[36]

The end of the war brought what the fearless runner Adolf Hitler had always feared: the return to civilian life, to the horror of the normality in which he, homeless, without profession, without family, without purpose, had no part. Life at the front had made him harder, given him experience and his first touch of self-confidence. But at bottom the war too was something outside ordinary life, even if he took it to be life itself and found in it confirmation of the philosophy of struggle that he had brought with him from the men's hostel. Up to the age of thirty he had never known anything but unreality, or a clouded view of reality. Already as a boy, he writes, 'I used to think it an ill-deserved stroke of bad luck that I had arrived too late on this terrestrial globe, and I felt sad at the idea that my life would have to run its course along peaceful and orderly lines.'[37] Now destiny proved kind after all. In the chaos of collapse, Germany assumed the shape of an enormously magnified men's hostel. Vast armies of people had been uprooted, threatened by the war or its economic and social aftermath. In the failure of a whole social order, the type of the failure had his chance of a fresh start. When society was thrown back to zero, those whose own lives were at zero had their historic opportunity.

This was Adolf Hitler's hour. The incubation period was over. In the brooding sullenness of the previous few years the fermenting elements – hatred, feverish fantasies, pathological delusions – had mysteriously settled. As Adolf Hitler puts it in the final chapter on the November Revolution: 'I decided to become a politician.'[38]

14

2 The Drummer

It was not out of modesty that I wanted to become a drummer. That is the highest thing, the rest is a trifle.

Adolf Hitler, 1924 before the Munich People's Court

In the anonymous mass of the beaten German armies returning from the front there shows up for the first time, blurred and indistinct, the face of the 'Unknown Soldier of the World War', Adolf Hitler. In one of the courses in 'national thinking' organised at the beginning of 1919 by the Education or Propaganda Department (Dept. Ib/P) of the Bavarian Reichswehr Group Headquarters 4 under the alert Captain Mayr, Hitler attracted attention as 'one of those everlasting barrack dwellers who didn't know where else to go, a lance corporal with a lean, yellow, crabbed face, who wore the Iron Cross First Class, a medal rarely won by private soldiers'.[1] He had spent the revolutionary days of 1918 in a military hospital in Pasewalk, his 'aching head buried between the blankets and pillow with bitterness and shame', as he writes. 'I had not cried since the day I stood beside my mother's grave. But now I could not help it. During those nights my hatred increased – hatred for the originators of this dastardly crime.'[2]

This hatred began to make itself heard in his first uncertain and not very effectual attempts at public speaking. His excitability, the vehemence with which he intervened in the discussions among others attending the course, soon attracted the attention of his superiors, and his name first crops up in one of the early lists of men charged with special assignments (V-men). Soon afterwards he received his first trial task. On July 22, 1919, in a list of members of a so-called Enlightenment Commando for the transit camp at Lechfeld, number 17 is the 'infantryman Adolf Hitler'. The task of the commando was to influence the returning soldiers of the transit army in an anti-socialist, patriotic direction. At the same time it was to be a 'practical course in public speaking and agitation' for the participants.[3]

Hitler was now getting his first psychopolitical experience. His 'doctrine', which he later attributed to ceaseless bitter struggle, a solitary illumination vouchsafed to him in dark hours of distress, in fact acquired its content here; here too the opportunism later embodied in what came to be known as National Socialism first emerged clearly. He read the resentment in the faces of the returning soldiers, who after years of war saw themselves cheated of everything that had given substance and greatness to their youth – the sacrifices, the victories, the heroism and the confidence – and he offered clearly defined enemies for their

15

still blind and aimless anger. His exercises in public speaking – the chief features of which, according to those involved, were a passionate 'fanaticism' and the 'easily comprehensible' nature of his ideas[4] – were consequently centred upon attacks on the 'Versailles disgrace', the 'Jewish-Marxist world plot', and that group which later, in a popular phrase, he called the 'November criminals'. From the same period also dates Hitler's first extant written utterance on political questions, a letter on the 'danger which Jewry today constitutes for our people':

Through a thousand years of incest, often practised within the narrowest circles, the Jew has generally preserved his race and its characteristics more sharply than many of the peoples among whom he lives. His power is the power of money, which multiplies in his hands effortlessly and endlessly in the form of interest and imposes upon the peoples that most dangerous yoke, whose original golden gleam makes it so difficult to foresee its later melancholy consequences. Everything which makes man strive for higher things, whether it is religion, socialism or democracy, is to him all a means to the end of satisfying his lust for money and power. In their consequences his activities become a racial tuberculosis of the peoples. And this has the following result: anti-Semitism for purely emotional reasons will find its final expression in the form of pogroms. The anti-Semitism of reason, however, must lead to the systematic combatting and elimination of Jewish privileges. Its ultimate goal must implacably be the total removal of the Jews. Of both these purposes only a government of national strength is capable, never a government of national impotence.[5]

The anti-revolutionary setting in which Hitler took his first tentative steps in the field of politics arose from specifically Bavarian circumstances; for in Munich in November 1918 certain well-meaning, radical but amateurish politicians of the extreme left had surprisingly seized power, quickly losing it again in chaos. There was a widespread feeling of guilt at having disloyally forsaken the royal house, together with indignation at rule by soviets, and the universal distress and anxiety of a society shaken to its roots. Blindly and bitterly determined to recover what they had unjustly lost, people were only too easily disposed, in their search for those responsible, to see the spokesmen of the revolutionary experiment, some of them Jewish, as commissars of a vast conspiracy. They were saddled with the guilt for everything behind the general malaise; for defeat, humiliation, the hopelessness of the future, people's fear of sinking to a lower social class.

Partly because of its role in crushing the soviets, but also as the representative of the civil authorities, who to begin with remained in hiding in Bamberg, Reichswehr Group Headquarters 4 at first appeared in Munich as the effective repository of power. Over and above military needs, it also claimed political and administrative jurisdiction. Its representatives kept a careful eye on the fifty-odd political parties and groups in Munich, whose numbers reflected the confusion of public consciousness at this moment of crisis, as did the sectarian programmes blazoned in many of their titles.[6]

As a trusted member of Headquarters, Hitler was ordered to attend a meeting of the German Labour Party (DAP) on September 12, 1919. The party had been founded by a machine fitter named Anton Drexler and a sports journalist, Karl

Harrer. Its small group of faithful followers – workmen, craftsmen, members of the lower middle class – assembled each week in the Leiber Room of the Sternecker-Bräu 'for the discussion and study of political matters'.[7] The trauma of the lost war, anti-Semitic feelings, and complaints about the snapping of all the 'bonds of order, law, and morality' set the tone of its meetings. It stood for the widespread idea of a national socialism 'led only by German leaders' and aiming at the 'ennoblement of the German worker'; instead of socialisation it called for profit-sharing, demanded the formation of an association for national unity, and proclaimed that its 'duty and task' was 'to educate its members in an ideal sense and raise them up to a higher conception of the world'. It was not so much a party in the usual sense, as a mixture of secret society and drinking club typical of the Munich of those years; it did not address itself to the public. Obscure visionaries would hold forth to the thirty or forty who had gathered together, discuss Germany's disgrace and rebirth, or write postcards to like-minded societies in North Germany.

On September 12 Gottfried Feder spoke on 'How and by what means is capitalism to be eliminated?' When in the ensuing discussion a visitor demanded that Bavaria should break away from the Reich, Hitler attacked him so violently that Drexler whispered to a neighbour, 'My, he's got the gift of the gab. We could use him.'[8] When Hitler soon afterwards left the 'dreary society', Drexler hurried after him and asked him to come back soon. He pressed into Hitler's hand a small pamphlet written by himself, *Mein politisches Erwachen* (My Political Awakening), and evidently arranged for him to receive unrequested, a few days later, a membership card numbered 555.[9] Having nothing else to do, Hitler attended a few more meetings. At his instigation, on October 16, 1919, the little party risked a meeting in the Hofbräukeller. A hundred and eleven people turned up, and Hitler rose to address his first public meeting as the second speaker of the evening. In a bitter stream of words the dammed-up emotions, the lonely man's suffocated feelings of hatred and impotence, burst out; like an explosion after the restriction and apathy of the past years, hallucinatory images and accusations came pouring out; abandoning restraint, he talked till he was sweating and exhausted. 'I spoke for thirty minutes,' he writes, 'and what I had always felt deep down in my heart, without being able to put it to the test, proved to be true.' Jubilantly he made the overwhelming, liberating discovery: 'I could make a good speech!'[10]

Hitler often later emphasised the superiority of the spoken over the written word, and with an eye on the great redeeming experience of the power of his rhetoric, one-sidedly attributed all the revolutions of history to the 'magic power', the 'burning brand of the word hurled among the masses'. He held to this principle from the beginning of his political activity, and its effect was apparent in the comparatively little importance that was to be attached to the NSDAP party press.[11] A list of meetings of the party in which he quickly rose to the top shows him as a speaker thirty-one times within the first year after his self-discovery. He appeared in public at increasingly shorter intervals. The list clearly reflects a growing intoxication, an urge to self-assertion through public appearances, which after years of continuous deprivation filled him with an orgiastic sense of fulfilment. He always spoke on the same subjects: twenty-two times the title of his lecture refers to the Treaty of Versailles and the Jewish problem.

This ceaseless repetition of identical themes was not merely the expression of his fixations, but also his deliberate technique:

The chief function [of propaganda] is to convince the masses, whose slowness of understanding needs to be given time in order that they may absorb information; and only constant repetition will finally succeed in imprinting an idea on their mind. Every digression in a propagandist message must always emphasise the same conclusions. The slogan must of course be illustrated in many ways and from several angles, but in the end one must always return to the assertion of the same formula. Then one will be rewarded by the surprising and almost incredible results that such a persistent policy secures. The success of any advertisement, whether of a business or a political nature, depends on the consistency and perseverance with which it is employed.[12]

It was ideas such as these, applied with increasing skill, that gained Hitler his first successes. Soon a poster announcing his appearance could offer this assurance: 'Since Herr Hitler is a brilliant speaker, we can hold out the prospect of an extremely exciting evening.'[13] The ingenuous, unworldly Anton Drexler saw the party unexpectedly change under this man's influence. He had always wanted to keep it small, well within his control amid the intimate haze of a beer hall; whereas Hitler, visibly growing in self-confidence, demanded an appeal to the people. The party's sociological face also began to change. The workers and small tradesmen were now joined by soldiers, many brought into the party by Hitler himself, others sent by Captain Röhm of the Reichswehr Group Headquarters. In the Munich barracks life for the majority was an aimless, day-to-day affair, since the war had alienated the soldiers from everything that gives meaning to a civilian existence. In many cases their whole lives had been disrupted by the war, a formative experience from which they could not find their way back to any other way of life; there were adventurers, officers whose energies had nothing to get a grip upon in the postwar period with its laborious return to normality. Baffled by the unfamiliar problems of earning a living in the civilian world, they yearned in their drab idleness after the heroic bustle that for so long had given direction and meaning to their lives and an outlet to their hunger for action. Their idea of 'trench socialism', derived from their experiences at the front and comradeship in the face of death, found no link with the complex reality of peace, with its passionate controversies. This, and the general mood of national indignation, impelled them towards radical ideas. With their help Hitler gradually gave the party a firm organisational structure, as a basis for the leadership he had worked for from the beginning, which he saw as the precondition for any political mass movement.

Records have been preserved of various meetings held during this developmental phase of the party, in which Hitler celebrated his first if modest triumphs as a speaker. They reveal the positively clinical primitivism that brought speakers and audience together. Behind the clumsy, inarticulate phrasing of the keeper of the records we glimpse again and again the emotionally charged figure of Hitler, who distorted with his own prejudices everything he took up as he endeavoured by pathological tirades of hate to find a way out of the 'inner ghetto of his individuality'.

The meeting began at 7:30 and ended at 10:45. The lecturer gave a talk on Jewry. The lecturer showed that wherever one looks one sees Jews. The whole of Germany is governed by Jews. It is a scandal that the German workers, whether with head or hand, let themselves be so harassed by the Jews. Of course, because the Jew has the money in his hands. The Jew sits in the government and swindles and smuggles. When he has his pockets full again he drives the workers into confusion, so that again and again he finds himself at the helm, and we poor Germans put up with all that. He also spoke about Russia and who did all that? Only the Jews. Therefore, Germans, be united and fight against the *Jews*. Because they will gobble up our last crumbs. The lecturer's concluding words: We shall carry on the struggle until the last Jew has been removed from the German Reich even if it comes to an insurrection or even to revolution. The lecturer received great applause.[14]

And elsewhere:

Herr Hitler then spoke on the subject, but he got into such a rage that people at the back couldn't understand very much. During Herr Hitler's speech one fellow kept shouting 'Shame' while the others approved the speech with cries of 'Hear, hear.' The fellow was given short shrift. He was thrown out of the hall; on the steps a policeman took him into his protection; otherwise he might not have got home in one piece. [Hitler] said that the time was coming when we should see whether Germany was united, but he hoped that Germany would soon open its eyes.[15]

In the seething beer cellars, heavy with smoke, the agitator who had now risen to be the party's 'recruiting chief' slowly talked his way upward; the record of a meeting in October 1920 states that there were almost five thousand listeners. It was probably at this time that Hitler finally decided to become a politician. Barely a year later we find by his name the remark: 'He is a businessman and is becoming a professional public speaker.'[16] In any case, he left the Army and once more went to live in a men's hostel, giving his profession as 'writer'. All the speeches that have come down to us show that he had no set programme but drew his slogans from the masses, whose resentments and moods of protest he identified all the more surely because they tallied with his own aggressive attitudes. The poverty of his ideology contrasted with the demagogic skill with which he turned to his own ends dissatisfactions sprung from a thousand sources. Hitler's radical rejection of existing society in favour of an unreal, ideal conception, for which at different times he claimed different omens, would bring the first contacts with his audience, a feeling of unity between himself and an assembly of people who were at first frequently hostile or inclined to laugh at him, but whom with increasing mastery he brought to the melting point of mindless intoxication.

Negative elements also largely determined the character of the party programme that Drexler had drawn up with Hitler and Feder, before Hitler announced it at a meeting on February 24, 1920; this occasion was later compared in National Socialist Party legend with Luther's nailing of his ninety-five theses on the Schlosskirche door at Wittenberg.[17] The programme contained twenty-five points, and was anti-Semitic, anti-capitalist, anti-democratic, anti-Marxist, and anti-liberal. Hitler himself never regarded 'positive' formulas – those advocating nationalist ideas or the protection of the middle classes, for example – as imposing constructive obligations, but always as slogans to stimulate and intensify resentment and cupidity. In a phrase that unconsciously betrayed his tactical opportunism, he later called his twenty-five points his 'publicity campaign' and declared, 'The ideas of our programme do not oblige us to behave like fools.'[18] At the same time the party's name was changed; it was now called – on the basis of existing groups, but also in response to an as yet inarticulate, but widespread need – the National Socialist German Workers' Party (Nationalsozialistische Deutsche Arbeiterpartei: NSDAP). By the end of 1920 it numbered some three thousand members, and six months later the prolonged and bitter struggle for the leadership ended with total victory for Hitler. On December 7, 1921, the *Völkische Beobachter* for the first time called him the 'leader of the NSDAP'.[19]

The acquisition of this paper was made possible by influential and wealthy patrons, who now visibly began to take an interest in the up-and-coming politician. The revolutionary upsets of the previous few years had shocked leading conservative circles with the spectacle of the irresistible dynamic of the masses, which had come to appear alien and sinister; Hitler seemed to these people to be the man to tame and master the masses. Hitler himself, however, was seeking contacts in high places – besides the favour of the street, he was systematically wooing government offices and the salons. The soviets had not been forgotten in Bavaria, and the officially fostered anti-republican mood had turned the province, by reaction, into a centre of conspiratorial activity by the extreme right. The Munich Chief of Police, Pöhner, when asked whether he was aware of the existence of rightist political murder groups, gave the famous reply, 'Yes, but there aren't enough of them yet!' His subordinate, High Bailiff Frick, asserted, 'We held our protective hand over Herr Hitler and the National Socialist Party [because] we saw in it the seed of a renewal of Germany, because we were convinced from the beginning that the movement was the one suited to bring the workers back into the nationalist camp.'[20] Hitler's rise to be Munich's celebrated local agitator would have been unthinkable without the patronage of the German nationalist politicians who largely controlled the governmental apparatus of Bavaria; National Socialism did indeed soon become 'the naughty, pampered darling of the state'.[21] These politicians, and also the 'National Field Marshal' Ludendorff, high-ranking Reichswehr officers, Freikorps* leaders, and many others who, in the city's government offices, barracks and beer halls, were hatching their private and often rival plots for a coup d'état, lent this nationalist

* 'Free corps' – armed bands, principally composed of ex-servicemen excluded from the Reichswehr by the limiting terms of the Versailles Treaty, that sprang up throughout Germany after the war.

figure their sometimes overt, sometimes covert support in order to harness him to their own purposes.

The poet Dietrich Eckart, who had joined Drexler's party before Hitler and had contacts with all the rightist circles, introduced him to Munich society, and the half curious, half repellent figure had its effect in the traditionally liberal stratum with its weakness for oddities. All accounts describe Hitler as awkward, fawningly polite, 'noteworthy for his hasty greed when eating and his exaggerated bows'.[22] His lack of confidence remained for a long time, and his sometimes eccentric efforts to show off mirrored the irreparably disturbed relationship to polite society of the former occupant of the charity ward and inmate of the men's hostel. He is reported to have made a habit of arriving late and leaving early; loud, ostentatious outbursts against the Jews or political opponents alternated abruptly with phases of introspective withdrawal. Obviously still dominated by the feeling of being an outsider, he was continually thwarted in his desire to shine by the fear of social slights, a fear which the numerous women, mostly elderly ladies who took him under their wing with belated maternal eagerness, were unable to soothe. Together with the prejudices dating from his Vienna days, he also clung to his habits, in particular to the irregular mode of life in which his earlier dreams of being an artist had found their only expression; and over his torn or carelessly worn clothes there lingered the smell of the men's hostel. When Pfeffer von Salomon, who was later to become his supreme SA leader, first met him, Hitler was wearing an old morning coat, yellow shoes, and a rucksack on his back, so that the flabbergasted Freikorps leader at first renounced personal acquaintance.[23] Of course, the fascinating reputation that preceded him always ensured interest in him, an interest that often wilted at close quarters. There are striking reports of the extraordinary difficulty people had in remembering what he looked like. Even at this time there was to be seen the curious phenomenon of Hitler's two faces: as an orator before large masses, he was exceptionally self-confident and persuasive, with an unerring instinct for triumphal effects and the means of producing collective intoxication – in the society of individuals he seemed unsure of himself, was rarely able to meet others on equal terms, and repeatedly flouted the rules of conversation in a monologue that soon tired and bored the listener. Asked once to say a few words to a circle of friends, he refused: 'I must have a crowd when I speak. In a small, intimate circle I never know what to say. I should only disappoint you all.'[24]

It was in Munich society that he made the acquaintance of a large proportion of his closest followers, among them Hermann Göring, the last commander of the Richthofen Fighter Squadron; the stiff, admiration-hungry Rudolf Hess; the Baltic German architect Alfred Rosenberg; and Max Erwin von Scheubner-Richter, who died on November 9, 1923, outside the Feldherrnhalle; all of these, and the many adherents of the second rank, were not workers, as the party's name implied, but representatives of an intellectual Bohemia, members of a middle class economically affected or mentally disorientated by the war. On the journey to the 'German Day' in Coburg in October 1922 Hitler travelled in the same compartment with Max Amann, Hermann Esser, Dietrich Eckart, Christian Weber, Ulrich Graf, Alfred Rosenberg, and Kurt Lüdecke, and it has been pointed out that this group almost exactly represented the party's sociological face: 'a painter, a commercial clerk, a journalist, a "horse trader", a poet, a butcher, an architect, and (including Lüdecke), another man of commerce – this was the mirror image of Hitler's movement'.[25]

The people who now packed Hitler's meetings in growing numbers came from the same social classes. Certainly workers also found their way into the party, but as a rule not into the leadership, the hard core of which was made up of men from the academic or industrial middle class. Even before the war, panic had stirred among the petty bourgeoisie at the prospect of being overwhelmed by large-scale industries or department stores. Now, in the critical postwar situation, the petty bourgeoisie was drawn to the NSDAP, whose programme took express account of these fears, at the same time as giving voice to a far more comprehensive malaise in its categorical rejection of the whole existing order. The failure of the Weimar Republic – its birth in the aftermath of a lost war and the victors' uncomprehending policy of punishment for the crimes of the Kaiser's Germany – the humiliation, hunger, chaos and collapse of the currency – all this made it profoundly difficult for the middle classes to develop a patriotic attachment to the new order. The lower, as well as the upper middle class had always had a marked attachment to the state, a loyalty to authority, and, now feeling leaderless, refused to accept a former master-saddler over whom hung the 'putrid odour of revolution' in a position formerly occupied by the Kaiser in his still-remembered radiance. Moreover the sense of identification with state order and authority, to which the middle classes owed part of their consciousness of social worth, had become thwarted since the concept of order itself had been called in question; 'national values' had been laid open to disrespectful attack not, as it seemed to the middle classes, by the postwar confusion but by the Constitution itself with its party strife, democracy and freedom of the press. These were the origins of the call for order and morality, loyalty and faith, bizarre as they might seem against the background of Bavarian politics and in the mouths of the spokesmen of National Socialism.

Similar motivations were decisive in the party's striking popularity among university students, from these same middle classes. Here championship of the economic interests of their parents was reinforced by patriotic revanchism, the bleakness of their professional prospects, and youthful protest. 'In the banqueting hall of the Hofbräuhaus yesterday,' wrote the Social Democratic *Münchener Post* of a meeting of the NSDAP, 'one saw people of every kind – except workers. By contrast, there were student *claqueurs*, swastikaed youths, Munich beer swillers.'[26] The first industrialists soon joined the party; a few were owners of large-scale undertakings, but mostly they were proprietors of small or medium-sized factories looking to the party to protect them against trade union pressure. Then came civil servants, and later peasants. It was significant that the movement gathered on its fringes people of every background, every sociological hue. All they had in common was disappointment and discontent, an unbalanced, neurotic frame of mind attracted by the NSDAP's ill-defined programme and the noisy extremism of appeals based on revanchism. The NSDAP, they felt, understood them.

Hitler was carried along by the collective malaise, by irrational longings and ideals which he was able to articulate into aggressive protests – and there could be no mistaking an element here of the typical Bavarian liking for uproar and *Gaudi* (noisy revelry). More and more effectively he came to act as the 'drummer' setting the masses in movement. This was still his own view of his mission: he saw himself as a forerunner, as the herald of that leader-figure who from earliest times in German political mythology had always been a focal point for virulent dissatisfaction with reality.[27] Here and there, however, he was already himself being hailed as the saviour, which swelled his self-confidence. The almost blind Houston Stewart Chamberlain, whose racially orientated philosophy of history had profoundly influenced Hitler, declared after a visit from him that he was now reassured: 'The fact that at the hour of her deepest need Germany has given birth to a Hitler proves her vitality.'[28]

The country's growing misery helped his rise, and he was already a leading figure in Bavarian politics when, in 1923, Germany was overwhelmed by crises. In North Germany there was a quickly repressed military putsch; in the Rhineland the separatist movement gained fresh impetus; in the Ruhr, France's narrow-minded policy provoked a struggle for that region; Saxony and Thuringia came increasingly under the influence of the radical left; and as the value of the mark plunged hunger riots broke out everywhere. A revolutionary situation had arisen, charged with the moods and expectations of civil war.

In Bavaria, an inextricable tangle of conspiracies and intrigues, all directed against the Republic, now broke out into open conflict with the Reich government. The 'nationalist opposition' fell broadly into three main camps: the monarchist white-and-blue followers of General State Commissioner von Kahr; the units of the Freikorps and the Vaterländische Kampfverbände (Fatherland Fighting Leagues), more or less closely grouped around Ludendorff but so fluid in their aims and sympathies as to defy categorisation; and Hitler's movement which, in autumn 1923, with more than 55,000 adherents, was not only numerically the strongest group but also the most tightly knit. In an atmosphere of mutual agreement and support, but also of suspicion, the three groups watched each other, not yet resolved on action and the much-discussed 'march on Red Berlin'. After this march had taken place the most diverse ideas were to arise, ranging from a military dictatorship, through the restoration of the Hohenzollerns, to vague ideas of a socialist people's state with a nationalist hue. On one point there was unanimity; in no circumstances would any of the three leave action to its rivals. As the chief of the Army, General von Seeckt, commented at the time, each of the three groups was determined not to appear at all 'if the performance turned out to be a comedy', but to appear in the third act 'if it turned out to be a drama'.[29]

At this critical point Hitler, still unsure of himself but intoxicated by his hold over the restless masses behind him, at first lost patience and ventured too far. In the mistaken belief that Kahr was ready to strike, he attempted a dramatic coup on the evening of November 8, seeking to place himself at the head of all anti-republican groups in the Bavarian capital. Brandishing a pistol, he burst into the midst of a gathering of dignitaries, leading politicians and picked citizens of the province, who had been invited by Kahr to the Bürgerbräukeller. After firing a shot into the ceiling he announced the National Revolution, declared the Bavarian government deposed, and proclaimed a provisional Reich government under his own leadership. But the attempt failed. Hitler was torn between rage, despair and nervous breakdown. His sequence of hysterical moods foreshadowed the later convulsions and fits of frenzy of the defeated war leader and clearly demonstrated the failure of a basically unstable neurotic in a critical situation. At first he determined to offer furious resistance, then, suddenly resigned, he agreed to a demonstration march next day: 'If it succeeds, very well; if it fails, we'll hang ourselves.'[30] This too anticipated his perpetual oscillation in later years between the extremes of victory or suicide, world power or total collapse. On the following day (November 9) he placed himself, together with Ludendorff, at the head of a growing crowd that finally numbered several thousands. In the Odeonplatz, directly beside the Feldherrnhalle, there was an exchange of fire with a numerically weak police cordon. Hitler and the majority of his companions in the front rank fell or threw themselves to the ground; only Ludendorff, trembling with rage, walked on with heedless heroism and was arrested. Hitler then fled, leaving behind a few thousand followers and sixteen dead. The legend, obviously put about later by himself, that he had carried a helpless child out of the firing line – he even produced the child in support of his statement – has been proved false.[31] Whilst he was hiding at Uffing am Staffelsee, in a house belonging to the Hanfstaengl family, he declared that he must end it all and shoot himself, but the Hanfstaengls succeeded in making him change his mind. Soon afterwards he was arrested and taken to the fortress prison at Landsberg am Lech, 'with a pale harassed face over which fell a tangled strand of hair'.[32]

The course of the ensuing trial, which began on February 24, 1924, was determined by the tacit agreement of all those taking part not to 'touch upon the "essence" of those events',[33] so that the hearing was reduced to a farce in which Hitler unexpectedly ceased to be the accused and became the accuser. Admittedly, the projected treasonable undertaking had been discussed for months in a twilight atmosphere of half approval and concealed encouragement and the embarrassed and transparent attempt of the leading Bavarian politicians, with Kahr at their head, to put all the blame on Hitler made it very much easier for him to turn the tables on his accusers. At the same time, the intuitive and provocatively assertive self-confidence with which, so soon after a serious defeat, Hitler confronted the court and deliberately took all the blame upon himself, and then immediately disclaimed all guilt on the grounds that he had acted from lofty patriotic motives, was 'one of his most impressive political achievements'.[34] In a concluding speech, which accurately mirrors his confident attitude during the trial, he declared:

[He who] is born for politics must practise politics, whether he is free or in prison, sitting on a silk-upholstered chair or forced to content himself with a hard bench; the fate of his people will exercise him from early morning till late at night. The man who is born to be a dictator is not compelled; he *wills* it, he is not driven forward, but drives himself. The man who feels called upon to govern a people has no right to say: If you want me or summon me I will cooperate. No, it is his duty to step forward. The army which we have formed is growing day by day. I nourish the proud hope that one day the hour will come when these rough companies will grow to battalions, the battalions to regiments, the regiments to divisions, that the old cockade will be taken from the mud, that the old flags will wave again, that there will be a reconciliation at the last great divine judgment which we are prepared to face. For it is not you, gentlemen, who pass judgment on us. That judgment is spoken by the eternal court of history. What judgment you will hand down, I know. But that court will not ask us: Did you commit high treason, or did you not? The court will judge us, the Quartermaster General of the old Army [Ludendorff], his officers and soldiers, as Germans who wanted only the good of their own people and Fatherland, who wanted to fight and die. Pronounce us guilty a thousand times over: the goddess of the eternal court of history will smile and tear to pieces the State Prosecutor's submission and the court's verdict; for she acquits us.[35]

In fact the verdict of the Munich People's Court, as has been aptly remarked, corresponded almost exactly to the heavenly verdict predicted by Hitler. The president of the court had the greatest difficulty in persuading the three lay judges to find him guilty at all. They agreed only on his assuring them that Hitler would unquestionably be granted an early pardon. The sentence, the preamble to which once more emphasised the accused's 'purely patriotic spirit and noblest intentions', was the minimum punishment of five years' imprisonment with the prospect of serving the term on probation after six months in prison. When the court announced its decision not to make use in Hitler's case of the legal provision for the expulsion of undesirable foreigners, there were cheers in court. After this Hitler showed himself to the cheering crowd from a window of the law courts.

Nevertheless his rise – he had advanced within a short time from V-man of a Reichswehr Group Headquarters to a leading figure in Bavarian politics – seemed to have been finally interrupted. The party, without the unifying force of his magical and Machiavellian talents, split up within a few months into insignificant groups engaged in jealous and embittered backbiting. The chances of his agitation succeeding – relying as it did almost exclusively upon public discontent – diminished further as, by the end of 1923, conditions in the Reich became noticeably more stable and the period of the 'happy year' began, under the Republic whose rule had started so inauspiciously.

But the way Hitler turned defeat to advantage, the way he could scent the propaganda, psychological and tactical opportunities hidden under the disaster and transform them, provided one more demonstration of his political skill. He himself later referred to the failure of November 1923, not without reason, as 'perhaps the greatest piece of good fortune in my life'. In complete agreement, Theodor Heuss remarked in a study of 'Hitler's way' written in 1932: 'What would all this – the sympathy of the German public, martyrdom as a means of recruiting followers, insurance against having to take concrete decisions, the fight against "persecution", the fostering of the incipient legend – what would all this have been without November 8, 1923? The putsch, its outcome, its consequences, were fate's greatest gift to Adolf Hitler.'[36] In any case this failure was the starting point for a struggle for power in entirely new conditions and by new methods. Of decisive importance in this struggle was Hitler's realisation that force was not the way to capture the modern state apparatus, that power could be seized only on the basis of the Constitution itself. This certainly did not mean that he accepted the Constitution as a binding limitation on his future efforts; it meant that he resolved, and rigorously held to his decision throughout the rest of his struggle for power, regardless of dissensions within the party and revolts by the impatient, to steer towards illegality under the protection of legality. Behind the protestations of loyalty to the Constitution which Hitler, following his new tactics, so readily made during the following years, there was never anything more than the desire – clearly shown in the scornfully formal character of the protestations – to avoid facing the gun barrels of state power until such time as he had those same gun barrels at his command. The contemporary catchphrase 'Adolphe Légalité' revealed an instinct that this much-vaunted legality amounted to no more than a 'moratorium on illegality',[37] yet the authorities noted these assurances with a deluded satisfaction that barely hid their lack of authority, their vacillation and impotence.

The unsuccessful putsch marked the end of Hitler's political apprenticeship. The understanding of power that enabled him to rise during the following years was based on an ability to adapt to those in power, adroit handling of tactical compromises, and growing familiarity with the techniques of psychological domination and the principles of party organisation. This last he increasingly directed towards his own person, elevating himself from the role of drummer to the pseudometaphysical concept of the 'Führer'. The figure of the agitator carried away by events and his own impulsive reactions moved into the background, to make way for the technician of power acting with calculated opportunism, disloyal even towards 'granite' principles, devoid of moral or intellectual inhibitions, ready, in his own words, 'to swear six false oaths every day'.[38]

Naturally none of this liberated him from the complexes and hysterical fixations of his formative period. On the contrary, he now began to show clearly that bewildering coexistence of rationality and *idées fixes*, of craftiness and stupid fanaticism, which poses so many riddles and is one of the inexplicable features of his make-up. Any attempt to explain this strange juxtaposition of incompatibles risks stopping short at a description of symptoms. We run the same risk when we approach the most important question of all: what inner motive force made it possible for this former failure suddenly to forsake the life of the down-at-heel art student clinging hungrily to his wild eccentricities, to hold sway over Germans and most of Europe?

3 The Führer

Where he comes from, no one can say. From a prince's palace, perhaps, or a day labourer's cottage. But everyone knows: He is the Führer, everyone cheers him and thus he will one day announce himself, he for whom all of us are waiting, full of longing, who feel Germany's present distress deep in our hearts, so that thousands and hundreds of thousands of brains picture him, millions of voices call for him, one single German soul seeks him.

Kurt Hesse, Feldherr Psychologos, *1922*

The break forced on him by the failure of November 9, 1923, and his imprisonment at Landsberg helped Hitler to find himself – to find faith in himself and his mission. As the turmoil of emotions quieted down, the role of leader of a putsch, attributed to him throughout the trial by his adversaries, took on the contours of the messianic, the unique Führer. The uncertainty with which he at first demonstrated his growing feeling of being 'called', within the circle of his fellow-prisoners, did not hide the consistency with which he strove to gain acceptance for his claim to be regarded as specially chosen. From now on he adopted the consciously distant, icy front which no smile, no casual gesture, no self-forgetful attitude ever breached. More and more he struck the rigid, statuesque pose in which he found the style for his conception of greatness and leadership. A striking repetition of the dark past – he was to rise once more from anonymity by winning over the masses and gaining the favour of those in power, before once again gambling everything on a single insane decision and losing everything, as in 1923. But now he was vouchsafed a breathing space to carry out a comprehensive stocktaking; he tried to rationalise the chaotic ferment of impulses, prejudices and hatreds and to combine the jumble of half-digested ideas picked up from books into a 'coherent' system of thought. He once referred to the months of his imprisonment as his 'university at the expense of the state', and possibly he also tried now to broaden his knowledge by reading books whose ideas had hitherto reached him boiled down and at second or third hand. He has mentioned Nietzsche, Chamberlain, Ranke, Treitschke, Marx, Bismarck and others in this connection; but in all these works he discovered only himself, and what he called the 'art of reading' was never anything more than a hectic search for formulas with which to support his own rigid prejudices. 'I found the correctness of my long-term views confirmed by a study of world history and natural history, and was content in myself.'[1]

The result of his stocktaking was the book *Mein Kampf*, the first part of which he produced soon after his release from prison. Partly a biography, partly an ideological tract, partly a plan of action, in spite of all its demonstrable dishonesty, contradictory myth-making and transfiguration of its author, it nevertheless contains much involuntary truth and gives, as a contemporary description written in characteristically fulsome style states, 'important information regarding the nature and methods of this man who in many respects is reminiscent of the prophets of the Bible, the conscience-stirrers and leaders of their people'.[2] In fact, the work contains an exact portrait of its author: the high-falutin disorder of its ideas; the random knowledge posing as scientific objectivity; the lack of self-control and the constant lapsing into the extreme opposite; the cramped rigidity of dammed-up energy; the maniac egocentricity and utter lack of humanity throughout the whole of its great length; the monotony of its obsessions. No doubt realising the extent to which he had revealed himself, Hitler later tried to dismiss *Mein Kampf* as 'fantasies between bars'. 'If I had had any inkling in 1924 that I should become Reich Chancellor, I should never have written the book.'[3]

This confession referred primarily to the work's unspeakable foulness, exemplified above all in the feverishly obscene chapter on syphilis: the axioms of his view of the world and mankind he did not disavow. The central idea, around which all the other conceptions were grouped, is a vulgar Darwinism which sees the fundamental law of life as a merciless struggle of each against all, as the victory of the strong over the weak. With obsessive energy Hitler applies this law to nature and animal life, and finally to the human community itself, trumpeting the idea of the superiority of the ruthless over the conscientious, of the tough over the sensitive, of brute strength over moral values.

This central idea determines the book's whole range of references and attitudes: the anti-Semitically slanted race myth; the idea of the selection of the best, with its aggressively nationalist emphasis; the aristocratic leader-principle inspired by the author's consciousness of being personally chosen; and the theory of the Germans' right to extend their *Lebensraum*. This leads to tactical instructions for arousing the fanaticism of the masses; the fusion of a multiplicity of individual interests into one single community of action; the organisation of the movement and its most effective structure and mode of operation, and after the capture of power, the organisation of the nation and its expansive energy under a unified leadership. Throughout, there is a fundamental inability to respect or even to grasp the rights of others and their claim to happiness. Behind a veil of randomly acquired learning runs an arrogant conviction of the omnipotence of the individual will, the idea of an 'everlasting, brutal struggle', a primitive belief in force sneeringly convinced of its superiority over all 'religions of pity' and exulting at the practice of running amuck as the ultimate meaning of history – such is the repetitive, paltry content of an ideology presented in inflated and semi-educated verbiage through almost eight hundred pages.

Fate answered the question for me inasmuch as 'it led me to make a detached and exhaustive inquiry into the Marxist teaching and the activities of the Jewish people in connection with it. The Jewish doctrine of Marxism repudiates the aristocratic principles of Nature and replaces the eternal privilege of vigour and strength by numerical mass and its dead weight. Thus it denies the individual worth of the human personality, impugns the teaching that nationhood and race have a primary significance, and by doing this it takes away the very foundations of human existence and human civilisation. If the Marxist teaching were to be accepted as the foundation of the life of the universe, it would lead to the disappearance of all order that is conceivable to the human mind. And thus the adoption of such a law would provoke chaos in the structure of the greatest organism that we know, with the result that the inhabitants of this earthly planet would finally disappear.[4]

Not the least of the purposes of this work, to the writing of which Hitler devoted himself with exceptional seriousness, was an attempt to substantiate on literary and philosophical grounds his personal claim to leadership within the movement. Behind the resounding verbal façade lies an uneasy fear that the reader may suspect the writer's intellectual authority. Not one single sentence is free, relaxed and natural. The stylistic solecisms, which were noticed almost as soon as the book was published, show the author's lack of confidence, which he seeks to hide by a chatty tone – 'the hard blow of Fate, which opened my eye', 'the flag of the Reich rising from the womb of war'. There are unfortunate metaphors: 'This [journalistic] pack fabricates more than two-thirds of so-called public opinion, from whose foam the parliamentary Aphrodite then rises.' Rudolf Olden has pointed out the absurd linguistic contradictions of this sentence on poverty: 'He who is not himself in the clutches of this strangulating viper never gets to know its venomous fangs.' Olden writes: 'A few words like these contain more errors than can be corrected in a whole essay. A viper has no clutches, and a snake that can coil itself around a man has no fangs. And if a man is strangled by a snake this will never result in his getting to know its fangs.'[5] And just as mistakes like these betray the fake scholar's ceaseless anxiety for applause, so in the pathos of the book we can clearly see the distrustful defensiveness, the nagging fear of disregard, irony or disparagement. The very fear of self-revelation is self-revealing. *Le style c'est l'homme*:

If for a period of only 600 years those individuals were to be sterilised who are physically degenerate or mentally diseased, humanity would not only be delivered from an immense misfortune but also restored to a state of general health such as we at present can hardly imagine. To achieve this the State should first of all not leave the colonisation of newly acquired territory to a haphazard policy but should have it carried out under the guidance of definite principles. Specially competent committees ought to issue certificates to individuals entitling them to engage in colonization work, and these certificates should guarantee the racial purity of the individuals in question. The racial idea embodied in the racial State must finally succeed in bringing about a nobler era, in which men will no longer pay exclusive attention to breeding and rearing pedigree dogs and horses and cats, but will endeavour to improve the breed of the human race itself. That will be an era of silence and renunciation for one class of people, while the others will give their gifts and make their sacrifices joyfully.[6]

The theory that Hitler had a morbid fixation against his own image is based upon this and innumerable similar passages foreshadowing the studbooks of the Central Office for Race and Settlement. According to this theory, it is precisely because of its insane exaggeration that Hitler's conviction 'that the Nordic-Germanic blood is the only really great, splendid creation of God in the human sphere',[7] can be seen as an expression of his certainty that he too suffered from the 'morbidity of corrupted blood' and was forever excluded from the 'brotherhood of the truly pure and noble'.[8] The physical characteristics he persecuted were for the most part easily recognisable in his own face and body, and for his description of the 'universal enemy' he drew upon his own personal traits: from his still obscure origins to the weakness and ineffectiveness of his early years, and the dress and appearance of that period which made him, in the words of a fellow inmate of the men's hostel, 'an apparition such as rarely occurs among Christians'.[9] Similarly Hitler's own principles, practices and aims – as he described them himself – are virtually identical with those for which he attacked his opponents, in whom he secretly recognised and hated himself. In his propaganda techniques, the organisational shape of his movement, and finally his plans for world conquest, he always had a cover for his behaviour, whether it was enemy war propaganda, Marxists or Jews. Admittedly this does not suffice to build a psychological interpretation, but the phenomenon of the *Homo alpinus* with the strands of black hair hanging over his face acting as the guardian of the Holy Grail of Nordic blood[10] cannot be simply explained as the opportunist tactics of the popular leader. National Socialist opinion, in so far as it did not simply ignore this dichotomy in accordance with its usual technique for reconciling the irreconcilable, solved it to its own satisfaction by straightforwardly declaring Hitler 'a pure Aryan-Germanic type'. A treatise published by Alfred Richter, a 'specialist' in 'racial characteristics', 'with the approval of the police and the office of the NSDAP' described Hitler as follows: 'Facial expression: that of a genius, a creative, spiritual leader, powerful, tenacious, filled with great love, unspeakable pain, and renunciation.' It read in the upper part of the head 'universal love, lofty religion, beauty and nobility of nature', gave an assurance that the forehead was 'of Nordic type', called the hair 'blond', and finally decided: 'In the left ear the external part stands out clearly. Hitler can therefore be a very tough fighter. The back of the head is also very strongly developed, from which we may see his feeling for home and children.'[11] In contrast to this, of course, there is the statement of Max von Gruber, Germany's so-called leading 'racial hygienist', when called as an expert witness before the People's Court in Munich:

I saw Hitler from close to for the first time. Face and head bad racial type, crossbred. Low, receding forehead, ugly nose, wide cheekbones, small eyes, dark hair; facial

30

expression not that of one in full self-control, but of one who suffers from insane excitement. Finally, an expression of complacent self-satisfaction.[12]

While Hitler, in respectable retirement in the fortress of Landsberg, was dictating to his follower Rudolf Hess the prolix results of his meditations, the movement disintegrated without Hitler 'lifting a finger',[13] as one of his supporters remarked at the time. Shortly before his arrest he had entrusted Alfred Rosenberg with the leadership of the movement on a 'scrap of paper', and Rosenberg, lacking authority and slow to make up his mind, surmised quite rightly that this was a tactical move deliberately aimed at the collapse of what was ostensibly the great common cause, as a means of maintaining Hitler's own claim to leadership. 'After this [his release],' Hitler frankly admitted later, 'I could say to all those in the party what otherwise it would never have been possible for me to say. My answer to my critics was: Now the battle will be waged as I wish and not otherwise.'[14]

His first concern, after his return from Landsberg on December 20, 1924, was the removal of the ban on the party. The quick success of his negotiations was partly due to the adroitness with which he worked his way back into the 'front of the parties standing for law and order', employing, according to circumstances, protestations of respect for legality, anti-Marxist, pro-Catholic, or monarchist attitudes.[15] But it must also be understood as the payoff for the tacit agreement 'not to touch upon the "essence" of those events [of November 8 and 9, 1923]' during his trial. By February 26, 1925, the *Völkische Beobachter* was appearing again, and the following day Hitler held a meeting with his remaining loyal followers and his rivals. In a two-hour speech devoted almost entirely to consolidating his position as leader he declared:

If anyone comes and tries to make conditions to me then I say to him: friend, wait and see what conditions I have to make to you. I am not wooing the masses. After a year you shall judge, my party comrades; if I have not acted correctly, then I shall place my office in your hands again. But until that moment this is the rule: I lead the movement alone, and no one shall set me conditions so long as I personally bear the responsibility. And I once more bear entire responsibility for everything that happens in the movement.[16]

Where he had failed previously, in countless private conversations, he now succeeded. Against a background of wild cheering from the crowd of four thousand, who jumped onto the tables and embraced one another, a reconciliation took place between the warring members of the party. While the leading contenders demonstratively shook hands on the platform, Streicher called Hitler's return a 'gift from God', and the leader of the Bavarian splinter group, Dr Buttmann, announced that all the doubts with which he had come 'melted away within me as the Führer spoke'. After this declaration, which repeated a title already used before, though this time without the lapidary, conspiratorial undertone, Hitler was henceforth invariably known as 'der Führer'. This success lent force to his decision to purge the party, which was refounded at this same meeting, of all the democratic relics of its early period and to give it the tightly

31

authoritarian character of a party with a single leader – himself. Once more he demonstrated his gift for tactical manoeuvring and the upshot was the elimination of his only two serious rivals. While the activities of Gregor Strasser were diverted to North Germany, the embittered Ernst Röhm found himself, without any explanation, expelled.[17]

His own power within the party re-established more firmly than ever, Hitler set about building up the NSDAP within the framework of the Constitution. He had already explained at Landsberg his decision never again in future openly to break the law, but to bend it to his will under the pretence of legality:

When I resume active work it will be necessary to pursue a new policy. Instead of working to achieve power by an armed coup we shall have to hold our noses and enter the Reichstag against the Catholic and Marxist deputies. If outvoting them takes longer than outshooting them, at least the results will be guaranteed by their own Constitution! Any lawful process is slow. But sooner or later we shall have a majority – and after that Germany.[18]

Meanwhile, times were not favourable. The Bavarian government quickly realised that 'the beast' was not 'tamed'[19] – as Minister-President Held had prematurely assured his cabinet colleagues – and consequently banned Hitler from making speeches. Most of the major *Länder* of the Reich did the same. In spite of tireless activity in arranging rallies – there were almost six thousand meetings in 1925 – the party itself failed to achieve even minor successes. Not only the enforced silence of its sole demagogic talent, but far more the growing stability of the Republic, pushed it into the shadow of political life. In 1926 it still had no more than 17,000 members, a year later only about 40,000; and whereas in 1928, after the lifting of the ban on Hitler, the number had risen to 60,000, at the Reich elections the same year it gained only twelve seats – less than half its goal. The flow of foreign capital into Germany ensured rising production, and in 1927 the national income had reached the prewar level with low unemployment. Hitler's passionate attempts to invoke catastrophe, his appeals against the 'ruthless blackmail of the poverty-stricken people', failed to mobilise the masses, and instead of the state it was the movement which found itself in a crisis. Tenacious and unyielding, Hitler used his ability to transmit self-confidence to hold the majority of his followers together and, by continually appointing his lieutenants to fresh positions, manoeuvred them into energy-consuming rivalries that left him in uncontested control.[20] He finally succeeded in completely subjugating Gregor Strasser – who had built up a relatively strong organisation in North Germany which, unlike the Munich centre, was markedly socialist in character – and yet keeping him in the party.

But Hitler did not use the years of stagnation merely to build up a totalitarian leadership structure and a reliable and effective élite striking force. During this same period the foundations were laid for what amounted to a shadow state. In *Mein Kampf* he had already demanded as a precondition of the planned revolution a movement that would not only 'be in a position to serve as a guide for the future State, but have its own organisation such that it can subsequently be placed at the disposal of the State itself'.[21] He rapidly set up numerous offices and institutions which, in addition to their potential for keeping power within the party divided, also served to contest the competence and legality of the state institutions in the name of the true representatives of the supposedly unrepresented people. The departments of the shadow state came into being in parallel with the structure of ministerial government, for example the NSDAP had its own foreign, agricultural and defence offices. Provincial and district leaders increasingly laid claim to the status of ministers and local presidents; at public meetings the SA and SS took over police duties; and Hitler had himself represented at international conferences by his own 'observers'. Similar aims lay behind the party symbols: the swastika provided the shadow state's national emblem, the Horst Wessel Song its national anthem, while the brown shirt, orders and badges created a sense of solidarity in opposition to the existing state and rationalised the fondness for 'decorations that were a profession of faith'.[22]

Beyond this systematic preparation for the conquest of power, Hitler himself was now leading the relatively withdrawn, unremarkable life of a South German provincial politician; his eccentric ways were hardly taken seriously and were readily explained by the baroque style of Bavarian politics. It took two distinct but favourably timed events to lift him from the narrowness of his South German domain into the front rank of the nationalist opposition within the Reich. The first was a move by the German Nationalist Party leader Alfred Hugenberg, who in 1929 gathered the extreme rightists for a massive campaign against the new reparations arrangements envisaged by the Young Plan. He was looking for a gifted agitator who could bring the conservative cause, now fixed in its assumption of superiority, into contact with the lost masses, and he hit upon Hitler. With the shortsighted arrogance of the 'gentleman' dealing with the leader of an undisciplined party of the rabble, he reckoned that when the time came he could outmanoeuvre Hitler and use the people he had stirred into motion for his own political purposes. As a result of this error, of which the Bavarian politicians had already been guilty once before, the pattern of 1923 was almost exactly repeated. The difference was that Hitler had long outgrown his modest self-assessment of that time and, supported by the almost religious adulation of his followers, had more and more consciously assumed the role and behaviour of the 'Führer'. Blindly, Hugenberg put at his disposal the vast apparatus of his press empire and arranged contacts, which Hitler had previously sought in vain, in a few influential wealthy circles of heavy industry.

The publicity resources of the Hugenberg organisation not only made Hitler's name known at a stroke throughout Germany, but also offered an unparalleled journalistic springboard when, that autumn, the world economic crisis spread to Germany. The number of unemployed, which rose with stupefying rapidity to over a million, was only the most spectacular feature of a collapse that dragged down every social class. Especially among the petty bourgeoisie, whose pronounced class-consciousness had always interpreted poverty as a humiliating index of social degradation, the economic crisis was instantaneously transformed

33

into a crisis of the national spirit. Tired of everlasting difficulties, their mental resistance shattered by war, defeat, and inflation, the unstable masses gave themselves up to their emotions. Through the thin veneer of a rather formal attachment to the state there broke impulses which, though always present, had been neither recognised nor utilised by the laborious everyday competence of the spokesmen of the Republic: flight into myth and utopianism, search for an evocative image of the future; protest against fossilised institutions, against capitalism, materialism and political formalism; demand for a comprehensible interpretation of the feelings of malaise that had never quite evaporated; and finally a longing for powerful leaders. All these desires, so long neglected, now broke out in aggressive form.[23]

It was everyone's misfortune that the parliamentary institutions failed almost immediately in the face of this test, which confirmed the general mood of dull indignation. While the crisis demanded a willingness to shoulder responsibility, the parties, unable to think broadly for reasons that were partly ideological and partly concerned with their selfish interests, rushed hurriedly into opposition. The Great Coalition broke up in spring 1930, even before the first climax of the crisis. The pusillanimous flight into opposition by almost all political camps, with the exception of a few centre parties, meanwhile proved to have been a miscalculation. The elections, which took place at increasingly short intervals, gave the NSDAP, the loudest and most obviously consistent voice in the prevailing chorus of negation, an opportunity to improve its representation. 'National Socialism,' ran the demagogic slogan, dispensing with long-term explanations, 'is the opposite of what exists today.'[24]

In the centre of the storm stood Adolf Hitler. With his background in the masses of déclassés and his unerring nose for the fear and indignation amid the social dissolution, he recognised the now-or-never hour of his life. When, writing in 1924 in *Mein Kampf*, he had admiringly praised the Mayor of Vienna Karl Lueger for having 'devoted the greatest part of his political activity to the task of winning over those sections of the population whose existence was in danger', he had shown an insight into the secret of his own success with the masses during the first few years after the war. But it was only now, in the infinitely severer distress resulting from the world economic crisis, that this insight dictated the methods he employed as an agitator. He arrived at them with an unwavering logic in which every detail was important and nothing left to chance: the size of the gathering, the precisely calculated composition of the crowd, the time of day, or the artificially delayed appearance of the speaker while tension was worked up by theatrically arranged processions of banners, military music, ecstatic shouts of 'Heil!' Suddenly, to the accompaniment of a blaze of light, he would emerge before a crowd systematically whipped up in its excitement to see him and primed for collective rapture. The 'elimination of thought', the 'suggestive paralysis', the creation of a 'receptive state of fanatical devotion': this culminating psychological state, the preparation of which Hitler had expressly described as the purpose of a mass meeting, had here become the aim of its stage-managing and the speech itself served no other purpose – the style, the arguments, the calculated climaxes, the modulation of the voice as well as the carefully practised threatening or imploring gestures. 'The masses are like an animal that obeys instincts', he declared. In accordance with this principle he prescribed the maximum primitiveness, simple catchphrases, constant repetition, the practice of attacking only one opponent at a time, as well as the dogmatic tone of the speeches, which deliberately refused to give 'reasons' or to 'refute other opinions'. All this amounted, as Hitler put it, to 'a tactic based on the precise calculation of all human weaknesses, the results of which must lead almost mathematically to success'.[25]

It was to these tactics that the party, profiting from the derangement, the wildly proliferating emotions and delusions of public opinion, owed its surge forward. The figure of Hitler, systematically elevated to pseudo-religious heights by irrational appeals to the emotions, soon became, for thousands upon thousands, the point of fusion of their feelings of revolt, hate and longing, a figure in which the ancient leader-myth of the Germans combined with the current need for order, security and unity. With his demagogic virtuosity, against which the other parties, in bewilderment, could offer only the sober routine of traditional mass meetings, went a far more active agitation. In the five summer months of 1931, for example, 4,135 mass meetings were organised by the political parties in the province of Hessen-Nassau; of these almost half were conducted by the NSDAP, whereas the SPD (the Socialist Party) appeared a bare 450 times and the Centre only 50 times.[26] Tirelessly, often travelling by plane, Hitler descended like a saviour to the seething crowds of despairing people; on one day alone he would address several hundred thousands, sweeping them into a 'forward-thrusting hysteria', as he called it himself. The collective feelings, the fascination of the vast mass, of which each individual could feel himself a part, gave people a sense of power which they had long lacked and which found fulfilment in Hitler's rhetoric in this atmosphere of rapturous emotion: extreme self-elevation was brought about by extreme self-surrender. On his first flight across Germany Hitler visited twenty-one towns in seven days, on the second flight twenty-five towns in eight days, and on the last two flights fifty towns each in sixteen and in twenty-four days. True to his principle that 'only the fanaticised masses can be guided', he gave them the things that helped to release their fanaticism: primitively abbreviated, plausible formulas of guilt, lashing catchphrases of indignation, vague recipes of power, Fatherland, honour, greatness and revenge, indifferent to the fact that this whipping up of emotions merely aggravated the chaos which he so accusingly and angrily deplored. This too was part of his comprehensive strategy for the conquest of power, which along with demagogic obfuscation included terrorism in the streets, the obstruction of Parliament, and the refusal of all loyal collaboration, as deliberate means of intensifying the crisis. All those who found themselves in need through no fault of their own – the unemployed, youths on street corners, pensioners, small shopkeepers, poverty-stricken academics, the whole of the middle class that was breaking down in the economic crisis – all those who helplessly or bitterly asked the reason for their distress and had lost their willingness to judge, abandoned themselves to the seductive power of this voice. Whereas the other parties addressed themselves predominantly to individual classes or groups of the population, the NSDAP uninhibitedly appealed to everyone, and just as its name 'did not rest content with the amalgamation of National and Socialist, but to be on the safe side attached to these the right-wing label "German" and the left-wing "Workers",' so it also filched from the other parties their 'political content and pretended to incorporate all of them'.[27]

For hundreds of thousands, soon for millions, Hitler became an idol whose rise they applauded with convulsive emotion. Photographs have been preserved in which he strides down streets lined with shouting, sobbing people, a '*via triumphalis* of living human bodies*', as Goebbels enthused,[28] women to the fore, and he himself solitary, closed, withdrawn from this lust for psychological rape, still 'in his right mind', a commonplace, misshapen figure of moral destitution. This was the other, the true side of his protean personality, the laboriously posing outer case of a man ready with the gifts of a medium to let the energy proclaimed in the crowd's shout of anticipation fill him and carry him aloft. Only when he had mounted the podium and his first exploratory words fell in the breathless silence did he seem to change and to achieve what seemed to be a compelling genius that carried him far above the inferior levels of his own individual personality. 'He begins in a low, slow tenor voice,' noted a contemporary observer, 'and after about fifteen minutes something occurs that can only be described by the ancient, primitive metaphor: the spirit enters into him.'[29] He himself confessed on one occasion that in front of a jubilant crowd he became 'another person'.[30]

To understand the origin of this phenomenon we need only look at the pages of *Mein Kampf* dealing with the masses, at the virtually erotic passion which the idea of the masses aroused in him, liberating his language for the only passages that are effusive and free. In the mass meetings which he sought out ever more avidly, the solitary man whose ability to make contact was severely disturbed and who 'avoided all encounters with [individual] people'[31] found sublimation. The masses – whom he habitually identified with 'woman' – provided him, in the orgiastic collective delirium which he pushed to ever new heights, with a substitute for the emotional experience that had remained closed to him in all his monstrous ego-fixation. The poet Rene Schickele described Hitler's speeches as 'rape and murder'. Some things seem nevertheless to support the idea that only in his rhetorical raptures, when 'the spirit entered into him', did he find his way to the other self, normally buried beneath the deformation that had taken place in his earlier life. 'Speaking was the element of his existence,' one of his followers stated:[32] only ever-renewed rhetorical outbursts offered an escape out of the cataleptic constriction of his nature. 'When he was not speaking he relapsed into his brooding twilight, his spirit temporarily departed, buried within himself and unable to reach a decision or to act – *post coitum triste*';[33] no longer the Führer, but simply Hitler, Adolf, an early failure, a copier of postcards, marked by his experiences at the men's hostel. An observer who once came upon him in this state, exhausted and with glazed eyes, was kept away by his adjutant Brückner with the words, 'Leave him in peace; the man's all in!' Hitler himself said that after his major speeches he was 'soaking wet and had lost four or six pounds in weight'.[34]

The turmoil unleashed by his agitation would not, of course, have brought him to power by itself. At no election did Hitler ever get more than 37.3 per cent of the votes. The way was opened by the governmental procedure introduced into Germany in 1930. Since normal parliamentary majority government had been rendered impossible, not least by the crisis fanned by the National Socialists, the state had recourse to the Reich President's authority to issue emergency regulations. Inevitably the centre of gravity of political power increasingly shifted onto the Reich President and his small group of advisers; and the President's son Oskar von Hindenburg was not the only one of those who, in the words of a popular jibe, was 'not provided for in the Constitution'. Hitler, with his support among voters and his Brown Shirt detachments behind him, stubbornly wooed the power group. His unrelenting courtship was characterised, in bewildering alternation, by threats of revolution on the one hand and promises of loyal cooperation on the other. While he was still waiting in vain and with growing restlessness, for a chance of making a bid for the Chancellorship, the party suffered its first severe setback in the elections of November 1932. A month later the party went through a serious crisis in the course of which Hitler, amidst outbursts of rage, convulsive weeping and wild accusations, threatened suicide yet again. This crisis once again clearly demonstrated the cracks in the structure of a party of divergent outlooks and ideals and with no clear programme. It required not only the myth of the Führer but also the myth of his invincibility, because at bottom precisely this was its programme. At the same time this crisis offered opponents an opportunity of continuing the publicly initiated process of 'removing the magic from the NSDAP'.[35]

The opportunity was not taken and the leader of the NSDAP found himself opposed no longer by a republic resolved to preserve its existence, but merely by a collection of frightened and divided democratic politicians lacking all conviction of the historical justice of their cause. The few conservative spokesmen, bombastic, naïve and deep in the illusion that 'the role of leaders had been conferred upon them by history', allowed themselves to play Hitler's game. In the midst of an intrigue that had arisen largely out of the personal motives of the participants, these conservatives gave the leader of the demoralised, despondent, financially embarrassed NSDAP a completely unexpected opening; and by astutely exploiting the class-conscious, anti-trade-union and nationalistic prejudices of the groups who commanded the vacillating mind of the Reich President, Hitler at last had his way. On January 30, 1933 Hindenburg bestowed on him the chancellorship, the key position for the acquisition of that power which, once in his possession, as he had publicly stated, he would never allow to be taken from him again, 'so help me God'. 'It all seems like a fairy story,' noted Goebbels in his diary.[36]

An astonishing career lay behind him, some stretches of it almost incomprehensible when analysis is attempted. His road to the Reich Chancellery had run not from the Kaiserhof, for years his Berlin headquarters, but from the men's hostel in the Meldemannstrasse, Vienna. Swept along by his own dynamic and unleashing new forces, new accelerating factors, he continued ever more impatiently in his impetuous onrush – for he did not consider his goal attained as the chancellor of a coalition cabinet with only three National Socialist members. His aim was a one-party totalitarian state. The slogan for the next stage in his career, upon which he embarked immediately and with no consideration for his partners in the government, was proclaimed by Goebbels: 'Power has to be conquered with power.'[37]

4 The Reich Chancellor

That is the miracle of our age, that you have found me, that you have
found me among so many millions! And that I have found you, that is
Germany's good fortune!

Adolf Hitler

What luck for the rulers that men do not think.

Adolf Hitler

Hitler appeared on the political scene on January 30, 1933 with all the triumphal
ceremonial of the historical victor. The grandiose setting with mass marches
and torchlight processions was out of all proportion to the constitutional
significance of the occasion, which technically speaking had merely brought a
change of government. However, the public duly noted that the nomination of
Hitler as Reich Chancellor was not like cabinet reshuffles in the past, but a new
departure. In spite of the boastful arrogance of Papen, who dismissed all
warnings about Hitler's determined hunger for power with the assurance,
'You're wrong; we've hired him,'[1] the safety measures taken by his German
Nationalist partners in the coalition – who trusted to their influence over the
Reich President, the economy, the Army and the civil service, and all the key
positions in society – proved completely ineffective in a matter of weeks. The
tactical singleness of purpose of the National Socialists and the tidal wave of
enthusiasm for the 'work of national unification', guided and intensified by
systematic stage management, developed a force which simply swept away all
plans for 'damming up' Hitler. To this force his conservative coalition partners
had no answer. Their amateurish efforts to join in the speeches and celebrations
and to take part themselves in directing the masses played into the hands of the
National Socialists. Hitler left no doubt that this was his promised hour, the hour
of his will and his power. Even the first signs of terrorism could not mute the
jubilation but rather added to it. The brutal behaviour with which the regime
celebrated its entry into office was widely seen as merely the expression of an
energy that was striving to manifest itself as much on the governmental plane as
in the street, and hence earned respect and even trust; for public feeling, perverted
by a mood of depression, valued even brutal activity higher than the state's past
inaction. Once again it was proved that in revolutionary times public opinion is
easily won over and perfidy, calculation and fear carry the day.

It was not only opportunism and lack of character, however, that lay behind the extraordinary reversals of political allegience during those turbulent weeks of spring, and the flood of desertions to the National Socialist camp from both left and right; often it was a secret desire, released as though at a cue, to throw old prejudices, ideologies and social barriers into the revolutionary fire and embark upon a new approach to a better form of state organisation. Mighty parties and associations rich in tradition collapsed, leaving only unmanoeuvrable debris even before they were forcibly dissolved. The old order was dead. The fast vanishing minority of those who did not succumb to the urge to embrace the new, which was spreading like an epidemic, found themselves isolated, hiding their bitterness, their lonely disgust, in the face of a defeat manifestly inflicted upon them 'by history itself'. Violence for opponents, and for supporters the great experience of a new sense of solidarity – these were the most striking features of this phase. Opponents were swept off the streets and into concentration camps, and then came demonstrations by hundreds of thousands with mass oaths under searchlight domes, addresses by the Führer, beacons and the Netherlands Prayer of Thanksgiving. Hitler, who once attributed all historical revolutions to the emergence of great popular speakers, also declared forthrightly that 'human solidarity was imposed on men by force and can be maintained only by the same means'.[2]

Nevertheless the strong-arm methods employed in the process of seizing power, which began immediately after January 30, should not be overestimated. There is a core of truth in the phrase, soon to become part of the basic rhetorical vocabulary, about the 'most bloodless revolution in world history'.[3] In fact, one of the chief features of this new type of revolution was that violence was directed largely against the mind. Murder and bloody outrages were seen as an indispensable but more or less auxiliary form of demonstration. The decisive effects were achieved by a cunning system of psychological violence, which on the one hand won support by the seductive notion of the 'National Awakening', and on the other, paralysed opposition by the concept of the 'legal revolution' which not merely restricted the use of terrorist methods but actually ruled them out on ideological grounds. Immediate success in gaining control of all the mass media created the technical preconditions for the imposition of a programme of thought and feeling that now disciplined the nation as a single unit. At its centre, in endless and at times grotesque variations, stood the theme of the Führer. The growing clamour of propaganda backed by all the resources of the state celebrated Hitler as the 'People's Chancellor', the 'national liberator', the 'renewer of the German blood', and presented him with tireless inventiveness as everything from the greatest of all Germans to the children's friend. He soon rose to almost mythical stature, and before the platforms which he mounted the artificially stimulated rutting cry of the masses rose more voraciously than ever. It was 'Hitler the great magician,'[4] far more than any event, person or group among his followers, who was responsible for the overwhelming level of the jubilation that quickly drowned the screams rising from the 'heroes' cellars' of the SA head-quarters. It was his combination of tactical skill with a sure grasp of the masses that within a year not only gave the NSDAP almost complete power but also roused the majority of the German people to a pitch of excitement that was a curious mixture of self-deception, idealism, fear, self-sacrifice and credulity, exuberantly celebrated as the 'miracle of Germany's emergence as a nation'.[5]

From his sense of personal victory Hitler then claimed the right to remould the state entirely according to his own judgment – which meant, according to the autocratic structure of the NSDAP leadership. In a revealing phrase, he once called the German people his 'instrument',[6] and this naked principle of subjection was stylised into a sworn bond between Führer and people. If National Socialism, apart from certain racial and expansionist fixations, ever did have a binding ideological or day-to-day political programme, this was finally abandoned in the course of seizing power and preserved only by a few eccentrics who were ridiculed or eliminated. The mass of former militants, many of them rewarded with benefices and offices, were steered onto the 'official' course, now quite openly aimed in the direction of Hitler's personal rule, and National Socialism revealed itself as what fundamentally it had always been: the ideological justification for its leader's will to power. 'The new Chancellor,' remarked a contemporary National Socialist essayist, 'entirely understandably from his point of view, has so far refused to present a detailed programme ("Party Member Number 1 doesn't answer," as the current Berlin joke has it).'[7] The public also saw in the events of those months the seizure of power not so much by the NSDAP or National Socialism as by Hitler himself. What held them captive, overwhelmed them, or swept them along with it was not the patchwork of National Socialist ideology, which had never been taken seriously and was an affront to common sense and every ethical principle, but the figure of this man; he was the ideology, the focal point of fluctuating expectations and the desire for self-surrender and subjection. It was from this popular reaction that the well-prepared transformation of National Socialism into Hitlerism received its real confirmation and the legitimation of its autocracy.[8]

Hitler's path to absolute power, which has since been variously imitated, remains in its several phases the classic model for the totalitarian capture of democratic institutions from within, that is to say with the assistance of, not in opposition to, the power of the state. Briefly, the technique consisted in the tactic of so linking the processes of revolutionary assault with legal actions that a screen of legality, dubious in individual cases and yet convincing as a whole, hid the illegality of the system from view. The concealed manner of the conquest of power, which took place behind the façade of old institutions deliberately preserved for that purpose, was the crucial feature and the one that had the gravest consequences. National Socialism adopted and perfected the practices of the Bolshevik and Fascist states, and developed its own version of the so-called 'period of struggle'. It was part of the plan that certain areas of public life were provisionally spared; thus, for example, civil law was initially allowed considerable independence. Islands on which the rule of law prevailed were left amid an ocean of lawlessness, reassuring preserves in which traditional ideas of order continued apparently undisputed, and this made it harder to assess the legality or illegality of the regime and decide whether to support or oppose it. In so far as the institutions and individuals responsible for constitutional integrity felt any concern at all over these acts on the boundaries of legality, and did not simply dismiss the partial encroachments with the crude formula that you can't make omelettes without breaking eggs, the almost universal reaction was one that only served to assist the National Socialists to gain power. Not a few people hoped by willing cooperation to prevent the 'worst excesses', the open transgression of legal bounds. They hoped to domesticate the revolutionary will, which Hitler was forever using as a bargaining counter and holding over their heads as a threat – above all as embodied in his brown-shirted stormtroopers. A smoke screen of nationalism fostered these illusions and persuaded the civil service, the army, the political parties and trade unions, and above all the simultaneously nationalist and law-abiding legal profession, to support precisely those totalitarian aims which some of them at least were trying to avert.

Furthermore, the public was confused not only by this brilliantly applied technique for concealing the facts but also by the breakneck speed at which, one after the other, opponents' positions were captured, leaving them no time to gather and regroup their in any case small and discouraged forces. Hitler later stated that it was his intention 'to seize power swiftly and at one blow'.[9] From the decree 'for the protection of the German People' of his first week as Chancellor,[10] the action against the Land of Prussia taken a few days later, and the so-called Reichstag Fire Decree, which established a permanent state of emergency, through the Enabling Law to the unparalleled decree declaring the murders carried out in connection with the Röhm affair* to have been legal – which concluded the process of seizing power – each step was a consequence of the one before, and created the factual, technical or legal preconditions for the next. It was precisely Ernst Röhm's lack of understanding of this concept of the gradual revolution carried out under the cloak of legality that led to his death and that of his followers. Naturally, Hitler's brutal action against Röhm lifted for one moment the carefully constructed backdrop and revealed what was going on offstage, where he and the rest of the leading actors of the 'legal revolution' were disclosed, without any disguise, in their unconditional determination to gain power. At the beginning of August 1934 Hitler had all the powers of the state in his hands before, in an act giving institutional status to the fact of his power, he followed Hindenburg as President of the Reich. 'For the next thousand years,' he proclaimed at Nuremberg, 'there will not be another revolution in Germany.'[11]

Hitler had reached his goal. In the 'years of construction' which followed he skilfully ran before the wind of the incipient world economic boom. With the instinct peculiar to him he sensed that the masses, and also the economy, were hungry for a forward thrust. And it was to his credit that he gave them what Brüning's government above all, excessively inhibited by its sense of responsibility, had failed to give. The decisiveness with which he was able to issue instructions

* See the chapter, 'Ernst Röhm and the Lost Generation'.

42

gave his policy an added effectiveness scarcely possible for democratic institutions, with their multiple control mechanisms. The large-scale stimulation of production not only rapidly reduced the number of unemployed, but also opened the way to considerable and effective activity in the socio-political field. The regime strove to temper the rigorous imposition of its ideas of order, as expressed in the compulsory regulation of tariffs or the establishment of a state trade union, by showing conciliation towards the workers. While the new holders of power did not carry out a single 'socialist' measure in their party programme, comprehensive welfare schemes served to organise the workers by means of holiday trips, sports festivals, factory celebrations, folk dancing, evening entertainments, and political education. At the same time, alongside the avowed aims of the 'Strength Through Joy' and 'Beauty of Labour' movements, these schemes performed the functions of control and pacification. The benefits to the individual scarcely concealed the true nature of these entertainments, which were merely compensations for a considerable deprivation of political rights. They reflected a contemptuous attitude towards the workers who, in Hitler's words, demanded nothing more than bread and circuses and had 'no understanding of any ideal'.[12] The intention to buy from the worker his right to social and political self-determination was always clear, however energetically these schemes were presented as manifestations of a sense of national community. Socialism in the Third Reich, according to Robert Ley's succinct phrase, was everything that served the interests of the German people; and since their interests were consistently identified by the National Socialist leaders with their own personal power aims, the rigid totalitarian permeation of every sphere of life was indeed 'socialism'. Moreover the regime's exceptional ability to spotlight its spectacular projects led to an overestimate of its successes. Any realistic judgment of this as of all other matters concerning Hitler's policies will also have to take account of the ruthlessness in the choice of means, as for example, that with regard to the policy for raising money, revealed by Hitler's cynical remark that 'no country has ever been ruined on account of its debts'.[13]

Finally, we must bear in mind the link between these achievements and the outbreak of war. Rearmament led to full employment, but the unrestrained expansion of production and credit was always linked with speculation on the future, the conquest of new *Lebensraum*, and was only feasible on this basis, if it was not to end in national economic disaster.[14] However, these implications were difficult to grasp at the time; moreover, few Germans, still shaken by the horrors of the economic crisis, were willing to reflect on these problems, and in 1937 and 1938 the popularity of Hitler and his government, reinforced by the success of their foreign policy, reached its zenith.

Nevertheless there was a dark side. There were persistent rumours about the concentration camps; and the defamation of minorities, the race cult, the policy towards the churches, the pressure on art and science, the arrogance of office holders and the sometimes intolerable over-organisation of individuals also caused unrest. This of course appeared solely in cautious expressions of discontent that had no practical effect. The widespread expectation that power and the compulsions inherent in it would have a moderating influence on Hitler proved illusory; he remained, despite all popular appearances, the most radical National Socialist, whose personal initiative was one – indeed the chief – source of the violent elements in the regime. But the astounding abilities which he had displayed during his rise to power were now supplemented by his capacity, used again and again with stimulating effect, to embody power now that he had it. In response to the needs and aims of the moment he could wield power threateningly or grandiosely, demonstrate it sombrely or intimidatingly, or from time to time jovially lighten the terror that regularly penetrated public consciousness – in high spirits among film actresses, eating stew at a field kitchen, at gala performances at Bayreuth, or as the simple man among children or old party militants. The principle of duplicity, which had always guided his tactics and given them their equivocal character, continued to set the pattern of his behaviour and that of his followers: barbed wire and steamer outings, 'mercy killings' and community get-togethers, dark cells and backslapping with the man in the street went hand in hand. But there was always one thing at stake: power, the ceaseless increase of which for its own sake alone was the obsession of his life.

Any demands of his office that did not offer opportunities for increasing his power were soon neglected. He had always hated the discipline of regular work; 'a single idea of genius is worth more than a whole lifetime of conscientious office work', he used to say.[15] It was only during the first month of his chancellorship that Hitler could be induced to take his duties seriously. Back came the old bohemian traits, the dependence upon emotions and the abrupt changes of mood. Irresolutely – according to unanimous witnesses – he frittered away his disorderly days by sudden changes of interest, putting off important decisions and pursuing others with disproportionate zeal. 'The efforts we are constantly trying to make,' wrote Goebbels in his characteristically Byzantine phraseology, 'have become in him a system of world-wide dimensions. His creative method is that of the authentic artist, no matter in what sphere he may operate.'[16] Meanwhile whole areas of the state's functions went to rack and ruin because of his lack of interest, while the uncertainty of the various institutions as to their jurisdiction – an uncertainty which was, of course, to some extent deliberately fostered – at times led to chaos. Energetic and vigorous as the state appeared from the activities of individuals in the foreground, on closer examination it proved muddled and disorganised. From 1937 onwards there were no meetings of the Reichsleiters or Gauleiters. Departmental ministers had for months and finally for years on end no opportunity to make their reports; and in his distaste for the pressure of duties inescapable in the capital – and also from a dislike for Berlin and the Berliners – Hitler withdrew more and more frequently to Munich or to his mountain retreat at Berchtesgaden.

He secured agreement for his measures from the yes-men immediately about him and from the masses. In addition to the manipulated plebiscites it was above all the storms of enthusiasm aroused by his rhetorical appearances that were held to demonstrate the agreement of the nation with the policy of the government. These he contrasted, as the expression of 'true' democracy, with democratic methods that had degenerated into formalism and liberalism. It has been calculated that in the course of his life Hitler spoke before almost 35 million people. At the party gatherings held every autumn he regularly delivered between fifteen and sixteen speeches, as dependent as an addict upon the opiate of communication with the masses and furious if he failed to receive the expected ovation.[17] It was entirely in character that at the same time he isolated himself and from 1938 onwards admitted people to his presence solely as a mark of favour.[18] He hated discussions; unaccustomed to contradiction and long since reduced to expressing himself only in monologues, he preferred the hoarse exaltations of the public platform to the stricter rules of private argument. On the occasion of Mussolini's state visit, after a meal Hitler addressed his anguished visitor uninterruptedly for an hour and a half, without giving him the opportunity, which he strenuously sought, to reply. Almost all his visitors or colleagues had similar experiences, especially during the war, when the restless man's flood of words grew ever more excessive. The generals of the Führer's headquarters found themselves forced to listen in helpless deference, fighting back sleep, night after night and mostly till early morning, to endless tirades on art, philosophy, race, technology or history. He always needed listeners, receivers, never interlocutors, and any occasional objection that might be raised merely incited him to further wildly proliferating digressions, without bounds, without order, and without end.

His impatience took increasingly violent forms. Even as a child, on his own admission, Hitler had once had a fainting fit when he 'failed to get the last word in an argument with his father'.[19] Now he had the power to get it all the time. After describing himself to the British journalist Ward Price as 'one of the most musical people in the world', he whistled a tune wrong. When a member of his entourage pointed this out he retorted, 'It's not I who am whistling it wrong, but the composer who made a blunder here.'[20] This episode, harmless in its infantility, contrasts with others where his claim to infallibility was linked with the 'argument' of vulgar force; he once challenged his lawyer Hans Frank to test the power of law against the power of his bayonet. Criticism he found intolerable; completely overlooking its constructive function, he saw in it only carping discontent and an outdated freedom which, he claimed, merely led people to behave 'like apes'.[21] His growing obstinacy and arrogance increased the void around him and made the expression of disagreement increasingly rare.

In his egocentricity Hitler naturally took this silence as a sign of dumbfounded admiration for the overwhelming grandeur of his visions and for his person. If the assertion of infallibility had originally been assumed for propaganda purposes, intended to gain him authority both in the party leadership and in the eyes of the masses, he now began to see himself wrapped in the aura of the Leader free from the weakness of human fallibility, his wishes consecrated by concurrence with the will of Providence itself. 'When I look back upon the five years that lie behind us,' he exclaimed during a speech in summer 1937, 'I can say, this was not the work of human hands alone!'[22] In order to live up to the dimensions of his self-portrait he forced himself into the mould of a monument, at the price of what self-mutilation one can only guess. 'Throughout his life there was something indescribably distant about him,' Ribbentrop noted later, and the observation that he had 'a horror of appearing ridiculous', is merely the reverse side of the same complex.[23] One of his secretaries reports that he always scrupulously avoided being surprised playing with one of his dogs; the moment he knew he was being watched 'he roughly drove the dog away'. When his personal photographer Heinrich Hoffmann photographed him playing with Eva Braun's terrier, Hitler remarked, 'You mustn't publish this snap, Hoffmann. A statesman does not permit himself to be photographed with a little dog. A German sheepdog is the only dog worthy of a real man.'[24] It was just this fear of showing himself without the pose of statesmanlike monumentality that made him so impersonal, so inhuman. Journalists and others often asked for information about his personal life; this was always refused. He never laughed without holding his hand across his face, apparently for fear of showing any natural human reaction. He tried to persuade Göring to give up smoking, using the highly revealing argument that as a monument one could not be portrayed 'with a cigar in one's mouth'.[25]

The state, over which he held absolute power, quickly took the shape of his own personality in countless respects: the naked dependence on power in relationships with people and things, coupled with a growing deterioration in all fields not connected with power; the boastful brutality of public manifestations of his will; the degradation of law; the theatrical and grandeur-seeking coldness which characterised all public announcements and all buildings representative of the state; the rigid constraint, followed from time to time by sudden discharges of energy; and finally the lack of relaxation and self-control. The special German form that all this took was not so much the expression of characteristics inherent in totalitarian systems as such as the faithful reflection of the mind of a psychopath in the institutions of state and society.

Within this larger pattern the widely canvassed view that Hitler gradually turned towards evil – which figures so prominently in the attempts at self-justification made especially by his accomplices from the conservative camp – becomes untenable. The popular version of the same argument, according to which the National Socialist state, with a few reservations, proved itself competent, effective and devoted to the public good, is also quickly shown to be an illusion. In this argument the war is presented as an avoidable deviation, and the extermination of the Jews, for example, as the inexorable consequence of an extremism that arose out of the bitterness caused by the 1939 war. But the will to force, the extremism, indeed the war itself, were from the very beginning rooted alike in the convictions of the rulers and in the nature of the regime; they were inseparable from its energetic measures for creating 'order'. We need not even look at the brutal incidents of its exercise of power – the murders, the 1935 Nuremberg

46

[margin handwritten note: he was afraid to show any human emotion]

Laws against the Jews, or the growing number of concentration camps – to realise what the hectic policies and the continual striving for fresh goals make clear. Action, an unruly, turbulent dynamism that shook off all restraint, was among its characteristics and was bound to lead to aggression abroad as soon as there was no internal resistance left to overcome. The conditions which helped the system to success were the very conditions which caused its excesses, its acts of injustice, and finally its collapse.

This has recently been demonstrated by study of the Third Reich's economic policy. The economic upsurge, in so far as it was attributable not to the world economic boom but to the programme outlined in Hitler's memorandum for the Four-Year Plan, was mainly a false flowering achieved by destructive exploitation. True, it produced a considerable concentration of forces, but it brought the regime 'into a continually more acute state of emergency from which in the end war offered the only means of escape, if the National Socialist leaders were not prepared to sacrifice their ideological postulates to a realistic attitude to foreign policy'.[26] Hitler himself later put this succinctly during one of the table talks at his headquarters. 'Particularly in the case of this war,' he explained to his hearers, 'one must never forget that if we lose it, we lose everything. There can therefore be but one slogan: Victory! If we win, the billions we have spent will weigh nothing in the scales.'[27]

The overstraining of the economy was simply one sign of the inescapable interrelation between 'success' and injustice in the National Socialist system; it was only one of the elements pushing the country towards war. In the centre there still stood the few primitive principles on which Hitler based his conception of human social life: life is struggle, the stronger kills the weaker, morality is stupidity or decadence. In his own words: 'The duel between intellect and strength will always be decided to the advantage of strength'; 'He who has, has'; 'Cruelty impresses'; or 'Everlasting peace will come to the world when the last man has slain the last but one.'[28]

Translated from the context of a general judgment of man and the world into that of concrete political policy, this becomes, for example:

I shall give a propagandist reason for starting the war, no matter whether it is plausible or not. The victor will not be asked afterwards whether he told the truth or not. When starting and waging war it is not right that matters, but victory.

Close your hearts to pity. Act brutally. Eighty million people must obtain what is their right. Their existence must be made secure. The strongest man is right. The greatest harshness.[29]

Hitler made this declaration to his military commanders a few days before the outbreak of war, when the pact with the Soviet Union had placed Poland 'where I wanted it'. The right of the 'biologically valuable' nation to subjugate, suppress and exterminate 'inferior' races seemed to him incontestable, and quite apart from his contempt for 'negrified' France or his later disparagement of 'degenerate' Britain, he always took for granted this assessment of the relative values of the

47

German nation and its neighbours to the east. His concept of nationalism – which always had an imperialist tinge – always directed the thrust towards the East. 'We shall put an end to the perpetual Germanic march to the south and west of Europe,' he writes in the famous passage in *Mein Kampf*, 'and turn our eyes towards the lands of the East. We shall finally put a stop to the colonial and trade policy of prewar times and pass over to the territorial policy of the future.'[30] The conquest of new *Lebensraum* in the 'heartland of the world', alongside the first-stage aim of wiping out the Treaty of Versailles, was the constant goal of Hitler's foreign policy, concealed at times for tactical reasons but never abandoned. On November 5, 1937, when he first disclosed his aggressive plans to a small group of top leaders, he described this conception as his legacy to the nation, in case he should die before it was realised.[31]

The idea of an early death, combined with the idea of his personal irreplaceability, perturbed him continually from this time on. This is indicated in numerous declarations referring to the need for rapid action, and swift and sudden actions that have been interpreted as springing from cold-blooded calculation were in reality also an expression of the disquiet that sprang from his premonitions of death. He stated in a speech at the end of 1937:

According to human calculations he, Hitler, had not very much longer to live. In his family people did not live to a great age. Both his parents had also died young.

Hence the problems that had to be solved (*Lebensraum!*) must be solved as soon as possible, so that the task could be done during his lifetime. Later generations would no longer be able to do this. Only he personally was capable of it.

After severe inner struggles he had freed himself from childhood religious ideas which he had continued to harbour. 'Now I feel as fresh as a foal in the meadow.'[32]

Naturally his astounding series of successes in foreign policy changed his original timetable. On November 5, 1937, he had named the years 1943–45 as the most favourable for the attack; but in fact he resolved upon war as early as 1938. In foreign policy he repeated his tactics for the conquest of internal power. By regularly linking acts of aggression with assurances of peaceful intentions and brilliantly exploiting the widespread tendency to self-deluding passivity, he continually duped and paralysed his opponents. Before their partly horrified, partly helpless eyes, clouded by the same unchanging illusions and self-reassurance, he succeeded in everything he undertook, from the withdrawal from the League of Nations in October 1933 through the introduction of universal military service and the occupation of the Rhineland to Vienna, Munich and Prague. His success was due to luck, calculation and a readiness to risk everything which enabled him to stake all on even limited individual goals, and made him not only 'Europe's greatest actor', as he called himself with cynical pride,[33] but also its greatest gambler. Unlike his opponents, who believed themselves to be at peace, he considered himself permanently at war and knew pretty clearly what he wanted, whereas they only knew what they did not want: war.[34]

'Seized by the intoxication of success,'[35] he trod dizzy heights. In 1938, at the mystical collective intoxication of the Nuremberg Party Rally, the personality cult approached pure idolatry. Robert Ley described him as the only human being who had never made a mistake; Hans Frank called him lonely like everything strong in the world, like God himself; and an SS Gruppenführer Schulz from Pomerania asserted that he was greater than Jesus Christ, for the latter had had twelve disloyal disciples, while the Führer stood at the head of a nation of seventy million sworn to loyalty.[36] In spite of occasional ironic asides, Hitler accepted the utterances of the cult that was springing up around his person in the growing certainty of his superhumanity and at times himself lapsed into an exalted, hymnlike tone that was a travesty of religious phraseology:

How could we not feel once again at this hour the miracle that brought us together! [he cried in a 1936 speech to political leaders]. You once heard the voice of a man, and it struck your hearts, it awakened you and you followed this voice. You followed it for years, without even having seen the owner of the voice; you merely heard a voice and followed it.

When we meet here we are all filled by the miraculous quality of this meeting. Not every one of you sees me, and I do not see every one of you. But I feel you, and you feel me! It is the faith in our nation that has made us small people great, that has made us poor people rich, that has made us vacillating, despondent, frightened people brave and determined; that has given us blind wanderers sight and brought us together!

So you come from your little villages, your market towns, your cities, from mines and factories, away from the plough on one day to this city. You come from the narrow environment of the struggle of your daily lives and your struggle for Germany and for our nation in order to have the feeling: 'Now we are together, we are with him and he is with us, and now we are Germany! It is a wonderful thing for me to be your Führer.[37]

And at about the same time as his 'intuition' had once more proved itself, contrary to the ideas of the experts, in a crisis of foreign affairs, he asserted, 'I go the way that Providence dictates with the assurance of a sleepwalker.'[38]

Now, however, this assurance began to forsake him. Alan Bullock has rightly pointed out that Hitler was favoured by success only so long as he used the belief in his infallibility as an instrument of his policy, but that his destiny changed when, blinded by the effortlessness of his victories, he began to believe in it himself and to take deification seriously: 'No man was ever more surely destroyed by the image he had created than Adolf Hitler.'[39] Pampered, puffed up with his good fortune, he began to underrate his opponents, to set before them, more and more arrogantly, dishonourable alternatives, to blackmail them in ever swifter sequence, and finally pointblank to provoke military involvement. He declared to the dumbfounded British Premier Neville Chamberlain at Berchtesgaden in 1938 that he 'didn't care whether there was a war or not', and after the Munich Conference he complained, 'That fellow Chamberlain has spoilt my entry into Prague' – by his willingness to compromise,[40] although the war that Hitler wanted[41] had not been adequately prepared for politically, psychologically or militarily. In spite of the massive efforts of the controlled press, the people were not ready to 'call for force', as Hitler had demanded of the chief editors of the national press in his speech of November 1938.[42] When on the afternoon of September 27 the same year, at the height of the Sudeten crisis in Czechoslovakia, a motorised division passed through the streets of Berlin in marching order, the people looked on in profound silence before turning away. 'I can't wage war with this nation yet,' Hitler is said to have exclaimed angrily.[43]

But he was determined to 'compel the German people, who are hesitating before their destiny, to walk the road to greatness'.[44] Peace, which in September 1938 had once more been preserved, a year later had no chance left. For in the meantime the world felt itself challenged to the limit by the so-called Crystal Night (on which windows of Jewish shops were smashed throughout Germany) and the swallowing up of Czechoslovakia, by the spectacle of Hitler's tearing up the Munich Agreement before the ink was dry. As though intoxicated, alternately pursuing his actions and being dragged along by them, seeking refuge in rhetorical delirium before the masses and with his judgment clouded by emotional exaltation, Hitler diligently arranged the preconditions for the catastrophe. 'Our opponents are little worms,' he scoffed. 'I saw them in Munich.' And he refused to believe they would take risks. When, at the end of August 1939, Göring tried to halt his insane behaviour and asked him to abandon his desperate gamble, Hitler replied excitedly that he had gambled desperately all his life.[45]

At this period, at the latest, it became evident that in sheer personal calibre he fell far short of the demands of the power he exercised and that he had gained nothing in the way of real knowledge, but simply increased his skill in the techniques of power and the overcoming of opposition. Despite all the tactical adroitness and cold-blooded superiority to which he owed his momentary triumphs, he remained the prisoner of his past with its prejudices and provincial limitations; although a statesman of Machiavellian cast, he was no more than a beer-cellar agitator of demonic proportions, who discounted all moral evaluation and saw the harassing problems that had been placed in his hands in the hazy perspective of the Munich local politician. So he continually compared the war with his struggle for power in Germany and tried to deduce certainty of victory from the processes of history. But this war was a disastrous departure from the recipe for tactical success which he had followed in the past. Fundamentally, he repeated in autumn 1939 the very mistake he had made in November 1923. With so much in his favour, he could probably have got most of what he wanted by that tactic of semi-'legality', of pursuing individual goals stubbornly and by more than one route, of fraudulent assurances, which had served him so extraordinarily well in his domestic policy and so far in his foreign policy too. Now he forsook this way, out of arrogance and impatience, corrupted by the success of the politician grown great in protest and accustomed to making 'indispensable demands', but deceived by his own foolish and trite platitudes. He reverted to the 'putschist solution' that had failed once already. 'Only he who lives dangerously lives fully,' he used to quote from Nietzsche, adding on one occasion, 'He wrote that for me.'[46]

Years before he had said in one of his bloody and misanthropic prophecies to Hermann Rauschning:

We must be prepared for the hardest struggle that a nation has ever had to face. Only through this test of endurance can we become ripe for the dominion to which we are called. It will be my duty to carry on this war regardless of losses. The sacrifice of lives will be immense. We all of us know what world war means. As a people we shall be forged to the hardness of steel. All that is weakly will fall away from us. But the forged central block will last forever. I have no fear of annihilation. We shall have to abandon much that is dear to us and today seems irreplaceable. Cities will become heaps of ruins; noble monuments of architecture will disappear forever. This time our sacred soil will not be spared. But I am not afraid of this.[47]

In these few sentences lies the epitaph of almost fifty million people.

5 Victor and Vanquished

In my will it will one day be written that nothing is to be engraved on my tombstone but 'Adolf Hitler'. I shall create my own title for myself in my name itself.

Adolf Hitler

And in the last analysis, success is what matters.

Adolf Hitler

At 4.45 on the morning of September 1, 1939, the German battleship 'Schleswig-Holstein' opened fire on the Westerplatte, the fortress on the Gulf of Danzig. At the same time, troops rose from their positions all along the German-Polish border, while squadrons of bombers flew over them in grey swarms towards the east. He was afraid, Hitler had told his commanders eight days earlier, that 'some dirty dog will present me with a mediation plan at the last moment'; now he was free of his fears. War had begun.[1]

In the streets of Berlin and the other German cities, however, there was neither jubilation nor that mass intoxication of men lusting for death so dear to totalitarian manipulators of the popular mood. In the depression which marked the outbreak of this war, people went about their business quietly, in dull resignation,[2] and lined the street only thinly when Hitler drove to the Kroll Opera House soon after 10 o'clock to explain his decision in a speech to the Reichstag. He seemed nervous and ill-assured; vacillating between forced arrogance and desperate attempts to justify himself, he heaped reproaches on Poland and solemnly stated that he had no quarrel with the West, but rather a desire to reach an understanding. Towards the end he stressed that he would not take off his soldier's coat until victory had been secured, or he would not survive the outcome. 'I therefore want to assure the whole world: there will never be another November 1918 in German history.'[3] Two days later, when the declarations of war by Britain and France had reached him, he went to the front.

To the last he had vaguely hoped the Western powers would not honour their guarantee to Poland. Wrongly advised, but also the victim of his own crude Machiavellianism, he could not believe that a world power would fulfil an agreement without the prospect of concrete gain, merely to keep its word, to maintain its honour, and because its patience had reached breaking point. He had never bothered to test this. For the first time, three days after fighting began, his contempt for reality, his renunciation of diplomatic methods, and his trust in his own intuition, to which he deferred all the more stubbornly the more it deceived him, now avenged themselves on him.

This lack of psychological and political planning went hand in hand with inadequate economic and military preparation. In fact, war had been launched, in a striking example of the Hitlerian policy of risk, not least in order to create the economic and military conditions necessary for its pursuance. But many of the preparations had not gone beyond the earliest stages. Of the planned four months' stockpile of armaments and reserves of all kinds, for example, on an average only 25 per cent was in existence.[4] Although Hitler had assured the Reichstag in his speech on September 1 that he had spent ninety thousand million marks in six years on building up the Wehrmacht, too much had been done under pressure of time, too much left to improvisation. There was too little of the methodical seriousness required in the face of Germany's provocation of almost the whole world, the implications of which had evidently never been fully appreciated. Nor had the various alternative contingencies been thought out: the possible battle-fronts, the course of the fighting and the measures to be adopted. The then Chief of Staff, General Halder, commented angrily, 'Incredible as it may sound, Hitler did not even have a general plan for the war.'[5] Torn this way and that between choleric elation and exhaustion, Hitler lashed out savagely in all directions, threw his armies over ever new frontiers, ceaselessly conquering fresh territories, none of which was large enough to satisfy his egomania. Anyone probing the root cause of the war and the manner of waging it is continually led back to considerations of Hitler's character; for, much as the war looks like a predatory excursion necessitated by the Third Reich's ruinous economic policy, great as was the influence of outdated nationalist, ideological or missionary motives, it was the purely hegemonic aims that overlay all others. The urge to dominate Europe, and ultimately the world, although backed by ideological and racial arguments, was at bottom nothing more nor less than the desire to exercise sovereignty. 'The question,' Hitler himself once laconically put it, 'is not the fate of National Socialist Germany, but who is to dominate Europe in the future.'[6] Only in this light can we understand the orgy of expansionism, at first sight as senseless as it is impressive, which placed Hitler's flag on the General Staff maps from the Volga to the Atlantic, from the North Cape to the Nile, with no economy of forces. 'The foreign policy of the national bourgeois world has in truth always been a border policy; as against that, the policy of the National Socialist movement will always be a territorial one,' Hitler had written in 1928 in an essay on foreign policy.[7] In this and similar formulas he proclaimed his restless will to power, which knew neither halt nor satisfaction. After the consolidation of his internal power, it broke out in an extravagant hunger for space and, guided by his vulgarised Darwinist axioms, sought new goals, new confirmations and aggrandisements of itself. 'I have to choose between victory and destruction. I choose victory.'[8]

The first phase of the war consisted of a series of breathtaking lightning campaigns which, from a professional military point of view, were undoubtedly remarkable achievements. Poland, whose military men in vainglorious illusion had seen themselves already in Berlin, was overrun in nineteen days; Denmark and Norway in two months; Holland, Belgium, Luxembourg and France in six weeks; Yugoslavia, Greece, the island of Crete in about the same time; and finally Cyrenaica, after being lost by Germany's greedy but feeble Italian allies, was recovered in nine days. Once it had been discovered, the recipe for success remained almost unvaried, based chiefly on the advance of massed tanks straight through the enemy lines, followed by a pincer movement and encirclement. The German superiority lay less in a preponderance of men or materials than in unswerving application of the principle of the rapid mobile operation which, combined with sudden air attacks and commando and paratroop assaults behind the front, had the effect not so much of 'defeating' the enemy in the classical sense as of so confusing him that he became incapable of fighting and ready to capitulate.

The so-called 'scythe cut' strategy was so strikingly successful, especially in the West, that Hitler became intoxicated by the possibilities it opened up and took more and more part in the military conduct of the war. His unbridled self-confidence swelled still further on the strength of his not inconsiderable share in the development of this strategy, so that he soon came to regard every victory as solely the result of his personal inspiration, wealth of ideas and brilliance as a general. Every fresh success distorted his vision still further, till finally he felt himself infinitely superior to the despised generals. 'This little affair of operational command is something that anybody can do,' he said after dismissing Brauchitsch and taking over command of the Army,[9] while Goebbels extolled him more and more extravagantly as the 'greatest general of all time'.

At the same time few would deny that he possessed certain military qualifications which were only strengthened by his autodidact's freedom from preconceptions.[10] In addition to his feeling for the potentialities of modern warfare – it was Hitler, for example, who instigated the creation of motorised and armoured units – he had an exceptional ability to see into the mind of his enemy, well proved in well calculated surprise attacks, in his accurate prediction of tactical countermeasures, and in his lightning seizure of opportunities. These qualities were offset by his failure to distinguish between the possible and the impossible, his at first grandiose and later hysterical contempt for facts, and his inability to reconcile large-scale plans conceived in a flash with concrete situations and requirements. Admittedly, he had his staff to cope with the detailed work, which remained alien to him to the last; but both his nature, in which a superior during the First World War had recognised the characteristics of a 'completely intolerable faultfinder, know-all and grumbler',[11] and his complex-ridden attitude towards the officer class, which was never free from the resentment of the man risen from the ranks and the former Munich putschist, made any calm collaboration based on objective principles impossible. 'He wanted believers, who obeyed without asking

54

questions. Independent minds were anathema to him,' commented one of his former colleagues. When the war took a turn for the worse, he began, in apparently pathological outbursts of emotion, to reprimand his generals, to dismiss them, recall them, and then repudiate them again. This moodiness and lack of self-control introduced a destructive element of unrest into all operations and, just as much as his excessive distrust, disqualified him for any sort of generalship. In the end he fell back on stubborn poses.[12]

The disaster already foreshadowed in such behaviour was accelerated by a growing lack of flexibility and tactical mobility. His supreme adaptability to changing situations, unhampered by any programme, in which the believing minority of his fellow-fighters of the past had seen so much treachery and betrayal, gave place to a rigidity compounded of arrogance and ideological fanaticism. Under the influence of his initial success, he abandoned the well-tried principle of pursuing two lines at the same time, which had so often confused his opponents, rendered him unassailable and smoothed his way, in favour of a policy of overbearing directness that was nothing but the total renunciation of political means. This trait was already discernible in the clearly fraudulent 'appeal to reason' – the peace offer to Britain after the conclusion of the campaign in the West – and it was further provocatively displayed in his treatment of the occupied countries. Not merely incapable of generosity, but also scorning all counsels of wisdom in his conviction of invincibility he knew only the one unchanging precept of 'grab and hold'. True, his decisions were no longer free; just as his economic policy had forced him into war, so now, in the face of the increasing strain on Germany's economic resources, he was forced to adopt a policy of exploitation which in turn continually reduced the area of his freedom of decision. Nevertheless, it would have been possible to prevent every increase in the area of his power from necessarily enlarging the circle of his enemies, but for his arrogance and deliberate advocacy of the policy of force. For a time the idea of the 'European nation', intentionally kept vague, came to the fore, the only attempt that he made to drape crude and stupid suppression with an ideological cloak of partnership. But in view of the terrorist practices provocatively aimed at demonstrating German superiority, the idea of a Greater German Reich, which in any case seemed fantastic, found no lasting response among the Belgians, the French, the Baltic peoples or the Ukrainians.[13]

The National Socialist plan for power, ordered and continually reinforced by Hitler himself, was seen at its most revolting in those regions of Poland incorporated into the Reich, where that biological 'cleansing' of all alien 'trash' and ensuing Germanisation which Hitler, in his indescribably vulgar language, had also announced for the so-called Old Reich, was already in full swing.[14] The administration of these provinces derived its barbaric character (in spite of the function of routine and sometimes in opposition to it) from rival groups of torturers and dreamers, murderers and stock-breeders of human beings. They became the 'new ground not merely for national and territorial expansion', but also for 'National Socialist self-realisation'.[15] It was not a case of the degeneration of earlier ideal programmes, as Alfred Rosenberg and Hans Frank were to complain in their cells at Nuremberg, but of their systematic fulfilment.

The idea of territorial conquest in the East, of the 'great Germanic march', remained the imperial leitmotiv in Hitler's life, and he turned to it as a saving solution in his indecision as to the further conduct of the war after the victorious conclusions of the campaign in the West; for in the meantime the lack of concrete aims that gave this war so largely the character of a blind dynamic aggression, had turned a series of impressive military successes into a series of useless victories. Britain's power remained unbroken, and among the motives for the renewed assault on the East quickly worked out by Hitler, with his capacity for finding plausible justifications for his impulsive decisions, was the idea that the destruction of Russia would mean the destruction of Britain's last hope of continuing the war with any prospect of success. We gain some idea of the extent to which Hitler overestimated his own abilities from the fact that, after the defeat of Russia, he planned to shatter the foundations of the British Empire by a vast three-pronged attack via North Africa, the Balkans and the Caucasus, and as early as 1941 gave the Wehrmacht General Staff the order to prepare plans for an invasion of India through Afghanistan.[16] Equally important to his decision to attack Russia was the conviction, never entirely concealed, of the inevitability of the 'final conflict with Bolshevism'. Cynically suppressed after the conclusion of the Moscow Pact, it was now revived as Hitler found himself increasingly entangled in his own ideology. One must 'never conduct more than *one* struggle at a time', he had once stated. 'One struggle after the other; really the proverb ought not to be "Many enemies, much honour" but "Many enemies, much stupidity." ' If he had boasted after the pact with Russia that he had saved Germany from the danger of a war on two fronts, he now wrote to Mussolini that his partnership with the Soviet Union had always been irksome to him: 'I am happy now to be delivered from this torment.'[17]

Not least of the calculations behind his decision had been the idea that he could bring Russia to her knees in the course of one summer. At a meeting of Gauleiters beforehand he assured his audience, with the grandiose air of the man spoilt by successive victories, that he would be in Leningrad within three weeks,[18] and the image of the Russian bear that was already dead but refused to lie down became, after the initial swift successes, a popular metaphor inspiring confidence. Only the premature winter halted the German advance. In the unparalleled catastrophe caused by the cold during the ensuing months, for which, significantly, the troops were totally unprepared, the veil of arrogant certainty seemed suddenly to tear and Hitler appeared for the first time to grasp the possibility of defeat. Between wild orders to hold on, which actually did lead to the stabilisation of the front, he exclaimed in desperation that the mere sight of snow caused him physical pain. He made a 'shattering impression' on Goebbels, who visited him at his headquarters; Goebbels found him 'greatly aged' and did not remember ever having seen him 'so grave and so withdrawn'.[19] In the gloomy mood of that winter he first made the remark that cropped up again at the end of his career:

he was left 'ice-cold. If the German people were no longer inclined to give them-selves body and soul in order to survive – then the German people would have nothing to do but disappear!'[20]

When spring set the frozen German advance in motion again, Hitler was seized with exaltation once more and at times actually complained that destiny had given him only second-rate opponents to wage war upon. 'The habit of underestimating the potentialities of the enemy, which he had always had,' the then Chief of the General Staff, General Halder, noted in his diary on July 23, 1942, 'is gradually assuming grotesque proportions. There can be no further talk of serious work. This so-called "leadership" is marked by pathological reactions to momentary impressions and a complete inability to judge the possibilities open to the High Command.'[21] In Hitler's unrestrained overestimation of his own capacities one of the essential causes of the defeat that could already be discerned in the midst of victory became increasingly apparent. It led him, especially in the southern section of the front, not only to disperse his forces, against all the principles of strategy, but also to renounce any policy for gaining the approbation and collaboration of the Russian peoples. He countered all attempts – by no means all hopeless – to stir up latent hostility to the Bolshevik regime by the preservation of certain autonomies or more humane treatment, with empty phrases drawn from his *Herrenvolk* ideology and his deep-rooted belief in the power of brutality. 'The idea of treating wars as anything other than the harshest means of settling questions of very existence,' he once said, 'is ridiculous. Every war costs blood, and the smell of blood arouses in man all the instincts which have lain within us since the beginning of the world: deeds of violence, the intoxication of murder, and many other things. Everything else is empty babble. A humane war exists only in bloodless brains.'[22] In such maxims the primitive fascination of a consciousness stuck fast in its own formative period survives in crude analogies of the right of the stronger. Their effect was to ensure approval in the highest quarters for the policy of suppression now being practised with increasing savagery. They also lent support to demands for the ruthless use of the German forces themselves. When the loss of young officers was pointed out to Hitler, he replied uncomprehendingly, 'But that's what the young men are there for!'[23]

Hitler's attitude, attaching no value to human life except as an instrument for the satisfaction of his own ambition for power, was one of the reasons for the exceptionally heavy losses in the defeat that symbolised the turning point in the war – and in his own life – Stalingrad. Since 1919 when, as a returning soldier with no trade, he had embarked upon his ambitious career, destiny had led him higher and higher. The greater initiative, the more reckless courage, and finally luck, had always been on his side: he had won first the party, then Germany, and finally almost the whole of Europe. Now all of these deserted him at the same time and he had to pay with an unparalleled disaster for demands that had again and again been pushed to the extreme limit, to victory or disaster, but had at last been pushed too far.

He no longer seemed to succeed in anything, although – or because – with growing impatience he took over more and more and even involved himself in tactical details. 'Everything is as though under a spell,' he complained in exasperation.[24] And while his foes, who since the active intervention of the United States had over 75 per cent of the world's manpower, industrial capacity and sources of raw materials at their disposal, overran the outer bastions of his empire – North Africa, Sicily and the Ukraine – gained mastery of the air, and forced the collapse of the German U-boat campaign, Hitler buried himself in the solitude of his headquarters. There in almost manic impersonality, with security zones, barbed-wire and lines of outposts which on both Jodl and Goebbels produced the impression of a concentration camp, an embittered man, visibly deteriorating physically and in his own words tortured by melancholy,[25] ever more deeply entangled in the hatreds and complexes of his early years, organised between attacks of convulsive screaming and pathological rage the continued prosecution of the war and the frenzied murder of whole peoples.

It was the old outbreak into total anathema, the old unbridled reactions of the unsuccessful art student to all resistance from outside, only now horrifyingly translated from the impotent attitudes of puberty into reality. And just as nothing but technical reports came to break the monotonous austerity of his days, so he himself began to avoid public life. As soon as the war began, he moved into the background, and all propaganda efforts to exploit his withdrawal for the construction of a myth could not fill the place of that old feeling of his omnipresence, with the help of which the regime had released a latent superabundance of energy, spontaneity and readiness for self-sacrifice. Hitler appeared in public more and more rarely; after Stalingrad, only twice more. Faith in the power of oratory to sweep all before it had reached its limit in the face of a hostile world closed to all attempts to shake its resolution with words, even though Goebbels once noted in his diary that after a speech by the Führer the English had 'become decidedly more modest'.[26] And if consciousness of his own lack of assurance was one of the reasons why Hitler shunned the platform, the result was to intensify it. He had often enough pointed to the increase in self-confidence which he derived from communication with the masses. Now he lost himself more and more in wild and yearning fantasies, which he spoke of to those immediately around him: the rebuilding of Berlin as the world capital Germania, the establishment of a museum for his favourite painters, Makart and Defregger, whose works he passionately collected, or the development of his 'home town', Linz, into the cultural metropolis of the Danube region, which was to receive a university and become a centre at which the 'three cosmologies of Ptolemy, Copernicus and Hörbiger (glacial theory)' – would be taught.[27]

During strategic conferences Hitler's overwrought nerves sought release in explosive outbursts of rage, often with little cause. His unstable moods, which reduced to chaos all the work of conducting the war, vacillated between stubborn resolution and disdainful resignation. Repeatedly he was seized with a self-pitying longing for death. 'It is only a fraction of a second and then one is freed from everything and has one's quiet and eternal peace,' he said.[28] As early as spring 1943 Goebbels noted with concern Hitler's growing inability to make decisions as well as his mistaken way of treating people, and observed that 'the Führer now uses the phrase "When this war is over at last!" with increasing frequency'.[29] About the same time Rommel heard him say that the war could scarcely be won now, but that none of the other powers would make peace with him. Now he would wage war to the end. But in the alternating hot and cold of Hitler's emotions despair again and again yielded to fresh confidence. When summer brought partial military successes, the Foreign Minister suggested peace feelers to Moscow. He was told: 'You know, Ribbentrop, if I come to terms with Russia today I shall only attack her again tomorrow – I simply can't help it.'[30]

Hitler was now completely buried in the mad world of his system of underground bunkers. It was 'tragic', noted Goebbels.[31] From the bearing of those around him, a mingling of fanatical believers and men without character, who moreover had strict orders to take an optimistic view of the situation, he built for himself an unfounded and illusory certainty of victory. But it was this ability to despise and ignore reality which alone enabled him to continue the struggle. Even before the war he had forbidden 'warning memoranda'; now he regarded all sober assessments of the situation as a 'personal insult'.[32] When Halder told him that the Russians were producing six or seven hundred tanks a month, Hitler thumped the table and said it was impossible, 'The Russians are dead.'[33]

He showed the same contempt for facts in his catastrophic inability to organise a retreat. The mere thought of it was repulsive to him, and all factual considerations were blocked by the rigid and unvarying formula that the troops were to stand firm 'to the last man'. His much-vaunted talents as a general were now seen to apply, at best, to offensive situations. To the last, with empty hands and caught in his own world of ghosts, he kept on planning new offensives. The prospect of defence showed up all the failings of this man who had always prided himself on his 'iron will' and scorned readiness to yield as weakness. 'The successful offensive strategist was devoid of ideas on the defensive,' wrote one of his closest colleagues, 'talentless to the point of disaster.'[34]

Disaster came inexorably closer. Since the Allied landing in Normandy the Reich had been fighting on three fronts, and with the increasing activity of the partisans of resistance movements, it was soon fighting on all fronts simultaneously. Germany was being squeezed in from all sides and pressed from above by almost continuous air attacks. A chain reaction was set up. The loss of sources of raw materials reduced production and shortened the life of the weapons already in use; this in turn contributed to further territorial losses, which then enabled the enemy to move his air bases even closer to the Reich itself. Even if the effects of the air war, as recent investigations have disclosed, were far below expectations and neither critically reduced the country's economic potential nor broke the nerve of the people, they nevertheless helped to foster a sceptical attitude towards the outcome of the war. To be sure, one side of the German character

59

remained effective: credulous subordination amounting to self-abandonment, as well as an almost pathological devotion to discipline, stimulated with absolute calculation by National Socialist propaganda. But it was now the fatalistic obedience of a majority who, though incapable of revolt, were not willing to follow the regime any further along its chosen path. After the elation, mingled with disquiet, of the victorious phase, people now began to shut their ears to the calls to hold firm and the fulsome phrases of the propagandists and to prepare themselves for defeat. 'The yearning for peace, widespread among Germans, is also to be discerned elsewhere. Everyone is human.'[35] By contrast, there reigned in the magically distorted atmosphere of the Führer's headquarters an absurd certainty of victory, kept alive by Hitler with renewed exhortations and threats. He actually drew encouragement from the attempt of the conspirators of July 20, 1944, to save the honour of their country and establish a basis for its continued existence before total disaster supervened. Hitler attributed the failure of the attempt on his life to the will of Providence and inferred that he was chosen by Providence to bring the war to a victorious conclusion.

In the growing confusion produced by contradictory orders from the Führer, the last elements of the defensive system broke down. Soon after the unsuccessful Ardennes offensive, which had come to grief in a thousand incompetencies, Hitler returned to Berlin, to the bunker under the Reich Chancellery. Here, protected by twenty-six feet of concrete as much from reality as from enemy bombs, to the accompaniment of attacks of rage, senseless orders to attack, and convulsive weeping, he once more constructed his world of delusions, which included miracle weapons, ultimate victory, and great buildings to go up after the war. His body ruined by drugs, at the mercy of the storms of his temperament, and tortured by distrust, he looked by all accounts like a figure from the kingdom of the shades.[36] He gestured wildly over maps, planned attacks, directed with a trembling hand armies that no longer existed, and as encirclement began described to his entourage the joy of the battle before the gates of Berlin which was going to decide the war. During the night-long brooding monologues, which reflected both the final stage of his intellectual decay and his bitterness at the 'cowardly failure' of the German people, he spoke 'almost exclusively of the training of dogs, questions of diet, and the stupidity and wickedness of the world'.[37] Almost daily he took counsel from the horoscopes of an astrologer, and while the attacking Russian armies were already clashing with the hastily assembled remnants of the shattered German forces, fantastic hopes flickered again from the conjunction of planets, ascendants and transits in the square. Only when the ring had closed around the government district, and he ruled over nothing but a few million cubic yards of rubble, did he begin to give in.

On the night of April 29, after he had begun the process of ending his exist-ence with a scene of macabre pedantry and married his companion of many years, Eva Braun, he dictated his political testament. It contained protestations of his own innocence, accusations of foreign treachery and of undeserved dis-loyalty, and in its repetition of the old formulas demonstrated his lifelong inability to learn. He had never outgrown his first prejudices, hatreds and complexes, and remained to the end fixed in a monotonous sameness of thought and feeling. After nominating his successor he concluded, in an empty embittered gesture: 'Above all I charge the leaders of the nation and those under them to scrupulous observance of the laws of race and to merciless opposition to the universal poisoner of all peoples, international Jewry.'[38] The following afternoon, with Russian troops only a few blocks from the Reich Chancellery, Hitler prepared to take his life. 'He sat there,' an orderly officer wrote later, 'apathetic and distractedly brooding, indifferent to everything going on around him, tormented, lifeless, a man dying slowly and with difficulty who was bound indissolubly to his destiny and was now being strangled by it. Then I knew that this was the end!'[39] Shortly after 3 p.m. he retired with Eva Braun to his private rooms. At this moment, a contemporary report says, a dance began in the canteen of the bunker, in which the weeks of nervous tension sought a violent release; it seemed like a final theatrical effect staged by the underworld as it called back its servant. Not even the thought that the Führer was in the very act of dying had power to interrupt the dance. In his last hour the word of a man who had once forced a continent to obey did not reach beyond the walls of his underground cell.

A single shot rang out. The commander of the SS guard, Rattenhuber, who had been waiting with a few others in the corridor, went in and found Hitler lying on the sofa, which was soaked in blood. Beside him lay Eva Braun, an unused revolver in her lap; she had taken poison. Rattenhuber had the two bodies taken into the garden, and petrol poured over them, then sent for the mourners: Goebbels, Bormann, General Burgdorf, Hitler's valet Linge, and a few others. A burst of Russian firing drove them back into the bunker, and one of those present threw a burning rag on the bodies. As the flames shot up they all stood to attention with hands raised in the Nazi salute. A member of the guard who passed the spot half an hour after the ceremony 'couldn't recognise Hitler because he was already pretty burnt'.[40] On the evening of the following day Radio Hamburg announced that 'our Führer Adolf Hitler died for Germany in his command post in the Reich Chancellery this afternoon, fighting to his last breath against Bolshevism'.

Even this last announcement still suggested a claim to the greatness at which this man had ceaselessly, violently grasped and tried to make a tragedy of what was in fact much more like the trite horror pictures of his favourite painter Makart. But we do not need to read a symbolic background into the manner of Hitler's death to note its revealing features. The unique mixture and contrast of banality and significance, of the commonplace that yet had historic status, seems one further example of the dialectic and driving mechanism of this dissonant character, which took its most powerful drive from the tension between what he was and what he wished to be. Hitler was undoubtedly great and a figure of historic significance. There is tragedy here too; the tragedy is that of his victims, and the greatness stems almost exclusively from destructiveness. In the sum total of this life, constructive achievements are lacking to an extent scarcely paralleled among the most savage figures of history. What his contemporaries saw as constructive achievements were either counterfeits devised for effect with the aid of compulsion, deception, and propaganda tricks, or were intended solely to give him the means to further his all-embracing destructiveness. Even in the account given by the man who was the first to join him, this motive keeps showing through the descriptions of outbursts of hate, contemptuous emotional coldness, frenzied self-seeking; and in retrospect Hitler's career seems to follow the same monotonous theme of destruction, played out on an ever larger stage and with ever growing means and power. Everything that may be associated with his career – his excesses in the use of power, the war, his systematic attempts at genocide – in the end merely conforms to the same inner consistency.

It is the same despairing man who failed every constructive task and test, the hopeless prisoner of his own negative impulses, the man who at an early age had 'felt chagrined at the idea that my life would have to run its course along peaceful and orderly lines' and was aware that history, if in no other way, also measures a man's greatness by the magnitude of the catastrophes he causes. This monstrous desire 'one day to read my name in the history books' led him far beyond the limits of his murky, amorphous personality which, with its deformities, dullness and *petit bourgeois* drabness, ensured shattering failure every time he devoted himself seriously to any occupation. Only respect for the dead and the ruins he left behind forbid us to dismiss this life as no more than a nauseating, vulgar and bloody horror story, which fundamentally is all it amounts to; not without justice the epoch of his rise and power has been called 'the age of the demonic nonentities'.[41] The historian who studies this figure is continually up against the difficulty 'of making the catastrophic magnitude of the events tally with the inconceivable commonplaceness of the individual who set them in motion'.[42]

To equate the obviously inferior features of Hitler's personality with lack of intelligence or actual stupidity would be to make the same mistake as so many of his self-confident partners and opponents. The elements of his biography which have been set forth within the scheme of this study prove the opposite often enough. On the basis of a few primitive notions fixed at an early stage in complex aggressive attitudes, he generally reacted with extraordinary acuteness and, to use one of his own favourite expressions, with 'icy coldness', with no counterbalancing sense of compassion, of morality or of responsibility – a familiar phenomenon in psychiatry. It was just this manic and unflinching concentration on the one aim of increasing his personal power which for so long ensured the superiority of his tactics over all his opponents within the country and the majority of those outside, until, in the wilful provocation of almost the whole world, it revealed the primitive narrowness of outlook that was his essential characteristic.

In the end not only Hitler the tactician but also Hitler the demagogue was destroyed by his one-sidedness and overconfidence in his methods. One witness at the trial before the Munich People's Court, asked about the discussions which took place the night before the march on the Feldherrnhalle, replied, 'Herr Hitler kept shouting all the time: Propaganda, propaganda, all that matters is propaganda!'[43] With no sense of proportion he saw events in history, the rise or fall of its leading figures, essentially in terms of greater or lesser skill in propaganda, and tried to prove this by citing Mayor Lueger, the First World War, or the nationalist movement. His own triumphs as an agitator, with their subjective emotional uplift and ecstatic self-liberation, reinforced his overestimation of the effect of propaganda. There was a core of truth in his view of the rise of great mass movements through the power of eloquent orators to inspire emotional fervour; but his basic error was to mistake the intoxication of the moment for conversion, frenzy for a sworn purpose, and systematically aroused shouts for the Führer for evidence of unconditional loyalty. By mistaking the result of careful manipulation for reality, he became a victim himself. His experiences in the so-called period of struggle, where his skill as a propagandist had had its greatest successes, served him ever after as a model. Incurably confined within the narrow outlook of the jumped-up provincial party leader, he was unable to see even a world war as anything but an election campaign expanded to global proportions. 'Hitler thereupon pointed out,' notes a commentator on the table talk at the Führer's headquarters, 'that this war was a faithful copy of conditions during the period of struggle. What then took place among the parties within the country was today taking place as a struggle between the nations outside.'[44]

In actual fact, frequently renewed outbursts of propagandist emotion were necessary if he was to maintain his hold on Germany. The advantage during the period of struggle had been that Hitler could see real aims, real obstacles, real opponents to fire his rhetorical energy and concentrate it in an integrated effort. The war, after a short phase of bewilderment, brought similar conditions, though at a far more demanding level and with less attractive prospects, especially as Hitler himself upset the approximate balance which he had hitherto maintained between the importance of his opponents and the level of his propaganda effort. When he abandoned the role of the demagogue for that of the general the intensity of public emotional attachment to his person immediately diminished, not least for this very reason. This showed once more how far the Third Reich, terrorist pressure aside, was an unreal construction held together by the power of Hitler's rhetoric. Having renounced true conviction in favour of the momentary self-surrender of emotional intoxication, it found its cohesion perpetually threatened by apathy.

When Hitler gave up speaking in public, his power over men's minds deteriorated, and so too, in a curious parallel, did he. 'Everything I am, I am through you alone,' he once cried to the masses. It was true, not merely as regards his acquisition of power, but also in a deeper, almost physiological, way.[45] His rhetorical excesses throughout his life from his earliest appearances in Munich beer halls to the laborious and exhausted struggles of his last years served not simply to whip up other people's energies, but also to stimulate his own. Above and beyond all propaganda considerations, they were a means of self-preservation. During the final phase of the war he complained in a depressed mood that he would never again be able to deliver a great speech. The idea of the end of his career as an orator was linked with the idea of the end altogether.[46]

Only the rhetorical ability that enabled him to turn so many adverse circumstances to his advantage, his power of persuasion over men's minds, can entirely explain this man's rise and career. It was far more significant to his success than his Machiavellian, statesmanlike or even military capacities, the limits of which became clear quite early on and served rather to ensure his downfall. He himself once said that his whole life could be summed up as 'a ceaseless effort to persuade people', and the irresistible effect of his persuasion is attested by the unbroken chain of individual and collective capitulations that line his path. There were the early opponents and rivals within the party, the masses of the late 1920s and 1930s and even a foreign diplomat who once confessed that in the face of Hitler's rhetorical power it had 'repeatedly happened' that 'for a few minutes he became a convinced National Socialist'.[47] No doubt Valentin's famous saying that the story of Hitler was the story of his underestimation is correct; but so is the opposite. Contemporaries who saw in Hitler 'merely a demagogue' were just as wrong as those who paid homage to his 'extraordinary personality' or 'greatness'. In the particular conditions of the time the ability to mislead gave a demagogue exceptional power. At the same time, Hitler's case showed how this ability may go hand in hand with an extraordinary primitiveness. This has been denied by people who met Hitler personally, but not very convincingly. In so far as their judgments did not merely disclose the perverted criteria of the time or were not blurred by the theatrical brilliance of Hitler's display of power, they always projected features of the transcendent mass agitator into the personality as a whole, although the vulgar traits in that personality were plain for all to see and recorded in innumerable accounts and in the texts of speeches and writings. The automatic fascination exercised by the mediumistic powers of Hitler the speaker distorted people's judgment. It helped to conceal the nakedness of his fundamentally squalid personal make-up and gave even his tritest utterances an aura of importance; and again and again it contributed to his success as a statesman. An entirely comparable automatic reaction is shown in the resistance, still widespread today, to accepting such an inexpressibly commonplace figure as Hitler as the man behind events of such extraordinary magnitude. But we need only take one look at his profession of faith, *Mein Kampf*, or his *Table Talk* to become aware of his real nature. In both documents, which mark the beginning and the end of his political career, he reveals himself without the irritating effects of the demagogue; he is not 'beside himself', as he was during his speeches, but despite all his masquerading entirely his normal self; and he shows in page after page, with an exhausting shrill monotony, a platitudinousness, an inability to rise above his own complexes, a human, moral and intellectual inferiority that explodes all myths to the contrary.

He once said that his philosophy of life had not changed since his Vienna days, and in fact at the zenith of his success he remained the inmate of the men's hostel, the pathological semigenius from the Twentieth District to whom, for a terrible moment of history, power was given over individuals and nations. His definition of politics bears unmistakable traces of those early experiences. It was, he said, 'the attainment of a goal by all conceivable means: persuasion, cunning, astuteness, persistence, kindness, slyness, but also brutality'. The power which he ensured for himself by these means he conceived only in its most primitive form as the use of force, extermination, war; and all the extremes to which he went in the exercise of power were intended solely to provide ever renewed confirmation of his personal, unlimited possession of that power. 'Genius of an extraordinary stamp,' he remarked with one eye on himself, 'is not to be judged by the normal standards whereby we judge other men.'[48] To the 'era of personal happiness', whose end he once proclaimed, he opposed an exclusively functional vision of man in which the sum of the individuals, far below the claims of the 'geniuses' to grandeur and historical fame, appeared merely as 'planetary bacilli'.[49]

This idea also set the tone of his relationship with the German people. He tried to justify transforming society into a closed, totally manageable unit, available for all his personal power aims, with the revealing phrase that 'monkeys put to death any members of their community who show a desire to live apart. And what the apes do, men do too, in their own manner.'[50] There was more to this than a desire to subjugate his own people; his will to power felt itself threatened by anyone else's freedom, and cramped in its ego-obsession by anyone else's self-determination, and quite logically sought nothing less than world domination.[51] The destruction of opponents and those who held aloof within Germany was necessary for two reasons: opposition and neutrality were not merely a challenge to the totalitarian demand for power but also constituted a disturbing element in the attempt to weld the German people into a cohesive whole, with the maximum striking force, in preparation for their expansionist mission. Hitler liked to describe the earth as an 'elusive trophy' reserved for the strongest in the struggle of races and nations – and he was determined to win that trophy.[52] The idea that this might hopelessly overtax the strength and resources of the country neither worried nor deterred him. 'The German people,' he retorted in 1938 with his own peculiar brand of irony, evidently to a warning someone had given him, 'once survived war with the Romans. The German people survived the Migration of the Peoples . . . the later great struggles of the early and late Middle Ages. Then the German people survived the religious wars of more recent times. Then later the German people survived the Napoleonic Wars, the Wars of Liberation, they even survived a world war, even the Revolution [of 1918] – they will also survive me!'[53] Similarly later, during the war, the suggestion of the end of Germany, which he had so thoughtlessly provoked, drew from him merely the comment – but this time without irony – 'that the fat was in the fire'.

Remarks Hitler made to Albert Speer in March 1945 show his view of his relationship with the German people as strictly that of user and used: if the war were lost the German people would also be lost; there was no need to worry about ensuring their continued existence even on a primitive level, for they would have proved themselves the weaker. Germany was not his 'bride', as Hitler once remarked, but – as Napoleon said of France – his mistress. She was indeed too weak for the sweeping plans for world domination which he had had in mind for her, and among the many reasons for Hitler's failure this violent overtaxing of Germany's strength, in the face of the facts, including the relative power of the protagonists, is one of the most important. He was always waiting to 'turn up nineteen points with three throws of the dice', and in his obstinate contempt for reality he stuck to the belief that he had succeeded in doing so right down to the death agony in his bunker underworld. Even if it is not true, as cynics say, that history judges men by results, Hitler's life does deserve to be 'measured solely by its one and only criterion, success'.[54] Of the grand and premature aim of an empire that would last for a thousand years, nothing was left. Neither the structure of his state nor a residue of his ideological system nor even his territorial conquests survived him, and the 'struggle against Bolshevism', which had been a central point of National Socialist ideology, brought the enemy deep into the heart of Europe. It was appropriate that a power structure built exclusively for himself and shaped exclusively by himself should collapse when he collapsed. All he left behind were ruins, and nothing else.

However, something remains unexplained when we consider how it was that Hitler, in spite of such a personality, could achieve not only dominion over Germany but also hegemony over Europe, before he was toppled by the united strength of almost the whole world. It is true that we must first establish the criteria of a century before we can take the measure of the man who ruled this century. The still visible traces of his legacy prevent our underestimating Hitler; but we can judge his calibre only if we take account of the period and its susceptibility both to the demagogue's power to lead it astray and to its own weaknesses and fears.

We must look beyond the mere failure of the German people. It is true that every nation bears the responsibility for its own history. But the emergence of Hitler, the conditions for his rise and his triumph, depended on circumstances far beyond the narrower framework of conditions in Germany. We need not mention Versailles, nor Munich, nor Moscow. We may confine ourselves to the common inner characteristics of which these and countless other comparable stages on the road were only symptoms: the turning away of almost all European powers from reason and realism; the disenchantment with traditional values and ethical standards, accompanied by a lack of will to defend any moral and legal principles whatever; a shortsighted striving for advantage and security as well as, in particular, a susceptibility to illusion – the fatal characteristic of the epoch. He was setting out to do battle with an evil beast, said Chamberlain before taking off for Bad Godesberg in September 1938,[55] but we know how unprepared he was for that battle, and how far he was concerned to find fresh justification for his own pusillanimous and absurd optimism, although Hitler's tactics and his aggressive resolution had been demonstrated not only in his conquest of power within Germany but also in his switch to an expansionist foreign policy, which he had long since abandoned any attempt to disguise. Hitler was the outcome of a long process of degeneration not confined to a single country, the end result of a development that was as much European as it was German, a common failure. This does not diminish the responsibility of the German people, but it divides it.

Similarly, Hitler did not destroy Germany alone, but put an end to the old Europe with its sterile rivalries, its narrow-mindedness, its selfish patriotism, and its deceitful imperatives. He put an end too to its splendour, its grandeur, and the magic of its *douceur de vivre*. The hour of that Europe is past and we shall never see it again. By the hand of the man whom it brought to power, the lights were really and finally put out over Europe.

PART TWO

Practitioners and Technicians of Totalitarian Rule

Hermann Göring – Number Two

Do you wish to fight? To kill?
To see streams of blood?
Great heaps of gold?
Herds of captive women?
Slaves?

Gabriele d'Annunzio

I am what I have always been: the last Renaissance man, if I may be allowed to say so.

Hermann Göring

At its roots National Socialist ideology contained only one tangible idea: the idea of struggle. This determined the classifications, the values and the terminology both of the early movement and of the Third Reich. It not only gave Hitler's written confession of faith its purposeful title but also so deeply marked the content and tone of the book that at times even the idea of race, the other cornerstone of National Socialist ideology, had to take second place.[1] All history is a story of struggles: thus Karl Marx's famous formula – forgetting its ideological slant – might be altered to define the National Socialist view of history and society. Struggle set the course of National Socialism throughout, and it supplied the most effective patterns for all its excursions into civil war, psychological and terrorist warfare, social imperialism, and finally total war followed by total collapse. Preference for violent methods is not to be explained by the impatient radicalism of a group of revolutionaries eager to implement an idea; violent struggle was itself an ideology, and if it had a goal above and beyond mere self-assertion it was the power that beckoned at its end.

Not everyone who joined Hitler's movement on its way to power accepted at first this renunciation of ideology for the sake of power. As always in times of upheavals, the widest variety of indictments and recipes for salvation were put forward and the mass party, as it grew, swallowed them all unselectively, planning gradually to neutralize them ideologically and subordinate them to the purpose of achieving naked power for a small, resolute élite. The top leadership of the party can be divided into two types according to the way they came to adopt a self-sufficient, completely unideological dynamic: those who were born National Socialists and those who became National Socialists. Joseph Goebbels

71

was the prototype of the latter. At the beginning of their careers this type always longed, more or less articulately, to change existing conditions according to a preconceived ideological plan. Certainly they wanted to conquer and rule Germany, but they also wanted to bring her new codes of law, to 'redeem' her, however vague and confused their schemes for doing so may have been. They saw violence and struggle, fundamentally, as only the means to carry out this ideological re-education; they abhorred bloodshed, though they did not of course shrink back 'from the graves' at the crunch, when the revolutionary 'cause' was at stake. They were radical, but their radicalism had a definable goal. Hitler, however, soon gave them the choice: either be pushed into the group ironically referred to within this self-seeking Machiavellian community as the 'serious-minded', the 'bigots', or take the plunge with an opportunist about-face and become true National Socialists – that is, supporters of the principle of struggle and power with only relatively binding ideological premises. Only then would the innermost circle of the party leadership be open to them.

In contrast to this type there were the 'born' National Socialists, men with a spontaneous urge to prove themselves in struggle, and an unreflecting, elemental hunger for power. Such men had never had any theoretical conceptions to give up. They were 'fighters' and in most cases marked by their experiences at the front during the war, modern mercenaries who would change flags and views for an appropriate 'reward'. For them there was now an opportunity extending beyond the war and the chaos of the collapse to use their military talents in civilian life, coupled with the promise of power. Ambitious, straightforward and ruthless, they did not suffer at the hands of the world like the ideological type, but wanted to possess or enjoy it. They did not, like the ideologist, think of future generations, but at best of the next day, or even the next hour. Their prototype was Hermann Göring; a contemporary called him 'the great representative of the National Socialist movement'. He said himself, 'I joined the party because I was a revolutionary, not because of any ideological nonsense.'[2]

Unlike those who had 'become' National Socialists, whose ideological impulses, even if concealed and sometimes unrecognisably distorted, always remained at work, so that after coming to power they returned restlessly to their old ideas and secretly longed to see them adopted, the more robust 'born' National Socialists were for the most part quickly satisfied with the privileges of power. In this respect, too, Hermann Göring was true to type. What governed him from the beginning and led him to follow Hitler was simply his absolute will to power. He made his name and acquired his status because he knew how to fight resolutely for power as almost no one else did, and he almost lost them both because he enjoyed them as almost no one else did: shamelessly, naïvely and greedily, always in too large draughts. Pompous and on the verge of ridiculous, he was a mixture of *condottiere* and sybarite. He was as vain, cunning and brutal as any other follower of Hitler, and yet he was more popular than any of them and for a time actually more popular than Hitler himself. With some justice, he declared at Nuremberg: 'I was the only man in Germany besides Hitler who had his *own*, underived authority. The people want to love, and the Führer was often too far from the broad masses. Then they clung to me.'[3]

In the eyes of the people he was what it was the limit of his ambition to be – the Second Man – long before Hitler officially appointed him so. And there he remained long after this election had been tacitly revoked and he had become merely a passenger, because the stir his fall would have caused had to be avoided in view of the tense war situation – the 'greatest failure', as Hitler called him. Corrupted by power and the temptations of good living, he lapsed visibly into the pitfalls of aging rulers, indolence and megalomania. In the end he was incapable of initiative, not to be diverted from his gross pleasures by any military disasters, a 'perfumed Nero',[4] playing the lyre and withdrawn from reality while Rome was in flames.

His massive figure and extraordinary vitality suggested, even to contemporary writers, the attributes of classical heroes. A life written on his orders in 1933 praised his 'Cato-like inflexibility', and a biographical sketch from the same period called him a 'rare iron man of action of Caesarian calibre' and compared him to an 'iron knight', whose figure seemed to burst the walls of a room.[5] To be called 'iron' or 'the Iron Man' was to him the most moving confirmation of his popularity. It was the picture he tried to live up to. The more he sacrificed his former hardness and forceful delight in taking decisions to his passions, the more strenuous his efforts became to simulate the old qualities in numerous heroic disguises. No longer the 'hero', as he had begun, winning the respect of the man in the street, he became no more than an actor playing the part. Devoid of all ideas except that of being the Second Man in the state, his blatantly personal ambition was quickly satisfied and he was happy and delighted simply to hold the insignia of power in his hands.[6]

He was popular mainly because he was the only leading figure in the Third Reich who had qualities with which the masses readily identified. He was manly, without seeming sombre or arrogant; intelligent and yet patently honest and without sophistry; and the inhumane traits of his personality lay concealed behind a moody jollity. His bluff equilibrium bore no trace of the complexities of a damaged personality structure of the sort that has rightly been seen behind the caustic temperament of Goebbels, the narrow-minded fanaticism of Himmler, or the sourness of Hess, Rosenberg or Ribbentrop. By the end of the war in 1918 he was commander of the Richthofen Fighter Squadron, which was rich in tradition. He combined the romantic aura of the much-decorated fighter pilot with the rough unaffected intimacy of the boon companion, at one and the same time hero and hail-fellow-well-met. And although as an orator he lacked both propagandist subtlety and a feeling for the undefined emotions at work in a mass audience, he nevertheless knew how to take a crowd as it wants to be taken – roughly, humorously, without beating about the bush. His aristrocratic background, which he emphasised with the deliberate intention of setting himself apart from the rest of Hitler's followers,[7] spared him any feelings of inferiority, the feelings of petty bourgeois who had come down in the world which were so characteristic of the men who later became the leaders of the National Socialist Party. Unlike them, he also proved himself at the end of the First World War perfectly capable of coping with the problems of civilian life, finding employment in Denmark and Sweden as a show flier and pilot. In the process he met the Baroness Karin von Fock-Kantzow, whom he married in February 1922 in Munich and who dominated his life, at first directly and later, after her early death, as a sentimental shadow. It was due not least to her influence, and not to 'ideological nonsense' that in the autumn of the same year he found his way to Hitler, who seemed to promise him what, as his life grew more bourgeois and settled, he longed for: freedom, action, comradeship and romanticism, as well as the satisfaction of his desire to be important. As for remarks like his 'ideological nonsense', they certainly covered something of the self-conscious charm of the swashbuckler, with his unconcern for the intellect. At the same time, they also conveyed the sober directness of the man of action who had always felt a total lack of contact with the world of ideas and regarded it with a mixture of admiration and dislike. At Nuremberg, Göring angrily demanded not to be questioned about the party programme, saying he did not know it;[8] the verbal and intellectual poverty of an attempt which he made in 1933 to explain the National Socialist ideology may remove natural scepticism at such a remark.

How often I have been asked [says the central passage of this exposition], 'Well, what actually is your programme?' I have been able to point full of pride to our simple and good SA men and say, 'There stand the bearers of our programme; they bear it upon their clear, free brows, and the programme is called: Germany! All the principles that can serve the rise and preservation of Germany are acknowledged as the only points in our programme. All others, which may damage the Fatherland, are rejected and are to be destroyed.'[9]

To begin with, however, it looked as if the link with the National Socialist movement was merely an episode in Göring's life. It is true that in 1923 Hitler had been able to obtain his services as leader of the SA and had exclaimed with calculating enthusiasm, 'Splendid! A war ace with the *Pour le Mérite* – imagine it! Excellent propaganda! Moreover, he has money and doesn't cost me a cent!'[10] But the march on the Feldherrnhalle, in the course of which Göring was wounded, temporarily brought their collaboration to an end, especially as the shattered movement no longer offered Göring any scope for action. After escaping into Austria he quickly went on to Italy, then to Sweden, and only when Hitler offered him a promising candidature before the Reichstag elections of 1928 did he once more, but this time resolutely, link his future with this man and this cause. Göring's assertion that he fell for Hitler 'from the first moment lock, stock, and barrel'[11] is therefore contradicted by events themselves. Doubtless it was said simply to support the general picture of a loyal follower of the Führer. When he stated in 1933 that 'no title and no distinction can make me as happy as the designation bestowed upon me by the German people: "The most faithful paladin of the Führer," '[12] there can be no doubt what he valued by far the most;

the legitimation as Second Man which this formula afforded him in his struggle with his rivals Röhm and Goebbels. But it is also true that the backbone of his personality gradually disintegrated under Hitler's influence and he lapsed into undignified subservience. This, to begin with, he celebrated in wildly emotional terms. 'I have no conscience! Adolf Hitler is my conscience!' he once exclaimed. On another occasion he said:

If the Catholic Christian is convinced that the Pope is infallible in all religious and ethical matters, so we National Socialists declare with the same ardent conviction that for us too the Führer is absolutely infallible in all political and other matters. It is a blessing for Germany that in Hitler the rare union has taken place between the most acute logical thinker and truly profound philosopher and the iron man of action, tenacious to the limit. [And again] I follow no leadership but that of Adolf Hitler and of God![13]

Such declarations, however, could never quite conceal the effort it cost Göring to copy Goebbels' extreme idolisation of the Führer, and it sounded totally implausible when this robust, burly man reflected 'It is not I who live, but the Führer who lives in me.'[14] Nor did he ever quite lose his sense of humiliation at such self-abandonment, and after the period of triumphal joy in subservience was over, he suffered increasingly from his servile dependence on his Führer. At the beginning he was making confessions like this one, to Hjalmar Schacht: 'Every time I face him [Hitler], my heart falls into my trousers,'[15] and at the end there was the horror of those terrible stormy quarrels in the Führer's headquarters, which he tried to avoid with schoolboyish anxiety because, in the words of an eyewitness, he always came away from them 'utterly beaten down'. 'Often,' Göring said, 'I couldn't eat anything again until midnight, because before then I should have vomited in my agitation. When I returned to Karinhall at about nine o'clock I actually had to sit in a chair for some hours in order to calm down. This relationship turned into downright mental prostitution to me.'[16] Entirely consistent is State Secretary von Weizsäcker's addition that Göring always 'puffed himself up' tremendously before these encounters. From another source comes evidence that his subservience finally took positively grotesque forms; he sometimes sprang to attention when he received a telephone call from the Führer's headquarters; and he occasionally sent a liaison officer to the headquarters to bring him back a detailed account of everything Hitler had said, so that at the next meeting he could put Hitler's utterances forward as his own ideas.[17]

Such debasements doubtless arose out of the bitter realisation that since his connection with Hitler he had abandoned every demand of his own personality or individuality. 'Anyone who knows how it is with us,' he remarked, 'knows that we each possess just so much power as the Führer wishes to give. And only with the Führer and standing behind him is one really powerful, only then does one hold the strong powers of the state in one's hands; but against his will, or even without his wish, one would instantly become totally powerless. A word from the

Führer and anyone whom he wishes to be rid of falls. His prestige, his authority are boundless.'[18]

Such humiliations were at first hidden under the impression created by the successes won jointly during the conquest of power, especially as it was Göring who decisively smoothed the path for the triumph of January 30. It was no coincidence that it was he who on January 29 brought Hitler the news that agreement on the new cabinet had been reached. Hitler owed not only a decisive step on his path to Hindenburg but also his contacts, in particular with conservative circles, to Göring, who, to anyone who was deeply class-conscious, differed so pleasantly in his origins and 'way of life', and as an officer and a bearer of the *Pour le Mérite*, from the other 'nonentities' of the National Socialist leadership. Göring's energy was also responsible for certain important interim successes on the way to power. Hitler's reward for the 'movement's diplomatist' was a seat in the cabinet and the portfolio of Prussian Minister of the Interior.[19] While outwardly Göring continued to use his stout joviality to increase his popularity, he showed from day to day the most brutal energy in seizing power, blustering, terrorising, crushing opposition, and creating order in accordance with his own ideas. His was the task of ruthlessly applying force, and hence that part in the National Socialist revolution which was concealed, with a profusion of words and gestures, behind bustling pseudolegalities and Hitler's protestations that this was 'the most bloodless revolution in world history'.

A technically legal basis for 'the great clearing up', as Göring called it,[20] was provided by the 'Decree for the Protection of the German People', promulgated by the Reich President on February 4 and the 'Emergency Decree for the Protection of People and State' of February 28 (the Reichstag Fire Decree). Under the pretext of the threat of a Communist coup the party was paving the way for its own coup. Only one week after taking up office, Göring assured the Prussian police that 'during the next few months you must expect another hard struggle at the front'. Ten days later he ordered them, in the notorious shooting decree, 'to establish the best possible agreement with the nationalist formations' (SA, SS and Stahlhelm), but against the left, 'if necessary, to make ruthless use of your weapons'. 'Every bullet,' he said later in a speech expressly confirming this decree, 'that now comes out of the barrel of a police pistol is my bullet. If people call that murder, then I have murdered, I have ordered it all, I shall defend it, I bear the responsibility for it and have no need to shrink from it.'[21] For the 'relief of the ordinary police in special cases' Göring arranged for the setting up of strong auxiliary police units made up of SA and SS, thus dropping the pretence of police neutrality and giving them terrorist duties in the service of the party. With rigorous consistency he personally combed through the ranks of the police force, so that, as a contemporary biography of Göring puts it, 'the System big shots were thrown out. This ruthless cleansing process extended from the supreme police chief to the doorkeeper.'[22]

His speeches at that time, with their positively delirious profession of faith in violence, afford a graphic view of his convictions and measures, as for example

when he declares: 'My measures will not be enfeebled by any legalistic hesitations. My measures will not be enfeebled by any bureaucracy. Here I have not to
exercise justice, here I have only to destroy and exterminate, nothing else!'[23] On
May 11, 1933, he said in a speech at Essen:

I have only just begun my purge; it is far from finished. For us the people are divided
into two parts: one which professes faith in the nation, the other which wants to poison
and destroy. I thank my Maker that I do not know what objective is. I am subjective. I
repudiate the idea that the police are a defence force for Jewish department stores. We
must put an end to the absurdity of every rogue shouting for the police. The police are
not there to protect rogues, vagabonds, usurers and traitors. If people say that here and
there someone has been taken away and maltreated, I can only reply: You can't make
omelettes without breaking eggs. Don't shout for justice so much, otherwise there might
be a justice that is to be found in the stars and not in your paragraphs! Even if we make a
lot of mistakes, we shall at least act and keep our nerve. I'd rather shoot a few times too
short or too wide, but at least I shoot.[24]

Carl Jacob Burckhardt, after a visit to Göring, aptly remarked that unrestrained outbursts were typical of 'the style of the whole National Socialist
movement' and that frenzied raging, with a total loss of self-control, was
considered masculine.[25] In fact much of the emphasis, many turns of phrase in
such speeches, must be attributed to this perverted ideal of masculinity, whose
adherents gained self-awareness only in unthinking frenzy. Göring's behaviour
during the seizure of power really does not permit us to see him as 'this upright
soldier with the heart of a child', which was the way Goebbels described him in a
spirit of unmistakably malicious comradeship.[26] And if he had once been the
object of a vague and imperceptive hope in conservative circles,[27] this hope now
collapsed along with many other conservative illusions. Wherever his moderating
influence might have been expected, Göring failed and increasingly left the field
to the more radical Goebbels. He proved his aggressive brutality once again when,
at the conclusion of the seizure of power, he appeared as an ambitious principal
in the Röhm affair. Together with Heinrich Himmler he took control of the
murders in North Germany and Berlin and, on his own admission, expanded the
'circle of duties' entrusted to him in order, as he thought, finally to ensure for
himself that position as Second Man blocked for so long by Röhm. There is a
revealing story that shows the sort of reputation he had at that time. It happened
shortly after June 30, 1934. Göring arrived late for dinner with the British
Ambassador, Sir Eric Phipps, explaining that he had only just got back from
shooting. Sir Eric replied: 'Animals, I hope.'[28]

For Göring, the goal was now achieved. The myth of the strong but also
popular man brought him official positions and tasks. One of the 'giants of
jurisdiction' of the Third Reich,[29] he performed or assumed in the first two years
alone the duties of President of the Reichstag as well as of Reich Minister for
Aviation; he was Prussian Minister of the Interior, head of the Gestapo, President
of the Prussian State Council, Reich Forestry Commissioner and Controller of
the Hunt, Commander in Chief of the Luftwaffe, and Commissioner for the

Four-Year Plan. Yet in each of these positions, which formally gave him enormous power, he was soon interested only in the decorative side. After a few fitful efforts at the beginning he generally left his duties to their own devices, with the result that there was 'paralysing disorder'.[30] What had been intended as a concentration of forces turned out the exact opposite, and his hunger for office began to look like nothing more than an eccentric extension of his mania for collecting. He yielded himself ever more extravagantly to the enjoyment of power, which he understood mainly as a source of wealth; he organised feasts, state hunts and birthday celebrations of almost oriental splendour. He was forever bringing home to Karinhall, the imposing manor house in the Schorfheide named after his first wife, paintings, statues, jewels and tapestries. These were sometimes forced gifts from industrialists or the great German cities after he had specified the presents he expected on birthdays or other occasions.[31] And while he devoted himself more and more to self-gratification and pleasure, his cooler rivals – in particular Goebbels and Himmler, who was unmistakably on the way up – took over little by little the real power whose trappings he clung to so blindly and vainly. 'Let him be, he's a Renaissance man!' Hitler used to say whenever his attention was drawn to Göring's compromising behaviour.[32] But he represented only one side of the Renaissance: the lack of scruple, the insatiable greed, the clear conscience of a beast of prey. In his beefy hedonism, however, there was more of the other side of Renaissance man: the supreme sense of style, the refined feeling for life. His first press officer at the Prussian Ministry of the Interior has recalled that Göring quickly began to hate the irksome routine of the Ministry and rarely turned up there. A biography published in 1938 by one of his closest colleagues nonchalantly lists the tailor, barber, art dealer and jeweller (in that order) as Göring's first visitors in the morning of a working day.[33] With a love of luxury like that of some voluptuous courtesan, he was always changing his suits and uniforms – as often as five times in a day. At a reception for the Diplomatic Corps in the Schorfheide, in the words of an eyewitness, 'he wore a rust-brown jerkin and high green boots and carried a six-foot spear'.[34] According to another account:

> Göring presents a grotesque picture. During the morning in a jerkin with white puffed shortsleeves, changing his clothes several times during the day, in the evening at table in a blue or violet kimono with fur-trimmed bedroom slippers. In the morning a gold dagger at his side that has been changed several times already, at his throat a brooch with gems that have also been changed, around his fat waist a broad belt also set with precious stones, to say nothing of the gorgeousness and number of his rings.

At a meeting in June 1937, Carl Jacob Burckhardt found him 'in a white uniform lying on an ottoman; he was already very corpulent in those days. His left leg, of which the trouser was rolled up above the knee, lay supported and raised on a cushion; he wore red silk stockings like a cardinal.' Besides soft, lascivious costumes he affected, especially at his hunting parties, an archaic Old German style: 'Fifty foresters in parade uniform blew the hunting horns when the chief, in his fantastic hunting dress, entered the car with measured step. In green leather

78

jackets and medieval peasant hats and armed with boar spears, whose flashing tips were protected by tasselled leather sheaths, the beaters and dog leaders with their dogs dragging at the lead marched past him in step.'[35]

The infantile side of his personality, to be seen in his naïve mania for dressing up, his delight in medals and tinsel, his monstrous egocentricity and such transports of delight as those he showed over an electric railway installed at Karinhall, were clearly obstacles to his ambition. During the first phase of his career he had shown aggressive adroitness in violently seizing power, but asserting this power by intrigue and slowly and cautiously extending it would have been foreign to his temperament, which demanded distraction and stimulus and gorgeous display. What he was looking for now was not power but theatrical effect. As a result the areas of his influence were eroded away: the Prussian position, control of the police, and later also the authority which he tried to build up for himself over the economy and the Wehrmacht. In comparison with Hitler, his well-fed joviality did have the advantage of drawing attention away from the gloomy and neurasthenic obsessiveness of his partner in the leadership, and his popularity, which was at its peak shortly before the war, owed much to his weaknesses, behind which people imagined they could sense human warmth.[36] In a last acknowledgment of this popularity, which no longer represented his real influence, Hitler appointed him on September 1, 1939 his first successor and later President of the Reich Defence Council as well as Reich Marshal.

As Hitler awarded Göring these nominal marks of distinction, relations between the two men were steadily growing cooler. At the end of 1936, Hitler had still been able to say of Göring's work in carrying out the Four-Year Plan: 'The words "It can't be done" do not exist for him. He is the best man I have for this task.'[37] About a year later, however, he refused to allow him to enjoy the fruits of an intrigue that would have brought him once more to the top. Contrary to Göring's hopes, he was not appointed to succeed the Reichswehr Minister von Blomberg, whom he had helped to bring down. Even behind Göring's very amateurish efforts to avoid war at the last moment, Hitler so clearly sensed the wish to be left in undisturbed enjoyment of his personal gains that it only increased their incipient estrangement.[38] The first failures, which soon occurred, did the rest. Göring's biographer of 1938 tells how when playing with lead soldiers the young Göring tried to increase the apparent number of his troops by the clever use of mirrors. In much the same way now, after the first quick triumphs in Poland and France, he tried to make up for the success that had been expected with a grandiose pose instead. After his boasting had actually contributed to the successful British withdrawal from Dunkirk,[39] his arrogant predictions about the air battle over Britain and then the bombing attacks on Germany were also proved wrong at great cost. He himself declared at Nuremberg, referring to the catastrophe of Stalingrad, which was also a catastrophe for the Luftwaffe and the turning-point in its supremacy, that 'since 1942 I have been a scapegoat for Hitler'. Yet there is a good deal of evidence that Hitler had dropped him considerably earlier.[40] Even the plans for the Russian campaign were revealed to him at a comparatively late stage. By the end of 1942 he found himself in a position of complete isolation and had lost to the steadily advancing Bormann such territory as had been left to him by his rivals Goebbels, Himmler and Speer. The rare sallies in which something of his old brutal consistency seemed to flare up, as for instance in his so-called 'plunder speech' before the Reich Commissioners for Occupied Territories,[41] could not hide his growing attitude of resignation. When the bombing of Germany, the danger of which he had so provocatively denied, began to show devastating effects he let things drift, and even in spring 1943, as Goebbels noted with amazement, 'was still not fully aware of the extent of the damage to property and life'.[42]

Because of his preoccupation with external show, the Luftwaffe, which idolised him, got little more than purely decorative benefit from the much vaunted 'comradeship'. He would visit airfields and front-line units, slapping backs, beaming, confident; at the same time there would be mounting disorganisation in neglected offices, and all the efforts of his colleagues to check the chaos and mount a new programme of technical development came to grief through his incorrigible illusions and lack of foresight. Deeply entangled in his romantic 'archaic ideals of life', he was sceptical of all technical developments and liked to think that ramming enemy aircraft was really 'the most dignified way of fighting'.[43] Neither General Ernst Udet's suicide nor that of General Jeschonnek, whose despair was largely attributable to Göring's indolence, could wrench him out of his self-deceptions. When General Galland informed him in 1943 that enemy fighters were accompanying the bomber squadrons further and further into German territory, Göring forbade him to report the matter.[44] He rarely took any part now in strategic or other conferences and was often sought in vain when his chief of staff required instructions. Instead he devoted himself as before to his pastimes and private passions. The Essen Gauleiter Terboven tells of a visit to Karinhall: 'It was Sunday and the sky over Germany was once more black with American bombers.' Göring merely made sure from his duty adjutant that there was no air-raid warning in force for Karinhall and then remarked, 'Fine, let's go hunting.'[45] At the height of the war, when Goebbels tried to enlist the Reich Marshal's prestige and authority for the efforts of a group that was trying to curb the excessive influence of Bormann, he found to his amazement that 'Göring's prestige with the Führer had suffered immensely'. Nevertheless he did not abandon his efforts until he realised the hopeless lethargy into which Göring had sunk. Finally, faced with the ruins of Dresden, he demanded angrily that 'this stupid and useless Reich Marshal' should be brought before the court.[46] Göring soon became isolated, even his most minor requests brusquely rejected. Significantly, his last personal achievement was to stop the intended closing of the Berlin luxury restaurant Horcher in 1943.[47] Henceforth not a trace remained of his former power and authority within the top leadership. When he fell ill in 1944 Hitler, to his chagrin, paid no attention. He was finally out of the game; he was left his rank and position solely as an act of charity.

An analysis of his inability to fill responsible positions purposefully must take account not only of the corrupting effect of good living but also of that wasting away of the personality which began at an early stage, leaving only the heavy and bloated shadow of his former self. The significance of his drug addiction, a consequence of the wounds he received during the war and later at the Munich Feldherrnhalle, is all the more difficult to assess because personal deterioration was not confined to Göring alone but spread like a disease among almost all Hitler's closer entourage. Only Göring's profound self-deception concealed from him the extent of his individual regression. There remains, of course, the question how far the one affected the other. Undoubtedly his hankering for self-display reflected a deep need of his theatrical temperament. But beneath this may have lain an unadmitted desire to conceal the progressive disintegration of his personality behind baroque ostentation. He may have attempted to use his boisterous way of life to camouflage his own atrophy, of which he was aware at the unconscious level and which reacted upon his consciousness in the form of restlessness. His unreflective nature rendered him incapable of subjecting his personal life to an act of conscious stocktaking, facing up to his failures, and the bitterness of continual self-reproach for his own weakness and willingness to capitulate. So he sought and found in a thousand disguises a means of hiding from himself the steady shrinking of his own stature. And, if his facility in self-deception could not prevent occasional humiliating flashes of insight, it became second nature to live in his own counterfeit world.

In the final phase of his life he suffered from profound illusion. In April 1945 he had been dismissed with ignominy from all his posts, arrested, and bequeathed a curse. But when he heard of Hitler's death, he was, his wife recalled, 'close to despair' and exclaimed, 'He's dead, Emmy. Now I shall never be able to tell him that I was true to him till the end!'[48] In much the same way as Himmler, he hoped to be accepted by the Allies as a partner in negotiations. As General Bodenschatz has testified, soon after his capture by the Americans his main concern was the proclamation which he intended to make to the German people as soon as he had reached a satisfactory agreement with Eisenhower.[49] His claim to the leadership of the Reich after Hitler's death was indisputable in his view. Even at Nuremberg he compelled his fellow prisoner the Grand Admiral Dönitz to admit that he owed his own 'nomination as the Führer's successor solely to coincidence'.[50] And if Göring defended himself before the International Court of Justice with striking skill and some aggressiveness, behind which some of the old elemental force of his personality could be felt, it was because of his conviction that his role as leader placed greater responsibility upon him than upon the other prisoners. Obstinately and at times not without success, he tried to command them, to influence their statements, and to establish a regime which Speer referred to angrily as 'Göring's dictatorship'. At last, after so many years, so many blows and humiliations, for a brief and fruitless span he had reached his goal: to be the First Man and 'Nazi Number One', as he called himself.[51]

The conditions of his personal rise to power were at the same time those of his failure. His rise and fall were rooted in an egocentricity devoid of all control mechanisms, an egocentricity that knew no criteria of behaviour beyond the satisfaction of its own desires and, in all its naïve greed, gave him the character of a large and dangerous child. In a speech which in its way is a contribution to the psychology of totalitarian governments, he explained to one of the Nuremberg defence lawyers:

If you really want to do something new, the good won't help you with it. They are self-satisfied, lazy, they have their God and their own pigheadedness – you can't do it with them. 'Let me have men about me that are fat.' An anointed king can say that, but not a leader who has made himself. Let me have men about me that are arrant knaves. The wicked, who have something on their conscience, are obliging, quick to hear threats, because they know how it's done, and for booty. You can offer them things, because they will take them. Because they have no hesitations. You can hang them if they get out of step. Let me have men about me that are utter villains – provided that I have the power, absolute power over life and death. The sole and single leader, whom no one can interfere with. What do you know of the possibilities in evil! Why do you write books and make philosophy when you only know about virtue and how to acquire it, whereas the world is fundamentally moved by something quite different?[52]

Possibly this is the key to his stubborn hope for posthumous fame. Germany needed for the future 'a personality that is strong enough to provide a focal point for the Germans', he said. 'Then people will think of me again! But by then unfortunately I shall be dead.'[53] But even his death he wanted to see only as the vehicle for his historical resurrection. All his utterances in the Nuremberg cell were pervaded, in a final act of illusory self-overvaluation, by the idea that he would one day be celebrated as a martyr. He was glad he had been condemned to death, he stated shortly before the end, because the man condemned to life imprisonment had no chance of becoming a martyr. 'In fifty or sixty years there will be statues of Hermann Göring all over Germany,' he remarked, and added, 'Little statues, maybe, but one in every German home.'[54]

Joseph Goebbels: 'Man the Beast'

I want to be a hero!

Joseph Goebbels

A revolutionary must be able to do everything!

Joseph Goebbels

Propaganda was the genius of National Socialism. Not only did it owe to propaganda its most important successes; propaganda was also its one and only original contribution to the conditions for its rise and was always more than a mere instrument of power: propaganda was part of its essence. What National Socialism meant is far less easily grasped from the contradictory and nebulous conglomerate of its philosophy than from the nature of its propagandist stage management. Carrying it to an extreme, one might say that National Socialism was propaganda masquerading as ideology, that is to say, a will to power which formed its ideological theorems according to the maximum psychological advantage to be derived at any given moment, and drew its postulates from the moods and impulses of the masses, in the sensing of which it was abnormally gifted. In view of its capacity for mediumistic communication with the 'mind' of the masses, it seemed not to require any real idea, such as had served to gather and hold together every other mass movement in history. Resentments, feelings of protest of the day and the hour, as well as that mechanical attachment which arises from the mere activation of social forces, replaced the integrative effect of an idea, in conjunction with a gift of handling crowds that made use of every technique of psychological manipulation. The majority of the ideological elements absorbed into National Socialism were nothing but material, assessed at varying degrees of effectiveness, for a ceaseless pyrotechnical display of propagandist agitation. Flags, Sieg Heils, fanfares, marching columns, banners and domes of searchlights – the whole arsenal of stimulants, developed with inventive ingenuity, for exciting public ecstasy was ultimately intended to bring about the individual's self-annulment, a permanent state of mindlessness, with the aim of rendering first the party adherents and later a whole nation totally amenable to the leaders' claim to power. The relative status of ideology and propaganda is shown more clearly than anywhere in that phraseology employed by numerous

83

contemporaries that referred to National Socialism as 'experience', a term that tacitly outlawed any cognitive or critical approach. In fact this ideology was literally indisputable and evaded all objective analysis by retreating into the unimpeachable realms of pseudo-religious feelings, where the Führer reigned in solitary metaphysical monumentality. To be sure, this flight into the irrational, into regions where politics became a matter of faith, of *Weltanschauung*, answered a vehement need of the disoriented masses; nevertheless, there was a purposeful Machiavellian guidance behind the direction and forms it took, so that on closer inspection the apparently elemental demand proves to be the planned and repeatedly reawakened irrationalism to which the modern totalitarian social religions owe their support and their existence.

Joseph Goebbels was the brain behind this manipulation of minds, 'the only really interesting man in the Third Reich besides Hitler'.[1] One of the most astonishingly gifted propagandists of modern times, he stood head and shoulders above the bizarre mediocrity of the rest of the regime's top-ranking functionaries. He was one of the few real powers in the movement's leadership, not merely a figurehead drawn into the light of history 'in the wake of the victorious cause'. These two, Hitler and Goebbels, complemented each other in an almost unique manner. For Hitler's sombre, complex-determined visions, his intuitive, ecstatic relationship with the masses, Goebbels found the techniques of persuasion, the rationalisations, the slogans, myths and images. It was from Goebbels that *der Führer*, the term by which Hitler appeared as redeemer, demiurge and blessed saviour, received its visionary content. He astutely turned the initially irresolute Adolf Hitler into *der Führer* and set him on the pillar of religious veneration. With strenuous Byzantinism, consciously mingling the sacred with the profane, he spread around Hitler that messianic aura which so appealed to the emotions of a deeply shaken nation. The cult of the Führer, whose true creator and organiser he was, not only exploited the need for faith and security, as well as the German's latent urge to self-abandonment in the face of a world stripped of its gods, but also gave the rising NSDAP the solid backbone of a hierarchical structure. The evidence of this cult is overwhelming. In *Der Angriff*, the paper he founded as Gauleiter of Berlin, Goebbels wrote, with a significant imitation [in the original] of biblical cadences and alliterations:

Works of talent are the result of diligence, persistence, and gifts. Genius is self-creative by grace alone. The deepest force of the truly great man is rooted in instinct. Very often he cannot even say why everything is as it is. He contents himself with saying: It is so. And it is so. What diligence and knowledge and school learning cannot solve, God announces through the mouths of those whom he has chosen. Genius in all fields of human endeavour means – to have been called. When Hitler speaks, all resistance breaks down before the magical effect of his words. One can only be his friend or his enemy. He divides the hot from the cold. But lukewarmness he spits out of his mouth. Many can know, even more can organise, but he alone in all Germany today can construct the political values of the future out of fateful knowledge through the power of the word. Many are called, but few are chosen. We are all unshakably convinced that he is their spokesman and guide. Therefore we believe in him. Over his inspiring human figure we see the grace of destiny at work in this man and cling with all our hopes to his ideal and are thereby bound to that creative force which carries him and all of us forward.[2]

Elsewhere Goebbels described his feelings for the Führer as 'holy and untouchable'. He stated after a speech by Hitler that he had spoken 'profoundly and mystically, almost like a gospel', and affirmed in a protestation of loyalty: 'An hour may come when the mob rages around you and roars, "Crucify him!" Then we shall stand as firm as iron and shout and sing "Hosanna!" '[3] In one of his regular birthday addresses on the eve of April 20, Goebbels declared, 'When the Führer speaks it is like a divine service',[4] while in his early journal, whenever he conjures up the image of Hitler, we find passages in the most unbearably sentimental style, reminiscent of an adolescent's diary:

We drive to Hitler. He is having his meal. He jumps to his feet, there he is. Shakes my hand. Like an old friend. And those big blue eyes. Like stars. He is glad to see me. I am in heaven. That man has got everything to be a king. A born tribune. The coming dictator.

Or elsewhere:

Hitler is there. Great joy. He greets me like an old friend. And looks after me. How I love him! What a fellow! Then he speaks. How small I am! He gives me his photograph. With a greeting to the Rhineland. Heil Hitler! I want Hitler to be my friend. His photograph is on my desk.[5]

Hitler's position in the mass party that was being formed was enormously reinforced by and received a positively metaphysical endorsement from such idolatry. The cult developed around his personality destroyed those beginnings of internal democracy which had characterised the party in its old form, and fostered its centralist, authoritarian structure. Hitler now finally became the exclusive central will, 'to whom were directed the party's members' desire for self-surrender, service and subordination, their weariness with responsibility, who alone knew how to pick up this desire and translate it into the redeeming political act'.[6] He rewarded his 'faithful, unshakable shield bearer', as he once called Goebbels,[7] by exceptional advancement at the beginning of his career and by giving him the distinction of being the partner and organiser of his private social life. Later a perceptible reserve entered their relationship. In so far as it was not due to purely tactical considerations – the wish to undermine the Minister of Propaganda's patently excessive self-confidence by the well-tried method of the cold shoulder – this reserve may have sprung from Hitler's distrust of the practised adroitness with which Goebbels always managed to adapt himself to circumstances.

In fact, these overemotional declarations are by no means to be taken as honest statements of Goebbels' feelings; the exaggeratedly demonstrative accent alone is enough to make them profoundly dubious. All too often Goebbels 'met his Damascus', and his various conversions were never dependent upon an inner voice but upon an opportunist eye for the bigger battalions. 'I am an apostate', he once confessed.[8] It was first and most consistently to himself that he applied that conviction of man's total guidability which later enabled him to organise whatever was asked of him: cheering and riots, pogroms, trust in the Führer, and the will to resist. The only clear brain within the party Old Guard, he was at the same time the least independent, and lacking in any personal core.

> I am only an instrument, / on which the old god
> Sings his song. / I am only a waiting vessel,
> Into which Nature pours the new wine / with a smile,

he wrote as a student.[9] Destitute of any inner conviction himself, he merely knew how to place the convictions of others decoratively and effectively on display. He once admiringly confessed that the reason why Hitler was so dangerous was that he believed what he said.[10] He himself, on the other hand, was never in his life able to believe what he said and concealed this shortcoming – which he fully understood to be a weakness – behind a front of cynicism. The soft, sentimental interior side of his nature, which yearned for dull but cosy certainties, was overlaid by a sober scepticism, and nothing that his longing for faith could construct stood up to the probing of his inquisitorial intelligence. The occasional cry of jubilation of the early days, 'I believe again,' or the formula *credo ergo sum* expressed all too clearly the hunger of the rationalist for a share in the heightened emotions and the self-forgetfulness of others, and significantly what the object of his hunger for faith might be was a matter of complete indifference to him. 'What matters is not so much what we believe; only that we believe.'[11]

That the son of a strictly Catholic working-class family from Rheydt in the Rhineland[12] should have found his ostensible certitude of faith, after years of agonising indecision, in the National Socialist movement is a stroke of historical irony. Highly gifted, he was subjected from an early age to a tormenting feeling of physical inadequacy; he had a weak constitution and a crippled foot. When he appeared in Geneva in 1933 as representative of the Reich, a caricature in a Swiss newspaper showed a crippled little man with black hair. Under it was written: 'Who is that? Oh, that's the representative of the tall, healthy, fair-haired, and blue-eyed Nordic race!'[13] This joke throws light on some of the difficulties Goebbels found himself up against in the midst of the old followers of Hitler, especially the rough SA. As a man with a physical deformity and an intellectual, he was something of a provocation to a party that regarded, not intellectual ability, but muscular strength and racial heritage, fair hair and long legs, as qualifications for genuine membership. The designation 'our little doctor', which quickly established itself, shows the sort of contemptuous esteem in which Goebbels was always held by his well-built, feeble-brained fellow fighters of the early days. In spite of their admiration for his demagogic brilliance, they were always suspicious of him. To their coarse slow-wittedness his rationality, his coldness always appeared strange and even 'un-German', and for a long time he was looked upon as a 'pupil of the Jesuits and a half Frenchman'.[14] It was almost as a challenge to the human type demanded and moulded by the movement when he wrote: 'We are not content with opinions. We seek to confirm and deepen these opinions. We want clarity, clarity. Faith moves mountains, but knowledge alone moves them to the right place. In knowledge we seek clarity and the definition of our feelings.'[15] Sentences such as this mark his intellectual distance from the type of mind predominant in the NSDAP, who, as Goebbels once said, 'has in his heart that which he does not have in his head, and, which is the main thing, has it *in his fists*'.[16]

Undoubtedly Goebbels suffered from not being like everyone else. Above all, at the beginning of his rise to power, as Gauleiter of Berlin – when he depended upon the absolute loyalty of an SA detachment whose criteria of merit were an uncritical activism, an athletic taste for violence and the dullest 'normality' – he found his authority repeatedly subjected to irritating curbs.[17] Like Mirabeau (and equally in vain) he may at times have asked God to bestow upon him that mediocrity from whose simple raptures he felt himself excluded. This was the source of his hatred of the intellect, which was a form of self-hatred, his longing to degrade himself, to submerge himself in the ranks of the masses, which ran curiously parallel with his ambition and his tormenting need to distinguish himself. He was incessantly tortured by the fear of being regarded as a 'bourgeois intellectual' and hence disqualified. His shrill anti-bourgeois complex[18] sprang from this problem, as did his painfully exaggerated attitude of loyalty to the person of Adolf Hitler: it always seemed as though he were offering blind devotion to make up for his lack of all those characteristics of the racial élite which nature had denied him. Because his intellectualism and his physical deformity combined to make him particularly vulnerable among his rivals for power, he developed into an uninhibited opportunist with an exceptional nose for the power relationships in his circle. In the internal conflicts of direction within the party Goebbels, by virtue of his temperament and his intellectual consistency, often found himself on the ideological wing, yet he always managed to switch in good time to the side of the majority.[19]

Tactical moves merely camouflaged the dichotomy, however, and with all his aptitude for self-deception he could not in the long run refrain from calling himself to account, even if more or less involuntarily. 'Everything within me revolts against the intellect,' he wrote early on. And then, betraying the real cause of all his tensions and awkwardness: 'My foot troubles me badly. I am conscious of it all the time, and that spoils my pleasure when I meet people.'[20]

He also tried continually to offset the bitter consciousness of his deformity. His hunger for status and prestige and the strained style of his early literary efforts, based on the language of military commands, bear witness to this. He liked to see himself as hard and manly, but it was the forced hardness of a sensitive young man – who once made a pilgrimage to lay a bunch of wild flowers on the grave of the poet Annette von Droste-Hülshoff. Only in unguarded romantic moods, as for instance in his helplessly sentimental poems, did he allow himself to depart a little from his stern ideals. His whole literary and propaganda output displays three curiously contrasting layers: alongside the stylistic and intellectual succinctness of his day-to-day political contributions is the foolishly strained pose of the fighter and finally the stammering bombast of his private jottings. 'In them dwells a poet and a soldier,' he makes the girl Hertha Holk say in his juvenile work *Michael*,[21] after he himself had been graded 'fit for non-combatant duties only' and had just seen his first literary works fail. The very name of the hero, Michael, to whom he gave many autobiographical features, suggests the way his self-identification was pointing: a figure of light, radiant, tall, unconquerable. He too is the son of a peasant, who strides over 'steaming clods' and feels the blood of his forefathers rising 'slow and healthy' within him. 'I don my helmet, draw my sword and declaim Liliencron. Sometimes I am overcome by a sort of spasm. To be a soldier! To stand sentinel! One ought always to be a soldier,' wrote Michael-Goebbels.[22] The fraudulent claim to having fought at the front which he made in this book, as in his later speeches when he used the phrase 'We who were shot up in the World War,' was intended to suggest that his crippled foot was the result of a war wound. The deception seems to have been successful for an astonishingly long time.[23]

No doubt the same feeling of physical inferiority also provided the essential impulse behind his erotic activity. Both the wide range of his various affairs, as revealed by those parts of his private diary that have been found, and the tone of these confessions very clearly betray the desire to appear 'a hell of a fellow', even if only in his own eyes. 'Alma sends me a postcard from Bad Harzburg,' he notes in his diary. 'The first sign of life since that night. Alma, the teaser and charmer. I quite like this girl. First letter from Else from Switzerland.' (August 14, 1925.) 'Little Else, when shall I see you again? Alma, you lithe, lovely flower! Anka, I shall never forget you.' (August 15, 1925.) And a little later: 'Yesterday Hagen together with Else. Celebrated my birthday together. She gave me a nice coloured cardigan. A sweet night. She is a good darling. Sometimes I hurt her bitterly. What a budding, bursting night of love. I am loved! Why complain!' (October 28, 1925.) But a few days later his mood changes: 'Over me and women there hangs a curse. Woe to those who love you! What an agonising thought. One is ready to despair.' (November 10, 1925.) And finally he comes to the conclusion: 'Such is life: many blossoms, many thorns, and – a dark grave.' (July 18, 1926.) In any case: 'Marriage would be torment. Eros raises his voice!' (July 29, 1926.)[24] Such outpourings by a man who after all was twenty-eight years old contrast with countless affirmations of an excessive self-confidence, which at all times turns abruptly into self-pity or, through a trivial demonisation of his own ego, threatens a plunge into the void. Then he writes, for example:

I am reading Gmelin's *Temudchin* (the Lord of the Earth). Every woman rouses my blood. I run hither and thither like a hungry wolf. And yet I am shy as a child. Often I can hardly understand myself. I ought to get married and become a philistine! And then hang myself after a week![25]

The Lord of the Earth, the feelings of a wolf, satiety and a profound insecurity. In so far as it was not sheer necessity, such impulses undoubtedly helped to persuade this academic, whose professional career had so far been a failure, to enter the NSDAP at the end of 1924. To reassure his worried parents he worked for a short time in a bank, after completing his studies, and then took a job as caller on the stock exchange, before finally, as secretary to a nationalist politician, he came into contact with the National Socialists. As a collaborator of Gregor Strasser he belonged first to the social-revolutionary North German wing of the party which, in its 'proletarian' anti-capitalist tendencies, differed markedly from the 'Fascist' South German wing. In Goebbels it found one of its most consistent spokesmen. 'I am the most radical. Of the new type. Man as revolutionary,' he noted, almost ecstatically, in his diary of those years,[26] and in his 'Letters to Contemporaries' he passionately dissociated himself from the bourgeois half-heartedness of the politicians of the German National People's Party. 'Tools of destruction they will call us,' he wrote in that characteristic tone of self-regarding revolutionary fervour. 'Children of revolt, we call ourselves with a poignant tremor. We have been through revolution, through revolt to the very end. We are out for the radical revaluation of all values'; people would 'take fright at the radicalism of our demands'.[27] Even at that time he announced, 'In the last analysis better go down with Bolshevism than live in eternal capitalist servitude,' and thought it 'horrible that we and the Communists bash in each other's heads'.[28] In an open letter to 'My Friend of the Left' he listed a whole catalogue of convictions and attitudes in common, among them fundamental agreement on the need for social solutions, common enmity towards the bourgeoisie and the 'lying system', as well as the fight 'for freedom' waged 'honestly and resolutely' by both sides, so that ultimately the only division remained the tactical question of the most appropriate means. 'You and I,' Goebbels finished his letter, 'we are fighting one another although we are not really enemies. By so doing we are splitting our strength, and we shall never reach our goal. Perhaps the last extremity will bring us together. Perhaps!'[29]

These questions raised by the socialist wing of the movement brought Goebbels into violent conflict, above all, with the so-called 'Munich group', the 'Munich big shots', as he called them.[30] During this controversy, at a party congress in Hanover early in 1926, he made the famous demand 'that the petty bourgeois Adolf Hitler shall be expelled from the National Socialist Party'.[31] But three weeks later, at a meeting called by the 'South Germans' in Bamberg, when he compared the external trappings, the prosperity and the great domestic power around Hitler with the material poverty of the Strasser group, he began for the first time to waver. True, he found Hitler's talk on Bolshevism, foreign policy, redemption of the rights and holdings of the princes and private property 'terrible' and spoke of 'one of the greatest disappointments of my life'; but when Hitler publicly embraced him shortly after a speech, Goebbels called him in gratitude 'a genius' and noted emotionally in his diary: 'Adolf Hitler, I love you'.[32] Six months earlier he had asked himself who this man really was, 'Christ or St John?' Now, notably under the influence of a generous invitation to Munich and Berchtesgaden, his last doubts vanished, while simultaneously his ambition recognised the outlines of the role he might play. If Hitler was really 'Christ', then he wanted to be the one to take the part of the prophet; for 'the greater and more towering I make God, the greater and more towering I am myself'.[33] In this sense it really was apt when he wrote that the days in Munich with Hitler had shown him his 'direction and path': the organiser of the Führer myth had found his mission. During his stay, he wrote in his diary:

The chief talks about race problems. It is impossible to reproduce what he said. It must be experienced. He is a genius. The natural, creative instrument of a fate determined by God. I am deeply moved. He is like a child: kind, good, merciful. Like a cat: cunning, clever, agile. Like a lion: roaring and gigantic. A fellow, a man. He talks about the state. In the afternoon about winning over the state and the political revolution. It sounds like prophecy. Up in the skies a white cloud takes on the shape of the swastika. There is a blinking light that cannot be a star. A sign of fate?[34]

From this point on he submitted himself, his whole existence, to his attachment to the person of the 'Führer', consciously eliminating all inhibitions springing from intellect, free will and self-respect. Since this submission was an act less of faith than of insight, it stood firm through all vicissitudes to the end. 'He who forsakes the Führer withers away,' he would say.[35] Three months later in the autumn of 1926 Hitler rewarded him for this change of front by making him a Gauleiter 'with special mandatory powers' at the head of the small, conflict-riven party organisation in Berlin. The hectic, noisy atmosphere of the city particularly suited Goebbels' quick, street-urchin nature. Very early on he had realised that 'history is made in the street' that 'the street is the political characteristic of this age'.[36] Now, by following this maxim to the limit, he rose within a few months to be the city's most feared demagogue. First of all, in order to get himself talked about, he and a tough bodyguard organised beer-hall battles, street brawls, and shooting affrays; one chapter in which he described this period carries the title 'Bloody Rise'. Shortly before this he had written: 'Beware, you dogs. When the Devil is loose in me you will not curb him again.'[37] His practice of stirring up fights was the logical application of a new, completely Machiavellian principle of propaganda. The blood which the party's rise cost among its own members was regarded, not as an inevitable sacrifice in the struggle for a political conviction, but as a deliberate means of furthering a political agitation which had recognised that blood always makes the best headlines. As he stated in a speech of this period:

That propaganda is good which leads to success, and that is bad which fails to achieve the desired result, however intelligent it is, for it is not propaganda's task to be intelligent, its task is to lead to success. Therefore no one can say your propaganda is too rough, too mean; these are not criteria by which it may be characterised. It ought not to be decent, nor ought it to be gentle or soft or humble; it ought to lead to success. If someone says to me, 'Your propaganda is not at a well-bred level,' there is no point in my talking to him at all. Never mind whether propaganda is at a well-bred level; what matters is that it achieves its purpose.[38]

With the aid of these maxims directed exclusively towards success, Goebbels made considerable breaches in the massive front of so-called 'Red Berlin'. In the foreword to a collection of the essays which he had published during this period in his newspaper *Der Angriff*, he speaks with astonishment of the 'incredible freedom' he was allowed by the Republican authorities; and this volume is indeed one of the most damning pieces of evidence of their lack of the will to assert themselves, their infinite helplessness in the face of their sworn enemy. 'Put pressure on your adversary with ice-cold determination,' he says, describing his own demagogic tactics. 'Probe him, search out his weak spot; deliberately and calculatingly sharpen the spear, hurl it with careful aim where the enemy is naked and vulnerable, and then perhaps say with a friendly smile, Sorry, neighbour, but I can't help it! This is the dish of revenge that is enjoyed cold.'[39]

There are countless examples of his method of fighting. For months on end he concentrated his attacks on the Berlin Police President Bernhard Weiss, whom he continually referred to as 'Isodore Weiss'. When the courts forbade him to use this name, he simply attacked the 'Isodore System'. He called Police President Karl Zörgiebel the 'publicity *goy* in the Police Praesidium'; the Reich Chancellor Hermann Müller, who had formerly been in the earthenware industry, a 'traveller in water closets'; Philipp Scheidemann a 'salon simpleton' – all without ever being seriously called to account. When a friend criticised him for his malicious attacks on Bernhard Weiss, who had been a gallant officer and was a man of integrity, he explained cynically that he wasn't in the least interested in Weiss, only in the propaganda effect. 'For our agitation we use whatever is effective.'[40] Through middlemen he circulated scandalous rumours against Carl Severing and was delighted when the democratic press 'fell into the trap'. During the campaign against the Young Reparations plan he openly admitted that he had never read what he was so passionately attacking. 'Propaganda has absolutely nothing to do with truth!' In one article he called the Reichstag a 'stinking dungheap' and blatantly stated that the parliamentary mandate merely served to allow the NSDAP 'to equip itself with democracy's own weapons from the democratic arsenal'.[41] With the same frankness he described the purpose of an election as 'to send a sabotage group into the exalted house', and finally, during the legislative period of 1928, he wrote: 'I am not a member of the Reichstag. I am an IdI. An IdF. An *Inhaber der Immunität* [possessor of immunity], an *Inhaber der Freifahrtkarte* [holder of a free-travel ticket]. What do we care about the Reichstag? We have been elected against the Reichstag, and we shall use our mandate in the spirit of those who gave it to us.' He concluded 'Now you are surprised, eh? But don't think we're already at an end. This is only the overture. You will have a lot more fun with us. Just let the play begin!'[42] A classic example of his mastery of propaganda comes in an article of May 31, 1931, entitled 'The Marshal President':

The presidency of the man to whom we here turn our attention was a deadly tragicomedy; it was based on a fundamental lack of character and an inability, cloaked in a dignified gravity, to see things as they really were. It is indeed painful to have to register the existence of a man merely because he was President of the Republic, a man whose grotesque insignificance raises in us the astonished question: How was it possible for this nincompoop to become Commander of the Imperial Army and President of the Republic?[43]

Only at this point did the article reveal that the man referred to was not, as everyone was bound to think and meant to think, the Reich President von Hindenburg, but the French President MacMahon. When Brüning refused a challenge to a public debate, Goebbels had one of the Chancellor's speeches recorded and refuted it paragraph by paragraph in the Sportpalast, to the accompaniment of yells from his followers. One of his admirers aptly called him the 'Marat of Red Berlin, a nightmare and goblin of history' who wanders 'around the house of this system like a crow around a carcass. A ratcatcher. A conqueror of souls.'[44] With the coming of the world economic crisis the masses flocked to him, and he showed extraordinary skill in mobilising their fears. As early as 1926 he declared in his pamphlet *Die Zweite Revolution* (The Second Revolution): 'We shall achieve everything if we set hunger, despair and sacrifice on the march for our goals. It is my will that we light the beacons in our nation till they form a single great fire of Nationalist and Socialist despair.' Now he openly welcomed the collapse,[45] and did all he could to add fuel to the fires of despair. 'To unleash volcanic passions, outbreaks of rage, to set masses of people on the march, to organise hatred and despair with ice-cold calculation': this was how he saw his self-imposed task.[46] And he succeeded. With diabolical flair, continually thinking up new tricks, he drove his listeners into ecstasy, made them stand up, sing songs, raise their arms, repeat oaths – and he did it, not through the passionate inspiration of the moment, but as the result of sober psychological calculation at the desk. Once he had got the reaction he wanted he stood there, small but erect, generally with one hand on his hip, above the tumult, coolly assessing the effect of his stage management. In truth, the 'little Doctor' with the tormenting feeling of physical inadequacy was capable of bending the masses to his will and making them available for any purpose; he could, as he boasted, play upon the national psyche 'as on a piano'.[47] Out of Horst Wessel, the SA leader who was shot by a rival, at least partly for reasons of jealousy, in a fight over a whore, he created the movement's martyr; after a meeting-hall battle in the Pharus rooms in North Berlin he created the heroic type of the 'Unknown SA Man'; with a kind of underworld pride he made the name 'Chief Bandit of Berlin', applied to him by hostile agitators, his honorary title; he invented slogans, hymns and myths, and made capital out of every defeat. Tireless, tenacious, stubborn: propaganda has absolutely nothing to do with truth! Its success rested rather, as he provocatively confessed, on an appeal to the 'most primitive mass instincts'.[48] He played a decisive part in the NSDAP's election successes wrung from the honest routine propaganda of the democratic parties. Immediately after January 30, 1933, he boasted that 'his propaganda had not only operated directly by winning over millions of supporters; equally important was its effect in paralysing opponents. Many had become so tired, so fearful, so inwardly despairing as a result of his onslaughts that in the end they regarded Hitler's chancellorship as fated.'[49] His reward came in the middle of March 1933 when Hitler openly broke the coalition agreement to bestow upon him the long-planned Ministry for National Enlightenment and Propaganda. On taking office Goebbels cheerfully announced that 'the government intends no longer to leave the people to their own devices'. It was the task of the new ministry 'to establish political coordination between people and government'.[50]

Skilfully riding the crest of a wave of consent made up of countless misunderstandings and blindnesses, he achieved this coordination in an amazingly short time and maintained it through all the phases of the regime right up to the end. Certainly the terrorist threat in the background effectively helped, but then the very essence of totalitarian government always lies in the combination of propaganda and terrorism. It is these two together that alone make possible that thoroughgoing psychological and social organisation of man which reduces the scope of individual freedom to the point of immobility. But we must not overestimate the part played by compulsion, and even such a critical observer, not subject to terrorist intimidation, as the American journalist William L. Shirer, has confessed that this propaganda 'made a certain impression on one's mind and often misled it'.[51]

From the way the role of Goebbels in the further history of the Third Reich, after his promising beginning, at first continuously fell in importance and then, towards the end of the war, suddenly and significantly rose again, we can clearly see to what extent he – and with him National Socialism – had made his way to power by mobilising moods of protest and resentment; indeed, it shows the extent to which the totalitarian propagandist needs an enemy. So long as the young minister's energies were absorbed in building a flawless apparatus of propaganda and surveillance and the fight against internal political resistance still furnished the required material for the psychological manipulation of the masses, the problem remained concealed. Then, however, it emerged all the more distinctly, especially as resort to the creation of outside enemies was barred for a long time while the government strove to win recognition for itself.

In consequence Goebbels was pushed into the background, at first almost imperceptibly. His writings at this time also remain curiously dull and empty. He may have realised this, since he did not publish them in a collected edition, as he did his writings during the period of struggle and later during the war years. Explaining his waning influence at that time, he once stated that he often looked back with longing to the years before the seizure of power, when there was something to attack.[52] Only when inner and outer political consolidation had progressed far enough for the control hitherto exercised to be abandoned did Goebbels find in the increasingly unrestrained practice of anti-Semitism by the state new possibilities into which he threw himself with all the zeal of an ambitious man worried by a constant diminution of his power. Thus the man who in earlier years had frequently mocked the primitive anti-Semitism of nationalist politicians now became one of the most relentless Jew-baiters. Unquestionably, personal motives also played a part; possibly his hatred of the Jews was an externalised form of self-hatred. A man who conformed so little to the National Socialist image of the élite and whose fellow pupils are said at one time to have called him 'the Rabbi'[53] may have had his reason, in the struggles for power at Hitler's court,

93

for offering keen anti-Semitism as a counterweight to his failure to conform to a type: ideological rectitude to counterbalance typological deviation. His attitude may also have had something to do with the fact that shortly before the onset of the great wave of anti-Semitism in 1938 he had risked his own prestige and that of the party by a passionate love affair, and was obsessed by the urge to rehabilitate himself. But whatever his real motives, it is fairly certain that Goebbels himself did not take the race theory seriously; one of his colleagues reported that during his twelve-year period in office Goebbels never once 'so much as mentioned it' inside the Ministry.[54] The opportunist and tactical motives behind his anti-Semitism are also evident from the fact that the measures he took to purify German culture of foreign influences were directed predominantly against the representatives of a spirit far nearer his own inclinations than the oppressive National Socialist approach to art, which he himself now propagated. Lastly, everything seems to indicate that in Goebbels' anti-Semitism, over and above individual motives, we must see an example of that dialectic common to all totalitarian propaganda: the need for a barbarically exaggerated image of the opponent. This helps to harness the aggressions within a society while attaching the latent positive energies to emotional idealisations of its own leader figures. Only in this way could propaganda regain that vehemence which had once brought it such success, even if there was always an obvious element of strained artificiality about the demonised figure of the Jew as presented by Goebbels with ever more breathless efforts. All his attempts to paint the universal enemy as a wirepuller at work from Moscow to Wall Street were shattered by the reality of the frightened and harassed human beings wearing the yellow star, who for a time wandered the streets of German cities before suddenly vanishing forever.

How much Goebbels' propaganda owed to the friend-enemy stereotype is also shown by a comment of Hitler's, which he proudly noted in his diary in 1943, to the effect that he 'is one of the few who today know how to make something useful out of the war'. The important thing about this first word of praise from Hitler for a long time is that it coincided with the turning-point in the war; for up to that time Goebbels, for all his efforts, had not succeeded in winning back the ground he had lost. Even towards the end of 1939 his rival Rosenberg had noted with satisfaction a statement by Hitler that for the duration of the war the Propaganda Minister must be kept as far as possible in the background.[55] With the first crises and setbacks, on the other hand, when propaganda abandoned the unprofitable tone of confidence in victory in favour of a growing bitterness, and switched from contempt for the enemy to hatred, Goebbels made his long-prepared comeback. He showed once again his old impudent adroitness, his cynical art of sowing confusion, and with an enemy to hate he also regained that great rhetorical fervour which had once won him the reputation of being the party's best speaker, superior even to Hitler.[56]

This was proved not only by his articles in the periodical *Das Reich*, in which he adopted the principle of at least *one* surprising concession to truth each time, but also by the inventiveness with which he wore down the enemy's nerve by

94

broadcasts over the front lines, by mobilising fear of an imaginary fifth column, and other means. He invented new terms, such as 'Coventrisation', and later, according to the state of the war, the formula of the 'advantage of the inner line'. He deftly usurped the enemy's V-sign as a symbol of Germany's own confidence in victory, discouraged undesirable behaviour by the creation of easily understood characters like the 'coal grabber' or that threatening black shadow-man who announced from every wall that the enemy was listening. Finally, faced with the growing hopelessness of the military situation, he invented the 'secret weapon'. The astonishing effect of his ideas once more confirmed Hitler's assertion 'that by the clever and continuous use of propaganda a people can even be made to mistake heaven for hell, and vice versa, the most miserable life for Paradise'.[57] Preoccupied as he was with propaganda, it was, as one of his colleagues confirmed, 'almost a happy day' for him when famous buildings were destroyed in an air raid, because at such times he put into his appeals that ecstatic hatred which aroused the fanaticism of the tiring workers and spurred them to fresh efforts. He strove for hours after the Stalingrad disaster to get Hitler's permission to stage a spectacular requiem, which finally took place in vast and sombre splendour. He achieved one of his greatest triumphs as a speaker when shortly afterwards he put his famous ten 'evocative questions' to an invited audience in the Sportpalast, raising them to a consciousness of being representative of the nation, and 'in a turmoil of wild emotion', as he wrote afterwards, won agreement to total war. Every sentence, every effect, every heightening of the emotional temperature in this speech, down to the electrifying final phrase, 'Now, nation, arise – storm, break loose!' had been carefully calculated days in advance. Even before he set out for this gathering he had confidently predicted: 'Today there will be a demonstration that will make the thirtieth of January rally look like a mothers' meeting.'[58] But he took every care not to allow himself to be carried away, to see to it that he remained the organiser, never the victim, of his own propaganda effects, even if he did not always succeed in this, and occasionally found himself caught in the grip of his own demagogy. When later, faced with the enemy's approaching front, he played on the spectre of the 'Asiatic hordes' with all the means at his disposal, he at the same time called Soviet propaganda 'the best horse in the stable' and toyed with the idea of a separate pact with the East:[59] a Machiavellian through and through, he desired power in exactly the same degree as he despised its objects.

In fact, Goebbels' career can be explained only on the basis of a deeply rooted contempt for humanity. Again and again the revealing expression 'man the beast' (*Canaille Mensch*) occurs in his private jottings,[60] a favourite formula to express his humiliated personality. Opponents, friends, supporters and finally the whole nation never meant more to him than raw material for achieving successful effects and bolstering his self-exaltation and power. The tirades of hate and the festive Sportpalast – they all came from him and in purpose and execution were nothing but cynically admitted gimmicks. He could speak to the hearts of millions although not one word came from his own heart; he manipulated souls and ideas and himself: it was all one. As the coldest and most unscrupulous calculator among the top leadership, he was entirely free from that 'burden of conscience' the removal of which from the whole nation Hitler had announced as his historic mission.[61] What urged him on throughout his life was the hatred felt by the weak, crippled and deformed which found satisfaction only when he could drive 'with ice-cold calculation' the healthy, those who were not crippled, through all the stages of delusion, intoxication and exhaustion. He seemed always anxiously trying to prove to the world that intelligent deformity was superior to dull-witted normality. In a report on a political discussion he noted, 'I dominated'. All his life he sought this consciousness of power. And if his physical weakness was the source of so many sufferings and tensions, it was certainly also one of the essential factors in his rise. He once recalled with amusement the statement of his old form master after his valedictory address that although he was gifted he was not cut out to be an orator,[62] which only proves the point that a shortcoming may be the cause not only of great failure but also of great achievement.

Just as he himself only used other people, so he allowed himself right up to the end to be used without demur, without a thought of revolt. During the last phase of the war, he not only regained and actually heightened his power and prestige but also to a great extent recovered his personal position of trust with Hitler, so that there was no feeling of having been slighted which might have prompted him to follow an independent line. True, he showed a certain tendency to think for himself after realising that Hitler was beginning to lose his earlier intuitive certainty; but the attachment retained its strength, and up to the last he extolled 'the height of good fortune that allowed me to be his contemporary'.[63] Even out of the ruins of the shattered Reich Chancellery he brought up again insanely and against his better knowledge the myth which he had once created that 'together with this man you can conquer the world'.[64] The attempt had failed. But true to his principle that the propagandist must never contradict himself he continued – with Russian tanks already in the suburbs of Berlin – to call Hitler the only man who could point the way to a new and flourishing Europe.[65] If the German people never shouted over Adolf Hitler the dreaded 'Crucify him!' it was largely due to Goebbels. But he himself, when all was manifestly lost, stood among the smoking debris and shouted 'Hosanna!' as he had once predicted, the paradoxical picture of an opportunist who at the last proved to be the most loyal follower. But what looked like loyalty was merely the realisation of his own lack of substance, which all his life, despite all his gifts, forced him into the role of substitute. He liked to hear himself referred to as the movement's Talleyrand, but he was certainly not that. 'I never pursued a policy of my own,'[66] he repeatedly asserted. Very true!

Unhesitatingly he accepted Hitler's end as his own. Unlike the former comrades in arms who ignominiously fled – Ley, Ribbentrop, Streicher – but also without the naïve self-deception of Göring or Himmler, he had no illusions as to how intensely they had provoked the world. 'As for us,' he wrote in *Das Reich* of November 14, 1943, 'we have burnt our bridges. We cannot go back, but neither do we want to go back. We are forced to extremes and therefore resolved to proceed to extremes.' And later: 'We shall go down in history as the greatest statesmen of all time, or as the greatest criminals.' He was level-headed enough to accept responsibility for the final verdict. For this reason he pressed Hitler, who as always was shrinking from important decisions, to await the end in the Reich Chancellery and add the crowning apotheosis to the artificially constructed myth. His last concern, to which he devoted himself with alert and tenacious resolution, was with a practised hand to make the end itself a spectacle of breathtaking grandeur. His remarks in his farewell conversation with Hans Fritzsche, in which, following Hitler's example, he ascribed the collapse to the failure of the German people, and at the same time the way he strove to intensify the process of destruction, were like a final seal set upon his contempt for humanity. 'When we depart, let the earth tremble!' were the last words with which, on April 21, 1945, he dismissed his associates.[67] What he seemed to fear more than anything else was a death devoid of dramatic effects; to the end, he was what he had always been: the propagandist for himself. Whatever he thought or did was always based solely on this one agonising wish for self-exaltation, and this same object was served by the murder of his children, on the evening of May 1, 1945. They were the last victims of an egomania extending beyond the grave. However, this deed too failed to make him the figure of tragic destiny he had hoped to become; it merely gave his end a touch of repulsive irony. A few hours later he died, together with his wife, in the gardens of the Reich Chancellery.

'The essence of propaganda,' he once remarked, 'consists in winning people over to an idea so sincerely, so vitally, that in the end they succumb to it utterly and can never again escape from it.'[68] By this standard, he undoubtedly failed; for the idea of National Socialism has been forgotten, or is at most only a memory. However, on closer inspection this maxim of propaganda proves to be itself no more than propaganda; in reality, totalitarian propaganda does not count on exercising a permanent influence. It bears witness to its own knowledge of the futility of its efforts in the capricious abruptness with which it alters watchwords and 'granite principles', demands damning judgments or oaths of loyalty, hails the deadly enemy of yesterday as the faithful ally of today, brands the friend a traitor, revokes, annuls, rewrites its history, and obtains from the people protestations of faith in each of its erratic changes of course, wiping out at each switch all previous truths and oaths of loyalty. There can be little doubt that Goebbels was occasionally aware of this, and his early words 'But scratch our names in history, that we shall do,'[69] now sound like an anticipatory reply. Certainly he succeeded in this aim. It was probably a matter of indifference to him whether he figured in history as a criminal or a statesman, but how wretched is his fame compared with what it cost.

Reinhard Heydrich – The Successor

We all suffer from the disease of mixed, corrupted blood. How can we purify ourselves and make atonement? The eternal life bestowed by the Grail is only for the really pure and noble!

Adolf Hitler

In Reinhard Heydrich, National Socialism seemed to be confronting itself. The true architect and brain behind the concept of the future SS state, he seemed to embody in its purest form everything that could be discerned behind the front of irrational 'magic' aimed at the masses and their need to believe – the rationality of its will to subjugate, the perfectionist objectivity, free from humanitarian restraints, of its striving for domination as decided by the inner circle of the leadership. He was a man like a whiplash. In his Luciferian coldness, amorality and insatiable greed for power he was comparable only to the great criminals of the Renaissance, with whom he shared a conscious awareness of the omnipotence of man. In his case this took the form of the conviction that by the methodical application of technology and organisation everything was possible: the construction of a government, the establishment of an empire, the re-creation of a race, the purification of blood over wide areas. And he intended these means to be directed to one single end: power. In his funeral speech Hitler called him 'the Man with the Iron Heart', and from among Himmler's own entourage comes the statement that beside the obtusely romantic figure of the Reichsführer of the SS himself, Heydrich seemed 'like polished steel'.[1] In his outlook, unencumbered by either ideologies or emotions and accustomed to assessing and using feelings, convictions, individual people and whole nations as merely means and instruments, he seemed the epitome not merely of National Socialist totalitarianism but of modern totalitarianism as a whole; and if he left the world a legacy before he had come fully into his own, it was that he taught man to fear man more comprehensively than ever before. The traditional idea of evil, which is linked with the concepts of possession by spirits, uncontrollable outbursts of emotion, and an attachment to the dark instincts, breaks down before the transparent sobriety of this type. So does the concept of the demonic, which has metaphysical overtones inappropriate to the unwavering realistic conception of power of this totally secularised phenomenon. At the same time the portrait is not free from murky patches; against its overall background we see the outlines of individual complications, and if he seemed, as almost no one else, to possess all the National

98

Socialist virtues, the lies of National Socialism lay on him more heavily than on others.

At the core of National Socialism, the foundation of its belief in its own superiority and at the same time the 'state philosophy' of the Third Reich,[2] lay the idea of race. Whatever aspect of ideology or practical policy was uppermost at any given moment – whether nationalist, socialist, monarchist or other tendencies – it only served to a greater or lesser degree to distract attention from the all-powerful racial doctrine. It has rightly been pointed out that 'the doctrine of the racial enemy is as essential to National Socialism as the doctrine of the class enemy is to Bolshevism'.[3] It welded together old emotions and prejudices which had been given a pseudo-scientific veneer during the nineteenth century and now, linked with nationalist, socialist and economic grievances, became a programme for political struggle of extraordinary explosive power. In itself, the mythological exaltation of their own race above the so-called lower or opposed races served the tactical purpose of increasing the masses' self-confidence and mobilising their will to violence. The lack of any clear scientific authority made racism all the easier to use as an instrument of power, and no attempt was ever made to define it more precisely, since its very vagueness lent it more readily to terrorism. It was directed at will against whatever groups those in power wished to destroy and applied with ever-increasing radicality, beginning with the sterilisation and euthanasia programmes and ending with the 'Final Solution' of the Jewish problem.

Nevertheless the race theory contained a utopian element that gnawed into the ideology of Hitler and his closer followers with the force and exclusiveness of an obsession. Hitler was influenced above all by the theories of the nineteenth-century social Darwinist school, whose conception of man as biological material was bound up with impulses towards a planned society.[4] He was convinced that the race was disintegrating, deteriorating through faulty breeding as a result of a liberally tinged promiscuity that was vitiating the nation's blood. And this led to the establishment of a catalogue of 'positive' curative measures: racial hygiene, eugenic choice of marriage partners, the breeding of human beings by the methods of selection on the one hand and extirpation on the other. The guiding aide of the 'race-attached soul' made all cultural and creative achievements dependent on external appearance and at the same time linked the ability and hence the right to found states and empires with biological preconditions. This is what gave National Socialist racism that imperialistic aspect, and its consciousness of mission, that thought in terms of vast areas and whole populations, that hybrid streak. After Hitler had spoken at an early stage within the narrower circle of his intimates of the need to develop a 'technique of depopulation',[5] he made an unconcealed demand in his speech to the Reichstag of October 6, 1939, for the rearrangement of nations and races in Eastern Europe.[6] Behind this lay the vision of 'a closed central area of people of pure blood', inhabited and defended around its frontiers by a human type whose appearance had been described by the race theorist Hans F. K. Günther as 'blond, tall, long-skulled, with narrow faces, pronounced chins, narrow noses with a high bridge, soft fair hair, widely spaced pale-coloured eyes, pinky-white skin colour'.[7] The efficacy of this racial image, however, was so repeatedly undermined – particularly by the physical appearance of most of the leading National Socialists – that it must not be seen as too binding. Yet there were frequent attempts to reconcile the leaders of the Third Reich to this racial picture, some of them so outrageous as to be comic, as when one writer stated:

Hitler is blond, has pink skin and blue eyes, and is therefore of a pure Aryan-Germanic character, and all contrary statements concerning his appearance and personality have been sown in the people's soul by the Black and Red press, which I hope herewith to have corrected.[8]

Reinhard Heydrich seemed to be the exception. With his combination of abilities and physical characteristics he seemed to confirm the theory of the race-attached soul: to anticipate that type of new man who was to be distilled by a process of interbreeding designed to suppress undesirable characteristics out of the murky biological material of the German people, and by education in special schools; 'the man who', as Hitler once declared, 'is master of life and death, of human fear and superstition, who has learnt to control his body, his muscles and his nerves but remains at the same time impervious to the temptations of the intellect and so-called "free" thought'.[9] Heydrich was tall, blond, athletic, and combined high intelligence with a metallic streak in his nature which was regarded as the proof of a special racial grace. 'A young, evil god of death,' as Carl Jacob Burckhardt said after meeting him, he was sometimes called by his subordinates, with a mixture of fear and admiration, 'the Blond Beast', while *Das Schwarze Korps* wrote of him: 'Even in his outward appearance he was an SS man as the people picture him, a man all of one piece.'[10]

Heydrich was actually a deeply split personality. This menacing figure with its apparently well-knit, compact inhumanity concealed a nervously irritable individual, subject to secret anxieties and continually plagued by tension, bitterness and self-hatred. His cynicism, the sign of complex weakness and vulnerability, alone betrayed what his elastic youthfulness concealed. His hardness and imperviousness were founded less in a tendency to sadistic brutality, as is popularly believed, than in the forced absence of conscience of a man who lived under continual constraint. For Reinhard Tristan Eugen Heydrich was besmirched by an indelible stain and in a melancholy state of 'mortal sin': he had Jewish ancestors.

He tried to destroy all the evidence. As soon as he was in a position to do so, he had all the documents brought to him from register offices and church records, but he was unable to prevent enemies and rivals, to whom such knowledge meant real power, from getting hold of documentary evidence of his racially impure parentage. Martin Bormann's much-feared secret card-index was never found after the war; nevertheless Bormann's personal file on Heydrich, which included his family tree, has been preserved. This family tree goes back only one generation on his mother's side and omits the name, parentage and place of origin of his

100

grandmother. After an investigation ordered during 1932 and 1933 by Gregor Strasser, at the instigation of Rudolf Jordan, the Gauleiter of Halle-Merseburg, a report was submitted by the information office of the NSDAP centre in Munich. However, it dealt only with the parental line, since Jordan's suspicions were based primarily on the fact that the father, Bruno Richard Heydrich, an exceptionally gifted and versatile musician and founder of the First Halle Conservatory for Music, Theatre and Teaching, was described in Riemann's musical encyclopedia of 1916 as 'Heydrich, Bruno, real name Süss.' The report came to the conclusion that the name 'Süss' was not incriminating and that Bruno Heydrich's son, born on March 7, 1904, was free from any Jewish blood.[11]

Nevertheless, rumours continued, and up to 1940 Heydrich had repeatedly to bring legal action for racial slander. As Chief of the Political Police, he won with ease, but this did not spare him the tormenting consciousness of racial inadequacy. Hitler and Himmler also knew of the doubts of Heydrich's pedigree, and took advantage of them in their own way, with a characteristic mixture of opportunism and blackmail. They received the first hints soon after the unemployed naval officer, who had been cashiered after a court-martial at the end of 1930 for an affair with a young girl, joined the SS.[12] Whereas Himmler, with the bigoted simple-mindedness of the strict believer, seemed at first in favour of expelling Heydrich, Hitler decided after a long private conversation, as reported by Himmler, 'that Heydrich was a highly gifted but also very dangerous man, whose gifts the movement had to retain. Such people could still be used so long as they were kept well in hand and for that purpose his non-Aryan origins were extremely useful; for he would be eternally grateful to us that we had kept him and not expelled him and would obey blindly.' 'That,' said Himmler, self-confidently adding his own comment, 'was in fact the case.'[13]

However, Himmler saw this relationship in his own biased way, and like everything he said about Heydrich after the latter's death, the above words bear traces of his attempt to wipe from his memory the inferiority and even fear he felt for years on end towards his own subordinate; for Heydrich was certainly too cold and controlled for emotional acts of submission and not made for either blindness or obedience. Nevertheless he had to pay all his life for the fact that his ambition had carried him into an élite Aryan order. He became entangled in the contradiction between his origins and the demands of ideology, and his destructive dynamism is only to be understood in terms of constant attempts to burst out of the trammels of a situation where he repeatedly faced ultimately insoluble problems. 'He suffered constantly,' Himmler said. 'He never really found peace; something was always upsetting him. Often I've talked to him and tried to help him, even against my own convictions, pointing out the possibility of overcoming Jewish elements by the admixture of better German blood, citing himself as a case in point. For the time being, it is true, he was very grateful to me for such help and seemed as if liberated, but nothing was any use in the long run.'[14]

The truth is that Heydrich was beyond help. To be sure, there is no doubt that he too had that opportunist attitude towards National Socialist ideology which saw in such theoretical constructions solely a welcome cover of respectability for a selfish lust for power and despised ideological zeal as evidence of lack of talent. Reasons of inner self-assertion alone induced his ideological nihilism, and just as he himself till his entry into the SS 'knew nothing about politics and had never shown any great interest in them', so his wife said later, in choosing even his closest collaborators he attached far less importance to their devotion to an idea than to their devotion to him personally.[15] But in the long run he could not escape the influence of the pervading ideology. With his inward-looking analytical turn of mind he had no more hope of learning to live with his contradictions than of finding consolation in easy phrases of the sort that helped people like Robert Ley over the problems of a questionable pedigree.

Out of such personal constrictions Heydrich developed or strengthened qualities that show all too clearly the desire to take revenge on life. The coldness and contempt with which he viewed human beings and human life may give us a hint of the way in which, during hours of solitary self-confrontation, he treated himself. Only alcohol and the pleasures of night life enjoyed with forced intemperance – outings on which he ordered his subordinates by turns to accompany him – could bring him brief respite from a life in which he was constantly being tested to breaking-point. The span of opposites that separates this picture from that other one which shows him as the head of a family, an anxious father and a passionate music-lover who devoted his free evenings to chamber music and especially to the music of Haydn and Mozart, was not based, as with so many SS members, on an ability to combine the incompatible; it was a case rather of a desire to suppress that which he had recognised as incompatible. One of his colleagues has described the haunting and profoundly revealing occasion when Heydrich came home at night to his brightly lit apartment and suddenly saw his reflection in a large wall mirror. In an attack of cold rage he 'whipped his pistol from his holster and fired two shots at this double', the ever and tormentingly present negation of himself, from which he could free himself in liquor and in the splintered glass, but not in reality. He was the prisoner of this figure of negation, he lived in a world populated by the self-created chimeras of a hostile distrust, scented behind everything treachery, intrigue or the snares of hidden enmity, and thought only in terms of dependence – the most impressive embodiment of that vulgarised Darwinist principle in whose light the world was revealed to National Socialist ideology: life seen exclusively as struggle. Himmler said of him that he was 'the embodiment of distrust – the "hypersuspicious", as people called him – nobody could endure it for long'.[17]

From the outset of his career, after he had recognised the value of the personal files initiated by Himmler, Heydrich collected information 'about servant girls as much as about ministers', convinced that only the knowledge of other people's weaknesses created loyalties. Unmoved by complexes of loyalty conditioned by emotion, which he regarded as weakness, he actually kept a dossier on Hitler and Himmler. In Berlin he had an intimate salon specially constructed for this purpose with double walls, microphones and monitoring equipment, which recorded every word and conveyed it to a listening post.[18] His burning desire for revenge is revealed in the unanimous reports that he explored particularly avidly the antecedents of other leading personalities. He was well informed about both Hitler's unexplained origins and the traces of Jewish blood among the relations of Himmler, about Goebbels' private affairs, Göring's debauches and bribe-taking, and Rosenberg's letters to his Jewish mistress.[19] As no-one else among his colleagues and rivals, he was a master of indirect methods of gaining influence, of bringing about the almost imperceptible shifting of power which only became visible at the moment of a rival's downfall. With the exception of Bormann, who thanks to his personal position of trust with Hitler felt unassailable, everyone feared him, however high above him they might stand in the official hierarchy, and they watched his apparently inexorable rise with a mixture of fascination and impotence, like an approaching doom.

In fact, he had set his sights high. Treating any secondary position as either a step towards the rank above or as a failure, he is said to have aimed at nothing less than the actual leadership of the Third Reich, and certain high functionaries of the regime asserted after the war that he would have had a chance of attaining this goal.[20] This may be an exaggeration, but it does confirm the direction and level of his aspirations, which were all of an utterly selfish nature. Unlike most of his fellow-leaders, who built up their careers on ruthlessness, courage and luck, he was not a gambler who had drifted into politics, but a calculator, and to him power was not a matter of taking chances but a technical problem entirely susceptible of solution by rational means. Just as he despised ideological ties, so, more comprehensively, he rejected all aims beyond power; for him, power was an aim in itself; any need to orient will and actions by notions of value that went beyond goals immediately in sight was alien to him. In this too he represented in almost unadulterated form the type of the modern technician of power who subordinates ideologies to tactics. He did not feel himself the servant of a cause, nor even the servant of an idea of the state that encroached upon all spheres of existence; his entirely Jacobin radicalism was not the outcome of reasons of state to which no bounds were set but the sign of a purely private greed for power. If Machiavelli's famous letter to Vettori of 1517, in which he set the fatherland above the salvation of the individual's own soul, really announced the emergence of a new era, then a figure like Heydrich marked a new subdivision of it. For him the salvation of his own soul was worth less than the exaltation of a power that desired only itself.

He was clever enough to keep his ambition in another's shadow, and destiny displayed remarkable perspicacity in bringing Heydrich together with the fussy, narrow-minded Himmler, whose disastrous mixture of energy and dependence made him the ideal steward of other people's purposes. The assertion that Himmler was only Heydrich's creature, or, as Göring put it, that 'the brain was called Heydrich',[21] is true in so far as the sinister features in Himmler's colourless philistine profile were lent by Heydrich. Whatever the motives for their alliance, each certainly regarded the other as an instrument of his personal striving for power. Whereas the leader of the still unimportant SS, which was then sub-ordinate to the SA, felt that in his highly gifted but racially tainted henchman he had found a partner who could smooth his path to the inner circle of the power-holders without ever becoming his rival, he himself probably already figured in Heydrich's plans as an aid of only passing value.

It was a singular partnership, which proceeded, beginning with the seizure of power in Bavaria, to set up the firing lines on the internal political scene from behind which they sooner or later drove all opponents of their personal ambition. Himmler was formally the superior, but was filled with petty bourgeois admira-tion for the other's smooth viciousness and unscrupulous dash. Eccentric, loquacious, full of aimless fervour, and so unsure of himself that to an observer he used to look 'as though he had been raped' after listening to Heydrich force-fully putting his viewpoint, he not infrequently first yielded and then tried to countermand his premature consent by issuing what purported to be an order from the Führer.[22] As for Heydrich, he was humiliatingly at Himmler's mercy because of his origins, but was always superior, dynamic, concentrated, unsenti-mental, at once dangerous and indispensable. The cranky projects to which Himmler devoted himself with obstinate conviction met with nothing but critical or sarcastic reserve from Heydrich, and often the discussion ended, as Frau Heydrich later reported, with Himmler bursting out excitedly and revealingly, 'You and your logic. We never hear about anything but your logic. Everything I propose you batter down with your logic. I'm fed up with you and your cold, rational criticism.'[23] On the other hand, it was obviously Heydrich who, even before 1933, drew Himmler's attention to the potentialities open to the SS Reichsführer. He was the originator of the plan to 'develop the police force of the Third Reich out of the SS'.[24] For himself, Heydrich demanded control of the Party Security Service (SD).

Heydrich clearly saw that in a modern totalitarian system of government there is no limit to the principle of state security, so that anyone in charge of it is bound to acquire almost unrestricted power. Within a year, always in agreement with Himmler, he gained control first of the Munich police, then of the Bavarian, and in turn of each of the political police of the German *Länder*. The last was Prussia, whose chief, Rudolf Diels, was astute enough and had enough friends in high places to resist until April 20, 1934; then he and Göring had to yield. Heydrich himself became head of the Secret Police (Gestapo) as well as of the SD, and in 1936, when Himmler became Chief of the German Police, Heydrich was also given control of the Criminal Police. He was then, at thirty-two, one of the most powerful men in the country. From the various areas of authority which he had acquired he organised in 1939 the Reich Central Security Office (RSHA) and therewith at last emerged at the top of the security services. Although still nominally subordinate to Himmler, he gradually began to secure the independence of his offices and activities. In a labyrinth of countless reports he evolved a system of surveillance whose huge, suspicious eye took in first the whole of Germany and later large parts of Europe, while not only the scope but also the intensity of his activities continually increased. As one of the few leaders of the Third Reich whose actions were not guided by a will to power acting instinctively but were rationally controlled and thought out, he evidently realised that the task of a consistently totalitarian police apparatus does not end with the elimination of all opposing forces and tendencies, but only at this point really begins to develop its special function. While the negative security functions of the initial period diminish, the terrorist omnipresence of the secret police increasingly works towards the establishment of total domination, the essential feature of which is not the absence of all opposition but 'the power to realise the current totalitarian fiction'. The secret police's purpose here is not to eradicate doubt but to foster faith or ceaselessly spur on the public to ostensibly spontaneous enthusiasm.[25] Only by recognising these principles, which were never fully put into practice in the Third Reich although the first phase was achieved, can we grasp the high aims of Heydrich's conception of the technique of power.

The make-up of his character and the insecurity due to his origins led Heydrich to take a particular interest, out of all the functions of the RSHA which he took over, in that of intelligence. Even in earlier years this ambition had caused friction between himself and the chief of the military secret service of the German High Command – the Abwehr – Admiral Canaris, although Heydrich, since their shared experience in the Navy, had close personal ties with his former superior and patron. An attempt to lay down their respective areas of jurisdiction in a ten-point plan quickly came to nothing, since the agreement meant no more to Heydrich than a tactical move to tie the hands of his rival. Moreover Canaris too seems to have succumbed like others to a complex of fear and fascination which immediately placed him in an inferior position in dealing with the ice-cold Heydrich. He was able to halt the inexorable diminution of his powers only when he had succeeded in obtaining photocopies of documents proving his adversary's Jewish antecedents and placing them in safe keeping abroad.[26]

After Heydrich had given such an impressive demonstration of his cunning and adroitness in the elimination of Röhm and the destruction of the power of the SA, he became almost indispensable wherever any dirty business had to be arranged. He had a hand in the Tukhachevsky affair, which led to the liquidation of the top military leaders of the Soviet Union,[27] and in the dismissal of the traditionalist Army leaders Blomberg and Fritsch following fabricated scandalous 'revelations'. His work behind the scenes helped to prepare the way for the Austrian *Anschluss* and the piecemeal incorporation of Czechoslovakia. In some way that is still obscure he was behind the attempt on Hitler's life in the Munich Bürgerbräu; he organised the nation-wide anti-Semitic demonstration that came to be known as the 'Crystal Night', conceived and staged the 'attack' on the German radio station at Gleiwitz which was to provide a pretext for declaring war on Poland, and finally was the initiator of Project Bernhard, the attempt to undermine the British currency by means of forged Bank of England notes.[28] As though under a compulsion, he always thought in terms of underhand methods,

105

intrigue, bribery or blackmail, and he believed that the most devious routes were quickest. His pessimistic and thwarted outlook on life was at the bottom of his idea that men were base, cowardly and selfish but also easily deceived. He seemed curiously incapable of understanding unselfish attitudes, and his deep-seated conviction of the total impotence of morality persuaded him that power could be achieved only by understanding and exploiting the meaner side of human nature. Honesty was not only alien to him but basically incomprehensible, and just as he had no friends, so he also avoided making open enemies – not out of fear, but because straightforward relationships were not in his nature. His curious preference for getting rid of opponents he disliked by poisoning was not so much an inconsistency based on romantic memories, as it may appear by contrast with the rationality of his mentality, as simply an expression of his deviousness. No less characteristic was his plan for destroying the churches: to send young, unshakably fanatical National Socialists into the seminaries for priests in order to begin their work on sedition from within.[29]

Hence he probably received with somewhat divided feelings the order for the so-called Final Solution of the Jewish Problem, which was given to him on January 24, 1939 (and, with the further order to supervise the 'zone of German influence in Europe', again on July 31, 1941). True, he never shrank from any task, and to this too he immediately devoted himself with that tendency to perfectionist, large-scale solutions and the apocalyptic thoroughness typical of the organisational thinking of National Socialist officialdom. But cunning was more in his line than brutality, and for an opponent to step unsuspectingly into an artistically constructed trap gave him a satisfaction he never derived from any aggressively brutal act. It has been reported that he tried to keep his criminal activity secret; he was to a great extent the author of the bureaucratic and commonplace terminology in which the business of mass murder was disguised. And Himmler's remark in his funeral address that Heydrich had scruples about organised genocide is all the more plausible because such feelings were strictly at variance with the principles of hardness governing the SS.[30]

These scruples found no outward expression, however, and with an inflexibility that gave no hint of inner conflict, Heydrich set about seizing and herding together the Jews of Europe and sending them to their death, partly by 'natural reduction', that is to say by hunger, exhaustion, or disease, and partly by physical destruction, either with the aid of murder squads or by the so-called 'special treatment' of mass gassing. He conceived the overall plan which, over and above extermination of the Jewish race, was to make vast areas of the East available as 'experimental fields' for eugenic breeding. He evolved the methods to be employed and, characteristically, such play with perfidiousness as the idea of forcing the Jewish communities themselves to organise the Final Solution at its lower levels.[31] It was not solely because of his position that he was entrusted with this task; and if the extraordinary thoroughness with which he set about it was due to the wish to wipe out the stain on his own pedigree by ruthless action, this was entirely in line with the considerations that had led Hitler and Himmler to choose him. As early as 1936, in an essay entitled *Wandlungen unseres Kampfes* (Metamorphoses of Our Struggle), he had declared himself with almost frenzied emphasis in favour of the 'historical task' of combating and defeating the 'Jewish universal enemy' and his shrill tone made clear the motive of self-purification which was the desperate and senseless basic striving of his life. He once remarked despondently to Walter Schellenberg that it was 'sheer madness to have created this Jewish problem', while Himmler remarked:

> He [Heydrich] had overcome the Jew in himself by purely intellectual means and had swung over to the other side. He was convinced that the Jewish elements in his blood were damnable; he hated the blood which had played him so false. The Führer could really have picked no better man than Heydrich for the campaign against the Jews. For them he was without mercy or pity.
>
> For the rest it will interest you to know that Heydrich was a very good violinist. He once played a serenade in my honour; it was really excellent – a pity that he did not do more in this field.[32]

This utterance, which is as useful a contribution to an understanding of the psychological structure of the Reichsführer of the SS as to that of his subordinate, also reveals the impulses behind Heydrich's desire to prove himself. Over and above the calculated power aims that were the essential objects of his ambition, Heydrich was imbued with a restless desire to distinguish himself. From early in his life a nervous energy drove him to seize everything, to know everything, to excel in all fields, not merely those of the intellect. As an athlete he was above average; he was a good fencer, shot and rider, and he also tried to distinguish himself in war. Soon after the beginning of the war he persuaded Hitler, who was at first reluctant, to let him go on active service as a pilot, and would not rest until, on the strength of a certain number of operations against the enemy – on one of which he had to make a forced landing behind the Russian lines – he received the Iron Cross First Class.[33]

This urge to prove his ability in various fields probably played some part in his decision in autumn 1941 to leave his headquarters in the Prinz-Albrecht-Strasse and go to Prague as Deputy Reich Protector ('Duke of Alva', as Hitler commented). This decision has been interpreted as an attempt to demonstrate his ability in public administration, especially as the new post did not raise his position in the power structure. It is also possible, however, that an additional motive was temporarily to avoid his adversary Admiral Canaris,[34] who shortly before had come into possession of the compromising document on his antecedents. Finally, there may have been some pressure from another quarter: Himmler and Bormann, whose jealous concern had finally been aroused, had joined forces to delay the menacing rise of their young colleague. Heydrich repeatedly referred at this time to his 'continually deteriorating relationship' with both of them, and on his last visit to the Führer's headquarters learnt that the machinations of his rivals had had some success. It is true that even after leaving Berlin he remained, as his title in official correspondence indicates with a lengthy brevity mysterious and intimidating, 'ChdSPudSD' (Chief of the Security Police and Security Service), but nevertheless he was removed, at least for a time, from the real centre of power. Heydrich himself may have been all the more willing to accept these disadvantages in return for the possibility of henceforth dealing with Hitler direct, instead of through the jealous Himmler.

Contrary to the reputation that preceded him, he acted in Prague, after a brief phase of open terrorism, with considerable tactical and psychological skill. He was surprisingly successful in his efforts to isolate the intelligentsia as the traditional spokesmen of an uncompromising nationalism and to win over the workers and peasants by partially genuine, partially simulated concessions, at least to the extent that they would place their undiminished labour power at the disposal of the regime. He improved social conditions to a great extent by introducing the social order that prevailed in the Reich itself, had the big luxury hotels and spas opened up to the working people, and actually received their representatives as his guests at Hradcany Castle. If despite all these measures he did not succeed in making himself popular, he was nevertheless able to turn the people's opportunism, based on the experience of generations, to his advantage and engender a state of 'political apathy'[35] in which individual attempts at effective resistance were easily suppressed. Ultimate aims apart, his behaviour was a considerable improvement in the eyes of the inhabitants of the Protectorate on that of his immediate forerunner, Neurath, whose indecision and lack of determination had delivered the country up to arbitrary, antagonistic and ambitious underlings. Hence it was not mere provocative recklessness that prompted him to do without the usual cohort of armed escorts and drive to Prague from his residence at Brezany every day in an open car; it was an albeit arrogant expression of the sense of security of a successful governor.

Hence the attack which cost him his life was planned and prepared by Czechoslovak exiles in London, who had noted the success of Heydrich's pacification measures with growing disquiet; not the least of their purposes in ordering the assassination was to provoke the regime into taking such brutal countermeasures that a more widespread resistance would be sparked off. The three young men who waited for Heydrich's car near the city boundary on May 27, 1942 had been dropped by parachute shortly before not far from Prague. As the car slowed down to take a sharp bend one of them, Jan Kubis, threw a bomb, which exploded under the vehicle. Heydrich was seriously wounded. He managed to jump out of the car and fire a few shots at his fleeing assailants, but then collapsed. Doctors were sent by Hitler and Himmler, but he died a week later.

Hitler exclaimed bitterly that Heydrich's death was like a 'lost battle',[36] and the regime reacted with the savagery displayed by primitive peoples at the graves of their tribal chiefs and demigods. In the punitive measures that followed no fewer than 936 people were condemned to death by court-martial at Prague and 395 at Brno.[37] Although no connection was established between them and the assassination, all the inhabitants of the village of Lidice were sacrificed to the manes of Reinhard Heydrich. And as if to make the terror emanating from his name live on after his death, the circumstances of his death provided the final impetus for the experiments with sulphonamides on human beings at Ravens-brück concentration camp.[38] Operation Reinhard, by which the property of murdered Jews was sequestered, was named after him.

Nevertheless Himmler seemed secretly rather relieved and stated darkly that fate had 'knowingly snatched Heydrich away at the zenith of his power'.[39] In his funeral eulogy, which contained countless referrences to Heydrich's supposedly sound racial heritage, Himmler called him one of the 'best educators in National Socialist Germany', a 'master by birth and behaviour', and stated towards the end: 'As he has continued the line of his ancestors and done them nothing but honour, so he will live on with all his qualities noble, decent, and clean in his sons, children who are the inheritors of his blood and his name.' But to his masseur, Felix Kersten, Himmler remarked that 'he had felt a bit funny following the coffin holding two mongrels by the hand'.[40]

The sum of this life is difficult to add up. Heydrich was far more than a leading henchman of Hitler remarkable for intelligence and extremism. He was a symbol and perhaps *the* representative figure of the Third Reich at the peak of its internal and external power. In this sense it was entirely apt when in the inner circle he was spoken of as Hitler's successor, who 'sooner or later' would have become Germany's 'Führer'.[41] He had already entered into this succession in the background through his place in the growing SS state which was mercilessly asserting itself.

Heydrich has been compared with Saint-Just. He did indeed share with him an utter lack of feeling, however much of an effort it may have cost, and like Saint-Just, Heydrich considered circumstances were difficult only for those who shrank from graves. But there were many differences between them. Heydrich was coarser and more frivolous, and in his hunger for a power devoid of any purpose but itself, more unconstrained than the sensitive Saint-Just with his rigid attachment to ideas. And whereas the latter made morality the measure of his revolutionary absolutism, the former held that morality was a matter purely of illusion or sentimentality. Nor was Heydrich a revolutionary; he wanted not to change the world but to subjugate it. Consequently the terrors with which Saint-Just burdened his time were of a different kind and had the melancholy justification of a humanitarian impulse gone bloodily astray. The difference between evil that is good gone astray, and evil that is simply evil, is to be found in murder which no longer seeks reasons but merely methods and is no longer trammelled by idealism.

Even this evaluation of Heydrich's personality, of course, needs qualifications. The disrupted background of his life defeats categorical judgment. On his dizzy rise to power he seems at times to have stopped and thought, before encouraging himself with cynicism or a piece of cheap ideology that his intelligence did not take seriously. 'It is almost too hard for the individual,' he once said, 'but we must be as hard as granite, otherwise the work of our Führer will perish.' Carl Jacob Burckhardt, who has passed down this remark of Heydrich's, noted the 'two totally different halves of the sharp, pale, asymmetrical face' and interpreted this as an expression of the profound, incurable split in this man who was at one moment 'tough and then again soft and morbid'.[42]

Whatever he did and became was marked by this fissure; no matter what he was, he was at the same time its opposite. The stereotyped picture of the executioner, which his figure has suggested, was shot through with the truly forlorn features of a man who was his own executioner. The legend that during the days of his death agony he turned away from the former excesses of power and tried to take back his hatred, his self-assertion, and his contempt for mankind has at least some psychological probability. Hitler once demanded that as National Socialists 'We must regain our clear conscience as to ruthlessness,'[43] but Heydrich had not this clear conscience, nor the iron heart which Hitler extolled after his death. Himmler undoubtedly knew him well: it was his opinion that Heydrich was 'at bottom an unhappy man'.[44]

Heinrich Himmler – Petty Bourgeois and Grand Inquisitor

I know that there are many people in Germany who feel sick when they see this black tunic; we can understand that.

Heinrich Himmler

It really makes no odds to us if we kill someone.

Heinrich Himmler

Two death masks were made of Heinrich Himmler after he had hastily swallowed the cyanide capsule that ended his life within a few minutes while he was undergoing a medical examination by a British military doctor on May 23, 1945. One of them shows a face twisted into a grotesque grimace, brutal, curiously impudent, its diabolical structure emphasised by the contortions of the death struggle, particularly by the pinched mouth. The other is an inexpressive, rather calm face with nothing frightening about it. It is as though death itself were trying, yet again, to demonstrate the strange combination to which it owed one of its most terrible and diligent servants in this world.[1]

The features of the first mask are more in keeping with the popular idea of the man. Widely identified with the SS state and the extermination factories, Heinrich Himmler seems like the civilised, or at least contemporary, reincarnation of a mythical monster. The feeling of menace, of omnipresent yet intangible terror, which once emanated from him has become attached to his name and to his personality, which is all the more sinister for its lack of personal colour. Even in his lifetime there was a Himmler 'myth', which distorted the features of the Reichsführer of the SS in a way that made him all the more terrifying and turned into an abstract principle the man who was unrecognisable as a human being. Entirely in this sense Himmler said of himself that he would be 'a merciless sword of justice'.[2] The methods of his terrorism, based upon modern principles of organisation, and the rationalised, 'industrial' extermination processes which he employed, the whole businesslike practicality of his fanaticism, have curiously intensified the aura of terror surrounding his person, beyond all actual experience.

However, as soon as we peel off a few layers from the demonised image we lay bare the far simpler features of a romantically eccentric petty bourgeois who, under the specific conditions of a totalitarian system of government, attained

111

exceptional power and hence found himself in a position to put his idiocies into bloody practice. Those who met him personally are unanimous in describing him as utterly mediocre, indistinguishable from the commonplace by any special trait of character. A British diplomat commented that he had never been able to draw from the Reichsführer of the SS 'a remark of even the most fleeting interest', and Speer's judgment, 'half schoolmaster, half crank', neatly sums up what many people have said.[3] Walter Dornberger, who was in charge of the rocket centre at Peenemünde, graphically described Himmler's appearance:

He looked to me like an intelligent elementary schoolteacher, certainly not a man of violence. I could not for the life of me see anything outstanding or extraordinary about this middle-sized, youthfully slender man in grey SS uniform. Under a brow of average height two grey-blue eyes looked out at me, behind glittering pince-nez, with an air of peaceful interrogation. The trimmed moustache below the straight, well-shaped nose traced a dark line on his unhealthy, pale features. The lips were colourless and very thin. Only the inconspicuous, receding chin surprised me. The skin of his neck was flaccid and wrinkled. With a broadening of his constant, set smile, faintly mocking and sometimes contemptuous about the corners of the mouth, two rows of excellent white teeth appeared between the thin lips. His slender, pale and almost girlishly soft hands, covered with blue veins, lay motionless on the table throughout our conversation.[4]

In fact, anyone who tried to see behind the slightly bloated smoothness of this face the disruption of a monstrous character was deluding himself. In the light of the millionfold terrors he inspired, there was a temptation to search for 'abysses' in which at least a pale gleam of some 'human' reaction might be visible, and it was that that misled people. In reality Heinrich Himmler was exactly what his appearance suggested: an insecure, vacillating character, the colour of whose personality was grey. His lack of independence was concealed by a desperate and stupid overzealousness. What looked like malignity or brutality was merely the conscienceless efficiency of a man whose life substance was so thinly spread that he had to borrow from outside. No emotion either carried him away or inhibited him; 'His very coldness was a negative element, not glacial, but bloodless.'[5] A capable organiser and administrator, he possessed that inhuman mixture of diligence, subservience and fanatical will to carry things through that casts aside humane considerations as irrelevant, and whose secret idols are closed files of reports of tasks completed; a man at freezing-point. Hence it required great psychological perspicacity to discover in personal contact – before the hasty construction of imaginary psychic abysses – the true basis of his existence, to find him sinister, more sinister than Hitler himself, as an observer wrote, 'through the degree of concentrated subservience, through a certain narrowminded conscientiousness, an inhuman methodicalness about which there was something of the automaton'.[6]

It was these qualities which, more than anything, laid the foundations for his rise and saved him from sharing the fate of the sectarians within the movement. For this character, almost abstract in its colourless impersonality, gained a certain individuality from Himmler's eccentric views, which opposed to a world heading for destruction a crude mixture of racial theories, runic beliefs and sundry doctrines of natural healing. With naïve certainty Himmler considered himself the reincarnation of Heinrich I, who had done battle with the Hungarians and Slavs. He recommended a breakfast of leeks and mineral water for his SS, would have only twelve people as guests at his table, following the example of the Round Table of King Arthur, and was occasionally to be found in the company of high SS officers all staring fixedly into space in an attempt to compel a person in the next room to confess the truth by their 'exercises in concentration'.[7] His peasant superstitions naturally, after the fashion of the time, had pseudo-scientific trimmings. He had archaeological excavations carried out in search of the original pure Aryan race and studies made of the skulls of 'Jewish-Bolshevik commissars', in order to arrive at a typological definition of the 'sub-human'. It was this same side of his personality that was reflected in the almost religious ceremonial practised in the SS.

Hitler undoubtedly watched these efforts with the greatest misgiving. In *Mein Kampf* he had already come out against pseudo-academic folkish occultism,[8] and finally at the cultural conference during the Reich Party Congress of 1938 he publicly repudiated all such goings on, which 'could not be tolerated in the movement':

At the pinnacle of our programme stands not mysterious premonition, but clear knowledge and hence open avowal. But woe if, through the insinuation of obscure mystical elements, the movement or the state should give unclear orders. And it is enough if this unclarity is contained merely in words. There is already a danger if orders are given for the setting up of so-called 'cult places', because this alone will give birth to the necessity subsequently to devise so-called cult games and cult rituals. Our 'cult' is exclusively cultivation of that which is natural and hence willed by God.[9]

Possibly these declarations were also directed against Himmler. Albert Speer, in any case, said Hitler was in the habit of 'criticising and mocking' the ideology of the SS;[10] but obviously he recognised and valued the skill in handling power that lay behind it. And if Himmler himself would have liked to give free play to his eccentric longings, the example of the SS shows more clearly than anything else how fully his irrational tendencies could at any time be checked by a purposeful sense of reality. 'In calculations I have always been sober,' he stated.[11] For the liturgy of self-presentation practised by the SS was never just show, a solemn but faded accessory. It was something that held them together, and one of the most effective means for establishing a sworn brotherhood of the elect. Participation in the mystic ritual not only conferred a special distinction but also placed them under a special obligation. Without a doubt the rituals which Himmler staged on the Wevelsburg, and at other places dictated by his faith, had the additional purpose of overwhelming those present with a melancholic shudder at his innate demonism. Over and above this, they were intended to inspire those states of rapture which are so easily transformed into brutal and merciless violence. But none of this belies the initiatory character of these solemn hours, which amounted to a repeated act of consecration and total commitment to a community above all traditional ties, one that seriously demanded 'unconditional liberation from the old social world of caste, class and family' and 'proclaimed its own "law" as springing unconditionally from the mere fact of belonging to the new community'.[12] In its aims the SS went far beyond all the overt considerations of militant political groupings. Leading SS officers appeared not merely as instruments of domination within the 'internal battleground', but as the nucleus of a new state apparatus. The goal of the SS was to permeate and dissolve the old order, and it was also to be the hard core of an imperial dominion aiming at 'organising Europe economically and politically on a basis that would destroy all pre-existing boundaries, with the Order in the background'.[13]

The setting of these tasks and the first steps towards their achievement once more reflected the dual character of unreal fantasy and rational planning which was Himmler's most personal contribution to the regime. It was his conviction that by systematically pursuing his policy, 'on the basis of Mendel's Law', the German people could in 120 years once more become 'authentically German in appearance'.[14] To this end he put forward and partially implemented an alteration in the marriage laws to do away with monogamy. He had various plans for establishing a privileged SS caste, eliminating traditional standards of value and working out a system of graduated educational and developmental opportunities for subjugated peoples. Within national frontiers pushed three hundred miles to the east, towns were to be pulled down and that 'paradise of the Germanic race' created of which splendid visions were continually conjured up by the Reichsführer of the SS, and those of his followers who enjoyed his special confidence. A widespread network of defensive villages was also envisaged, not merely to make it possible for the members of the Order, the 'New Nobility', to maintain their dominant position by force and government, but also to re-establish the ancient contact with the soil. The police functions which in actual fact the SS largely assumed paled beside these romantic visions of the future. These latter were the 'Holy of Holies', and Himmler described as the 'happiest day of my life' the day on which Hitler gave his consent to the plan for the creation of soldier-peasants (*Wehrbauern*).[15]

Crazy ideas of this sort exist on the lunatic fringe of every society in almost every epoch, exercising varying degrees of practical influence. Stable social orders absorb those who hold them relatively unharmed and allow them a certain limited field of activity as founders of sects, quack doctors or pamphleteers. It is only in a hopelessly disrupted society that a figure like Heinrich Himmler can acquire political influence; and only under a totalitarian form of government offering universal salvation could he come to hold the power that offered some prospect of putting his ideas into practice. His sobriety and apparent common sense, which deceived outsiders, were precisely what made his career possible. 'I am convinced that nobody I met in Germany is more normal,' an English observer wrote in 1929.[16] The basic pathological characteristic of the National Socialist movement, so often and so erroneously sought in clinically obvious psychopaths like Julius Streicher, showed itself rather in the curious amalgam of crankiness and

114

'normality', of insanity and sober administrative ability. Thus Streicher was pushed further and further to the sidelines, while Heinrich Himmler, who possessed the *arcanum imperii* of this system of government, quickly reached the highest power, a calculating man of faith who without doubt or challenge trampled over millions, leaving behind him a trail of blood and tears, the most dreadful combination of crackpot and manipulator of power, of quack and inquisitor, that history has ever known. Concentration camps and herb gardens, such as he had planted at Dachau and elsewhere: these are still the most apt symbols of his personality.

His loquacity has left behind a wealth of documents that all support this analysis. In his speech to the SS Group Leaders on October 4, 1943 in Poznan, one of the most horrifying testaments in the German language, he declared:

It is absolutely wrong to project our own harmless soul with its deep feelings, our kind-heartedness, our idealism, upon alien peoples. This is true, beginning with Herder, who must have been drunk when he wrote the *Voices of the Peoples*, thereby bringing such immeasurable suffering and misery upon us who came after him. This is true, beginning with the Czechs and Slovenes, to whom we brought their sense of nationhood. They themselves were incapable of it, but we invented it for them.

One principle must be absolute for the SS man: we must be honest, decent, loyal and comradely to members of our own blood and to no one else. What happens to the Russians, what happens to the Czechs, is a matter of utter indifference to me. Such good blood of our own kind as there may be among the nations we shall acquire for ourselves, if necessary by taking away the children and bringing them up among us. Whether the other peoples live in comfort or perish of hunger interests me only in so far as we need them as slaves for our culture; apart from that it does not interest me. Whether or not 10,000 Russian women collapse from exhaustion while digging a tank ditch interests me only in so far as the tank ditch is completed for Germany. We shall never be rough or heartless where it is not necessary; that is clear. We Germans, who are the only people in the world who have a decent attitude to animals, will also adopt a decent attitude to these human animals, but it is a crime against our own blood to worry about them and to bring them ideals.

I shall speak to you here with all frankness of a very serious subject. We shall now discuss it absolutely openly among ourselves, nevertheless we shall never speak of it in public. I mean the evacuation of the Jews, the extermination of the Jewish people. It is one of those things which it is easy to say. 'The Jewish people is to be exterminated,' says every party member. 'That's clear, it's part of our programme, elimination of the Jews, extermination, right, we'll do it.' And then they all come along, the eighty million good Germans, and each one has his decent Jew. Of course the others are swine, but this one is a first-class Jew. Of all those who talk like this, not one has watched, not one has stood up to it. Most of you know what it means to see a hundred corpses lying together, five hundred, or a thousand. To have gone through this and yet – apart from a few exceptions, examples of human weakness – to have remained decent, this has made us hard. This is a glorious page in our history that has never been written and never shall be written.[17]

The man who wrote some of the most terrible chapters in German history was born in Munich on October 7, 1900. His family atmosphere and all the main impressions of his years of development were evidently decisively influenced by the personality of his father, who, as the son of a police president, a former tutor to the princes at the Bavarian court, and a headmaster, also applied authoritarian principles in his own household. He was austere, precise and pious. No doubt it would be going too far to see in the son's early interest in Teutonic sagas, criminology and military affairs the beginnings of his later development, but the family milieu, with its combination of 'officialdom, police work and teaching',[18] manifestly had a lasting effect on him. His opposition to his father's discipline and upbringing may have engendered a kind of dependence that later expressed itself as a complex need to look up to someone and surrender himself to that person. His fanatical concern with education, which led him continually to try to teach and impart axioms for living, was doubtless also largely the outcome of his early years. The doctor Felix Kersten, who treated him continuously from 1939 onwards and enjoyed his confidence, has asserted that Himmler himself would rather have educated foreign peoples than exterminate them.[19] During the war he spoke enthusiastically – looking ahead to peace – of establishing military units who were 'educated and trained, once education and training can be practised again'.[20]

It was at first intended that Himmler should become a farmer, and this was the source of the peasant ideas which later infused his ideological conceptions, especially in relation to the SS. But his poor physical constitution would in any case have made him unfit for a farmer's life. During the celebrations which he organised in Quedlinburg Cathedral in July 1936 to the accompaniment of ancient German horns, to celebrate the thousandth anniversary of the death of Heinrich I, he extolled the latter as a 'noble peasant of his people'; in a speech the same year he described himself as 'a peasant by ancestry, blood and nature'.[21] But after the First World War, in which he had taken part at the very end as an ensign, he came via a rightist-radical soldiers' association to Hitler's party. A photograph of the November Putsch of 1923 shows him as a standard-bearer at the side of Ernst Röhm. Soon he emerged as a colleague of Gregor Strasser in the social-revolutionary wing of the NSDAP; undoubtedly this association sprang not so much from ideological motives as from the fact that he and Strasser were compatriots. In fact his ideological position, which later seemed so resolute, remained for a long time vague and indefinite. In 1926 he met Margarete Boden, the daughter of a West Prussian landowner. She had served as a nurse in the war and later had built up a modest private nursing home with her father's money. She was seven years older than Himmler, fair-haired and blue-eyed in complete conformity with the supposed Germanic type. Two years later he married her, and it was she, it was revealed later, who aroused his interest in homeopathy, mesmerism, oat-straw baths and herbalism.[22]

On January 6, 1929 Himmler, at the same time running a chicken farm at Waldtrudering near Munich, was appointed head of the then barely three-hundred-man-strong SS. He proved his abilities as an organiser by expanding the force to over 50,000 men by 1933. He was still a marginal figure in the top leadership; it was only during the seizure of power that, along with his superior assistant Reinhard Heydrich, he methodically and patiently worked his way up and gained control of the Political Police.[23] June 30, 1934 was the crucial day of his career. After he had worked in the background on the construction of the scenery before which the clumsy Röhm, for whom he had once carried the banner, advanced to his own execution, his SS units provided the murder commandos for the three-day massacre. From the rivalry between the Reichswehr and the SA he emerged alongside Hitler as the true victor. Only three weeks later the SS, hitherto subordinate to the SA, was raised to the status of an independent organisation.[24] When on June 17, 1936 Himmler was finally appointed head of the now unified police forces of the Reich and confirmed as Reichsführer of the SS, he seemed to have reached the peak of an astounding career. He now controlled a substantial portion of the real power and also, thanks to the terror that he spread, an even greater part of the psychological power.

This appointment provided him, in fact, with a springboard for a process of expansion which largely determined the future face and history of the Third Reich, and in the course of which the real power visibly shifted towards himself and the SS. What he had been secretly preparing for a long time, egged on by Heydrich restlessly working in the background, now took shape step by step as the conquest of positions of solid power. The SS mobile troops, the economic and administrative head office of the SS, the concentration camps, the SS security service, the Head Office for Race and Settlement, and finally the Waffen SS soon grew from small institutions with limited functions into powerful organisations. The economic empire of the SS, which eventually spread over Europe, and the Waffen SS with almost forty divisions were merely particularly striking sides of an expansionist urge which must be seen as a whole, an urge which revealed not simply an insatiable desire for office but rather the structural law of the National Socialist regime in transition to the SS state. This process is not to be understood merely by considering the SS state from its most obvious side, the police empire or the system of concentration camps and extermination factories.

In fact, the aims of the enormous SS apparatus were far more comprehensive and concerned not so much with controlling the state as with becoming a state itself. The occupants of the chief positions in the SS developed step by step into the holders of power in an authentic 'collateral state', which gradually penetrated existing institutions, undermined them, and finally began to dissolve them. Fundamentally there was no sphere of public life upon which the SS did not make its competing demands: the economic, ideological, military, scientific and technical spheres, as well as those of agrarian and population policies, legislation and general administration. This development found its most unmistakable expression in the hierarchy of the Senior SS and Police Commanders, especially in the Eastern zones; the considerable independence that Himmler's corps of leaders enjoyed *vis-à-vis* the civil or military administration was a working model for a shift of power planned for the whole area of the Greater German Reich after the war. This process received its initial impetus following the so-called Röhm

Putsch, and it moved towards its completion after the attempted revolt of July 20, 1944. The SS now pushed its way into 'the centre of the organisational fabric of the Wehrmacht', and Himmler, who had meanwhile also become Reich Minister of the Interior, now in addition became chief of the Replacement Army. On top of his many other functions he was thus in charge 'of all military transport, military censorship, the intelligence service, surveillance of the troops, the supply of food, clothing and pay to the troops, and care of the wounded'.[25]

Within this picture of consistent and soberly planned extensions of power, individual eccentricities were not lacking. While the majority of Himmler's organisations, foundations and acquisitions served realistic power aims, others merely satisfied his private fantasies – like the Mattoni mineral-water factory, the Lebensborn eV (the state-registered organisation for the promotion of human propagation), the Nordland Publishing Company, the cultivation of Kog-Sagy's roots, or the SS Association for Research and Teaching on Heredity, whose task it was 'to investigate the geographical distribution, spirit, deeds and heritage of the Nordic Indo-Germanic race'.[26]

Himmler's comprehensive and unitary organisation provided the totalitarian government with the systematic control that now enabled it to operate to its full extent. No sooner had Himmler, in the course of capturing power, seized control of the police than a perceptible tightening of the regime could be felt. The spontaneous acts of violence that had marked the initial phases of the Third Reich lessened and then ceased altogether with the final removal of power from the SA. The 'emotional' terrorism practised by Ernst Röhm's shock troops with a blend of political and criminal techniques gave way to its rational counterpart, a central bureaucracy systematically employing terrorism as an institution. The new type of man of violence recruited by Himmler was concerned with the dispassionate extermination of real or possible opponents, not with the primitive release of sadistic impulses. Whatever sadism occurred, particularly in the concentration camps, was included by Himmler among those 'exceptional cases of human weakness' of which he had spoken in his Poznan speech quoted above; they occurred in contradiction of the 'idea' of the type. His perpetually reiterated moral admonishments are in no way a merely feigned moral austerity not 'meant seriously'; they are founded in the principle of rational terrorism. He took ruthless measures in cases where corruption, brutality or any other personal motives were apparent, and even trusted henchmen were not spared.[27] As he once emphasised:

The wealth which they [the Jews] had, we have taken from them. We ourselves have taken none of it. Individuals who have offended against this principle will be punished according to an order which I issued at the beginning and which threatens: He who takes so much as a mark shall die. A certain number of SS men – not very many – disobeyed this order and they will die, without mercy. We had the moral right, we had the duty to our own people, to kill this people that wanted to kill us. But we have no right to enrich ourselves by so much as a fur, a watch, a mark, or a cigarette or anything else. I shall never stand by and watch the slightest rot develop or establish itself here. Wherever it

118

forms, we shall burn it out together. By and large, however, we can say that we have performed this task in love of our people. And we have suffered no damage from it in our inner self, in our soul, in our character.[28]

It was not so much a sign of moral callousness when the numerous members of the SS leadership who were present failed to be repelled by the terms of this speech; rather, it was that they felt confirmed in their hopelessly perverted idealism. If the system of concentration camps mainly served the purpose of destroying opponents, it also and to an increasing extent fulfilled the task of educating the members of the Order according to the ideal of the new aristocracy of the Germanic *Herrenvolk*, of training them above all in hardness towards themselves.[29] Unlike the SA, rightly described as recruited from the urban labour exchanges,[30] the élite SS succeeded, at least to begin with, in attracting a type who sought scope for his idealism, his readiness to serve, and his vague need for faith. According to Himmler's ideas its 'inner values' comprised loyalty, honesty, obedience, hardness, decency, poverty and courage. But this ethos, though ceaselessly preached and reinforced by torchlight celebrations, lacked genuine ethical roots and therefore ended by being a scantly romanticised call to murder, addressed to a mentality that had ceased to ask questions but silently and obediently killed, and actually compared the justice of mass murder with the injustice of a stolen cigarette. With its principles of behaviour removed from any system of moral standards and linked to the aims of power, it ceased to be an ethos. It became an instrument of total domination aimed directly at a man's inner being and wearing the mask of morality, though misconstrued by some of the rank and file as a 'new morality' and not infrequently – at the cost of individual conflict – put in the place of traditional values. Precisely the effort that it cost the non-criminal, 'idealistic'-minded type of SS man to achieve total lack of feeling, the ability literally to walk unmoved over corpses, often enabled him to delude himself into thinking that he was engaged in an ethical struggle, from which he then drew a sense of self-justification. In the hopeless confusion of all criteria under the influence of a totalitarian ethic, harshness towards the victims was held justified by the harshness practised towards oneself. 'To be harsh toward ourselves and others, to give death and to take it,' was one of the mottoes of the SS repeatedly emphasised by Himmler. Because murder was difficult, it was good, and justified. By the same reasoning he was always able to point proudly, as though to a Roll of Honour, to the fact that the Order had suffered 'no inner damage' from its murderous activity and had remained 'decent'. It was entirely consistent that the moral status of the SS rose with the number of its victims. As Himmler declared to the officer corps of the 'Adolf Hitler' SS Bodyguard on September 7, 1940:

Exactly the same thing happened at forty degrees below zero in Poland when we had to carry off thousands and tens of thousands and hundreds of thousands, when we had to be so hard – as to shoot thousands of leading Poles. When we had to be so hard, because otherwise vengeance would have fallen upon us later. It is a great deal easier in many

119

cases to go with a company into battle than to operate with a company in some region suppressing a rebellious population at a low level of culture, carrying out executions, transporting people away, taking away howling and weeping women.[31]

However, it was not merely the ethos of hardness that gave such utterances by Himmler their decisive twist, but rather the vulgar and calculating pride in his own capacity for inhumanity with which the pedant and the former model pupil of the King Wilhelm Gymnasium in Munich sought to establish his leadership among his murder-and-battle-hardened subordinates. In fact it is difficult even now to understand to what individual qualities and advantages he owed his relatively uncontested position within the SS. He was the most colourless personality in the inner circle of the leaders of the Third Reich; he possessed no natural authority and his 'charisma' was that of a head teacher. The long years of screening by Heydrich, and Hitler's personal trust, which lasted to the end and which he paid for with extreme docility, clearly assisted him greatly. In addition, the Order's stringent principles of obedience and duty helped to keep his position uncontested, and its members were always being involved in new tasks imposed by its continuous expansionist drive, which gave them sufficient goals to exercise their rivalry outside the SS. But independently of this, he himself was always concerned to reinforce his influence, not merely institutionally but also psychologically, by proving both to those above him and those below him that he was the most extreme SS man among the Führer's followers. Indeed, totalitarian systems in general owe their inhumanity more to competition between rivals jealously striving for power than to the principle of contempt for human beings as such.

It is true that from the time when the SS became more and more exclusively engaged in mass murder and extermination, Himmler's extremist protestations frequently took on strained undertones. 'We must forswear and renounce false comradeship, falsely conceived compassion, false softness, and a false excuse to ourselves,' he once cried out almost passionately to his listeners.[32] The observation that in his purposeful coldness he was beyond reach of all feeling is undoubtedly correct.[33] All feelings of guilt, of individual responsibility, were warded off and 'dealt with' partly by his pseudo-moral values, partly by interposing those bureaucratic mechanisms that gave his character its specific stamp, so that they did not reach the foundations of his personality. Nevertheless we may surmise that the ever louder admonishments to harshness and ruthlessness were intended to drown elements of unrest which in the end he could not fail to hear. The scope of the terrorist activity made it inevitable that occasionally he should face the consequences of what he had thoughtlessly set in motion at the conference table or by putting his signature to documents. But he himself did not have the hardness he demanded from his subordinates, any more than he had the rest of the élite characteristics of the SS man, the external racial features, the physical height, the hair colour, or the so-called Great Family Tree (*Grosse Ahnennachweis*) going back to 1750.[34] There is no evidence that he was conscious of these problems or suffered from them. Only once does he seem to have submitted himself to the sight

120

of what he demanded from others. SS Obergruppenführer von dem Bach-Zelewski has attested that in 1941 in Minsk, Himmler ordered a hundred prisoners to be assembled for a model execution. At the first salvo, however, he almost fainted, and he screamed when the execution squad failed to kill two women outright.[35] In significant contrast to his abstract readiness to commit murder was the heartfelt emotion, described elsewhere, which overcame him at the sight of blond children,[36] and his positively hysterical opposition to hunting. His lunch was ruined if he was reminded that animals had been slaughtered. He once protested to his doctor:

How can you find pleasure, Herr Kersten, in shooting from behind cover at poor creatures browsing on the edge of a wood, innocent, defenceless, and unsuspecting? It's really pure murder. Nature is so marvellously beautiful and every animal has a right to live. It's just this point of view that I admire so much in our forefathers. They, for instance, formally declared war on rats and mice, which were required to stop their depredations and leave a fixed area with a definite time limit, before beginning a war of annihilation against them. You will find this respect for animals in all Indo-Germanic peoples. It was of extraordinary interest to me to hear recently that even today Buddhist monks, when they pass through a wood in the evening, carry a bell with them, to make any woodland animals they might meet keep away, so that no harm will come to them. But with us every slug is trampled on, every worm destroyed.[37]

The almost incomprehensible distortion of all standards of judgment revealed when this observation is set beside what he said about experiments on living prisoners or the 'treatment of other races in the East'[38] can be understood only in the context of his utopian fanaticism, which in its narrow-minded obsessionalism undoubtedly contained an element of insanity, and in the context of his world of ideas that was totally divorced from human reality. At an early stage he had shown that he could attribute idealistic motives to his behaviour. In 1921, when he was active in student self-government, he wrote in his diary: 'In actual fact I did not originally do it for idealistic reasons. Now that I have done it, I shall do it idealistically.'[39] This ability to make 'decent' motives seem plausible according to changing needs prepared the way for a further abstraction of all activity from categories of individual guilt and made possible, not only for him but for a large number of his subordinates, a clouding of all personal responsibility. The human experiments in the laboratories of the concentration camps, which displayed a horrifying amateurism, yielded not the slightest useful result because their real purpose was merely to act as a blind; in the words of one of the doctors involved, Himmler wanted to prove 'that he was not a murderer but a patron of science'.[40] Any remaining feelings of guilt were removed by the assertion, delivered with the pseudo-tragic pose of provincial demonism, that it was 'the curse of the great to have to walk over corpses'.[41] Behind this, conjured up more zealously than ever, lay that concept of a Greater German postwar empire which, beyond the extermination which he carried out with routine conscientiousness, he was planning and preparing. The nature of these plans is disclosed by the terms in which he expressed himself on this 'theme of his life', by means of which he hoped to escape from the constraints of his dry and colourless existence to a position of leadership in idealised territories. '*Herrenmenschen*' were contrasted with 'working peoples'; there was talk of 'fields of racial experiment', 'nordification', 'aids to procreation', 'the foundations of our blood', 'fundamental biological laws', 'the ruination of our blood', 'the breeding of a new human type', or 'the botanical garden of Germanic blood' – truly the visions of a poultry farmer from Waldtrudering! Meanwhile Himmler devised plans for an SS State of Burgundy, which was to enjoy a certain autonomy as a racially and ideologically model state under his personal leadership, to be a sort of gigantic Nordic boarding school; this idea gave his narrow-minded pedagogic temperament the cold happiness for which it longed.[42] As it has been said of the spokesmen of the French Revolution that they confused politics with a novel, so it may be said of Himmler that he confused politics with the obscure and fanciful tracts that had been the first stage in the educational career of his Führer.

The ultimate indissoluble residue of Himmler's make-up rests upon his devotion to the person of Hitler, to whom he subordinated himself in a positively pathological manner. His dependent nature and need of emotional support, demonstrated both by his choice of a wife seven years older than himself and by the dogmatic pedantry of his beliefs, culminated in an exaggerated loyalty towards the 'Führer of the Greater Germanic Reich', as he liked to call Hitler in anticipation of the future. Once when Felix Kersten was treating Himmler, Kersten answered the telephone; Himmler turned to him, his eyes shining, and said, 'You have been listening to the voice of the Führer, you're a very lucky man.'[43] The head of the German Intelligence Service, Walter Schellenberg, who was his adviser towards the end of the war, reports that after every conversation with his Führer, Himmler used to imitate his speech and mode of expression.[44] Kersten says that Himmler saw in Hitler's orders 'the binding decisions of the Germanic race's Führer, pronouncements from a world transcending this one', which 'possessed a divine power':

He [Hitler] rose up out of our deepest need, when the German people had come to a dead end. He is one of those brilliant figures which always appear in the Germanic world when it has reached a final crisis in body, mind and soul. Goethe was one such figure in the intellectual sphere, Bismarck in the political – the Führer in the political, cultural and military combined. It has been ordained by the Karma of the Germanic world that he should wage war against the East and save the Germanic peoples – a figure of the greatest brilliance has become incarnate in his person.[45]

Kersten himself adds: 'Himmler uttered these words with great solemnity and effect. Now it became clear to me why Himmler had sometimes pointed to Hitler as a person whom men would regard in centuries to come with the same reverence that they accorded to Christ.'

If the devoutly exaggerated absoluteness of his loyalty towards the Führer-god corresponded to a deep need on Himmler's part for security and something to hold on to, it is also understandable that his faith barely stood up to the strain of the final phase of the regime. For when, with the turn of the tide in the war and

122

Hitler's increasingly obvious failure, the first cracks and fissures began to show on the idol, he instantly relapsed into his fundamental vacillation. Today we may take it as proved that from 1943 onwards he had loose, informative contacts with the Resistance Movement and even played a still unclarified but unquestionably dubious role in the events of July 20,[46] before entering in the spring of 1945 into secret negotiations with a representative of the World Jewish Congress and finally with Count Folke Bernadotte. In so far as he was not forced into these negotiations against his will it remains questionable whether he ever intended to commit an act of conscious disloyalty. It is more probable that in a corner of his pathologically adoring heart he maintained the altars of his idol-worship to the last and that this was why his actions were irresolute and unplanned. But the inherent weight of the enormous power which he had gathered together during the last few years – not least with an eye on the succession to Hitler – now forced him to act.

The steps he took, however, indicate an almost incredible divorce from reality. He greeted the representative of the World Jewish Congress, who came to see him on April 21, 1945, with the unbelievable words: 'Welcome to Germany, Herr Masur. It is time you Jews and we National Socialists buried the hatchet.'[47] He indulged in speculation upon what he would do as soon as he came to power, and seriously hoped, up to the day of his arrest, that the Western Allies would greet him as a partner in negotiations and even as an ally against Soviet Russia. When he visited Grand Admiral Dönitz, who had just been appointed Hitler's successor, on May 1, he spoke of his 'widespread reputation' abroad.[48] Having bid farewell to Dönitz he was still planning on May 5 to create a National Socialist government under his personal leadership in Schleswig-Holstein, to provide him with the legal right to negotiate with the Western Allies.

In the last analysis it was this stupendous lack of realism which determined this man's life and character. Once, in the panic turbulence of those days when, after shattered hopes, he became aware of reality in the shape of the approaching disaster, he told one of his colleagues, 'I shudder at the thought of everything that is going to happen now.'[49] And if it was only fear that he felt now, this too was something he had obviously never considered, because it had never appeared either in documents or reports, or in his daydreams of future projects. They did not mention the fact that man is afraid of death.

Indeed, during these weeks of the collapse of the Third Reich the SS Reichsführer Heinrich Himmler was an opportunist fighting stubbornly to delay the end. In vain did those around him press him to declare himself and assume responsibility for the SS.[50] On March 19 he was still conjuring up apocalyptic visions of a last-ditch stand to the last man 'like the Ostrogoths on Vesuvius';[51] now he thought only of disguise and flight. 'One thing can never be forgiven among us Germans: that is treachery,' he had assured his followers a few months earlier. No small number of the SS, especially members of the élite groups, committed suicide when they realised Heinrich Himmler's treachery. In Bohemia, in May 1945, according to a contemporary report, SS officers lit a fire one night, stood in a circle around it singing the SS oath song 'Wenn alle untreu werden' (When all become untrue), and thereafter all took their own lives. What caused their disillusionment so suddenly and with such shock was not so much the betrayal to which Hitler was referring when he repudiated Himmler in his testament and stripped him of all his offices because of his independent peace feelers with the Western powers. In so far as their motives related to the SS leader's actions, it was rather his betrayal of the shared 'idea of the SS', in which they had believed through all battles, all victories, defeats, and crimes. Its collapse left only a senseless, filthy, barbaric murder industry, for which there could be no defence. Rudolf Höss, for many years commandant of Auschwitz, became 'quite mute' when Himmler, 'radiant and in the best of spirits', advised him to go underground.[52]

Evidently the mechanism that produced illusion did not break down even now. On May 21, 1945, when Himmler left Flensburg under the name of Heinrich Hitzinger, his moustache shaved off and a black patch over his left eye, he had chosen for his disguise the uniform of a sergeant-major of the Secret Military Police, a subdivision of the Gestapo. Not grasping the terrifying reputation of all organisations associated with his name, he had no idea that he had thereby laid himself open to automatic arrest. The very same day he was taken prisoner by a British control post.

He put an appropriate end to his life. Suicide erased whatever justification he had advanced for the sufferings he had caused. 'My behaviour is more important than what I say,' he had declared in his Poznan speech, and added, 'This Germanic Reich needs the Order of the SS. It needs it at least for the next few centuries.'[53] Now his behaviour contradicted it all. There is no legend.

Martin Bormann – The Brown Eminence

Admittedly it is not honesty which in real life overcomes dishonesty. In the harsh struggle for existence the stronger, the harder capacity for self-assertion daily gains the victory – and yet it is bitter if this capacity is based upon intrigue and a burning ambition as in the case before us.

Martin Bormann

But you know, don't you, that in my dictionary *DUTY* is written in capitals.

Martin Bormann

From too great a distance, as from too close, a totalitarian system of government looks like a single tightly knit block whose massive structure towers over society, as vast as it is impenetrable. However, this impression, based upon the determination and the merciless energy with which such governments achieve their purposes, is an illusion. What the observer sees as a block is often enough merely the reflection of his own anxiety, which has clothed this arbitrary and unrestricted power in a compact mental image. In contrast, the National Socialist regime had a curious and at first sight astounding lack of structure, which was not the result only of the laziness about establishing an orderly system which continually betrayed the leading National Socialists' urban bohemian origins. This structural untidiness is the expression of one of the basic principles of totalitarian government: the maxim of the unreliability of all authority, which, paradoxically, is the leadership's most reliable instrument for the establishment of an intimidating, continuously threatening superauthority. The effect of this is that power itself recedes into the background and becomes curiously intangible.

By keeping the jurisdiction of the various authorities intentionally vague and their hierarchical positions inextricably involved, it was possible to play a double game, leaving the individual in a state of utter helplessness like that experienced by Kafka's heroes and producing the same psychological reactions. The individual in the National Socialist state gradually lost all human certainty and dignity in the crushing encounters with a power that could not be located and yet was everywhere.

The duplication and finally the 'multiplication'[1] of authorities, which gave this feeling of insecurity a basis in institutional organisation, began with the separation of party and state. Every state function was balanced against a party office of equal status, and the result was a chaos of rival institutions, all of which considered themselves competent in such matters as foreign policy, intelligence, administration or law. This dichotomy was largely a reflection of the principle that lay behind the rise of National Socialism, as of every totalitarian movement. Such movements do not see themselves as a party in the literal sense, that is to say as the representative of a part within the framework of an accepted order, but as the spearhead of a bid for total domination which 'is developed and realised in express and open hostility to the state'.[2] It is true that after the law of December 1, 1933 official pronouncements repeatedly stressed the unity of party and state; in fact, however, the dividing line was sharp. The state soon degenerated into a mere 'technical apparatus' with purely executive functions. It still had the task, as representative of the civil principle, of inspiring trust and appearing to preserve bourgeois standards, but the party gained wide scope for the expression of its emotional drives and the achievement of its aims. The top leadership, in its single-minded and opportunist pursuit of power, could waver from side to side, play off one against another, and if necessary betray all. The preponderance of power, and above all the role of formulating and realising its own totalitarian aims, always lay with the movement, just as in his own eyes Hitler was always the 'Führer' rather than Reich Chancellor. Beyond its purely technical functions the state, visibly deprived of its sovereignty, had no importance except as a façade. Its task was to represent a power which it did not actually possess, a power that stood behind it and appropriated to itself, for its own legitimation, a deep-rooted popular attachment to the state which drew on common national experience, tradition and respect. Hidden and secret, the real centre of power, by its very aura of anonymity, appeared to its opponents, as well as to the merely refractory, all the less vulnerable, all the more terrifying, all the more omnipotent – an earthly *deus absconditus*.[3]

From this situation Hannah Arendt has deduced the principle that within a totalitarian system 'real power begins where secrecy begins'; she suggests that this is 'the only rule of which everybody in a totalitarian state may be sure'.[4] The representation of power already indicates the loss of power; it is effective and unhindered in so far as it remains invisible.

If this is correct, it applies not only to institutions but also to a considerable degree to the individuals in power. Martin Bormann, whose career and leading role in the Third Reich strikingly confirm this principle, wrote in autumn 1943 to his wife that he had always 'deliberately avoided' every kind of public notoriety, such as was sought by other party leaders; whereas they wrote articles addressed directly to the people, his instructions reached only the leadership. 'I,' he continued self-confidently, 'am accomplishing more, considerably more.' He added, 'If ever there is a memorial ceremony after my death, there must under no circumstances be a cheap exhibition of cushions with rows of medals and so on. These things give a false impression.'[5]

He got his wish. At the end of his life he received a distinction which undoubtedly meant more to him than the honours of a state funeral. The phrase 'my most loyal party comrade, Martin Bormann', with which Hitler, seeing nothing but treachery and disloyalty all around him, referred to him in his last utterance, marked the culmination of a career in which he had always been content with apparently modest titles, so long as his sphere of influence was at the same time expanded. When Hitler appointed him executor of his will, Bormann attained his ultimate ambition of complete identification with the central will of the National Socialist power structure.[6] Sober, calculating and coldly diligent, he had always sought power alone, never its insignia. The latter seemed to him mere foolishness and evidence of a misdirected cupidity that clung to externals. Almost unnoticed, with his characteristic silent persistence, he had risen step by step within a short time. He was never called more than 'Director of the Party Chancellery' and 'the Führer's secretary', and yet during the declining years of the Hitler regime no one was more powerful. His dark and clumsy shadow fell across the stars of those who had been among Hitler's closest followers long before him: Göring, Ribbentrop, Ley, indeed even Goebbels and finally Himmler. He was the 'Brown Eminence', mute and dangerous in the background, holding the threads in his hands and also the thunderbolts which, during Hitler's uncontrolled outbursts in the final phase, Bormann was able to direct adroitly towards those whom he felt to be his rivals. In one sense he eventually became more powerful than Hitler himself, and he was a classic embodiment of the dictator in the antechamber, a type that is gaining more and more influence within modern political and economic power concentrations. His views and the way in which he presented facts were almost the only picture which Hitler, buried in the deluded world of his underground shelter, received of the world outside. But up to the concluding stage of the war not even his name was familiar to the public. He was a man in the background, a man of 'darkness and concealment', as Richelieu called Père Joseph, who is still the prototype of all such anonymous power-seekers. Incapable as he was of articulating a few coherent sentences in a speech of greeting,[7] Bormann was at home with the bureaucratic apparatus and mastered its mechanisms with extraordinary skill. His short, squat figure in the badly fitting civil servant's uniform, briefcase under arm, always listening, weighing up the situation or with an expression on his peasant face of being ready to pounce, was part of the picture of the Führer's headquarters during the last years. He has been called 'Hitler's evil spirit', but this phrase does not by any means permit us to conclude that he forced a benevolent Hitler onto the path of evil;[8] he was, rather, the Devil's Beelzebub.

No one was more hated. The contempt aroused by the Neronic pomposity of Göring, Ribbentrop's absurdity, or even Himmler's bloodthirsty reputation, all the mutual antipathies that built up within the top leadership through years of rivalry, were of a different kind and not to be compared with the intensity of the bitterness his countless enemies felt towards this Machiavelli of the office desk. Hans Frank, who called him an 'arch-scoundrel', remarked that the word 'hate' was 'far too weak',[9] and even his personal colleagues and secretaries – who in every other case, without exception, could find a good word for their superior – expressed only aversion at Nuremberg.[10] 'A few critical words from Hitler and all

Bormann's enemies would have been at his throat,' Albert Speer states.[11] But in all his moody unpredictability, that of an oriental despot, Hitler to the last never uttered these few critical words. 'I know,' he said, dismissing occasional remonstrations from those around him, 'that Bormann is brutal. But there is sense in everything he does and I can absolutely rely on my orders being carried out by Bormann immediately and in spite of all obstacles. Bormann's proposals are so precisely worked out that I have only to say yes or no. With him I deal in ten minutes with a pile of documents for which with another man I should need hours. If I say to him, remind me about such and such a matter in half a year's time, I can be sure that he will really do so.'[12]

Much as his enemies and rivals gradually learned to fear Bormann, equally they underestimated his abilities. At times it seems as though his drab, unpretentious appearance was merely a means of slipping unobserved into the control points of power. For with all his sergeant-major's dreary triviality he evidently possessed qualities which gained him not merely the undiminished trust of Hitler but also the lead over all his competitors. The tone of incredulous amazement in the comments of so many of those who were Hitler's companions in the early stages of his career[13] clearly expresses the inability of the so-called Old Guard to understand an advancement that proceeded, not by way of the street or beerhouse battles, but the office desk. For in appearance and temperament Bormann belonged to that 'second generation' which in every revolution follows the Old Guard of faithful fighters: the generation of practical men devoid of fervour, calculators without ideological ballast and without the drive of emotional indignation which gave the old-fashioned revolutionaries of the past their inner justification and their success with the masses. 'Bormann is not a man of the people,' noted Goebbels, 'He has always been engaged in administrative work and therefore has not the proper qualifications for the real tasks of leadership.'[14]

The misunderstanding is significant, for the men of the people have no guarantee that they will hold on to the power which is theirs during the earlier phase of the conquest and consolidation of government; that power gradually passes into the hands of those with the technique of organisation and control and the ability to administer the possessions acquired by the first-generation revolutionaries.

Martin Bormann was a 'functionary' who derived his power solely from the office he held. His personality was not compelling, nor had he a record of legendary services in the party's period of struggles. He had no domestic power, no prestige, no friends, in short nothing to fall back on if he should ever lose Hitler's trust. He was a man who had absolutely nothing to draw upon. But precisely this lack of background, as well as his lack of distinctive personal qualities, made him an adaptable, uninhibitedly 'functioning' instrument in the hands of those who utilised him. He was the prototype of the 'follower' thrown up in times of shattered values, always on the search for some cause, some person, to attach himself to; this cause, this person, has only to appear strong enough and imperious enough to give directions to this type's aimlessness and enlist his readiness to serve. And if he was the functionary type, he was at the same time

128

the type of totally malleable man, knowing neither moral nor intellectual inhibitions, but ready to carry out directives without argument, without vacillations of mood, any picture of the suffering he was causing lying far beyond the range of his vision. Bormann described himself as the 'narrow party man', not without an undertone of pride.[15] Even his extraordinary distrustfulness is in keeping with the rest of his personality, for within the smooth-functioning mechanism of his bureaucratic apparatus, man was the only element not entirely calculable, a latent deviation, the element of an unreliability that he knew he alone did not share. According to the available evidence he did not smoke, did not drink, ate with moderation, and possessed no inclinations of his own, no interests, no hobbies, but probably there was here, not a consciously austere attitude of renunciation, but merely the puritanism of an impersonality that was without needs because it knew no needs. His peculiar advantages derived from just this lack of personality-forming factors. He was eager to serve, unobtrusive, down to earth, and even his enemies have always stressed his unparalleled diligence. In bureaucratic routine he was readily adaptable and could take over other people's ideas without distorting them by any subjective emphasis of his own, and interpret them accurately.

His colourless past only underlines this side of him. The early years in the life of this son of a petty bourgeois Saxon family[16] display the classic pattern of the homeless rightists who found their way, via a lost war they had not got over, the postwar period, membership of the Freikorps and nationalist secret societies, into the rising Hitler party. Significantly, there is not a single event in Bormann's life that bears an individual stamp, not a single scene that reveals a personal trait. First working as a steward on an estate in Mecklenburg, he joined the Rossbach Freikorps, and the only incident that gives a special, if repellent, note to his development is the sordid murder of Kadow, his former teacher at elementary school.[17] And this period already shows him as a man in the background looking after the cash box, dropping hints and supplying the technical means. In the foreground, with the blind zeal of the man born to take orders, is one Rudolf Höss, who crops up again later as commandant of the extermination camp at Auschwitz; Höss strikes his victim 'on the skull with all his strength with a broken-off maple sapling'. The difference in the roles that each man played in this affair is profoundly significant. In the NSDAP Bormann held various posts: regional press officer, district leader and gau general secretary in Thuringia, then on the staff of the SA headquarters, and after 1930, administrator of the fund which he himself created for the assistance of comrades injured in the bloody fights that marked the party's rise to power. In these positions he acquired the formal qualification of the model secretary: the mute attentiveness towards those above him and the unfeeling energy towards those beneath him, but also administrative skill and the ability to flatter that served him so well later.[18] In July 1933, when Hitler promoted him to Reichsleiter and appointed him chief of staff to his deputy, Rudolf Hess, Bormann took the first step towards that lofty eminence which he then proceeded to conquer for himself. He first made himself felt in the realm of organisation, where on the pretext of unity he noticeably reduced the influence of the old party leaders, chiefly by altering plans and areas of jurisdiction. It was during this ruthless re-allocation of powers that the treasurer of the NSDAP, Franz Xaver Schwarz, described Bormann as 'the worst egotist and enemy of the old party'; he even considered him capable of the liquidation of all his old comrades.[19] Unable to see that his own position too was being undermined by Bormann's machinations, the unsuspecting Rudolf Hess backed what he was doing in the hope that he would be the one to benefit from the improved status of the offices. The tactics Martin Bormann used to create the conditions for his personal promotion have been vividly described by Alfred Rosenberg:

> Whenever I visited Hess, he was often present; later on, almost always. When I had dinner with the Führer, Bormann and Goebbels were usually there. Hess had obviously got on the Führer's nerves, and so Bormann took care of the queries and orders. Here is where he began to make himself indispensable. If, during our dinner conversation, some incident was mentioned, Bormann would pull out his notebook and make an entry. Or else, if the Führer expressed displeasure over some remark, some measure, some film, Bormann would make a note. If something seemed unclear, Bormann would get up and leave the room, but return almost immediately – after having given orders to his office staff to investigate forthwith, and to telephone, wire or teletype.[20]

Meanwhile the former steward also found other well-tried means of proving himself indispensable. Gradually he took all Hitler's financial affairs into his hands and on top of this bought his way into Hitler's private life via the administration of the 'Adolf Hitler Contribution from Industry', by purchasing not merely the house of Hitler's birth at Braunau and his parents' house at Leonding, but also the whole complex of properties on the Obersalzberg which in 1945 were still entered in the Land Register in his name.[21] The growing scope of his influence, founded partly on personal arrangements and partly on his official posts, naturally remained largely hidden from even the leading figures. As late as 1941, when he had been for almost three years adjutant on Hitler's personal staff, he was referred to in the diary of a close colleague of Goebbels as 'a certain party comrade named Bormann'.[22]

Probably no higher tribute could have been paid to his surreptitious will to power, and when he finally reached the pinnacle, the same year, it was in the most unobtrusive manner. On the very day Rudolf Hess's spectacular flight to Britain was officially announced, the newspapers published the following statement with no additional explanation:

> The former post of Deputy to the Führer will henceforth bear the title of Party Chancellery. It is directly subordinate to me. It will be directed as heretofore by Party Comrade Martin Bormann.
>
> *(signed) Adolf Hitler*

The modest wording concealed the importance of a change whose significance lay in the intangible area of personal relationships. It is true that Bormann did not take over the post of Führer's Deputy, which now formally lapsed; but the functions and rights that the Party Ministry, till then directed by Hess, exercised especially in relation to the state authorities, now largely devolved upon him. The apparent reduction of the influence of the Ministry, in that it no longer acted as representative of the movement as a whole, in reality perfectly suited Bormann, who, forced into the shadow of power, had never wanted to represent anything but merely to run an office.[23]

The influence of the party, which had considerably diminished under Hess's weak and aimless leadership, now gained ground again, especially as Bormann himself, through his experience, his contempt for human beings, and his own peculiar stubborn energy, quickly worked his way up and only a year later was appointed 'Secretary to the Führer'. Within a short time he thrust aside the senior aide, Brückner, and, in accordance with one of the basic principles of the bureaucratic acquisition of power, filled all the key posts with men who owed their position not to their own past service or qualifications, but to unexpected favouritism. Through his supervision of the lists of Hitler's visitors he kept a suspicious watch over the Führer's contacts with the outside world and, in the words of an observer, 'erected a positive Chinese wall through which people were admitted only after showing their empty hands and explaining in detail to Bormann the purpose of their visit. By this means he had absolute control over the whole machinery of the Reich.'[24] In cautious doses he nourished Hitler's self-satisfaction and took advantage of the latter's hysterical outbursts against objective facts that ran counter to his own fantasies in order to reinforce his own personal position. Towards the end of the war Hitler positively thanked him for, in effect, closing the doors more and more tightly against everyone who tried to bring the cold air of reality into the musty world of insane delusions and fantasies that prevailed in the Führer's headquarters. His intimate knowledge of Hitler's weaknesses and personal peculiarities gave him an advantage over all his rivals. Even Goebbels, when early in 1945 he sent an album of photographs of ploughed-up streets and shattered architectural monuments to the Führer's headquarters, received it back from Bormann with the comment that the Führer did not want to be bothered 'with such trivial matters'.[25]

He divided people into two categories: those he could win over and subordinate to himself and those he had to fear, and he distrusted everyone. In order to know everything about everyone, he ceaselessly collected information for his personal card-index and showed himself a master of methods of secret intrigue among favourites such as characterise despotic courts. Hints, half-voiced suspicions, double-dealing, usurpations of authority now more than ever dominated relations between the top leaders, and even Heydrich, himself well informed on all the secrets of the intrigues tirelessly plotted by Bormann, began to respect his underhand ingenuity.[26] By all accounts, the Führer's secretary not infrequently passed on as firm instructions from Hitler what were really no more than casual remarks at table or inventions of his own which could not be checked, all of them serving his own ends.[27] The very vagueness of the boundaries of his authority, which he increasingly manipulated to suit himself on the pretext of the will of the Führer, ensured him virtually unrestricted freedom of movement and made him in fact 'Germany's secret ruler',[28] while Hitler was glad to be relieved of the burden of administrative routine. Bormann's circular of April 2, 1942, on the 'sphere of duties of the Party Chancellery', which purported to give his office administrative and representative functions related solely to the party, did not nearly exhaust the catalogue of his real jurisdiction and once again followed the principle of minimum publicity. 'Silence,' he noted in a letter to his wife, 'is usually the wisest course. And one should by no means always tell the truth, but only when sufficient reasons make it really necessary.'[29] The truth was that, apart from his indirect influence on Hitler's person, he came increasingly to dominate the whole party apparatus. He deprived Rosenberg of part of his ideological authority and Ley of his jurisdiction over political personnel, and Reich Minister Lammers, head of the Reich Chancellery, found himself deprived of important responsibilities. Bormann dismissed and appointed party officials or the Gauleiters subordinate to him personally, made massive use of his right to a voice in appointments and promotions in all state and even military departments, gave or withdrew his favour, praised, bullied, eliminated, but stayed in the background and always kept up his sleeve one more suspicion, one more piece of flattery than his opponent. His nebulous position has been fairly compared to Stalin's powers during Lenin's last days.[30]

Before the ideology of National Socialism he was as helpless as before intellectual matters in general. He was a controller of power, the type whose field of activity was execution, not origination, and the ideological comments which occasionally crop up in the accessible part of his correspondence are not to be taken too seriously; often they simply echo the ideological zeal of his wife. They manifestly imitate a style and an emotion of which he was incapable; National Socialism meant to him not so much a faith as an instrument of his ambition. His coarse worldliness was incapable of the sustained fervour so dear to a Heinrich Himmler, and behind his thick skull there was not one iota of demonism, but only a robust will to power that found its justification within itself.

It was this will to power too, and not any ideological opposition, that made him one of the most extreme opponents of the churches. He was concerned less with the burdensome ideological competition of Christianity than with the claims upon people with which the churches opposed the Third Reich's bid for total power. His directives on policy towards the churches refer repeatedly to 'diminution of power', 'possibilities of exercising influence', and the 'right to lead the people'; and when, in his famous order to the Gauleiters of June 6–7, 1941, on the 'relations between National Socialism and Christianity', he tried with dreary impertinence to place an ideological cloak around ideas relating purely to the acquisition of power, he could not avoid eventually revealing the true cause of this hostility:

National Socialist and Christian conceptions are incompatible. The Christian churches build upon men's ignorance; by contrast N[ational Socialism] rests upon *scientific* foundations.

When we [National Socialists] speak of belief in God, we do not mean, like the naïve

132

Christians and their spiritual exploiters, a man-like being sitting around somewhere in the universe. The force governed by natural law by which all these countless planets move in the universe, we call omnipotence or God. The assertion that this universal force can trouble itself about the destiny of each individual being, every smallest earthly bacillus, can be influenced by so-called prayers or other surprising things, depends upon a requisite dose of naïvety or else upon shameless professional self-interest.[31]

Only then does Bormann pass over to arguments based upon the crucial considerations of power. Since Adolf Hitler himself has the leadership of the people in his hands,

all influences which might restrict or even damage the leadership of the people exercised by the Führer with the aid of the NSDAP must be eliminated. The people must be increasingly wrested from the churches and their instruments the priests. Naturally the churches, looking at matters from their point of view, will and must resist this diminution of power. But never again must the churches be allowed any influence over the leadership of the people. This must be broken totally and forever. Only then will the existence of nation and Reich be assured.[32]

There was probably an additional, tactical, element in Bormann's anti-ecclesiastical pronouncements. Along with physical domination over the party, he also wanted to ensure its claim to ideological infallibility – not because he combined the striving for orthodoxy with the ambition of the scribe, but simply because this too meant power and fundamentally every alien authority represented a challenge. Furthermore, as always where there is such emphatic hostility, personal motives were also at work; and there were also ideological forms to be considered – he paid tribute to these as a matter of course, like the atheist who teaches his children the evening prayer. National Socialism was everything that played into the hands of his varying personal needs and impulses: ambition, will to dominate, career, brutal instincts, even his little pieces of erotic libertinism. This is the explanation for the embarrassingly comic exchange of letters between Bormann and his wife after he had told her in January 1944, with triumphant frankness, that he had at last succeeded in seducing the actress M. Gerda Bormann at once bravely accommodated this information to her philosophy and assured him that she was neither angry nor jealous, but ready to accept M into the common household and, in view of the terrible decline in child production brought about by the war, to work out a system of motherhood by shifts, 'so that you always have a wife who is usable'. His reply was appreciative, but in the tone of one for whom the sole function of ideologies is to act as a mask for the instincts: 'You are of National Socialist stock; as a child of Nazism you are, so to speak, dyed in the wool.'[33]

It was his declared intention largely to crush the churches even while the war was in progress. In 1941, when he found himself in tactical opposition on this point to Hitler, who considered such a clash inopportune in view of the strains and stresses of the war, he continued to pursue his plans in secret;[34] for the war seemed to him a suitable opportunity, which would never recur, for carrying the regime's ideological aims to their logical conclusion. Here as always Bormann was resolved to go to extremes, the 'advocate of all harsh measures', as he has been called.[35] The ramifications of his office do not alone explain the way his name crops up again and again in connection with the introduction of a number of increasingly harsh measures during the last years of the war, whether relating to race policy, the treatment of the Eastern peoples or prisoners of war. What lay behind this was rather the odd extremism of the subordinate official who seeks to preserve his power by constantly exercising it. He shows his harshness and his moral insensitivity, which went hand in hand with a bullying meticulousness, characteristically in an order to Alfred Rosenberg that he is not merely to encourage abortions in the Eastern occupied territories, to reduce the level of education and to liquidate the health services, but also to see that 'on no account are the towns to be in any way rebuilt or even beautified'.[36] In a memorandum of August 19, 1942, he wrote:

The Slavs are to work for us. In so far as we do not need them, they may die. Slav fertility is undesirable. They may possess contraceptives or abort, the more the better. Education is dangerous. We shall leave them religion as a means of diversion. They will receive only the absolutely necessary provisions. We are the masters, we come first.[37]

Anyone who, like Bormann, thought exclusively in terms of rivalries could never escape from the net of tactical considerations. Such utterances indicate an abysmal coarseness, but they also indicate an attempt to push everyone else – and toward the end the three remaining rivals, Himmler, Goebbels and Speer – out of the game of power politics by extreme methods that followed the example of Hitler's ever more unrestrained manner. Whereas the Reichsführer of the SS, in his continued blindness, still clearly underestimated his adversary and provided him with so many points to attack that within a short time he had to capitulate,[38] Goebbels put up a bitter resistance before he too gave in or at least had to admit his inferiority. Goebbels' plan to take control of the intensification of the war, in collaboration especially with Göring, Speer and Ley, came to nothing; his complaints to Hitler had no effect, and Bormann filed away unread in the rear compartments of his safe his great memorandum on the political situation, from which he had hoped to derive a decisive initiative.[39] When the two of them drew together again in the final phase of the Third Reich, this was due less to their common efforts to intensify the war and destruction than to Goebbels' intelligence and tactical adroitness in finally recognising and respecting the advantages of Bormann's position at court. The influence of Speer alone Bormann was unable to undermine despite all his efforts; when Speer departed it was on his own initiative, in horror at a wilful end terrifyingly inspired by hatred, a longing for destruction, and romantic memories of Wagner's operas. 'We must not be downhearted,' Bormann wrote in April 1945 in his last extant letter to his wife. 'Whatever comes, we are pledged to do our duty. And if we are destined, like the old Nibelungs, to perish in Attila's hall, then we'll go to death proudly and with our heads high!'[40]

Even then he still intrigued, stubbornly playing his Diadochian game and pursuing with senseless tenacity even rivals he had already eliminated. It was to Bormann's fondness for setting traps that Himmler owed his appointment to supreme command of Army Group Vistula, which was offering utterly hopeless resistance east of Berlin – an appointment that could no longer be put into effect; and it was Bormann who tampered with Hitler's order for Göring's arrest, turning it into a death sentence. His position was most powerful and most uncontested when the Third Reich held sway only over a few heaps of rubble and a bunker twenty-five feet below ground in the centre of Berlin: then he at last reached his goal.

Fundamentally only one man was safe from his hunger for power: Hitler himself. Bormann needed him, because he could not do without the great order-giving authority and its instructions, and because only the shadow which Hitler cast was wide and deep enough to provide him with the darkness that was his element. 'He [Hitler] towered over us like Mount Everest,' he wrote. 'When all is said and done, the Führer is the Führer! Where should we be without him?'[41] The question shows that at times at least he felt the inadequacy of his own personality, and possibly his straining ambition was an attempt to replace his lack of individual substance by the substance of the power with which he so ruthlessly identified himself. This alone would explain why a man who coldly and calculatingly sought his own advantage stayed at Hitler's side to the end, the 'most loyal party comrade'. He signed Hitler's political testament, acted as witness to his marriage, and stood in the courtyard of the Reich Chancellery, along with Goebbels, General Burgdorf and a few others, under the fire of Russian shells as Hitler's corpse went up in flames.

During the night of May 1–2, with the other occupants of the bunker, he made an attempt to break out. Thanks to his insensitive rigidity, and through clinging tightly to the routine of his office, he had hitherto known neither doubt nor uncertainty. Now, with the breakdown of the organisational system which he had dominated so firmly, and with no one to satisfy his need for subordination after the death of Hitler, he began for the first time to lose his sense of direction: 'Where shall we be without him?' The mood of resignation, which had overshadowed the thought of the irrevocably approaching end, broke out openly in the leaderless functionary. In letters during the last few months he had outlined petty bourgeois daydreams for the postwar period which included a house, a garden and life away from politics. 'You know, I've come to know too well all the ugliness, distortion, slander, nauseating and false flattery, toadying, ineptitude, folly, idiocy, ambition, vanity, greed for money, etc. etc., in short, all the unpleasant aspects of human nature. I've had enough!'[42] Now he said to his secretary, 'Well, then, goodbye. There's not much sense in it any more. I'll have a try, but I won't get through.'[43] Behind him the flames rose in the air from the Führer's abandoned bunker.

Since then he has vanished. Between the Weidendammer Brücke and the Lehrter Station all trace of him was lost behind fountains of dust and crashing walls in that anonymity which he always sought.

Ernst Röhm
and the Lost Generation

So far from fear,
So close to death –
Hail to you, SA!

Joseph Goebbels

Ernst Röhm once declared that he always took the opposite view.[1] In saying this he was not merely acknowledging his spirit of contradiction and his self-confidence. The representative of a truly lost generation, he spoke in this self-revelation for those who came together after the First World War with vague but consistent feelings of opposition, of protest, in the Freikorps and armed nationalist associations, in order to transmute their incapacity for civilian life into extremist adventurism and criminality masquerading as nationalism. Active unrest, readiness to take risks, belief in force and irresponsibility were the essential psychological elements that lay behind the organised nihilism of those whose formative experience had been the war, with its underlying sense of the decline of a culture, and whose heroic myth was the spirit of the front-line soldier. Agents of a permanent revolution without any revolutionary idea of the future, they had no goal, but only restlessness; no idea of values that looked to the future, but only a wish to eternalise the values of the trenches. They fought on and marched on beyond the Armistice and the end of the war, not towards any vision of a new social order, but for the sake of fighting and marching, because the world appeared to them a battlefront and their rhythm was that of marching feet. 'Marching is the most meaningful form of our profession of faith.'

It only required the combination of this blind dynamism with a purposeful revolutionary will to make this group all but irresistible. The SA was this combination. It arose on the one hand because a 'pure driving force' wandering aimlessly in political space needed aims and tasks, and on the other because Hitler's plans for gaining power were, after vague beginnings, acquiring a sharper outline. Like a magnet drawing iron filings, to use one of his favourite metaphors, Hitler attracted these men who had been irrevocably thrown off course early in life. He was one of them himself, and he fitted their extremism, their moral brutalisation, into his tactical system for the conquest of power. It was not only because there were natural points of contact here, not only because he found in these people a human type perfectly prepared to serve his purposes, that he directed his propaganda so expressly towards the militant groups. The truth was rather that he quickly saw the propaganda advantages to be gained from intimidating his opponents by the parade of uniformed groups ready and willing to use violence, and here more than anywhere else he showed his psychological astuteness. Contrary to civilised expectations, he put his trust in the propaganda value of terror, the attraction of terror spread by the most brutal methods. 'Brutality is respected,' he once stated, enunciating this principle. 'The people need wholesome fear. They want to fear something. They want someone to frighten them and make them shudderingly submissive. Haven't you seen everywhere that after the beerhall battles those who have been beaten are the first to join the party as new members? Why babble about brutality and get indignant about tortures? The masses want them. They need something that will give them a thrill of horror.'[2] The SA's mobilisation of the coarse instincts released by the war, intensified by the introduction of unequivocally criminal elements, of thugs and riffraff, was not an inevitable aspect of a revolutionary outbreak, nor, as was at times stated in an unmistakable attempt at excuse, was it made necessary by the organisation of similar militant formations by political opponents; it was planned psychological exploitation. With growing tactical assurance Hitler ever more carefully appreciated the advantages of strong-arm bands over rhetorical and liturgical propaganda as a means of winning recruits; he expressly advocated combining 'activist brutality' or 'brutal power with brilliant political planning'.[3]

In spite of the difficulty of distinguishing the meaning and function of the SA within the movement as a whole, we may now see the true task of the Brown Shirt detachments, in contrast to that of the Political Organisation, to have lain in emphasising the belligerent element in the setting up of an all-embracing system of coercion. The rise of the NSDAP and its conquest of power show the combination demanded by Hitler, although theory was continually complicated by practical difficulties because there were two distinct, though curiously interwoven, power groups with competing demands both struggling for independence. In general, however, the system proved practicable and successful so long as there was a firm goal and an accepted authority at the top, to whose tactical moves both blocs unprotestingly adapted themselves. But once power had been achieved the ambitions of the SA for independence, previously smouldering more or less underground, strove for open expression. Hitler solved the structural problem of the 'double party' with bloodshed.[4] On June 30, 1934 and the following two days he arranged the liquidation of his old follower and friend Ernst Röhm, together with the homosexual element within the SA that had lent not merely the brown terrorist army but the whole of Hitler's movement some of its most striking and repellent features.

Death before the firing squad against the walls of Stadelheim prison and the Lichterfeld Military College meant for most of the high SA leaders, from Ernst Röhm through Edmund Heines down to August Schneidhuber, the identical conclusion to almost identical careers.[5] Service as an officer in the war and in the Freikorps or the right-radical defence associations had in most cases been followed by half-hearted attempts to get a foothold in civilian life, as a traveller, commercial employee, estate manager or simply head of household. At intervals they cultivated the old contacts; there was a deeply ingrained longing for male companionship, for the trade of arms, for the unconstrainedness of the soldier's life, and finally, for unrestrained indulgence in eating and drinking. These men were merely hibernating behind a bourgeois façade which they felt to be alien and 'civilian'; meanwhile they conspired, joined in enterprises that amounted to high treason, in the assassination of Republican politicians, in vehmic murders. Almost every one of these careers includes a period of imprisonment, a symptom of the inability to adapt on the part of men who, in fruitless resentment, always took 'the opposite view', opposed in any case to that despised and hated bourgeois world whose values and concepts of order had irrevocably perished for most of them in the course of their wartime experiences. Suddenly, with entry into the emergent SA, this empty, self-alienated life regained its central system of reference: now in all their unrest, their love of adventure, their feelings of hatred, they once more stood shoulder to shoulder with others; their feeling of meaninglessness was shared with comrades and thus, in the blurred reasoning of revolutionary irrationalism, acquired meaning.

There were various reasons for this generation's extraordinary inability to adapt to civilian life. For some it was the excessive psychic and intellectual demands made upon them by war and its aftermath. This was true above all for the mercenaries, whose outlook often swung from right to left extremism, but it was also true for the 'idealists', who imagined they had grasped in the 'fires of the war of equipment' the hem of a new, still vague meaning of life which they sought in vain to rediscover in the drab normality of peace. It was these who formed the true revolutionary core of the SA. For others economic ruin or social decline threatened or had already been suffered. The petty bourgeois stratum, which provided the main manpower of the SA, was joined by another category, former professional soldiers who felt themselves socially reduced, deprived of their livelihood, and on top of this morally defamed by the Versailles Treaty, and were consequently full of resentment. Common to them all, in varying degrees, was the longing for new forms of community, aroused even before the war by the youth movement and confirmed and reinforced by the legendary comradeship of the front, and now neither absorbed nor adequately represented in existing parties that followed the methods of civilian organisations.[6] It is no statistical coincidence that the top leadership of the SA in the early days was made up almost exclusively, not of the dregs of the urban masses, but predominantly of failures who had started life with every advantage, an uprooted bourgeoisie which found its way to crime as a result of lost honour, lost faith, or lost social status, but took care to cover itself by orders from above, ideological pretexts and formal safeguards. Destined in normal times for the middle ranks of society and with a rather conservative outlook on life, these men were pushed, by the combination of a past they had been unable to cope with and multiple aggressive impulses, on to a revolutionary course outside and in deliberate opposition to every form of order except the military. Instead of the moderate social privileges they had once looked forward to, they now noisily and demonstratively claimed the privileges of force that go with the soldier's life. In the inimitable words of a toast proposed by one of the leaders of the Freikorps, making lofty claims to patriotism at the time of the battles in Upper Silesia: 'There's nothing better than a little war like this! God preserve the theatre of war. I'm threatening to become sober.' And Ernst Röhm wrote: 'Since I am an immature and wicked man, war and unrest appeal to me more than the good bourgeois order.'[7]

The fat little man with the bullet-scarred, always slightly red face was the typical representative of this group, which had gone off the rails and only found its way back in Hitler's army of brown-shirted terrorists; it was obviously more than a caprice of fate that this man should provoke the spectacular trial in the course of which Hitler thrust the prototype of the robust and popular trooper with the blustering self-confidence out of the top leadership of the movement. Coming from an old Bavarian family of civil servants, Röhm shared not only the sociological values but also many of the psychological values common to a number of Hitler's leading followers: above an intense attachment to his mother there rose the commanding shadow of his father, who was 'harsh towards himself, righteous and thrifty'.[8] Röhm was a fanatical soldier and officer, though without the arrogance and strained intensity that put a touch of martial demonism into the blank face of the General Staff officer of the old school. Although from childhood he had had 'only one thought and wish, to be a soldier', and towards the end of the war was actually on the General Staff and a magnificent organiser, he was much closer to the type of the field officer. He was a daredevil who had come out of the war with numerous wounds and even in his memoirs he expressed a curiously exalted aversion for the word 'prudent' (*besonnen*).[9] He divided men simply into soldiers and civilians, into friend and enemy, was honest and without guile, coarse, sober, a simpleminded and straightforward swashbuckler who liked 'the noise of the camp and the bustle of the quartermaster's stores'.[10] Wherever he appeared, one of his comrades from the period of illegal military activity noted, 'life came into the place, but above all *practical* work was done'.[11] His robustly practical Bavarian mind, to which all brooding was alien, had no time for profound cults, for emotional enthusiasm for the Nordic ideal, or insane race fantasies, and he openly mocked the complex philosophical mysticism of Rosenberg, Himmler and Darré. His successor, Viktor Lutze, later remarked reproachfully that he had never been able to get on friendly terms with Röhm because he 'did not take sufficient interest in questions of *Weltanschauung*'.[12]

At the same time, Röhm was a brutal boss, who gathered around him a dissolute crew who did not shrink from a bad reputation and actually prided themselves on their corruption, perverse debauchery and crimes of violence. Admittedly the functions and aims of the SA quickly brought out the criminal energies liberated by the First World War, but only under Röhm was there that ostentation which, so to speak, institutionalised them and finally stamped the SA as a kind of wrestling club with a political bias. Röhm had no qualms of conscience; murder did not worry him, and whereas Captain Weiss wrote that wherever Röhm appeared 'life' came into the place, often enough precisely the opposite was the case. When his close friend Edmund Heines was condemned by a court of law for murder, he called this, in angry ignorance of legal standards, 'an encroachment by formal justice upon a soldier's right to be 'consciously one-sided'',[13] as he proudly proclaimed. In his memoirs he spoke with enthusiasm of the time when the soldier was 'everything', and openly demanded special privileges for his caste, 'the primacy of the soldier over the politician'.[14] His view that those in the opposing, un-uniformed camp consisted exclusively of 'draft-dodgers, deserters and profiteers' was based on the argument that the only man entitled to lead was the one who, free from private interests, was ready to die for his principles – 'an outlook of staggering naïvety', as has rightly been said, 'a kind of total military resentment against the civilian environment'.[15] He once stated that, since they shared the same activist attitude, he had more in common with the Communists than with the 'bourgeoisie', and in 1933 he told a British diplomat that he 'would reach an understanding more easily with an enemy soldier than with a German civilian; because the latter is a swine, and I don't understand his language'.[16]

Conditions after the First World War were extraordinarily favourable to Captain Röhm of Reichswehr Group Headquarters 4 in Munich. He was one of a large group of ambitious captains and majors who, after their return from the front, exploited the helplessness of public institutions and, with the real power at their disposal, occupied a growing area where no one was in control. Not least of their reasons for being the most resolute in refusing to recognise the revolutionary new democratic state was their almost traumatic self-reproach for having failed to defend the monarchy in November 1918. In Bavaria above all they were all the more free to develop their counter-revolutionary activity against the Reich and its legality because here, as a result of the more radical revolutionary events and the resultant chaos, they found wide popular support reaching up into the highest echelons of the government. Röhm himself rose, through various positions the precise sequence of which we cannot examine here, to be master of a secret cache of weapons in Bavaria, and accordingly one of the most powerful men in the province.[17] The activities of the Freikorps and armed associations would have been inconceivable without the restless initiatives of this man who, less by virtue of his rank than through his actual influence, became one of the key figures on the political scene. Guided by the idea of the soldier's right to leadership, he first organised a special intelligence department for the General Staff, with whose aid he kept watch over the political groups and thus made contact with the 'V-man' Adolf Hitler. Impressed like almost everyone else by the young agitator's oratorical genius, Röhm obtained for him his first valuable links with the politicians and military leaders of the province. In his efforts to promote the party, one of whose early members he was and which enjoyed many special favours thanks to his initiative, he brought it numerous supporters from among his own friends or the ranks of the Reichswehr and also supported it during the founding and building up of the SA. But whereas Hitler, the tactician out to achieve unrestricted authority, envisaged the SA purely as a terrorist organisation to assist the party leadership, Röhm's intention, after his discharge from the army enabled him to take an active part in the movement, was to create an armed military force for the revolutionary conquest of the state.

Vague as the two opposing conceptions were at first, a silent conflict, fought with growing stubbornness, soon broke out between them and was not resolved until June 30, 1934. To begin with, Hitler was at a disadvantage. His position was difficult not only because of the far greater power Röhm held at that time, but also because of the large number of soldiers who were joining the SA. There was an increasing tendency, for reasons of organisation, for the SA to develop military forms, which in turn increased the self-confidence with which the Brown Guard demanded wider functions. From 1923 onwards Röhm succeeded more and more openly in imposing his ideas, so that the NSDAP visibly developed into a 'double party' made up of two rival blocs: the SA, or Storm Troops, as Hitler had christened them after a beerhall battle that became a party legend;[18] and the Political Organisation, abbreviated to PO and contemptuously dubbed 'P-Zero' by the SA. Hitler at this period was little more than an expert speaker recruiting for a movement whose true core was the paramilitary organisation led by Röhm, and if everything indicates that the leader of the NSDAP was at this time content with such a distribution of roles, subsequent events proved that it had its effect on his desire for self-assertion. At the latest after the unsuccessful enterprise of November 9, 1923, which saw Hitler on his knees before the authority of the state on the steps of the Feldherrnhalle, he realised that Röhm's crude idea of a head-on conquest of power was hopeless and that consequently the building up of a great military party organisation was fundamentally wrong. Whereas Röhm, released on probation immediately after the trial, at once tried to reassemble the shattered nationalist armed organisations, Hitler, even while still in Landsberg prison, began to dissociate himself from Röhm, to drop the military presuppositions of his plans for seizing power, and, as he proudly stressed later, remained 'immune to advice'.[19] Various halfhearted attempts by both sides to reach an understanding came to nothing, so that soon after his release Hitler brought about the break that robbed Röhm of all further opportunities for activity. Repudiated by Hitler, whose position and prestige within the movement had been greatly strengthened largely because of the course taken by the trial, and dismissed from the Reichswehr, Röhm was 'nothing now but a private individual';[20] his name carried no more weight. On April 17, 1925 he withdrew from political life. According to entirely credible interrogation findings, he lived 'the life of a sick animal',[21] removed from the excesses and irregularities of a soldier's life and from most of his comrades. He wandered restlessly, stayed here and there with friends, became a travelling salesman for a patriotic publishing company, and worked for two months in a machine factory, until finally he was invited to go to Bolivia as a military instructor; he accepted almost precipitately 'within twenty-four hours'.

141

Meanwhile Hitler was attempting a complete reconstruction of the SA. 'The purpose of the new SA,' as the 'General Instructions for the Re-establishment of the NSDAP' of February 1925 had already declared, would be 'to steel the bodies of our youth, to educate them in discipline and devotion to the common great ideal, to train them in the organisational and instructional service of the movement'. Together with Franz Pfeffer von Salomon, the newly appointed leader of the SA, Hitler developed the principles of an organisation which was to be freed both from the character of the defence corps and from its limited and fragmentary role as the bodyguard of local party leaders. Instead, it was to become a rigidly controlled, powerful instrument of mass terror in the hands of the political party leadership. 'The training of the SA,' Hitler wrote in a letter to Pfeffer, 'must be carried out, not according to military principles, but according to the needs of the party. In so far as the members are to be made physically fit, the chief stress should be placed not upon military drill but upon athletic activities. Boxing and ju-jitsu have always appeared to me more important than any ineffective, because incomplete, rifle practice.' 'In order also to divert the SA,' the letter continues, 'from any temptation to satisfy their activism by petty conspiracies, they must from the very beginning be completely initiated into the great idea of the movement and so fully trained in the task of representing this idea that the individual does not see his mission as eliminating some great or petty rogue, but as committing himself to the establishment of a new National Socialist people's state. Thereby the struggle against the present state will be raised out of the atmosphere of petty acts of revenge and conspiracy to the grandeur of a philosophical war of annihilation against Marxism, its constructions and its wirepullers. We shall not work in secret conventicles but in huge mass marches; the way for the movement cannot be opened up by dagger or poison or pistol, but by conquest of the street.'[22] In a series of so-called SA orders and decrees, Pfeffer later further differentiated the principles governing the activities of the SA and, especially fascinated by its potentialities for influencing the masses, stated:

The only form in which the SA appears to the public is that of the closed formation. This is at the same time one of the most powerful forms of propaganda. The sight of a large number of inwardly and outwardly calm, disciplined men, whose total will to fight may be unequivocally seen or sensed, makes the most profound impression on every German and speaks to his heart a more convincing and inspiring language than writing and speech and logic can ever do. Calm composure and matter-of-factness underline the impression of strength – the strength of the marching columns and the strength of the cause for which they are marching. The inner strength of the cause leads the German emotionally to deduce its rightness: 'For only the right, the honest, the good can release true strength.' Where whole hosts purposefully (not in the welling up of sudden mass suggestion) stake life and limb and existence for a cause, the cause *must* be great and true!

The same SA order contains the following statement on the demarcation of the functions of the SA and the PO:

The SA man is the sacred freedom fighter. The Pg [Parteigenosse – member of the NSDAP] is the instructor and skilled agitator. Political propaganda seeks to enlighten the adversary, to dispute with him, to understand his viewpoint, to go into his ideas, up to a certain point to agree with him – but when the SA appear on the scene, this stops. They are out for all or nothing. They know only the motto (metaphorically): Strike dead! You or me![23]

Beyond such maxims of a general programme of fighting and killing, the SA did not in fact develop any marked ideological profile, and when Hitler saw in it the 'fanatical fighting unit of a great idea', here too the absoluteness of their fanaticism was more important to him than their strict ideological orthodoxy. The 'proletarian' attitude so often attributed especially to the early SA, in contrast to the petty bourgeois political organisation of the party, meant at bottom no more than the plebian lack of ties of men who had burnt their bridges and stylised their nihilism into the selflessness of the political fighter. It was precisely this indistinct outlook, determined by vague national and social elements, which allowed SA members to attach to their organisation the most varied personal predilections, instinctual attitudes and interests. Matched with the ideology of the National Socialist movement, so exactly made to measure for the individual restlessness of these failures, it had a powerful attraction and went far to meet the need of the German soldier, the predominant type in all ranks of the SA, for a leadership and a rank-and-file both equally devoid of ideas. Unlike the common criminal, such a man demanded an ideological motive for his actions,[24] but this demand was generally satisfied by the empty phrases of a demagogically exalted collective feeling of value, in so far as it was not satisfied in advance by the semimilitary structure of the SA itself. There is a curious misconception, rife in a society stamped by militarist traditions, which leads it to believe that a 'cause' is being represented and 'idealism' practised wherever the possessors of individual emotions and resentments form ranks and march in step. Pfeffer's order quoted above is vivid evidence of this. The ideology of the SA was activity at any price, with the background of a general, totally undifferentiated readiness to believe, and its seductive power upon the generation of those who had been pushed off the rails by the war was further reinforced by the romantic notion of the 'Lost Band' claiming to be defending the nation's value and dignity against a world of enemies, at a time when the nation had forgotten its honour and society was concerned only with its own selfish advantage – a notion deliberately fostered to attract recruits. At this point, with these fundamental principles clear, it must be stated that this overall picture consisted of various hues. For example, non-ideological dynamism was especially characteristic of the South German core of the SA. In the North German wing certain leftist, anti-capitalist ideas were rife, even if they were vague and never raised to the level of an intellectually elaborated concept and were overridden and finally liquidated through the growing predominance of the central office in Munich. In accordance with the homosexual stamp of the SA, its members' devotion was aroused far less by programmes than by persons, by 'born leaders', the centre of a passionate admiration that was in strange contrast to the strikingly barbaric style of all other expressions of emotion. The general force of these observations is underlined by statistical evidence that crimes of violence of a non-political nature notably decreased in number during those years: the activity of the paramilitary formations evidently absorbed a part of the country's criminal energy.[25]

The so-called 'good' years of the Republic, which cost all the extreme groups on both political wings considerable loss of support, left the SA largely unaffected. Whereas the movement as a whole, as a political party, found itself squeezed into almost hopeless-looking fringe positions, the SA was able not merely to maintain its membership but actually, thanks above all to recruits from the camps of the dissolving Freikorps and private defence formations, to increase it to approximately 70,000 men by autumn 1930. Conflict and friction, arising both from recurrent difficulties over the demarcation of jurisdiction between SA and PO and from the jealousy of many party functionaries for the visibly more self-confident SA leadership corps, finally led to Pfeffer's resignation. Shortly after the NSDAP's great electoral victory of September 14, Hitler therefore recalled Ernst Röhm from Bolivia, though not without first himself assuming the post of Supreme Leader of the SA and demanding from every SA leader 'an oath of unconditional allegiance' to his person, as an assurance against future insubordination.[26]

Röhm immediately obeyed the call, and the passion with which he devoted himself to his new task as Chief of Staff of the SA seemed to contain some conviction that, in spite of all contrary assurances, his former conception of the paramilitary organisation and of direct action for the seizure of the state had gained ground. Attracted by the SA hostels and kitchens, there flocked to the Brown Shirt formations during the world economic crisis, in a second wave, countless unemployed as well as the socially *déclassés* whose hatred against society reacted in conjunction with that of the adventurous activists and led to extreme aggression. Nine months after Röhm had taken up his duties, the SA already numbered 170,000 men. He brought with him the whole notorious company of his friends, whose entry finally ensured the dominance of the criminal element within the SA. This left no more room for selfless devotion to the cause, which had in any case been only a faint and fitful impulse. Röhm, it soon came to be said, was building up a 'private army within the private army', while Hitler rejected reports of criminal activities within the top leadership of the SA 'utterly and vigorously' as an 'impertinence'; the SA, he said, was a 'gathering of men for a political purpose, not an institute for the moral education of young ladies but a band of rough fighters'. The crucial question was 'whether or not the SA leader or man did his duty in the SA. A man's private life can be an object of consideration only if it runs counter to essential principles of the National Socialist *Weltanschauung*.'[27]

Confident in the knowledge of its ceaselessly swelling numbers, the SA now became for the first time the instrument of calculated mass terrorism which Hitler had intended. Battles in meeting halls and in the streets, propaganda trips, the blowing up of buildings and murder spread paralysis and fear, and caused a complete breakdown of morale among the Republican forces. According to investigations by the police, its arsenal contained the 'classic' weapons of criminals: blackjacks, brass knuckles, rubber hoses, etc. while 'as for the pistols – likewise in the established manner of criminals – "girls" were employed where necessary as ever-ready "arms bearers" '. Above all in the big cities, 'a permanent underworld war was carried on between the SA and the Red Front (RF), in which both sides made use of low taverns as bases', not without occasional tactical alliances and, following National Socialist reverses at the end of 1932, frequent desertions from the SA to the RF, which in the spring of 1933 were offset by whole units of the RF going over to the SA. The underworld style is also reflected in SA slang: Munich units in the early period referred to a pistol as *Feuerzeug* (cigarette-lighter) and a rubber truncheon as *Radiergummi* (eraser), and the Berlin SA of the early 1930s, with the perverted pride of gangsters, took nicknames which showed up all talk about the supposed political-revolutionary impulse behind these fighting units as propagandist eyewash. One SA unit at Wedding was called *Räubersturm* (the Robber Band), a troop from the central district *Tanzgilde* (Dance Guild), one of the men *Mollenkönig* (King of the Beer Barrels), another *Revolverschnauze* (Revolver-muzzle), and yet another *Schiessmüller* (Müller the Shot).[28]

While the SA were winning the freedom of the streets for Hitler and thus opening his road to power, the question of what was to happen to its formations after the seizure of power was becoming ever more urgent. Röhm, his self-confidence immeasurably swollen by success, now returned more provocatively than ever to the old solution: a duumvirate with Hitler as political leader and agitator and himself as generalissimo of a vast armed force in which the whole nation was to be organised.[29] Hitler at first kept his options open by giving the SA, after January 30, 1933, the most varied tasks in an unparalleled tangle of tactical directions. Within the framework of the double revolution from above and below, it was given the role of expressing the popular anger that could no longer control itself; some of its units were now permitted, free from all the restrictions of the preceding years, to hunt, torture and murder and, in the first unsupervised concentration camps, to give vent to all the sadistic ingenuity of inhibited petty bourgeois feelings. The number of murdered within the first nine months of the regime has been estimated at 500 to 600, the number of those sent to the concentration camps already announced by Frick on March 8 at about 100,000.[30] The elimination of the protection of the law and its replacement by private vengeance had the most varied motives, as a list of some of the victims of this phase makes clear: along with the anarchist poet Erich Mühsam others murdered include the philosopher and pacifist Theodor Lessing, the Jewish theatrical agent Rotter and his wife, and Horst Wessel's murderer, Ali Höhler. As always when we come to analyse the complex structures of National Socialist behaviour, we see an almost inextricable tangle of political motives, satisfaction of personal instincts and cold calculations. In the individual explanations given for terrorist activity National Socialism revealed itself as precisely that high school for the disguise of individual impulses behind ideological pretexts which for the majority of its supporters it fundamentally was – as for example when the ingenious tortures were justified on educational grounds. The SA, wrote Gruppen-führer Ernst at the beginning of 1934, has in the concentration camps the 'major pedagogic task' of 'helping misled fellow citizens against their will but in their own best interests to political reflection and the ethos of work'.[31] Other units were employed soon after January 30 as auxiliary police, or, in order to complete the confusion during the seizure of power, had to parade for church services on Sundays, act as stewards at meetings, or go out into the streets with collection boxes. Hitler called his tactical method 'a unique, wonderfully elastic interplay between the impulsive popular movement and carefully thought-out guidance by the leadership'; this corresponded almost literally with what he had demanded in the past.[32]

Nevertheless the SA were dissatisfied. They felt they had been cheated of their real wishes, and in their violent urge to action they were not prepared to let the promised 'Night of the Long Knives' be suddenly explained away as a rhetorical metaphor. The vague promise that after victory Germany would belong to them had largely become for them the tangible prospect of a comprehensive 'sacking of Germany'; occasional permission to break into private homes or plunder Jewish shops was not by any means the same thing. For others the dawn of the new era was linked with the hope of an officer's commission, a district president's office, a post as forest administrator, or whatever else met their demand for social elevation. Very soon cases came to light where members of the SA had used force to gain positions for themselves in industry and commerce, and in May 1933 Göring had to attempt to pacify disquiet over the Brown Shirt leadership's hunger for office; he attempted to justify this as a claim to 'restitution' and by saying that it was an eternal law that 'he who has fought for and won a position will occupy it'.[33] In general, however, it was rather the officials of the party's Political Organisation whose demands were met, and in any case the expectations of the SA were not fulfilled. It was their determination not to be pushed aside without a struggle that lay behind the slogan 'Second Revolution', so often misinterpreted as indicating a predominantly socialist programme, whereas in reality it was merely an expression of the aim of many individuals to enrich themselves or to regain a place in society.

These upheavals finally revealed how the SA had been transformed into an organisation with a petty bourgeois class structure under the impact, especially, of the world economic crisis. Unlike its early composition, which had taken its stamp from the basic extremism of the war generation and the Freikorps, it was largely dominated now by the type of man who was an extremist only till he got what he wanted, the man whose trauma and formative experience was not the 'war of equipment' but unemployment which led to loss of social status and individual self-respect. Not the downfall of a world, but his exclusion from a world was his decisive experience, and his extremism was based largely on an uninhibited desire to reconquer while at the same time leaving the fabric of this world's order untouched. He did not want to change the world by revolution, but merely to obtain for himself a place in it, if possible with greater security and greater social prestige than before and with more opportunity of exercising influence. Konrad Heiden coined the unforgettable phrase 'SA class' for those classes whose aim was a secure existence through state aid and who, instead of claiming the state for their own, as the workers did at the time of their greatest self-confidence, were content to make claims upon the state[34] – desperados in search of a pension.

Most dissatisfied of all was Ernst Röhm himself, who saw the dream of a soldiers' state fade after a few months. With an unmistakably threatening undertone he declared, referring to the many mass proclamations of the victory of the national revolt, that he 'preferred to make revolutions rather than celebrate them',[35] adding that the goal 'was far from being reached'; the national revolt represented only 'a partial stretch' along the road 'to the National Socialist State, our ultimate goal'. Deeply offended, he accused Hitler of being nothing but 'a civilian, an "artist", a dreamer'.[36] From the summer of 1933 onwards he demonstratively revived the SA's old militaristic tendencies and organised huge parades all over the Reich, voicing his discontent in numerous critical utterances on foreign policy, anti-Semitism, the destruction of the trade unions, or the suppression of freedom of expression. He turned bitterly against Goebbels, Göring, Himmler and Hess and moreover, with his plans for amalgamating the Reichswehr and the SA into a National Socialist militia, antagonised the generals, who were jealous of their privileges. 'The grey rock,' he would say, 'must be submerged by the brown flood.'[37]

Thus he gradually arranged the stage upon which his own fate was to be decided. Undoubtedly no revolt was in progress when on the morning of June 30, 1934, drowsy and bemused, he was arrested by Hitler himself; for fundamentally, despite all his impulsive rebelliousness, he had always demanded leadership and offered obedience. In the early years of the movement he had already begged Hitler 'not to bother to spend a long time explaining any political or military measure. "It is enough if you say: at such and such a time you will be at the Siegestor with such and such a number of men; then I shall be there." '[38] But at least he wanted to be at the Siegestor with his band, if possible after a battle at the barricades, the smoke of gunpowder and bloodshed. His complaint was that Hitler never called him there. In his dull-witted simplicity he had no understanding of the crafty tactics for the seizure of power employed after January 30, 1933. When the Bavarian Minister of Justice, Hans Frank, visited him in his cell in Stadelheim prison on June 30 he told Frank with resignation, 'All revolutions devour their own children.'[39]

In fact, there died with Ernst Röhm only those children of the revolution who, like himself, wished to achieve in a swift assault what Hitler, in his own words, sought 'slowly and purposefully, in tiny steps'.[40] Röhm's conviction, held to the last, that he was in full agreement with Hitler was entirely correct, as is shown by the evolution of the SS, the true victor in this bloody story. For its influence, its power, later attained that all-embracing extension which Röhm had planned for his SA. And if his ambitious lieutenants had dreamt of an SA state, now the SS

147

state became a reality. Its key positions were largely occupied by the survivors of just those radical activists of the war and Freikorps generation whose revolutionary nihilism had been smothered in the course of the SA's development by the petty bourgeois type with its material ambitions. Those who perished in the three days of murder died in the last analysis merely because of their impatience, for victims and victors were both unconditional revolutionaries; the reproaches which Hitler had made in his major speech of justification of July 13, 1934 applied to both sides:

[This] group of destructive elements arises out of those revolutionaries who, in 1918, were shaken and uprooted in their previous relationship to the state and hence have lost all inner relation to the human order of society. They have become revolutionaries who worship revolution as revolution and wish to see in it a permanent condition. Among the countless documents which it has been my duty to read through during the past weeks I found a diary containing the jottings of a man who in 1918 was thrown on to the path of resistance to law and now lives in a world in which the law as such seems to inspire resistance; a shattering document, an everlasting conspiracy, an insight into the mentality of men who, without suspecting it, have found in nihilism their last faith. Incapable of any real collaboration, determined to adopt an attitude of opposition towards all authority, their unrest and disquiet find satisfaction only in continual intellectual and conspiratorial preoccupation with the destruction of whatever exists.[41]

In fact this picture, apt as it may appear in detail, is incomplete. War, the postwar period and the consequences of each certainly played an extraordinary part in the wasted lives of this generation. But the great corrupting force which opened to their aimless searching, after the wretched years of the Freikorps, the path to a gangster's existence (disguised of course by ideological pretexts) and finally liberated their already dangerously unconstrained impulses by bestowing upon them the halo of a political struggle – the great corrupting influence of their lives was Hitler himself.

What so fascinated them and drew them under his spell was the promise of irresponsible violence, the terror of which they had long spread abroad, before they themselves now became its victims. In its casual brutality Hitler's retribution conformed to the maxims that had been practised for years by the SA. Strictly speaking, it is not that revolutions devour their own children: it is the principle of violence that destroys revolutionaries.

PART THREE

Functionaries of Totalitarian Rule

Franz von Papen
and the Conservative Collaboration

These men are ghosts.

Adolf Hitler

The face of the Third Reich was from the beginning a double face. That principle of duality which was Hitler's essential tactical device, which characterised the regime's initial rise to power and meant that all structures combined terror and legality, strict order and chaos, Machiavellian open-mindedness and dull-witted instinctiveness, was also expressed, quite overtly, in physiognomic terms. The type of the 'Unknown SS Man', the muscular but frankly heartless and brainless hero forever tearing chains apart and smashing barriers on countless posters – for example, those by the designer Mjoelnir – was counterbalanced by the figure of the respected privy councillor of conservative stamp, who 'placed himself confidently behind the new leadership'. The strong-arm and the respectable elements marched side by side and supplemented each other. While the half-light of the background was populated by wholly criminal characters such as troop-leader 'Rubber Leg' from the Berlin Central District or the Neuköllner SA unit which, with underworld self-confidence, called itself the *Ludensturm*, the 'Gang of Rogues'.[1] the regime presented a legalistic façade of reassuring types who guaranteed its middle-class respectability: Konstantin von Neurath, Hjalmar Schacht, Franz von Papen.

It needed them especially at the beginning. The National Socialist leadership had realised that a complicated modern administrative system was not to be overcome in open attacks in the street, but rather by the gradual capture of key points in the political, economic and bureaucratic organisation; now it defined its own steps towards the conquest of the state, not as a revolutionary break, but as the final attainment of the true nationalist Germany which had remained hitherto suppressed, or at least had failed to take over government. What was presented by skilful propaganda and enthusiastically acclaimed as the emergence of the people, the rebirth and liberation of the national honour, bore in reality all the marks of a revolutionary change.

A multitude of factors enabled this aspect to be widely and effectively concealed at least at the beginning. Of crucial importance was the fact that the National Socialists were able to play with overwhelming success upon the weakness of character and susceptibility to totalitarianism of the spokesmen of

151

national conservatism, who allowed themselves to be thrust into the foreground and exploited as figureheads in the great deception. In the wider sphere of the conservative middle class the decision to support the 'national cause' did not spring solely from blindness and opportunism; but also from the short-sighted argument that by collaborating they could 'avert something worse' and block Hitler's path to autocratic rule. This complex of illusions and fallacies contributed essentially to the success of the National Socialist bid for power, but what weight it carried was the result not least of the collaboration of leading representatives of conservatism, and for them these considerations possessed no significance whatever. Their personal support gave a spurious appearance of legality to the ecstatic emphasis upon the nationalist element; they were men of straw in the seizure of power, who distracted attention from the terrorism and violence, providing a murderous enterprise with an honourable veneer. Their attempt, based on an overestimate of their own importance, to enlist the regime in the service of their own aims, in themselves not very dissimilar from those of the National Socialists, lasted only until Hitler knew that he was firmly in the saddle. Then they found themselves eliminated, and for some humiliating dismissal was their first intimation of the mistake they had made in entering into this partnership.

With all his self-righteous lack of conscience Franz von Papen, of course, never achieved this insight. Nevertheless particular circumstances made him the representative of these nationalist conservative circles: his historical role itself and the characteristics and qualities which shaped him for it; his claim, in which he persisted throughout, to belong to the 'upper stratum authorised by history'; his unhesitating identification of the interests of his class with the interests of the state; his socially reactionary attitude, which he disguised behind a pseudo-Christian vocabulary; his sprinkling of monarchist ideas; his nationalistic jargon; his tendency to think in long-outdated categories; in short, his anachronistic profile and finally the hint of caricature which hung over his whole person. All this makes him a perfect model of that type of the ruling class which on January 30, 1933 placed itself at the disposal of National Socialism, because with an almost unparalleled blindness it imagined itself to be once more called upon by history to assume leadership.

Franz von Papen came of an old Westphalian noble family, had served in a feudal cavalry regiment, and achieved a certain publicity in 1916, during the First World War, when he was expelled from the United States for conspiratorial activities while military attaché. While crossing to Europe he allowed important documents relating to his secret service activities to fall into the hands of British intelligence, a piece of carelessness which seemed typical, for a similar misfortune befell him a little later on the Turkish front. A few years after the end of the war he entered politics and became a member of the centre group in the Prussian Landtag, evidently as representative of the agrarian interests of his district. His marked rightist tendencies induced him in 1925 to canvass during the Reich presidential election not for the candidate of his own camp but for Hindenburg, and he found himself on several occasions in open conflict with his party, within which he enjoyed no particular influence. He was more highly thought of among the anti-parliamentary, anti-republican right, whose representatives mourned the end of the monarchy and with it their own opportunities for prestige and influence, and who were striving for the recovery of power by means of confused, naïve, reactionary and unrealistic plans.

Although unsuccessful in attempts to gain a seat in the Reichstag, Papen did achieve a certain political influence over the centre newspaper *Germania*. Together with the industrialist Florian Klöckner he acquired a majority of the shares in the paper and eventually became chairman of its management committee. His marriage to the daughter of a leading Saar industrialist had brought him both a considerable fortune and good connections with industry. If we add to this the fact that he had links with the high clergy as a Catholic nobleman and contacts with the Reichswehr as a former General Staff officer, we have the picture of a man who supplemented his personal inadequacies with a network of connections and achieved some importance in the intermediate realms of politics as the point of intersection of numerous interests. Occasional lectures to rightist clubs and cliques, as well as newspaper articles, show him as a man who addressed himself with a forceful superficiality to a conservatism which labelled itself national, above parties and Christian. In fact, this conservatism acted on behalf of massive interests, with class-political, industrial and agrarian basis, and in advocating an authoritarian regime linked nostalgia for the past with rejection of the present. Papen had practised politics more in the dilettante form of establishing and exploiting contacts and had no experience of administration or leadership when on May 31, 1932 he was appointed to succeed Brüning as head of a crisis-shaken modern industrial state. The change of government was based solely on personal whim and Papen's appointment, the then French ambassador in Berlin, André François-Poncet, wrote, 'was at first greeted with incredulous amazement; when the news was confirmed, everyone smiled. There is something about Papen that prevents either his friends or his enemies from taking him entirely seriously; he bears the stamp of frivolity, he is not a personality of the first rank. He is one of those people who are considered capable of plunging into a dangerous adventure; they pick up every gauntlet, accept every wager. If he succeeds in an undertaking he is very pleased; if he fails it doesn't bother him.'[2]

Precisely these qualities no doubt contributed to the making of a Chancellor out of a political nonentity. The power groups that had brought about Brüning's downfall and now arranged this appointment may have been less interested in Papen himself than in his political position between centre and right.[3] They evidently saw in him, with his insouciant activism, a suitable front man for the elimination of the severely damaged parliamentary system in the interests of an authoritarian class regime. Furthermore the decision of General von Schleicher, who as Hindenburg's confidant and 'Chancellor-maker' very largely controlled this affair, was undoubtedly greatly influenced by the idea that the inexperienced

Papen, with his concern for outward trappings, would find his vanity satisfied by the post itself and the representational functions connected with it, and for the rest would prove a pliable tool. This was very much to the liking of Schleicher, who combined ambition with an aversion from publicity. When astonished friends protested that Papen had no head for administration, the General replied, 'He doesn't need a head, his job is to be a hat.'[4]

If Schleicher imagined that the real head of the new government was going to be himself, he was soon disappointed. Lacking any natural respect for the traditions and problems of his high office, Papen took up his duties, and it was no mere polemical exaggeration when his opponents repeatedly accused him of carrying over into politics the outlook of a riding gentleman: he himself confirmed the parallel in his memoirs when he advocated riding as a school for political character-building on the grounds that it offered 'no concern for broken bones'.[5] Again and again he acted on his basic idea that a difficulty, like an obstacle confronting a rider, was overcome once one had easily and boldly jumped it. In any case, he broke free from his dependence upon Schleicher and began, with growing self-confidence, to pursue his own aims and the interests of those circles whose representative he was, so that the General was forced to the admission: 'What do you say to that, Fränzchen has discovered himself!'[6]

The new Chancellor owed the opportunity of evolving a policy of his own mainly to the backing of the aged Reich President, who took a fatherly pleasure in the adroitness and frivolous charm of Papen, the man of the world. The mutual attraction sprang from their respective characters and matched the close relationship between their prejudices, political tendencies and interests, in which, across the generation gap, a sterile conservatism bogged down in out-of-date ideas found expression. 'Both had in common, in spite of the great age difference, the fact that they failed to recognise that times had changed,'[7] and in particular, the fact that they ignored the social problem and any possible solutions, or evaded the problem with hollow phrases revealing patriarchal and aristocratic attitudes. Their anachronistic thinking still reflected the imperial period's false alternatives of socialist or nationalist, in which every group to the left of centre was tainted with the odium of anti-patriotism; it blindly overlooked the fact that the dominant antithesis of the age had long been between democratic and totalitarian. The aim of achieving, in an imaginary halfway house between these two, something expressed by the formula of 'a constitutional dictatorship', a new state 'between democracy and totalitarian dictatorship', was nothing but the thoughtless and confused coupling together of contradictions. It made no sense but in the course of historical evolution had the effect of preparing the way structurally and psychologically for Hitler.[8] When Walther Schotte, the ideologist of Papen's reformist idea, asserted that the new state 'must be a strong state free from sectional interests, just in itself, independent of the parties', each of these formulas was merely a lofty synonym for a demand for domination on the part of the social classes which stood behind this project. A 'strong state' meant merely an anti-liberal state; 'free from sectional interests' meant free from any right of the trade unions or any other public institutions to participate; the demand for justice was intended to legitimise the ostensibly 'naturally' determined claim of these classes to have the state at their disposal; and 'independent of the parties' really meant independent of the left. It has been rightly pointed out that it was no coincidence that many representatives of this brand of conservatism 'saw the Middle Ages as their ideal, not only because at this period men were rooted in a firmly established order and had faith, but also because political rights were at that time possessed only by the few'.[9]

From the socially reactionary emergency decrees of mid-June 1932, which gained the administration the mocking title 'the cabinet of barons', through the coup d'état against Prussia, to the openly proclaimed intention to bring society back to its class foundations and wipe out the 'so-called achievements of the Revolution',[10] every measure of Papen's administration betrayed a fixation with out-of-date ideas. Its aims and programme gained the support of only a minute fraction of the public, whose personal interests they represented; otherwise the regime remained highly unpopular. If Papen was appointed Chancellor in the hope of replacing the SPD's toleration of the government's line by toleration on the part of the NSDAP, this hope quickly proved ill-founded. Even the hazardous credit which the government extended to the Hitler party, ruthlessly fighting its way to power by the method of civil war but nevertheless a good nationalist and anti-liberal party, did not bring it the hoped-for period of toleration. Amid loud expressions of public disapproval and supported only upon the narrow foundations of the President's trust, it slipped into isolation. No other cabinet in German parliamentary history ever suffered, like this one, a defeat by 42 to 512 votes. Astonishingly enough, in spite of growing failures, the Chancellor lost all his former doubts[11] as to his fitness for government office. Only tremendous pressure by Schleicher compelled him to resign at the end of 1932, just as he was about to carry out a large-scale coup. In a touching scene, which conveyed to the departing Chancellor the certainty of his undiminished influence at the presidential court, Hindenburg handed him his photograph with the inscription 'I had a comrade.'[12]

Papen used his influence for an altogether disastrous intrigue. In spite of all assertions to the contrary, it was he who took the initiative in establishing an alliance with Hitler, who was already beginning to despair of attaining power. Any hesitations he may have had about entering into this suicidal partnership were doubtless swept aside by his natural recklessness, his arrogant assumption of his own right to lead, and an itch for revenge upon his rival Schleicher, now Chancellor in the new cabinet. At all events, the offended Papen cleared away the last personal obstacles to a partnership between the nationalist right and the NSDAP, thereby restoring the Harzburg alliance, but this time with real chances of achieving power.[13] The fragility of this alliance had already been clearly demonstrated several times, but no experience could cure Papen, Hugenberg or the German nationalist circles around them of their illusions. The curious mixture of personal vindictiveness, blindness and arrogance which had brought about this alliance shows how far the leading elements in German conservatism had come in the long process of degeneration, and it is undoubtedly more than a coincidence that its thinking led it to Hitler.

Agreement went far beyond tactics, not merely negatively in a common antagonism to democracy, liberalism and all freedom, but also positively in the vision of an authoritarian, nationalist class order with militarily orientated structures and the idea of a national community welded into a single disciplined entity. The nationalist and the National Socialist visions only gradually parted company. 'Papen spoke on the radio,' Goebbels noted in his diary in August 1932. 'A speech that sprang from beginning to end from our ideas.'[14] Long since shorn of all humanist and religious values, but also devoid of the critical consciousness of tradition, the position of the conservatives no longer had any vitality or any ideas relevant to the future. It contained nothing but the rigid demand, linked with the memory of past privileges, to entrench and wait for the hour to strike. Such conservatism could boast no intellectual or practical result that was not lost in the catastrophe it brought about. It stood immobile on all fronts; defensively it staked everything on the negation of the Revolution of 1789 with its political and social consequences, while offensively it had nothing to show but the concept of the nationalist authoritarian state; and whatever it presented as conservative ideology, the overwhelmingly predominant ideas were nothing but variations on these two uninspired motifs.

This was the point at which the national conservative and the National Socialist ideologies met. It was not so much the voters' lack of discrimination, as Papen later reproachfully claimed, as the largely identical points of departure which led the greater part of the population to vote for Hitler instead of for the 'conservative programme'.[15] Strictly speaking, all attempts to differentiate the conservative ideology and programme from the National Socialist failed, and the verbiage expended in the effort reveals precisely what it seeks to conceal. 'If I were not a German Nationalist, I should like to be a Nazi,' Oldenburg-Januschau declared at a public meeting.[16] A remark of this kind tells us more than the most extensive analysis could about the degeneration of the conservative spirit in Germany. Fundamentally, he and his kind admired the consistency and ruthlessness of the National Socialists, and only the more helpless and stilted manner in which the German Nationalist movement expressed its aims distinguished it from the other camp. Whereas Hitler was able to set masses in motion, the turgid conservative proclamations, together with the recurrent assumption of arrogant superiority, prevented their having any effect whatever. In January 1933 as in Harzburg, a crucial attraction of the alliance with Hitler was the hope that the 'officers without an army' in the ranks of the NSDAP might at last come to lead those masses that had refused their allegiance to the conservative cause as such.[17] The hate-filled demagogy, naked barbarism and evil impulses that filtered up to the top were indulgently ascribed by these gentlemen to what they called the basically good-natured young and to the movement's excessive revolutionary impetus, which they confidently expected to tame. With such a wide range of agreement on practical points, they believed the points of disagreement were mainly about differences of method, and the forms in which the claim to social exclusivity was made.

That even here the divisions crumbled away is shown by the reaction to the Potempa murder case. In this Upper Silesian town, in summer 1932, five SA men dragged a Communist worker out of bed after a drinking bout and literally trampled him to death in front of his horrified mother. When the murderers were condemned to death, it was not only Hitler and the other National Socialist leaders who declared their solidarity with them, but also various conservative groups, including the Stahlhelm and the Königin Luise Bund, who petitioned for clemency to the Reich President,[18] while Papen, as Chancellor, hastened to put the pardon into effect. Hermann Rauschning wrote, vividly summing up the conservative Nationalist–National Socialist convergence:

In judging violence there is no contradiction between reaction and revolution. Hence the German Nationalist viewpoint was in essence merely a politically more moderate but fundamentally equally as nihilistic a doctrine of force as that of the National Socialists. This is the basic reason for the combination of bourgeois nationalism, of reactionary pseudo-conservative forces with revolutionary dynamism, and it is the essential reason for the later capitulation of those bourgeois forces before National Socialism, because the more consistent expression of any viewpoint always triumphs over the more irresolute. There had for a long time been no conservatism left in Germany, but only a bourgeois form of the doctrine of force coexisting with the consistent revolutionary form.[19]

It was in fact widely believed in the conservative camp that they all, including the Hitler party, belonged to a great common movement with great common aims. Edgar Jung, one of the spokesmen of conservatism and a close colleague of Papen, stated in 1933, in complete agreement with this view, that the 'German revolution' had conservative roots alongside its National Socialist roots.[20] No doubt this comment had the tactical aim of stating the conservatives' own claim to a part in the fashioning of the new state; but it confirms the thesis advanced here, and is moreover an expression of the illusory conviction of their own value that finally led the conservatives around Papen, Hindenburg and Hugenberg to the fatal government reconstruction of January 30, 1933. Despite all warnings, Papen, Vice-Chancellor in the new cabinet, arrogantly declared, 'What are you worried about? I have Hindenburg's confidence. In two months we shall have Hitler squeezed into a corner so that he squeaks.'[21]

Even if both sides entered the alliance of 'national coalition' with treacherous intentions, it soon emerged that only one side was resourceful, skilful and unscrupulous enough to turn this 'system of perfidy'[22] to its own advantage. In spite of the composition of the cabinet – eight German Nationalists to only three National Socialists – the former were unable to resist Hitler's power lust, pursued by himself and his followers with every means at their disposal. Many conservative interests were simply seized and swept away by adroit manipulation of the current of national rebirth. All the nervous efforts of Papen and his aides to assert their own image beside that of the National Socialist mass movement were simply not taken seriously by the public, in fact were totally disregarded, so that support for the new state was expressed almost exclusively as support for the dominant personality of Hitler. Another weakness of the German Nationalist members of the cabinet was that they were unable to present a united front to the National Socialists, who themselves acted in close and systematic concert. Hence in Hitler's lightning conquest of power every step led to success, while the other side lapsed first into paralysis and then into disintegration. Hindenburg was led by the nose, Papen tricked, the *Länder* forced to toe the line, while the Reichswehr leadership swung over into Hitler's camp and so was no longer available as a bastion for a conservative counter-attack. Papen and his friends owed it solely to a magnanimous leadership confident of victory that for a little while longer they were allowed to believe they had achieved their hopes; for the more Hitler secured for himself the true positions of power, the more he left the symbols of power to the others together with the illusion that their cause was advancing. As late as April 1933 Hugenberg called himself and the German Nationalist groups guarantors for the order and legality of the 'German resurrection', dismissing National Socialist excesses with the comment that you couldn't make omelettes without breaking eggs.[23] The summit of conservative blindness and error was reached on March 21, 1933, the day of the carefully staged ceremonial opening of the first Reichstag of the Third Reich, which brought together partners in a supposedly common cause at the tomb of Frederick the Great at Potsdam in a welter of national emotion; the deceived and the triumphant deceivers, Hindenburg and Hitler, Papen and Göring, Hugenberg and Goebbels. Immediately afterwards 'the veil of illusion was torn, affording a full view of the reality of the National Socialist autocracy'.[24]

With the State Act of Potsdam, which National Socialist propaganda celebrated as the 'hour of birth of the Third Reich',[25] together with the Enabling Law passed two days later, the conservative partners in the cabinet had largely fulfilled their function in the National Socialists' scheme for seizing power: namely, to cover up the break that marked the transition from the constitutional to the illegal state and at the same time to foster in the still hesitant, vacillating mass of the people the misconception of the common cause of all Germans under the 'Chancellor of Unity', Adolf Hitler. There is no doubt that up to the collapse of their deluded hopes, and in some cases even beyond it, the conservatives performed their part perfectly. Papen's assurance that in the electoral campaign prior to March 5, 1933 he had sufficiently proclaimed the distance between Hitler and his own camp by his reference to the coalition character of the government was useless, and it is contradicted by the observation of his close ally Edgar Jung that on this day 'real government elections were carried out in Germany for the first time'.[26] He also hoped that by stressing their common interests he would benefit from that wave of new confidence which was so patently carrying Hitler aloft. There were in fact very few members of the nationalist-minded bourgeoisie who were not led astray by the slogans of unity and the intoxication produced by the apparent realisation of the 'community of the nation'; but the demonstrative fraternisation between the spokesmen of conservatism and the National Socialists confronted many of them with a genuine dilemma and finally, as a national 'duty', they accepted trends which they regarded with aversion. Among the documents of the Nuremberg trials is the diary of a senior Bavarian judge from the years 1933–34, who was clearly fully aware of the terrorist, anti-legal and anti-cultural character of National Socialism and yet joined the party and even the SA in order to place his energies at the service, not of the NSDAP, but of the 'movement for national rebirth'.[27]

In the same way holders of public or semi-public office were not infrequently willing actively to collaborate with the new order with a view to damping down the National Socialist Party's extremism and moves towards exclusive rule. In so far as they exercised any moderating influence at all, this was entirely in line with the aims of Hitler, who in the stage of transition to full power was particularly dependent upon the specialist knowledge and tutelage of the bureaucratic, technical and economic élite in order to maintain the fiction of the regime's legality.

It bears all the marks of brazen impudence when Papen denies all understanding of this problem, which he himself largely caused, and when he of all people, who did more than anyone else outside the Nazi Party to help Hitler to power, reproaches the German people with 'lack of intelligence' and 'intellectual laziness' because they did not show greater reserve towards Hitler and National Socialism.[28] He himself was for a long time content, on his own admission, to pin his hopes on the 'work of education in the cabinet'. Notwithstanding all the acts of resistance which he subsequently claimed, he announced his own reservations at a rather late stage, when Hitler had long since seized power and scornfully shouted after the partners he had brusquely dismissed that they were bourgeois 'who choose a dictator for themselves, but on the tacit conditions that in reality he will never dictate'.[29] Papen's famous Marburg speech of June 17, 1934, written by Edgar Jung, which occupies so much space in Papen's apologia, was not so much the outcry of a sense of justice outraged by the aims and methods of the National Socialist conquest of power as the outcry of an infuriated accomplice finally brought to realise that he had no chance of putting his own plans into effect and that if he had been given any role at all it was purely as a decorative element in a state which, after a fourteen-year interregnum, he considered as belonging once more to himself and his class and which he had intended to govern. It was not least this claim behind Papen's words that caused Hitler's harsh reaction to the speech and gave the bloodbath of June 30, 1934, a fortnight later, its double intention. We should still be blinded by National Socialist pronouncements if we looked upon the events of that day as solely a showdown between Hitler and Röhm, between party and SA. Far beyond this, the blow was simultaneously aimed at the last remaining claims to power of the conservative and bourgeois interests. Papen himself was kept under house arrest for a time, while two of his closest colleagues, one of them Edgar Jung, were murdered, so that the Vice-Chancellor 'stood like a melancholy king skittle among blood and corpses'.[30] It is true that like a man of honour he thereupon offered his resignation, but he did not follow the path to resistance which a considerable group from the conservative camp took after this moment of disillusionment. On the contrary, a few weeks later he again offered his services to Hitler, the murderer of his friends, and one wonders whether this decision was the easier because Hitler was at the same time the murderer of his bitterest enemy, General von Schleicher.

Ambition and an insatiable self-importance, however, undoubtedly played a greater part in Papen's decision. He found it intolerable, one of his conservative cabinet colleagues later wrote, 'not to be in the game, even if he did not like his fellow players'.[31] Ostensibly after a severe inner struggle, he went to Vienna as an envoy on a special mission – to prepare the way for the Anschluss; but we have only to read what thoughts filled his mind when he was called by Hitler to know how willingly he allowed himself to be defeated in this struggle with himself.[32] Again in 1938, when for the second time one of his closest colleagues was murdered at his side, he remained willing to serve Hitler and shortly afterwards assumed the post of ambassador in the Turkish capital, as ever incorrigibly convinced that in so doing he was serving not the illegal National Socialist regime but the German Fatherland. 'The man of true spirit,' Papen declared in his Marburg speech, 'is so full of vitality that he sacrifices himself for his convictions.'[33] But neither he himself nor German conservatism as a whole displayed the vitality that would have led them to sacrifice themselves, or even their opportunism and self-importance, for the convictions which they later claimed to have; the few exceptions do not disprove this. Instead they all fell back upon the idea of service to the Fatherland, blindly accepting as 'service to the Fatherland' service to a murderous regime that flouted the law and broke its word.

Papen's personal experience and his unusually great opportunities for true insight into events make it clear that in his case, at least, the arguments which he produced were simply self-justification. Even if we accept that the realisation he voiced at Nuremberg that Hitler was 'the greatest murderer of all time' had not come to him earlier, it involves the admission of a serious and long-standing error. In fact, Papen retained to the last his self-righteous attitude and criticised lack of intelligence, discrimination and insight on the part of others only – the German people, the Allies, and even, in a particularly shocking manner, the murdered Edgar Jung.[34] Moral insensitivity, a fundamental lack of intellectual honesty, and that class-conscious mode of thinking which dealt with the truth like a master with his servants, always made such inconsistency easy for him. Justice Robert H. Jackson, in his speech for the prosecution against Schacht, vividly summed up the contradiction in the behaviour of the conservative collaborators. 'When we ask him,' said Jackson, 'why he did not halt the criminal course of this government in which he was a minister, he says he had absolutely no influence. But when we ask him why he remained a member of a criminal government, he tells us that he hoped to moderate the programme by remaining there.'[35] In fact this contradiction, to which, in various shapes, all later attempts at self-justification by the regime's conservative collaborators ultimately lead, cannot be resolved. It indicates at the same time the homogeneous nature of the motives which, beyond all purely personal interests, caused the majority of conservatives to cling to the alliance with Hitler regardless of humiliations: the will at any price to regain the leadership of the nation, or at any rate certain leading positions. Behind this lay the feeling of being naturally called upon to govern, which had never left them, and the trauma suffered by the loss of the state in 1918, both permeated by the outwardly denied but inescapable realisation of their own weakness, which made their urge to participate as undignified as it was tenacious. 'Have you noticed how people tremble, how they try to say what will please me?' Hitler asked contemptuously in 1934, looking at Papen and the German Nationalist group.[36]

Thus the collaboration with National Socialism revealed how incompetent and utterly burnt out conservative nationalism was. No other social group failed so abysmally in face of the challenge. The case does not need to be reinforced by reference to the personal and financial support which Hitler received, in particular during the years of his rise to power, from landowners, leaders of heavy industry and other interested parties. Some predominantly Marxist interpretations[37] unwarrantably shift the emphasis and make Hitler appear a mere front man for alien forces in the background, whereas in reality it was precisely the specific failure of German nationalist conservatism to have allowed itself, for the sake of shortsighted aims, to be misused for the purposes of others. Edgar Jung declared in 1933: 'Revolutionary conservatism is sacrificing temporal values in order to save eternal values.'[38] The truth is that this type of conservatism had long abandoned 'eternal values' and, in its desperate and vulgar hunger for power, threw away temporal values too when it fraternised with Hitler. The lack of any feeling of personal guilt, continually evident in the memoirs of the conservative partners in the regime, may be subjectively entirely honest; it merely shows the extent to which consciousness of the existence of obligatory values had atrophied, for the degree of sense of guilt is always dependent upon the degree of consciousness of value, and only where binding norms are no longer recognised is their betrayal no longer felt. 'Dear lady, we have fallen into the hands of criminals, how could I have suspected that?' wrote Schacht in summer 1938.[39] Actually, anyone capable of sober, uncorrupted thought would not merely have suspected this but known it without a shadow of doubt long before 1938. It was above all the loss of integrity, the intellectual corruptibility and the capacity to close its eyes that led conservatism first into Hitler's company and then inevitably into alliance with him. When a documentary film on the concentration camps and mass extermination centres of the Third Reich was shown in the Nuremberg courtroom, Papen covered his face with his hands. It was more than a spontaneous gesture of horror: it symbolised an attitude. 'I did not want to see Germany's shame,' he declared later.[40] He had never wanted to see it, though he had helped to bring it about.

Any analysis of the role of Papen and the conservatism he represented must lead to indictment for his share in the rise of National Socialism, his work in

161

preparing the way. Unembarrassed by his disastrous activities, by his speeches on the 'National Revolution' which mark him as a driving force in the coalescence of the nationalist right, by the 'high degree of responsibility for the alliance',[41] which he joyfully assumed at the time, Papen vigorously denied this historical guilt and even at Nuremberg provocatively described himself as the spokesman 'of the other Germany'.[42] Meanwhile the degree of his responsibility has been clearly demonstrated, and his transparent attempts to diminish his own part in the formation of the government of January 30, 1933 do not exculpate him, for they miss the essential point of the accusation against him, that he was the 'stirrup-holder' of the new regime. It is not on his mere attachment to Hitler, mainly from base personal motives, that the indictment of Papen rests, but rather on his preparation of public opinion for the ideals which conservatism shared with National Socialism, upon which he embarked before 1933, and his stirring up of anti-republican feeling and systematic undermining of the constitutional structure of the Weimar state.

'History is waiting for us,' Papen cried at the end of his Marburg speech, 'but only if we prove ourselves worthy of her.'[43] With all circumstances taken into account, even bearing in mind the resistance offered by isolated groups of bourgeois conservatives when they belatedly realised the truth, German conservatism as a whole cannot be said to have stood the historical test. For the decision to resist did not spring from a newly acquired consciousness of the binding force of a once-valid conservative idea, which had long since been devalued in opportunist manoeuvres, bargains with power and parasitic class egotism; it was a case of individual decisions the impulses to which lay 'outside ideology', so that conservatism did not even master the one task Hitler had left to it: 'to die gracefully'.[44] Ultimately it was probably the sense of its own dessication and anaemia, together with a desperate desire for power and 'historical authority', that set German Nationalist conservatism on its downward path. It hoped, by joining with the secretly despised but at the same time admired upstart Hitler, to share in the force and vitality of the National Socialist mass movement, and with its support to regain a status of which history, not without reason, had already deprived it. 'I desire a great and strong Germany and to achieve it I would enter into an alliance with the Devil,' Hjalmar Schacht once declared.[45] But rarely in history has the old proverb proved so true, that he who sups with the Devil needs a long spoon.

As Thomas Mann remarked, however, the Devil is already present 'where intellectual arrogance is wedded to an antiquated and restricted frame of mind'.[46] This raises the question which side of the table the Devil was actually sitting in this alliance. But this is one of those questions that only grow more complicated, and finally insoluble, the longer one thinks about them.

Alfred Rosenberg – The Forgotten Disciple

National Socialism stands or falls by its *Weltanschauung*.
Alfred Rosenberg

The ideas behind our programme do not oblige us to act like fools.
Adolf Hitler

It was Alfred Rosenberg's tragedy that he really believed in National Socialism. The pedantic certainty with which he saw himself as the scribe of a new gospel of salvation made him something of an oddity among the top leadership of the NSDAP, an object of covert smiles – the 'philosopher' of a movement whose philosophy almost always boiled down to power. Rosenberg himself never realised and certainly never admitted this, and so in the course of the years, as the idea of power itself visibly outweighed its ideological drapings, he came to be the forgotten disciple: scarcely taken seriously any longer, insolently overlooked and pushed around, a prop from the party's recruiting phase when ideology determined action. For a long time he failed to realise that the philosophy he so fervently advocated carried no weight, at least at the centres of power. With heavy consistency he treated the fool's paradise of his faith to the last as the political, social and religious answer to the problems of the time and saw in National Socialism, as he wrote in his 'confession' in the Nuremberg cell, 'the noblest idea to which a German could devote the strength he has been given'.[1]

The relation of National Socialism as a whole to its own ideology is difficult to unravel. It was not a programme exclusively determined by tactical considerations and aiming at success and power, which set itself up as an absolute and used ideological props whenever they served its purpose – as the formula has it, 'the revolution of nihilism'.[2] On the other hand it cannot be interpreted as part of the history of ideas, isolated from its dependence upon the technique of gaining power. It was at one and the same time the practice of domination and a doctrine, inextricably interwoven together, and even, in the shameless admissions that have come down to us, a drive for power divorced from any other purpose. Hitler and his close associates always reveal themselves as at bottom the prisoners of their own prejudices. Just as National Socialism never absorbed any ideological motives without first inquiring into their value as aids to power, so its crucial manifestations of power are not to be understood without reference to an ideological motive, however fleeting and impalpable.

163

The leading National Socialists, in so far as they observed or even directed this interplay of ideology and power-seeking, always avoided committing themselves on the subject, emphasising, like Goebbels for example, that in its totality National Socialism was indefinable, since it was 'subject to continual changes and transformations'.[3] Undoubtedly at its roots were certain views to which it remained indissolubly wedded, but with the exception of the idea of struggle and the maxims of the Führer, there was scarcely any article in its creed that it would not have willingly abandoned or set aside at least temporarily for the sake of gaining or holding power. This tactical opportunism was reflected in the arbitrary way the rising movement took over the most diverse ideological elements, and its lack of loyalty towards ideas matched the calculating spirit in which they had been picked up. It had absorbed racial, anti-Semitic, biological and pan-German concepts along with others of an emotional pro-peasant, anti-civilization, militaristic and pseudo-religious nature. Among them flitted the shades of the German Romantics, Wagner, Nietzsche and Paul de Lagardes; the mood of the time was reflected in nationalist, monarchist, federalist and socialist ideas. Down to eccentric reformers like the new pagans and believers in the Garden of Eden, there was scarcely a trend of those years that did not, at least for a time, make its contribution to the conglomerate of National Socialist ideology. 'We have picked our ideas from all the bushes along our life's path,' Hitler once declared, 'and we no longer know where they came from.'[4]

Not only the heterogeneous character of this philosophy, but also the varying weights of the individual elements and their greater or lesser importance to the fight for power, make it difficult to determine the relationship of National Socialism to its own ideology. Just as National Socialism's lack of unity and its inner inconsistency compel us to mark off the limits of its ideological value in the power struggle case by case, so we can do no more than outline the attitude of individual leaders towards individual ideological postulates. Göring's ideological indifference, for example, was strikingly distinct from Rosenberg's cranky adherence to the ideological letter, and Himmler's sentimentally exaggerated relation to ideology was in the greatest possible contrast to that of his subordinate Heydrich. Hans Frank stated: 'The formula: National Socialism is exclusively what So-and-So says or does, by which the representative who happened to be speaking meant himself, gradually replaced the assumptions of the party programme. Fundamentally there were as many "National Socialisms" as there were leaders.'[5] Consequently the idea of power and purpose inevitably moved into the foreground, but underpinned by changing personal obsessions and resentments that were restricted only by unconditional obedience to the Führer. This situation largely explains why the type of the strict believer was relatively rare in the top leadership. Those whose convictions were not moulded by a resolute will to success and capable of being activated in the direction of the aims set by Hitler were soon isolated. Put in a different way, National Socialism had room for every cynical contempt for ideology that was coupled with a will to power, but not for the ideological will that was coupled with contempt for power.

Hitler expressed this situation in the words: 'National Socialism is a movement of the people, but in no circumstances a cult movement.'[6]

The fate of those of his followers who set faith above power emphatically confirmed this. If Alfred Rosenberg was the paradox of a leading National Socialist who felt obliged to maintain allegiance to his ideological premises with the utmost stubborn consistency, he is also the clearest demonstration of the ludicrous position of all serious-minded people within the movement. A note in his diary on May 7, 1940, evidently so important to him that he repeated it later elsewhere, makes his orthodox convictions unmistakably clear and at the same time furnishes a key to his nature. The note repeats what he once told Walther Darré, who was trying to persuade him to take part in a struggle for power within the party. 'I told him,' writes Rosenberg, 'I would adopt a standpoint, irrespective of whether someone was for or against it, if I felt deeply that it was right for the movement. I would do that even if in the end I remained *alone*.'[7] In fact, it was not merely 'in the end'. Again and again humiliated and passed over, he sought compensation in casting the contemptuous glance of the true believer on apostate former fellow-fighters who, hungry for power and booty, formed themselves into continually changing packs. His helpless foolishness rewarded with insultingly uninfluential positions, he was a prophet without honour in his own country and with even less outside it. Goebbels ironically called him 'Almost Rosenberg', because 'Rosenberg almost managed to become a scholar, a journalist, a politician, but only almost'.[8] This phrase expressed the contempt of the adroit technician of power for a man whose cumbersome convictions forever stood in his own way. As he lost more and more power, Rosenberg shut himself up in his intellectual arrogance and stuck with increasing obstinacy to that overriding 'philosophy' to which he devoted his narrowminded loyalty until the end – 'the noblest idea'. While, entrusted with tasks of ideological supervision, he guarded the heaven of racial bliss, other, tougher characters set about erecting those hells which Rosenberg later incredulously regarded as a falsification of the pure doctrine. If, as Wilhelm Raabe put it in a phrase which Rosenberg quotes in his last notes, the German spirit draws a third of its strength from philistinism, the German anti-spirit does so no less.

Originating from a petty bourgeois background in Reval (Estonia), Rosenberg was one of the numerous expatriate Germans whose Germanity complex gave the rising NSDAP much of its character.[9] 'The opponents of the National Socialist movement,' we read in Richter's contemporary work on racial characteristics, 'insist on seeing a foreigner in Rosenberg, because of his Baltic origins; but anyone who looks at his skull with a trained eye will immediately recognise him as a Germanic man who can with every right claim his place in the ranks of Adolf Hitler. The clearly defined long skull tells us that we are dealing with a man of pure emotion and sensibility. But there is a certain pain in the overall expression of the eyes.'[10] This character study, which unconsciously verges on irony, tends to reveal what it seeks to conceal; for in fact among the robust, tough followers of the period of the party's struggle, a type better represented by figures like

Streicher, Dietrich Eckart or Röhm, Rosenberg was regarded from the outset as an outsider. He was made a 'foreigner', not by the movement's opponents, but by his own introverted temperament and by his fellow-fighters. A man in whose hands everything became difficult and complicated, he never found the uncomplicated practicality of Hitler's 'South German' followers, who were precisely the ones who set the movement's tone, and on occasion he remarked himself that he had hardly any friends in the party.[11] His one-sidedly ideological tendencies, which ran counter to the nature of the party old guard with their emphasis on activist self-assertion, increased the distance still further. He was 'the buffoon, the stuck-up crackpot ninny', the 'bohemian', as Max Amann said of his editor-in-chief on the *Völkischer Beobachter*,[12] when Rosenberg was accused of arrogance on account of what was no doubt really inhibition and intellectual prejudice.

In conversation [a former National Socialist has reported] one had the impression that he was not listening properly at all. Every now and then he would purse his lips when critical remarks were made or attempt a supercilious smile, which naturally gained him the reputation of arrogant unamiability. Undoubtedly this was doing him an injustice, as was the accusation that he wished to be a dictator of opinion. He was merely so cramped within his acquired ideas and egocentric dreams of the Baltic noble, the English lord, the scientific genius of Copernican stamp, that he had entirely lost his in any case underdeveloped capacity for making contact and entering into conversation with other people.[13]

Fundamentally, therefore, it is hard to say what combination of circumstances led the heavy-blooded, pedantic architectural student and art master to see his vocation in politics at all, let alone in the NSDAP; and even his written statement at Nuremberg does little to clarify this disputed phase of his development. Manifestly it was originally neither the typical resentments of the 'German Balt', nor the desire to further a political vision of the future, but rather the result of chance; for on whatever else his account of his life may keep silent, it at least reveals a weakness in his character that allowed him to be led or driven almost exclusively by arbitrary external pressures. Even for his move to Germany in 1918 he could produce no more impressive explanation than his own irresolution: 'Life drew me and I followed it.'[14]

Rosenberg followed life to Munich, where to begin with he lived laboriously by taking odd jobs. He quickly found his way into Russian émigré circles and made contact with the Thule Society, a nationalist secret society with an occult tinge that practised a sectarian Aryan and Germanic cult – chiefly against a background of sinister horror stories and shabby 'revelations' about Jews, Freemasons and Bolsheviks – before becoming for a time the centre of counter-revolutionary activities in Bavaria. Both encounters left an indelible impression in the soft wax of Alfred Rosenberg's personality. Soon after his meeting with Hitler, arranged by Dietrich Eckart, and his entry into the party, he fostered émigré discontent through the Lebensraum idea, the basic foreign policy concept of the Hitler movement, while the impressions received in the Thule Society marked the direction and style of his secondary philosophical undertaking. The very titles of his first publications make this clear enough: 'The Tracks of the Jew Through the Ages' and 'Immorality in the Talmud' (1920), 'The Crime of Freemasonry' (1921), 'The Morass, or Plague in Russia' (1922). He was also one of the main disseminators of the famous forgery 'The Protocols of the Elders of Zion and Jewish World Politics' (1923), which with all his naïve-courageous readiness for self-committal he had republished in 1940.[15] In this and all his subsequent writings he revealed himself as a man of profound half-culture, acquainted with countless apocryphal sources and theories and all the cranky tract literature of pathological nationalist fanaticism, a reader who assimilated his mass of reading rapidly, uncritically, and inaccurately, so that the result was always in line with his preconceived opinions. His growing literary output, which brought him the over-valued status of 'chief ideologist' of the NSDAP, culminated in 'The Myth of the Twentieth Century' in 1930 – according to a contemporary bibliography 'the most important book of National Socialism next to Adolf Hitler's *Mein Kampf*'.[16] It attempted to combine the mutually contradictory historical and emotional elements to which the movement owed its success into a systematic National Socialist philosophy. After the grandiose opening, 'Today world history must be written afresh', it interprets history in terms of race conflict, inspired by Houston Stewart Chamberlain, Gobineau and their followers, but also by a misconstrued Nietzsche:

A new interrelated, colourful picture of human and terrestrial history is beginning to reveal itself today if we reverently recognise that the conflict between blood and environment, between blood and blood, represents the ultimate phenomenon accessible to us, *behind* which it is not vouchsafed us to seek and investigate. But this realisation immediately brings with it recognition of the fact that the struggles of blood and the dimly felt mysticism of living events do not represent two different things but one and the same thing in two different ways. Racial history is therefore natural history and the mysticism of the soul at one and the same time; but the history of the religion of the blood, conversely, is the great world story of the rise and downfall of peoples, their heroes and thinkers, their inventors and artists.[17]

The whole work, in its vehemence and attempted profundity, was based on emotional arguments like these, safeguarded against any objective, logical refutation. Consistently with this, Rosenberg evolved his theory that cultural and state-creating genius was peculiar to Nordic man, not by demonstrating the presence of Nordic blood in the peoples distinguished by such achievements, but by the opposite method, which is difficult to contest; wherever he saw an important culture-creating force at work, as in Greek antiquity, he took this as proof of his incontrovertible initial thesis. In his basic pessimism he saw Germanness, the priceless sediment in the bowl of Nordic blood, and thereby the whole world, as threatened by downfall and destruction. As a symptom of disintegration he lamented the 'psychic bastardisation of our people' and linked with it the 'loss of natural good sense' as well as of 'will-determined Nordic aesthetics'.[18] In a cosmic system of evaluation and devaluation he proclaimed the dissolution of the Christian-Syrian-liberal world idea and contrasted it with the new values which naturally required for their full development the acquisition of new *Lebensraum*. Action and struggle took the place of compassion and humanity, the 'beautiful' was contrasted with the 'good', 'love' was displaced by the masculine Germanic concept of 'honour', and all this in turn was placed under the heading of a blood-determined interpretation of existence:

Today a *new* faith is stirring: the myth of blood, the faith that along with blood we are defending the divine nature of man as a whole. The belief, incarnate with the most lucid knowledge, that Nordic blood represents that mystery which has replaced and overcome the old sacraments.[19]

It was basically from its assault upon Christianity and all that it stands for that 'The Myth of the Twentieth Century' gained its reputation. In a 'catechism' of the National Socialist ideology which summarised the views expressed in the book, Rosenberg did emphasise that Christianity was 'ennobled solely by the fact that Germans have believed in it'; but this in no way diminished the resolute harshness of his declaration of war on Christianity. He wrote:

From education by the Church to education by Germanic values is a step of several generations. *We* are the transition from one education to the other. We are the conquerors of one era and the founders of a new – also religious – epoch. We bear a heavy and therefore a great destiny. To destroy images is something every revolution has been able to do. But to establish its cause upon nothing and yet not to burn all bridges behind it: that is the nobility of character of the National Socialist era.

The German people is not marked by original sin, but by original nobility. The place of Christian love has been taken by the National Socialist, Germanic idea of comradeship . . . which has already been symbolically expressed through the replacement of the rosary by the spade of labour.[20]

The wearisome, declamatory mysticism that characterises 'The Myth of the Twentieth Century', as it does everything the author published, evidently rather repelled his fellow-leaders; it certainly did not strengthen Rosenberg's position. Hitler found the book 'derivative, pastiche, illogical rubbish! Bad Chamberlain with a few additions!' At the same time he assured the author that it was 'a very intelligent book'.[21] During the war he admitted, moreover, that he 'had read only very little of it', because it was 'written in too unintelligible a style', and attributed its great popularity solely to its attacks on the Catholic Church.[22] And while Goebbels dismissed it half in amusement, half angrily, as an 'ideological belch', the accused at the Nuremberg Trial later stated without exception that they had never read the book.[23] Among the public too it found few readers, though thanks to a sales campaign using every trick of the trade it had run to 1,100,000 copies by 1944. Rosenberg's proud entry in his diary for January 19, 1940 that 'gradually hundreds of thousands have been inwardly revolutionised by my book'[24] was no doubt an expression of his need to compensate for an unsuccessful political career by convincing himself of his philosophical success.

For by this time it had long been evident that Rosenberg had little or no political influence and no voice in the real decisions. His original ambition, which was not merely ideological but at least equally directed towards foreign policy, had brought him during the so-called time of struggle into the top leadership as Hitler's adviser on foreign affairs and chairman of the NSDAP's committee on foreign policy. After the unsuccessful putsch of November 1923, Hitler actually put him in charge of the movement, but only, as Rosenberg rightly surmised, to hasten its disintegration and thus ensure a favourable starting-point for his own recapture of the leadership.[25] With the beginning of the seizure of power Rosenberg found himself being pushed aside; it did not need the painfully unsuccessful trip to England, which was intended to demonstrate his claim to leadership in foreign affairs, to undermine the position which he had laboriously built up for himself. His rigidity of principle, which saw the movement's ideological heritage as being in constant danger, made him an inflexible opponent of all tactical compromise, such as Hitler's compromise with the Church in spring 1933. No doubt he was also disqualified by his positively neurotic ideological suspiciousness, which scented the conspiratorial activity of Jews, Marxists, Freemasons or Jesuits behind every movement of opposition. Thus at the beginning of the 1930s he was 'seriously of the opinion that the Chancellor [Brüning], as the emissary of the Vatican, had only one task: by his policy of emergency regulations and the consequent inevitable impoverishment of ever-widening circles of the population to deliver up Protestant North Germany to Communism, in order by the purgatory of this affliction to leave it ripe for a second counter-revolution with the restoration of the Catholic princely houses'.[26] The world of his ideas was dominated by a pandemonium of dark powers, which he saw as being in full assault on the 'world of light'. Behind all obscure movements in the present, whether economic, financial or merely organisational, he surmised the spectral operations of demons, the activities of priests, or the cabalistic work of the Devil. When he asked who were the men secretly behind a newspaper and was told 'No one', he declared with utter conviction, 'There is always someone in the background.'[27] Rarely has there been a clearer example than Rosenberg of modern man's tendency, brilliantly exploited by Hitler himself, to blame anonymous powers for his helplessness and his fear of life; and the obstinacy with which Rosenberg sought to mobilise ancient bloodlust against these imagined powers merely reveals his essential ineffectiveness of character.

Rosenberg was soon outdone by his more adroit rivals in the struggles for power at the top of the movement, and forced into the thankless role of the man who has continually to point to merits and rights recognised earlier, and this was due not only to their greater ruthlessness but also to his own narrow-mindedness. He pursued Goebbels, Ribbentrop and Ley with deep and earnest hatred after they had forced their way into departments for which, as the ideological high priest, he considered himself alone competent. He was a jealous, intolerable grumbler who could play the part of a particularly fanatic racist or, if circumstances demanded, of a mouthpiece for Jewish interests.[28] He set his heart on taking over the foreign ministry in any cabinet formed by Hitler. Consequently he never got over the fact that he was passed over in 1933 and, apart from functions connected with ideology and political education, was entrusted solely with the Foreign Department of the NSDAP. In spite of all the activities upon which he immediately embarked, in spite of all his quarrels with the German Foreign Office over the scope of his authority, his department had little to do but look after foreign visitors, and Göring stated in Nuremberg that it 'was never once listened to in matters concerning foreign policy'.[29] His ambition therefore turned vigorously in compensation to the aesthetic programme outlined in 'The Myth of the Twentieth Century'. In 1929, well before the party came to power, he had set up the Kampfbund für Deutsche Kultur (Fighting League for German Culture) with a view to the establishment of racially orientated criteria of beauty, from which his offensive against the 'bastardised mestizoism' of so-called degenerate art could now be carried on without restraint and with all the resources of the state behind it. From now on the assumptions and stylistic principles of 'the art of the national community' were dictated by a narrow-minded zeal in whose petty bourgeois nationalist scale of values Dürer's 'Hare', or, as the then director of the Folkwang Museum declared, the 'Steel Helmet', appeared as the unsurpassable expression of 'inspired' or great German art.[30] Entirely in keeping with this, one of the new cultural officials celebrated 'the thunder of cannon at Sédan and Mozart's *Eine Kleine Nachtmusik*' as 'expressions of the same cultural capacity of the Germans', while Professor Ewald Geissler declared that only art that was easy to remember could prove its 'Germanness'.[31] The call for the 'great destruction of the images throughout the German land', which had been heard for years,[32] now reached its height in the demand that 'all productions showing cosmopolitan and Bolshevist symptoms shall be removed from German museums and collections' and burnt; 'the names of all those artists who have been swept along by the flood of Marxism and Bolshevism must never be mentioned again in public'; for here 'we must proceed according to Old Testament morality: an eye for an eye and a tooth for a tooth'.[33] And while the Reich Centre for the Advancement of German Literature, presided over by Rosenberg, operating later with 1,400 editors, imposed the dictatorship of the taste of the man in the street on literature as well, the new folk aesthetic was popularised by the National Socialist Cultural Community, also under Rosenberg's direction, in pronouncements of pathetic narrow-mindedness and banality.[34]

Rosenberg's boast that he possessed 'sovereignty over the judgment of all intellectual institutions'[35] did not allow him to forget what he had lost in the process. The personal documents he left behind are dominated by the marks of a deeply humiliated sense of his own worth: by bitterness, envy, persecution mania and an almost unparalleled vanity. Thus he confides in his diary that on the occasion of his visit to Brunswick the whole town 'was in joyful mood as never before'; declares 'the whole youth of the movement swears by me', or notes 'with inner satisfaction that my struggle for the soul and outlook of the party has already fundamentally triumphed'. Elsewhere he congratulates himself that his 'Myth' is the 'success of the century' and sees all the forces of the Catholic Church mobilised against it by Rome: 'The evil Cardinal Faulhaber spoke in Munich and among other things venomously attacked my book; since they do not *yet* dare to kick the Führer, they are trying to run down his most dangerous colleague. The man will not go unanswered.'[36] He avidly wrote down every casual compliment paid him by Hitler. In his notes written in Nuremberg he still happily recalled the mysterious accord the two of them had attained at certain times,[37] and through which he felt raised up from the horde of fellow-suitors for the Führer's favour. It may have been some satisfaction to him to observe that his bitterest rival, Goebbels, missed the opportunity of the last word in their long-drawn-out quarrel. He stated in retrospect, with pedantic finality:

Hitler naturally knew that I had a deeper understanding of art and culture than Goebbels, indeed, that the latter was scarcely able to see below the surface. Nevertheless he left to that man the direction of this sphere of German life which he loved so passionately. Because as I later had only too often to tell myself, the latter was able to surround the Führer with an environment such as I would never have created. He fed the theatrical element in the Führer.[38]

But immediately back comes the feeling of having been slighted.

In the evenings the Führer often used to invite this man or that for a long fireside discussion. Apart from the usual guests at his table, Goebbels, Ley and some others were favoured in this respect. I can say nothing on this subject, as I was not once invited.[39]

Rosenberg's bitterest disappointment, however, came in spring 1938, when Hitler, in appointing a new Foreign Minister, once more passed him over in favour of the despised careerist Ribbentrop. His worst premonitions were confirmed in summer 1939 when Ribbentrop concluded the Moscow Pact, the political advantages of which did not offset its ideological lack of principle in his eyes, especially as he doubted whether the clash with Poland was inevitable. 'History will perhaps one day make clear,' he wrote, '*whether* the situation that had arisen *had* to arise.' With unconcealed horror he noted that 'the Soviets are said already to have selected a delegation to the Nuremberg Party Rally' and huffily registered Ribbentrop's remark on his return from Moscow, that 'the Russians were very nice; among them he had felt as though *in the midst of* old party comrades'.[40] Summing up, he concluded:

I have the feeling that this Moscow Pact will at some time or other exact vengeance upon National Socialism. That was not a step taken out of a free decision but an act imposed by a difficult situation, a petition on the part of one revolution to the head of another, the overcoming of which has been the ideal held up to inspire a twenty-year struggle. How can we still speak of the salvation and reformation of Europe, when we have to ask Europe's destroyer for help?[41]

The Moscow Pact struck a decisive blow against Rosenberg's naïve loyalty to his Führer, maintained till then in spite of all humiliations. Thenceforth he believed that the backbone had been torn out of National Socialism and Hitler himself had apostatised to the camp of the opportunists who betrayed an epoch-making cause to the needs of day-to-day politics. Deeply wounded by National

Socialist realities, he henceforth withdrew more and more into his confused world of National Socialist ideas, lonely but with his feelings intact. At the beginning of 1940, at his own suggestion, he was appointed by Hitler 'Representative of the Führer for the Furtherance of the National Socialist View', and in the same year he actually succeeded in what he referred to with satisfaction as an 'historical' act of foreign policy, by arranging an ominous personal contact between a leading Norwegian 'National Socialist' named Quisling and the German government. But successes like this merely raised his self-esteem, not his prestige. Again and again he had to remind people of his identity; his burning ambition was ultimately stronger than his readiness to rest content with the role of doctrinal guardian. After the French campaign he asked Hitler's permission to search the libraries and archives, as well as 'ownerless Jewish cultural property', for valuable material, a task which, by means of 'Reichsleiter Rosenberg's Temporary Staff', he extended to cover blatant robbery.[42] For the first time, long after his rivals in the leadership, the theorist and 'philosopher' found himself in a position to practise his extremism, which till then had remained purely literary; he devoted himself to his task with a ruthlessness in which euphoria at suddenly finding himself in a position to give orders combined vigorously with the aggressions left over from his disappointment in the field of foreign affairs. At bottom, however, this activity too was already part of his retreat from executive politics; for the expropriated material, notably 55,000 books, was earmarked for the so-called Higher Schools, the postwar 'central institutions for National Socialist research, teaching and education', of which he was preparing not only the curricula and administration but also – with models of grandiose bad taste – architecture. Here he believed that he was dedicating himself to pure doctrine, unsullied by compromise and tactical concessions, and instead of the real exercise of power, which had been refused him, assuming unrestricted dominion over the spirit.[43]

In these circumstances even the outbreak of the war with Russia could not heal what was broken within him. It was true that appointment as Reich Minister for the occupied Eastern regions restored to him the feeling of being indispensable as a political specialist which he had so long missed; but he was soon forced to recognise that his appointment was purely formal, made no doubt partly because of his Baltic origins and partly to avoid further troublesome claims. His powers were pathetically limited from the outset. Göring as General Supervisor of the Four-Year Plan, Himmler as Special Commissioner in the Army Operational Zone, Chief of Police and Reichsführer of the SS as well as Reich Commissar for the Consolidation of German National Identity (*Volkstum*) and responsible for resettlement measures, Sauckel as Commissioner for the Labour Force, and finally the Wehrmacht High Command: all these ate away his authority to the point where little was left but the title. Since he rejected Hitler's primitive and short-sighted ideas for the Eastern Region, his subordinates Hinrich Lohse and Erich Koch were soon able to push to the fore. Koch built up in the Ukraine a grandiose and bloody slave state far closer to the spirit of Hitler's Eastern policy than Rosenberg's lone efforts to win over the population by such things as the elimination of the kolkhozes and the preservation of some degree of self-government. In the stubborn conflicts that ensued he remained alone or was a pawn in the game for tougher and cleverer rivals, and his appeals, ignored by Hitler, were increasingly lost in the void. Soon the rival authorities no longer bothered to inform him of their measures or plans; Hinrich Lohse was even able to propose to Hitler the dissolution of the Ministry for the East to which he himself was answerable[44] – the Ostministerium, or 'Cha-ostministerium' (Ministry of Chaos), as Goebbels aptly called it in view of Rosenberg's clumsiness in organisation and handling of power. Rosenberg, the Minister of Propaganda declared, reminded him of a 'monarch with neither country nor subjects',[45] and in truth the function of his office was becoming visibly reduced to writing pleas which no one read, memoranda which were circulated only within his own office, protests which no-one took notice of any more: a forgotten man at the head of a forgotten institution. Despised, tricked and ridiculed, finally in autumn 1944 he resigned. Even then he failed, of course, to find the right words for the slights he had suffered and, presumably, his indignation; the only note he could strike was one of demoralised ill-humour, behind which the feelings of an indissoluble attachment to the Führer were clearly visible. In his letter of resignation of October 12, 1944 he wrote:

I beg you, my Führer, to tell me whether you still require my services; since I have not been able to report to you orally, but the problems of the East are being brought to you and discussed with you by various parties, in view of this development I must yield to the assumption that perhaps you no longer consider my activities necessary.[46]

It seems that he was not spared the final humiliation; for there is no sign that this appeal was ever answered by Hitler. Rosenberg was no longer a force to be reckoned with.

He never really had been, and it was his personal misfortune always to have stood above his station, however low it may have been. In his clumsy handling of power, his laborious German tendency to complication and his superstition he was not only hopelessly inferior to all his rivals, but in no way was he the figure of a modern totalitarian leader. He was a follower, material for the technicians of irrational modern social religion to work upon. If, in a phrase of Pareto's, the art of ruling consists in exploiting emotions instead of wasting time on vainly attempting to destroy them, this was precisely what he never understood in his excited missionary zeal. Goebbels mocked the ideologue who believed 'that when a member of a U-boat crew comes filthy and oily from the engine room, what he reaches for in preference to anything is a copy of 'The Myth of the Twentieth Century'' ';[47] in his warped pseudo-intellectuality Rosenberg did believe this, or at least wanted to. The world as a Walpurgis Night of dark powers and himself in the midst of it, conscious of his mission and unconquerable, side by side with the Führer holding the sword in front of the Holy Grail – in such images he sought and found the heroic compensation he needed; this was the real content of the *Weltanschauung* that sprang from his sickly and distorted personality.

He was infinitely overvalued, especially as to his 'evil influence'. The American military doctor and psychiatrist in the Nuremberg prison, Douglas M. Kelley, called him brutal and cruel; that is certainly wrong.[48] It would be much more accurate to say that he was intolerant and given to the petty bullying that is a sign of inferiority. Like many intellectuals of his time he was a lover of old-fashioned stupidities, only he had the opportunity to proclaim them solemnly in public places and gain currency for them, even if greatly restricted. But this remained pure theory with him. He did not think things out to their logical conclusions, like so many who expressed a literary contempt for reason and humanity and mused upon folk truths in fashionable intellectual twilight. Very little in his hazy constructions, which defy translation into any practical programme, entered the real world of the National Socialist dictatorship, beyond the restricted areas placed under his personal influence. True, the accusation against him in the Nuremberg courtroom related not to what he had thought but to what he had done. But everything he did was rather that which was done in his name, because he was incapable, either personally or in administrative technique, of living up to his own unfortunate predilection for executive activity. He remained 'Almost Rosenberg'. The evidence before the Nuremberg Court, which unequivocally proves that he knew about and indirectly took part in the measures for the extermination of the Jews, makes his horror over Auschwitz and Theresienstadt highly incredible. But if it was genuine, so certainly was the dull-wittedness with which he lied his way out of it, speaking of a 'great disease of National Socialism', a temporary degeneration for which he blamed above all Goebbels, Himmler, Bormann and officials like Erich Koch.[49] To the end he never realised that the injustices of National Socialism were inherent in it, that the terrible practice grew in the soil of a terrible theory. Within this broader framework, ideology and reality ultimately did correspond. And if Rosenberg, shortly before his death, expressed the hope that the idea of National Socialism would never be forgotten and would be 'reborn from a new generation steeled by suffering', this too merely indicates that he never grasped the largely false nature of totalitarian ideologies, which as they lose the external power in which they embody themselves also lose their power over men's minds.[50]

Thus no one so mistook the character and significance of National Socialist ideology as this man who considered himself one of its founders and authoritative exponents. The final sentence in the notes written in his Nuremberg cell admits, characteristically, his inability 'to *understand* all that in its deepest meaning'.[51]

Joachim von Ribbentrop
and the Degradation of Diplomacy

Ribbentrop is a genius.

Adolf Hitler

I assure you, we are all appalled by all these persecutions and atrocities.
It is simply not typically German! Can you imagine that I could kill
anyone? Tell me honestly, do any of us look like murderers?
Joachim von Ribbentrop in Nuremberg

Among the few ideas that Hitler held to throughout his life, unaltered by any
compromise demanded by the tactics of power, was the conviction of the
supremacy of force. He took up the old dictum that struggle is the father of all
things, which the popular philosophy of the nineteenth century had interpreted
in the tritest possible way, and construed it as meaning that murder, cruelty,
cunning or brutality were the right of a higher humanity and proof of an unspoilt
morality. Totally ensnared in analogies between nature and human society, which
gave both his first and his later pronouncements their characteristic mark, he
carried over the laws of the jungle into the lives of individuals and of nations.

How deeply such an outlook – not consciously and firmly, but as a vague
underlying feeling – pervaded the masses is proved by the echo it aroused when
Hitler made his debut as a demagogue. From the deep German subconscious, his
extravagant appeals touched in particular that type of petty bourgeois behind
whose philistine respectability, soulfulness and vague romanticism could be seen
the outlines of a harsh belief in force. Blood and iron, as the current phrase had it,
ruled the course of the world; history was unsentimental; the world spirit rode its
tall steed through battlefields littered with corpses and cared nothing for the
rights of others. It would be a mistake to regard this perversion of values as being
confined to the German situation; it represented an upsurge of long standing
with its origins in Europe as a whole. But the combination of this distorted viewpoint with specifically German problems proved a highly inflammable mixture.

The universal phenomenon involved has been aptly described as 'mass
Machiavellianism'. It resulted from the increasing participation of all levels of the
population in politics. Whereas in past ages only the leading groups had been
conscious of the conflict between the norms of accepted morality and the
demands of the state, now, in a way quite different from that anticipated by the

175

liberal and democratic spokesmen of the twentieth century, awareness of this conflict became infinitely widespread without creating any feeling of tension. What had been held out as liberation from dependence on uncontrollable old-style power politics, and as the elimination of the 'double morality' of power politics, proved on the contrary to be the point at which precisely this double morality entered into the whole of society. The new situation was marked by the increasingly unashamed disparagement, by ever-widening circles of the population, of all forms of public ethics, which were condemned as a 'soft morality of sentiment and renunciation'. This meant nothing less than that morality per se was considered an attitude of soft emotionalism and of cowardly renunciation of the nation's essential claims. The conviction that the state had a morality of its own had hitherto been held only by those in positions of leadership and acted on only after weighing up all the factors involved. Now it became the 'everyday morality of the little man', as Karl Mannheim wrote, 'who today practises power politics such as we find in the past only in the secret documents of leading statesmen',[1] and practised it, moreover, without the control provided by a rational consideration of the facts. The urge towards participation in politics degenerated into an urge towards participation in the contempt for moral sanctions within politics.

This development coincided with the peculiarly pathological assumptions current in the political consciousness of the German people at the dawn of the era of the national state. The aspiration towards a German national state, never satisfied and never relaxed; the widespread feeling of having arrived too late at the colonial partition of the world; the vision of a German mission in the heart of Europe, as romantically sentimental in conception as it was aggressive; the urge for German hegemony culminating rapturously in the idea of the Reich; and a willingness to sacrifice to the outward goals of domination an inner freedom that had never really been experienced – in short, the unstable equilibrium of a nation which had almost never in its history felt at one with itself – created a combination of circumstances ripe for the swing to an all-or-nothing imperialist adventure.

One may or may not see German participation in the First World War as a first step in a truly Napoleonic dream of dominion, a grasping at world power. In any case, such dreams came to a head with the end of the war and its aftermath. The Hitlerian thesis 'world power or destruction' had its precursors and contributors, who placed the emphasis on many different aspects, in every camp from the centre to the right and running right across the established political fronts. Treaties, tracts or circular letters, significantly always dealing with foreign policy, whether they were put out by scholars, businessmen or journalists or by the wildly proliferating sectarian nationalist groups, revealed not merely a passionate desire for a say in public affairs but also an ambition to rebuild the deeply wounded national spirit on the foundations of future imperialism. The widespread humiliation gave these projects an extreme note and a sense of being above all consideration for others both in setting their aims and in choosing their means. No matter if the world 'fell in fragments', as a later popular National

Socialist fighting song put it, expressing the thrilling shudder that so warmed petty bourgeois hearts with a taste for the apocalyptic. Faith in force, in unscrupulous violence, rapturously proclaimed by Hitler, worked on these groups and classes like magic and had a far more lasting influence than hazy National Socialist ideology. Here the 'natural law' traditionally surrounded by a zone of silence was openly stated, the formula for success openly displayed with its promise of satisfying all the nation's needs at one blow. The 'Machiavellianism of the masses' had culminated in the appearance of Hitler and now became a political force.[2]

With his divorce from the standards of wider responsibility, the typical man of power who rose to the top among Hitler's followers certainly recognised the explosiveness of the mixture that made him what he was, but he admired himself in this situation and mistook his predilection for catastrophe for the demonic quality of historical grandeur. The logical consequence of all this was that in the course of the history of the Third Reich control of foreign policy was always more violently fought for than any other. Here practical incompetence had the greatest chance of success, national bitterness could be most effectively worked off and an understanding of power and faith in force could most readily take effect in aggression. And here too was the logical point at which the spirit of the tavern crashed into the world of high-level politics, knocking over all the players, and before the eyes of a dumbfounded world displayed its bombast, its greed for prestige, and its desire to impress in a way that was both pathetic and shattering. The representative of this type was the Third Reich's Foreign Minister, Joachim von Ribbentrop.

The circumstances in which he found his way to Hitler in the early 1930s are revealing in themselves. In response to a chance remark by Hitler that he could not follow the foreign press because of his ignorance of foreign languages, Ribbentrop, the wine and spirits importer, was recommended to him as a reader. Ribbentrop not only had a good knowledge of languages but had also been the author of a political newsletter which was sent to business contacts at home and abroad and which took a nationalist and anti-Bolshevik line. Hitler accepted him, influenced not least by his outward appearance as a man of the world.[3] This was the start of a rapid rise in a career of astounding incompetence. For Ribbentrop, who shared Hitler's habit of indulging in great visions expressed in endless monologues, it led into those realms where the megalomaniac word loses its innocence and unexpectedly influences the destinies of nations; where self-assertive coarseness brings the reputation, not of a swashbuckler among neighbours and boon companions, but of a disturber of the peace before the bar of history. Ribbentrop evidently never grasped the difference between these two roles and confronted it during the Nuremberg Trial with that same strained mien which a lifelong intellectual helplessness had forced him to adopt. He was condemned as the pothouse politician whose bombastic utterances were suddenly fulfilled as by a malevolent fairy, whose words, dictated by a hunger for self-importance, suddenly became flesh and, even more, blood.

177

It was no doubt his inflated busybody arrogance that also made him the target of so much negative criticism. From the French Foreign Minister Bonnet and his Italian and Spanish counterparts, Count Ciano and Serrano Suñer, through the leading functionaries of the Third Reich to the court psychologists at the Nuremberg Trial the verdicts differ in tone, never in substance. Representative in this sense is the sketch by the former French ambassador in Berlin, Robert Coulondre:

Hitler launches into monologues when carried away by passion, but Herr von Ribbentrop does so when he is ice-cold. It is futile to challenge his statements; he hears you just as little as his cold, empty, moonlike eyes see you. Always speaking down to his interlocutor, always striking a pose, he delivers his well-prepared speech in a cutting voice; the rest no longer interests him; there is nothing for you to do but withdraw. There is nothing human about this German, who incidentally is good-looking, except the baser instincts.[4]

State Secretary von Weizsäcker referred to Ribbentrop's disqualifying inability to submit to the rules of conversation. The Reich press chief, Otto Dietrich, called him 'witless and undiplomatic, touchy and subservient', while Goebbels sarcastically explained the contempt for the Foreign Minister by almost all the top leaders of the Third Reich by saying that whereas each of the leading men had at least one praiseworthy side, Ribbentrop had none.[5] The lone weak voice raised in his favour among the hostile chorus is that of his secretary; but she too emphasised Ribbentrop's unconditional subservience, thereby indicating the obvious reason why he for so long retained the esteem of Hitler, who on one occasion called him a 'second Bismarck' and on another 'a genius'.[6] For whatever Ribbentrop accomplished to win the admiration of his contemporaries, he paid for it with servitude, and his later State Secretary von Steengracht actually spoke in Nuremberg of 'a certain hypnotic dependence upon Hitler'.[7] But it would doubtless be more correct to say that Byzantinism was merely part of the ambitious efforts of a man who sought dependence and fell on his knees before he was asked to. It matches the picture of this character ready-made for totalitarianism in its intellectual dishonesty, brutality and longing for subjection that in August 1939, after his spectacular trip to Moscow, he 'went into raptures before anyone who would listen about Stalin and his fellow "men with the strong faces" ', and even in his last notes written during his imprisonment in Nuremberg he commented that he had spent 'a harmonious evening with them'.[8]

It was his great desire, which he pursued beyond the limits of the ridiculous, to appear himself as 'a man with a strong face'. Hence the forced toughness which he assumed; the artificial, screwed-up pose of the statesman filled with cares for the future; the laboriously furrowed brow; in short all the Caesar-like grimacing which, in all his highfalutin obtuseness, so often verged towards *buffo* comic opera. Eyewitnesses said he almost fell on the rails of the Gare des Invalides when he visited Paris in 1938, through holding his head high, as he always did.[9] The vanity, the provocative self-assertion and continual self-dramatisation, were merely the reverse side of his very ordinary personality; on the sleeves of the fantastic diplomatic uniform which he had designed for him there was embroidered a terrestrial globe dominated by an eagle. His desire to please and his ambition were as great as the ruthlessly fraudulent means by which he sought to satisfy them.

These elements crop up over and over again in his undistinguished career up to the beginning of the 1930s. He came from a middle-class officer's family, went to Canada as a merchant in his youth, and returned to Germany shortly after the outbreak of the First World War. That he was awarded the Iron Cross First Class only retrospectively and in response to a petition has been disputed, but it would be in keeping with his mentality.[10] After the war he belonged 'to the lower ranks of café society',[11] until marriage to the daughter of a well-known champagne manufacturer gave him the entrée into high society which he had been striving for. He later tried, falsely, to explain his elevation to the nobility as a reward for bravery in the war; for his name was originally Joachim Ribbentrop and he exploited a change in the law after 1918 to get himself adopted by a distant noble relative of the same name. Goebbels commented contemptuously, 'He bought his name, he married his money, and he swindled his way into office.'[12]

The emphatic hostility of the Minister of Propaganda was due not merely to rivalry in the sphere of foreign policy but to a considerable extent also to Ribbentrop's having joined the party late and rather by chance. Also his dubious nobility and ostentatious snobbery, which earned him the nickname 'Ribbensnob',[13] together with his forced gentility and exclusiveness, irritated the older supporters of the movement, especially those who, like Goebbels, remembered its former proletarian impulses and spirit. True, Ribbentrop's house in Berlin-Dahlem, Lentze-Allee 7–9, had served as a meeting-place during final negotiations over the formation of the cabinet of January 30, 1933; but such predominantly social activities did not count among Hitler's early followers. They regarded him as a parvenu, and these men who had risked their lives for the movement never entirely lost their distrust of the upstart who was using it as a springboard for his undisguised personal aims. The *Führerlexikon* (the Who's Who of leading Nazis) of 1935 did not even mention his name.[14]

It may be that it was this total lack of support within the party that finally placed him in that attitude of unconditional servility, already present in his personality, which determined his future career and made him such an undignified and despised shadow of Hitler. It is also said of him that he sometimes sought to discover Hitler's views through go-betweens and then presented them as his own. 'Foreign policy for him consisted in being the first to present some important report to Hitler and to sense in advance how Hitler would evaluate it. To Ribbentrop a thing was important if it was likely to be regarded as important by Hitler. If he turned out to have been mistaken about this, he immediately lost all interest.'[15] In the so-called Ribbentrop Bureau, which he provocatively set up opposite the German Foreign Office in the former house of the Prussian Minister-President, he created in spring 1933 a staff, at first small but soon numbering more than 300, to satisfy his ambitions in the field of foreign policy. He later explained that the function of this office was restricted to the creation of 'good will' abroad.[16] In fact, however, he used it to carry on a stubborn and ruthless war with the Foreign Office. He found himself emphatically supported in this by Hitler, who fostered such rival claims to jurisdiction not only because they made it easier for him to maintain his own power, but also out of a deep-seated aversion for the Foreign Office, that 'omnium-gatherum of creatures', as he once called it. Its fundamentally conservative outlook, its traditional objectivity and recalcitrant stiffness, coupled with its lack of enthusiasm and its bureaucratic pedantry, were anathema to him. 'The dreary embassy reports' did not interest him, he once declared and gave his own idea of the new-style diplomat of the National Socialist school: 'An efficient ambassador must be able to act as a *maître de plaisir*; in any case he must be able to pander and prefabricate. What he should be least of all is a correct civil servant.'[17] Ribbentrop himself hardly measured up to this ideal, but Hitler was obviously impressed by his brutal directness, and his curt, domineering tone was in keeping with Hitler's views on the style of National Socialist foreign policy.

Nevertheless, the apparatus of the Foreign Office remained for the time being largely intact, particularly as Hitler seemed to be trying to carry on the revisionist policy of continual willingness to negotiate that had been the foreign policy credo of the Weimar Republic. The carefully preserved appearance of moderation and constancy were entirely tactical. He wanted to soothe foreign fears that the men now in power in the Reich might embark on the boundless ambitions proclaimed, for example, in *Mein Kampf* and in countless threatening speeches. This would give the regime a breathing spell in which to eliminate internal opposition and consolidate. The first aim of foreign policy, as stated in detail by Hitler in his speech to the Düsseldorf Industrial Society in 1932, was to mobilise and unify the militant energies of the people within the framework of plans for future expansion. Only total control and unification internally – this was the burden of his declaration – guaranteed complete freedom of action externally.[18]

Apart from occasional intervention, then, Hitler did not interfere in the work of the Foreign Office until the process of seizing power was completed and stability largely assured. Then, however, its influence on the moulding and formulation of foreign policy was noticeably curbed, in so far as it was not voluntarily abandoned. The old officials of this department, in working for Hitler's immediate aims – the undermining and dissolution of collective security as represented by the League of Nations, and its transformation into a multiplicity of bilateral relationships – had shown a lethargy that was not in keeping with the versatile ruthlessness of the new style: when it came to carrying out his strategic ideas they were quite useless. Plans for the revision of the Versailles Treaty, the creation of a unified Greater German Reich and imperialist solutions to the problems of *Lebensraum* in the East all involved breaking agreements, and using blackmail, duplicity or the threat of war, and these plans were confined to a very narrow circle. Soon the Foreign Office became a mere 'technical apparatus'[19] required for purely routine tasks, but for the rest more and more obviously bypassed and ignored.

In one of these special tasks, now increasingly entrusted to reliable followers in the first moves towards cold-shouldering the Foreign Office, Ribbentrop achieved an astonishing success in the early summer of 1933 with the conclusion of the Anglo-German Naval Agreement. It was of course due less to his tactless and blackmailing conduct of the negotiations than to the vacillations of British policy, to wavering in London and Paris. In neither city could the authorities make up their minds whether the dynamism of Hitler's regime was to be halted by cautiously meeting him halfway or by vigorously opposing him. In both they veered between distrust and attempts to minimise the danger. Thus they found themselves facing precisely that problem which had dominated the political situation inside Germany before 1933 and they confronted it in the same deluded and contradictory manner, handing Hitler his successes and then disputing them with him ever more helplessly and nervously.[20]

Despite assertions to the contrary,[21] Ribbentrop manifestly felt it a setback, in summer 1936, to be appointed German ambassador to London. As a mere courtier, far from the capital Berlin, with its struggles for power and its cabals, he probably feared for his position. With provocative negligence he did not go to London until three months after the appointment, and thereafter made so many trips home to Berlin that *Punch* christened him the Wandering Aryan, while a leading official of the British Foreign Office indignantly complained that Herr von Ribbentrop apparently regarded his activity at the Court of St James as a 'part-time job'.[22] Nor were his humourless and officious nature and the frosty solemnity with which he surrounded himself calculated to win him even the personal success which he so much desired. 'When I questioned Ribbentrop's ability to cope with British problems,' Göring later commented, 'Hitler explained to me that Ribbentrop knew "Lord So-and-So". I replied, "Yes, but the trouble is that they also know Ribbentrop." '[23] At a reception at court in 1937 the Ambassador committed the famous gaffe of greeting the King with the Nazi salute, a faux pas that has become the classic example of amateurish and unfitting diplomacy. Rejection by English society, which in his eyes held the ultimate decision on some imaginary social rank, offended him deeply and perhaps confirmed him in his conviction of the irreconcilable nature of Anglo-German antagonism even more strongly than the failure of his policy, which varied between attempts to curry favour and arrogant demonstrations of strength. 'Every day,' he wrote in a secret memorandum shortly before his recall, 'on which in future our political reflections were not fundamentally determined by the idea that England is our most dangerous adversary would be a gain for our enemies'.[24]

The disastrous consequences of this aversion, which was in total opposition to the Third Reich's initial policy of an alliance of interests with Britain, were first disclosed in 1938 when Hitler, in the great spring reshuffle, appointed him Foreign Minister. According to an eyewitness it sometimes happened that 'Hitler fundamentally opposed Ribbentrop's Anglophobia and commented upon it sarcastically. But in practical terms Ribbentrop's one-sided instructions had a clearly observable effect on him.'[25] According to everyone except the ex-Foreign

Minister himself, he gave Hitler misleading information, especially on British policy, during all the crises of 1938–39, creating the picture of a nation basically so resigned that for the foreseeable future it would accept every act of violent conquest by the Reich.[26] Hitler acted on this catastrophic and shortsighted thesis all the more readily because it was in line with his own ideological preconceptions about the humanitarian weakness and political degeneracy of the Western democracies. Ribbentrop's prestige and influence grew still further when this prediction was apparently confirmed in the course of the Austrian and Czech crises, when the British Prime Minister left the unhappy Czechoslovakia to her fate after his disastrous reference to 'these countries which we scarcely know'. Certainly Ribbentrop did not decisively determine the Reich's foreign policy at this or at any other time. 'The policy I pursue is not mine but the Führer's,' he frankly told the French ambassador, Coulondre.[27] But Ribbentrop added many characteristic details to that policy and, at least between the Munich Agreement of autumn 1938 and the Moscow Pact of August 1939, was at the height of his political career, more than ever the 'foreign-political secretary', as he was described at Nuremberg.[28] He more than anyone reinforced Hitler in the hazardous policy that gave its stamp to the hot and hectic summer of 1939; he in particular circulated the foolish theories that Germany 'had not exploited the Western powers' fear of war to the full' and that 'at Munich Britain was only out to gain time in order to strike when better armed'.[29] Göring's remark in 1943 that 'this war is Ribbentrop's war' was going too far,[30] but demonstrably Ribbentrop did everything he could to frustrate last-minute peace moves. The account by the Swedish businessman Birger Dahlerus of his efforts in summer 1939 to prevent the threatened war contains not merely a mass of indications of Ribbentrop's activity in exactly the opposite direction, but also the surmise, admittedly originating from Ribbentrop's personal rival Göring, that the Foreign Minister had been after his life.[31] Over and above this he refused to allow the head of the London mission to see Hitler when he came to Berlin in response to a request for an urgent report on the situation; he forbade the ambassador in Warsaw to return to his post, although German-Polish relations were heading for a crisis; and he pushed aside unconsidered the warning reports from the ambassador in Washington because they contradicted Hitler's preconceived opinion. State Secretary von Weizsäcker once had to warn his leading colleagues of a directive from Ribbentrop ordering him to have any of his officials who expressed an opinion of his own running counter to the line ordered by Hitler shot in the office on his personal responsibility – the ultimate absurd exaggeration of the methods of a 'personal foreign policy' that was now fully established.[32]

These methods could claim certain striking successes and, as Hitler said, had ruthlessly exploited the advantages of knowing 'no pedantic and sentimental scruples'.[33] The tactics were always the same: an initial announcement of unconditional demands, immediately followed by a surprise attack, and then a peace offer coupled with the assurance that no further demands would be made, until the game began all over again. At first they bewildered the adversary and put the

European powers in a state of paralysis which was further intensified by the constant threat of war, but it was to be expected that this diplomacy by challenge must soon reach its natural limits. As early as 1937 Weizsäcker noted in the margin of an embassy report from London that this was a policy of 'accelerating the Last Judgment'.[34] Ribbentrop, however, seems never to have been aware of this. When he was reminded after the Austrian Anschluss of Bismarck's cautiously gradual policy, he retorted, 'Then you have no idea of the dynamic force of National Socialism.'[35] Dynamism was here nothing but a synonym for the readiness continually to go the whole hog. The Italian Foreign Minister, Count Ciano, wrote in his diary:

It was at his Schloss Fuschl, while we were waiting to sit down to dinner, that Ribbentrop informed me of the decision to throw the tinder into the powder barrel, exactly as though he were talking to me about the most unimportant and ordinary administrative matter. Well, Ribbentrop, I asked him as we strolled in the garden, what do you want? Danzig or the corridor? Not any more – and he stared at me with those cold Musée Grevin eyes – we want war! The will to fight is unalterable. Any solution that might satisfy Germany or avoid war, he rejects. I know for sure that the Germans, even if all their demands were met, would attack just the same, because they are possessed by the devil of destruction.[36]

It may be that Ciano was exaggerating; but the impression of resolute barbarity that actually prides itself on its own brutality and greed is authentic. Undoubtedly this was all nothing but talk and 'war' merely another word in Ribbentrop's swashbuckling vocabulary; nevertheless it made history. A close colleague of Goebbels overheard a conversation between Ribbentrop and Hitler that reveals the inconceivable cynicism of this policy. 'When the war is over,' boasted the Foreign Minister, 'I shall have a finely carved chest made for myself. I shall put in it all the state agreements and other contracts between governments that I have broken during my period of office and shall break in the future.' Hitler replied jokingly, 'And I shall send you a second chest when the first one is full.'[37] And if it was not a resolute will to war that guided Ribbentrop during the great world crisis, it was a sly arrogance that persuaded himself and others that Britain and France would intervene only formally in order to save face in a cause – as he assured his listeners, posing as a man in the know – for which they had no serious intention of taking real action. The first inkling of what he had started may have come when the British ultimatum reached the Reich Chancellery on September 3, 1939, and Hitler spat out that furious 'What now?' which Ribbentrop could answer only with a meaningless rhetorical flourish.[38] The rapid triumphs of the early phase of the war, which carried the Third Reich to the zenith of its power, swept away all hesitation; and when the first difficulties arose with the breaking off of 'Operation Sea Lion', the principle of flight forward into new adventures, new campaigns, helped to stun any lasting realisation of the truth. On June 22, 1941 the most disastrous step on this path was taken: German armies launched an invasion of Soviet Russia. Among his closest confederates Hitler said, 'I feel as though I were pushing open a door into a dark room I had never seen – not knowing what lies behind the door.'[39] This, fundamentally, was how they had always conducted foreign policy.

By the time they had pushed open the doors to almost all the dark rooms, convinced of the truth of Ribbentrop's arrogant 'We are far stronger than we ourselves believe!'[40] the Foreign Minister's personal fall began. True, he continually travelled around in the wake of headquarters and kept himself in readiness within easy reach, but he could do nothing to revive his waning influence. This was partly because of Hitler's view that in time of war the Foreign Office had no function, since questions of power 'could not be decided by diplomatic means'.[41] Behind this lay not merely the memory of the rejection of the 'peace offer' that Hitler in his usual way made shortly after the successful conclusion of the Polish campaign, but also an insight into the nature of this war. It was becoming more and more clearly a bitter ideological conflict and hence acquiring the character of a 'crusade', which indeed left little room for diplomatic activity. At the same time, the neglecting of contacts with neutral and Allied powers clearly revealed the limits of a purely expansionist 'diplomacy', which could impose from a position of power but could not genuinely negotiate because of its basic hostility to compromise.

However, Ribbentrop's inflexibility and lack of imagination also certainly played a part in the final phase of the withdrawal of power from the Foreign Office; now, as events became increasingly unfavourable to him and threats of force no longer achieved anything, he lapsed into pugnacity. It is reported that in spring 1943 'he received no further support from Hitler, who derided him as a busybody'. As his influence waned, his desire to extend his jurisdiction increased, so that according to his secretary he was soon devoting 'at least 60 per cent of his time' to futile conflicts with rivals.[42] He tried to regain part of his influence, following the well-tried method of his rivals, by taking an active part in the policy of exterminating the Jews and urging Germany's allies to speed up the evacuation of their Jewish populations; naturally this attempt had no lasting effect.[43] His offer of resignation, later such an important part of his attempts at self-justification, was an obvious expression of wounded pride, and though he drew attention later to the fact that Hitler called him his 'most difficult subordinate' and his department the 'house of difficulties', this certainly referred not to any practical resistance he had offered, but to the purely procedural difficulties he caused. A typical incident underlines this. When Rumania began to back out of the coalition with Hitler he did not bother to look into conditions in Bucharest, but devoted his whole energy to quarrelsome investigations into who could have handed in a memorandum on this subject to the Führer's headquarters without going through the proper channels.[44]

Helplessly he watched the gradual dissolution of his department, whose influence he had once been so keen to reduce. By 1944 his name crops up only occasionally and in trifling contexts in documents and memoirs. One such was when he commissioned a colleague to demonstrate in a memorandum the indispensability of the Foreign Office. Or there was that grotesque scene on July

20, 1944, when an argument broke out in the exasperated atmosphere of head-quarters. In the course of it Göring, evidently without first addressing him in the proper terms, went for him with his marshal's baton and was shrilly put in his place with the words, 'I am still Foreign Minister and my name is *von* Ribbentrop.'[45] This was all that was left: a reference to his title of nobility, to which strictly speaking he had no claim, and to a post which he had long since ceased to hold. His last months were filled with nervous hopes of conflict among the enemy, with unrealistic fantasies of uniting with the Western powers against the danger from the East, which the Nazis themselves had conjured up and introduced into the heart of Europe. Yet he still maintained an outward show of bold self-confidence. Count Folke Bernadotte found him in April 1945 as vain as ever and with his old unpleasant tendency to self-righteous monologues. Time after time he assured the Count that nothing was lost yet.[46] His career came to an end on May 1, when Dönitz informed him that he was dismissed from the post of Reich Foreign Minister. 'In order to avoid a long argument he invited Ribbentrop to ring him back if he thought he could name a suitable successor. After an hour Ribbentrop was on the line. He had thought the matter over at length and with a good conscience he could only suggest *one* man to Dönitz: Ribbentrop.'[47] A few weeks later he was taken from his bed in a Hamburg flat by British soldiers.

Birger Dahlerus, who saw him as head of the 'inferior elements' around Hitler, overestimated his personal importance. Certainly his activities were disastrous, but at bottom he was not really evil, but only base and heartless and of an unparalleled moral insensitivity that caused him to refuse to the last to withdraw his bloodthirsty phrases. Even in the face of death he could not see the extermination of millions of people as anything but 'an additional burden on foreign policy'.[48]

In their cold impersonality the notes he wrote in the Nuremberg prison are among the most agonising documents left by the chief actors of that epoch. There is not a word of remorse or even of understanding, nothing but the wearisome platitudes of an indoctrination supervisor, as when he seeks to justify his policy, blames the German opposition and the British government alternately for the war, and tells the world with a silly fake honesty that 'seriously, there was no joint action directed by world Jewry from Moscow, Paris, London and New York'.[49] In his total poverty of conscience he never grasped the moral considerations which, beyond all the dubious legal technicalities, gave the trial its decisive legitimation; rather, seeing everywhere the triumph of force and neither knowing nor acknowledging anything beyond it, he saw this trial too as purely a question of power. 'Everyone knows that the verdict is utterly untenable,' he wrote in one of his last letters. 'But I was once Adolf Hitler's Foreign Minister and politics demands that for this fact I shall be condemned.'[50]

The only argument he ever understood was who had the greater number of divisions, airplanes, tanks, factories or raw materials behind him. He was nothing in himself, and whatever he achieved he owed to Hitler's favour and power. Once he was deprived of their support and they no longer lent their terrible weight to his words, he was quickly reduced to the wretched proportions of the pothouse politician with the Nietzschean will to power which fundamentally he had always been. 'Since Hitler's death I have been done for,' he said at Nuremberg.[51]

His subservience endured, for it was the precondition for his rise to a position of historical importance. He was an example of that paradox, a million times repeated – the 'totalitarian man' who achieves the longed-for feeling of self-elevation only in a state of total subservience. 'Do you know,' he admitted to the Nuremberg court psychologist, G. M. Gilbert, 'even with all I know, if now in this cell Hitler should come to me and say, "Do this!" I would still do it.' In his attempt at self-justification he kept returning to the idea of loyalty, which is an old mythological concept from the emotional world of the German petty bourgeois, who has been taught to measure the value of loyalty not by the value of its object, but isolated from all reasons and hence from all meaning. 'We Germans are a peculiar people; we are so loyal,' asserted Ribbentrop.[52]

G. M. Gilbert advanced the theory that each of the leaders of the Third Reich at Nuremberg possessed a kind of 'second line of defence'. The diplomats and military men took refuge in their social standard, Göring adopted an attitude of self-conscious heroism, Hess escaped into hysteria, others identified themselves with certain ideas, traditions or rediscovered certainties of faith; only Ribbentrop had nothing left to retreat to after Hitler's death. He possessed neither a conviction nor the support of an aristocratic origin, and in the narrow sobriety of his nature even escape into a psychopathological condition was barred to him. The world of Hitler, which for a while had inflated and maintained his insubstantial ego, now after the collapse left a vacuum in which he could no longer keep himself erect.[53] This is the only explanation for his spinelessness, the tearful tone of his statements, and his degeneration even outwardly in clothing and bearing. Eyewitnesses all agree with shock about his performance in court. He had transformed his once brash arrogance into an undignified, anxious servility, by which he seemed to hope to gain something. He disputed everything at great length, unimpressed by proof, in wearisome monologues. We are told that he failed 'even to gain the ear of the court. He did not succeed even in arousing the listeners' curiosity. He failed to convince. People felt ashamed. The feeling of shame grew, it proliferated, strangled, and cut off the breath.'[54]

Rudolf Hess:
The Embarrassment of Freedom

Hitler is simply pure reason incarnate.

Rudolf Hess

All modern systems of order based on a totalitarian ideology contain a pseudo-religious claim. The end or at least the erosion of the authority of Christianity helped to prepare the way for states themselves to appear with growing emphasis as the bearers of a compulsory secular ethic. The Enlightenment and the French Revolution, the concepts of a 'civic religion', and the idea of virtue started the shift from the religious plane to that of social reality, which has been further and further intensified up to the present day. In their certainty of promise, their intolerance, the inexorable alternative of subservience or damnation, but also in the order constituted by a favoured élite and a hierarchic structure, totalitarian systems in modern times have copied and still copy, to some extent consciously, the metaphysical or sociological structures of Western religious societies. 'The Revolution could not tolerate a Church,' Michelet stated, looking back at the events of 1789. 'Why? Because it was itself a Church.' Dostoyevsky in *The Brothers Karamazov* commented that the Church nowadays showed no tendency to become a 'state', but on the other hand the state did all it could to become a 'church'.[1]

The liquidation and capture of heaven, as practised by the rival secular religions with zealous seriousness and growing support from the masses, was certainly in line with modern man's lack of religious orientation and his consequent search for fresh metaphysical attachments inside or outside the traditional content of faith; to this extent the trend merely reflected the re-establishment of identity between the state of consciousness on the one hand and reality on the other. But the totalitarian systems, in doing away with 'heaven', did not simultaneously do away with hells, but actually established them for the first time, because however far and however consistently the parallels with religion were drawn, they did not possess the power of grace and forgiveness. On the other hand their demands went far beyond all traditional forms of dictatorial rule. While the dictators' urge to power was basically satisfied with the elimination of all opposition movements, totalitarian systems continually seek positive manifestations of faith; they demand, not the loyal servant of the state, but the idolator. It is not a demand solely for exclusive outward power, but a demand by the state for dominion over souls, the ultimate key to power, which alone guarantees total power over the social body.

'National Socialism and Christianity have this much in common, that they lay claim to the whole man,' one of the leaders of the Third Reich once said, and a questionnaire once asked the young leaders of the BDM – the German Girls League – whether God or the Führer was 'greater, more powerful, and stronger'.² Just as the National Socialist movement on its way to power strangled the Weimar state by means of a so-called shadow state which duplicated almost every state institution with a corresponding party institution, so the National Socialist *Weltanschauung* also envisaged a shadow church. The attempt to detach the masses' desire to believe from existing creeds in favour of a political ideology brought its own dogmas, places of sacrifice and liturgy; there was a God and a vision of the Devil that led to the bloodiest exorcisms in history. True, as an ideology National Socialism never had the scholastic rigidity of Communist theory; it was vague, imprecise, and deliberately left the greatest possible scope for irrational needs. Its followers owed allegiance less to the orthodoxy of a doctrine than to the person of the Führer. But the lack of clarity in the ideological reference-points has no bearing on the intensity of the emotions called for or aroused. Within the inner circle of the National Socialist community there emerged men prepared only for utter subservience, men who, as Hitler put it, in thoroughly religious terms, 'set themselves free from their environment, who put everything far behind them, all the petty things of life that are apparently so important, who turn once more to a greater task'.³ This type was to be found, above all, among the followers of the movement in its early days and among the middle ranks of the leadership; but few typified it so unequivocally as Rudolf Hess, who took the Führer's call more seriously than almost anyone else and fell to his knees before lowly shrines more ardently than others, seeking for the strength to utter the prayer used in National Socialist day nurseries: 'Führer, my Führer, my faith, my light!'⁴ – until, in response to an insane decision, he tried his strength in disobedience and immediately came to grief. Far from his God and the dispensation of blessings, for which he had always been so avid, he was a mere ghost of himself. Those who met him again at Nuremberg saw a face burnt out by its former ecstasies and the torture of excommunication.

Sola fide, by faith alone, Rudolf Hess rose from depressed, introverted student to deputy leader of a great power; no-one, as the weekly magazine *Das Reich* said in an article of December 1940, 'sang at his cradle that he would one day become the third man in a mighty empire'.⁵ He did not have, to recommend him, demagogic talent or tactical adroitness, or striking intelligence, brutality or ideological skill. Shy, in many ways inhibited, and so modest as often to seem a positive backwoodsman, he was nothing but believing and strenuously loyal. 'I want to be the party's Hagen von Tronje!'⁶ Expressions of unconditional and ardent devotion mark his path from the day of his first meeting with Hitler, when he felt, in his own words, 'as though overcome by a vision',⁷ down to his closing words at Nuremberg, when he escaped for a moment from his fantasies and dreams and gazed for one brief, ecstatic instant into the world outside: 'It was granted me for many years to live and work under the greatest son whom my nation has brought forth in the thousand years of its history.'[8] For all its devouring vehemence his faith remained rather mute; by comparison with his rhetorically adroit partners in the leadership, he has left few testimonies behind. But whatever he did say or write, though stammering and clumsy in both word and thought, was a canticle to subservience and a cry of jubilation at having cast aside freedom. If the actively totalitarian man is characterised by the consciousness that everything is possible,[9] Hess was the type of the passively totalitarian man with whom it is possible to do anything, because he loves to feel he is wax in the hands of another, and his ambition is to intensify his impersonality, voluntarily to renounce criticism, judgment and self-determination, under such ideological pretexts as loyalty, duty or obedience: in short, to be nothing, or only a particle, and accordingly to experience the high-points of existence in intoxications of enthusiasm, in moments of melting emotion, of total extinction of personality. 'One must want the Führer,' Rudolf Hess used to say.[10] In a speech a few days before June 30, 1934, clearly shaking a warning finger at the insubordinate SA Chief of Staff, Ernst Röhm, he said revealingly:

With pride we see that one man remains beyond all criticism, that is the Führer. This is because everyone feels and knows: he is always right, and he will always be right. The National Socialism of all of us is anchored in uncritical loyalty, in the surrender to the Führer that does not ask for the why in individual cases, in the silent execution of his orders. We believe that the Führer is obeying a higher call to fashion German history. There can be no criticism of this belief.[11]

Albert Krebs, one of the so-called Old Guard of the NSDAP and one-time Gauleiter of Hamburg, accused Rudolf Hess, not without reason, of having given the youthful movement a decisive push in the direction of a fascist-totalitarian, quasi-military party and, thanks to his greater reliability, of having been more effective even than Goebbels in erecting altars to the cult of the Führer which, in its efforts to set Hitler in the place of God, feared neither blasphemy nor ridicule.[12]

In his unbalanced approach to authority Hess strikingly resembles many National Socialists who, like him, had 'strict' parents. There is a good deal of evidence that Hitler profited considerably from the damage wrought by an education system that took its models from the barracks and brought up its sons to be as tough as army cadets. The fixation on the military world, the determining feature of their early background, shows not only in the peculiar mixture of aggressiveness and doglike cringing so typical of the 'Old Fighter', but also in the lack of inner independence and the need to receive orders. Whatever hidden rebellious feelings the young Rudolf Hess may have had against his father, who emphatically demonstrated his power for the last time when he refused to let his son go to a university but forced him, against his wishes and the pleas of his teacher, to train as a businessman with a view to taking over his own firm in Alexandria – the son, whose will was broken over and over again, henceforth sought fathers and father substitutes wherever he could find them. One must want the Führer! It fits into the picture of this complicated relationship that, of all the Hohenzollern kings, Rudolf Hess felt a particular admiration for Friedrich Wilhelm I, a blustering *roi sergent* with a fatherly roughness and strictness who has been interpreted in literature as a father figure.[13] When Rudolf Hess volunteered for the Army at the outbreak of the First World War he was seeking to escape not only from the hated commercial career, but above all from the demands of his own father figure. He could not, of course, escape from himself.

What military service with its clear-cut relationships of dependence gave him, Hess later sought and found again in dependence upon his teacher Karl Haushofer, before his meeting with Hitler in 1920 created that 'almost magical' attachment of which his wife has spoken.[14] She has left a description of an evening when Hess came back from a meeting at which Hitler had spoken; Hess, who in his despair at the lost war and the downfall of the Fatherland seldom laughed and 'really was a string taut to the point of snapping, on which the fateful song of Germany's distress was unendingly played', rushed into the *pension* in Schwabing in which they were living and kept on shouting, 'the man, the man', laughing ecstatically. Another account, written later, still gives a hint of the hysteria that went with this overwhelming, almost religious experience. 'He was like a new man, lively, radiant, no longer gloomy, not despondent. Something completely new, something stirring must have happened to him.'[15] This description reveals the inequality of the two sides to the encounter. On the one hand, the demagogue sure of achieving the desired effect; on the other, the unstable neurotic who has nothing with which to counter the man he faces, however hard he tries to hide his own lack of substance behind the pose of rugged solidity.

Characteristically, the first articulate sound in Hess's political career is a hero-worshipping defence of Hitler, who had been accused of embezzlement and dictatorial egotism in a pamphlet issued as part of a factional dispute inside the party. Soon afterward Hess won a prize for an essay on the subject 'What must the man be like who will lead Germany back to the heights again?' In it he described the future great dictator according to his idealised picture of Hitler:

Profound knowledge of all matters of state and of history, the ability to learn from it, faith in the purity of his own cause and in ultimate victory, and an indomitable will to give him the power to carry away audiences with his speeches and cause the masses to cry out to him in jubilation. For the sake of the salvation of the nation he will not shrink from employing the weapons of his opponents, demagogy, slogans, marches through the streets. He himself has nothing in common with the masses, is all personality like every great man. The power of personality radiates something that puts those around him under its spell and spreads in ever-widening circles. The people are yearning for a real leader, free from all party fraud, for a pure leader with inner truthfulness . . .

On every occasion the leader demonstrates his courage. This produces blind trust in the organised power; through this he achieves dictatorship. When necessity demands he does not shrink from shedding blood. Great questions are always decided by blood and iron. He has nothing in view but to attain his goal, even if he has to trample on his closest friends in order to reach it. . . .

190

Thus we have the picture of the dictator: sharp of mind, clear and true, passionate and yet controlled, cold and bold, thoughtful and conscious of his aims when making decisions, uninhibited in swiftly putting them into execution, ruthless towards himself and others, mercilessly hard and then again soft in his love of his people, tireless in work, with a steel fist in a velvet glove, capable last of all of conquering himself.

We do not yet know when 'the man' will intervene to save us. But millions feel that he is coming.[16]

Soon after their first meeting, Hess had allied himself personally very closely with Hitler; his attachment to Hitler was henceforth 'set above' all other relationships.[17] While they were both imprisoned in Landsberg, Hitler dictated to him parts of his ideological testament *Mein Kampf*, and it was no doubt here that the dominating idea of *Lebensraum* found its way into National Socialist ideology; for through Karl Haushofer, who kept up a lively contact with the prisoners, the original idea of a political geography under the catchword 'geopolitics' had undergone an imperialistic transformation into a 'pseudo-scientific expansionist philosophy'.[18] It offered the humiliated national spirit the idea that the destiny of Germany would be decided in the East and thus added a fundamental ideological category of National Socialism, that of 'space', to that of 'race'. These two ideas, linked by that of struggle, constituted the only more or less fixed structural elements in the intricate tactical and propagandist conglomerate of the National Socialist *Weltanschauung*.

Acting as intermediary between Haushofer and Hitler was the most important and virtually the only personal contribution Rudolf Hess made towards the birth and shaping of National Socialism. Up to 1932 he held no rank in the party but belonged rather to Hitler's personal retinue, as head of his private chancellery. As was his wish, he stood in the Führer's shadow, high enough for his secretly burning ambition and yet as concealed as his insurmountable shyness demanded. To most people's surprise, in December 1932, after the fall of Gregor Strasser, Hitler thrust him a little out of this shadow to head the newly formed Political Central Commission, and very soon afterwards, in April 1933, appointed him his deputy. 'Up to then,' as the *Frankfurter Zeitung* wrote, 'he had been credited only with the tasks of an adjutant, or more accurately, absolutely no mental picture has been connected with his name.'[19]

His image remained blurred, even after he had entered the cabinet at the end of 1933 as a kind of minister for the party. His innocence kept him from joining his former colleagues in the wholehearted intrigue for power; he simply wanted to be loyal and to serve the Führer. He was often called 'the conscience of the party', but in his undemanding readiness to serve he was grossly overestimated.[20] He was incapable of taking any moral initiative, since for him the highest morality lay in the 'blindly trusting subservience' of which he had spoken, and he regarded himself as a tool of 'the man', for whom he was prepared to make any sacrifice of conscience. Even during the so-called period of struggle he had said nothing to Hitler about the excesses of the brown-shirted columns, for fear of paralysing his 'working energy and joy in taking decisions'; expressions of concern he dismissed with the revealing reproach that they sprang from 'an intellectual tendency to criticism'.[21] Now he reacted in exactly the same way. Because of his powerlessness and his hungry loyalty to his Führer, he soon found himself downgraded to a channel for petty grievances, and after he had failed to get into the political power game by means of moves to reform the Reich, nothing was left to him but subordinate representative functions. He was allowed to deliver the annual Christmas speech, to welcome VDA (German expatriate) delegations, to give coffee parties for mothers of large numbers of children, and alongside charitable duties to preside over second-level congresses. It was also his privilege to announce the Führer from the tribunal at mass meetings, and this is the picture most of his contemporaries have of him: Hess standing there with his arm outstretched, watching his Führer mounting towards him, his eyes wide with happiness at so much power in another, enjoying his own subservience. His hunger for faith, which took its pretexts and stimulants where it could find them, drew additional satisfaction from the pseudo-sciences and occult wisdoms that flourished upon the contempt for reason energetically fostered by National Socialism. He was convinced the stars ruled human destiny, had diagrams worked out for him by an old soothsayer, and devoted himself earnestly to the tortuous efforts of the practitioners of terrestrial radiations, animal magnetism, pendulum diagnosis, and the various means of foretelling the future.[22] When he flew to Britain his pockets were filled with medicaments and drugs, mostly of a homeopathic nature, among them an elixir supposed to have been brought from Tibet by Sven Hedin.[23]

He was saved from being ridiculous, in the high office he held with such a total lack of knowledge of the mechanics of power, solely by his personal integrity, which he maintained in the face of every temptation. With his own peculiar fondness for lapidary profundity he once declared, 'He climbs highest who does not know where he is climbing to.'[24] By following this precept, which merely clothed in a phrase his own uncertainty in handling power, he had thrown away the influence he had acquired more or less by chance, and he carried no further weight within the top leadership. With his concealed ambition, this undoubtedly pained him; Hans Frank said he was always waiting 'for the Führer to recognise his reticence' and give it preference, especially, over the noisy 'courting of publicity' by Göring, who as the 'Second Man' was displacing the nominal 'Deputy' in public favour.[25] 'Decent, but sick and indecisive,' was Rosenberg's verdict on Hess, and his secretary frequently caught him gazing into space with a blank look in his eyes.[26] With his deep-set eyes in a lumpy, almost rectangular face, the sombreness of sleepless nights and the zealot-like hint of ecstatic rapture, which all his artificial hardness and simplicity could not hide, he looked rather like a master of devotional exercises who has had dealings with demons and has fought down his doubts and fears in long-drawn-out penances. At the end of 1940 *Das Reich* published a character study of Hess which naturally deduced 'energy', 'self-discipline' and 'austere firmness' from his features, but also stated, 'Hess can be silent and keep secrets.'[27]

In fact, the neglected deputy of the Führer was already preparing for the enterprise that dumbfounded an incredulous world on May 10, 1941. With a kind of confused heroism he secretly flew to Britain in the middle of the war with a personal peace proposal to the Duke of Hamilton, about whom he knew nothing. The essence of the plan was that Germany should be given a free hand for its *Lebensraum* politics within Europe and in return would guarantee the undiminished continuation of the British Empire.[28]

While the British noted these proposals without comment, and shut Hess up as a prisoner of war, Hitler was profoundly shocked and announced that if Hess returned he should be 'put in a madhouse or shot'.[29] During a conference on May 13 Hitler was 'in tears and looked ten years older', while Goebbels intimated that Hess's flight was 'more serious than the desertion of an army corps'.[30] A party memorandum published the same day spoke of 'an illness that has been going on for years', of 'traces of a mental breakdown' and 'hallucinations'; yet Hitler only eighteen months before, in his speech of September 1, 1939, had called upon the German people to place 'blind trust' in his successor-designate as Führer.[31] By a personal call from his Foreign Minister he had his Italian allies informed immediately that 'he and his colleagues had been utterly taken aback by Hess's enterprise. It was the act of a madman. Hess had been suffering for a long time from a gall-bladder complaint and had fallen into the hands of naturopaths and mesmerists, who had caused his condition to become progressively worse.'[32] Meanwhile those left behind vied with one another in casting ridicule and contempt upon their ex-fellow leader. Rudolf Semmler, a member of Goebbels' immediate staff, has given a revealing description of this process from within the Propaganda Minister's private circle, which at the same time throws light on the mutual relationships of the National Socialist leaders:

Goebbels spoke of Hess's mental illness and then described the comedy of Hess and his wife, who had been trying for years to produce an heir. No one knew for sure whether the child was really his. Hess was alleged to have been with his wife to astrologers, cartomancers, and other workers of magic and to have drunk all kinds of mixtures and potions before they were successful in begetting a child.

Frau Goebbels remembered that Frau Hess had told her for five or six years in succession that she was at last going to have a child – generally because some prophet had predicted it. When the child arrived, Hess danced for joy. All the Gauleiters were instructed to send the Deputy Führer a sack of earth from each Gau. This earth was scattered under a specially made cradle, so that the child symbolically started his life on German soil. Goebbels added that he himself had seriously considered – as Gauleiter of Berlin – whether he would not do best to send a Berlin paving stone.[33]

The contemptuous or bitter comments on Hess's action concealed rather than revealed his motives. Now it may be taken as almost beyond question that he had a whole series of motives, virtually all of them of a depressive character. According to the Nuremberg court psychiatrist Douglas M. Kelley, Hess as early as 1940 was in a mental state 'not far removed from a severe nervous breakdown'.[34] Hess himself declared in England that he had reached this 'most serious decision of his life' after 'an endless series of children's coffins with weeping mothers behind them' had repeatedly appeared before his eyes.[35] It is possible that dismay at the ruthless extermination policy in Poland may also have played a part.[36] The psychologists have further pointed out that the flight may be attributed to the discovery 'that his "father-substitute", Hitler, was not a god but a cruel and violent man';[37] but against this, it is certain that Hess did not think of treason. It is much more probable that the motives first mentioned condensed among the wild phantasmagoria of his emotional life into a decision to perform an act of self-sacrifice for Führer and Fatherland in a deed of constructive disobedience. Also his self-esteem, which after the first unexpected rise to eminence had been for so many years repeatedly wounded in the ambiance of prolific 'mothers' and VDA treasurers, may have been partly responsible for an action through which – as Baldur von Schirach commented – he would hope to become 'the most important man in the world'.[38]

Meanwhile his sober reception by the British government, who totally ignored the sensational nature of the event, quickly shattered such hopes. This disillusionment, which comes through clearly in Hess's written account of his stay in England, manifestly brought into the open the paranoid elements long present in his personality. According to one of his doctors, Hess declared in extreme agitation after barely a fortnight that he felt he was surrounded by murderers, and a week later his paranoia had constructed out of the normal day-to-day events around him a catalogue of devilish torments, from which he tried to escape at the end of July by attempting suicide.[39] Hess's own description of his stay in England makes it sound as though the author had found his way into Dr Bondi's cabinet of horrors. In conformity with his in any case hypochondriac nature, he suspected poison at every meal so that at table he would sometimes quickly change plates with a neighbour.[40] In sealed envelopes he preserved pieces of blotting paper saturated with remains of food.[41] He hid scraps of paper all over his room and from time to time lay with his fingers in his ears, smiling to himself, and saying, 'I'm thinking.'[42]

'When the signs of poisoning mounted up,' Hess wrote, 'in my desperation I scratched the lime from the walls in the hope that this would neutralise the effect of the poisons, but without success.' In his food he analysed not only 'soap, dishwater, dung and rotten fish', but also 'petroleum and carbolic acid'. 'The worst thing,' he continues, 'were glandular secretions of camels and pigs. The crockery was full of bone splinters, and thousands of little splinters of stone were mixed with the vegetables.' He was allegedly submitted unprotected to the scorching rays of the sun, and as a torture he was made to stand 'for hours' in the smoke of fires. Mountains of stinking fish heads were tipped out in front of his window, and after he one day discovered a shady bench nearby, where he went to sit for several days away from all the noise to read, a dead bull with its throat cut was suddenly lying there. 'They put substances in my evening meal that robbed me of sleep,' and 'Outside my garden moonstruck men wandered up and down with loaded guns – moonstruck men surrounded me in the house, and when I went for a walk moonstruck men went before and behind me.'[43] From this ghostly world Rudolf Hess fled in autumn 1943 into the night of amnesia, after having previously shown isolated signs of loss of memory and diminished concentration.[44] According to his own statements, even the things closest to him had vanished from his memory: his family, his role in the party, his parents' house in Alexandria, his father, Haushofer, Hitler. He did not awake from his amnesia until February 4, 1945, when he declared to the doctor who had been summoned that he had an important statement to make to the world. The Jews, he announced, possessed a secret power. They were able to hypnotise people. Their magical influence led the victim to commit criminal actions against his will. Among those hypnotised were Winston Churchill, the men responsible for the attempt on Hitler's life on July 20, 1944, the King of Italy, the doctors and his guards, and himself, Rudolf Hess. 'In order to gain propaganda material against Germany,' the Jews had actually gone so far as to 'cause the guards in the German concentration camps, by the use of a secret chemical, to treat the inmates after the manner of the GPU.'[45] A few hours later he made a fresh attempt at suicide.

Then things became even more confused. Again and again the shadows he tried to grasp eluded him. From the churned-up depths he dredged the intelligence that the Jews had instigated his attempted suicide because he had revealed their secret. Then he claimed triumphantly that his loss of memory had only been simulated, 'a big act', as he later wrote from Nuremberg.[46] Four days later he went on hunger strike and published a declaration to the German and British governments that he wished to die and to be conveyed to Germany in full Luftwaffe uniform.

Whatever he did or said from this moment on was devoted to the attempt to gain the attention that everyone denied him. His renewed assertions at Nuremberg that his claim to have lost his memory and regained it, and all the rest, were nothing but bluff, part of a helpless attempt to escape from the chaos of inner conflicts that he could no longer master. His unbroken faith in the Führer, his own branding as a traitor and madman, the discovery of the regime's crimes, the meeting with his former colleagues: he could not stand up to these contradictions and emotional conflicts. But his stubborn silence before the court and his occasional announcement of a 'great disclosure' were unquestionably the belated dramatic gestures of a man who found himself taken seriously by no-one but his doctors. In writing of his stay in England he concluded that the war of nerves to which he was subjected was an attempt to wring out of him an anti-German declaration, but he had stood fast against all temptations and blackmail.[47] Here too he deluded himself that he had an importance which the British government was by no means prepared to accord him. It looks as though all his actions from his flight to Britain to the gesture of demonstrative contempt with which he received his sentence at Nuremberg sprang from a desperate attempt to regain, by the most spectacular means available, that personal foundation which he had once given up, to re-create the lines of an individual personality that had vanished in the blaze of his faith in the Führer. But whatever he regained added up, significantly enough, only to fragments of a second-rate imitation of the Führer. The Führer, the world was supposed to understand, would have behaved in just this way if he had ever appeared at Nuremberg, just as proud, just as reserved, just as full of imperious rejection; and he, Hess, was still his legitimate deputy, in spite of the self-important, theatrical behaviour of Göring, who could not abandon his histrionics and aspired to the level of his judges. Meanwhile Rudolf Hess remained silent, his burnt-out eyes gazing contemptuously over the scene; at times he covered them with his hand or stared dreamily at the same page of a book lying on his knees.[48]

Only during his final speech did he return once again from his silent world, to deliver his monologue with his eyes and voice directed towards some distant interlocutor in the void: fragments of a banal revelation about Jewry, secret chemical preparations, the Moscow Trials, and the glassy eyes of his guards in England. When Göring whispered to him to stop, he exclaimed out loud, 'Don't interrupt me.' Then he said:

> It was granted to me for many years of my life to live and work under the greatest son whom my nation has produced in the thousand years of its history. Even if I could I would not expunge this period from my existence. I regret nothing. If I were standing once more at the beginning I should act once again as I did then, even if I knew that at the end I should be burnt at the stake. No matter what men do, I shall one day stand before the judgment seat of the Almighty. I shall answer to him, and I know that he will acquit me.[49]

He did not regain his lost self. The last sentence reiterated almost verbatim a phrase with which Hitler had ended his final plea to the Munich People's Court in 1924.[50] The desire for rehabilitation, for reinstatement in the community of the faithful, from which he knew he had been ejected by Hitler himself, dominated him with a power that can be comprehended only in religious terms. On his ravaged features, which mirrored the hunger for 'the man', after the horrors and exaltations which he had experienced at his side, he bore the visible signs of rejection. 'Why don't they let me die?' he asked one of the guards after the verdict.[51] Life was henceforth devoid of meaning for him, after he had tried in his final attempt to appear as Hitler's successor to wrest some meaning from it once more.

And then, unexpectedly, he found himself accepted once more into the fold after all. From Erich Kempka, Hitler's chauffeur, he learnt that shortly before the end, speaking of his former deputy, the Führer had said 'that at least in all these years it had been possible to introduce *one* idealist of the purest water indelibly into history'. Hess had to 'summon up all his manliness in order not to weep', he wrote afterwards.[52]

He was forgiven; he was once more with his father.

He embodied one of the fundamental weaknesses of the type susceptible to totalitarianism: he was incapable of living on his own. Without the support and certitudes of ethical or religious ties in his early life, he continually sought substitute satisfaction for his irrational needs, and he finally found a new orientation and a new faith in the overwhelming apparition of 'the man'. For him freedom and independent existence meant terrifying exposure. There is much to suggest that the confusion into which he lapsed after his independent trip to Britain was rooted in this constitutional servitude; that he took flight into neurosis from the isolation into which he was plunged by the loss of his Führer-god, for the symptoms of his mental illness evidently lasted no longer than the feeling of having been repudiated by Hitler. A psychiatric report of May 27, 1948 states that 'Hess at the present time is not suffering from any mental disturbance' and is 'perfectly normal'.[53] The letters to his family which he wrote during his imprisonment in Spandau confirm this. It is possible, therefore, that what we see in him is nothing other than an exemplary failure of self-determination, the psychopathology of bewilderment in the face of freedom. This alone would make him, beyond all politically sensational aspects, the 'most famous psychiatric case of the first half of the century', as he has been called.[54]

The American court psychiatrist Douglas M. Kelley reported from Nuremberg that his French colleague, in order to have a specimen of his handwriting, asked Hess for his signature. Thereupon Hess 'wrote his name and immediately crossed it out again'. 'This,' we learn, 'happened several times.'[55]

Albert Speer
and the Immorality of the Technicians

The task which I have to fulfil is an unpolitical one. I felt comfortable in my work so long as my person and also my work were valued *solely* according to my specialist achievement.

Albert Speer
in a memorandum to Hitler

The processes of a people's demoralisation usually take place imperceptibly, concealed in the social structure. It is only in great upheavals that the seemingly firm shell of a society's self-assurance is broken and in the real state of its general consciousness laid bare. In the course of its breathtaking advances during the past hundred years technology has developed, along with its own ideology, its own morality, based upon earlier ideas of the autonomy of the scientific spirit. Not only technology itself but all technological work came to be held exempt from value-judgment, and just as there were supposed to be no 'evil' discoveries or inventions, so the technological genius remained untouched by the moral aspect of any relationship in which it might be involved. The fundamental and tacit assumption developed that technology does not serve any alien power; it is now itself power. Having long outgrown its original function as a tool, it is now no longer an instrument of power but the bearer of power.

Behind such convictions an ethical subjectivism was at work which looked down contemptuously upon public affairs and saw morality exclusively in the context of private life. Profoundly involved in the world of ends, its vision and thought were concentrated solely upon its self-given aims and left the management of the state to whoever wanted to bother with it. The satisfaction of personal good conduct within the narrowly restricted zone of individual action went hand in hand with renunciation of any knowledge of the effective environment within which all activity takes place. This attitude, which might be justified in an orderly world based upon unified convictions and criteria, became involved with the maelstrom of problems raised by the modern totalitarian systems beneath the surface of all traditional ideas. It became clear that there was something unsatisfactory about the sort of political naïvety that went with keeping oneself to oneself, doing whatever duty or professional code seemed to require, and taking no responsibility for the framework of force within which even strictly specialized

198

activities must operate;[1] the more so since totalitarian regimes specifically counted on that naïvety and depended on it for a good deal of their success.

The self-chosen isolation of the technological mind is one of the keys to its total readiness to serve, and the specialist who sees himself solely as a function in an environment which he neither sees nor wishes to see as a whole meets totalitarianism half-way. Hitler's vision of the future as a termite state[2] originated in this picture of the totally isolated man concerned exclusively with his limited objectives, and he carried this vision to its logical conclusion: an élite consciousness perpetually susceptible of being thus perverted. The first stages were seen in 1933, when countless people placed their technological and organisational skills at the service of the new masters without the slightest trace of disquiet, enabling the transition to the Third Reich to take place without friction in key social sectors – a striking illustration of that 'clicking into place' of the bureaucratic mechanism which Max Weber has described in his writings as the prerequisite for the seizure of power in a modern society.[3] It was a crucial step in the establishment of National Socialist power.

As almost no-one else under the Third Reich, Albert Speer, Hitler's architect and later Minister of Armaments, represented this type of the narrow specialist and his technocratic amorality, until both met their refutation in him. For it was not so much ambition, the lure of an exalted career, and the almost unlimited creative possibilities open to a court artist which kept him for so many years tied to a regime whose methods were bound to be repulsive to a man of his origins and character. It was predominantly his belief that the terrorism, of which he was well aware, the persecution of minorities, arbitrary decisions, concentration camps, aggression against other countries were not his business; all this was 'politics', whereas he was an architect, a technologist, an artist. Even at Nuremberg he still maintained that his 'task was a technological and economic one', not political, and to the question did he not, as an educated man, realise that the forcible transportation of foreign workers was contrary to the law of nations, he replied that he was an architect and all he knew about law was what he read in the papers.[4] It was entirely in keeping with this that although he regularly and credibly, before the Tribunal, repudiated the use of violence, he based this repudiation not upon humanitarian considerations but upon the practical point that it hindered his constant ministerial efforts to increase output.[5]

To see a figure like Albert Speer as an example of the work-obsessed artist's alienation from the world and his times would be a fundamental misunderstanding of the problems involved. For all his exceptional gifts, he was no *génie bête*, nor was he insensitive, unimaginative, or deaf to conscience. On the contrary, he was intelligent, life-orientated, and no doubt also sensitive, but imbued with the traditional anti-social indifference of the artist and technologist, which left him dead to all challenges of political origin. At the same time he sought to keep the imperious demands of the regime at a distance by pointing out that his was a non-political profession, and no doubt this was partly why he refused honorary rank in the SS.[6] Towards the end of the war, however, when he found himself faced with the self-destructive extremism of Hitler, Bormann and Goebbels, this argument manifestly would not do. For a time Speer tried to avoid a decision: his memoranda from that time ceaselessly reiterate that he wants to keep out of politics and emphatically document the untenable situation of a man who has sought to evade the consequence of a political policy which he has simultaneously played a prominent part in and ignored. It is true that he later stated privately at Nuremberg that in the end it was Hitler who transgressed against the principles of selfless expertise and pursued only his own self-interest and desire for fame;[7] but this was the fallacy that, in a far more dishonest form, permeated the apologia put out by Hitler's bourgeois-conservative partners. From the day he set out to gain dominion over Germany until his withdrawal into the concrete cavern deep under the Reich Chancellery, the slogan 'a war of ashes', and his end in 200 litres of blazing petrol, Hitler was always consistent, never once deviating from his chosen path. Albert Speer, on the other hand, broke away at the turn of the year 1944–45, when in joining the resistance movement and the preparations for the assassination of Hitler he sought to correct the fallacy of his life: that one can simultaneously sit at the table of power and not sit at it.

This equivocation is typical of Speer's actual position among Hitler's henchmen. He always seemed a stranger, as though he had wandered in by mistake among all these Machiavellian or booty-hungry petty bourgeois, and even his appearance showed how far he was from the type that embodied the National Socialist movement at all levels: the brown-uniformed political leader who, with broad neck and seat, stood firm in his own toughly trained fat and noisily, humourlessly and violently pursued his own interests along with those of the 'National Revolution'. Education, intelligence and also unusual firmness of character made Speer a genuine exception. Although his career contained all the preconditions that lead to corruption of character, he maintained his personal integrity to the end as well as a readiness to say what he thought. The historian H. R. Trevor-Roper, for all the harshness of his general evaluation, says it is a 'mystery' that Speer, after so many personal triumphs, never renounced his objective and critical-intellectual attitude.[8] With some justification he has been credited with the rare virtue of civil courage,[9] which emphatically distinguished him from Hitler's muted and subservient entourage. In fact Hitler's stuffy demonism invariably tried its power in vain against Speer's practical expertise and clear-headedness.

Speer's exceptional quality comes out in an account by one of his former colleagues, Dietrich Stahl, of their first meeting in autumn 1944. 'For the first time,' Stahl stated at Nuremberg, 'I found to my complete surprise a leading and responsible man who saw the real situation soberly and clearly, and who not only had the courage to say things that put his life in danger but was also prepared to take resolute action.'[10]

Despite a rationalism that was fired by concrete objects rather than ideologies, Speer was capable of the sort of enthusiastic belief out of which devotion to high (and often horrible) ideals grows. He never, of course, lent himself to the undignified Byzantine fawning that Hitler increasingly demanded and which his company of favourites so readily offered. He seemed always to be conscious that he was not like the rest of them, and nothing demonstrates his position as an outsider among Hitler's henchmen more clearly than Göring's remark at Nuremberg: 'We ought never to have trusted him!'[11] It was undoubtedly the whole range of these qualities and circumstances that gained him the respect of many, including many opponents. Thus for example the conspirators of July 20, 1944 placed Hitler's minister on their cabinet list, although he had never sought contact with them, and even in the cross-questioning by the chief American prosecutor at Nuremberg, Justice Robert H. Jackson, an element of personal respect comes through.[12] Speer was almost the only one of the accused to confess his own failure, without prevarication and without transparent excuses, openly to admit his responsibility, and to answer with a simple 'No!' the question: did he wish to plead that he was carrying out the Führer's orders? 'In so far as Hitler gave me orders and I carried them out, I accept responsibility for them; however, I did not carry out all his orders.'[13]

Unlike the majority of his fellow-accused, he declared a residue of loyalty to Hitler, in spite of all the contradictions in their relationship, and even after their bitter clashes during the last months. In fact he owed a great deal to Hitler, who had taken an intense personal liking to the young architect after meeting him through Goebbels. Speer came of an old family of master-builders, had joined the NSDAP in 1931, and in addition to a few minor undertakings as a private architect, had carried out two commissions for the Berlin Gauleiter's office the following year.[14] At the beginning of 1933 the technical arrangements for the staging of the major rally of May 1 on the Tempelhofer Feld were entrusted to him. Here he first showed his skill in improvisation, using rapidly erected flagpoles and, in the final display in the evening, inventive lighting effects to create the atmospheric pageantry desired by his employers. He thereby gave to National Socialist mass rallies a style he continued to develop for the demonstrations at the harvest festivals on the Bückeberg, during the Tannenberg celebrations, and finally during the parades that formed part of the Reich Party Rallies. He showed exceptional insight into mass psychology in perfecting the NSDAP's style of public parade, which had hitherto relied too much on sheer size and concentration of effort. He combined block-line buildings, stairways, pylons, walls of banners and the famous domes of light – circles of searchlights around the arena that created a moving spatial effect as they shone up under the night sky – with arrangements of human masses to create a monumental liturgy which stylised petty bourgeois longing for the impressive and perfectly mirrored the psychology of the movement. He still has his imitators, particularly in the communist world.

These successes launched Speer on a soaring career which brought him, still under thirty, a multitude of offices and commissions. In 1934 he was commissioned to design the Reich Party Rally grounds at Nuremberg. The same year he became head of the 'Beauty of Work' Department, and at the beginning of 1937 he was appointed General Architectural Inspector for the Reich capital, responsible, as Hitler stressed, for systematically 'turning Berlin into a real and true capital of the German Reich'.[15] Together with Speer, Hitler, now catching up with his earlier dreams of becoming an architect, planned the redesigning of the other German cities with huge buildings and parks in an imitative style in which pseudo-classical elements, excessive in size, and lack of charm combined to create a solemn emptiness. The Königsplatz in Munich or the New Reich Chancellery, said by a contemporary to be 'the first state building to have foreshadowed the shape of all future buildings', as well as countless sketches, designs and half-finished works, gave and still give an oppressive idea of these plans.[16] Speer proved a brilliant executant of the line inspired by Hitler, that of insane monumentality. The same writer speaks of 'buildings of faith', in which 'the Führer's word is converted into a "word of stone" '. Speer willingly transferred his personal admiration for his patron and Führer to the latter's architectural ideas, of which it might rightly be said, as the wife of party architect Paul Ludwig Troost said of Hitler's views on art in general, that he had got stuck at the year 1890.[17] Hitler's taste for the pompous decadence of a painter like Hans Makart was in keeping with his liking for the vapid classicism of the Vienna Parliament Building which, together with the Opera House and the insignificant but ostentatious buildings on the Ringstrasse, he recalled as the most powerful architectural impressions of his youth in Vienna. He could stand and admire them for hours, he wrote.[18] The ornate and forced, the smooth, undemanding and technically precise, Richard Wagner and the allegory 'The Sin' by Franz von Stuck, a student of Piloty, were pointers to his artistic taste, which, with the vengefulness of the failed art student, he elevated to a norm both in governmental cultural politics and in official buildings.[19]

At times there were evidently open differences of opinion between himself and Speer; for when Wilhelm Furtwängler once remarked that 'it must be wonderful to build in such a grand style according to one's own ideas', Speer is said to have replied ironically, 'Just imagine someone saying to you: It is my unshakable wish that henceforth the "Ninth" shall only be performed on the mouth organ.'[20] All planning was monotonously and indistinguishably determined by 'gigantic' proportions, after the traditional ambition of dictators to create in huge buildings monuments that would outlast the short-lived dominion of their own persons. This aim rings out over and over again in Hitler's speeches. At the Reich Party Rally of 1937, he stated:

Because we believe in the everlasting continuance of this Reich, in so far as we can reckon by human standards, these works too shall be eternal, that is to say they shall satisfy eternal demands not only in the grandeur of their conception but also in the lucidity of their ground plans, the harmony of their proportions.

Therefore these buildings are not to be conceived for the year 1940, nor for the year 2000, but are to tower up like the cathedrals of our past into the millennia to come.

And if God perhaps makes today's poets and singers into fighters, then at least he has given these fighters architects who will see to it that the success of their fight receives everlasting substantiation in the documents of a unique great art. This state shall not be a power without culture nor a force without beauty.[21]

Such considerations were reflected in the designs prepared under Hitler's sustained and fervent influence. He once said that if the First World War 'had not come he might have been – indeed probably would have been – one of Germany's leading architects, if not the leading architect'.[22] The extant plans show every sign of arrogant megalomania. A domed hall was to be erected a hundred feet high to seat 100,000. Among the party buildings designed to give the city of Nuremberg 'its future and hence everlasting style' was a congress hall for 60,000, a stadium 'such as the world has never seen before',[23] and a parade ground for a million people. The excavations alone would have called for 40 miles of railway track, 600 million bricks would have been required for the foundations, and the outer walls would have been 270 feet high. Hitler paid particular attention to the durability of the bricks and other materials, so that thousands of years later the buildings should bear witness to the grandeur of his power as the pyramids of Egypt testified to the power and splendour of the Pharaohs.[24] 'But if the movement should ever fall silent,' he declared as he laid the foundation stone for the congress hall at Nuremberg, 'then this witness here will still speak for thousands of years. In the midst of a sacred grove of ancient oaks men will then admire in reverent awe this first giant among the buildings of the Third Reich.'[25] And he remarked effusively to Hans Frank, 'They will be so gigantic that even the pyramids will pale before the masses of concrete and colossi of stone which I am erecting here. I am building for eternity, for, Frank, we are the last Germans. If we were ever to disappear, if the movement were to pass away after many centuries, there would be no Germany any more.' The desire to convey to those distant millennia the impression of his own greatness, when 'perhaps the Huns or the barbarians will rule over Europe', also revealingly prompted him to order a sketch to be made showing the projected congress hall as a vast ruin.[26]

In spite of the growing number of offices he held in the progress of his career, Speer's position and influence were based exclusively on his close personal relationship with Hitler; and in the knowledge that he had no institutional power but only a position of confidence, he kept well out of the rivalries of the leading office-holders. His ambition remained non-political, and up to 1942, when he was appointed a minister, he had 'never made a speech in his life'.[27] At the same time he was by temperament more unselfish than the warring holders of top-level power, more attracted by the tasks than the power.

During all these years Hitler's relations with Speer had a remarkably sentimental character in striking contrast to the coldness and self-interest of his other human contacts. Perhaps he saw in the young architect, with his energy, brilliance and ability to achieve extraordinary results with apparent ease, his other self, freely developed and without the twists placed by a malevolent destiny to which, in his all-pervading self-pity, he still ascribed the failure of his early ambitions. In an essay written in 1939 Hitler paid Speer an unusual compliment; he described him as 'an architect of genius' and along with his 'artistic talent' praised especially his 'unparalleled organisational ability'.[28] It has rightly been pointed out that Speer was one of the few exceptions to Hitler's deeply rooted suspicion of men of middle-class origin, and Speer himself stated, 'If Hitler had had friends, I should have been his friend.'[29] Moreover he was not untouched by the numerous expressions of personal favour Hitler so openly showed him. He clearly revered Hitler at this time and, in his unworldliness as an artist and technologist, saw no reason to distrust his emotions. In so far as reality contradicted the somewhat fanciful ideas he had of it, he simply shut it out. There was nothing of which, in his mixture of political innocence and restricted specialist outlook, he was less aware than that he had become the accomplice of a criminal regime and that Hitler's friendship was a highly dubious distinction. In his first public speech, on February 24, 1942, he declared almost dejectedly that he was making a great sacrifice. 'Until recently I have been moving in an ideal world.'[30]

He was thirty-six when, after the mysterious death of Fritz Todt, he took over the Ministry for Armament and Munitions. He had already from time to time been concerned with problems of organisation and transport, and he set about his new tasks energetically and with unorthodox solutions, quickly overcoming the first critical hold-ups in the mechanism of the German armaments industry. Improvising with typical courage, he bridged over transport links that had been destroyed, rebuilt factories, established new industries, went personally to the front to find out for himself the advantages or weaknesses of the weapons and equipment used by the troops, and, as Goebbels noted in his diary, 'rode rough-shod over the high military gentlemen'.[31] He combined an unbureaucratic breadth of vision with an 'instinct for the right way' which he recognised he possessed.[32] He reshaped his ministry according to his own unconventional ideas, replacing the hierarchy of civil servants by the so-called 'typical Speer set-up', a qualified group of relatively independent experts with initiative, vigour and specialised knowledge. His efforts quickly bore fruit. He not only succeeded, despite air raids of increasing violence, in keeping the transport system as a whole functioning right up to the end of the war, but production rose from month to month and, in face of all difficulties, reached its peak in summer 1944. Aircraft production climbed from 9,540 front-line machines in 1941 to 34,350 machines in 1944, and production of heavy tanks rose from 2,900 to 17,300.[33] Admittedly not all the statistics published by Speer are reliable; at the end of 1943, when the Red Army had just crossed the Dnieper, Goebbels asked suspiciously what had happened to all the extra production.[34] But Speer's successes spoke for themselves, and Hitler said his youngest minister was at the same time his 'most efficient minister'.[35] Without the efforts of Speer, who by 1943 had concentrated more than 80 per cent of German industrial capacity in his hands, Hitler would unquestionably not have been able to continue the war so long and might possibly, as Speer himself conjectured, have had to admit defeat as early as 1942 or 1943.[36]

This consideration clearly demonstrates the whole dubious nature of these efforts, and undoubtedly Speer gradually came to see this dichotomy, even if, in his technocratic self-assurance, he may not have sensed it personally. In his speeches at this period he forever quotes production figures, output, productive capacity, as though intoxicated by these deceptive credit balances, and the pseudo-military jargon in which he described industrial production – 'the mobilisation of output reserves', 'the breaking down of bottlenecks', and so on – played with figures that were entirely detached from political reality and left no room for intrusive thought.[37] Not until spring 1944, when he was ill for several months, does he seem to have broken away from his specialist fixations and cast off the habit of thinking exclusively in terms of achievement and efficiency. For it was obviously these months that released in him those elements of inner conflict which from now on never left him. According to his own statement, he had already, at the height of his success in summer 1940, recognised the first signs of the inner flaws and despicable characteristics of National Socialist rule: its boastful arrogance, its greed, and the excesses of the bad winner.[38] Nevertheless he had kept up his expert's indifference, had continued to satisfy his ambition in the midst of people whom he was beginning to despise, and to build for the regime the temple of its millennial expectations. Now he began to discover that the economic and technical power at his disposal brought with it political responsibility. He may have come to this point through the realisation that in the meantime every increase in production consumed the nation's basic substance and could only be maintained for a limited time. Moreover, at this stage of a war that was being waged by ever more total methods, he must have been persuaded predominantly by concrete facts; he must have had a technocrat's concern over the past and threatened destruction of so many factories, mines, roads, bridges and transport installations. Doubt was increased still further when he saw Hitler, after summer 1944, begin 'to lay the main blame for the course of the war upon the failure of the German people and in no case upon himself', and under the slogan 'victory or annihilation' take steps to convert the increasingly senseless prolongation of the war into preparations for total self-destruction. With this discovery Speer entered the 'crisis of his life'.[39]

Loyalty struggled with his sense of responsibility. He had a lot to thank Hitler for. The distinction of personal affection, the generous provision of artistic opportunities, influence, fame: all this had meant a great deal to him. But he had always preserved an idealistic readiness to place the cause above persons, and his sober, calculating temperament was permeated by a very German, romantically tinged enthusiasm that felt behind trite, sentimental sayings the whole weight of a categorical imperative. His later memoranda to Hitler prove this very clearly; in one of them he confessed that he could work only with a feeling of inner decency, with conviction and faith,[40] preconditions which Hitler now palpably placed in question. For a short time he attempted to blur the alternatives and avoid a decision between personal emotional attachments and the interests of the country and its people, for example in his memorandum of September 20, 1944. But a few weeks earlier he had already begun to circumvent the measures which Hitler had ordered for the destruction of areas threatened by the advancing enemy.[41] In an effort to make the Führer more reasonable and alert him to the breakdown of the war effort, now inevitable for economic and technical reasons, Speer wrote innumerable memoranda. In one dated January 30, 1945 beginning 'The war is lost' he tried to combat the illusions of the fantasy world of the Führer's headquarters. He made a comprehensive analysis of the situation, but without achieving anything more than the henceforth unconcealed hostility of Bormann and also of Goebbels, who for a long time had stood by him.[42] Hitler, on the other hand, in view of the opening sentence, refused to read the memorandum at all.[43] Speer slipped into disfavour and thereupon, with typical independence, he began systematically to work against Hitler's plans for the annihilation of Germany. In spring 1945 the conflict took a dramatic turn. On March 18, when Speer handed in to the Führer's headquarters a memorandum predicting 'with certainty' the imminent 'final breakdown of the German economy' and stressing that it was the Führer's responsibility to ensure the conditions for the continued existence of the German people, there was a violent quarrel. The crux of it was summed up by Speer in a subsequent letter to Hitler:

When I handed you my memorandum on March 18 I was firmly convinced that the conclusions which I had drawn from the present situation for the preservation of our national strength would definitely meet with your approval. For you yourself once stated that it is the task of the government, in the event of losing a war, to preserve the nation from a heroic end.

Nevertheless you made statements to me in the evening from which, if I have not misunderstood them, it emerges clearly and unambiguously that if the war is lost the nation too will be lost. This fate is inescapable. It would not be necessary to take any account of the basis which the nation needs for its survival on the most primitive level. On the contrary, it would be better to destroy even these things. For the nation would have proved itself the weaker and then the future would belong exclusively to the stronger nation of the East. Those who remained after the struggle would in any case only be the inferior; for the good would have died. After these words I was deeply shaken. And when a day later I read the demolition order and shortly after that the evacuation order, I saw in them the first steps towards the carrying out of these purposes.[44]

While Hitler's egocentricity clearly took the form of disappointed hatred of his own people, Speer went to work openly against his plans. Although his authority to give orders was expressly withdrawn, he travelled to zones near the front, convinced the local authorities of the senselessness of the orders they had received, had explosives immersed in water, and supplied the controllers of important undertakings with submachine guns with which to protect themselves against the demolition squads. When eventually called to account by Hitler, he repeated that the war was lost. Hitler gave him twenty-four hours to think it over. But instead of an assurance that he had regained his faith in victory, Speer handed him a detailed memorandum analysing their mutual relationship and demanding withdrawal of the demolition order of March 19.[45] Nevertheless, he finally succeeded in propitiating Hitler to the extent of regaining his official powers. Exploiting the general confusion of orders, Speer then issued numerous instructions, some in the name of other authorities such as the Army High Command or the Reich Railways, some in his own name, which he withheld from Hitler and which at times merely served the purpose of intensifying the chaos and paralysing the work of destruction. At the same time he took steps to circumvent the intention of leading officials to escape responsibility by fleeing abroad.[46] Finally, in his 'despair', as he said, he evolved a plan to kill Hitler, along with the self-centred company that had buried itself in the bunkers of the Reich Chancellery in a mood of apocalyptic doom, by feeding poison gas into the underground ventilation system. Hitler, in Speer's view, 'had originally been called upon by the people', and 'he had no right to gamble away their destiny along with his own'.[47] But a last-minute alteration to the ventilation shaft carried out on Hitler's own instructions frustrated this plan. Once again Hitler had escaped an attempt on his life.

And yet this was not the end of their curious relationship. Many factors were involved. According to Speer's own confession, he feared to appear a coward; at the same time, no doubt, some isolated impulses of loyalty remained; and finally there was the psychological phenomenon that every period of enlightenment was succeeded by a relapse into the protective darkness of the old blind faith. In any case on April 23, 1945 Speer, filled with 'conflicting emotions', as he himself stated, flew into encircled, burning Berlin in order to say farewell to his colleagues and 'after all that had happened, to place myself at Hitler's disposal'.[48] Unhesitatingly, he admitted what he had done to circumvent the order of March 19. But instead of the expected outburst of rage, Hitler remained calm and seemed impressed by Speer's candour. He let him go unharmed, though his name disappeared from the cabinet list which Hitler drew up a few days later as part of his will.

'They were all under his spell,' Speer said of Hitler's leading henchmen. 'They obeyed him blindly, with no will of their own, whatever the medical term for this phenomenon may be.'[49] But he was the exception, the only man in Hitler's immediate entourage who refused to sacrifice either his own will or the guidance of his own reason and character, as the majority did so eagerly. The apologetic nature of the memoirs and autobiographical notes the others wrote at this time set forth the thesis of Hitler's compulsive power and the ostensibly irresistible magic of his will. Speer's example proves that it was rather the weakness and insignificance of the men who made up his entourage that ensured the 'Führer' his unchallenged superiority right to the end.

However, in spite of all his distinguishing qualities, human and moral, Hugh R. Trevor-Roper has called Albert Speer 'the real criminal of Nazi Germany, for he, more than any other, represented that fatal philosophy which has made havoc of Germany and nearly shipwrecked the world. For ten years he sat at the very centre of political power but he did nothing.'[50] But this judgment is as mistaken about the structural characteristics of a highly industrialised society as it is about the nature of totalitarian regimes and the individual's power to work against them. In fact, until 1942 Speer neither sat at the real centre of political power in any relevant sense, nor did he 'do nothing'. But he did represent a type without which neither the National Socialist nor any other variety of modern totalitarianism could have succeeded: the expert who sought to guarantee himself an irreproachable existence by retreating into the ostensibly unpolitical position of his profession, confining himself to his work in order to glorify his inaction as 'doing his duty'. In so far as such men, however influential, kept their distance from the events of the day, wore no uniform, indulged in no acts of violence, promulgated no laws, and arrested no-one, they remained from a technical legal point of view free from tangible guilt. Nevertheless, having regard to their positions and potentialities, they did not do enough to prevent the establishment and spread of violence; they are open to the reproach of having refused to accept responsibility for what was going on. For a plea of duty amounts to very little in a state where uniforms are worn, acts of violence performed, and people arrested and killed. He who can appeal only to his own irreproachable behaviour cannot claim, however much personal satisfaction he may derive from doing so, that he has emerged from times like this uncorrupted. Furthermore, heroes are rare and in bad times weakness and blindness are for many a technique of survival. Such people are not on that account criminals.

Albert Speer admitted this failure. It took him a long time to appreciate this personal guilt, not merely from a specialist's traditional contempt for politics, but also because of the exceptional complexity of moral insights in a world of partial and divided responsibilities. Nevertheless he did not evade the final confrontation, and if he had greater power than others he also showed greater resolution.

He was sentenced at Nuremberg to twenty years' imprisonment. But his attempt to escape responsibility behind his role as a technocrat was not mentioned in the explanation of the verdict; for this is not a matter that lies within the jurisdiction of the criminal code, but one of conscience. Both under interrogation and through his defence counsel, he kept returning in a strangely compulsive manner to the problem of responsibility, which he emphatically admitted in a kind of belated reckoning up to be his 'self-evident duty':

> In my view there are two kinds of responsibility in the life of the state. One kind of responsibility is for one's own sector; for this one is, of course, entirely responsible. But over and above this I am of the opinion that for quite decisive matters there is and must be a collective responsibility, insofar as one is one of the leaders, for who else should bear responsibility for the course of events?[51]

Speer was found guilty on the grounds of his participation in the forced labour programme.

Hans Frank – Imitation of a Man of Violence

The German carries in his racial character a feature that must be taken infinitely seriously: an unusual need for justice and sensitivity concerning justice.

Hans Frank

We must not be squeamish when we hear the figure of 17,000 shot.

Hans Frank

Hans Frank was one of the most equivocal figures among the National Socialist top leadership, weak, unstable and full of strange contradictions. Behind the bloody image of the 'slayer of Poles' and the party's leading jurist we see, on closer inspection, an insecure and vacillating character; Frank's unrestrained veneration for the person of Hitler and for the party programme of the NSDAP – which throughout his life he completely misinterpreted in keeping with illusions rooted in theatrical idealism – carried him to the most abysmal depths of criminality. Governed by emotions and cranky ideas, ready to surrender himself and at the same time subject to sudden spells of self-destructive obstinacy springing from an awareness of normal standards from which in the last resort he could not escape, he seemed among all those cold manipulators of power as though made for the role of a sectarian, whose usual fate he actually avoided only with some difficulty. What prevented him from offering the ultimate challenge was solely a deeply rooted subservience and a remnant of devotion to the 'glorious shaper' Hitler, which he preserved even 'in sight of the gallows'. 'While I sit here in the solitude of Nuremberg [Adolf Hitler] goes striding through my earnest, profound thoughts as a concentrated, rich personality whose influence has attained gigantic proportions.'[1]

He never belonged to the innermost circle of the leadership; the stigma of middle-class origins, which only Speer and Ribbentrop really succeeded in overcoming, no doubt prevented that. Admittedly, any sociology of the National Socialist movement would be incomplete without a consideration of the educated man of upper middle class origin; this type certainly had its role to play, especially in the early phase of the party's history.[2] Nevertheless men of this stamp always stood a little outside the movement's true centres, which at no time received their decisive impulses from the Rauschnings, Darrés or Franks, but almost exclusively from the petty bourgeois prophets of violence and the extremist members of the war generation. The function of the 'middle class' leaders was solely to provide a backcloth of respectability and various forms of ideological cover for the movement's ruthless will to power. Prepared, for reasons outlined elsewhere in this book, to be fascinated by any romantically decked barbarism, they fluttered around this revolutionary movement, magically attracted by its strength and brutality and intoxicated by the new principles of order announced by the marching feet of the brown columns. Whatever pseudo-rational structure they contributed to the National Socialist ideology, strictly speaking they had no say in practical policy, and Hitler, to whom 'being educated and being weak' meant the same thing,[3] made little effort to hide his contempt for them.

Sensitive to the humiliations that went with a sense of belonging on sufferance, Frank hungered after acknowledgment and acceptance with full rights into the inner circle. He liked to boast of his special confidential relationship with Hitler and would claim, for example, that the Führer 'freely confided in him everything which he kept from even his closest political associates'.[4] Unstable and unsure of himself by nature, the prey of his own emotions, and with a markedly feminine character, Frank gazed with secret admiration at the men of violence around him, who obviously carried out every task entrusted to them without a moment's hesitation. Greedy for their approval, he imposed their role on himself, at times showing himself harder, more cynical and more merciless than they, Hitler's vassal who as Governor-General of Poland actually turned the country entrusted to him, both literally and figuratively, into that 'vandal Gau' of which he had once spoken. At the same time he lacked the tough nerves of the swashbucklers he imitated, the professional murderers – the Globocniks, Stroops and Krügers – repeatedly fell back on 'bourgeois' standards and, as Hitler contemptuously observed, was 'merely a lawyer like all the rest'.[5] He burned behind him bridges such as the others had never crossed, to the accompaniment of dreadful mental contortions intended to drown the inner voices that disturbed him.

From this situation of conflict sprang the obvious disharmonies of his personality: the millionfold murderer, as others saw him; the servant and almost the martyr of justice, as he saw himself. The man who cried to the ruthless advocates of the overriding claims of the state that when justice is not supported 'the state too loses its moral backbone, it sinks into the abyss of night and horror. You can depend on it that I would rather die than give up this idea of justice,' and who, on the other hand, at almost the same time, considered it only worth a marginal note that in consequence of measures taken by him '1.2 million Jews will perish'.[6] The man who, in the vulgar phraseology characteristic of the officials responsible for the Final Solution, described his task as being to cleanse Poland of lice and Jews, and who then, in four sensational university lectures in summer 1942, stated in criticism of Hitler that 'no empire has ever been conceivable without justice – or contrary to justice'.[7] Although Frank's liking for highfalutin phrases repeatedly concealed his real convictions, it cannot be denied that behind this exhortation to respect justice there lay at least an emotional honesty. Frank the man of violence, on the other hand, was the result of the urge to imitate felt by a

210

weak eccentric who was as ashamed of his own weakness as he was filled with admiration for self-confident brutality. Characteristically adopting one of Hitler's favourite expressions, he had a predilection for the term 'ice-cold', although this was something he never managed to be, and he repudiated the suspicion of weakness often enough to take care not to provoke it, until he finally confessed 'And then I am such a weak man'.[8] At Nuremberg he admitted to the court psychologist G. M. Gilbert that at times 'It is as though I am two people – me, myself, Frank here – and the other Frank, the Nazi leader. And sometimes I wonder how that Frank could have done those things. This Frank looks at the other Frank and says, "Hmm, what a louse you are, Frank! – How could you do such things?" '[9]

The problems of the intellectual with a longing for contact with the idealistically misconstrued world of the primitive man of violence – the 'noble savage' returned in a barbaric modern guise – led thousands of members of the educated classes to take the way of National Socialism. Not in every case did individual insecurity and weakness play such an important part as in Frank's, but without exception there was always a profound dissatisfaction with the whole basis of the established order and its 'mechanical', 'soulless', 'rationally diluted' structures. Where personal inadequacy and discontent with things as they were supplemented each other as drastically as they did in Frank's case, the path to revolutionary nihilism was almost inescapable.

For Hans Frank the jurist, the decisive impetus to his discontent came from the gulf between law and real life so much complained of at the time, which had laid the judiciary open to the reproach of critical inadequacy; 'justice divorced from the people' was the popular slogan. With the collapse of the monarchy and the foundations of order which had remained till then unchallenged, people suddenly saw the end of the era of legal positivism. Into the vacuum left by the collapse of ideas there poured a plethora of idealist theories, most with a romantic tinge, which sought to give new life to law by linking it with mystical concepts like nation, national community, national soul, history, and so on. However much they differed over details, these new systems agreed in repudiating the liberal constitutional state, whose complex structure was denounced as a danger to the homogeneous mythological ground upon which the 'people' stood. Critics of the law and legal practice waxed indignant, for example, over the prevailing 'formalism', over the degeneration of law into a technical legal procedure in which the idea of real justice was lost, and also over the antithesis between 'alien Roman' and 'indigenous German' legal principles. From this starting-point there arose many cross-links with National Socialism, though here as elsewhere they were frequently based on misunderstandings.

Undoubtedly Hans Frank too, after joining the National Socialist movement, believed for a long time that he had found in Adolf Hitler a partner for the realisation of those dreams in which he saw himself winning immortality as the creator of a legal system linked to the people and based on ancient Germanic ideas. When he exclaimed at the proclamation of the founding of the 'German

211

Legal Front' in June 1933, 'Germany has always been the saviour of mankind', the implication was that the event was of an epoch-making significance extending far beyond Germany alone.[10] Despite all experience to the contrary, he was incapable of recognising his misunderstanding about this. Hitler's innate hostility to law, and his failure to see the necessity for ordering life according to the dictates of law in a civilised community, deprived all Frank's plans for reform of any chance of success. Starting from the maxims of struggle derived from social Darwinism, Hitler could see nothing in law or the institutions of justice but instruments for combating political foes. This view was later embodied in the formula that criminal law was a law of struggle and annihilation,[11] and the scope of the law was extended in principle only to the point where it did not restrict the permanent freedom of the Political Police to take what measures they wished. Consequently Hitler felt fresh bitterness every time unpolitical – that is to say, juridical – concepts came into play and set limits to totalitarian self-assertion, until finally all lawyers were to him nothing but 'traitors to the nation', 'idiots', 'utter fools'. In his memorable speech to the Reichstag of April 26, 1942 he declared that he 'would not rest until every German sees that it is a disgrace to be a lawyer'.[12] While Frank, still undeterred and with his taste for resounding phrases, announced that 'National Socialism is carrying out a secular revolution to resurrect German popular law and replace the dead law of jurists', Hitler stated that 'There is no one to whom the lawyer is closer than to the criminal,' adding that the lawyer really deserved, like actors in the past, to be buried in the knacker's yard.[13] Frank lectured with emotion about Germany as a 'refuge of security for all members of the nation' and constructed his sentimental compromises between the idea of law and the totalitarian state, while Hitler commented that, if necessary, he would unhesitatingly disregard the jurists.[14]

The various drafts of a new legal code, particularly the revision of criminal law, never went beyond the first stages, even though they were tailored to suit the demands of the National Socialist regime. This was because the regime's continued practice of intervening by force in the legal system, whenever it wished – a practice which it established while still in the process of seizing power – guaranteed it greater freedom of manipulation than even a National Socialist legal system would have done if it had had binding force. The legal uncertainty engendered by this method itself created the certainty of power.

Frank was willing at any time to banish from his mind his discouraging experiences of Hitler's hostility to law. He created for himself an ideal world in which, even during the days immediately preceding his execution and in stubborn alienation from reality, principles and concepts held sway which Hitler had either acknowledged or had thrown overboard at the very beginning of his career. In dismay Frank appealed to the party programme which 'did not contain the very slightest reference to any extermination of the Jews' as proof 'that the party had nothing whatever to do with these events either ideologically or practically'. Similarly he repeatedly invoked article 19 of the party programme, as though the utterly empty demand for a 'German common law' was enough to provide the

212

National Socialist regime or at least its old fighters with a veneer of his lachrymose nostalgia for the early phase of the movement; 'honest tears' came to his eyes at Nuremberg at the thought of 'the Hitler of those days' and of that revolution which he had helped to make with such confidence in the future.[15]

Even as a student Frank, who in 1919 had belonged for a few weeks to the Epp Freikorps and then to the Thule Society, had come into contact with the NSDAP before entering the SA in September 1923 as a twenty-three-year-old junior barrister, like so many others 'positively spellbound' by Hitler's personality. In November 1923 he took part in the march on the Feldherrnhalle and finally, soon after settling down as a barrister, he became the NSDAP's legal adviser and star defence counsel; up to 1933 he had represented the party in more than 2,400 out of approximately 40,000 actions brought against it.[16] He had left the party in 1926 in the course of a controversy over the case of South Tyrol, which was abandoned by Hitler and the leadership for opportunist reasons; but it is clear that even as early as this he could not escape Hitler's sway. In any case, he rejoined the NSDAP a year later. A second attempt at a break also came to nothing. In 1929, when he wanted to withdraw for a career as a legal scholar, Hitler made a personal appeal to him. 'And I had embarked upon the new, strong, radiantly refulgent path into Adolf Hitler's world,' Frank wrote retrospectively in his high-flown style. 'An infinitely serious and difficult, sparkling, ultimately night-grey course.'[17] At an early stage, this course brought his career to its high-point. Head of the NSDAP's legal office since 1929, he became in 1933, in the course of the capture of power in the *Länder*, Bavarian Minister of Justice and soon afterwards 'Reich Commissioner for the Standardisation of Justice in the *Länder* and for the Renewal of the Legal Order,' as the official title ran. The Association of German National Socialist Jurists, led by himself and till then rather obscure, swelled during those months, as a result of the opportunist rush to join, into a mass organisation which, by the end of 1933, already numbered 80,000 members and could certainly have lent its weight to the isolated attempts made to assert the independence of law. Frank, however, regarded such attempts with total incomprehension, and it was merely characteristic self-dramatisation when he later claimed that the Association had been 'a genuine fighting organisation against Himmler and Bormann'.[18] It became, rather, not merely an important instrument within the framework of legal and personal politics for imposing the party line, but also an ideological weapon for facilitating the breakthrough of totalitarian concepts into wide areas of the legal profession. The effects here were all the more devastating because the tactic of disguising the revolution as both legal and national caught the legal profession, as it had the civil service as a whole, at its weakest point. Such concepts of legal positivism as remained made it difficult to resist a seizure of power that was formally guaranteed and supported by the law; on the other hand the nationalist claims of the new power-holders paralysed all thought of counter-measures on the part of the traditional conservative class, enclosed within its own caste outlook, although its attitudes of mind and its solidarity had enabled it to come almost unscathed through the Republican era. It was possible, therefore, for the National Socialists to steer a course towards a permanent state of emergency without any particular difficulty and to effect almost without friction the transition from the constitutional principle of the stability of legal institutions to that of their total 'mobility'.

It was merely the logical last stage on this gradually descending path into what Frank, looking back, lamented as the 'night of law' when in a public speech he assured his hearers: 'In the Third Reich we must, as it were, remove the well-known blindfold from the eyes of justice, so that she may see clearly into life.' In the same context he demanded 'only one total jurisdiction – the Führer's'.[19] Similarly he proclaimed in 'Guiding Principles for German Judges' in 1936: 'The judge has no right of review over the decisions of the Führer as embodied in a law or a degree.' And it is no proof of the resistance which he subsequently so emphatically claimed to have offered when, one paragraph later, he adds: 'In order to fulfil his task in the community of the nation the judge must be independent. He is not bound to follow instructions.'[20]

However, soon after the conclusion of the struggle for power, Frank noted a 'positively systematic persecution of jurists'.[21] His personal prestige in the eyes of Hitler and the top leadership was severely reduced after he had raised certain formal objections at the time of Röhm's murder. In any case, as he himself said with good reason, he was 'after 1934 a slowly but steadily declining political force'. Once having achieved his goal, Hitler no longer needed the law and Frank's complaint that 'never once in all these years' had Hitler received him in audience 'on legal matters' merely showed his naïvety.[22] His attempts to compensate for the steady erosion of his power found expression in a cult of the Führer that attributed to him everything that a bombastic vocabulary could produce in the way of extravagant flattery. As late as 1944, after all the humiliations, defeats and clashes, Frank fulsomely celebrated the feeling 'of being truly lifted aloft in happiness' at having been called upon 'to be the first to prepare the way for this man'.[23] Naturally this intoxicated grandiloquence did nothing to win back his continually diminishing authority. Hitler was manifestly unable to separate the person of the Reich legal chief from the hated subject which he represented. As the 'most unimportant area of the party leadership' the Reich Legal Office of the NSDAP was soon afterwards moved out of the national headquarters of the party, the Brown House in Munich.[24]

It was all the more of a surprise when, in the middle of September 1939, Hitler recalled him from an army unit in Potsdam and appointed him civilian administrative chief with the Commander-in-Chief East and, with effect from October 26 of the same year, Governor-General of the occupied territory of Poland. The post seemed tailor-made for Frank's histrionic thirst for prestige, and with the ostentation of an oriental despot he moved into the old royal palace in Cracow, set on a rocky plateau falling steeply to the Vistula. Here he resided with the extravagant ceremonial that went with his nature, regarding himself 'with audacious romanticism as a vassal king set by Hitler over Poland',[25] lord of life and death, unpredictable in magnanimity or brutality, carrying on a patriarchal, arbitrary rule, the principles of which were manifestly gleaned at random from reading of the ways of supermen, the style of a world power, German consciousness of mission, and cheap literature on Slav psychology. In his first conferences with Hitler individual measures were agreed for the future lines of policy towards the occupied zone, including the razing of Warsaw Castle, the removal of art treasures, and the liquidation of Poland's intellectual leaders. Behind this stood the goal of that 'process of re-Germanisation' of which Frank had occasionally spoken, the 'absolute permeation of the area by Germanness' and its cleansing from 'alien races that are no longer required'. Overwhelmed that now 'the greatest hour of Germanness is striking', he announced rapturously that the territory he governed 'has an immense world historical task to accomplish'. In Berlin government circles Poland under Frank soon came to be known as 'Frank-Reich ['Frank's kingdom' – a pun on 'Frankreich', France] in the East'.[26]

Over and above this Poland was to provide an area for the practical application of that 'technique of state' whose systematic elaboration and perfection was one of Frank's pet ideas. This is, in fact, what it did become, as has since been demonstrated,[27] though in a sense diametrically opposed to Frank's own conception. The subjugated Polish territories became a model police state and a high school for the cadres who were to exercise totalitarian power. But it was the SS who here, inexorably and almost unhindered, developed the technique and the technicians of the SS state, and what emerged was later used to perfect the totalitarian apparatus inside Germany.

This also explains what Frank meant when he called his period as Governor-General of Poland 'the most terrible years' of his life and repeatedly pointed out that, contrary to appearances, he was 'an isolated, powerless man who had no influence on events'.[28] In fact, from the very day of his appointment his jurisdiction was eroded from all sides, and it casts a revealing light on the disloyal duplicity of Hitler's policies towards his followers that from the outset he failed to give Frank any support in his struggle for authority, in particular support against the bid for autonomy by SS Obergruppenführer Krüger, who was in overall control of the SS and the police in Poland. Hitler actually fostered the rival independent authority, though Krüger was formally subordinate to the Governor-General. The system of half-jurisdictions that were combined into total jurisdiction only at the summit, in the person of Hitler as the final arbiter – a system which we can observe throughout the Third Reich – subsequently resulted in a total disorganisation that was quite obviously accepted as a necessary price to pay; it was also made the pretext for continual exhausting conflicts in which Frank, a man at the mercy of uncontrollable emotion, proved hopelessly inferior to the cold intriguer Krüger. While Frank, obviously in increasing desperation, invoked his exclusive competence to give orders at sittings of the government, Krüger, under Himmler's protection, simply went ahead with his, or at least the SS's, conception of a policy for Poland. Frank tried alternately to counteract this policy by one of relative leniency and reason towards the Poles, with occasional rudimentary attempts at cooperation, or to outdo the SS by even

215

greater harshness, hoping by acts of terror and mass extermination to gain a reputation with Hitler and his entourage for National Socialist ability in dealing with the East. His famous diary, which he handed over during his imprisonment in May 1945, contains in thirty-eight volumes, along with minute descriptions of the events of every single day during his period of government, countless passages designed to impress by their brutality. For example, when asked by a correspondent of the *Völkischer Beobachter* named Kleiss what was the difference between the Protectorate of Bohemia and Moravia and the government in Poland, Frank replied, 'I can tell you a graphic difference. In Prague, for example, big red posters were put up on which could be read that seven Czechs had been shot today. I said to myself: If I put up a poster for every seven Poles shot, the forests of Poland would not be sufficient to manufacture the paper for such posters.' At a session of his government he declared in one of those countless speeches which were his passion: 'As far as the Jews are concerned, I will tell you frankly, they must be done away with by one means or another. Therefore I shall approach the Jews exclusively in the anticipation that they are going to disappear. They must go.' And on another occasion, with nauseating humour: 'What's all this? There are said to have been thousands and thousands of these Flatfoot Indians [the Jews] in this city; now there are none to be seen. Surely you haven't used unkind methods against them?' – and the record adds: 'Laughter.' Exactly four weeks later to the day, on the other hand, Frank noted in a memorandum: 'The power and the certainty of being able to use force without any resistance are the sweetest and most noxious poison that can be introduced into a government. In the long run this poison is absolutely lethal, and history teaches that systems based on law last for thousands of years, but systems based on force barely for decades.' Himmler, who was naturally unaware of utterances of this kind, once commented angrily that Frank was a 'traitor to the Fatherland who was hand in glove with the Poles' and whose downfall with the Führer he would bring about in the very near future.[29]

These almost unresolvable contradictions, however, originated not only from Frank's bloody style of government but also from the lack of a unifying concept of how to rule the East. The idea of a Polish constitutional state, which seemed originally to be the guiding principle, was soon abandoned, as were projects tending towards protectorate status and Frank's own vague 'idea of a German multi-national empire'. Hitler shied away from any clear commitment all the more because at a very early stage he had allowed the idea to get about that he would never give up this territory. Frank had to be content with the formula, which had no precise meaning in international law, that Poland was to be a 'secondary country (*Nebenland*) of the Reich'; this kept all the options open while it gave the office of Governor-General a certain sovereignty.[30] Hitler's original instructions to him read, 'to assume the administration of the conquered territories with the special order ruthlessly to exploit this region as a war zone and booty country, to reduce it, as it were, to a heap of rubble in its economic, social, cultural and political structure'.[31]

The destructive basis of these instructions, however, was too much at variance with the necessary mechanism of every method of governing – which always tends towards the establishment of order – to be put into practice. Furthermore Frank recognised that such principles worked diametrically counter to the needs of the Reich, especially as regards agricultural produce and labour; Hitler, deeply entangled in his racial resentment, was demanding the impossible – to exploit and to exterminate at the same time. Only after his repeated suggestions to Hitler had fallen upon deaf ears did Frank, who wanted a policy of practical utility, begin to steer a cautious course in the opposite direction to Hitler's demands. However, this policy was continually frustrated by the terrorist line of SS Obergruppenführer Krüger and by Frank's own alternative policy of harshness in reaction to this. In this chaos of opposite or competing aims and ideas all real possibility of settling for either one or the other disappeared, along with the principles of reason and humanity. 'Humanity,' Frank reflected in his diary in July 1942, when the word inadvertently slipped into something he was dictating, 'a word that one often does not dare to use, as though it had become a foreign word.'[32]

In view of the perpetual quarrels over jurisdiction and the lack of stability in the administration of his territory, Frank's position appears to have been severely undermined by 1942. When on top of that he laid himself open to the charge of privately enriching members of his family, he was forced to submit to a 'comradely interrogation' and to accept a painful diminution of his authority, which worked out to the advantage of his adversary. As State Secretary for Security, Krüger received ministerial rank and moreover, as deputy for Himmler (in his capacity as Reich Commissioner for the Consolidation of the German National Heritage), was given supreme jurisdiction over the great resettlement of Poles and Germans that was planned. The ever more open rivalry was clearly coming to a head when, that summer, Frank delivered four university lectures which, at the infuriated Hitler's personal orders, resulted in his being forbidden to make any further public speeches and dismissed from every party office. This seemed to foreshadow his imminent recall from the post of Governor-General, for which Himmler and Bormann were working, and within the SS they were already casting about for a successor. In his uncertainty about his position and his fate, Frank wrote a report which, in its verbose mixture of audacity, self-castigation, sentimentality and confused idealism, presents an extraordinarily revealing portrait of his character. Frank, Goebbels noted soon afterward in his diary, 'enjoys absolutely none of the Führer's esteem any more. I shall propose to the Führer in all seriousness that he must either get rid of Frank or re-establish his authority; for a Governor-General, i.e. a viceroy, in Poland without authority is naturally unthinkable in these critical times.'[33]

Surprisingly enough, Hitler decided to drop not Frank but his adversary Krüger, after the ruthlessly executed resettlement scheme had produced a wave of revolt. 'The province is, as it were, a simmering crisis,' stated Frank.[34] Even those among the Poles who had originally been prepared to cooperate had been

217

repudiated, and in so far as the population had not in the meantime joined in the resistance movement, whose cells had become focal points for the temporarily submerged sense of nationhood, they maintained a mute and stubborn indolence, ignoring all promises and attempts at a change of policy.

With Krüger's successor, SS Obergruppenführer Wilhelm Koppe, who till then had worked as a Senior SS and Police Commander in Poznan, Frank reached a tolerable relationship; but quarrels continued on all sides, since their origin was more inherent in the set-up than psychological, and up to the end of his term of office the Governor-General had offered his resignation fourteen times in all, naturally in vain. Outwardly he continued, in his insecurity, to boast of Hitler's special trust, and he assured a session of the government that his suggestions had earned him from Hitler 'the honorary title of the great realist politician of the East'.[35] In fact, his ideas, which had always been marked by distorted imaginative fancies, showed that particular lack of realism which became endemic, with the approaching end of the war, among officials of the Third Reich. He seemed to believe in all seriousness that the propagation of the idea of the Reich would help to reconcile the Polish population. While the war situation was visibly deteriorating and the front was drawing closer to the borders of his province, he proposed a policy of 'humanisation' and 'Europeanisation', but neither Hitler on the one hand nor the Polish population on the other were prepared for any such unconvincing and furthermore dishonest compromise. His rule came to an end among such delusions, a last flicker of hectic enthusiasm, and battles over jurisdiction, with abrupt, grandiosely phrased outbursts of contempt for humanity. On August 18, 1944 he informed Berlin of the 'complete collapse of the authority' of his administration and suggested the dissolution of the Governor-Generalship. In one of his last speeches in Cracow Castle he reminded his listeners of 'the organisms of the national being whose intoxicated and luminous blood must be preserved in its purity'.[36] Then he bade farewell to Cracow, to the royal residence overlooking the Vistula, to his vice-kingdom. The great hour of Germanness, as he had called it, was in many ways at an end.

At Nuremberg he said the aim of his policy had been 'to administer justice without detriment to the interests of the war'.[37] He felt at home in such contradictions, and the more so the more contradictory they were. But whenever in the course of his career a party interest or reason of state had clashed with justice, he had decided for party and state and against justice. His claim to have held aloft the 'banner of justice' does not count for much. Had he done so he would not have risen so high under a man to whom the law was an alien concept and the service of justice a 'disgrace'. 'Here I stand with my bayonets, there you stand with your law! We'll see which counts for more!' Hitler once told him scornfully, and it is hard to see how after that he could have persuaded himself that under Hitler law would ever count for anything besides the urge for prestige, ambition and vanity.[38] Did Frank believe in justice, or did he believe in force as he observed it in the person of Hitler and his power-hungry henchmen? The truth behind his life, paradoxical but more exact than his own explanation, was doubtless that he 'wanted to administer justice without detriment to the interests of force'. He admired law, morality and truth with the same enthusiasm – but also detachment – with which he admired force and the ideologically embellished horrors of 'historical grandeur'. Despite the extravagance of his apparent convictions, he really had no convictions at all, only moods, ecstatically exaggerated momentary leanings, blown this way and that by varying external stimuli. 'The half is worse than the whole,' he later stated with self-reproachful insight into his life. 'In that lay the curse. I said yes to Hitler's ideas, no to his methods. I should have said no to his ideas too. I remained caught up in this contradiction.'[39]

However, it was not merely through this single contradiction that he ultimately came to grief, dumbfounded at the way his life had gone astray and missed its purpose; it was through the whole contradictory structure of his personality, which was devoid of any firm foundation whatever. His aimless, emotionally directed readiness to surrender himself was at work to the last, as the inconsistency of the statement he wrote out in his Nuremberg cell vividly illustrates. 'I am seized now,' he wrote, 'as I prepare to say farewell to this earth in order to follow the Führer[!], by the most profound melancholy when I recall this tremendous setting out of a whole great self-confident nation that followed a strong voice as though to a celebration of the eternal Godhead himself. Why, why was it all lost, why did it all fade away, why is it all gone, destroyed? I am seized by uncomprehending horror at the senselessness of destiny.'[40]

Destiny, with pedantic consistency, had led him where subservience, weakness and dishonesty take a man. When he had just made his first appearance as defence counsel for National Socialist strong-arm bands, one of his teachers, the old Geheimrat von Calker, warned him: 'I beg you to leave these people alone! No good will come of it! Political movements that begin in the criminal courts will end in the criminal courts!'[41]

Now the movement was indeed ending in the criminal courts. Shattered and bewildered, he found himself in the courtroom facing the evidence he had produced himself, the documents of a life in which out of weakness he had fled into destructive extremism, the documents of a life which now – and he imagined he heard the 'angry laughter of God'[42] – brought him contritely to his knees. The repentance which he proclaimed, the visible sign of an inner conversion, certainly deserves attention, but there is a lot to suggest that it was only a passing mood; for basically, in a character such as his there is no room for truth. 'A thousand years will pass,' he said, overwhelmed during questioning by his counsel before the court, 'and will not take away this guilt from Germany.'[43]

In his final speech, on the other hand, he withdrew this. And so his last words were a contradiction. The end fitted the man.

Baldur von Schirach
and the 'Mission of the Younger Generation'

We simply believed.

Baldur von Schirach

To us Germans everything is religion. What we do we do not merely with our hands and brains, but with our hearts and souls. This has often become a tragic fate for us.

Baldur von Schirach

The National Socialist movement, especially before and immediately after the conquest of power, has been widely interpreted as an upsurge and victory of youth. Outside observers, like the spokesmen of National Socialism themselves, have claimed that the NSDAP, more than any rival political group, represented the 'mission of the younger generation' in contrast to the rotten and crumbling world of yesterday. At the end of the 1920s Gregor Strasser stressed this viewpoint in an article the title of which later became a slogan, 'Make Way, You Old Ones!'; Goebbels was eloquent in his efforts to activate the radicalism of the youth of the big cities; and Baldur von Schirach proclaimed succinctly, 'The NSDAP is the party of youth.'[1]

In such appeals to the younger generation, which coloured the style and subject-matter of its propaganda, National Socialism, here as everywhere else, was merely exploiting emotions which already dominated the political arena and were a symptom of the transitional character of the period. The idea that youth, free from all burden of proof, was a value in itself, which went hand in hand with a summary contempt for age, was part of the signature of this as of every revolutionary epoch. Youth, the style of youth, the youth movement, were expressions of the same idea on various planes, and had already been given a concrete political turn in the myth of the 'young nations' or the youth ideology of Italian Fascism, whose anthem was significantly called '*Giovinezza*'. Youth had right, hope and the future on its side: age had death. Like most of the central concepts of National Socialism, 'youth' was vague enough in meaning to be employed at will to defame or enhance the value of anything whose disparagement or commendation suited the tactical needs of the moment. Thus liberalism, the bourgeoisie, parliamentarianism or the democratic order could just as easily be condemned as belonging to an old and outworn era as values of a different kind could be usurped for the National Socialist cause in the name of youth. 'Faust, the Ninth Symphony, and the will of Adolf Hitler are eternal youth and know neither time nor transience,' proclaimed Baldur von Schirach.[2]

Although it had featured prominently in the jargon of the turn of the century, the myth of youth made its breakthrough in politics only with the First World War. Not least among the experiences of the war generation was the witnessing of the collapse, along with so many other values and positions, of the prewar antitheses liberal and conservative, national and social, left and right, which had given the prewar era its essential stamp; the true division now was between old and young. 'We see in the war the fall of the older generation and the rise of the younger,' wrote Max Hildebert Böhm in 1919 in a book with the significant title 'Call of the Young'.[3]

By the way in which it took up this call, answered it and repeated it the rising National Socialist movement once more demonstrated its extraordinarily effective manipulation of mass emotions. It made equal use of the expectations of the young themselves and of the widespread hopes placed in 'youth'. While all the other parties were attempting to carry on in the old way, in their programmes, membership and style of activity, the NSDAP arose as a party without, indeed opposed to, any past; its lack of tradition, and its denial of tradition, made it considerably the more attractive to a generation without links with the past. From the beginning its propaganda was directed towards this generation, for which, with persuasive eloquence, it offered tasks and aims, and a 'pioneer role'[4] that corresponded both to its members' personal ambitions and to their hunger for action. Along with a skilful emphasis on its antithesis to the 'old', this programme of promises was one of the decisive factors in the NSDAP's success in attracting a strikingly large membership of younger people, which in turn largely determined the membership structure and shape of the original militant movement, at least until its development into an amorphous mass party. There were many influences at work here: the difficult conditions of everyday life after the war; a longing for new, 'organic' forms of community aroused by the experience of comradeship during the war and in the *Bünde*, or youth associations, which the other parties were unable to exploit; an urge among the young to prove themselves; and various anti-bourgeois attitudes, for the most part reflecting the idea that 'times were changing' and so aggravating the widespread hostility towards the Weimar Republic as the 'state of the old'. These and other motives of similar origin pushed an ever-increasing section of middle class youth, especially among academic circles, towards the NSDAP and gave it the character of a youth movement of its own special type. 'Among youth,' a contemporary writer noted in an analysis of this phenomenon, 'social despair, nationalistic romanticism, and inter-generational hostility form a positively classic compound'.[5]

This observation was true not only of the younger generation that had taken part in the war and formed the determining element during the initial phase of the movement, but also of the whole postwar generation. Credulously, fanatically, unhesitatingly ready for extreme measures, they saw themselves mobilised for the aims of National Socialism and, right down to the teenagers, swarmed into the ranks of the party. 'What happens inside a boy like this,' asked an advertisement for Schenzinger's 'Hitler Youth Member Quex', 'when the great river catches him? What is it that sweeps him along, that draws him, that inspires him, that destroys him? How does a child of fifteen come to leave his mother, to hate his father, to despise his former friends? Norkus and Preisser [two young National Socialist 'martyrs'] were hardly older when they died for an idea whose greatness they could not yet understand, of which they had only a presentiment.'[6]

What was it, in fact? The commercial sentimentality of the advertisement should not blind us to the fact that this type of youthful absolutist aged between fifteen and twenty, radically different from later party members, did indeed exist. Postwar difficulties, or youthful radicalism, offer only a partial explanation of such a boy's blind, self-sacrificing idealism. There was, too, undoubtedly a romantic attraction about a party that always operated close to the edge of legality and under the urge to ruthless action stepped over it.[7] But over and above such explanations the particular susceptibility of the younger generation to Hitler's party indicates a faulty understanding of itself which cannot be explained in everyday political terms or in those of normal psychological development. For this generation had long been living and arguing on an irrational basis; turned towards the past instead of open to reality, it was introverted and hostile to society and civilisation and had embarked upon 'the retreat into Germany's forests' long before the National Socialist ideology came to show it the way. Here latent correspondences in attitude made it easier for National Socialism's demagogic power to lead these people astray even before the devastating effects of the 1918 collapse produced the great breakthrough.

All this was most clearly seen in the German youth movement, though as a universal phenomenon it was to be met far beyond it. It is not the case as defenders of the regime in search of precedents have claimed, that the National Socialist revolution started in the youth movement or the 'Wandervögel' who roamed the countryside.[8] Nevertheless this development around the turn of the century created an emotional climate that contained elements of the later evolution and left many of the younger generation ideologically open to the National Socialist programme. Despite all differences in detail, the common elements are repeatedly visible: the vague terminology, the pseudo-romantic cult of the past, the proclamation of membership of an élite association. Guided by other motives and certainly with other, well-meaning aims, the youth movement nevertheless developed the prerequisites for its own perversion by National Socialism. The SA, even more the Hitler Youth, and in a wider sense also the SS, were fundamentally the end products, distorted by totalitarianism, of a process which even at the outset had shown numerous pre-totalitarian features as it moved from the innocent days of the Wandervögel movement first to the Bünde and then with a certain inner logic, though also as the result of outside influence, to the forms created by National Socialism.

In spite of all revolutionary claims, the Wandervögel movement was fundamentally escapist. What purported to be a revolt against the dullness and dreariness of the bourgeois world was at bottom a retreat into a special state of mind not seeking to change the world but despising it. As the protest against society was confined to a turning away from society, it denied itself and devalued the 'wanderer's joy', the rediscovery of the homeland and its past, into acts of lonely self-gratification. Significantly, the Wandervögel movement, although its members were undoubtedly the country's élite, evolved no theories or concepts of social criticism and left only intoxicated protestations of its youthfulness, just as its whole reproach against society began not from concrete social phenomena but from its own malaise and remained stuck at its starting-point. Always 'what dwells beyond the mountains' seemed to this movement more important than what was happening in the factories, the centres of power, or the scientific laboratories. Its inability to articulate clearly, demonstrated in a plethora of proclamations, was merely the expression of its political, technological and social apathy, which a high-minded and impetuous, but at the same time self-satisfied idealism could not counterbalance. One cannot help a certain irritation on observing part of the intellectual avant-garde of a great industrial nation at the beginning of the twentieth century devoting itself with passionate enthusiasm to the revival of items of dead national heritage, the collection of *Landsknecht* songs, or the wilful return to an ideologically determined primitivism. In constant alternation between a narcissistic ego-cult and ecstatic groping in cosmic expanses, this generation withdrew its gaze from the near at hand and the necessary, and even the famous 'wrestling with problems' around night-time campfires – the prerogative of youth in search of an orientation – was always a form of escapism. The philanthropic enthusiasm which the movement aroused remained entirely uncommitted and devoid of any 'impulse to enlightenment'.[9]

Even in its own sphere the Wandervögel movement was unable to establish an alternative to the world of the previous generation, and its efforts, for example, to overcome religious, class or even racial prejudices scarcely made any headway. Its criticism of bourgeois society did not touch its foundations but merely opted for looking for a romantic way of life within it. Strictly speaking, this protest against the lies lived by the elder generation was, for all its striving after 'inner truthfulness', a demand by these young people for the right to live their own lies. They despised the celebration of Sedan and 'operatic Germanness', being led into the new century by the ideal of the sixteenth-century peasant mercenary Jörg von Frundsberg. Of all their literary productions, what survived for only a short while were, significantly, a collection of songs and above all Walter Flex's book 'Wanderer Between Two Worlds', whose hero in fact wanders exclusively towards that other world which he has built up in his daydreams out of 'theology, political irrationality and resignation to fate'.[10] To remain pure and become mature: this formula summed up the self-knowledge of that prewar generation which withdrew from the demands of its present to the 'investigation of being'. It was entirely consistent with this that the legendary gathering on the Hoher Meissner, shortly before the outbreak of the First World War, proclaimed retreat to 'inner freedom

223

and personal responsibility' as the answer to the contemporary situation, which it clearly felt to be an emergency. The best the Wandervögel movement had to offer was honesty, self-discipline and the capacity for enthusiastic faith, but all this remained largely self-centred, without anchorage in an objective system of values and hence wide open to abuse. There was always something curiously antiquated about the peculiar type developed by the youth movement, an Old Frankish uprightness, which only imperfectly concealed the youth's helplessness in the face of the world from which he had too long withdrawn. The 'search for roots' had not left him better fitted to cope with life, but rather unsure of himself, so that on entering a profession and ordinary life he 'landed all the more decisively in the critical zone of the long-avoided conflict with his environment' and was confronted 'either by a compromise that was contrary to his convictions or by a radical break with the existing order'.[11]

The First World War further reinforced the attitudes established by the Wandervögel movement. Experience with the weapons of war was no more successful in awakening the movement's followers to reality than the revolution and the beginning of democracy brought the awakening to politics which was their avowed historical purpose. 'First the new man, then the new state,' ran one of the current slogans, still calling for 'inner' responsibility.[12] Only about one third of the 15,000 or so Wandervögel who went to the front returned, and the exceptionally high casualty rate was seen as confirming their way of looking on selfless devotion, self-sacrifice and readiness to die as high virtues. But the old anti-civilisation attitude, too, remained and in fact emerged even stronger, imbued now with nationalist bitterness. It was no longer directed solely against the phenomenon of the city, against urban degeneration and overrefinement of life, but now also against the Allies as the representatives of the 'shallow West' and against imposed democracy, parliamentarianism, and the party system as products of that civilisation.[13] These and similar reactionary attitudes bore witness to a still disturbed relationship to reality that remained half self-reflection and half utilitarian political mythology. The will to join and to serve, the cult of community and leader, the myth of comradeship, the cultivation of ancient customs, the socialism of the *Bünde,* a mystical image of the nation: these were now the starting-points of a vehement controversy in which the protagonists were still concerned to achieve a divorce from existing reality. 'Does not political activity,' one publication asked, 'all belong to that urban civilisation of yester-day, from which we fled when we set up our community of friends out in the forests? Is there anything more unpolitical than the Wandervögel? Were not the Meissner festival and its formula a repudiation of the party men who were so anxious to harness youth to their political activities? Is not the sole task of the Free German communities to educate free, noble and kind people?'[14] In other publications the attempt at insulation was presented as a concern about 'uncalled-for politicisation [of youth], about premature, harmful submergence in organisa-tions, about the nervous modern activism dictated by immaturity and the urge to intrude', and they cited the educational monopoly of the Bünde.[15]

All this was far more dangerous in the new political circumstances than it had been before the war, because the youth movement now being formed, the so-called 'Bündische Jugend', soon became a mass organisation with a membership of hundreds of thousands, whose refusal of political responsibility withdrew an important source of energy from public life. The position was even more difficult because the Republic was far more dependent upon active participation than the prewar state. Whereas the imperial structure could not be shaken by the 'displeased reaction' of what was in any case only a small minority, 'the weaker Republic was bound to suffer considerably, if not to become impossible, through the refusal of the middle class to make use of its machinery'.[16] There was no help in the crude nostrums with which numerous representatives of the Bündische Jugend intervened in public debate, pointing the way to the 'rediscovery of heroic standards in politics' or complaining of the lack of 'struggle for the eternal in man' in everyday political life – a struggle which the Germans had to fight out 'between death and the Devil' – and demanding the establishment of a 'state of the young' or the 'conquest of the parties by the spirit of youth'. These merely recapitulated the same old refusal, compounded of arrogance and social immaturity, to accept political responsibility. The Bündische Jugend's public utterances were visionary and declamatory, not factual and analytical.

For the individual Bünde, however, the attempt to stand apart became increasingly difficult, and all their contortions could not prevent at least the echo of political conflicts from breaking into the anxiously protected circle. The increasingly obvious splitting up of the movement, which vividly mirrored the chaos of opinions in the narrower political sphere, emphatically bears this out. Nonetheless the Bünde held fast to the principle of apolitical self-preservation, and in the case of the liberal, socialist, nationalist, pacifist, Christian, folk, world citizenship and other factions, what was involved, apart from personal rivalries, was at bottom simply the particular style in which the refusal to cooperate in the state and society was stated. The self-defence leagues, fighting associations and youth formations of the radical parties, which the more openly political young people joined, were only another sort of escapism based on a romantic spirit of opposition.

Over and above this fundamental similarity, the groups of the Bündische Jugend had in common a comparatively strict form of organisation, instead of the loose, individualistic forms of association evolved by the Wandervögel. This reflected the influence of the war generation, and indeed the new situation was marked altogether by a certain swiftly developing militarisation. The soldier became the ideal figure, the command structure the model of organisation, and where prewar youth had wandered the Bündische Jugend began to march. It was in keeping with their divorce from reality that the idea of a 'soldierly existence' was based not on the real experiences of the war but upon vainglorious illusions; not upon dirt, disgust and the fear of death, but upon that myth of the front-line soldier with which the older generation compensated for defeat. The first steps towards a contempt for life developed by the Wandervögel, the battlefield romanticism with 'mounds of dead', the transfiguration of striking and stabbing

225

and throttling, the whole aestheticisation of violent death culminating in the intoxication of grandiose disasters, now underwent unlimited extension in an ignorantly blissful shudder before the Nibelungen and the Last of the Goths, before the Lost Warrior Bands of the Middle Ages, before Langemarck, Koltschak and the Samurai ideal praised by Tusk, the leader of the 'German Youth 1.11'. All this was not merely the expression of a historicising hero-worship but also a symptom of a deep-rooted tendency of German educational tradition to prepare the young for death rather than life. Rarely did the character of the Bündische Jugend, in its mixture of commonplace metaphysics, ego-assertion, and pseudo-military spirit, find for itself a more apt formula than in the 'German trinity' proclaimed by one of its members: 'God, myself and my weapon.'[17]

At this point some qualification is needed, for the development was by no means as straightforward and simple as this necessarily compressed survey may suggest. Also, there were important shades of difference in the make-up of the Bündische Jugend, above all between the so-called Free German groups, which for the most part tolerated the Republican state, and their *völkisch* counterparts, who thought in pan-German and anti-Semitic terms. It was not these differences of emphasis that determined the nature of the Bünde, however, but their fundamentally false, romantic attitude to reality, which left the youth of both sides incapable of asserting themselves intellectually and morally in the confusion of the time, above all during the great crisis at the end of the 1920s. The points of contact with the right which, despite all disagreements over details, had always been present, at least in the ideological foreground, now inevitably worked in favour of the powerfully advancing Hitler movement; and even if, at least in the case of some of the groups, there was not yet an amalgamation, this was only because they were more than ever jealous of their own individual existence, even if they could no longer convincingly define their distinction from National Socialism. Hence Hitler's speedy and progressive breakthrough took place less within the Bünde themselves than among the proletarian and petty bourgeois youth who till then had been excluded, or had kept their distance from the Bund Movement.[18] By the end of 1932 the Hitler Youth Organisation (Hitler Jugend) after a long period of stagnation, numbered almost 110,000 members. Quite unaware that an unpolitical attitude was in itself a form of political behaviour, the Bünde clung to their principle of isolation from political events. Even in its issue of February 1, 1933 the *Zeitung* of the Deutsche Freischar youth movement contained not a word on the real political situation.[19]

Inevitably the Bünde fell victim, after January 30, 1933, to the universal urge to toe the party line. The spontaneous acts of self-adaptation to the new masters were the result not so much of opportunism and apostasy as of that political naïvety in which the Bündische Jugend, with some arrogance, trained itself. Only isolated outsiders or small groups went into consistent opposition; apart from this, such resistance as was offered was less a struggle against the new holders of power and the Third Reich than an indignant effort to preserve the Bünde. At the beginning of April, Obergebietsführer Nabersberg, with fifty Hitler Youth members, seized the building of the Reich Committee of German Youth Associations in a surprise attack, giving the cue for an uncompromising elimination of all the other youth groups, even the *völkisch* groups, so that it was soon possible to announce the end of 'everything which in the past could be referred to as the German Youth Movement'.[20] The Hitler Youth organisation, rising quickly, through the influx of members from all camps, to a membership of millions, was given 'the task of becoming the most important educational force in National Socialist society and was developed into a system for including and influencing the whole of youth'. 'The fighting élite of the Hitler Youth must now become the national youth,' was the motto of the new phase.[21]

On June 17, 1933 the twenty-six-year-old Baldur von Schirach was appointed Youth Leader of the German Reich. Schirach did not come from the Hitler Youth in the narrower sense, but had first gained a reputation in the party as leader of the National Socialist German Students Union (NSDStB) with the mobilisation of an exceptionally large proportion of the academic youth for National Socialism, before Hitler called upon him in 1931 to become Reich Youth Leader of the NSDAP.[22] Burdened by his numerous official tasks, he never completed his studies, and this fact was of fundamental significance for his personal development. He always looked like a student, immature in both a good and bad sense: idealistic, lyrical, educated. He never managed to become a true representative of the Hitler Youth, and if he could not claim an origin in either the urban working class or the middle class, his outward appearance corresponded even less to the ideal type of the Hitler Youth. He was not hard, tough or quick, as demanded in the famous motto formulated by Hitler himself, but a big, pampered boy of good family who laboriously imitated the rough, forceful style of the boys' gang. His unemphatic, rather soft features held a hint of femininity, and all the time he was in office there were rumours about his allegedly white bedroom furnished like a girl's. His brown uniform always looked like fancy dress. He painstakingly stylised himself into the desired posture and tried to live up to the robust, swashbuckling ideal of the Hitler Youth boy which he himself had helped to create without ever being able to match up to it. Consciousness of this discrepancy finally warped his whole personality, introducing into it unauthentic, artificial elements. Both his pathetic aspect and the arrogance of which he was accused arose from this incessant disguise; even his comradely gestures seemed pretentious and smacked of forced affability. He enjoyed some esteem within the Hitler Youth, but he was never popular, especially with the lower ranks; he was regarded as a bit of a literary figure, and on many sides he met a contempt that was only held in check by his position as leader. His speeches too failed to inspire; they were full of sentimental enthusiasm but lacking in fire, 'a blend of academic lecture and lyrical poem'.[23] Nevertheless he took his ideals seriously, and within the narrow area which they left him he exercised his own judgment and gave evidence of open-mindedness and a certain amount of moral courage, as for example on the day after the so-called Crystal Night on which windows of Jewish shops were smashed throughout Germany, when he called

227

together the top leaders of the Hitler Youth in Berlin, spoke of a 'disgrace to civilisation', and forbade the Hitler Youth to take any part in 'criminal actions' of this kind.[24] His approach to ideology was innocent of cynical calculation; he 'simply believed', and saw acts of violence and terrorism as deviations from the pure idea, which he pursued to the end unwaveringly and true to his boyish concept of loyalty.

Baldur von Schirach came of an officer's family with artistic tendencies and a cosmopolitan background. Both his parents were born in the United States; his father had served in Germany as a regular officer, before obtaining his discharge in 1908 in order to take over the management of the Hoftheater in Weimar, later to become the Weimar National Theatre. After his dismissal during the post-1918 revolution, fear of becoming déclassé brought him in the early 1920s into contact with Hitler's followers and eventually into personal contact with the leader of the NSDAP himself, whose appearance made an indelible impression in particular upon his son, then eighteen. At Hitler's suggestion, the boy went to study in Munich, and if he was not already he now became 'one of his most loyal followers'.[25]

Looking back upon his youth in Weimar, Schirach declared at Nuremberg that it was above all 'the aura of classical but also of postclassical Weimar' that exercised a decisive influence upon his development. But in fact he was far more influenced by the spirit of a folksy, denatured romanticism that was much closer to the German Rembrandt (Julius Langbehn), Paul de Lagarde or the Nietzsche of Elisabeth Förster than to E. T. A. Hoffmann, Tieck or Heinrich Heine. The order, reason and humanity of the classical era were totally alien to him as to the whole of this postwar generation with its disturbed equilibrium and neurotic self-obsession, and classical Weimar gave him the empty sensations of national pride rather than sound standards of self-education. Henriette von Schirach, the Youth Leader's former wife, has described in her memoirs the group of student friends which met regularly in Munich beneath a picture of Napoleon to read Stefan George, discuss Talhoff's 'Monument to the Dead' poems, recite Rilke's 'Cornet' by candlelight, and quote Ernst Jünger.[26] The choice is extremely revealing of the circle's state of mind, especially when we add the works which Schirach himself said had exercised 'the most lasting influence' on his development: Houston Stewart Chamberlain's *Foundations of the Twentieth Century*, the writings of the nationalist, anti-Semitic literary historian Adolf Bartels, Henry Ford's *The International Jew*, and Hitler's *Mein Kampf*.[27] His own poems, which in the words of the Reich Theatrical Controller Rainer Schlösser introduced 'Year 1 of National Socialist poetry',[28] are a kind of summary of this cultural background, though free from the stuffiness and stale bombast of the majority of these works and containing instead the feeling of personal participation and an excess of emotion which for the most part far outstrips the author's poetic ability. Nevertheless, as poetry with a political purpose, they exercised considerable influence and guided his generation's self-assertiveness in the direction of flag, struggle, heroism and self-sacrifice. Of the fifty poems in the volume 'The

Banner of the Persecuted' almost all follow this theme, and more than half are variations on the idea of death, which was the great obsession of this nationalistic youth. In the name of his generation, which like him had not experienced the war at the front, Schirach wrote, 'We wish to give meaning to our lives: The war spared us for war!' Self-sacrifice, death in battle, flag-draped coffins, marble monuments, the 'celebration of the front' – this was the basic vocabulary in ever new, ever unchanged contexts. In keeping with his insincere nature, a high proportion of the content of these verses was purely literary emotion, a belles-lettres delight in disaster. But here literature was transformed into life; his formulas set the direction of Hitler Youth training and taught a generation of young people to believe, to obey and to die.

For with the seizure of power the ethos proclaimed in these poems became the core of a state education that was immediately organised with both all-embracing totality and extreme intensity. Of the slogans which Schirach now enunciated year by year in order to designate the points requiring special organisational or ideological emphasis, the first, that for 1934, was 'The Year of Inner Education and Orientation'. The assault on the individual, so characteristic of the totalitarian nature of the regime, was directed most consistently towards youth and aimed at including every individual, at every single phase of his development, within an organisation and subjecting him to a planned course of indoctrination. 'The Hitler Youth seeks to embrace both the whole of youth and the whole sphere of life of the young German.'[29] The movement thus provided the first step in an almost faultless system for the organisation and indoctrination of every individual.

This youth [Hitler declared in 1938, with some cynicism] learns nothing else than to think German, to act German, and if these boys enter our organisation at the age of ten and there often get and feel a breath of fresh air for the first time, then four years later they come from the Jungvolk [Young People] into the Hitler Youth, and we keep them there for another four years, and then we certainly don't give them back into the hands of the originators of our old classes and estates, but take them straight into the party, into the Labour Front, the SA or the SS, the NSKK [National Socialist Motorised Corps], and so on. And if they are there for another two years or a year and a half and still haven't become complete National Socialists, then they go into the Labour Service and are polished for another six or seven months, all with a symbol, the German spade. And any class consciousness or pride of status that may be left here and there is taken over by the Wehrmacht for further treatment for two years, and when they come back after two, three, or four years, we take them straight into the SA, SS, and so on again, so that they shall in no case suffer a relapse, and they don't get free again as long as they live. And if anyone says to me, yes, but there will always be a few left over: National Socialism is not at the end of its days but only at the beginning![30]

The majority of the preconditions for this programme requisitioning youth had already been set up in the course of seizing power. The elimination of the Bund groups and Hitler's decree of June 17, 1933, giving Schirach control of all youth work, cleared the decks for the construction of a state youth organisation. By the end of 1934 it had more than three and a half million members, by the end of 1936 around six million. This was due not merely to compulsion and the well-tried methods of psychological pressure, but also to a considerable extent to the wave of nationalist enthusiasm by which the young were seized and carried away, showing even more credulity than the rest of the population. The appeal to the younger generation which was now launched with all the weight of the state behind it certainly helped to bring about the impetuous change of allegiance, and the majority of young people followed the more easily because it was only in rare cases that the type of youth group evolved by the Bund movement felt the new forms to be a break with the past. Moreover, in keeping with Hitler's principle of the 'creeping revolution' in all fields, the Reich Youth leadership was at pains to carry out the transition as imperceptibly as possible. The organisation, style of activity and leadership principle of the Hitler Youth, as well as the travels, camps, uniforms and communal evenings, were in any case derived from the Bünde; the Hitler Youth was able to take over unchanged the songs, the rituals and a certain background ideological consciousness in order only later and piece-meal to adapt them in detail to its own aims. The Hitler Youth Law of December 1, 1936 merely legalised something that had really taken place long before, and two subsequent regulations put service in the Hitler Youth on the same footing as service in the Labour Corps and the Wehrmacht.[31] 'The battle for the unifica-tion of youth is at an end,' Schirach declared on December 1, 1936. He expressed the hope of also 'reconciling and inwardly winning over' the young people who were now being added, in particular those from the ranks of the remaining Catholic youth groups, which had managed to carry on until then in spite of endless harassing. In a second speech that evening, to parents, he supplemented his reference to the 'hard and uncompromising' unification campaign by an almost open invitation to political opportunism. 'Every Hitler Youth cub,' he assured them, 'carries a marshal's baton in his knapsack. But it is not merely the leader-ship of youth that stands open to him; the gates of the state are also open for him. He who from his earliest youth, in this Germany of Adolf Hitler, does his duty and is competent, loyal and brave need have no worries about his future.'[32]

The motives of calculation or fear nourished by such hints, often backed by pressure from worried parents, undoubtedly led many young people into the ranks of the Hitler Youth. But just as many were attracted by the leaders' ability to display ideals, arouse faith, and fill the imagination with an exciting utopia. To a degree hitherto unknown, young people were able to satisfy their spontaneous urge towards involvement, activity and demonstration of their worth. The National Socialist regime seemed to provide what they longed for: 'To throw oneself into a cause, to take responsibility for one's contemporaries, to be able to work for an ever stronger Fatherland in unison with equally enthusiastic comrades,' as one of its members wrote, looking back. 'Public acknowledgment and promotion to positions which previously had been unthinkable lay open.'[33] When Schirach repeatedly declared at Nuremberg that his aim had been the formation of a 'youth state within the state', it was at least true that an attempt had been made to give the nation's youth an awareness of its own self and its pre-eminent position. The problem of the generation gap, which was officially denied and was claimed to have been overcome in the national community, did seem to have been largely solved. On closer inspection, however, we see that it had merely undergone a remarkable process of reversal and that now it was the adults who had been largely forced into a condition of dependence. In this form the division was often deliberately kept alive and turned above all against the rival authority of parents, churches and teachers. Schirach once accused these of simply forgetting 'that in a higher sense the young are always right'.[34] To keep them aware of their own separateness and superiority the young had their own code of honour, their hymns, their leaders, and in Herbert Norkus and the twenty-one members of the so-called 'Immortal Band' their own martyrs. 'Youth must be led by youth,' was the formula coined by Hitler himself.

All this, however, could not conceal the fact that rarely had any growing generation been less independent than this one. Their independence was solely in relation to the bourgeois environment, and was a means of undermining the traditional forces of education. The rigid integration of the Hitler Youth into the party organisation made it totally amenable to the directives of the top leadership, and hence Schirach also called it the 'Youth Sector of the National Socialist Workers Party.'[35] With a barely concealed consistency the organised young were brought up as 'material' for the regime's plans for future expansion and taken into account in calculations of relative strength in considering foreign policy. Incapable, because of their whole apolitical education, of discerning the motives behind the measures adopted by the state, young people saw them only in the context of their own needs; even the ideological training, the 'service' activities, or the organisation of the Hitler Youth in structures taken over from the Wehrmacht, they saw for the most part only as concessions on the part of the leadership to young people's urge towards play and adventure, and naïvely interpreted as an appeal to a universal idealism what in fact served concrete aims of power politics. Although the disguise technique of the National Socialist leadership facilitated such misunderstandings, they would scarcely have been possible without German youth's traditional alienation from politics, which dated from the Wandervögel movement but reached its worst in the storms of enthusiasm that rose in front of Hitler's rostrum. These young people always imagined that the arguments were addressed to their 'sound understanding', not that they were part of imperialist manipulations. Unpolitical as fundamentally they still were, they imagined they heard moral imperatives in situations that involved human malleability before totalitarianism, the accumulation of central power, and war. Thus for example, when Hitler cried out to them:

We must be dominated by one will, we must form one unity, we must be held together by one discipline; we must all be filled with one obedience, one subordination. For over us stands the nation. You must practise today the virtues that nations need when they wish to become great. You must be loyal, you must be courageous, you must be brave, and among yourselves you must form one great, splendid comradeship. Then all the sacrifices of the past that had to be made and were made for the life of our nation will not have been offered in vain.[36]

231

The whole practical and ideological training of youth was subordinated to the regime's political aims. The year 1935 had already been designated as the 'Year of Training', thereby opening the floodgates of terminological inflation. There was talk of physical training, defence training, artistic, professional, racial and even domestic training (within the framework of the Bund Deutscher Mädel (BDM), the Association of German Girls). Side by side with this went a systematic defamation of reason, knowledge and the intellect, each of which was frequently coupled with the adjective 'cowardly'. 'We wish in the course of the year,' ran a speech by Obergebietsführer Dr Hellmuth Stellrecht, 'to reach the point where the gun rests as securely in the hand of German boys as the pen. It is a curious state of mind for a nation when for years it spends many hours a day on calligraphy and orthography, but not one single hour on shooting. Liberalism wrote over the school doors that "Knowledge is power". But we have learnt during the war and the postwar years that the power of a nation ultimately rests exclusively on its weapons and those who know how to use them.'[37] According to an achievement report issued by Schirach's successor as Reich Youth Leader, Arthur Axmann, in 1943, '30,700 Hitler Youth marksmen have been trained. 1.5 million Hitler Youth boys have done regular rifle practice. At the beginning of 1939 an agreement was reached between the Wehrmacht High Command and the Reich Youth Leadership concerning the training of the whole leadership in all aspects of defence in special training camps. While training in shooting and manoeuvre exercises was extended to all young men, the defence training of the Hitler Youth was expanded into special units. In 1938 the Naval Hitler Youth numbered 50,000 the Motorised Hitler Youth 90,000, the Air Force units 74,000, the model-airplane clubs of the German Youth 73,000, the Communications Hitler Youth 29,000.'[38]

This programme was supplemented by 'ideological training'. Hitler laid down its task as 'to bring up that unspoilt generation which will consciously find its way back to primitive instinct'.[39] The key ideas were struggle and race. As the two central concepts of National Socialist ideology, they accompanied and dominated the young person's development from the earliest moment. Even fairy stories were seen 'as a childhood means of education to a heroic view of the world and of life', and a volume of fairy tales forming part of the educational work 'Nation and Führer' bore the significant title 'People Fight'. For the so-called 'Robinson Crusoe' age groups, according to the directions of the National Socialist League of Teachers, descriptions of the World War and Hitler Youth literature were prescribed. 'From an early age youth must be able to face a time when it may be ordered not merely to act, but also to die,' it must 'simply learn to think like our ancestors again. A man's greatest honour lies in death before the enemy of his country.'[40] 'God is struggle and struggle is our blood, and that is why we were born,' sang the Hitler Youth. This line of verse reveals the close connection between 'heroic' and 'racial' complexes of ideas, to which all other education was subordinated. Germany was abundantly rich 'in philosophical systems, in excellent grammars, in beautiful poems'. But 'because in Danzig, Vienna or the Saar region, in Eupen and Malmédy, we are at present very poor,' was the explanation for the new line given in 1933, at first restricted to the immediate aims of foreign policy.[41] Behind this lay from the outset far more ambitious projects. The object of the education programme was no more and no less than 'one day to obtain the generation that is ripe for the last and greatest decisions on this globe', as Hitler stated:[42]

My pedagogy is hard. The weak must be hammered away. In my castle of the Teutonic Order a youth will grow up before which the world will tremble. I want a violent, domineering, undismayed, cruel youth. Youth must be all that. It must bear pain. There must be nothing weak and gentle about it. The free, splendid beast of prey must once more flash from its eyes. I want my youth strong and beautiful. In this way I can create the new.

There was a marked 'literary' flavour about such early utterances by Hitler, and the regime's education policy reflected this only in so far as these visions could be combined with the rigid theme of domination. The 'free, splendid beast of prey' was in reality a domesticated variety trained to react as required. Predictability, extreme effectiveness, all the functional qualities determined the image of the type that was called for. The capacity for independent decision and responsibility was developed only halfway and was kept to prescribed aims. The 'belief in the impossible' which, according to a phrase of Schirach's, youth was to acquire, simply meant credulous readiness to carry out seemingly impossible orders.[43]

The war, which put these educational maxims to the test, confirmed their effectiveness as expected and enabled the generation schooled according to them to achieve results whose splendour could not, of course, conceal the wretchedness of personal degeneration involved. At the beginning of 1940, which he had proclaimed as the 'Year of Testing', Schirach himself went to the Western front before being called to the Führer's headquarters in July of the same year and appointed Gauleiter of Vienna. Either because the intention from the outset was to get him out of the way, or because the influence of the still comparatively liberal and cosmopolitan city released him from his ideological fixations and aroused his first doubts, he soon found himself growing further and further away from the Führer whom he had once so vehemently admired. He had already adopted a sceptical opposition to the decision to make war; his family ties with America and his unorthodox cultural politics as a Gauleiter strained relations still further, and at the beginning of 1943 Hitler remarked to Göring that he felt 'a vague distrust' of Schirach.[44] When the former Reich Youth Leader organised an exhibition in Vienna at about this time, in which works of 'degenerate art' were included, Hitler felt challenged on his most intimate ground and accused him of 'leading the cultural opposition against him in Germany'. This excited outburst did not accurately describe either Schirach's real position or the direction and extent of his efforts. A few weeks later, during a visit to the Berghof, Schirach urged a more moderate policy towards the Russian peoples and, with the assistance of his wife, tried to draw Hitler's attention to the barbaric conditions of the deportation of the Jews, provoking a clash which led to the couple's premature departure. From this point on he found himself isolated, and if his subsequent statement that he had expected to be arrested and charged before the People's Court was probably simply self-dramatisation, it is nevertheless true, as he claimed, that after the controversy at the Berghof he was 'politically a dead man'. He retired into the background, partly out of personal fear and also no doubt out of the embarrassment of a man who saw his romantic ideals and fantasies of self-sacrifice, heroism and marble monuments contradicted by the reality of the war, even if he refrained from putting it into words, 'in order to maintain a foolish dream a little while longer'.[45] When the Hitler Youth went into action in the Breslau Fortress, when the Volksturm units made up the 'Third Levy', or when they defended the Pichelsdorf Bridge in Berlin, the boys of the Hitler Youth died in reality the death that he had celebrated in rhymes.

Schirach's defence counsel emphasised in his closing speech at Nuremberg that there was no blood on his client's hands. However true this may be in a strictly legal sense, it obscures certain relevant facts about the person and career of the Third Reich's Youth Leader. We misconstrue the problems and also the possible meaning of a figure such as this if we argue, from whatever point of view, for or against his guilt as a murderer; in fact what is involved is *suicide* in response to an irrational emotional impulse. Not the adversary's death, but one's own death, was the burden of Schirach's intoxicated utterances, and with him – and long before him – one of the major themes of the younger generation. This, far more than the brown Hitler Youth uniform he wore, makes him the representative of one type, or one widespread attitude – how widespread this investigation, in spite of its restricted frame of reference, has I hope already shown. 'We were born to die for Germany', was written over the entrance to one Hitler Youth centre; but the sentence might also have come from the diary of a member of the Wandervögel or one of the countless publications of the Bündische Jugend. What linked them all, along with numerous other common features, was their rapturous suppression of the instinct of self-preservation, their faith in the magic of self-sacrifice. It was a romantic attitude that was described and construed as heroic, when in truth it was only an ineptitude for life and a readiness to die.

It would be hard to deny that the Third Reich's youth programme represented, as the title in one of Schirach's books put it, a 'Revolution in Education'; but at the same time it also contained countless pre-National Socialist elements that had arisen out of lack of self-knowledge. Faith in authority, political irrationalism, the cult of the past, flight from reality into an 'inner' realm not of this world, resignation to destiny, a mystic readiness for death: these were motifs, long in the air, which National Socialism merely exploited and cynically put to its own purposes. When at his Nuremberg trial Schirach repeatedly called upon German youth to abjure anti-Semitism he demonstrated his misunderstanding of the complex character of the problem, whose solution demanded not merely the repudiation of extreme or criminal phenomena but a radically different self-interpretation on the part of youth. The first steps towards this are apparent in the transition from the credulous to the 'sceptical' generation.

General von X:
The Behaviour and Role of the
Officer Corps in the Third Reich

Oh, you know, one became such a blackguard.

Wilhelm Keitel

True heroism, contrary to military heroism, is always bound up with insults and contempt.

Theodor Fontane

On January 30, 1933 General von X, then still at the beginning of his career, placed himself alongside Lieutenant Count von Stauffenberg at the head of an enthusiastic crowd in the streets of Bamberg celebrating Hitler's appointment as Reich Chancellor. A few weeks later, at the ceremonial opening of the first Reichstag of the Third Reich at Potsdam, he willingly allowed himself to be overwhelmed by the make-believe reconciliation of the old Germany with the new. He had a hand in the elimination of Röhm and in the mid-1930s he devoted himself to the establishment of new divisions bearing the stamp of his energy and his precise expertise, until the events of 1938 sobered his illusory self-confidence. He conspired and, like Brauchitsch and others, accepted personal favours. He combined the enthusiastic blindness of Blomberg with Beck's morality, the narrow-minded expertise of Manstein with Keitel's undignified compliancy. He was, as was said of Major General Oster, 'a man after God's heart', and yet 'the Devil's General'.[1] The countless historical judgments passed against him, the 'Prussian-German officer', miss the reality of the relationship between Hitler and his generals since they miss the element of contradiction; for *the* German officer did not exist while Hitler was working for power or after it, any more than *the* officer corps existed as a homogeneous entity. General Ludwig Beck represented no-one as a human or moral type. The same is true of his antitheses: Keitel, Burgdorf or Jodl. The devastating effect of the explosive charges which Hitler set off deep in the social block of the officer caste allows only one summary assertion: they were all vanquished men. For in their differing or actually opposed attitudes we can read the defeat of a social group that had always watched jealously over both its inner and its outer solidarity.

The cleft began to show before 1933, while the National Socialist movement

235

was fighting for power; to begin with, it separated the generations. After the resignation of Seeckt, the commander in chief of the Reichswehr, who had used his authority to stop the developing schisms within the officer corps immediately after the war and had forced the Reichswehr into a state of solidarity by a rigorously one-sided policy, fissures began to show again towards the end of the 1920s. This was surprisingly and dramatically shown in the treason trial of the three young Nazi officers of the Ulm Reichswehr, when at times violently divergent attitudes appeared within the officer corps. Particularly among the young officers, a considerable minority clearly opted for the 'activist' NSDAP, not only for reasons of national temperament and because of the inactivity and weakness of the Republican authorities, but also from professional resentment at seeing themselves condemned to a 'career in the second rank' by the restriction to a hundred-thousand-man army.[2] The older generation, on the other hand, greeted the rising Hitler party with either reserve or with open rejection. Only a few, of course, opposed it out of genuine republican convictions; for the most part opposition sprang from intellectual and sentimental attachment to the imperial era as well as from disapproval of bad manners and a political rowdyism far removed from behaviour becoming to an officer and a gentleman. This rift between the generations, however, was for a long time bridged by a common antipathy towards the Weimar Republic. Right up to the last moment the Reichswehr served it with every sign of unwilling, forced loyalty, and Seeckt himself consistently worked against all attempts at reconciliation. His cold, impersonal attitude towards the political authorities, his ostentatious refusal to join in the annual celebration of the Constitution, his success – at least as far as the Reichswehr was concerned – in settling a dispute over flags in favour of the old black, white and red colours, as well as his stubborn refusal to accept the establishment of a Republican order of merit, all resulted from a fundamental and obstinate repudiation of a state with such revolutionary, socialist and pacifist features, whose existence was seen and tolerated only as provisional, as a 'bad patch'.[3]

Seeckt's efforts to keep the Reichswehr ideologically apart from all outside influences went hand in hand, at least before Hindenburg's presidency, with efforts to transfer the officer corps' traditional attachment to the monarch to the military leadership itself, since the abstract concept of the state was incapable of satisfying the persistent desire for personal loyalty, or at all events to prevent this loyalty from operating for the benefit of the democratic regime. Above this was elevated the idea of the 'unpolitical soldier', which was put forward as the principle of standing above the parties, but in reality was simply a tactical maxim designed to extend the army's autonomy and resist all demands for involvement in the defence of the Republic. The Reichswehr's responsibility for the events leading up to January 30, 1933 does not lie in active support for the NSDAP, or in more or less overt acts of intervention in favour of Hitler, as certain prejudiced interpretations would have it, but in the stubborn and incorrigible attachment to the idea of a separate 'state within the state'.[4] This attitude led to an unfortunate

236

corresponding indifference to the officer corps on the Republican side, so that in the end both proved incapable of bridging the old, tragic cleft between civil and military.

Furthermore, during the last days of January 1933 the Reichswehr, at least at the top, was a picture of confusion and division, as can be seen in what happened at the time of Blomberg's appointment as Minister for the Reichswehr. There were isolated feelings of resignation or revolt, voiced most strongly by the then Chief of the General Staff, General von Hammerstein, who informed the Reich President of the Army Command's doubts about appointing Hitler to ministerial office. But such feelings were outweighed by the readiness to see the change of Chancellor as the decision of Hindenburg, who alone represented the state which the Reichswehr served, beyond all parliamentary or cabinet changes, those of January 30, 1933 included. It was precisely this passive attitude that led Hitler in September 1933 to make the famous remark that has repeatedly been quoted as proof of the generals' guilt: 'If the Reichswehr had not stood at our side during the days of the revolution, then we should not be standing here today.'[5] But, regarded in historical context, this utterance can be seen to have been intended to bring about that very action for which it pretended to be thankful. It was part of that policy of friendly gestures and marks of favour which Hitler followed during his first few months of power, when his position was still shaky, in order to win over the manifestly sceptical generals. It was in line with the flood of lip service to nationalism, tradition, the Prussian spirit, Western values, or the spirit of the front-line soldier, ostentatious displays of respect for the person of the Reich President, and stress upon decency, morality, order, Christianity, and all those concepts which went with a conservative idea of the state. As part of the same propagandist effort Hitler had delivered a speech to the top ranks of the Army on February 3, 1933 which, according to Blomberg, he described as 'one of his most difficult speeches, because all the time it was as though he were speaking to a wall'.[6] The way in which, although he did not actually remove them at once, he nevertheless radically undermined the suspicions of the military leaders, which were in any case halfhearted, proved him once more a master of psychological calculation. He not only promised them the rearming of the Wehrmacht, the 'steeling of youth and the strengthening of the will to defence by all possible means', and powerful key positions in the state as against the rival claims of Röhm and the SA, but in addition presented his own counterdemands in such a way that they 'merely seemed to fulfil the wishes of the Reichswehr'.[7] The speech culminated in the declaration that the Wehrmacht was to remain 'unpolitical and above the parties', 'the struggle inside the country [was] not its affair, but the affair of the Nazi organisations'. Hitler seemed to be offering concessions and a return to the familiar practice of Seeckt with all the advantages of relief from decision-making and the secretly hoped for possibility of taking over the role of supreme arbiter at the right moment; in fact, he extracted from the unsuspecting officers a free hand for terrorism.

The decisive factor was that Hitler found in the Reichswehr Minister, Blomberg, and his closest adviser, Colonel von Reichenau, who was appointed head of the ministerial department on February 21, two partners who followed his course almost unconditionally. In spite of roughly similar points of departure, these two were nevertheless totally different from each other.. The freedom from the trammels of tradition, the flexibility and open-mindedness which they had in common arose in Blomberg's case from rootlessness and a lack of mental balance; he was a man of temperament, moods and impulses. Reichenau, on the other hand, was a calculating cynic who had discarded all moral criteria as potential hindrances to his power. Blomberg was a weak, easily influenced personality who had little to oppose to Hitler's forceful persuasiveness; he vacillated and abandoned himself in turn to democratic convictions, the cult of anthroposophy, Prussian socialism, then (after a trip to Russia) 'almost to Communism', and finally succumbed increasingly to authoritarian ideas, before falling victim to Hitler with all the excessive emotionalism of his enthusiastic but fundamentally insubstantial nature. He wrote in his memoirs that in 1933 things had fallen into his lap overnight which since 1919 he had ceased to expect: faith, respect for a man, and total support for an idea. He had subscribed to National Socialism because he found that in the core of this movement everything was right.[8]

Even during the time they spent together in East Prussia, Blomberg was reinforced in such beliefs, indeed probably led to them, by Reichenau, then his chief of staff. As head, too, of the ministerial department, Reichenau did not allow his ambitions to be confused by emotionalism but brought to them cold, purposeful, Machiavellian instincts. Although he had made contact with Hitler at a comparatively early stage and had exchanged letters with him, National Socialism was not to him, any more than anything else, a matter of inner conviction, but the ideology of a political mass movement whose revolutionary élan he planned to harness, and at the right moment tame, to further both his career and the interests of the Army. As sober as he was intelligent, delighting in taking decisions, magnanimous and yet not without a touch of frivolity, Reichenau embodied almost perfectly the type of the modern, technically trained and socially unprejudiced officer, who had resolutely thrown overboard the feudal blinkers of his class and extended his freedom from prejudice to moral principles as well. In February 1933 Reichenau, who by virtue of his personality was soon to become a crucial figure in the Reichswehr's policy-making at that period, told a council of commanding officers, according to the notes of one of those present:

We must recognise that we are in the midst of a revolution. What is rotten in the state must fall and it can only be brought down by terror. The party will proceed ruthlessly against Marxism. The Army's task is to order arms. No succour if any of the persecuted seek refuge with the troops.[9]

This dishonourable injunction which aroused 'great dismay' but significantly only one voice of protest, governed the actions of the Reichswehr leaders during the coming months. They stood aside with ordered arms while the Constitution was eroded piecemeal, the *Länder* overcome, the parties and political organisations suppressed, minorities persecuted, opponents of the regime arrested, maltreated or murdered, and justice and the law eliminated. They did so not under the pressure of external circumstances, nor from duty to their oath of obedience, which did not disintegrate until later, nor, finally, in obedience to traditional ways of thinking, which Reichenau's above-quoted speech violently contradicted. Their attitude was a deliberate political decision. And the Army leaders did not stir when Hitler sent out his murder squads on a three-day massacre in the Röhm affair. If public order, as Blomberg later claimed, was really threatened by rebels and conspirators, it would have been the Reichswehr leaders' duty to intervene; if this was not the case, then they should have put a stop to what was happening. But far from recognising any such duty, they actually lent the SS their weapons, and for the right to call themselves the nation's only arms-bearers they finally tolerated the crimes committed against them and held fast to the restricted political aims they had set themselves. This demonstrated above even the most elementary ties of comradeship that they were perfectly ready to 'barter the honour of the Army for the illusion of power'.[10] Non-intervention finally became a synonym for the renunciation of integrity and all moral claims, and with his unfailing nose for power relationships Hitler immediately discerned the underlying confession of weakness. When, immediately after Hindenburg's death at the beginning of August 1934, Blomberg and Reichenau rather overhurriedly compelled the Army to take an oath of unconditional obedience to the 'Führer of the German Reich and nation, Adolf Hitler, the Supreme Commander of the Wehrmacht', this was not so much, as has frequently been suggested, the beginning of a disastrous entanglement, but more accurately its first conclusive climax.

From this point on, however, the policy of the Reichswehr leadership no longer reflected the prevailing mood in the officer corps. But all of them, whether they shortsightedly regarded the June murders as a victory for the Reichswehr, prematurely saw them as the final conclusion of the revolutionary phase, as a dubious encroachment, or with indignation and disgust as naked murder, were agreed in the view expressed by a head of department in the Army High Command: 'A soldier has to do his duty, but not to bother about other people's affairs.'[11] It was the old formula, not erroneous in itself but, as always, erroneously applied, of the 'unpolitical soldier' that was now employed more intensively than ever before as an ideological mask for a fundamental fear of decision-making. With the difference, of course, that under the Weimar Republic this attitude had led the Army to withdraw its loyalty from the state, whereas now, under the growing power of Hitler, it was to the victims of the state that aid was refused. In other words, where before the Army had refused to say yes, now it refused to say no. This was the main factor in the attitude of the higher ranks of the officer corps, especially after the introduction of universal military service in March 1935. In so far as the higher-ranking officers took cognizance of political events at all, they welcomed the regime's rigorous and energetic enforcement of order, its resolute nationalism – so different from the readiness to yield and renounce which had characterised the Weimar period – its policy of rearmament and the enhanced status of the officer that went with it. Just as the officer corps had never learnt to think beyond its own aims, so now, restricting itself to the directly military tasks confronting it, it turned a blind eye to the disquieting occurrences outside, dismissing them as inevitable in a revolutionary fresh start. Where tendencies to opposition emerged at all, they occurred once again among the older generation; but here too they were more tactical than fundamental. The majority were grateful to Hitler for saving the soldier by entrusting him once more with the 'purely objective tasks of the service', as General von Choltitz wrote in retrospect.[12] A phrase widely current at the time described the Army as the 'aristocratic form of emigration'; many of the bourgeois class, resigned to the situation, sought refuge in military service from the repugnant reality of political activity, in order to satisfy their desire for individual achievement in tasks that were supposedly beyond moral evaluation.

Their motives were, however, not always unambiguous. It is difficult to distinguish, in this apparently homogeneous retreat to the objective demands of military life, the respective parts played by mute protest, escapism, pure careerism or a blind professionalism that saw moral objections as mere emotional weakness of character and unhesitatingly placed its expertise at the service of any partnership whatever. We need hardly refer to Hitler's resolution to tolerate politically halfhearted specialists within the Wehrmacht only for so long as he was dependent upon them for constructing an effective instrument for the attainment of his imperialist aims. As early as 1934 he told an interviewer that in his opinion there was 'absolutely no room for the unpolitical man'. Later, in the concluding phase of the process of ideological indoctrination of the Wehrmacht, which was now soon to be embarked upon with great vigour, he declared when dismissing Field Marshal von Brauchitsch: 'It is the task of the Supreme Commander of the Army to educate the Army in a National Socialist sense. I know no Army general capable of doing this. Therefore I have decided to assume supreme command of the Army myself.'[13] In fact the withdrawal of power from the generals was merely the end of a process. This had begun with, among other preconditions, the formula of the 'unpolitical soldier', reflected in countless utterances that have come down to us, as when the Chief of the Army High Command, General von Fritsch, remarked in a letter in May 1937, with an undertone of short-sighted self-satisfaction: 'I have made it a guiding principle to confine myself to the military domain and to keep aloof from all political activity. I lack all talent for it.'[14] Similarly Brauchitsch dismissed politics out of hand as a realm that was beyond his horizon, while Ernst Udet and others smiled at it as 'a comic din in the background',[15] though this din forced its way to their door and even across the threshold in the form of injustice, terror and murder.

If Blomberg and Reichenau had at first supported Hitler's totalitarian efforts because they calculated that the rearmament that was promised and begun, together with the increase in the number of troops, would inevitably augment the weight and influence of the military authorities, they were soon disillusioned. It was not that Blomberg, for all his ingratiating attitude, voluntarily abandoned

240

his position; rather the overhasty and almost unplanned rearmament had a disintegrating effect on the solidarity of the officer corps, since the existing strength was simply not in a position to impose its stamp upon the mass of young officers commissioned within a short space of time. Freiherr von Fritsch complained that Hitler was 'forcing everything, overdoing everything, rushing everything far too much and destroying every healthy development'. It remains an open question whether this side effect of the insistence on hurried rearmament was not intentional, but there can be no doubt that it suited Hitler's purpose, although he had ordered the chief of the Army Command, when he took office on February 1, 1934, to 'create an army of the greatest possible strength and internal compactness and homogeneity at the best imaginable level of training'.[16] In any case, what was supposed to be an instrument of the High Command became increasingly an effective weapon for Hitler against all internal political ambitions of the military leaders. Knowledge of this made it easier for him to take the unparalleled step with which, in spring 1938, he humiliated the Wehrmacht and put paid to the last remining illusions of a military claim to leadership or self-assertion.

As it happened, it was Blomberg who gave Hitler the opportunity after exasperating him by a reluctance to follow up his hazardous foreign policy measures and by allowing within the military leadership a spirit in which aversion to warlike entanglements was combined with ideological indolence. From Hitler's point of view an officer corps that approved rearmament but not war, the 'order' created by National Socialism but not its ideology, was bound to appear inconsistent. When the Chief of the Army High Command stated in a memorandum, 'Quite apart from the fact that the basis of our present-day Army is and must be National Socialist, an incursion of party-political influences into the Army cannot be tolerated,'[17] Hitler was not alone in trying in vain to resolve the contradiction. The repeated warnings and fundamental objections advanced by Blomberg and those around him, expressed in their most definite form in a famous discussion on November 5, 1937, convinced Hitler that the top military leadership was not made of the stuff which he required for his extensive plans for conquest. Therefore, when it became known at the end of January 1938 that Blomberg's recent remarriage was a misalliance of a character to concern the vice squad and necessitate the minister's dismissal, he seized the opportunity to get rid of Blomberg's natural successor, Freiherr von Fritsch, at the same time. In a scene that might have come out of a melodrama the unsuspecting Commander in Chief of the Army was accused in the Reich Chancellery of homosexual offences, an accusation which, although it soon proved absolutely unfounded, provided the excuse for the extensive reshuffle on February 4 that went far beyond the military sphere and forced the last remaining representatives of conservatism from their positions of influence. Hitler himself took over and surrounded himself in the newly formed Wehrmacht Supreme Command with yes-men who, in exact reversal of Marwitsch's phrase, 'chose favour, where disobedience did not bring honour'. Fritsch was succeeded by General von Brauchitsch, whose qualifications for the post were a weak character and the declaration that he was 'ready for anything' that was asked of him. In particular he gave an assurance that he would bring the Wehrmacht closer to National Socialism.[18]

At one blow, with not one hint of resistance, Hitler had eliminated the last power centre of any significance and, along with the whole civilian power, now held the military in his hand. Contemptuously he commented that he now knew all generals were cowards.[19] His contempt was reinforced by the unhesitating readiness of numerous generals to move into the positions that had become free, even before Fritsch's rehabilitation. This process also demonstrated that the inner unity of the officer corps was finally broken and that the solidarity of the caste, which had already failed to vindicate itself in the case of the murder of Schleicher and Bredow, no longer existed. General von Fritsch wrote despondently:

No nation ever allowed the commander in chief of its army to be subjected to such disgraceful treatment. I hereby place this on record, so that later historians may know how the Commander in Chief of the Army was treated in 1938. Such treatment is not only undignified for me, it at the same time dishonours the whole Army.[20]

Characteristically, the former Commander-in-Chief of the Army had historians in mind, not history itself. Both now and six months later he refused his support to a group of officers who, as they saw the way things were going, sought to make conspiratorial contact with him, with the fatalistic remark: 'This man is Germany's destiny, and this destiny will run its course to the end.'[21]

Nevertheless the crisis of spring 1938 became the starting-point for attempts, at the cost of personal sacrifice, to win back the honour of the Army, whose loss the General had only been able to lament. Elements of Hitler's belligerent policy, which till then had been thoughtlessly disregarded or simply overlooked, crystallised more and more into concrete fears. It may be taken as certain that the majority of the top-ranking officers were entirely critical of his hazardous plans for the future and by no means approved of a course that was leading towards war, though naturally not so much out of moral considerations as on the basis of a sober evaluation of the relative strength of the armed forces concerned. But a complicated system of assurances and self-deceptions again and again dissipated their objections and they got around their 'worried presentiment of his liability to disaster'[22] with the aid of various arguments, whether, like Blomberg, they refused for a long time to take Hitler's plans 'seriously', whether they trusted to the damping effect of the facts of power politics, which would soon enough show the limits of these extravagant fantasies of domination, or finally whether, especially after the astonishing triumphs of bloodless expansion, they put their faith in the 'Führer's genius'.[23] Only a minority refused to accept such dishonest excuses and took seriously both Hitler's person and his plans, as well as the challenge to a personal decision contained in them. As early as January 1937 Ludwig Beck, the Chief of the General Staff, wrote to his superior, General von Fritsch:

The Wehrmacht enjoys among our military-minded nation almost unlimited trust. The responsibility for what is to come rests almost exclusively with the Army. There is no avoiding this fact.[24]

From his position Beck did indeed do everything to thwart or at least delay Hitler's plans, without achieving anything to begin with but his own dismissal. 'What is the dog making of our beautiful Germany!' he exclaimed at the time,[25] and only slowly, with endless pangs of conscience, did he come to approve a project for a coup d'état again and again discussed and planned within a restricted circle. His despair, which was partly the helplessness of the individual in the face of a totalitarian regime, but clearly also the inner helplessness of a man caught up in the characteristic ideas of his caste, is a clear demonstration of the problems that faced almost all the officer conspirators. Respect for the now purely formal authority of the oath of obedience remained insurmountable. The realisation that Hitler had long since forfeited any claim on that oath and that an assassination had become a necessity could never break down that last emotional barrier; what he was planning appeared to him as mutiny and revolution, words which, as he himself said in a discussion with Halder, 'do not exist in the dictionary of a German soldier'. In this sense, right up to the end, he saw the day he took an oath to Hitler as the 'blackest day' of his life.[26]

The dichotomy revealed the limitations of rigid military thinking and feeling. Objective achievement and integration in an effective organisation were all: the subjective was something to be regarded with distrust. But behind this there had to be a social order that was accepted as binding. The ethos was viable only so long as the order itself was not called in question; in revolutionary times it broke down, even if its aim was to produce not the 'mechanical' but the disciplined character, which in its best representatives it did indeed achieve. But accustomed as they were to suppress their individuality and to deny all contradictions, all feelings, especially those of revolt against an established order, as captious arrogance, since there was 'no room for sentiment here', the officers' doubts of the dictator's right to rule constantly reverted to doubt of their right to doubt. This dilemma, devoid as it was here of any evasive secondary aims, commands our respect; here an educational principle came up against limits beyond which it had no answer to the problems confronting it. But we must also ask whether it was not this scrupulous attitude, hampered by constant inner worries and conflicts on the part of the officers of the opposition, from Hammerstein to Canaris, from Olbricht, Tresckow, Stieff and Schlabrendorff to Stauffenberg, that was responsible for the failure of the military resistance. Certainly there was too the discouraging compliance of Great Britain, followed by a technical failure, then again Hitler's ever renewed and astounding successes, and finally, again and again, a fatal mischance. But in the last resort it must also have been that lack of resolution in setting about a task which ran counter to everything all of them had been brought up to believe in, that turned all these obsessional, split-natured, endlessly arguing conspirators, inextricably entangled in their reasons and counter-reasons, into modern Hamlets.

243

Meanwhile their efforts also came to grief on the weakness and moral immobility of a large proportion of the generals and leading officers, who had to be won over to ever renewed conspiracies, only in the end to vacillate once more and burden every one of the actions, from summer 1938 to July 1944, with an element of uncertainty; this in the end the conspirators disregarded, less because of real prospects of success than because it was felt that even an unsuccessful assassination attempt would help to restore lost honour. 'We are purifying ourselves,' General Stieff replied in answer to a sceptical question about the probable outcome of one attempt.[27] Here the conception of being subject to a special imperative of duty, based upon traditional notions of the élite status of the officer, was still at work. Under the challenge of totalitarian government, however, the conviction of their special value felt by the military was shown to have been perverted into an empty claim to social privilege. There was nothing left but outward show; the conviction had merely the forms and formulas of that type of Prussian officer to whom it appealed and with whom it has often been confused. The extent of this degeneration becomes horrifyingly clear from the fact that, looking back after the disaster, one of the members of the officer caste, Keitel, showed himself incapable of recognising the conflict in which the conspirators of July 20, 1944 found themselves, and saw there nothing but injured pride, frustrated ambition and office-seeking![28] When former Field Marshal von Rundstedt was asked in Nuremberg whether he had never thought of getting rid of Hitler, he replied firmly and unhesitatingly that he was a soldier, not a traitor.[29] Here, as in many postwar references to the military resistance that are marked by the same confusion of ideas, we can see the consequences of the idea that a soldier can betray his country, his people, his honour and his responsibility for the lives of his subordinates, but not a man to whom he has sworn an oath, even if on his side this man has broken his word a thousand times over.

It is not difficult, then, to discern behind this defence, which employed pseudo-morality to stylise into an attitude of selfless devotion to duty what was really only a lack of moral fibre, the distinctive mark of a weak opportunism which characterised the overwhelming majority of the top-ranking German officers of the period and found typical expression in Friedrich Fromm and Günther von Kluge. The vacillation of these two men arose out of a split that could not be healed by ordinary military standards and modes of thought, but only by a degree of individual 'civilian' courage which they did not possess. In the conflict of values, after long-drawn-out wavering between promises to the conspirators abruptly alternating with professions of loyalty to the 'Führer', at the moment when they found themselves confronted with an irrevocable decision, the lives of both came to an equally revealing and memorable end. While Fromm had his partners in the plot of July 20, 1944 shot in the War Ministry yard after a hurried trial to avoid possible implication and save his own life, though he was later arrested and executed himself, Field Marshal von Kluge, relieved of his post and ordered back to Berlin, committed suicide in the train between Paris and Metz, leaving a letter of farewell once more proclaiming his personal admiration for

Hitler.[30] Many came to grief through the same inadequacy of character, if not in equally dramatic circumstances, and instead of performing a historically effective or at least memorable act, resignedly sought death. Keitel later asked regretfully why, on July 20, 1944, during the attempt on Hitler's life, fate had denied him a 'decent, honourable hero's death', thereby clearly showing how far disintegration had gone, when the only answer to the need to reach an unambiguous decision of conscience was a longing for fortuitous death.[31]

This almost universal weakness of character led in the course of the war to a loss of influence on the part of the military leaders in the sphere of the state as well as in that of their own operations. By bowing, often against their better judgment, to Hitler's orders as dictated by the whim of the moment, they themselves fostered the process of loss of power which began with the planning of the French campaign before Dunkirk, reached its climax with the dismissal of Brauchitsch and the battle of Stalingrad, and concluded after July 20, 1944 with the appointment of Himmler as commander in chief of the Replacement Army. It was this same feeble readiness to collaborate, even at the price of self-compromise, that finally entangled a considerable number of them in the regime's injustices and its extermination programme. We may be sure that the so-called jurisdiction order, the 'Night and Fog Decree' or the 'Commando Group Order' once again aroused 'intense dismay' among the high-ranking officers; but as before there was with a few exceptions a complete absence of any attempt at protest or counter-activity. Instead we see isolated efforts to preserve a merely formal integrity, as when Manstein's Chief of Staff requested Einsatzgruppenleiter Otto Ohlendorf to carry out the extermination measures away from Army headquarters, whereas Manstein himself, as well as Küchler, Hoth and Reichenau, even almost over-fulfilled such decrees when they issued orders in near-identical terms to the units under their command stating that 'the soldier in the Eastern zone is not merely a fighter according to the rules of the art of war, but also the carrier of an inexorable racial idea, who must have complete understanding for the need for harsh but just punishment of Jewish subhumanity'.[32] When Manstein later pleaded at Nuremberg that he could not remember any such order, this at best revealed the corrupting effects of continual collaboration in the unjust system; for nothing but an attitude of blind fundamental cooperation can explain how such a radical communiqué totally contrary to every soldierly tradition could have 'completely vanished from memory'.

Finally the appeal to the concept of obedience, which played such a great part in the attempts at self-justification made by all the generals, served merely to cloak their overriding weakness of personality. Obedience is basic to any military organisation, but like every moral obligation it has limits in supralegal standards that must remain its ultimate sanction. To set up dependence on orders as an absolute which degrades responsibility and conscience to the same levels as orders 'inseparable from commands' is indefensible either morally or legally, and if the Prussian tradition repudiated disobedience, it nevertheless left room for the refusal of obedience. There is support for this all the way from the general who snapped at one of his officers who had carried out an order without thinking: 'Sir, the King of Prussia made you a staff officer so that you should know when you ought not to obey!' to Generals von der Marwitz, Seydlitz or Yorck.[33] The Second World War offers comparable examples: Rommel's decision to withdraw his troops before El Alamein, although under express orders to pursue a strategy of death or victory, is by no means without parallel. But contrary examples preponderate by far. From Stalingrad to the senseless acts of self-destruction during the concluding phase of the war, the majority displayed an irresoluteness, a cowardice, a moral apathy incapable of individual initiative; bowing utterly to Hitler's orders, they finally marched at his side unmoved, despondent and helpless towards a defeat which they themselves had long prepared.

Yet even this requires some qualification. For some, particularly among commanders at the front, there were special circumstances that made the decision between obedience and refusal of obedience very much more difficult. Among these commanders the type of the 'unpolitical soldier' was particularly heavily represented, the officer who had been confirmed in his self-satisfied professionalism by the run of brilliant victories at the beginning of the war. Only the vicissitudes of the war made clear to him the incompetence and illegality of the regime, to which till then he had given a totally unideological loyalty inspired by its success. After the onset of the defensive phase, their basic readiness to resist was balked by various considerations. Some felt they were not entitled to revolt and thus shake the confidence of the troops entrusted to them; others felt it their duty first to bring the war to an end before taking the internal political action which they recognised as necessary; yet others feared the collapse of the front, with inevitable chaos, and tried to weigh up the sacrifices demanded by various possible decisions; and along with other similar arguments all were inhibited by the Allied demand for 'unconditional surrender'. However much blinkered professionalism or intellectual inconsistency may have played a part, many of those concerned were clearly agonisingly aware of this conflict, and certainly as the war went on the scope for decision was greatly reduced. It is possible that there was no other way out of this dilemma than that chosen by the mass of high-ranking officers at the front when they elected to fight on; for at this stage what was at stake was mitigation of the consequences. The causes lay much further back.

Anyone who looks back can name the decisive landmarks in the progress – not January 30, 1933, or an even earlier date, however much in this phase certain psychological stages on the road were prepared and occupied; not the frivolous arrogance with which the officer corps welcomed the regime's restoration of order and nationalist self-confidence, knuckled under to the mental act of violence of Potsdam, or deluded itself so long about its position of leadership; nor the mutual attraction of the 'Prussian military spirit' and the National Socialist hatred of the intellect. All these elements, so far as they play any part at all, are of only secondary importance. The significant signs were rather the gradual, unprotesting readiness to toe the line laid down by Reichenau's order-arms decree; ambiguous political neutralism and especially the order of June 30, 1930: 'Give arms to the SS if they want them'; the murders so openly celebrated as a victory by the military leaders that Blomberg had to remind them it was not fitting to rejoice over 'those ki..ed in battle', as he put it.[34] These acts of opportunism practised at first hesitantly and with a bad conscience, but then ever more uninhibitedly, decisively established the path and position of the military power-holders in the Third Reich. It sounds like an echo of Reichenau's own words in spring 1933 when we read Halder's note in his war diary of a remark by Canaris about the behaviour of the military leaders in the East: 'Officers too slack; no humane action on behalf of the unjustly persecuted.'[35] It was not only slackness, however, but a tactical principle that had long since become habit. The selfish calculation that more and more determined the actions of the top-level military leadership had merely served to gain short-lived initial successes or simply the illusions of victories, which were soon revealed as defeats. *Les institutions périssent par leurs victoires.* What happened on July 20, 1944 was not least the attempt of a minority to break out of the vicious circle by a courageous deed and turn away in an act of visible and decisive revolt from the errors and confusions of the past years in order to retrieve at least a part of the integrity that had been sacrificed to shortsighted goals.

Hitler's growing contempt for the military leadership had a complex foundation. But there is much to indicate that an important element in it was his recognition of the weakness shown in his generals' continual vacillations between fronts, at its most obvious in their attitude towards the war and National Socialism. Rarely has a military leadership been accused of aggressive desires with more inaccurate, fundamentally prejudiced arguments than the German General Staff of those years. From Fritsch and Blomberg down to Generals Wilhelm Adam and Georg Thomas they repeatedly expressed expert warnings and doubts, and tried to circumvent Hitler's intoxicated plans by their own pessimistic evaluations of the situation, and again and again they were proved wrong. The frequent changes in the leadership are a clear reflection of this resistance. Hitler himself remarked during the war:

Before I became Reich Chancellor I thought the General Staff was like a mastiff that has to be kept on a tight leash because otherwise it threatens to attack everyone else. After I had become Reich Chancellor I was forced to observe that there is nothing the General Staff less resembles than a mastiff. This General Staff always prevented me from doing what I considered necessary. The General Staff opposed rearmament, the occupation of the Rhineland, the invasion of Austria, the occupation of Czechoslovakia, and finally even the war against Poland. The General Staff advised me not to make war on Russia. It is I who always have first to urge on this mastiff.[36]

The top generals as a whole showed the same resistance towards National Socialism. In the then current division of the Army leadership into three categories, purely military experts, the officers of the resistance, and the so-called 'party soldiers', the last group was the smallest. The diary of one of these 'party soldiers', General Jodl, repeatedly laments that the General Staff refused to believe in the genius of the Führer, and describes it as 'deeply sad' that at the Party Congress at Nuremberg in 1938, for example, 'the Führer has the whole nation behind him, but not the leading generals of the Army'.[37] This attitude, a mixture of arrogance, scepticism and indifference, intensified the resentment which Hitler already felt to the point of open hatred of the whole body of generals, a hatred from which it seems even his closest colleagues in the Führer's headquarters were not spared. In any case Goebbels noted at the height of the war:

He [Hitler] passes on the whole body of the generals an annihilating judgment which is admittedly often prejudiced or unjust, but by and large no doubt accurate. He has also explained to me why he no longer eats his lunch at the big table in the Führer's headquarters. He can no longer bear the sight of the generals. All generals lie, he says, all generals are against National Socialism, all generals are reactionaries. They are disloyal, they don't stand by him, to a large extent they don't understand him at all. However, he feels that a general can no longer offend him. He feels alien to this class of person and will in future remain more than ever remote from them.[38]

In conclusion one cannot help measuring the results of this investigation of the behaviour and role of the officer corps in the Third Reich against the halo that surrounded the German military leadership at the time, in particular the General Staff. Its fame was legendary; but the secret of its soul, Hitler was to discover, was a humiliation; an opportunism that thought itself crafty, totally devoid of convictions, almost exclusively concerned with self-interest, 'ready for anything'. The German General Staff obviously shared Blomberg's conviction that the honour of a Prussian officer consisted in being correct and that it became the honour of a German officer to be cunning.[39] Such attitudes, and those others that have already been quoted, disclosed the final stage of a long process of degeneration against which appeals to oaths of obedience and the obligation of loyalty, as well as to the Prussian military tradition, possessed no more power. It is true that the failure of a nation cannot be blamed exclusively upon the military forces, and that 'a few Army generals, no matter how many tanks they have at their disposal', neither have a mission that goes beyond the limits of those in whom resides the political will, nor by themselves the means of making good such a failure.[40] But the special moral and national authority which the officer corps in Germany had for generations claimed as its own at least justifies expectations of a greater degree of initiative than the overwhelming majority displayed. Among the positive effects of those years we can include the dismissal of this claim to special authority. The somewhat reluctant respect felt today for the military resistance shows just how little it was able to assert this claim. Incidentally, it was not solely the National Socialist party officer who damaged the reputation and prestige of the Army. It was no less the obsequiousness of so many, the total lack of moral courage in so many, that dulled the lustre of undoubtedly real soldierly and professional virtues and did more to dishonour the image of the officer corps than all the reproaches of its bitterest opponents.

'Professor NSDAP':
The Intellectuals and National Socialism

I don't want any intellectuals!

Adolf Hitler

In every spiritual attitude a political attitude is latent.

Thomas Mann

'I say yes!' proclaimed Gerhart Hauptmann in spring 1933 in a public declaration. The upsurge of feeling that swept the nation and spread like an epidemic, sparing only those who stood very firm, let loose a wave of confessions of loyalty towards the new holders of power, in which the bitter protests and helpless disgust of those who were persecuted or actually driven out of the country went almost unheard. Faced with the thousands of spontaneous expressions of approval – fragments of a large-scale capitulation – one asks oneself in amazement what were the causes of the success which the blatantly anti-intellectual movement of National Socialism enjoyed among poets and thinkers. This success casts grave doubts upon the proposition that the high-ranking officers and big industrialists had shown themselves the weakest points in withstanding the regime's seduction and blackmail; for unquestionably 'National Socialism succeeded more rapidly and effectively in its assault on people's minds than in its seizure of political and social power.'[1] Setting aside pure opportunism, all sorts of misapprehensions played a part in this strange alliance, and many people were quickly forced to realise that they had hallooed before they were out of the dark wood. But that deeper common element, which alone makes possible misapprehension in the field of ideas, was doubtless also present here, and Thomas Mann had good reason to write to Ernst Bertram: 'The last thing you can be accused of is having turned your coat. You always wore it the "right" way round.'[2]

This weakness and readiness to capitulate can be understood only against a background of complex motivations connected with the whole position and function of intellectuals in modern society, which again and again explains the susceptibility of these classes to totalitarian solutions. Among these motivations are the ambivalent attitude of intellectuals to power and their tendency to embrace utopian systems or ideological concepts per se.[3] Even more important in the present case was the pervasive uncertainty about values, opinions and truths which gave the face of the age an unmistakably pretotalitarian look and was expressed, but at the same time threatened, by National Socialism. If the movement and later the regime was defined as 'the dawn of a new era' and a 'turning point in time', this was its own self-evaluation; yet there was a germ of truth in it. For National Socialism was a radical new departure yet with a history going back much further than the history of the NSDAP. It was not merely a ruthless exploitation of the fears of a nation which for the most part felt its loss of status, or the brilliant utilisation of the nation's 'emotional distress' for its own ends; it was not merely its slogans which secured the mass influx into the movement; rather it was the whole anti-rational uproar that accompanied it from its sectarian beginnings to the triumphant mass hysteria of the later years and, exactly like its totalitarian counterpart on the left, exercised such a stupefying effect on large sections of the intelligentsia.

Thereby National Socialism laid bare phenomena of which the movement itself was in turn only a symptom: the most consistent expression in the field of political power groupings of a multiplicity of pseudo-religious longings, a need for fundamental certainty, intellectual discontent, and impulses to escape from practical intellectual activity into the more hospitable semi-darkness of substitute metaphysical realms. These motivations in turn were permeated by the longing of the intellectual, isolated in his world of letters, for solidarity with the masses, for a share in their unthinking vitality and closeness to nature, but also in their force and historical effectiveness as expressed in the myth of the national community. Fundamentally National Socialism represented a politically organised contempt for the mind. Of course, it was not on that account that the anti-intellectual types, the beerhall battle heroes and the thugs in the brown shirts, won the masses to it. On its fringes, and visibly in its ranks too, were members of the educated classes who for the reasons cited, but also out of self-hatred, destructiveness, or simply the irresponsibility that springs from a feeling of pointlessness, committed that 'high treason of the spirit' to which Ernst Jünger confessed, not without pride,[4] and made available to the movement scraps of ideology which it swallowed indiscriminately and with total disregard for logic. In spite of the almost exclusively recondite elements in such ideology, National Socialism was able to rely not merely upon the confused utterances of obscurely fantasising eccentrics but also upon the authority of university lecturers, politicising lawyers, poets and literary-minded teachers. Its hostility to reason was intellectual, just as it was essentially a movement of failed intellectuals who had lost their faith in reason.[5] It was intellectuals above all who made possible that intellectual façade without which, in a scientific age, it is impossible to win over the petty bourgeois masses: even the denial of reason must be presented in rational terms. 'The spiritual preparation of the German revolution,' so Ernst Jünger, who had fostered it intellectually from the sidelines, wrote in 1953, 'was carried out by countless scientific works' and to these the German nation owed 'the undermining of the ideology of human rights upon which the edifice of the Weimar Republic was founded, as well as the destruction of belief in formal law, in dialectics and the intellect as such'.[6]

250

Such corrupting cultural and ethical criteria were the outcome of a long process reaching back far into the nineteenth century, in the course of which the mind turned away from itself in the name of a philosophy of life, of the will to power, of rough dynamic vitality, and continually renounced the European rationalist tradition. Generations of philosophers, historians, sociologists and psychologists had a hand in bringing the 'mind as the adversary of the soul' into disrepute and replacing it by intuition, blood, instinct, to which it gave a status that inevitably raised stupidity to the level of an authority and produced a moral indigence, a 'defeatism of humanity'[7] such as had never been seen before. Yet this was not lamented as a retrogression or a loss, but enthusiastically acclaimed as the rebirth of creative life forces. This vehement anti-enlightenment, fed by romantic impulses, was a phenomenon common to the whole of Europe; names like Carlyle, Sorel or Bergson underline this and at the same time indicate some of the main lines along which this reversal in the history of ideas moved. But nowhere did this critique of reason so fully expand into a 'destruction of reason', nowhere was it carried out with such a seemingly vengeful thoroughness as in Germany, where it was possible for a widely read work to brand reason as a 'villainy' and a 'sacrilege' and where lamentations over the situation of the 'man enslaved by reason', over his 'cerebralisation', met with approval.[8]

A combination of conditions peculiar to Germany combined to foster this process. Although Luther's extreme phrase 'the whore reason' – conditioned as it was by his own temperament, period and theological context – cannot justly be set up as a typical German utterance expressive of a constant opposition to the ethical norms of Europe as a whole, as has been attempted, it does at least indicate a long tradition of distrust of rational categories that has prevented the acceptance of reason as a self-evident authority. Reason has long remained curiously excluded in Germany, only half acknowledged and surrounded by an odour of profane superficiality.

One would have to go more deeply than is possible here into political and social conditions, and into the psychological structures which they produced and which in turn produced them, to grasp all the elements of this romantic basic attitude. Among such conditions was the centuries-old dilemma of German state organisation which constantly fostered the idea of the 'Inner Reich' and, linked with it, the tendency to romantic dreaming and confused political emotions. Of particular importance, too, was the German conception of education, in which anti-social arrogance and flight from reality were so strangely combined. Further, there was the traditionally unbalanced relationship between spirit and power, and then the role of the country's poets and writers in society, from which they found themselves continually excluded so that they were forced to retreat into their own garrets, where they preferred to meditate upon the Last Things, since the first things denied them any possibility of influence and effect.

Even the crudest texts of that trend of the 1920s generally referred to as the 'Conservative Revolution' contain hints of this. The vehemently inflated, categorical tone, impervious to the lessons of reality, reveals traces of the deviation

251

of a collective mind striving to escape from its nooks and crannies and provincial limitations into the 'eternal', a mind that wishes its thoughts on the political situation to be taken not as sociology but as a theological tract, not as analysis but as vision. 'The renewal of the German reality must spring not from the head but from the heart, not from doctrines but from visions [!] and instincts.'[9] The old German dissatisfaction with the existing form of state, which enjoyed a frenetically overintense relief during the brief period of the Empire and found itself thrown back upon its traditional positions in the Weimar Republic, emerged in countless shapes, and it was no more than a nuance when a few voices relieved the embittered metaphysical earnestness of the others by an affectation of cynical amusement. Common to all remained the ceaseless attempt, directed against the very foundations of the state, to discredit mind, ethics and humanity as from a loftier standpoint. In view of the dilution of life which leading intellectuals claimed to see on all sides, many of their followers were prepared to take part in the return to 'soulfulness', to the 'primordial forces of life', to the 'sacred darkness of ancient times', and to join the chorus of those who scorned the mind as the 'most fruitless of illusions'. Anti-rationalist feelings were inflamed by the very reality of the Republic which, in its sobriety and emotional aridity, seemed merely to confirm the failure of rational principles and intensified doubt even further, as it intensified the susceptibility to 'new solutions'. Even Max Scheler, in an essay written towards the end of the 1920s, though dissociating himself from the fashionable contempt for the mind, interpreted the irrationalist movements of the period as 'a process of recovery', 'a systematic revolt of the instincts in the man of the new age against the former sublimation, against the excessive intellectualism of our fathers and the asceticism which they have been practising for hundreds of years'.[10] The victory of the Hitler movement was then widely construed as a final breakthrough in this process, in that National Socialism seemed – entirely in line with its own self-interpretation – to be ushering in a new era that would bring to an end the rule of reason and restore life to its primordial rights.

It is only against this background that the widespread wave of approbation which, immediately after January 30, 1933, rolled towards the new regime is comprehensible. It was by no means only those names established as 'folk', 'nationalist', 'conservative' or 'authoritarian' who expressed their expectations in the same high-flown terms as Hans Friedrich Blunck, who proclaimed 'Humility before God, honour to the Reich, the golden age of the arts'.[11] As early as March 3 three hundred university teachers of all political persuasions declared themselves for Hitler in an election appeal, while the mass of students had gone over to the National Socialist camp considerably earlier. As early as 1931 the party, with 50 to 60 per cent of the votes, enjoyed almost twice as much support in the universities as in the country as a whole. The dominant influence of rightist tendencies was as evident in the teaching staff as in the self-governing student body, which was largely controlled by the Union of National Socialist German Students (NSDStB). It was no less noticeable on Langemarck Day, regularly celebrated from 1927 onward with nationalistic excesses and a lack of feeling for the tragic nature of the events, than in the style and speeches of the student congresses, the last of which, in summer 1932, was held significantly in a barracks.[12] In May 1933 a collective declaration of support for the new regime was made by the professors. This was accompanied by a welter of individual expressions of approval, some of them linked with concrete demands, such as those advanced by the well-known cultural sociologist Hans Freyer, who wanted the universities to become more political in keeping with the new spirit. On the eve of the popular elections of November 12 well-known scholars and scientists like Pinder, Sauerbruch and Heidegger called for an understanding attitude towards Hitler's policies.[13] An 'Oath of Loyalty by the German Poets to the People's Chancellor Adolf Hitler' was signed among others by Binding, Halbe, Molo, Ponten, Scholz and Stucken. Almost everyone invited to do so placed himself at the disposal of the regime, which was out to woo recognition and secure a list of decorative names, and which here and elsewhere concealed the aims of the National Socialist revolution behind a general screen of nationalism. The list included Richard Strauss, Wilhelm Furtwängler, Gustaf Gründgens, Heinz Hilpert and Werner Krauss. This fatal willingness to serve was paralleled by the ease with which the new holders of power overran existing institutions, such as the Prussian Academy of Poets. Undoubtedly many of those who entered into the pact could claim honourable motives; but more courageous was the attitude of Ricarda Huch, who resigned from the new Academy of the Arts on the grounds that her Germanness was not that of the government.[14] Faced with this mass conversion, Hitler issued in September 1933 a warning against those who 'suddenly change their flag and move into the new state as though nothing had happened, in order once again to have the main say in the realms of art and cultural policy; for this is our state and not theirs'.[15]

While the new rulers almost had to defend themselves against the influx of new supporters, comparatively few coercive measures were required, and finally all the cultural officials of the regime had to do was to set the institutional seal upon a spontaneous toeing of the party line over wide areas of the intellectual field. Only during a brief phase in a few universities did the well-tried combination of 'spontaneous expressions of will' from below with a subsequent administrative act from above have to be employed to create the necessary order, which was inseparably linked with the leadership's concept of power and of the Third Reich for which they were consistently working. For never was there the slightest doubt about the leadership's determination to extend strict control to the cultural sphere in particular.

The aim of this first period was defined by Reich Minister Frick in the words: 'An end must be put once and for all to this spirit of subversion that has gnawed for long enough at Germany's heart.'[16] Chief among the measures adopted to this end were the mass introduction of new professors into the universities, the suppression of unwanted artists by forcibly preventing them from working and legally banning their work, and the most spectacular gesture of resolute hostility to the intellect: the burning of some 20,000 so-called un-German writings in the public squares of German university towns to the accompaniment of SA and SS bands playing 'patriotic airs'. These measures were supplemented by the immediate establishment of the Reich Chamber of Culture, which organised everyone working in the artistic and journalistic fields into seven separate chambers in order, as Goebbels put it with cynical frankness, to relieve creative people of that 'feeling of forlorn emptiness' and give them the consciousness that the state was holding 'its protective hand' over them.[17]

Side by side with this, writers and artists were harassed and subjected to regulations that systematised the random interferences of the first phase. The victims, gradually realising what was happening to them, had no authority before which to state their case save their own secret diaries. Within those weeks no fewer than 250 writers left Germany, giving the cue for a process of unparalleled cultural wastage whose after-effects can still be felt. Others withdrew and fell silent out of disgust and helpless anger. But no gesture of indignation, of joint self-assertion, could be observed, and consequently whatever resistance was offered went unnoticed by those who found themselves put to the test individually and looked about for examples of how to act. Admittedly, totalitarian regimes care little about the disrepute into which their violation of the human spirit brings them. But if only for the sake of their own reputations one would have expected literature and science to make such a gesture. Many of those who had stayed behind, Blunck, Benn, Bäumer, Hauptmann, Molo or Seidel, and now occupied official positions in the academies and at official banquets, had friends among the emigrants; they were all, as one of them later recalled, one great community.[18] But the nationalist intoxication swept away such feelings, and where official intellectuals did not avert their eyes in embarrassment from the many tragedies of the outlawed and expelled, they mocked them in the full consciousness of their fine illusions. 'If the fulminations of world opinion strike us because we have ostensibly betrayed freedom, we can only smile wryly as they do who know the facts,' Wilhelm Schäfer declared in a speech in Berlin under the self-confidently ironic title 'Germany's Relapse into the Middle Ages'. And while Rudolf G. Binding in his 'A German's Answer to the World' defended the expulsions on the grounds of the national interest and stated: 'Germany – this Germany – was born of the furious longing, the inner obsession, the bloody agonies of wanting Germany: at any price, at the price of every downfall,'[19] Börries von Münchhausen justified the same process with the words: 'Once more the corn is being threshed on the threshing floor of the world – what does it matter whether a few handfuls of golden grain are lost when also the chaff is swept out, the holy harvest will be kept safe! Germany, the heart of the nations, is prodigal like all true hearts.' And when the newspaper *Der Nationalsozialist* proposed the deportation of all non-folk poets and writers, *Die Tat* raised its voice in approval.[20]

These and many other declarations revealed not least the perpetual dehumanising effect of literary activity. The burning of the books did not greatly worry

254

those who from their desks, with an artistically contrived shudder, had cast whole universes into the flames or had celebrated struggle, 'delight in everything that can destroy', as the typical mark of a heroic nationalism.[21] Emigration or persecution had no message for a writer accustomed to conjuring up cosmic catastrophes and lauding, for example, the 'splendid day when the Mont Pelées will smother these fertile settlements with their lava and the oceans will silently submerge this mud of amelioration'. Often the terrorist lived cheek by jowl with the aesthete, and at the beginning of the Third Reich Gottfried Benn reflected that everything which had made the West famous had come into being in slave states, and commented that history is 'rich in combinations of the pharaonic exercise of power with culture'.[22]

The story of the Third Reich clearly demonstrates the contrary. Rarely was a government's cultural ambition higher; never was the result more provincial and insignificant. The self-confident prophecies of the initial phase about 'an unheard-of blossoming of German art', a 'new artistic renaissance of Aryan man', gave way, in a retrospective assessment undertaken by Goebbels after five years of National Socialist cultural policy, to much more modest formulas, as when he states that literature is working, 'thoroughly cleansed, in great agony towards new light'.[23] Hitler, with the impatience of the failed artist, had already arrogated to himself the highest authority in artistic questions, and in his speech on the Enabling Act had already set the heroic and the racial criteria as the obligatory norms for artistic creation. In numerous subsequent outbursts, comparable in their furious exasperation only to his later anti-Semitic utterances, he had proclaimed the end of 'November art', of the 'trifling with art and destruction of culture', threatened to have 'cultural Neanderthalers' either placed in medical custody or imprisoned for fraud, and ordered their 'artistic stammerings', these 'international artistic scribblings' in German museums, the 'abortions of an impertinent, shameless arrogance', to be delivered to destruction.[24]

What took the place of the banned works, in spite of all the verbose embellishments, was nothing more than a projection of the artistic prejudices of the German nationalist man in the street, who now saw his intellectual backwardness and cultural narrow-mindedness sanctioned by the state itself as healthy common sense – a martial Biedermeier art which, despite generous aid, remained hopelessly caught in the narrowness of its own presuppositions, even if it celebrated lavishly organised triumphs every year in the House of German Art. The ambitious artistic efforts of the Third Reich never passed beyond classical imitations to an original aesthetic, although at the Reich Party Congress of 1933 Hitler had already enunciated the motto 'through ideological renewal and the consequent racial purification, to find a new style of life, culture, and art'. The project got no further than the principle of negative selection, as was vividly demonstrated in the fields of painting and sculpture by the admission procedure for the Munich art exhibitions presided over by Hitler himself.

In literature selection was entrusted to a censorship apparatus with wide powers. It caught and suppressed everything that had helped the country's literature to a new world reputation, and cleared the way for a dull poetry of blood and soil. This was the breakthrough of a pseudo-romantic undercurrent in German literature that had always existed but had never before achieved significant recognition; now, however, its productions gained recognition, along with the resentment of the unsuccessful, with the whole weight of state support. Shutting itself off from the world, proud of the narrowness of its own chosen realm, totally lacking in urbanity and intellectual receptiveness, this cult pursued its twilight and its earthiness, not with the sensibility, the poetic anguish and artistic refinement of German Romantic literature, but with a stubbornly defensive nationalism. Its neurotic relationship with the modern world narrowed its view and made it primitive; it was always the German fields, the German forest or glistening snow-capped peaks that were played off against the urban scene; the philistine existence of peasants was played off against metropolitan civilisation, the cult of Wotan against the conveyer belt, the ways of the Northmen against present-day social structures. It was with a false inwardness that it meditated upon essentials behind shuttered windows: plough, sword, and then in the evening happiness under the linden tree. No complicated psychological analysis is required to demonstrate the affinity between such 'inwardness' and totalitarian thinking. It will be enough to take a glance at a history of literature[25] and list the titles of the works of Max Jungnickel in chronological order: *Sorge* (Care), 1913; *Peter Himmelhoch*, 1916; *Jakob Heidebuckel*, 1917; *Der Wolkenschulze* (Mayor of the Clouds), 1919; *Michael Spinnler*, 1925; *Rutsch ins Mauseloch* (Journey down a Mousehole), 1929; and then in 1933, *Goebbels*; in 1935, *Junge lacht ins Leben* (A Lad Laughs at Life); in 1938, *Mythos der Soldaten* (Myth of the Soldiers); in 1939, *Kommando der Erde* (Commando of the Earth); and finally in 1940, *Fliegende Grenadiere* (Flying Grenadiers).

Iron and inwardness, this was the combination Goebbels had in mind when he asked for a 'steely romanticism'.[26] With this went the demand for the corresponding 'human attitudes', as expressed in the desire of the men in power, once more stressed by Goebbels, 'to breed a new type of German artist' or 'to create a new type of university teacher'.[27] The direction of these efforts became clear when a 'soldierliness of the spirit' was spoken of, when poetry was described as 'fighting power', scientists were referred to as 'comrades in the science services of the German nation', and 'muster rolls of authors' were introduced, 'comradeship evenings of the department of poets'.[28] The aim was to organise the arts and sciences in military categories so as to make them emphatically aware of their service function, in such a way that movements of individual revolt or scepticism became acts of desertion, which, in a nation with an ingrained respect for the military, was always regarded as especially heinous. The final stage of this policy was the elimination of all distinctions between poet and soldier in a nation welded into a single block, as glorified in the extravagant style of Reich Theatrical Controller Rainer Schlösser: 'Not: here poet and thinker, there soldier and politician, but: proud brows beneath steel helmets, high hearts in armour, and when the time comes to fight, German souls in the trenches.'[29]

256

The leading example of the soldierly spirit in the ideological field, at least until June 30, 1934, was the SA. There was talk of 'SA men of the mind', and while Göring and Rosenberg set up the artistic sense of the 'healthy SA man' as an aesthetic criterion,[30] rebellious art critics were told to emulate Horst Wessel and 'march in Adolf Hitler's brown battalions' in order 'to know better about German art today'.[31] So that 'the German scholar alienated from the people may soon belong to the past', Professor Ernst Storm, later Rector of the Berlin Technical University, held up Hitler in his role as Supreme Commander of the SA and Chief of Staff Ernst Röhm as models 'for every German university lecturer'. On December 1, 1933 the Reich Leader of the German Students Union and the National Socialist German Students' Union, Oscar Stäbel, intimated that 'the time is not far off when there will be no room in German universities for men who are too genteel to take their place in the community of the SA'. As though in support of this, the Prussian Minister of Education the same day issued a regulation making 'the completion of ten weeks' service in the Labour Corps or SA a condition for obtaining a teaching certificate'.[32]

To the institutional regimentation of the universities there was quickly added their material organisation. It was Hitler's conviction that the idea of a free science subject to no outside direction was 'absurd', that in the scientific as in the moral sense there was no truth, indeed that fundamentally science had, as he put it, a 'devastating' effect, because 'it leads away from instinct'.[33] Solicitous educational civil servants and also numerous university teachers, immediately set about spreading these ideas in the academic field. The efforts to put an end to the rule of intelligence are documented in the grotesque outbursts of an anti-intellectualism that was finally to come out into the open. 'Intelligence, what does that include?' asked the Bavarian Minister of Education, Hans Schemm. His answer was: 'Logic, calculation, speculation, banks, stock exchange, interest, dividends, capitalism, career, profiteering, usury, Marxism, Bolshevism, rogues, and thieves.'[34] And while the idea of scientific objectivity – in Hitler's view a 'slogan coined by the professors simply in order to escape from the necessary supervision by the power of the state' – was damned in a flood of directives and pamphlets as a symptom of a bourgeois-liberal epoch, the historians, for example, found themselves called upon 'to see German history only with German eyes, with the eyes of the blood'; the Nobel Prize-winner Philipp Lenard on the 550-year jubilee of Heidelberg University issued his unspeakable views on 'Aryan physics'; Professor Walter Poppelreuther glorified Hitler as a 'scientific psychologist'; and Professor Reinhard Höhn elevated the concept of the national community 'to the fundamental principle of science'.[35] The list could be prolonged almost indefinitely and would include the names of jurists, doctors, theologians, political economists, Germanists and musicologists.

Undoubtedly those who argued in this way did not do so against all conviction; for even the betrayal of reason takes place in its name, since man remains dependent upon reasons. The mechanics of 'misguided thinking' have been analysed in relation to the Communist world, though here the phenomenon takes place on an altogether more rigorous plane. However, even under National Socialist rule the *sacrificium intellectus* was given many opportunities for ideological evolution, especially during the initial phase with its manifold illusions. From the medieval idea of the Reich or the notion of the state evolved from German idealist philosophy to the expectation of an imminent consummation of Bismarck's Reich, the National Socialist seizure of power was accompanied by the most varied and often violent historical apologia, such as later enjoyed a remarkable revival in the process of 'revising' German history that took place during the upheavals of the postwar years. The ideas aroused by the anti-rationalist writings of the pre-totalitarian phase were now seen as manifested in current events, ideas related to the revolution of instinct, blood, primordial vital force against the rationalist and Western 'asphalt world'. Common to all these visions was the basic feeling of a long-awaited political advent, whose time had now come. It was from these visions that the measures involved in the process of seizing power, as well as individual behaviour, drew their ideological justification. Harshness, arbitrariness and the demand for obedience, for example, could be justified by reference to such semi-mythological concepts as order, Prussianism or Germanic democracy; pusillanimous silence, the closing of the eyes to violence, could be glossed over by notions of duty and self-discipline – concepts of exceptional weight for the ordinary German; or excessive nationalism could be interpreted and exalted as the reawakening of Germany to the historical present after sleeping for centuries and lapsing into a 'dullard's cosmopolitanism'. Over and above this the enthusiastic acclamations always contained an element of that peculiar German conception of destiny to which submission had been demanded since time immemorial. Objective knowledge was renounced, as the evidence cited above shows; and the renunciation was demanded and imposed in the name of the national community, whose realisation after age-old divisions in any case carried sacred significance in the country's tradition of political ideas. The state was acknowledged to possess not merely a historical but also an absolute right to trample on venerable standards, such as the objectivity of scientific thinking, so that acts which turned out to be betrayals of the human mind looked at the time like service to historical greatness.

At the same time many who capitulated more quietly, or sought to make their peace with the men in power, were also motivated by the illusions and dreams that permeated the nation as a whole, effectively fostered by the new masters. Among these were various universal if vague ideas of renewal; the usurped role of 'defenders of the West against Bolshevism'; and even, along with other tendencies in the German and European history of ideas which, grossly falsified and perverted, were confidently claimed for the National Socialist cause, the very idea of the 'Third Reich', which contained a magical promise that had existed for centuries. All impulses of any effectiveness were absorbed into the National Socialist philosophy, which, within a certain overall framework, was largely left by the leadership to its own devices. Surprisingly enough the inconsistency of this philosophy, far from pointing up its essential spuriousness,

258

actually constituted its specific attraction for many intellectuals. By giving free play to all nationalist, conservative or popular revolutionary ideas, it was largely whatever imagination at any given moment demanded of it. And those in whom the mechanism of self-deception broke down found their readiness to accept illusions reinforced by the terrifying example of what happened to those who attempted to assert themselves. Public defamation, surveillance by the party and the Gestapo, denial of the right to publish, could be seen to descend upon anyone who drew upon himself the disfavour of the authorities and was thereby rendered 'undesirable'. Finally it must be pointed out that here, as always in times of upheaval, characters were revealed and their most objectionable side laid bare: opportunism, ruthless ambition and intrigue triumphed in astounding careers. Thomas Mann noted in the pages of his diary in June 1933:

> The abysmal wretchedness of men is at times amazing. The *Simplicissimus* artists who declared that they had never shared the paper's outlook and had merely been led astray by Heine. – The Berlin sculptor who, for the sake of his professorship, or some other aspect of his career, admitted that his wife was a Jewess, but claimed that for five years he had had nothing to do with her.
> The German newspapers – horror.[36]

The oath of allegiance which the times demanded from every intellectual disclosed a deeply confusing situation. Only in those who fell silent, and in the emigrants, did there seem to live on some conviction that the spirit demands a readiness to make sacrifices from those who claim to be its representatives. The right to make mistakes is certainly fundamental, and there is nothing reprehensible about mistakes in themselves. It is also true that 'intellectual freedom and a sense of cultural values have never before been put to such a test'.[37] But what was revealed during those years was more than a mistake, and that 'unforgettable failure fatal to the honour of the German mind', of which Thomas Mann spoke,[38] was more than the result of a brief state of intoxication brought about by hands with the power to mislead. The weakness of the intellectual will to assert itself is comprehensible only on the basis of a prolonged corruption of all politico-moral values. To be sure, here too only a minority consistently followed National Socialism and its leadership; above all, the later evolution of the regime sobered many who had experienced exalted emotions at the beginning. And it was just this refusal of lasting adherence that aroused Hitler's reiterated rancour against the 'intellectual classes'. He declared in his speech to the German press on November 10, 1938: 'Unfortunately we need them; otherwise we might one day, I don't know, exterminate them or something like that. But unfortunately we need them.'[39]

Almost more staggering were the countless half-pacts with the National Socialist leaders, the attitude of those prepared to back any theoretical anti-intellectualism, who evidently persuaded themselves that barbarism was divisible and finally saw in National Socialism the degeneration of their folk, anti-rational ideals of a rebirth of the soul or whatever it might be. These were people like the literary historian and poet Ernst Bertram, who, during the first days of May 1933, set out to remove from the lists of works to be burnt the books of his personal friends Thomas Mann and Friedrich Gundolf, and after succeeding in this wrote happily that now he could 'participate in the solemn auto-da-fé' and actually had a poem to the flames, specially written for the occasion, read out in public.[40] Such behaviour, which is more horrifying than the believed idiocies uttered by Philipp Lenard or Reinhard Höhn, reveals something more than the dilemma of a scholarly mind specialised exclusively in its own narrow field and, lacking any idea of its own social position, remaining stubbornly in a state of political tutelage. It also shows up the comprehensive failure of a bourgeois educational ideal which was ostensibly 'unpolitical' but in reality always submissive to authority and willing to enter into a pact with authority. This is the source not only of the 'readiness of the bourgeois spirit in Germany to be politically misled',[41] but also of the lack of civil self-confidence and courage which plunged characters into such a discouraging twilight during this period. 'If only life would at last stop demanding solutions from us,' Gerhart Hauptmann exclaimed with his eyes on the moment of decision before which he was placed and which he repeatedly sought to evade.[42]

Finally, any inquiry into the causes and responsibility for the failure of the educated classes continually leads back to that crisis of consciousness whose protracted preparatory phase reached its climax in the infectious spiritual climate of the 1920s. Every intellectual knows an occasional temptation to fall for the charlatan; in each there lives an urge to the Black Mass, a desire to 'turn the world of the spirit upside down with an intellectual gesture, to interchange the signs that mark its whole system of relationships, as the practical joker switches all the shoes outside the doors of hotel rooms during the night'.[43] But when the charlatans and 'practical jokers' suddenly appear in droves and, not with the gesture of ironic detachment but the mien of dark wisdom, as though they were continually holding anguished converse with angels, then everything points to one of those crises of the spirit that precede politico-moral catastrophes. A culture whose mouthpieces, to the applause of the majority, had long since become the spokesmen for the defamation and negation of everything upon which this culture rested could no longer credibly oppose its own destruction. The Expressionist poet Hanns Johst, later President of the Reich Chamber of Writers, went to the heart of this crisis when he made the hero of one of his dramas say that he released the safety catch of his Browning as soon as he heard the word 'culture';[44] fundamentally, everyone did. F. G. Jünger wrote: 'Every new screw in the machine-gun, every improvement in gas warfare, is more important than the League of Nations.' Stefan George stated: 'We see in every event, every age, only a means to artistic stimulus. Even the freest of the free could not manage without the ethical blanket – we have only to think of the concepts of guilt and so on [!] – which has become to us quite worthless.'[45] Symptoms of the same condition showed in the contempt for man seen in literature and art, the brutality of style and expression which ran parallel with the mania for twilight and darkness, the delight in barbarism, downfall, myth and cynicism which were not confined to the political right. Looking back, as one who was for a time part of all this, Franz Werfel confessed in terms that are probably not universally valid but certainly largely apply to the situation at that time: 'There is no more consuming, impudent, mocking, more devil-possessed arrogance than that of the avant-garde artist and radical intellectual who are bursting with the vain hankering to be deep and obscure and difficult and to inflict pain. To the accompaniment of the amusedly indignant laughter of a few philistines we inconspicuously heated up the hell in which mankind is now frying.'[46] Keyed as they were to a mood of downfall and destruction, artists, writers and intellectuals as a whole failed to see that the culture which they were slandering included everything upon which their existence as artists, writers and intellectuals rested, and many eventually acclaimed the victory of National Socialism precisely because of the possibilities of barbarism and chaos which it brought with it – to the terror, as they thought, only of a 'cowardly and well-fed bourgeoisie'.

Too late they realised that the terror was directed against all of them. Many paid terribly for their blindness. To others, however, fate was kind: the consequences of what they had so emphatically called into being were not forced upon them. They merely fell silent, cowered in a corner, and remained untouched, while noting with secret bitterness the rule of the mob, the barbarisation of public life, the path to war and chaos – and found that this was not the mob, the barbarism, the chaos which they had once called down upon civilisation. With some justice Hitler complained of them:

Today the old wives of the literary world are everywhere croaking at me, charging me with 'betrayal of the spirit'! And they themselves have been betraying the spirit to this day in their fine phrases. So long as it was just a literary pastime, they prided themselves on it. Now that we are in earnest with it, they are opening wide their innocent eyes.[47]

It may be surmised that something of this astonishment was to be seen in Edgar Jung's eyes when the myrmidons of the SS broke into his home at the end of June 1934. Only a few months previously had he pointed out to those caught up 'in the notions of the constitutional state' and unduly perturbed 'by certain acts of violence' that 'violence is an element of life' and 'a nation that has become incapable of employing violence must be suspected of biological decline'.[48]

The story of the withdrawal of power from the intellectuals in a country is always the story of voluntary relinquishment, and if resistance is called for, it is mainly resistance to the temptation to suicide. Thomas Mann asked in 1930 whether it was possible at all, in an old, mature, experienced, civilised nation that had intellectual and spiritual exploits behind it like Germany, to impose the anti-mind, primitivism, complete national simplicity. In essence the answer was there before the question was asked, even if it was only later, in the conditions of totalitarian rule, that its definite character became clear, along with the realisation that the frontier of what man is capable of is boundless. The guilt of intellectual radicalism in helping to bring about National Socialism lies in the way it prepared public opinion for the regime's excessive claims in all fields, in its expulsion of reason, its devaluation of the image of man, its scorn for all those who still recognised truths or moral standards and its consistent denunciation of all ethical principles, these being presented under the guise of a fresh, undismayed, undeluded feeling for life. This is an incontestable fact, regardless of such questions as whether an intellectual attitude can be held responsible for what happens when that same attitude is fraudulently distorted and actually put into practice. 'Everything romantic stands in the service of other, unromantic energies,' wrote Carl Schmitt in 1925, involuntarily giving himself away.[49]

There were exceptions, men who took no part in the one trend or the other, either before or after 1933. The sculptor Ernst Barlach, the poet Friedrich Reck-Malleczewen, the painter Karl Schmitt-Rottluff. Pestered by petty officials, they saw themselves faced with 'slow strangulation', as Barlach wrote.[50] There was the not inconsiderable minority of scholars and scientists who fought hard to preserve the integrity of research and teaching: the historian Friedrich Meinecke, the philosopher Kurt Huber, the scientists Otto Hahn and Werner Heisenberg. And if what the regime was vouchsafed, instead of the expected cultural successes, was only impoverishment and stagnation, it remained so far behind the rest of the world in the military sciences, on account of the expulsion of the intellectual élite as well as the well-founded refusal of the country's leading specialist scientists to swear the oath of loyalty, that this was not the least among the factors that helped to seal its fate.[51] The anti-intellectualism that played a leading part in its rise was equally important among the causes of its downfall.

The poetic justice of this may satisfy the retrospective observer; it was little comfort to contemporaries. The unfortunate Oskar Loerke summed up the martyrdom of his experiences in the Third Reich – his pain at the undignified situations into which he was constantly forced, his bitterness at the conformity and opportunism of his friends, his despair at the boastful meanness of those in power – in the words: 'There is a disgust in the world that reaches beyond death and will last to eternity.'[52]

German Wife and Mother:
The Role of Women in the Third Reich

Never become ladies, remain German girls and women!

Julius Streicher

Who will ever ask in three or five hundred years time whether a Fräulein Müller or Schulze was unhappy?

Heinrich Himmler

The National Socialist movement, from the beginning a militant community of like-minded men, had almost no place in its ranks for women. The very first general meeting of members early in 1921 passed a unanimous resolution that 'a woman can never be accepted into the leadership of the party and into the governing committee'.[1] The *Führerlexikon*, or index of leaders, among countless names, often of third-rate people, does not list one woman; and during the subsequent years of the Third Reich, in spite of all the organisations of millions of both sexes, there was no true political representation of women. The misogyny of the initial phase, despite all mitigating assurances by the top leadership, remained a basic factor and emphatically differentiated the NSDAP from all other political groups and parties. The type of homeless man, profoundly incapable of bourgeois stability, who gave the movement its shape during the early phase, generally despised attachment to a wife and family along with all other ties. The decisive influences in his life, experience at the front, the years of the Freikorps, the militant alliances in the big cities, had always had the character of a men's society, and the feelings of comradeship from those years further reinforced this masculine exclusiveness. In the idea of a carefully fostered élite and hierarchy, particularly in the SA and later in the SS, in the ecstatic admiration for the 'indomitable leader', the 'heroic friend' and the 'self-sacrificing comrade' we see a repeated tendency to homosexuality also revealed in the soft, vaguely sentimental tone used to embellish acts of brutality.

It is no coincidence that for years no-one found his way into the movement's top leadership who had a family or whose family life matched the image of National Socialist ideology. In countless and tirelessly presented metaphors, pictures, monuments, as well as in the amateurish but officially fostered 'genuinely national poetry',[2] the type is pictured as a heroic figure, preferably on his own

263

land, gazing boldly into the rising sun or standing with legs apart as he offers his strong bare chest to the turbulent waves of life, and leaning against him is his tall, full-bosomed wife; she too is doughty and valiant, but at the same time fervent, profound and gay amid the children to whom she has tirelessly given birth. This erect blond idyll with the unmistakable aura of male sweat and nobility of soul was peculiar to all stylisations of National Socialist ideology, in whatever sphere. Behind the stilted heroism of these pictures there always lurked the sober considerations of power politics, which saw marriage as a 'productive relationship' and graded women according to their 'childbearing achievements'.[3] Naturally, the prevalent military vocabulary spoke of 'throwing woman into the struggle', of battles fought 'not in the social but in the erotic sphere. The fulfilment of love, happiness in love, conception, and birth are the heroic high-points of female life.'[4] The woman who 'voluntarily renounced motherhood' was a 'deserter', and Hitler even proclaimed: 'Every child which she brings into the world is a battle which she wins for the existence or non-existence of her nation.'[5]

For the origin and content of National Socialist ideology in respect of women, however, we must look beyond simple considerations of power to Hitler's own problematic attitude to the opposite sex. We can be fairly certain that his personal deviation from the ideal which he set up, like all his decisions and even his private behaviour, was determined in the first place by considerations relating to the psychology of power. As early as 1919 his later mentor, Dietrich Eckart, giving his idea of the future saviour of Germany at the table of a Schwabing tavern, demanded, 'He must be a bachelor! Then we shall bring in the women.' And later Hitler himself admitted that in view of the decisive importance of women in the elections he could not afford to marry.[6] One of the determining factors in his 'unorthodox' behaviour, however, was undoubtedly his own emotional coldness and inability to make human contact, which emerges clearly in the account given by his youthful friend August Kubizek of his relations with the girl 'Stefanie'. Possibly the already complex tangle of his personal relationships with women was further complicated by the unhappy affair of his niece Geli Raubal; she seems to have sought escape from the oppression of his presence by sudden suicide, although we cannot and should not decide here which factor was the prime cause and which merely reinforced her decision. In any case, according to a witness from his immediate entourage, Hitler's characteristic fear of all spontaneous human attitudes included a constant fear 'of entering into conversation with a woman', and there are good grounds for the supposition occasionally put forward that his later carefully concealed relationship with Eva Braun, far from being a natural sexual bond, was intended solely to provide a strained confirmation of his manhood in his own eyes and those of his closest followers.[7]

There is an element of speculation in such theories. More revealing and reliable is Hitler's *Mein Kampf*, which involuntarily lays bare the essential elements in what is clearly a pathological attitude to women, above all in the endless and almost unbearable chapter on syphilis, in the whole of his curiously debauched vocabulary, and also in that ever-recurring repulsive nightmare that

264

evidently obsessed him throughout his life and to which Julius Streicher – whom he again and again protected against every attack – later gave such squalid publicity. In it the cruelly chained naked Germanic woman is approached from the background by the lurking, black-haired Jewish butcher, while he himself, a cowardly, inhibited, ever-failing Saint George, does not set the maiden free but leaves her to the 'dragon'. There is reason to believe that his so-called *Weltanschauung* was largely the rationalisation of the hatred and vengeance aroused by such humiliating dreams, and the ideological frame in which he sought to place women contained features of this vision, marked by both transfiguring and depressive ideas, which was never subjected to the corrective experience of a normal sexual relationship.

However, as has been explained already, in his public appearances as a speaker before large crowds Hitler sought and to a great extent found what was denied him in contact with a single individual. Moreover the unmistakable element of self-gratification here, as well as the clear evidence that he was suffering from frustration, had a special attraction for women, whose enthusiastic reactions in the early days of the movement 'were usually decisive for the success' of Hitler's speeches.[8] Friedrich Reck-Malleczewen once compared him, after a chance meeting, to a marriage swindler out to catch love-hungry cooks and Hitler himself admitted that women had 'played a not insignificant part in my political career'. Quite simply they discovered, chose and idolised him.[9] Long before the *Münchener Post* stated in April 1923 that there was talk of 'women infatuated by Hitler', Countess Reventlow proclaimed him 'the coming Messiah'; he was surrounded by motherly women friends who 'instinctively scented the unsatisfied male'[10] in the sombre, profoundly strange young man. In particular there were Carola Hoffmann, a headmaster's widow; the wife of the publisher Bruckmann, who was descended from the highest European nobility; and the wife of Bechstein the piano manufacturer. They above all, joined in later years by this or that successor or rival, opened the doors of so-called better society to him. They largely represented, not the respectable right, but a class grown blasé and weary of the refinements of life, who sought precisely those sensations which Hitler had to offer: his extremism, the hair-raising consistency of his views, but also his social awkwardness and his bad manners. The total effect of his personality was the delight of a society with time on its hands, which took its stimulants where it could find them. At the same time the gloomy strain, the depression from which he seemed to suffer, suggested all sorts of tensions waiting to be released, and there was a great deal of sombre desire involved in the motherly care. Hannah Arendt has noted the 'continually growing admiration of good society for the underworld' in the nineteenth century, 'its gradual yielding in all moral questions, its growing predilection for the anarchic cynicism of its offspring'. She has drawn attention to the astounding affinity between the political ideology of the mob and the ideology of bourgeois society, beneath all its hypocrisy, an affinity that was at its closest in the Munich salons of the early 1920s or later in the famous circle of Frau von Dircksen.[11]

Almost more effective than the social and abundant material assistance which the young agitator increasingly received from this quarter[12] was its importance for the cult that developed around his person. Certainly the elements of immoderate veneration in the 'masculine movement' were no less effective. But the over-excited, distinctly hysterical tone that quickly spread in all directions sprang in the first place from the excessive emotionalism of a particular kind of elderly woman who sought to activate the unsatisfied impulses within her in the tumult of nightly political demonstrations before the ecstatic figure of Hitler. 'One must have seen from above, from the speaker's rostrum,' wrote one of Hitler's closest followers, 'the rapturously rolling, moist, veiled eyes of the female listeners in order to be in no further doubt as to the character of this enthusiasm': the 'role of eroticism in modern mass propaganda' has rarely been more effectively documented.[13] And in just the same way that skilful stage-management perverted political demonstrations into purely instinctual processes by the use of subtle stimuli, so Hitler visibly degenerated from an orator in the true sense to an impulse-object before whom the neurotic petty bourgeoisie gathered for collective debauch, waiting lustfully for the moment of escape from all inhibitions, of the great release, when the crowd's yell strikingly revealed the pleasurable character of these proceedings and their resemblance to the public sexual acts of primitive tribes. Hitler himself declared that in his speeches he had 'systematically adapted himself to the taste of women', who from the beginning had been 'among his most enthusiastic admirers'; and even during the war he tried to counter moods of criticism with rhetorical arguments 'addressed above all to the female mind'.[14]

Whether we hold political considerations or Hitler's personal fixations responsible for this mass eroticism, in either case woman is treated solely as an object and specific female qualities, such as capacity for self-surrender or demand for authority and order, are seen and evaluated solely as making woman more susceptible to psychological manipulation. Here, then, lies the point of intersection between Hitler's individual tendencies and the few clear outlines of National Socialist ideology concerning women; for although in the main this ideology merely revived theories advanced in popular writings, it nevertheless gave them a particular direction, and behind the deceitful homeliness of its words and images appeared the murderous reality of its aims. It was never anything other than a pseudo-romantic disguise for political, imperialistic purposes – herein revealing a characteristic feature of all National Socialist ideological practice.

The self-confident claim that National Socialism would finally solve the question of women's emancipation was based on the notion that the uncertain position of woman in modern society was entirely the result of the liberal idea of the equality of the sexes. As soon as the natural difference between man and woman – on the face of it denied by the ideology of human rights – was restored and a return made to origins, to the primordial will, all the problems 'artificially created by an intellectualism of the most depraved kind' would become meaningless.[15] According to this view, woman was the preserver of the tribe and of biological inheritance, the guardian of the unadulterated racial fountainhead, of domestic virtue and eternal morality. Unlike man, as Alfred Rosenberg once put it, woman thinks 'lyrically' and not 'systematically', 'atomistically' and not 'synoptically', whatever that may mean; and while he saw it as one of woman's main tasks 'to preach the maintenance of the purity of the race', the Reich Women's Leader Gertrud Scholtz-Klink, in full agreement, complained especially of the absence in sober modern times of the sacred racial function and significance of women and called upon them 'to become once more the priestesses of the family and nation'.[16] In the light of such ideas, the women's rights movement of the nineteenth century appeared as a 'symptom of decay', like democracy, liberalism or parliamentarianism, 'a phrase invented by the Jewish intellect' as part of the systematic destruction of the Aryan race, as Hitler put it.[17] A popular exposition of National Socialist ideology stated: 'German women wish in the main to be wives and mothers, they do not wish to be comrades, as the Red philanthropists try to convince themselves and women. They have no longing for the factory, no longing for the office, and no longing for Parliament. A cosy home, a loved husband, and a multitude of happy children are closer to their hearts.'[18]

The hostile attitude towards the modern world peculiar to National Socialism, its overheated, romantic protest against the big city and against civilisation as such, and its ludicrous attempt to impose agrarian models on a highly techno-logical industrial society, which went as far as an open demand for the 'creation of a peasant mentality in the nation',[19] also found expression in the ideal which it postulated for women. The directives for the guidance of National Socialist writers vividly demonstrate this. Ministerial quarters suggested the following themes for the 'creators of literature': 'The seizure of land by the peasants; the idea of the clan; the law relating to the entailed farm; resistance to urbanisation; the testing of men in a new popular order subject to the racial idea; the life of soldiers and settlers linked with the soil; the technical equipment and cultural independence of the village.' In a newspaper article proclaiming 'order in German writing', Reich Theatrical Controller Rainer Schlösser wrote: 'Do we not all await the resurrection of that genuine German eroticism which distinguished a Goethe, a Kleist, a Storm, or a Mörike? Our writers must be drawn as by little else to confront the raving alien sexual speculations springing from Asiatic soil, now happily stamped out, with the exalted song of the blossoming blood of the German who is close to the soil!'[20] Common to these and many similar declara-tions was condemnation of the so-called Ibsen woman, who had cast off the motherly qualities of the 'primordial woman, the peasant woman' and 'instead of children [had] psychological conflicts',[21] and of the whole urban type of the 'lady', whose attributes were held to be red lips, lacquered fingernails, high heels and the enjoyment of nicotine. In the early years of National Socialist rule in parti-cular, there were numerous persecutions inspired by a bullying puritanism whose sour narrowmindedness was in striking contrast to the regime's contempt for morality and worship of rough and vital force in other fields; even Goebbels was stung to protest. Police chiefs of numerous German cities put up posters in all public restaurants forbidding females to smoke, and the Erfurt police chief actually invited the population to stop women who were smoking and 'remind them of their duty as German women and mothers'.[22] In the prevailing image, which inextricably mingled the type of the Frisian peasant woman with traits of Queen Luise, 'German' and nicotine, 'German' and lipstick, or 'German' and fashion were incompatible concepts. As Curt Rosten's pamphlet 'The ABC of National Socialism' put it:

But German men want *German* women again, and quite rightly. Not a frivolous plaything who is superficial and only out for pleasure, who decks herself with tawdry finery and is like a glittering exterior that is hollow and drab within. Our opponents sought to bend women to their dark purposes by painting frivolous life in the most glowing colours and portraying the true profession allotted to woman by nature as slavery.[23]

This profession was exclusively that of motherhood and 'guardian of the hearth', and the 'lady' was always suspected of not taking this task with the seriousness proper to a consciousness of her duty to the race based on solid ideological convictions. She, the devastating example of her kind, was held responsible for the disturbing 'twilight of the family'. It was she too who withdrew from the simple and unwavering reproduction upon which all the medley of theories ultimately converged; in the jargon, she was guilty of 'treason against nature' by taking part in the 'childbearing strike'.[24] 'The healthy is a heroic commandment,' was the maxim of this human ideal proclaimed by Hans Johnst.[25] In *Mein Kampf* Hitler had already promised 'to do away with the idea that what he does with his own body is each individual's own business', and the tendency to treat marriage as a breeding institution foreshadowed what were later called 'practices of elimination based on the laws of heredity'. 'A popular state will have in the first instance to raise marriage from the level of a constant racial disgrace [*Rassenschande*] in order to give it the consecrated character of that institution which is called upon to beget the image and likeness of the Lord and not monstrosities halfway between men and monkeys.'[26]

Any idea of withdrawing from women all functions, interests and rights was always denied by National Socialist ideologists, who asserted that 'the mental and spiritual struggle of women has its rights and its tasks alongside the advancing struggle of men'. As Gertrud Scholtz-Klink rather quaintly put it: 'Even if our weapon is only the wooden spoon, its striking power shall be no less than that of other weapons.'[27] Motherhood stood at the core of such attempts to raise the status of women. 'Can women imagine anything finer than to experience centuries and millennia with the beloved husband in the cosy home in reverent attention to the inner workings of creative motherhood?'[28] And while Goebbels gave the assurance that 'woman is being removed from public life' only in order 'that her essential dignity may be restored to her',[29] Hitler stated frankly: 'If in the past the liberal-intellectual women's movements contained in their programmes many, many points arising out of the so-called "mind", then the programme of our

268

National Socialist women's movement really only contains one single point and that point is: the child.' Such propositions claimed to solve the problem while in fact simply ignoring it along with all the ideas behind it, and Hitler would follow them up with a threadbare vision of the harmony of the sexes in the National Socialist state: 'Then conflict and quarrels will never be able to break out between the sexes, but they will go through this life hand in hand and fighting together, as was intended by Providence, which created them both to this purpose.'[30]

The aphoristic and often incomprehensibly generalised nature of National Socialism's numerous references to the place of women was in keeping with the leadership's lack of concern with ideological precision, which contrasted of course with its acute instinct for the actual facts of power. While the new leaders, after January 30, 1933, resolutely seized upon effective means of influencing women and the family, they left all elements of a woman-and-family ideology, already widely treated in popular literature, suspended in a state of vagueness or self-contradiction. Their claim to total control, to which the existing women's associations fell victim at the very beginning of the National Socialist reorganisation measures, yielded them bases for power in an incalculable multitude of organisations: the National Socialist People's Welfare Organisation, the National Socialist Women's Club, the German Women's Organisation with its ancillary groups, the Mother and Child Relief Organisation, the Women's Office of the German Workers' Front (DAF). 'We alone are entitled,' cried Hitler, 'to lead the people as such – the individual man, the individual woman. We regulate relations between the sexes. We mould the child!' And elsewhere he declared that children 'belong to their mothers as at the same moment they belong to me'.[31]

To ensure that these demands were met, a comprehensive list of 'national-biological' measures was proposed and planned from 1933 onwards, though only the anti-Semitic parts of it were actually put fully into practice, the remainder getting no further than the thoroughly barbaric first steps. The multiplicity of offices, committees, expert advisers and ministerial departments claiming future jurisdiction over population, racial and health matters was in keeping with the new laws designed to raise the birth-rate and improve eugenic standards. Among these were the 'Law for the Encouragement of Marriage' of July 5, 1933 (with a new version on February 21, 1935), whose main provision was marriage loans with exemption from repayment as a reward for a large number of children; the 'Law for the Prevention of Hereditarily Sick Offspring' was publicly acclaimed as the 'beginning of state measures for the elimination' of the biologically inferior; and there were projects for 'making the establishment of young civil servants dependent upon their being married'.[32] Other measures in the same category included the attempts to introduce the genealogical tree (*Ahnenpass*), and the transformation of register offices into family offices which were to be entrusted with the task of elucidating 'the blood relationships of all Germans' with the aid of photocopies of all church registers. Then came the euthanasia programme and finally the establishment of the Motherhood Cross, to be awarded on each August 12 – 'the birthday of our Führer's mother', as the explanatory preamble stated – and based upon the idea that 'the German mother of many children should hold the same place of honour in the national community as the front-line soldier, for her risk of life and body for people and Fatherland was the same as that of the front-line soldier in the thunder of battle'.[33]

Real influence was also assured by gathering women together in strictly regimented, uniformed compulsory organisations such as the female Hitler Youth or the institutions of the Women's Labour Corps, the founding of which strikingly resembled a popular counter-measure to the supposed Jewish-liberal masculinisation of women and is impressive evidence of the way ideology could be twisted in National Socialism. As always when ideology came into conflict with its concern for power, the National Socialist leaders came down on the side of power, and the attempt to justify this act of ideological self-contradiction by invoking the idea of the national community was all too transparent.[34] Over and above this there was an evident attempt to develop in the female in the Reich Labour Service (RAD) the new type of ideal woman, who was to be contrasted with the 'protesting, demonstrating "suffragettes" of other countries who ludicrously aped male ways' to act, by virtue of her ideological and biological predisposition, as a 'living example' of National Socialism.[35]

This type possessed its fixed characteristics, and only later, in particular through the more urbane influence of Magda Goebbels, wife of the Propaganda Minister, was it possible to introduce some cosmetic improvements on the coarse, peasant contours of this female image. But the ideal remained of a blonde apotheosis beneath hair tied in a bun or plaited in a diadem; of the heavy-hipped, athletic woman in a long full skirt, wearing flat heels and freed from the prohibited stays, a figure lacking all intimacy and looking, for all its stylised naturalness, strikingly unnatural and radiating a discouraging pseudo-rustic jollity. In her every movement, this woman seemed actually conscious of her 'duty to the blood' and of carrying within her the 'necessary self-control in the interests of service to the race'.[36] A marriage advertisement dating from 1935 gives a graphic picture of this type:

52-year-old, pure Aryan physician,
fighter at Tannenberg, wishing to settle down,
desires
male offspring through civil marriage
with young, healthy virgin of pure Aryan stock, undemanding,
suited to heavy work and thrifty,
with flat heels, without earrings, if possible without money.
No marriage brokers. Secrecy guaranteed.
Letters to box number AEH 151,094, C/o M. Neuest.[37]

Outside such fantasies, the ideal type of National Socialist woman found its purest incarnation in Gerda Bormann, the wife of Martin Bormann. In addition to her family background, her outward appearance, and the great number of her children, she had an imperturbable attachment to the person of the Führer that went hand in hand with a simple, literal, ideological seriousness open to every intellectual claim, no matter how unreasonable. Her correspondence with her husband, part of which has been published, makes absolutely clear the basic psychological pattern of this type of woman: the yearning for subjection and self-surrender that lacks neither the features of personal unselfishness nor the shrill tones of hysterical faith; the blatant prejudices and the ability to fit all obviously contradictory facts into her philosophy without any intellectual embarrassment, to canonise stupidities, and to surrender blissfully to the densest obscurity. 'O Daddy,' she wrote once towards the end of the war in a characteristic tone of homespun extravagance, 'every word which the Führer said in the years of our hardest struggles is going round and round in my head again.' And a little later: 'On the radio they are singing the song "And if the world were full of devils." Without knowing it Luther wrote a real Nazi song!' She worries about the meaning of history for life, about Charlemagne's responsibility for the intrusion of Christianity and Jewry into Central Europe, about the deleterious effects of Christian morality as such, and about racial characteristics, and immediately accepts instruction from educational speakers or Gauleiters which makes 'everything clear at once'. Her zeal was always ready for ideological devotional exercises or tests and quite willing to be taken at its word, in fact glad of every sacrifice demanded 'for the cause'. Only in this light can we understand why when her husband told her of his finally successful seduction of the actress 'M' her only reply was to suggest that he brought 'M' home with him, that they worked out a system of shift motherhood and finally 'put all the children together in the house on the lake, and live together, and the wife who is not having a child will always be able to come and stay with you in Obersalzberg or Berlin'. Then she assures him:

Of course I'm not angry with the two of you, nor am I jealous. This was something that overcame you, just as you are often assailed by an idea or a desire and then carry it out immediately in your headlong, resolute fashion. I'm only worried whether you haven't given that poor girl a frightful shock with your impetuous ways. (AT FIRST NO DOUBT I DID.*) Does she really love you, then?

The incident suggests a practical step in accordance with ideology:

It would be a good thing if a law were to be made at the end of this war, like the one at the end of the Thirty Years War, which would entitle healthy, valuable men to have two wives. (THE FÜHRER IS THINKING ON SIMILAR LINES.*) So frighteningly few valuable men survive this fateful struggle, so many valuable women are doomed to be barren because their destined mate was killed in battle – Should that be? We need the children of these women too! (ABSOLUTELY, FOR THE STRUGGLES TO COME, WHICH WILL DECIDE THE NATIONAL DESTINY.*)[38]

With this and with her further ideas on the 'National Emergency Marriage', which was to annul the principle of monogamous marriage and permit secondary wives in the interests of child production, Gerda Bormann's train of thought was

* Bormann's comment.[38]

in keeping with numerous official proposals. Certain popular aspects of National Socialist family policy have partially concealed the fact that state assistance measures were aimed exclusively at creating the population requirements for the German people's 'imperial mission', that is to say for war. While Bormann demanded that 'for the sake of our nation's future we must practise a positive mother cult',[39] Walther Darré remarked with the carefree indifference of the ideologist who takes catastrophes in his stride that 'with a healthy land law and healthy marriages a war has never damaged the Nordic race in a biological sense'.[40] On the same lines, Himmler stated that 'without multiplying our blood we shall not be able to maintain the Great Germanic Empire that is in the process of coming into existence'.[41] And if the Director of the Party Chancellery in a memorandum on 'The Safeguarding of the Future of the German Nation' described the 'fertility of many age groups of millions of women' as the 'most precious capital', it was nevertheless from the outset capital amassed only to be squandered: the purely aggressive character of the National Socialist outlook rarely emerges more openly. Thus Hitler declared: 'That we have an excess of children will be our good fortune, for it will cause us want [!].'[42]

The high losses of the war, which were obviously not reckoned with in this deliberate planning for want, inspired in the top leadership from about 1943 onwards a flood of ghastly projects in which the pretentious narrowmindedness of small-animal breeders was unhesitatingly applied to the human world in a mixture of amateurish fantasies, lasciviousness and an excruciating philistine 'wit' masquerading as the exacting seriousness of statesmanship conscious of its debt to the future. Hitler and his closest advisers started from the assumption that after the war three to four million women would have to remain unmarried, a loss which, reckoned in divisions, as Hitler commented in the course of a discussion, 'cannot be tolerated by our nation'. Consequently these women too must be given the opportunity of having children. Since, however, as Bormann's memorandum puts it in the language of the tavern, 'they cannot receive their children from the Holy Ghost, but only from those German men who are still left', the state had to see to it that 'the decent, strong-minded, physically and psychically healthy men reproduce themselves increasingly'. A special procedure of application and selection was to make it possible for them 'to enter into a firmly established marriage not only with one woman but also with another, in which without more ado the second woman takes the name of the husband, her children the name of the father'.[43]

Similar ideas were put forward by Himmler. In the 'SS Order for the Combined SS and Police' of October 28, 1939, following earlier pronouncements, he had called for the procreation even, and especially, of illegitimate children, and taken the first practical steps by setting up the state registered brothel organisation, the Lebensborn, as well as by the systematic drafting of so-called 'conception assistants'.[44] Now, along with Bormann, he became the driving force in these projects. To safeguard the privileged position of the first wife he proposed for her the title 'Domina', and advocated that the right to enter into a second marriage should initially be bestowed 'as a high distinction upon the heroes of the war, holders of the German Cross in gold as well as the holders of the Knight's Cross'. Later he said that 'this could be extended to holders of the Iron Cross first class as well as those holding the silver and gold close-combat bar';[45] for 'the greatest fighter is entitled to the most beautiful woman', as Hitler used to say. The clichés of a romantic view of history, the dream of Saint George of his early years, and the fruits of reading the tracts on social Darwinism that had formed the basis of Hitler's education combined into an unspeakable amalgam:

If the German man as a soldier must be unconditionally prepared to die, then he must also have the freedom to love unconditionally. Fighting and love belong together. The bourgeois can think himself lucky to get what is left over.[46]

The projected new law envisaged the possibility of dissolving a marriage that had remained childless for five years, 'since a childless marriage is not of the slightest interest to a state that is concerned with the procreation of as many children as possible'.[47] According to a statement by Kaltenbrunner, citing similar ideas put forward within the top leadership of the SS, 'all single and married women up to the age of thirty-five who do not already have four children should be obliged to produce four children by racially pure, unexceptionable German men. Whether these men are married is without significance. Every family that already has four children must set the husband free for this action.'[48]

Kaltenbrunner linked these ideas with comprehensive future plans for extermination and thereby once more clearly revealed the dual motive behind them. For alongside the immediate objective of increasing Germany's power, there was always the aim of achieving that 'new man' whose birth Hitler once described as the true historic task of National Socialism.[49] To the numerous projects put forward with this object National Socialist theorists devoted themselves with passion and a verbosity intended to create the impression that they were initiates with special knowledge – the more so since this limited field of anthropology, with its largely untested assumptions and its tendency to pseudo-scientific speculative obscurantism, left them every conceivable freedom. There was already available from the social Darwinist schools of the nineteenth century a whole arsenal of ideas relating to being unworthy to live, a quantitative population policy, compulsory segregation and sterilisation of those unqualified to reproduce themselves, principles of selection and the idea of aristocratic polygamy. All this had been discussed long ago and merely required a few terminological modifications before being applied to the new conditions. Pseudo-romantic passion for nature and exaltation of country life, based upon the idea that cultural and social advance worked against natural selection, rested upon earlier ideas. Himmler's Lebensborn organisation had a forerunner in the 'Human Garden' of the Mittgart-Bund,[50] and personal files setting out the heredity of individuals had already been introduced for a section of the population in the card-indexed breeding-points system of RuSHA, the SS Head Office for Race and Settlement. From the nineteenth century dated the conviction that by 'favourable combinations of genes' the overall level of humanity could be raised to that of the genius 'and we may therefore expect that the distinguished poets and philosophers of the future will radically excel a Homer or a Shakespeare, a Goethe or a Humboldt'; Himmler's comment on the same lines had one significant variation, that 'Nietzsche's Superman could be attained by means of breeding.'[51] With the 'Engagement and Marriage Order' for the SS of December 31, 1931 he acquired the means of influencing his followers' choice of a partner; in the RuSHA he created the instrument for systematic breeding control; and by the subsequent nomination of Munich as the 'capital of the New Order and the family' he staked his personal claim in the execution of future comprehensive plans.[52] The next step was the methodical planning of so-called 'Women's Universities for Wisdom and Culture'. Starting from the conviction that the German people lacked 'the great, strong, purposeful woman such as the Romans possessed in their Vestals and the Teutons in their Wise Women', he proposed to gather together in schools a politically, biologically and intellectually selected élite of young women. After an education that was to extend from courses in cooking and housecraft through sport and revolver-shooting to the basic rules of the Foreign Service they would be given the title 'High Woman'. It was Hitler's idea that they should first of all replace 'the wives of most of our National Socialist leaders', who were merely 'good, trusty housewives who were entirely in place during the time of struggle but no longer suit their husbands today'. Such systematic coupling of people of high value to form 'National Socialist model marriages', Himmler enthused, 'is a unique phenomenon and can be the basis for a new advance of the Germanic race'.[53]

The enlightenment of the public on all these projects, however, as Bormann urged, should 'for obvious reasons not begin until after the war'. Nevertheless psychological preparation was begun. In future no novels, short stories or plays were to be permitted 'which equate "marital drama" with "marital infidelity" ' or present 'conflicts between a "lawful wife" and an "unlawful rival"'. On the contrary,' Bormann's memorandum continues, 'we must skilfully and unobtrusively indicate that, for example, as genealogical investigation reveals, very many family trees of famous scholars, statesmen, artists, economists and soldiers show the birth of illegitimate children.' Moreover, the word 'illegitimate' itself must be 'totally eradicated'; rather 'it is necessary for us to eliminate and forbid the various designations for a "relationship" that now have a more or less disreputable ring' and instead 'find good friendly names for it'.[54]

The good friendly names were not found, and if not all, then at least most of all this remained at the project stage in the blood cult of the fanatical planners. The ideological concepts of National Socialism still give off an almost palpable effluvium, an obscene odour of ideological poverty. The view of woman as never more than an object of ambitious struggle for political power becomes nakedly clear in the plans to multiply the Germanic race, to 'freshen and renew its blood'. Quite consistently, what had begun as a protest against the 'masculinisation' of woman ended with the eradication of all differences under the totalitarian system, which finally recognised only sexless 'operational units'. The degradation of woman under Hitler and National Socialism was never fully appreciated by contemporary public opinion, corrupted as it was with the help of popular measures designed to foster the regime's plans; even today its extent has not been fully recognised. It was surely a reflection of this degradation, intensified by the conditions of private life, that of the six women who were close to Hitler in the course of his life five committed or attempted suicide.[55]

Rudolf Höss –
The Man from the Crowd

> I am completely normal. Even while I was carrying out the task of extermination I led a normal family life and so on.
>
> *Rudolf Höss*

Present-day systems of totalitarian government have opened up many new insights into the nature of man. By testing him to the limits of endurance, they have demonstrated not only what man can do but also what can be done with man. The concentration camps with their manifold functions of combating, excluding and destroying the opponent of the moment on the one hand, and of training a chosen 'élite' to hardness on the other – intended in either case to destroy all human qualities – fundamentally challenged accepted estimates of what a human being is capable of doing and also of suffering. In Chelmno, Treblinka and Auschwitz there persished both the last remnants of an optimistic view of man based on the value of the human personality, and the whole system of logical psychology. The camps brought the discovery that there was 'an absolute evil which could no longer be understood and explained by the evil motives of self-interest, greed, covetousness, resentment, lust for power and cowardice; and which therefore anger could not avenge, love could not endure, friendship could not forgive'.[1]

This radical evil appears most clearly when viewed in its least obvious aspect. What are referred to as the barbaric features of the regime, to use a conventional phrase that falls far short of their true horror, were not based primarily upon the savagery of brutes systematically utilised by the leadership, upon elemental cruelty or sadism. It is true that in every society there are elements with whose aid a ruthlessly open reign of terror can be established and for a time maintained, and the National Socialist regime also made use of them, especially during the initial phase. But their number is limited, and moreover there are limits to the numbers that can be killed by hate, brutality or blood lust. To the industrially organised death factory, such as was perfected later, murder is limited solely by technical capacity. What happened in the extermination camps of the Third Reich is therefore not to be adequately explained in terms of the mobilisation of destructive and criminal energies. The new, disturbing experience lay precisely in the fact that it did not need such means and impulses. It was the appeal to idealism, to the readiness for self-sacrifice to a historic mission, and the perpetually reawakened

276

devotion to a utopian world which placed at the regime's disposal those forces without whose willingness to serve, self-discipline and sense of duty neither the proportions nor the cold perfectionism of the extermination system would have been possible. Despite differences in individual cases, it was preponderantly a credulous normality, devoted to its ideology and ideas of loyalty, that stamped the features of this horror. It has shattered the image of man more lastingly than ever the collective outbreak of base passions could have done.

It is part of the essence of totalitarian rule that it turns all concepts upside down, perverts all standards of judgment. It owes its support less to the attraction of satisfying impulses without fear of punishment than to the systematic confusion of moral values, accompanied by the proclamation of a new morality of its own. Freed from any overriding frame of reference, totalitarianism has no morality but opportunism designed to assist in gaining and keeping political power. In the name of history, the race, the national community or similar concepts beyond logical explanation, the totalitarian system arouses the latent willingness of disorientated people, hungry for certainty, to subordinate themselves to a 'higher law' and identify themselves with an 'iron necessity'. Countless simple, conscientious Germans during the years of the Third Reich were the less able to refuse the call of those in power because the regime's ability to present aims and arouse faith met their own longings, reinforced by a weariness of individual responsibility. They were filled with the need to be given commands, the need for order, for dependence, the desire for 'community' that goes largely unsatisfied in a plural society, and the hunger to prove themselves that had been thwarted during the critical years just past. Gripped by the ringing phrases of the new élite ethos, they followed this ethos selflessly, with discipline, and still with the subjective feeling of serving a just cause long after its criminal character had become manifest. A minority, more or less by accident, had become directly involved in criminal activity. But the ideology of the 'higher law', the maxims of the new morality and mission in conjunction with the system's all-embracing structure of allegiance, made it possible for them patiently and dutifully to perform the most inhuman tasks without any consciousness of personal guilt.

This state of affairs is demonstrated with extreme and dreadful clarity in the person of one of the regime's second-grade officials, Rudolf Höss. During the period of the Third Reich his name was unknown outside a comparatively restricted circle. Moreover, not only his character, education and intelligence but also his origins and career make him a truly representative phenomenon of his generation. The individual stages and turning-points of his life are typical of the development of many who passed through war, Freikorps, Vehmgericht, prison, and finally the general attachment to National Socialism. The inner journey, a constant search for dependency arising from restlessness, emptiness and aimlessness, is also typical, even if it rarely appeared in such an extreme form. His life demonstrates in a dreadful ideal case the dilemma of the man who has surrendered his independence, the abjectness of total servitude.

Rudolf Höss was the type of a functionary in the true sense: the exemplary product of a combination of the urge to renounce individual self-determination and totalitarian training in obedience. The suppression of personal 'spontaneity' and the absolute, reliable automatism of thought and action that are the models of every form of totalitarian training succeeded so completely in this case because Höss had from an early age, through his own character and circumstances, felt at home only in a world of commands and found the consciousness of merit and self-confirmation only within this framework. 'Believe, obey, simply fight!' In this motto of the SS he saw his deepest needs recognised and understood.[2] In him the capacity for rational and responsible action had atrophied to an almost unique degree, and the only doubt which ever shadowed his docile face was whether any measure that was ordered was covered by the authority of the moment. If life had led him upon a different path, he might have handled dossiers or run the farm that he dreamt of with the same reliability with which in the end he murdered human beings by the hundred thousand. Rudolf Höss was the commandant of the concentration and extermination camp of Auschwitz.

Still with the feeling of being called to service, he made every effort, offering his observations and experiences, 'in an almost repellent manner to be helpful'[3] to the investigating authorities in Nuremberg and also later in Poland. With the same willingness with which he had become the executive of mass murder he placed the documents needed to condemn him at the disposal of his judges, and entirely in keeping with the pattern of commands to which he was firmly attached, he saw the opportunity to write down his life story as a 'piece of homework' for which he was grateful.[4]

These notes are not only a revealing document on the system and practice of the Third Reich's machinery of destruction, but also an impressive proof of the state of affairs referred to above: the record of the seduction of an average man by the pseudo-moral claims of a totalitarian ideology. If Höss was not the type of the sadistic criminal, he also did not belong to that large socially inferior group who sought to enhance their self-esteem by membership of a privileged order. This type, whose energy and ruthlessness were merely the manifestations of a primitive nature drilled to military smartness, did indeed lend its stamp to Himmler's camp commandants as a whole. Rudolf Höss differed considerably from this type. Among his most outstanding characteristics were strict attention to duty, unselfishness, love of nature, sentimentality, even a certain helpfulness and kindliness, simplicity, and finally a marked hankering after morality, an abnormal tendency to submit himself to strict imperatives and to feel authority over him. The dilemma which confronted him, along with a large number of his generation, was that this tendency remained largely unsatisfied in a society confused about its values and inclined to deny them or admit to them only shamefacedly. The military world alone seemed still to offer that firm and immovable world of concepts and values for which he yearned: comradeship, loyalty, honour, courage held good there in an absolutely direct and literal sense, unvitiated by differentiating glosses, which the simple, uncritical mind immediately felt to be 'subversive'.

It was this moral longing, as powerful as it was undirected, that made Rudolf Höss suitable material for the demands of the totalitarian ethic, because it contained everything he was seeking: simple formulas, an uncomplicated schema of good and evil, a hierarchy of normal standards orientated according to military categories, and a utopia. For him, unlike the majority of his fellow-SS leaders, the demands with which he found himself confronted lay on a different plane from his personal impulses. Precisely because what he had to do seemed to him for a long time difficult, it gave him a feeling of particularly meritorious achievement. Again and again he emphasises in his life story how extremely difficult it had been for him, especially at the beginning, to be harsh, to watch executions, to see those who 'had run into the wire', to observe acts of brutality. He added that he was 'not suited to concentration camp service'.[5]

In fact, however, this psychological feature was the very key to his particular suitability for his work, according to Himmler's principles of selection. Constant effort towards self-mastery continually stimulated his misguided idealism, so that in the 'cold, indeed stony' attitude which in his own words he demanded of himself, Höss could see the result of moral struggle. It was only through a continual process of hardening that he became the type of the passionless, fundamentally disinterested murderer to whom, beyond the given objective purposes, murder meant nothing. Hitler once stated that the expression 'crime' came from a world that had now been superseded, that there was now only positive and negative activity,[6] and Höss was the product of this conception, standing outside all traditional moral categories, all personal contact with his acts. All consciousness of individual guilt had been eliminated and murder was simply an administrative procedure. In the type represented by Höss evil takes the shape of the uninvolved book-keeper, pedantic, sober, accurate. Hate, he states, had always been alien to him, and in later sections of his autobiography when he repeatedly complains of his vain struggles with malicious, rough subordinates, there is no hint of retrospective self-justification. The man who attached so much importance to his bourgeois 'decency', who proclaimed his aversion from his comrades' alcoholic excesses, who stated that he had never personally hated the Jews and had repudiated the anti-Semitic paper *Der Stürmer* because it was 'calculated to appeal to the basest instincts', precisely because of all this succeeded in becoming the 'ideal type' of Himmler's camp commandant,[7] since any subjective impulse, from sadism to pity, would have disturbed the smooth functioning of the mechanism of extermination. 'As for me,' Höss told a comrade in 1944, 'I have long since ceased to have any human feelings.'[8] Such utterances were the realisation of the idea of the SS camp functionary aimed at by Himmler and endorsed in countless speeches, the man who in his immunity to emotion corresponded only too closely to the bloodless, bureaucratic fanaticism of the Reichsführer of the SS himself. If one reads the initials SS as standing for 'Societas Satanas', it is by no means clear from which type this order received its 'satanic' qualities: from the matter-of-fact, unemotional figures devoid of all personal impulses, such as Rudolf Höss, or from the criminal, 'abnormal' elements; at least behind the latters' enjoyment of brutality there lay an over-whelming social, intellectual or otherwise motivated personal reaction which, significantly, 'appears to us like a last residue of humanly intelligible behaviour'.[9]

Höss was born in 1900 in Baden-Baden, in a strict and unusually pious home. His father, whose dogmatic and overpowering figure furnished the rather oppressive experiences of Höss's early development, had taken a vow that his son should be a priest. The educational principles described in the first pages of the autobiography read almost as if deliberately intended to set him on his subsequent path as commandant of Auschwitz:

I had been brought up by my parents to be respectful and obedient towards all grown-up people, and especially the elderly, regardless of their social status. I was taught that my highest duty was to help those in need. It was constantly impressed upon me in forceful terms that I must obey promptly the wishes and commands of my parents, teachers, priests, etc., and indeed of all grown-up people, including servants, and that nothing must distract me from this duty. Whatever they said was always right.

These basic principles on which I was brought up became part of my flesh and blood. I can still clearly remember how my father, who on account of his fervent Catholicism was a determined opponent of the Reich Government and its policy, never ceased to remind his friends that, however strong one's opposition might be, the laws and decrees of the State had to be obeyed unconditionally.

From my earliest youth I was brought up with a strong awareness of duty. In my parents' house it was insisted that every task be exactly and conscientiously carried out. Each member of the family had his own special duties to perform.[10]

This establishes the basic theme that ruled his life, with increasing importance and increasingly catastrophic results. There was no phase in his development when it did not, under changing authorities, operate to compel obedience. At the end of his life, in the Nuremberg cell, Rudolf Höss summed up this situation with the words: 'I had nothing to say; I could only say *Jawohl*! We could only execute orders without thinking about it.' Asked whether he could not have refused a given order, he replied: 'No, from our entire training the thought of refusing an order just didn't enter one's head, regardless of what kind of order it was.'[11]

This characteristic was supplemented and reinforced by an equally early, extraordinary introversion and lack of contact with others, which was peculiar to many of the National Socialist leadership and explained not merely their blind acceptance of authority but also their lack of human sympathy, their inability to identify with others. 'I always preferred to be alone,' Höss stated. 'When I had troubles I tried to cope with them alone. This was what most saddened my wife. I never had friends or close relationships with anyone, not even in my youth. I never had a friend. I never had any real intimacy with my parents – my sisters either. It only occurred to me after they were married that they were like strangers to me. – I always played alone as a child.'[12] The sentimental love of animals which comes out again and again even in the description of his childhood, like his later, only briefly interrupted membership of military communities, was purely a search for compensation for the poverty of his personal relationships. Both were attempts to escape from the demands of his environment; in one case he turned to 'dumb friends', in the other to a protective anonymous institution where the individual no longer counted. It was just this removal of the individual element that constituted the attraction of military organisations and all-male associations for the inhibited solitary. Martin Broszat, in his introduction to Rudolf Höss's auto-biographical notes, remarks on the nature of 'comradeship': 'Quite apart from its positive side, it is not based on the personal and individual qualities of the partners, but is determined by the alleged situation of the group, by the purpose on which it is engaged, and is given indiscriminately to everyone who "belongs".'[13]

Immediately after his father's death in 1914 Rudolf Höss insisted upon becoming a soldier. After continual but fruitless requests to his mother and his guardian, the fifteen-year-old finally succeeded in secretly joining a regiment. After a brief training he was sent to the Turkish front. Like anyone else he experienced the fears and inner anguish of his first action, and glimpsed 'in fear and trepidation' his 'first dead man'. Praised by his captain, who now satisfied his need for authority and someone to look up to, he reflected: 'If he had only known how I actually felt deep down!'[14] Several times wounded, but also several times decorated and holder among other medals of the Iron Cross First and Second Class, he became at seventeen the youngest NCO in the Army. To avoid internment after the Armistice he set out with his platoon, on his own initiative, on a remarkable odyssey from Anatolia to Germany and after wandering for three months reported back with his complete unit, according to regulations, to his regimental reserve unit.

Naturally Höss, like his whole generation of homecoming soldiers uprooted by the war, at once found himself confronted by the problem of establishing himself in civilian life. He had meanwhile turned his back on the priesthood; his mother had died in 1917, and since he felt misunderstood by his relations he joined the East Prussian Volunteer Corps for the Protection of the Frontier. In his memoirs he makes the characteristic remark, which appears in this or very similar form in numerous biographies of men who later became officials of the Third Reich: 'In this way the problem of my profession was suddenly solved!'[15] And at the same time – the more urgent individual problem for a man who was to find his fullest release from his own lack of direction inside the military collective and in the language of military commands – his release from all questions and doubts. 'I became a soldier once more. I found a home again, and a sense of security in the comradeship of my fellows. Oddly enough,' he adds, confirming the foregoing analysis, 'it was I, the lone wolf, always keeping my thoughts and feelings to myself, who felt continually drawn towards that comradeship which enables a man to rely on others in time of need and danger.'[16] As a member of the notorious Rossbach Freikorps he took part in the battles in the Baltic region, where he witnessed, 'dumbfounded', the 'destructive madness' of these pitiless conflicts, and went through the battles at Mecklenburg and in the Ruhr and Upper Silesia. Nevertheless, it seems that this training in brutalisation had its effect on the

281

sensitive outsider. In any case, in 1923 his name crops up in the so-called Parchim Vehmgericht murder trial, when the State Court tried some former members of the Rossbach Freikorps, which had been declared illegal, who after a drinking orgy had carried off into the forest a young man whom they held to be a traitor, beaten him half dead with truncheons, and finally shot him. As one of the chief participants in this crime, Höss was sentenced to ten years' imprisonment. The analytical tone of his account of life in the Brandenburg penitentiary, written without any serious hint of personal distress caused by prison life and continually lapsing into sententious and knowing self-satisfaction, makes it clear that in the strict regimentation of prison he merely saw another kind of 'home', of 'protectedness', such as he had hitherto found in military organisations. 'I had been taught since childhood to be absolutely obedient and meticulously tidy and clean; so in these matters I did not find it difficult to conform to the strict discipline of prison. I conscientiously carried out my well-defined duties. I completed the work allotted to me, and usually more, to the satisfaction of the foreman. My cell was a model of neatness and cleanliness, and even the most malicious eyes could see nothing there with which to find fault.'[17]

The monotonous theme of his life, the cardinal, desperate question of his as of every dependent, empty life was: 'Where can I serve?' Later he was to employ exactly the same vocabulary – 'unconditional obedience', 'strictest order', 'conscientiousness', and 'fulfilment of the duties prescribed to me' – to describe his work in Auschwitz; the only philosophy of life he had with which to confront the monstrous conditions was that of the recruit who takes a naïve and foolish pride in a well-made bed and the look of satisfaction on an NCO's face. The exemplary prisoner Höss was the first of approximately eight hundred prisoners to be found eligible for probation, with a resulting alleviation of his prison existence and the prospect of early release. Nevertheless repeated applications for release proved fruitless, Höss remained in prison, and in his dreams the idea became more and more firmly established that later he would regain his lost contact with civilian life as a farmer with his own land.

After almost six years in prison he was unexpectedly released on the strength of the Amnesty Law of July 14, 1928, and soon afterwards joined the Bund der Artamanen, an organisation that combined reactionary hostility towards civilisation with a belief in runes and the soil, and reformist aims based on agricultural settlement. He resolutely resisted pressure from former comrades to take office, as an old party member, in the NSDAP, on the grounds that although he agreed with the aims of the movement, he was opposed to its 'bargaining for the good will of the masses', its 'appeal to the lowest instincts of the masses'. Höss wanted to settle on the land: 'There was for me only one object for which it was worth working and fighting, namely, a farm run by myself, on which I should live with a large and healthy family. That was to be the content and aim of my life.'[18] Soon after his release he married, then worked for several years in various land-service groups in Brandenburg and Pomerania, and was about to be apportioned the land he had longed for when once again he received a call from authority, and Höss was not the man to disobey. Heinrich Himmler, likewise a member of the Bund der Artamanen, invited him in 1934 to join the active SS. After long hesitation Höss finally decided to exchange the uncertainties of a civilian future for the familiar service in a firmly knit community. Characteristically, as he later stated, he gave no thought to Himmler's remark that he would be placed in a unit guarding a concentration camp. 'To me it was just a question of being an active soldier once again, of resuming my military career.'

The commandant of Dachau concentration camp, to which Höss was sent, was the then SS Standartenführer Theodor Eicke, a man who combined the energy and organisational vigilance of the former officer with the unscrupulousness of the brutalised private soldier and whose writing paper bore the heading: 'Only one thing is valid: orders!' For Höss this motto, which set him free from his indecision through the mechanism of unquestioning fulfilment of duty, was a golden phrase. This was what his father, this was what his captain, this was what the Freikorps leader and very much what the prison foreman had said. It was the foundation of his view of life, and it would be a mistake to see this reduction of existence to mere reaction to commands solely in terms of loss of dignity, and not to take account of the happiness it offered to many people tired of the burden of responsibility for their own existence. Remarkable, though clearly a first step towards that split in consciousness characteristic of adaptation to totalitarian conditions, is Höss's statement that he emphatically rejected Eicke's terrorist practices. When the numerous beatings were carried out he always, according to his own admission, placed himself in the rear ranks, because he could not bear to watch torture, and he confesses with naïve frankness that later too, as camp commandant of Auschwitz, he was 'rarely present' at the beatings to which he himself had condemned prisoners. Evidently quite oblivious of what little right he had to express indignation, he described his comrades who carried out the beatings in his stead as 'almost without exception sly, rough, violent, and often common creatures', adding almost unbelievably: '*They* did not regard prisoners as human beings at all.'[19]

Undoubtedly Höss, with his mental rigidity, never recognised the contradictions of his behaviour. Even if the tendency to present himself in a favourable light continually creeps into his autobiography, we need scarcely question the honesty of his claims to feelings: 'I never grew indifferent to human suffering. I have always seen it and felt for it.'[20] But it was the honesty of a man made deaf and blind by his pathologically restricted outlook and lacking genuine sympathy and moral standards, and also incapable of consciously realising what he was doing. His introversion reflected an inaccessible emotional coldness, and what he believed to be sympathy for his victims was nothing but sentimental pity for himself, who was ordered to carry out such inhuman acts. Thus he was able to claim merit for a completely self-centred sentimentality, which placed him under no obligation to take any action, and to credit himself with the mendacious self-pity of the 'sorrowful murderer' as evidence of his humanitarianism.

Like many of his kind he was helped to get over such paradoxes presented by the realities of camp life by an increasing ability to keep separate the various planes of experience: the 'service' from those zones of private life in which feelings dominate, wives and children are paternally cared for, and exalted emotions are experienced. It is true that the continual alternation between his simple off-duty emotions and the vexations of daily routine, between the deeply felt idyll of the quiet evening at home and the executioner's trade, was not possible without occasional complications, and occasionally no doubt his sub-conscious mind rebelled against the imposed split in his personality. But it was the inability to see his individual situation, whether historical, social or moral, critically and in context – an inability characteristic of the type of unthinking underling he represented – which erected that barrier behind which he performed the tasks allotted to him with such unimpeachable self-righteousness. Moreover, he was haunted by the fear of being accused of weakness. The desire, bred by the perverted image of the National Socialist ideal man, 'to be described as harsh,' as Höss remarked, 'in order not to be considered soft', nipped doubt in the bud. It helped when in 1938 he was transferred to Sachsenhausen, where as camp adjutant his functions were predominantly bureaucratic, so that he 'no longer came into such direct contact with the prisoners' and the smoke-screen of phrases and pseudo-emotions was scarcely touched by the sight of the squalid everyday reality. Significantly he praised the camp commandant, SS Standarten-führer Hermann Baranowski, whom he revered as his 'magnified mirror image', for his 'good nature' and 'kind heart', which were coupled with the ability to be 'hard and mercilessly severe in all matters appertaining to service'.[21]

This schizophrenic state of mind, which enabled Höss to keep his sentimental reserves in the midst of a world of brutal murder and to prescribe at the writing desk with unimaginative savagery measures he was too sensitive to watch being carried out, was something which he developed to an inconceivable degree two years later when, having proved himself in many different ways, he was given the task of building up Auschwitz. On almost every page of his life-story he speaks of having been 'completely filled, indeed obsessed' by his task, of how it was his 'whole preoccupation and endeavour' to create the maximum efficiency in the camp as requested. 'I had only one end in view: to drive everything and everyone forward so that I could carry out the measures laid down. The Reichsführer of the SS required every man to do his duty and if necessary to sacrifice himself entirely in so doing.'[22] At the same time, the remarks about his vulnerable inner life do not cease, and in spite of all restropective embellishments this coexistence of hectic diligence and perpetual self-pity provides a fairly accurate picture of his state of mind. The tragedies of the victims paled into a ghostly unreality that he no longer really noticed, leaving him the exemplary representative of that abstract approach which commits its murders methodically, with occasional private unease, but in general with patient disinterestedness. Asked whether he was convinced of the guilt of the murdered Jews, he said the question was unrealistic, 'he had really never wasted much thought on it'.[23] Far from his being tormented by the despairing screams of men dying in agony, the process was finally reduced to an administrative problem: a question of timetable conferences to arrange the smooth transport of human loads, a question of types of oven, gassing capacities, and 'potentialities of fuel technology'. It was precisely this mechanisation of the process of extermination which allowed him later to deny all personal responsibility and, what is so horrifying to the observer, to argue from the fact that he murdered without any personal emotion that he was free from guilt. Crucially revealing is his account of his relief that the use of gas made possible a method of killing as rational as it was bloodless and hygienic. 'I always shuddered at the prospect of carrying out extermination by shooting, when I thought of the vast numbers concerned, and of the women and children. The shooting of hostages and the group executions ordered by the Reichsführer of the SS or by the Reich Central Security Office had been enough for me. I was therefore relieved to think that we were to be spared all these blood-baths.'[24] The constant repetition of the personal pronoun reveals his intolerable self-centredness; the victims emerge only remotely as a burdensome and fundamentally annoying source of personal disquiet. Eloquently he describes his 'perpetual harassment', his private disappointments, the incomprehension of the responsible authorities towards his material and personal wishes, finally exclaiming at the end of one of these complaints, 'It was in truth not a happy or desirable state of affairs.'[25] It was these essentially practical difficulties, not the inhuman task, which, as he writes himself, brought him to despair and to that misanthropic bitterness of which he speaks with the offended mien of misunderstood virtue. In his moral lethargy the million-fold sufferings of the victims seemed as nothing by comparison with the technical difficulties of the executioner. 'Believe me, it wasn't always a pleasure to see those mountains of corpses and smell the perpetual burning.'[26] The same unshakable self-righteousness led him to adopt a tone of petty bourgeois moral arrogance when reporting thefts and sexual misdemeanours among camp inmates or to record with an unmistakable undertone of surprised disapproval that Jewish Special Detachments (*Sonderkommandos*) were willing, in return for a short extension of their own lives, to help with the gassing of members of their own race.

Some of the one-sided perfectionist pride of the expert comes out in Höss's statement: 'By the will of the Reichsführer of the SS, Auschwitz became the greatest human extermination centre of all time,'[27] or when he points out with the satisfaction of the successful planner that the gas chambers of his own camp had a capacity ten times greater than those of Treblinka. His descriptions of the individual stages in the process of extermination are also written entirely in the self-satisfied tone of a superior technician, even with a didactic touch, as though he wished to give the world the benefit of his experience in evolving the most rational methods of mass extermination. Thus, for example, after describing the outbreaks of panic when the first transports arrived, he writes:

With subsequent transports the difficult individuals were picked out early on and most carefully supervised. At the first sign of unrest, those responsible were unobtrusively led behind the building and killed with a small-calibre gun that was inaudible to the others.

The presence and calm behaviour of the Special Detachment served to reassure those who were worried or who suspected what was about to happen. A further calming effect was obtained by members of the Special Detachment accompanying them into the rooms and remaining with them until the last moment, while an SS man also stood in the doorway until the end. It was most important that the whole business of arriving and undressing should take place in an atmosphere of the greatest possible calm. People reluctant to take off their clothes had to be helped by those of their companions who had already undressed, or by men of the Special Detachment. The refractory ones were calmed down and encouraged to undress. The prisoners of the Special Detachment also saw to it that the process of undressing was carried out quickly, so that the victims would have little time to wonder what was happening.[28]

In the course of the years Höss developed the various phases in the extermination process, gassing, disposal of the bodies, utilisation of the things left behind by the dead, into a smoothly functioning system of linked procedures. It was in perfect keeping with the ambitious, cold hunger for organisation typical of a man of his stamp, revealing an uninhibited thoroughness that sprang from the absence of all human consideration. It was the consciousness of this special achievement which caused him to say, 'At first I felt unhappy at the prospect of uprooting myself,' when, after three and a half years, he was recalled from Auschwitz and made head of the Political Department of the Inspectorate of Concentration Camps.[29] This duty he carried out until the end of the war, visibly troubled by the desolate condition of most of the camps, which lacked the perfectionism of the Auschwitz model, but also unable, as the situation became increasingly acute, to do anything to improve matters. One final picture, typical in all its absurdity of this man's career and character, appears at the end of his account. He describes the termination of his work amid the chaos of total collapse. 'We ourselves had to flee,' he writes. 'We went first of all towards the Darss, then after two days we headed for Schleswig-Holstein. All this was in accordance with the orders of the Reichsführer of the SS. What we were supposed to do for him, or what duties we were still intended to perform, we could not imagine.'[30] Thus at the end of this unindependent life, lived throughout at second hand, there stands senseless compliance with a senseless order, an act of blind obedience.

In fact a great deal remained inexplicable to Rudolf Höss. Although in his statements he later admitted the criminal nature of his work, he seems never to have quite realised who he was and what his name meant in connection with the name of Auschwitz. It is impossible to avoid the suspicion that even in admitting his guilt he was merely making a final effort to obey, this time the investigating officials and the court, who now condemned organised genocide and whom, 'always in accordance with orders', he wished to please by repudiating his own actions. The American court psychologist G. M. Gilbert, from a conversation with Höss, gained the impression that the former commandant of Auschwitz 'would never have become aware of the monstrous nature of his crime if someone had not pointed it out to him'.[31] Not only countless passages in his autobiography, but far more their whole tone and style, prove that even as his end approached he was unable to see his actions in terms of guilt and responsibility. Instead, he remained fixated to the last on command and obedience, not because he hoped, by stressing his purely executive function, to justify or even save himself, but simply because he was incapable of seeing the situation in any other light. Like one of the executioners of the French Revolution, Höss considered himself merely the axe, and seemed always to be asking during his trial whether it was the axe that was being judged. No appeal, no shock could disturb his conviction that he had always done right, that he had done his duty 'conscientiously, attentively, and to everyone's satisfaction'. 'In prison,' he writes in that section of his account dealing with his arrival in Warsaw to be handed over to the Polish authorities, 'several of the officials came at me, and showed me their Auschwitz tattoo numbers. I could not understand them.'[32] Whatever had been done in his name had nothing to do with the solitary, nature-loving, soft-hearted Rudolf Höss who was affectionately devoted to his family and above all to his children. Fundamentally it simply was not his business.

Finally realising that the world would not recognise this distinction, he felt himself the victim of personal tragedy. He blamed fate for his plight, for having obstinately 'intervened to save my life, so that at the end I might be put to death in this shameful manner'. 'Unknowingly [!],' he wrote, 'I was a cog in the chain of the great extermination machine of the Third Reich.' With the characteristic twist of the introvert, in the final sentence of his autobiography he turned away from this world that had maltreated him, deceived him, left him alone with a responsibility that was not his, and finally had not understood him. Now and for the remainder of his life he abandoned himself to that self-pity which was one of the dominant features of his personality: 'Let the public continue to regard me as the bloodthirsty beast, the cruel sadist, and the mass murderer; for the masses could never imagine the commandant of Auschwitz in any other light. They could never understand that he, too, had a heart and that he was not evil.'[33] But if the most terrible page of history appears in the autobiography which he left behind, it is not terrible only because of the millions of murdered it lists. It is terrible no less because of the picture it presents of those organisers of mass murder who 'also had a heart', but whose blind obedience to orders and immunity to personal feelings involved greater guilt than any 'heartless' criminal ever brought upon himself.

The Polish Supreme People's Court, established to try war criminals, condemned Rudolf Höss to death on April 2, 1947. A fortnight later he was hanged at Auschwitz.

PART FOUR

The Face of the Third Reich:
Attempt at a Summing Up

The Face of the Third Reich:
Attempt at a Summing Up

There have never been better slaves, never worse masters.

Tacitus

The starting-point for a final discussion summing up certain essential findings of the studies in this volume presents itself at once. The attempt to unravel the psychologies of the leaders of the Third Reich has laid bare, to an extent exceeding all expectation, virtually the whole range of human weaknesses, shortcomings and inadequacies. The chronicler of this epoch stands almost helpless before the task of relating so much incapacity, so much mediocrity and insignificance of character, intelligibly to their extraordinary results. What confronts him is never greatness, rarely an outstanding talent, and in hardly one case a great obsession with a single goal. It is not even in the traditional sense a question of a base passion that is great by virtue of the intensity of the will at work behind it. On the contrary, it is in the overwhelming majority of cases petty weaknesses, egotisms, idiosyncrasies and impulses of an altogether insignificant, even if totally uninhibited character. The analysis of psychological elements in totalitarian forms of government, at least in the case of the leading National Socialists, is not, as has often been suggested, a task for demonology; it is rather a question of describing concrete individual failures. From Hitler to Heydrich, from Goebbels to Rosenberg, it was without exception from the starting-point of unconscious impulses or emotional disturbance that each of the figures sketched here pushed his way to power or allowed himself to be swept along by the movement that was already thrusting towards power, and the same is true of the mass of the nation itself, whose representatives in this sense the regime's leading men unquestionably were. Impelled towards politics in the first instance not by an overwhelming idea but by psychological conflict, whatever ideological constructions were erected to obscure this fundamental fact, they were all concerned not so much to realise a dream of the future as to work off an instinctual urge.

Nevertheless National Socialism, as we have seen, was not a self-enclosed will to power exclusively determined by the individual desires of its spokesmen; it did undoubtedly contain a utopian element. 'Gods and beasts, that is what our world is made of,' Hitler once exclaimed in one of his confidential disquisitions on the philosophy of power to his closest followers.[1] This lapidary sentence is probably

291

the most succinct possible summary of the essence of National Socialism, behind all ideological and tactical masks. It points to the foundations of its claim to govern, its image of man, its racial and expansionist aims, and the ultimate ground from which the manifold ideological elements evolved. The domineering and hybrid features in the face of the Third Reich, the coldness of its personality, its artificial stimulation of emotion, but also its desolate, contorted grimaces, its brutality, and not least its peculiar neurotic obstinacy, are contained in the basic principle formulated by Hitler that man does not equal man but is divided into gods and beasts.[2]

What did the gods look like – and possibly the beasts too, the ideal as well as the real? What interrelationships existed between them? Did the one need the other? By what signs can we recognise the man who establishes the modern rule of force – and the man with whose aid it can be established? Is there indeed such a thing as the type susceptible to totalitarian manipulation? These questions, which have been the subject of our investigation, reveal the concern of a 'burnt' age that has not merely learnt to fear the fire of totalitarianism, but seeks the necessary knowledge to counter its causes. Certainly, wide areas of the problem still lie in darkness or in the questionable zone of mass psychology. Nevertheless, elements may be gleaned from the study of the personalities of Hitler's followers, and from the shaping principles of National Socialism which circumscribe the type of National Socialist man and give him certain defining characteristics.

Every totalitarian government starts from a new image of man; this, by definition, is what distinguishes it from the classical forms of coercive government. Its revolutionary claims are not aimed solely at the reconstruction of the state; it not only prescribes new laws, demands new principles of order or new forms of mutual relationships, but also calls for a 'new man'. Unlike the great revolutions of past ages, it sets out to change not things but people, not structures but life itself: this is precisely what identifies it as totalitarian. Nothing demonstrates, in this strict sense, the totalitarian character of the Third Reich more unequivocally than the measures consistently taken on all social planes to mould a new human type, the creation of which National Socialism described as 'the task of the twentieth century'.[3] Hitler himself identified this project completely with the meaning of his struggle for power when he stated:

The selection of the new Führer class is what my struggle for power means. Whoever proclaims his allegiance to me is, by this very proclamation and by the manner in which it is made, one of the chosen. This is the great significance of our long, dogged struggle for power, that in it will be born a new master class, chosen to guide the fortunes not only of the German people but of the world.[4]

In countless speeches and proclamations Hitler again and again conjured up the image of the 'new man', and the many people who acclaimed the regime, who applauded every step it made and every point in its programme, celebrated the development of this man as the dawn of 'the truly golden age'.[5] As always with the National Socialist *Weltanschauung*, which was marked by very few original ideas, here too the return to older concepts, in this case those of the social Darwinist school of the nineteenth century, is unmistakable. The specific contribution of National Socialism lay not on the ideological but on the executive plane, in the hair-raisingly literal consistency with which these planned games with human nature were pursued in practice.

Parallel with the programme for destroying alien or opposing races were the efforts to 'ennoble' the blood of the German people itself. Behind this lay the postulated type of the racially pure master-human with his particular creative and cultural abilities and capacity for leadership; the orthodox characteristics of the type were excepted for the higher and possibly the middle ranks of the National Socialist hierarchy, who were racially legitimised simply by their rank and their allegiance to the person of the Führer. They represented the élite and the first stage towards that new species whose representatives were identical in appearance, expression and attitude. It was the greatness of the movement, Hitler proclaimed on one occasion, that 'sixty thousand men have outwardly become almost a unit, that actually these men are uniform not only in ideas, but that even the facial expression is almost the same. Look at these laughing eyes, this fanatical enthusiasm, and you will discover how a hundred thousand men in a movement become a single type.'[6] Hitler saw the situation they were striving for, in which the whole nation would correspond to this image as the result of a long biological and educational process. In his secret speech to the officers' passing-out class of 1939 he spoke of a development extending over a hundred years, at the end of which a majority would possess those élite characteristics with whose aid the world could be conquered and ruled. 'Those who see in National Socialism nothing more than a political movement know scarcely anything of it,' he said on another occasion. 'It is more even than a religion: it is the will to create mankind anew.'[7]

It was no doubt merely in one of those moods of exaltation which would come over Hitler during his endless nocturnal monologues in his most intimate circle that he painted this new man as possessing demonic features like those of a beast of prey, 'fearless and cruel', as he said, so that he himself 'shrank from him'.[8] The revolutionary attributes with which, for a time at least, this redesigned human being was equipped also prove on closer examination to be rhetorical accessories; for what the top leadership forbade in the interests of the maintenance of power and self-preservation is also undesirable vis-à-vis the inner structure of totalitarian rule itself. Totalitarianism aims at producing not the revolutionary but the aggressive type, whose aggression can be directed and used as required. Recognition of one's own social and personal situation, which is one of the conceptual prerequisites for the true revolutionary, was consistently obscured by National Socialism and replaced by the element of 'convictions'; theoretical clarity was replaced by 'experience in faith' and by that 'blindness' which came in various verbal combinations according to the National Socialist hierarchy of values: blind loyalty, blind courage, or blind obedience. The character-training principles according to which the young élite of the coming Greater Germanic

Reich were educated at the national political educational establishments or the SS 'Order Castles' aimed at producing an easily governed type: not absolutely fearless, but absolutely compliant; not cruel, but impersonal and perfectionist; at the same time bold when thrown into battle, disciplined, unselfish, and as willing to fulfil its function as it was inspired with the consciousness of its own masterhood. Robert Ley drew a vivid picture of the new man in his tract *Der Weg zur Ordensburg* (The Way to the Order Castle):

We want to know whether these men carry in them the will to lead, to be master, in a word to rule. The NSDAP and its leaders must want to rule. He who does not take up a total claim to leadership of the people, or is even willing to share it with others, can never become a leader in the NSDAP. We want to rule, to take pleasure in ruling, not in order to be a despot or to pay homage to a sadistic tyranny, but because we unshakably believe that in all things only one man can lead and only one can bear the responsibility. To this one man power also belongs. Thus, for example, these men will learn to ride on horseback, not in order to pay homage to a social prejudice, but to have the feeling of being able absolutely to master a living being. We want these men to be capable of dealing with every situation and not to be intimidated by anything in the world. These men, whom the Order of the NSDAP is thereby bringing to honour and power and giving everything which a real man can hope for from life, must on the other hand recognise and preserve in the depths of their hearts that they belong to this Order for better or for worse and must obey it utterly. So I want these men, who have the honour to become political leaders in Germany, and to whom the gates to the highest power and the highest leadership are opening – for they alone will one day rule Germany – to know and recognise that there is no more turning back for them. He who fails or actually betrays the party and its Führer, he who is unable to master the baseness in himself, the Order will destroy. He from whom the party removes the brown shirt – this each one of us must know and recognise – will not thereby merely be deprived of an office, but he personally, together with his family, his wife, and his children, will be destroyed. These are the harsh and implacable laws of an Order. On the one hand men may reach to the skies and grasp whatever a man can desire. On the other hand lies the deep abyss of annihilation.[9]

Supermanhood and depersonalisation, an autonomous sense of power and automatism, fearlessness and subservience, the type demanded reveals its true contours in such ambivalent states of consciousness. From the passage quoted we can analyse virtually the whole gamut of formulas for training the totally malleable functional man. The efforts of countless educational institutions were directed towards this end. At the same time the racial branch of the science of 'psychosomatics' evolved by National Socialism, which saw in the so-called optimum racial value the highest values both of character and intellect, led to systematic attempts to breed the new man. The beginnings of these attempts may be seen in the genetic and marriage laws as partly applied and partly planned for the postwar period.[10]

Against the background of these projects for the achievement of the ideal type, the facts of real life stood out in complete contradiction. It requires careful search to find even a hint of this supposed purity of blood among the leadership of the Third Reich, whose dominant type was more like the racially hybrid product of an Alpine province. And if, in accordance with the racial guiding image, 'the healthy' was proclaimed as a 'heroic command',[11] here too the real situation was rather the diametrical opposite. Apart from the acutely neurotic personalities of almost all the leading National Socialists which we have seen in the course of the present study, a large proportion were also sick in the narrower clinical sense, including Goebbels, Göring, Ley, Himmler, and not least Hitler himself. Hitler got over such obvious discrepancies with the fiction that racial values showed not so much in outward appearances as in reactions to the National Socialist idea and its Führer, undisturbed by the fact that this amounted to a denial of the whole racial theory. This, he proclaimed, 'is the infallible method of seeking the men one wants to find, for everyone listens only to the sound to which his innermost being is attuned'.[12]

Despite all assertions to the contrary – as for instance in a pamphlet entitled 'Our Führer in the Light of the Racial Question',[13] which stated that the representative National Socialists were 'predominantly Nordic men with very good character indications for leadership' – the extreme rarity of the 'figure typical of the species' within the so-called Old Guard is obvious. The explanation lies not only in the ideological poverty and admittedly propagandistic function of the party programme and outlook, but also in the movement's social origins.

The nucleus of the early membership was a militant minority of the disappointed and embittered of all classes. And even if hostility to 'the Jew' appeared relatively early, indeed was from the beginning one of the key slogans for attracting followers, it was a long time before the Nordic 'counterfigure' became the racially concrete, obligatory type: indeed, not only the biological but also the social and ideological 'whence' remained as much a matter of indifference to each individual as the 'whither' did to the movement as a whole. They were bound together solely by movement, by active protest, the same or similar origins of their basic 'anti' feelings, inability to surmount individually the military and political catastrophe of the nation. Fundamentally, beyond the basic maxim of 'hitting out', which drew its peculiar slogans from dubious Bavarian sources, there were no stricter ideological premises, even if members were required to believe that movement and hitting out were being performed 'for Germany', and Göring stated most significantly at Nuremberg that he had 'joined the party because it was revolutionary, not because of the ideological stuff'.[14] The so-called 'serious-minded group', who had some conception, whatever its nature, of an attempt to reconstruct society, always remained a minority, and in hardly a single instance did ideological aims provide the decisive incentive for any of Hitler's chief followers to join the party. In almost every case we can trace the extent to which personal difficulties of adaptation and inarticulate discontents, the whole great difficulty of living experienced by that generation, gave the decisive push towards politics, which in that restless epoch quickly became the classic 'profession' of the homeless and those lacking in capacity for human contact. It is precisely the exaggeratedly masculine bearing of the movement, its paramilitary forms of organisation, that betray the instability of men who could only repress their consciousness of individual impotence within serried ranks. Like Babeuf, they could almost all say of themselves that the revolutionary times had 'ruined them terribly', so that they had become incapable of following any other profession than that of the politician. They were men with unbalanced natures, their systems of values perverted by the war and the postwar troubles, uprooted people in whom the 'national distress' combined with individual failure and in some cases with manifestly neurotic personalities. Hitler himself is still the most graphic example, but Hess must also be mentioned in this connection, as well as Rosenberg and above all the seething mass in the second rank, including the members of the Freikorps and the Nationalist associations who quickly joined the movement.

The blind desire for a radical reversal of existing conditions, in which the divergent expectations found their common denominator, was perfectly summed up by Gregor Strasser in the statement that National Socialism was 'the opposite of what exists today', while Hitler stressed: 'Those people will never come to us who see in the preservation of an existing social order the ultimate purpose of their lives':[15] *rerum novarum cupidi*. Consequently the decisive distinguishing feature during the early phase of the movement was the almost total lack of qualifications for joining. The very fact that they possessed nothing, no ties, no traditionally determined reservations of respect, no 'origins', no support of family, religious or social ties, and even refused to accept convention and morality in a total, nihilistic purification of existence, made them in part the material, in part the spokesmen of totalitarian aspirations. Lack of habitual attitudes was their essential attitude, and with it went the readiness to use force and take 'direct action'. If this constituted a firm cement within the movement – because, as Hitler remarked, apart from common ideals nothing binds people together as firmly as 'common crimes'[16] – it appeared to those outside, who were also affected by the disaster, positive proof of the thoroughness of an indignation which, faced with a social order that had broken down, did not think of secret compromises but firmly burned its boats.

This combination of lack of ties and belief in force, which can be demonstrated in all the exponents of the National Socialist movement, is not merely among the most important conditions for Hitler's rise but is no doubt the crucial symptom of all pretotalitarian phases. What came to light here, amid the breakdown of a traditional order, was the Machiavellianism of the little man who no longer acknowledged his responsibility to any authority for his words and actions. Faced with an existence that had lost its certainties, he at once took refuge in crime. The halo which increasingly surrounded criminality, even if it was decked out with ideology and presented as political combat, the admiration for 'great men' and leaders together with widespread contempt for all standards of conduct, were, on the psychological plane, simply an attempt to identify with historical greatness as such, which was thought also to be above the law and to know no hesitation but always inexorably to follow its chosen path. Behind such reactions it was easy enough to see the aim of regaining a self-confidence lost in the war and all the economic and social degradations that followed. However, the attack on morality as 'petty bourgeois' disclosed the petty bourgeois character of the attackers themselves. This curious blend of provincial narrow-mindedness and Caesarist dreams, so typical of the majority of the leading National Socialists, was vividly documented by Rudolf Hess in a letter from Spandau prison: 'My activities towards achieving mental balance (*geistige Ausgleichstätigkeit*) have recently moved between Heinrich Seidel's *Leberecht Hühnchen* and Ranke's *Männer und Zeiten*, that is to say between the atmosphere of Monsieur Petit when he was still planting his cabbages in a Paris suburb, and that surrounding Napoleon on the hill overlooking Austerlitz.'[17]

Furthermore, the National Socialist movement drew a thousandfold advantage from the radicalism of its image, which gave it such a striking resemblance to Sorel's 'politico-criminal associations'. The bourgeois politicians who reproached the movement with its chain of acts of violence were incontestably in the right; but the arguments they used proved again and again that they did not understand the panic aspects of a time in which the bourgeois world with its ideas of order and morality was heading towards its demise. Certainly the totalitarian tendencies of a society are closely linked with political, social and economic conditions, but primarily they are a psychological problem. By trying to fight them exclusively on the political, social and economic plane the 'non-psychologists of Weimar' failed to appreciate their real structure. The attraction of the NSDAP lay precisely in the fact that it assuaged the need for aggression felt by the masses who had been reduced to despair by defeat, the power vacuum of the postwar years, the inflation, and later the world economic crisis. 'The men I want around me are those who, like myself, see in force the motive element in history, and who act accordingly.'[18] To see in force the motivating energy not merely of history but also of their own interests and in addition the cure for difficulties in life as a whole, became the characteristic reaction among ever-widening areas of the population, a reaction that, more powerfully than any events in the foreground, foreshadowed that crisis which might at any moment lead the country suddenly to embark upon a totalitarian adventure. The blind demand for happiness above all on the part of the petty bourgeoisie, frightened and déclassé, its secularised longing for faith, its tendency to see behind all the blows of fate the machinations of dark powers and to blame its own failures on others, its sentimentality, and finally its need to capitulate before force: all this found satisfaction before the rostra of the National Socialist speakers, even if it was shamelessly manipulated.

It was above all the figure of Hitler that delivered these vague demands from apathy. He seemed like the synthetic product of all the collective malaise of those years, and in him the hundreds of rival nationalist groups, and later the inconstantly fluctuating masses, first found their uncontested leader and thereby their hopes, their enemies, their aims, and their orders for tactical action. He made it possible for them to overcome the consciousness of their own weakness by equating themselves with a supposedly elemental force. Thanks to his superior talents, confirmed both in the struggle for power within the party and in his power of suggestion over men and masses, he quickly succeeded in welding the diffuse reactions together. And while the former impulses and programme now visibly paled, he himself became the most effective content of a movement that was fundamentally devoid of any programme. 'Everything,' Hans Frank asserted later, 'came exclusively from Hitler himself.' Even more succinctly the SA leader August Schneidhuber stated in a memorandum that the party's power to attract the masses 'is not due to organisers, but solely to the password "Hitler", which holds everything together'.[19]

The structure of command and submission imposed upon the party by Hitler naturally altered the principle of absence of specific qualities in the new élite. At the moment when his figure assumed the semi-mythological features of the 'Führer', the activism which till then had been its only characteristic was augmented by the demand for absolute obedience, upon which, according to Franz L. Neumann, all charismatic domination is based.[20] Until shortly before his death, even from the cell of his underground bunker system, Hitler was able to compel the strictest obedience. The members of his closest circle had to purchase their position at the cost of a thousand insults, constant sacrifice of their honour, and anyone still capable of a stab of indignation hid it even from himself, like Goebbels, with the formula that it was the greatest good fortune of a contemporary to serve a genius.[21] What is again and again manifest among the figures surrounding Hitler is an empty but dogged will to power, which is so often combined with extreme servility. Even Göring who, not without reason, boasted of having been 'the only man in Germany besides Hitler who had authority of his own derived from no one else', had to admit: 'When a decision is to be taken none of us counts for more than the stone on which he is standing. The Führer alone decides.'[22] And where Hitler did not simply punish opposition by expulsion or liquidation, as in the case of Gregor Strasser or Ernst Röhm, he adopted in varying degrees a demonstrative indifference or refusal of access to his presence. The effects of such measures can be seen, for example, in the cases of Rosenberg, Frank or Ribbentrop, of whose suffering and despair when they were no longer praised, esteemed or consulted by Hitler enough is known to make it clear that the character of Hitler's compulsive power over men's minds can only be understood in religious terms. It is reported of Himmler, Göring and Ribbentrop that after outbursts of criticism from Hitler they became so ill that they had to retire to bed, and when Frank exclaimed, 'Our constitution is the will of the Führer,' this was undoubtedly also true in the physiological sense as well. The lack of independence and poverty of personality of so many of his leading supporters was a prime means of preserving an attachment to Hitler's person through all humiliations, and a general search for a father figure found its deepest satisfaction in the consciousness of Hitler's close presence. The stringency and caprice with which he treated his entourage merely confirmed and strengthened this feeling. Ribbentrop protested at Nuremberg that the idea of killing Hitler would have appeared to him like patricide.[23] And there is Frank's grotesque but revealing declaration shortly before his execution that he was preparing to take his leave of this earth in order to follow the Führer.[24]

Whatever these facts tell us about Hitler's monstrous power over men's minds, they also reveal something of the mechanics of selecting the élite. Only the man who was prepared for Byzantine submission was ordained to enter the most intimate circle of the night-time table talks at which Hitler, full of contempt for the people – the scum – communicated his cynical principles of government. The top echelons of totalitarian movements have been compared to secret societies that establish themselves in the full light of publicity,[25] and what we know of the conspiratorial remoteness of these conversations supports this. Whereas the catalogue of 'granite principles' and the assurance of Hitler's own desire for peace or protestations of the regime's intention to establish order created a false impression of firm-principled benevolence upon the outside world, here, in his solitary monologues, Hitler revealed himself for what he was. His tactical opportunism, his disloyalty towards ideas and principles, his peculiar mixture of fanaticism and calculation, which coloured the most passionate outbursts of rage with a cunning purposefulness and set up his own claim to power as an indispensable maxim, all this was as manifest in these conversations as his barbarian hatred of culture, his grandiose plans for world conquest, his projects for racial 'weeding' or the reorganisation of society. The purposes of the leadership, Hitler commented, must 'never burden the thoughts of the simple party comrade', and he spoke of the 'quite special secret pleasure of seeing how the people around us fail to realise what is really happening to them'. The new social order, which he announced to the initiates, envisaged four classes: the National Socialist high aristocracy 'tempered by battle'; then the hierarchy of party members forming 'the new middle class'; then 'the great mass of the anonymous, the serving collective, the eternally disfranchised'; and finally 'the class of subject alien races; we need not hesitate to call them the modern slave class'.[26]

The cold, unscrupulous logic in the exploitation of human passions, illusions and expectations, the objectivity, totally devoid of any values, in the monstrous planning, have helped to obscure the realisation that Hitler and the whole National Socialist élite were themselves caught up in the dark corners of irrationality. It is certainly true that blind hatred is incapable of producing that technical perfection which characterised the execution of Hitler's murderous plans; but that sobriety was confined exclusively to method and did not reach down to the murky bed of emotional fixations. The conversations referred to above make this abundantly clear. Every time Hitler himself or the participants in his table talk imagine themselves high above the despised multitude in their ruthless Machiavellianism, the craziness of their next remark sends them crashing down to their true level. There is little that typifies the National Socialist variety of the totalitarian character more aptly than this coexistence of Machiavellianism and addiction to magic, cold calculation and dull-witted superstition, total freedom from prejudice and total mysticism.[27]

These intermingling elements marked not only the thought and action of the group at the top, but also the atmosphere of the whole movement. The type of National Socialist functionary who forced his way into key positions in the seizure of power in 1933–34 possessed for the most part an exceptional knowledge of how to impose his own demands, eliminate opponents or rivals, conquer zones of influence, or get a firm grip on office. The acuity which marked his analyses of situations and reactions from the point of view of power tactics, however, was in astonishing contrast to the vagueness of his ideological premises. His image of man, based half on the Naumburg cathedral 'figures of the founders', on Cesare Borgia and untroubledly combining lip service to ancient German nobility with robust self-seeking, bears witness in its own way to the same state of affairs. It is also one more proof that the ideological propositions were mere camouflage. In fact they were nothing else than the 'great landscape painted on the background of our stage' of which Hitler spoke.[28] In the lower and middle levels of the party hierarchy everyone was out for the naked satisfaction of his desires and the service of personal interests. The perpetual struggle for self-assertion, the compulsion to seek a complete understanding of power, consumed intellectual energy and resulted in the ideological indifference that was satisfied, beyond the most general terms of fatherland, honour, blood or loyalty, with the most blatant contradictions.

Certainly every revolutionary movement derives part of its dynamic from the principle of the *carrière ouverte aux talents*, but this does not adequately explain the phenomena of the initial phase of the Third Reich. Power was not so much conquered as looted. Hitler himself in no way opposed these activities on the part of his followers; he didn't 'give a damn'. 'Do anything you like, but don't be caught at it!' he said, but not without justifying this view in terms of power politics. 'Only he who can so link his own advance with the general cause that one cannot be separated from the other, upon him alone can I rely.'[29]

The parasitical supermen whose petty bourgeois greed for possessions was unmasked in this hunt for posts, livings and pensions proved, for the same reasons, absolutely incapable of coping with the real tasks they had shouldered. Those who, from the executive government down to the district presidents' offices and town halls and also in the Gau and Kreis offices of the NSDAP, threw their weight about with the crude affectation of power, had for the most part nothing with which to meet the administrative demands of their office but their revolutionary right and their long-frustrated desires. Goebbels aptly remarked of such ideologically disguised self-indulgence that these men needed only 'the old *jus primae noctis* in order to possess greater power than the most absolute princes of the seventeenth and eighteenth centuries'.[30] There were few exceptions; among those who followed the rule were countless second- and third-rate names, but also figures like Mutschmann, Brückner, Forster, Streicher, and Lutze. Some of them had to be dismissed for obvious incapacity or transferred to purely nominal positions; the majority, however, found themselves protected by Hitler, even against sometimes violent resistance from within their own ranks. Indeed, according to a statement by one of those closest to him, 'the "hard men", who were unpopular or hated by the people, enjoyed Hitler's highest confidence'; as an old revolutionary he always favoured the more ruthless.[31] Goebbels, who in his way was undoubtedly one of the exceptions, passed a devastating judgment on this old party élite towards the end of the war:

At best these are average men. Not one of them has the qualities of a mediocre politician, to say nothing of the calibre of a statesman. They have all remained the beer-cellar rowdies they always were. And in the course of twelve years of easy living many of them have destroyed with drink the little bit of intelligence that once brought them into the movement. This gang of spiteful children, each of whom intrigues against all the rest, whose only thought is of their personal welfare and their standing with the Führer, and who call the sum of all these actions of their 'ruling' – today they do and leave undone what they like, now that the Führer no longer leads them on a tight rein.[32]

However, the type of the brown-shirted official, once his interests had been satisfied, did not figure for long as an élite element. These lethargic figures, indistinguishable from each other, their faces expressing nothing but dull brutality, seemed to remind the party far too much of its past, when it was devoid of all ideological principles. After the Röhm affair the figure of the SA leader, which had for so long served as a model for the élite, quickly lost its exemplary character. Meanwhile efforts were begun for the first time, especially by Himmler, to bring the human type of the Third Reich into line with ideals, to create the 'order of good blood', the founding of which the Reichsführer of the SS had described as the 'unshakable overall goal' of his efforts.[33] Consequently the type of petty bourgeois *manqué*, as represented especially by the functionaries of the Political Organisation, soon saw itself dismissed and its solid, calculating worldliness replaced by the figure of the SS man, marked at first by rather high-flown, austere ideas. Deliberately basing himself upon the traditions of existing orders, Himmler set his whole sectarian ambition upon producing the National Socialist and Nordic ideal type by selection, training and breeding. In one of his countless communiqués on this subject he demanded that the SS man should possess 'the tradition of authentic soldierliness, the refined outlook, demeanour and good breeding of the German nobility, the knowledge and ability and the creative energy of the industrialist, and the profundity of German scholarship, all founded in racial preselection, combined with the ability to satisfy the demands of the present time'.[34] The increasing exercise of the SS terrorist and police functions, inevitable in a totalitarian regime, quickly reduced these demands to empty claims that served as a romantic embellishment to the business of common murder practised by modern executioners of a tyrant's commands. A high SS leader described this double function in the following words:

The selection of the new stratum of leaders is being carried out by the SS – positively through the National Political Educational Establishments (Napola) as a preliminary stage, through the Castles of the Order as the true universities of the coming National

Socialist aristocracy, and through the ensuing practical political training; negatively through the elimination of all racially and biologically inferior elements and the radical extirpation of all incorrigible political opposition.[35]

Not the least of the effects of the contradiction between claims and function of the SS was the remarkably heterogeneous character of its members. The question of whether and to what extent the methods of totalitarian systems actually require the type of the split personality cannot be examined further here. Nevertheless the SS, as the pioneering advance guard of National Socialism, owes to this type so much of the cold perfectionism of its vision of the future that such a link seems highly probable. Split psychology has already been analysed in connection with the various phenomena of 'double-think' and 'double-behaviour' relating to the Communist world. Figures like Rudolf Höss, Otto Ohlendorf or Adolf Eichmann represented, each in his own horrifying way, this type of the totally malleable man able to bring utterly incompatible elements into equilibrium without a hint of inner discomfort. The daily practice of murder and an almost tender family relationship, discussions of the technical improvement of the 'fuel capacity' of the incineration ovens and the almost legendary musical evenings by candlelight, senseless harshness and brutality towards the victims and a strict code of decent behaviour which, for example, could become deeply indignant over theft among the Jewish inmates of the camps: all this went side by side, and Rudolf Höss's declaration in his posthumous notes that he also had 'a heart' and was 'not wicked' is all the more horrifying because in a sense it is the truth. Extreme docility towards those above and unyielding harshness towards those below, uncertainty in making personal decisions and resolute cold-bloodedness in carrying out orders, sentimentality in private life and lack of feeling in official duty, the ability to split oneself and yet remain in harmony with oneself: these and numerous similar antitheses provide the starting-point for a psychological study of this type. Its need for something to lean on, which was the expression of an inadequacy of personality, was further reinforced by the deliberately fostered awareness of a constant threat, so that a sense of security, where it was present at all, depended on blind obedience. 'Human emotions,' Rudolf Höss commented, came to seem 'a betrayal of the Führer'.[36]

Contrary to the widespread idea that the power structures of totalitarian systems are monolithically compact, they are for the most part structurally chaotic. Behind the façade of conspiratorial solidarity they seethe with rivalries, hostilities, intrigues, as previous chapters of this book have amply demonstrated. The basic feeling of insecurity, especially in the higher ranks, drives each individual to basically futile efforts to secure his own position, efforts that are not merely tolerated but actually fostered by the top leadership. For where all jurisdictions become unimportant by comparison with the jurisdiction of the single leader, everyone is able to create his own sphere of influence to the best of his ability, the process being adequately held in check by the ambition and envy of rivals and also, if necessary, by shifting the centres of gravity of power. Even today it is sometimes difficult to disentangle the bizarre confusion in the relationships of the leading forces in the Third Reich and to decipher the various motives which lay behind the mutual aversions and ever-changing alliances. In the savage struggles for power before Hitler's throne everyone was at some time or other against everyone: Göring against Goebbels, Goebbels against Rosenberg, Rosenberg against Ley (he is out 'to cheat me of my life's work behind my back'[37]) and Bormann, Bormann against Frank, Frank against Himmler, and all against all. The constant and often grotesque feuds over authority within the fields of foreign policy or propaganda clearly show the results of this 'multi-Caesarism'. Charles Dubost, the deputy chief prosecuting counsel at Nuremberg, was reminded of 'the minor courts of the Italian Renaissance'.[38]

Hitler always fostered this anarchy of rivalries; from the outset of his career, it was one of his most successful devices for his own tactical success within the party. It was not least because of these rivalries that he remained to the end, as regards the question of power, the exclusive point of reference, the dynamic centre of the movement, the effective axis of a great centripetal force which determined the running of the satellites and established the system of counterbalances between them. Every change, every phase of movement, of rise or fall, took its orientation from him, 'their light was the reflection of his light'.[39] In relation to the figure of Hitler we can see more clearly than anywhere else the basic psychological fact that bound together his whole following, regardless of their outward differences: their personal emptiness, their lack of any firm individuality, of any human stature. The elements of the man willing to put himself at the disposal of totalitarianism may all be traced back: his poverty of personality, his lack of background, his weak contact with others and his emotional instability, his aggressive prejudices, his subservience to his impulses, his split mind, and his deification of the leader matched by his contempt for humanity.

All this is reflected not only in the lack of direction peculiar to most of the careers outlined in this book up to their meeting with Hitler, but also in the most idiosyncratic predilections. For example, in the widespread search for historic precursors, Himmler saw himself as the reincarnation of Heinrich I and rather liked to be referred to as 'the Black Duke' by his own rank and file, and Rosenberg had himself celebrated as the spiritual successor of Henry the Lion, Frederick the Great and Bismarck.[40] 'Why do the Germans love Hitler?' Robert Ley exclaimed in 1942 during a speech at the Sportpalast, and replied with a phrase which by no means applied to himself alone: 'Because with Adolf Hitler they feel safe – it's the feeling of safety, that's it!' The strong gestures and the big words, which they all knew how to employ, long disguised the fact that they were all of them nothing but projections of Hitler's will. In particular the generation that went through it all was repeatedly tempted to measure the individual importance of Hitler's followers by the power of the regime. It was the trials to which they were all subjected that first disclosed the truth, that their stature was entirely borrowed from Hitler. Before the bar of the court they all (with a few exceptions such as Göring and Speer) appeared a disrupted, faceless herd of nonentities to whom not even the millions of victims which their rule had cost could lend a fleeting weight. These men, who had subjugated first a nation, then a continent, and had challenged the world, had never been more than excrescences of their Führer Hitler. They were by no means great and cruel, as a superficial assessment had supposed. Also the judgments, for the most part polemically coloured, which have attributed to them intellectual rigidity or even stupidity, miss the core of the problem, for the indifference with which they accepted the most contradictory propositions of National Socialist ideology was due less to lack of intellectual ability than to the cynicism of practitioners of power who did not believe in ideologies but simply used them. Intelligence tests at Nuremberg showed in the majority of cases an above-average IQ.[41] In reality they were neither important nor primitive, but simply empty, open to alien purposes, and ready to let themselves be abused; washed-out characters, human husks, on whose weakness Hitler's domination was built. 'Everything was contained in a mightier destiny which swept me along with it,' stated one of the accused.[42] The course of the trials confirmed what has already been hinted: they did not even feel sworn to an idea, so that everything – violence, war and genocide – finally assumed the character of an error, a terrible misunderstanding, from whose consequences they wanted to slink away with a shrug of the shoulders. The predominant type, as it emerged above all in the secondary Nuremberg trials, lacked even unmitigated criminality; he had preserved the petty bourgeois attitudes and impulses of his origin; his fanaticism was expressed in unthinking efficiency. Pedantic, with a murderous 'love of his job', he always did only what he conceived as his duty, and, like Himmler or Höss, was completely incapable of understanding his terrible reputation. Instead of the 'beast from the depths' which the whole world expected, there rose from the benches of the accused merely dull 'normality'. During the first few years after the collapse of the regime, still at a loss for an explanation of its essential nature, people spoke of a 'Faustian crisis', thereby construing National Socialism as a phenomenon of superhuman revolt. Such phrases betray a fundamental misconception.[43] Not Faust but Wagner was the symbolic figure of the crisis.

The aim of this book in portraying the leading actors of those years is not, however, to create a group of scapegoats to carry the historical failure of a whole nation into the desert of oblivion. This collection of portrait studies from recent history must be supplemented by reference to a guilt that is not covered by the behaviour of the top National Socialist figures. 'Hitler,' Hans Frank averred at Nuremberg, 'was the Devil. Thus he led us all astray.'[44] Such turns of phrase do not reduce the general guilt; for the truth is that a people must first be in a condition to be led astray before it can abandon itself to the totalitarian adventure. In the realm of historical errors there is no 'Devil' who, under self-critical examination, does not reveal the physiognomy of the man in the street. The National Socialist leaders were fundamentally nothing more than particularly well marked examples of a type that was to be met throughout society, and in this sense the face of the Third Reich was the face of a whole nation. For it is never the artist with the gold paint but always the worshipper who makes the idol. Nothing would be more dangerous, a historian remarked recently, 'than now, when the mendacious legend *of* Hitler has been destroyed, to cultivate a new legend *against* Hitler at the cost of truth and justice. Not least important in this connection is that the whole guilt should not be attributed to him and National Socialism.'[45]

First among the conditions that made the events of those years possible was not the very real distress of the 1920s and early 1930s; this was the symptom rather than the cause of the failure. The preconditions of totalitarian rule in a country are to be sought at a deeper level, for they are 'the result of man's faulty understanding of himself'.[46] One does not have to support the view that German history represents a single consistent path to National Socialism in order nonetheless to see the elements of this failure foreshadowed in the chain of evolution that passed through various periods of historical development, some of them prolonged. Again and again we find ourselves thrown back, as the individual chapters of this book have clearly shown, upon the traditional German lack of a proper attitude to politics, in particular upon that fatal German concept of education which excluded politics, which made it the despised business of dubious characters or a matter for 'strong men'. It was an idea which compensated for lack of civil liberty by a retreat to 'inner freedom' and cultivated both a misguided political abstinence and a political consciousness saturated with heroic concepts. Not the parliamentary committee with its need to compromise but Dürer's 'The Knight, Death and the Devil' appeared in this political consciousness as the symbol of day-to-day political action. It celebrated its weakness of orientation as 'depth' or 'soul' and held itself up to the world as the 'German way and mission'. It understood the state not as a system of checks and balances for the protection of individual liberties but as an absolute quantity with extensive claims to submission, as a sacred entity, holy not only as a kind of German Roman Empire, but absolutely holy. These and many other intellectual circumstances, which have been discussed in the appropriate chapters, helped to create that ideological climate without which Hitler's efforts would have been in vain.[47]

This, then, is the point at which the much discussed 'overcoming of the past' enters the picture; it covers more than the recollection and analysis of those thirty years. A long and wretched tradition of German intellectual history, which managed to assert itself alongside humane developments and finally against them, ended in that phenomenon which we call National Socialism. Whole generations of university teachers, literary pseudo-prophets and presidents of nationalist societies helped to create the atmosphere in which hostility to reason, brutalisation of life and corruption of ethical standards required only to be crystallised in a political outlook and expressed by an eloquent speaker in order to unfold their destructive violence.

Hitler is now forgotten and the sterile philosophy with which he caused such turmoil has perished with him. Even the traces of his rule now terrify only a few.

Of the documents that bear witness to the psychic power which he exercised little is left but the impression of his voice, which arouses in the survivors a feeling of embarrassment rather than fascination. In Hannah Arendt's words:

This impermanence no doubt has something to do with the proverbial fickleness of the masses and the fame that rests on them; more likely it can be traced to the perpetual-motion character of totalitarian movements which can remain in power only so long as they keep moving and set everything around them in motion. Therefore, in a certain sense, this very impermanence is a rather flattering testimonial to the dead leaders in so far as they succeeded in contaminating their subjects with the specifically totalitarian virus; for if there is such a thing as a totalitarian personality or mentality, this extraordinary adaptability and absence of continuity are no doubt its outstanding characteristics. Hence it might be a mistake to assume that the inconstancy and forgetfulness of the masses signify that they are cured of the totalitarian delusion . . . The opposite might well be true.[48]

It is not easy to find evidence in the political reality of the present that would contradict the basically sceptical tone of these comments. It is true that the Hitler regime compromised itself to an extent surpassing all historical experience and to the majority of the nation, especially after its fall, revealed features that leave no room for sentimental attachments that would lead to its being seen in a favourable light. This cuts the ground from under that disastrous tendency to denigrate the present in the name of an idealised vision of the remembered past, which contributed so much to the emotional vacuum surrounding the Weimar Republic and finally made its existence impossible. Also we rarely meet any more those romanticised, aggressive ideas of flight into imaginary realms of the more distant past or future, which for so long left their disastrous mark on German political consciousness. The dream of the 'Third Reich' which, in many guises and under many names, has again and again excited the imagination of the nation, has perished along with the horrifying reality of its final form. The Germany of the post-Hitler era has adopted an up-to-date attitude of which earlier generations always seemed incapable and the lack of which was one of the chief weaknesses in the political life of the German people. The present Germany would deserve greater approbation if it showed more inclination to overcome the recent past by understanding what made it possible than to suppress it. The free examination of the content of German historical, political and social consciousness – free from both reaction and uncritical extenuation; clarification of the relationship between intellect and power, society and liberty; the problems of authority, obedience, the responsibility of citizenship, civil standards, and resistance to tyranny; and the structure of the modern constitutional state: all these and numerous similar problems posed by the experience of National Socialist rule have only begun to be examined, and it is not an encouraging sign that all these concepts have come to sound old-fashioned. True, Hitler is dead. But in spite of everything he was too large, too undeniably a symptom and consequence of specific faulty developments in our German history, too much 'within ourselves' for forgetfulness to be enough. The totalitarian infection survives its active phase in many, often apparently insignificant, manifestations. The worldwide political developments of the post-war period have given the German people, at least in the Federal Republic, a period of grace during which its changed consciousness has not been put to the test. Nevertheless it is possible that the new 'political rationality' of the German people, not infrequently pointed out with pride, is merely the reflection of 'rational' circumstances. The proof has yet to be given, but who can be blamed for awaiting it with trepidation?

NOTES
BIBLIOGRAPHY
INDEX

Notes

Where an English-language edition exists of a foreign work quoted in this book, the English title is given in the notes. However, the exact wording of the English text has not invariably been used.

Abbreviations used in these notes:
IfZ—Institut für Zeitgeschichte, Munich
IMT—*Trial of the Major War Criminals before the International Military Tribunal*, Nuremberg, 1947–1949
VJHfZ—*Vierteljahrshefte für Zeitgeschichte*

Part One

ADOLF HITLER'S PATH FROM MEN'S HOSTEL TO REICH CHANCELLERY

I The Incubation Period

1 Hans Frank, *Im Angesicht des Galgens. Cf.* 'The Face of the Third Reich: Attempt at a Summing Up,' the final chapter of this book.

2 Quoted in Hermann Rauschning, *The Revolution of Nihilism* (British title: *Germany's Revolution of Destruction*).

3 Grigoire Gafencu, *The Last Days of Europe. A Diplomatic Journey in 1939* (London, 1947; New Haven, Conn., 1948).

4 Johann von Leers, *Die geschichtlichen Grundlagen des Nationalsozialismus* (Berlin, 1938); also Rudolf Alexander Moissl, *Die Ahnenheimat des Führers* (St Pölten, n.d.).

5 Frank, *Im Angesicht des Galgens.* This paragraph in Frank's memoirs caused widespread, even wild, speculation. But there is no reason to suppose Frank's account as a whole untrustworthy or to suspect him of unserious motives, of sensation-mongering or notoriety-seeking. The loyalty that Frank maintained towards his Führer to the end supports this.

Nevertheless, in 1956 Franz Jetzinger, in the first critical study of Hitler's formative years, *Hitler's Youth*, cast the first doubts on Frank's version of Hitler's origins. In particular, he pointed out that it can by no means be assumed that the name Frankenberger is of exclusively Jewish origin. Up to now the most conclusive version of Hitler's family background has been that given by the historian Werner Maser, according to which Hitler had no Jewish ancestors but was the product of a particularly close-knit peasant interbreeding. Maser believes Hitler's father had no connection with either Frankenberger or Johann Georg Hiedler, the miller's apprentice whom Hitler's grandmother Maria Anna Schicklgruber married in 1842, but was the natural son of his 'foster father', Johann Nepomuk Hiedler (or

Hüttler). The latter, however, was not only Hitler's grandfather but also the grandfather of Klara Pölzl, Hitler's mother. Thus Hitler's father must have been the uncle of his wife and Hitler himself his mother's cousin. But Maser cannot produce the vital document showing that Johann Nepomuk Hiedler (Hüttler) was in fact the natural father of Alois Schicklgruber-Hitler. Also Frank's assurance about the paternity payments, which doubtless were not invented, is not satisfactorily explained in this version.

Yet whichever version seems the more credible, the fact remains that Hitler was unable to furnish the so-called 'Aryan' documentary proof to which he attached such lethal importance. He himself certainly felt this handicap and, despite all the ancestor investigations he instigated, never spoke of his origins. 'These people must not know who I am,' he said nervously to his nephew William Patrick Hitler. 'They must not know from where and from what family I come' (*Der Spiegel*, No. 31, 1967).

6 Jetzinger, *Hitler's Youth*.
7 *Ibid*. See also Hitler's own statement in *Mein Kampf*. Not only contemporary works during the Third Reich, but also some later historical accounts, uncritically accepted the description placed in circulation by Hitler. See particularly Walter Görlitz and Herbert A. Quint, *Adolf Hitler. Eine Biographie*.
8 August Kubizek, *The Young Hitler I knew* (British title: *Young Hitler. The Story of Our Friendship*), on Hitler's relationship to Richard Wagner. Parts of Kubizek's book have not stood up to serious original research such as Jetzinger's. Apart from purely technical discrepancies, one can discern in its psychological emphasis the author's continuous attempt to reassess along demonic lines the former friend for whom he still had a naïve, unreasoning devotion, and to project his later image of Hitler into his description of Hitler's early years. Nevertheless Kubizek provides important insights into this very significant phase of Hitler's development. I have incorporated them in so far as they are substantiated elsewhere or fit into the picture supplied by other descriptions or research. Kubizek is sometimes involuntarily sincere, out of the simplicity of his own character.
9 Hitler, *Mein Kampf*.
10 See Jetzinger, *Hitler's Youth*. For comparison Jetzinger notes that, during the first five years of service, a teacher earned 66 kronen (about $92 or £33) a month, a post office employee less than 60 kronen (about $84 or £30). See also Werner Maser, *Die Frühgeschichte der NSDAP. Hitlers Weg bis 1914* (Frankfurt, 1965).
11 On Hitler's spelling, see Kubizek, *Young Hitler*. Also Jetzinger, *Hitler's Youth*. On the young Hitler's dramatic and literary efforts, see Kubizek.
12 Kubizek, *Young Hitler*. The author also refers here to the 'dangerous depressions' to which Hitler was occasionally subject.
13 Jetzinger, *Hitler's Youth*.
14 Konrad Heiden, *Adolf Hitler. Das Zeitalter der Verantwortungslosigkeit*, Vol. I. For this period Heiden depends extensively on the remarks of Reinhold Hanisch, which also need to be read with caution. However, Hitler's depraved and dishevelled appearance is reported elsewhere in Heiden and also in Jetzinger, *Hitler's Youth*. In other respects Heiden's portrayal is factually largely out of date, since considerable source material more comprehensive than he had at his disposal has now come to light. Nevertheless, in its psychological analysis of Hitler's personality it still holds its ground among all later publications, which in many cases are based on it. However, toward the end it becomes strongly polemical, which is understandable in view of the circumstances when the book was written, but mars its effectiveness. There are no such limitations to Heiden's best book, *A History of National Socialism*, which is of a scope astounding for its time and still highly informative.

15 Rudolf Olden, *Hitler* (British title: *Hitler the Pawn*). See also Heiden, *Adolf Hitler*, Vol. I.

16 *Mein Kampf.*

17 *Ibid.* In his book Hitler made illuminating comments on 'the art of reading'. His was the attitude of total prejudice which only 'reads' what it already knows better, only absorbs what endorses its views, and resists any questioning of knowledge it has already absorbed. Evidently, moreover, he had read only Karl May, whom he even recommended to his generals as a model for the conduct of modern warfare, and Gustave le Bon, on whom especially he based the widely praised propaganda chapter of his book; see also Alfred Stein, 'Adolf Hitler und Gustave le Bon,' *Geschichte in Wissenschaft und Unterricht*, No. 6, 1955.

18 See Wilfried Daim, *Der Mann, der Hitler die Ideen gab*. Hitler's remark is from *Mein Kampf.*

19 Heiden, *Adolf Hitler*, Vol. I. Hitler's fear of proletarianisation is also mentioned by Kubizek, *Young Hitler*.

20 Olden, *Hitler*; also *Mein Kampf.*

21 Speech at Kulmbach on February 5, 1928, quoted by Alan Bullock in *Hitler. A Study in Tyranny.*

22 Hitler's praise for Lueger is found in *Mein Kampf*; his demand for cunning in *The Voice of Destruction* (British title: *Hitler Speaks*) by Hermann Rauschning; for his view of brutality as a creative principle see Walther Hofer, *Der Nationalsozialismus. Dokumente 1933–1945.*

23 *Mein Kampf.*

24 *Ibid.*

25 *Ibid.*

26 The suggestion that Hitler's anti-Semitism had at least one of its roots in sexual jealousy was probably first put forward by Rudolf Olden. In his book *Das Ende des Hitler-Mythos* (Zurich, 1947), which in many respects has not stood up to later findings of Hitler research, Josef Greiner reports a rather scandalous attempt by the young Hitler to approach a girl student employed as a model. This girl, who conformed to Hitler's specially favoured blond type, was later to marry a half-Jewish manufacturer. Because Greiner's reliability is somewhat in doubt there must be strong reservations about this episode, which shows signs of having been made up after the fact. On the reference to 'Stefanie' see Kubizek, *Young Hitler*, Stefanie, for whom Hitler was supposed to have composed 'countless love poems,' none of which she ever got to read, was big, blond, of Valkyrie-like appearance. If we are to believe Kubizek, Hitler waited each afternoon at an appointed place in the street which Stefanie and her mother used to pass on their walk, and gazed at her. In one of the poems, which is said to have had the title 'Hymn to the Beloved,' Stefanie, according to Kubizek, was described as follows: 'A high-born damsel in a dark blue, flowing velvet gown rode on a white steed over the flowering meadows, her loose hair fell in golden waves on her shoulders; a clear spring sky was above. Everything was pure, radiant joy.'

27 Herbert Lüthy, 'Der Führer persönlich,' *Der Monat*, No. 62, November 1953.

28 *Ibid.*

29 *Mein Kampf.*

30 This state of affairs, which Heiden had already come across during his researches, is now presented on the basis of all available data by Jetzinger, *Hitler's Youth.*

31 *Ibid.*

32 Greiner, *Das Ende des Hitler-Mythos*. The quotation on Hitler's vague hopes of a career as an architect is from *Mein Kampf.*

33 *Mein Kampf.*

34 Frank, *Im Angesicht des Galgens.*

35 Olden, *Hitler*. See also Otto Dietrich, *Hitler* (British title: *The Hitler I Knew*): 'In June 1940, when Hitler revisited his old frontline positions and resting areas in the vicinity of Lille, where he had been posted in 1915, several comrades from his old company pointed out to me the garden arbour of a certain house where the eccentric young soldier had poured forth his ideas to them, ideas which he later so forcefully developed to a larger public.'

36 See Görlitz and Quint, *Adolf Hitler*. Also Fritz Wiedemann, *Der Mann der Feldherr werden wollte* (Velbert, 1964). Wiedemann, for a time Hitler's chief in the First World War and later his personal adjutant, gives a mass of further detail which is highly revealing of Hitler's psychological make-up.

37 *Mein Kampf*.

38 *Ibid.*

2 The Drummer

1 Hanns Hubert Hofmann, *Der Hitlerputsch*.

2 *Mein Kampf*. Hitler maintained that he had been blinded, or nearly so, and later enlarged on this by saying he returned 'as a cripple' from the battlefield. His war record does not mention a loss of sight, only that he was 'gassed'. This injury seems to have had no lasting effects, for when he was released from military service on March 31, 1920, he made no application for a maintenance claim although, as the record shows, he had been informed about the 'notification of claims for maintenance and the appointed deadline'. At the time it was explicitly stated: 'No claim for maintenance was put forward by him'. Recorded by Ernst Deuerlein, 'Hitlers Eintritt in die Politik und die Reichswehr,' *VJHfZ*, 1959, No. 2, Document 1a.

3 Deuerlein, 'Hitlers Eintritt,' Document 4. Moreover, Hitler was not, as he later used to say, an education officer (*Bildungsoffizier*) but a V-man. In the documents referred to, this designation, possibly contrary to oral usage, is reserved for those of officer rank.

4 *Ibid.*, Documents 8 and 9.

5 One of those who took part in the education course, Adolf Gemlich, had addressed several questions to Captain Mayr, who passed the letter on to Hitler for reply. Hitler's letter to Gemlich is dated September 16, 1919, and is reproduced together with other letters in the papers of Ernst Deuerlein already referred to (Documents 10 *et seq.*). It is perhaps worth noting that Hitler's pronounced oratorical style (*Redestil*) is already apparent in this letter, particularly in the last sentence.

6 Deuerlein, on the basis of reports produced by the Munich Public Records Office, compiled a list of the political groups then under surveillance. Among these were the Berg-Partei, Bund Sozialer Frauen, Diskutier-Club, Freie Vereinigung Sozialer Schüler, Neues Vaterland, Nova Vaconia, Ostara-Bund, Rat Geistiger Arbeit, Siegfriedring, Schutz- und Trutzbund, and Universalbund.

7 The German Labour Party (DAP) had passed through several preliminary stages which we need not record here. To begin with Drexler's venture also had other names, and the meetings did not inevitably take place in the Sternecker-Bräu. On these details see Georg Franz-Willing's *Die Hitlerbewegung. Der Ursprung 1919–1922* which is factually excellent though the interpretation is sometimes questionable.

8 *Ibid.*

9 Hitler was not, as he misleadingly says in *Mein Kampf*, member number 7 of the DAP. This was his membership in the party's working committee. Also he was the 55th member, not the 555th. For the sake of its 'image', the DAP's membership list in fact began with number 501.

10 *Mein Kampf.*

11 The only exceptions were *Der Angriff*, edited by Goebbels, which on the whole was restricted to Berlin yet achieved considerable importance, and the *Völkische Beobachter*. The picture changes with the rise of the NSDAP in 1930. Up to this time, in addition to the papers already mentioned, the party had at its disposal 12 small daily newspapers (against the 170 of the SPD), 34 weekly papers, a few monthly magazines, an illustrated newspaper, and a parliamentary letter, with a total circulation of barely 700,000 copies. See Karl Dietrich Bracher, *Die Auflösung der Weimarer Republik*. The quoted words come from *Mein Kampf.*

12 *Mein Kampf.*

13 Franz-Willing, *Die Hitlerbewegung.*

14 Lüthy, 'Der Führer persönlich,' *Der Monat*, No. 62.

15 Deuerlein, 'Hitlers Eintritt,' Documents 19 and 23.

16 Record of the Munich Political Police – which had been charged by the Police Praesidium with the surveillance of political activity – on the DAP meeting of November 13, 1919, at which Hitler appeared as speaker; see Deuerlein, 'Hitlers Eintritt', Document 14. *Cf. VJHfZ*, 1963, No. 3.

17 Gottfried Griessmayr, *Das völkische Ideal* (printed in manuscript). Actually, Hitler's position within the party at that time was still completely second-rank; the organisational directives do not list his name once.

18 *Mein Kampf*; also speech of July 6, 1933, at a conference of *Reichsstatthalter* in Berlin, quoted by Cuno Horkenbach, *Das Deutsche Reich von 1918 bis Heute. Das Jahr 1933* (hereafter cited as *1933*).

19 A very detailed description of this appears in Franz-Willing, *Die Hitlerbewegung.*

20 Wilhelm Frick's statement at his trial before the Munich People's Court, recorded by Franz-Willing, *ibid.*

21 Olden, *Hitler.*

22 Heiden, *Adolf Hitler*, Vol. I. See also Bullock, *Hitler*; Görlitz and Quint, *Adolf Hitler*. The data, observations, personalities, etc. mentioned in this paragraph are drawn principally from these works.

23 Görlitz and Quint, *Adolf Hitler*. See also the description, quoted by Bullock, *Hitler*, of Hitler's appearance given by Friedelind Wagner, a granddaughter of the composer.

24 Heinrich Hoffman, *Hitler Was My Friend.*

25 Franz-Willing, *Die Hitlerbewegung*, draws this characterisation from a remark by Kurt Lüdecke in his book *I Knew Hitler.*

26 Quoted by Franz-Willing, *Die Hitlerbewegung.*

27 Hitler's casting at that time in the role of 'drummer' has been unearthed by Hanns Hubert Hofmann in his book on the Hitler putsch (see note 1 above).

28 Quoted by Heiden, *Adolf Hitler*, Vol. I.

29 Quoted by Hofmann, *Der Hitlerputsch.*

30 Similarly in his speech in the Bürgerbräukeller on the eve of November 9 Hitler said, 'Morning will find in Germany either a national German government or ourselves dead.' In his Nuremberg statement Hans Frank aptly pointed out that 'the story of Hitler's whole life was contained in a nutshell' in the events of November 8 and 9, 1923, that during this period the 'substance of his entire nature' had revealed itself.

31 Hitler himself had evidently been pulled down by Scheubner-Richter, the man next to him as they marched arm in arm, who fell dead at the first salvo. This, as the official doctor of the Landsberg prison confirmed two days later in the course of the admission examination, probably caused the break in Hitler's upper arm, as well as a painful dislocation of the shoulder joint. On the evidence of this diagnosis, the rescue which Hitler claimed would have been impossible.

Notes

32 An eyewitness report, quoted by Heiden, *Adolf Hitler*, Vol. I.
33 Ernst von Salomon reached this by no means exaggerated conclusion after a study of the proceedings; quoted by Hofmann, *Der Hitlerputsch*.
34 Helmut Heiber, *Adolf Hitler*.
35 *Der Hitler-Prozess*: record of the proceedings of the Munich People's Court at Hitler's trial in 1924.
36 Theodor Heuss, *Hitlers Weg*. Hitler's previously quoted remark comes from his speech of November 6, 1937, to the original party members. Similarly, in his speech on November 8, 1933, commemorating the same occasion, he had declared: 'This evening and this day made it possible for us afterwards to fight a battle for ten years by legal means: for, make no mistake, if we had not acted then I should never have been able to found a revolutionary movement, to form it and keep it in being, and yet all the time maintain legality.' (Norman H. Baynes, ed., *The Speeches of Adolf Hitler, April 1922–August 1939*).
37 Heuss, *Hitlers Weg*.
38 Rauschning, *Voice of Destruction*.

3   The Führer

1 Frank, *Im Angesicht des Galgens*.
2 Hans Wendt, *Hitler regiert*.
3 Frank, *Im Angesicht des Galgens*.
4 *Mein Kampf*. In his study *Hitlers Weg*, Theodor Heuss has said, not unfairly, of the anti-Semitic chapter what can basically be said of the book as a whole: 'In tone it is vulgar and brutal.'
5 Olden, *Hitler*. Elsewhere in the same work he says: 'The clumsy longwindedness of such sentences seems to bespeak an artless lack of confidence in language as such, a fear that it may not be equal to its task of statement and explanation, an anxious plea for understanding. An odd contrast to the blustering threats of violence, the sword, the gallows.' The stylistic errors quoted are taken from an anonymous, manifestly communist tract, *Das Selbstportrait Adolf Hitlers. Deutschland erwache!—Deutschland lache!* (Berlin, 1931).
6 *Mein Kampf*.
7 Frank, *Im Angesicht des Galgens*.
8 Rauschning, *Voice of Destruction*.
9 Statement by Reinhold Hanisch; see Heiden, *Adolf Hitler*, Vol. I.
10 Lüthy, in his study 'Der Führer persönlich,' *Der Monat*, No. 62. Lüthy also deals with this subject; comments on it can be found in Hans Frank and others.
11 Alfred Richter, *Unsere Führer im Lichte der Rassenfrage und Charakterologie*. The author describes himself on the title page as 'Director of the Private Institute for Practical Knowledge of Human Nature and Ethnology, Bärenstein'. The book, which analyses many of the movement's leaders under aspects similar to those indicated in the heading 'racial-characterological', includes the dedication: 'In deep spiritual alliance with all creative German race-sisters and race-brothers, who live and strive to be German.'
12 Quoted by Heiden, *Adolf Hitler*. Vol. 7. See also Frank, *Im Angesicht des Galgens*, who remarks: 'Gruber gave an essentially phrenological opinion, deducing both an absence of objective brainpower from Hitler's singularly receding forehead and an intellectually exceedingly subjective character from his strong occiput. Racially, Gruber characterised Hitler as typically un-Nordic, East Slav.'
13 Lüdecke, *I Knew Hitler*. On Hitler's efforts to remain aloof during his imprisonment,

see the memoirs of one of his fellow-prisoners, Hans Kallenbach, *Mit Adolf Hitler auf der Festung Landsberg*.

14 Hitler's speech of November 9, 1934, quoted by Bullock, *Hitler*; on his entrusting Alfred Rosenberg with the party leadership see the latter's *Letzte Aufzeichnungen*.

15 Hofmann, *Der Hitlerputsch*.

16 Quoted by Heiden, *Adolf Hitler*, Vol. I.

17 See the chapter 'Ernst Röhm and the Lost Generation'. For a description of the meeting of February 27, 1925, see Heiden, *Adolf Hitler*, Vol. I.

18 Lüdecke, *I Knew Hitler*.

19 Otto Strasser, *Hitler and I*.

20 On the economic and socio-political development of the Weimar Republic see especially Ferdinand Friedensburg, *Die Weimarer Republik*. For the data on party membership see Bullock, *Hitler*.

21 *Mein Kampf*.

22 Heuss, *Hitlers Weg*. Revealing is the speech given by Goebbels on November 7, 1933, at the Berlin Sportpalast in which he amplified: 'The party had its authorities, it had its leader, it had its conception, it had its organisational rules, its style, its beliefs, its faith. Everything that appertains to the state was already embodied in the party, and at that instant in which external power was transferred to it, it in turn needed only to transfer its rules, its belief in authority, and its conceptualisation to the state in order to bring the revolution to a practical conclusion. This – nothing more – has taken place since January 30' (Joseph Goebbels, *Signale der neuen Zeit*).

23 This catalogue of failures and omissions relies to a great extent on a self-critical expression of the socialist position: see Hendrik de Man, *Sozialismus und National-faschismus* (Potsdam, 1931), quoted in *Zwischenspiel Hitler*. He goes on to say: 'It is understandable after the disappointments of socialistic experiments in the early postwar years that socialism had no further utopia, that so many people allowed themselves, out of a dull feeling of indignation against the established order and unhampered by the vagueness of its ideas and the contradictions of its mythology, to be inspired by the Nationalist Fascist utopia of the Third Reich.' To this explanation, which brings out the intrinsic elements of failure of the Weimar Republic, the point must be added that, in spite of all shortcomings, this state still had great merit and while free to do so showed great achievements. The failure of its institutions was the fault less of any unsuitable structural conception than of the men who managed them. The architects of its constitution could point out that no one had or could have foreseen the unprecedented crises which impeded the Republic from its inception; but the earlier principal mistake probably lay in the overestimation of the human material, so that all good beginnings finally and unexpectedly came to grief. The most impressive example of this is still that liberal principles were consistently maintained in the face of mutual and bitter hostilities. Also, the utopian belief in the automatic rule of law stemming from liberal thought which makes leadership superfluous in a democracy is worth mentioning here: it was clearly refuted by Hitler, who knew how to stir up continual need for charismatic or at least personal rule.

24 Gregor Strasser, in a speech in the Berlin Sportpalast to the NSBO on October 20, 1932.

25 *Mein Kampf*. That Hitler also reached this conclusion by supposedly following the example of the opposition does not alter the validity of this formula so far as his own activities are concerned and only confirms the previously discussed complexity of his attitude. The remaining quotations and references to Hitler's propaganda technique are taken from Hermann Rauschning's book *Voice of Destruction*, as well as from various places in the text of *Mein Kampf*. In an interview on February

21, 1936 with the French journalist Bertrand de Jouvenel, Hitler mentioned another condition for his success: 'I will disclose to you what has raised me to my position. Our problems seemed complicated. The German people did not know what to do about them. In these circumstances the people preferred to leave them to the professional politicians. I on the other hand have simplified the problems and reduced them to the simplest formula. The masses recognised this and followed me' (quoted in French in Baynes, *Speeches of Adolf Hitler*). It should also be mentioned that Hitler managed to get attuned to his audience of the moment with extraordinary skill which certainly sprang in good part from an intuitive shrewdness. He always knew where the interests of his hearers lay, whether they were petty bourgeois, industrialists, peasants or generals, and how to find the arguments, or at least words, exactly tailored to their mood and needs.

26 The total of 4,135 rallies is for the period from April 1 to August 30, 1931. These are divided as follows: NSDAP 1,910; KPD 1,129; SPD 447; DNVP 73; Centre 50; DVP 30; and State Party 12. The rest are divided among small splinter groups. See *Frankfurter Zeitung*, December 4, 1931.

27 Hannah Arendt, *The Origins of Totalitarianism*. Also Kurt Sontheimer, *Antidemokratisches Denken in der Weimarer Republik*: 'In its name National Socialism united the two most powerful ideological impulses of the epoch. It already conceptually anticipated the synthesis which the era had yet to accomplish. The old-style socialist parties were not national, the national-bourgeois parties not socialist. But this seemed to be the party which was both and simultaneously the party of Germany's future.'

28 Joseph Goebbels, *My Part in Germany's Fight*.

29 Weigand von Miltenberg (i.e. Herbert Blank, who together with Major Buchrucker belonged to the circle around Otto Strasser), *Adolf Hitler Wilhelm III*, quoted in *Zwischenspiel Hitler*.

30 See Heiden, *Adolf Hitler*, Vol. I. On another occasion he asserted, 'If you pass through ten halls and everywhere men shout for you with enthusiasm – that surely is a sublime feeling' (see Görlitz and Quint, *Adolf Hitler*). Of the energising force which Hitler derived from his oratorical triumphs, Goebbels remarked in a diary during the war: 'It's good for the Führer to speak to a larger audience. He not only radiates strength, but becomes charged with it himself' (*The Goebbels Diaries, 1942–43*, entry for November 19, 1943).

31 Kubizek, *Young Hitler*.

32 Dietrich, *Hitler*. Here is also to be found a vivid description of the basic structure of a Hitler speech.

33 Lüthy, 'Der Führer persönlich,' who supports this view: 'Perhaps the discrepancy between the larger-than-life world historical figure and the poor amorphous personality with which his biographers grapple is no more than the discrepancy between the excited condition of the medium through which 'the spirit speaks' and the reversion to dullness of his own unprepossessing individuality.' Lüthy too borrows from demonology the formula of the 'spirit' speaking through Hitler, thus seemingly sharing the perplexity of the contemporary observer referred to.

34 Henry Picker, *Hitlers Tischgespräche im Führerhauptquartier 1941–1942* (hereafter cited as *Tischgespräche*). See also Lüdecke, *I Knew Hitler*. Henriette von Schirach, in *The Price of Glory*, reports: 'On another occasion I saw him, after he had completed his speech. He was wearing an army coat and waiting for fresh linen and another suit. He was tired and pale, exhausted and completely still.'

35 Lead article in the *Frankfurter Zeitung*, January 1, 1933, quoted by Bracher, *Auflösung der Weimarer Republik*.

36 Goebbels, *My Part in Germany's Fight*. The foregoing remark of Hitler's, which was made during a speech in Königsberg on October 17, 1932, runs as follows:

'What I strive for is power and not a title. . . . I want only power. Once we obtain power then we shall, so help us God, keep it. We shall not ever let it be taken from us' (quoted in Max Domarus, *Hitler. Reden und Proklamationen 1932–1945*, Vol. I).
37 Goebbels, in a speech on May 8, 1933, in the Hotel Kaiserhof, quoted in *Goebbels spricht. Reden aus Kampf und Sieg* (Oldenburg, 1933).

4 The Reich Chancellor

1 Lutz Graf Schwerin von Krosigk, *Es geschah in Deutschland*.
2 Picker, *Tischgespräche*, entry for April 11, 1942.
3 Hitler's speech of January 30, 1935, Domarus, *Hitler*, Vol. I: also Joseph Goebbels in a speech to the 1933 Reich Party Congress, 'The Race Question and World Propaganda,' reproduced in a collection of his speeches, *Signale der neuen Zeit*. During a commemorative address of January 30, 1937, in which Hitler boasted that the National Socialist revolution had 'not broken even a windowpane,' he added significantly, 'Don't misunderstand me, however. If this revolution was bloodless that was not because we were not manly enough to look at blood' (Baynes, *Speeches of Adolf Hitler*).
4 Frank, *Im Angesicht des Galgens*.
5 Horkenbach, *1933*. On February 10, 1933, Hitler, in a speech at the Berlin Sport-palast, had still spoken of 'the millions who curse us today'. Yet by May 1 the NSDAP already had to suspend all admissions to the party, following a massive run on party offices, and some time later the Reich party treasurer said that over two million new applications had been registered (*ibid.*).
6 An election speech of Hitler's at Essen on March 27, 1936.
7 Wendt, *Hitler regiert*.
8 This point of view is developed especially by Hans Frank, *Im Angesicht des Galgens*; also, and obviously basing themselves on Frank, by Görlitz and Quint, *Adolf Hitler*.
9 Hitler's speech of July 12, 1933, to the Gauleiters, the Treuhänder der Arbeit, and the Landesobleute der Betriebszellenorganisation, quoted by Horkenbach, *1933*.
10 Decree of February 4, 1933; it provided for restrictions on the freedom of assembly and the press, since – as the official explanation had it – the warning 'to avoid everything that could cause public unrest and endanger public safety . . . had not been complied with'. The decree was the first measure to be taken in the initial election campaign and was invoked almost exclusively against the SPD and KPD. See Horkenbach, *1933*.
11 Hitler's proclamation to the 1934 Reich Party Congress, quoted by Domarus, *Hitler*, Vol. I.
12 Strasser, *Hitler and I*.
13 Picker, *Tischgespräche*, entry for May 4, 1942. In this connection see also Gerhard Meinck, *Hitler und die deutsche Aufrüstung 1933–1937*; and especially René Erbe, *Die nationalsozialistische Wirtschaftspolitik im Lichte der modernen Theorie* (Zurich, 1958). The latter excellent study, free from polemical assessment, produces extensive evidence to show that National Socialist economic policy was carried on to the detriment rather than the benefit of the people. Already in 1934 49 per cent of public expenditure was invested in the armaments industry; by 1938, it was 79 per cent. To finance this, a method was developed which on one hand led to an inflationary development concealed by price controls and various compulsory measures, and on the other, brought about as a consequence the quiet dispossession of all savers and policy-holders. The advantageous general economic development was by no means reflected in a generally higher standard of living: for example,

in 1938 wages and salaries had declined to approximately 57 per cent of the national income. The core of the National Socialist economic policy was not, as had been unceasingly proclaimed, work and bread, but arms and war; at no time were work and bread a primary aim but only a concomitant.

14 See note 26 below.

15 Dietrich, *Hitler*; also Frank, *Im Angesicht des Galgens*, and Weizsäcker, *The Memoirs of Ernst von Weizsäcker.*

16 Joseph Goebbels, 'Wer hat die Initiative?' article dated June 28, 1942, in *Das eherne Herz. Reden und Aufsätze aus den Jahren 1941–42.*

17 Albert Zoller, *Hitler privat*; also Dietrich, *Hitler.*

18 Frank, *Im Angesicht des Galgens.*

19 Dietrich, *Hitler.*

20 Zoller, *Hitler privat*; the remark to Ward Price is repeated by Domarus, *Hitler.*

21 Picker, *Tischgespräche*, entry for April 11, 1942. At about the same time he noted that 'it won't do for the Supreme Leadership to allow criticism of its measures from below. The people themselves don't want privileges of this sort, only the grumblers among the people' (*ibid.*, entry for May 14, 1942). Also, his antipathy toward the Berliners was a reaction against the cutting criticism habitually indulged in by people of the capital (entry of March 30, 1942). Max Domarus' collection of Hitler's speeches shows impressively how Hitler was particularly overcome with anger at the critical attitude of the intellectuals.

22 A speech of Hitler's of June 27, 1937, at Würzburg, quoted by Domarus, *Hitler.*

23 Hitler's photographer Heinrich Hoffmann records this trait. Hoffmann also notes that before Hitler wore a new suit in public, he had himself photographed in it to see what he looked like. Hitler decreed in 1933 that all pictures showing him in *Lederhosen* should be taken out of circulation, and showed distaste at Mussolini's allowing himself to be photographed in his bathing suit: 'A really great statesman doesn't do that.' For Ribbentrop's comment see Joachim von Ribbentrop, *The Ribbentrop Memoirs.*

24 Hoffmann, *Hitler Was My Friend.* Also Zoller, *Hitler privat.*

25 Picker, *Tischgespräche*, and Dietrich, *Hitler.*

26 Wolfgang Sauer, in Karl Dietrich Bracher, Wolfgang Sauer and Gerhard Schulz, *Die nationalsozialistische Machtergreifung*; see in the same work the detailed description that follows.

27 Picker, *Tischgespräche*, entry for April 12, 1942. Compare this with Hitler's remarks in his speech to the commanders of the Wehrmacht on August 22, 1939: 'We have nothing to lose, only something to gain. As a result of our restrictions our economic position is such that we can only hold on for a few years. Göring can confirm this. There is no other course left to us; we must act' (*IMT*, XXVI, 798–PS).

28 The quotes are taken in this order from Picker, *Tischgespräche*, entries for January 27 and May 8, 1942; Rauschning, *Voice of Destruction*; Frank, *Im Angesicht des Galgens.*

29 Record of the address to the commanders of the Wehrmacht on August 22, 1939, the so-called second speech, IMT XXVI, 1014–PS.

30 *Mein Kampf.*

31 The so-called Hossbach Protocol, reproduced in Hans-Adolf Jacobsen, *1939–1945. Der Zweite Weltkrieg in Chronik und Documenten*; see also H. R. Trevor-Roper, *Blitzkrieg to Defeat. Hitler's War Directives 1939–1945.*

32 Gaupropagandaleiter Waldemar Vogt, recorded by Domarus, *Hitler*, Vol. I; see also Rauschning, *Voice of Destruction*, and Frank, *Im Angesicht des Galgens.* Hitler also made a similar remark to Chamberlain in Berchtesgaden: see Michael Freund, *Geschichte des Zweiten Weltkrieges in Dokumenten*, Vol. I. In his August 22, 1939, speech to the commanders of the Wehrmacht, Hitler gave this as a reason

for his determination to force a confrontation: 'My own personality and that of Mussolini. Essentially it depends on me, on my existence by virtue of my political abilities. Also the fact that no man will again have the trust of the whole German people to the extent that I do. In the future there will never again be a man who has more authority than I. Thus my existence is a fact of great importance. But I can at any time be eliminated by a murderer, an idiot' (see Freund, *Geschichte*, Vol. III). It can generally be accepted that the reference to an untimely death was also, at least in part, a tactical consideration; the remark was intended to underline his arguments. At the same time, in a verbal reference about this to the author, Albert Speer remarked that possible tactical motives were doubtless interspersed with a real fear of death. From 1938 onward this was, as Speer also observed, more and more evident.

33 Schwerin von Krosigk, *Es geschah in Deutschland*.

34 Thus Bullock, *Hitler*; see also Rauschning, *Voice of Destruction*, and Frank, *Im Angesicht des Galgens*.

35 Dietrich, *Hitler*.

36 See Görlitz and Quint, *Adolf Hitler*.

37 Hitler addressing the political leaders at the 1936 Party Congress, taken from *Der Reichsparteitag der Ehre vom 8.–14.9.1936. Offizieller Bericht uber den Verlauf des Reichsparteitages*. There is an abundance of similar remarks.

38 Speech of March 14, 1936, in Munich, referring to the successful entry into the demilitarised zone of the Rhineland.

39 Bullock, *Hitler*.

40 Hjalmar Schacht to the Nuremberg Tribunal, see *IMT*, XIII; also Bullock, *Hitler*, which quotes Kirkpatrick's record of Hitler's remark to Sir Horace Wilson on September 27, 1938: 'If France and England strike, let them do so. It is a matter of complete indifference to me. I am prepared for every eventuality. It is Tuesday today and by next Monday we shall all be at war.' Before he flew to Bad Godesberg, Neville Chamberlain aptly remarked that he was setting out to do battle with an evil beast (see Freund, *Geschichte des Zweiten Weltkrieges*, Vol. I).

41 'He wanted war,' was Hans Frank's concise opinion (*Im Angesicht des Galgens*), and one must give particular weight to the remark of a man who even in his Nuremberg cell still retained a considerable amount of loyalty and veneration for Hitler; this is especially necessary in the face of the most recent attempts to play down Hitler's share of blame for the outbreak of war. See Hitler's remark that 'the resolve to strike had always been part of me,' quoted by Schwerin von Krosigk in *Es geschah in Deutschland*.

42 The passage runs in full: 'It was by this time necessary gradually to convert the German people psychologically and make them increasingly aware that there are things which, if they can't be accomplished by peaceful means, must be accomplished by violence. The point was not to propagate violence per se but so to illumine for the German people certain political occurrences that the inner voice of the people itself began gradually to cry for violence.' The full text of this speech is published in *VJHfZ*, 1958, No. 2.

43 Walter Hewel records this remark; see Erich Kordt, *Nicht aus den Akten*, which generally gives more space to the proceedings. Also Paul Schmidt, *Hitler's Interpreter*. A. I. Berndt, the deputy Reich press chief, remarked in this connection: 'People in the street raise their arms to the troops as a greeting, but they are serious and silent. What goes on in their minds?' (*Der Marsch ins Grossdeutsche Reich*). See also William L. Shirer, *The Rise and Fall of the Third Reich*.

44 Rauschning, *Voice of Destruction*.

45 Weizsäcker, *Memoirs*. Reference should also be made to Hitler's many remarks at that time in which he emphasises his determination to take risks and indeed turns

this determination into the very criterion for statesmanship. See his speech to the commanders of the Wehrmacht of August 22, 1939, quoted by Freund, *Geschichte des Zweiten Weltkrieges*, Vol. III; also Franz Halder, *Kriegstagebuch*, Vol. I.

46 Frank, *Im Angesicht des Galgens.*
47 Rauschning, *Voice of Destruction.*

5 Victor and Vanquished

1 Note by a military aide (Schmundt?) on Hitler's speech of August 22, 1939, to the commanders of the Wehrmacht, quoted by Freund, *Geschichte des Zweiten Weltkrieges*, Vol. III. A similar note in Halder's *Kriegstagebuch*, Vol. I, about one of Hitler's speeches: 'Führer's worried that at the last moment England will make the final proceeding more difficult for him through an offer.'
2 Shirer, *Rise and Fall of the Third Reich*; see also Frank, *Im Angesicht des Galgens.*
3 *Dokumente der deutschen Politik*, Vol. VII, Pt 1.
4 See Jacobsen, *1939–1945*. Goebbels too agreed with the numerous complaints, especially from military sources (expressed for example in the report of General Georg Thomas reprinted in *IMT*, XXXVI, 028–EC) when he noted in his diary on April 17, 1942: 'We took the matter of arms and munitions production far too lightly and now have to pay for it' (*The Goebbels Diaries*).
5 Peter Bor, *Gespräche mit Halder.*
6 Hitler's speech to the supreme commanders of the Wehrmacht at the end of the Polish campaign; see *IMT*, XXVI, 789 PS.
7 *Hitler's Secret Book.*
8 *IMT*, XXVI, 789 PS. Hitler also believed his opponents to be exclusively motivated by considerations of naked power politics; see for example Picker, *Tischgespräche.*
9 Bor, *Gespräche mit Halder.* Hitler's contempt for the generals was due not least to his aversion for the calculated reluctance to take risks to which the officer corps inclined by temperament and education; he was irritated by arrogant professionalism and ideological reserve. So far as the Army was concerned, he explained that its unfinished tasks were not so much a question 'of professional ability as of the need for glowing professions of National Socialism' (*ibid.*).
10 Gert Buchheit's interpretation within the framework of his study *Hitler der Feldherr* is certainly more reserved; according to this 'the German Army . . . only scored military successes for as long as Hitler's activity as a field marshal remained minimal'. For the opposite point of view see for example Alan Bullock, *Hitler*, who tends to overestimate Hitler's military talents. Numerous opinions have been expressed on this question. In the majority of cases they reflect scepticism and support the point of view represented here.
11 See Frank, *Im Angesicht des Galgens.*
12 The remark quoted comes from Halder (Bor, *Gespräche mit Halder*). For Hitler's distrust of his generals, whom he hated because of their absolute necessity *au fond*, see the chapter in the present book 'General von X'; also Zoller, *Hitler privat*: 'The General Staff is the last Freemasons' lodge which unfortunately I have forgotten to dissolve.' The description of the General Staff as 'the last Freemasons' lodge' occurs elsewhere, for example Bor, *Gespräche mit Halder.*
13 See Paul Kluke, 'Nationalsozialistische Europa Ideologie,' *VJHfZ*, 1955, No. 3. 'As though by a magnet' – Hitler employed this image also on another occasion in his table talks – 'the best, as it were the metallic, iron-containing proportion of mankind, must be extracted by us from the Germanic peoples.' This, together with his unveiled expansionist policies, was basically his 'Europe Programme,'

about which he would not, as Goebbels noted in his diary on March 9, 1943, 'go into details'; see also Picker, *Tischgespräche*, entry for July 15, 1942.

14 Picker, *Tischgespräche*, entry for June 4, 1942. That Hitler not only knew about the extermination measures but had repeatedly encouraged their speedier execution is today proved beyond doubt, in spite of still powerful popular prejudice ('If the Führer had known that . . .'). See for example Zoller, *Hitler privat;* Dietrich, *Hitler; The Goebbels Diaries*; Carl Haensel, *Das Gericht vertagt sich.*

15 Martin Broszat, *Nationalsozialistische Polenpolitik 1939–1945.*

16 *Kriegstagebuch des Wehrmachtführungsstabes*, quoted in Jacobsen, *1939–1945.*

17 Bullock, *Hitler.* The quotation comes from Hitler's speech of February 2, 1934, taken from Hans-Adolf Jacobsen and Werner Jochmann, *Ausgewählte Dokumente zur Geschichte des Nationalsozialismus* (hereafter cited as *Ausgewählte Dokumente*). In his overall foreign policy Hitler had always adhered to the tactical principle of bilateral agreements and refused to join the system of collective security as exemplified by the League of Nations. In the process it emerged that one or another European power was prepared (Britain and Poland were the first) to make bilateral treaties with Hitler and thus not only abandon friends and allies but also disavow the concept of collective reponsibility. Accordingly, he had at first taken care to have on the military front only *one* chief opponent of equal stature. Then he became unfaithful to this principle, which he later violated once more by his declaration of war on the USA, thus furthering the coalition or system of collective defence in the camp of the enemy. When he later referred to these developments indignantly as 'monstrous', he was forgetting what he doubtless wanted to forget: his own part in them.

18 Noted by Halder in Bor, *Gespräche mit Halder.*

19 *The Goebbels Diaries.* When at the end of April 1942 Hitler went to the Obersalzberg for a few days rest, some late snow fell and Hitler felt compelled, as Goebbels noted, 'to cut short his holiday. It is, so to speak, a flight from the snow.'

20 Picker, *Tischgespräche*, entry for January 27, 1942.

21 Quoted by Jacobsen, *1939–1945.*

22 Frank, *Im Angesicht des Galgens.* Goebbels' Diary, which includes never-ending complaints about political inactivity in the East, also contains illuminating references to the politics of total subjection and exploitation with their damaging consequences; see among others the entry for April 25, 1942, also the remark about a report of Quisling's on the same subject (entry for April 14, 1943). Within this same framework belong the staunch efforts of the Propaganda Minister toward a so-called Proclamation on the East which Hitler, of course, always determined to avoid fixed positions, could not be persuaded to accept (see entry for April 15, 1943). An inquiry set up by the Americans in 1945 among 1,000 Russian Displaced Persons who had experienced the German occupation policy at first hand gives an illuminating example of the possibilities which would have been open to cooperative German policy in the conquered Eastern territories. The question whether the attitude of the population toward the Germans had changed between the time of the invasion and the retreat was answered with 728 yeses and 85 nos. Majority opinion was that the change of attitude began in 1942, when occupation policy allowed no more doubts as to the German objective; see Jacobsen, *1939–1945.*

23 Zoller, *Hitler privat.*

24 Recorded by Hans Frank; *cf.* Görlitz and Quint, *Adolf Hitler.*

25 Frank, *Im Angesicht des Galgens*; on Jodl's view see *IMT*, XV; also *The Goebbels Diaries.*

26 *The Goebbels Diaries*, entry for February 2, 1942. The extraordinary overestimation of rhetoric also finds vivid expression in an entry two days earlier covering Hitler's same speech: 'The address made a tremendous impression. . . . We may now rest

assured that the main psychological difficulties have been overcome. . . . The Führer has charged the entire nation as though it were a storage battery.'

27 Picker, *Tischgespräche*, entries for June 8, April 12, and April 26, 1942. See also Zoller, *Hitler Privat*, and Dietrich, *Hitler*. On the peculiarity of Hitler's artistic tastes see the chapter in the present book 'Albert Speer and the Immorality of the Technicians'.

28 See Hitler's remark in this connection in Bullock, *Hitler*; also *The Goebbels Diaries*. For a typical instance of Hitler's vacillating moods and outbursts of rage over trifles, see Dietrich, *Hitler*.

29 *The Goebbels Diaries*, entries for March 2 and 10, 1943; *Cf.* entry for May 10, 1943.

30 Ribbentrop, *Memoirs*. Rommel's remark is recorded by Görlitz and Quint, *Adolf Hitler*.

31 *The Goebbels Diaries*, entry for March 2, 1943: 'It is tragic that the Führer has become such a recluse and leads such an unhealthy life. He never gets out into the fresh air. He does not relax. He sits in his bunker, worries and broods.'

32 See Bor, *Gespräche mit Halder*; also *The Memoirs of Field-Marshal Keitel*, ed. Walter Görlitz. Keitel was, as he says, simply 'forbidden to publish the defeatist reports of General Thomas, which were fantasies'. The reference to Hitler's speech of January 30, 1939, to high-ranking officers in which he strongly objected to alarmist memoranda is also found in Keitel, *Memoirs*.

Hitler's contempt for facts is also repeatedly emphasised by other sources. When Rudolf Diels once referred to 'the objective falsehood of his premises,' Hitler replied, 'Then I must seek other premises' (Diels, *Lucifer ante portas*). See also Speer's evidence at Nuremberg, *IMT*, XVI; and Weizsäcker, *Memoirs*: 'It seemed as though he could forget facts or contradict them as occasion demanded.'

33 Franz Halder, *Hitler as Warlord* (London, 1950). On another occasion Hitler attacked the speaker and would not permit such 'idiotic babble' (*ibid.*).

34 Dietrich, *Hitler*; also Bor, *Gespräche mit Halder*, where a revealing and tragic episode of Hitler's 'withdrawal strategy', a mixture of dilettantism and fanatical endurance, is described.

35 *The Goebbels Diaries*, entry for March 29, 1943.

36 See for example Gerhard Boldt's account in *In the Shelter with Hitler* (London, 1948); also Zoller, *Hitler privat*, for a highly graphic description of the atmosphere in the bunker.

37 Zoller, *Hitler privat*.

38 See *IMT*, XLI, 3569–PS. In a 'codicil' to his testament Hitler wrote: 'In this long and hard struggle the people and the Wehrmacht have given of their best. The sacrifice has been enormous. But my trust has been abused by many. Throughout the whole war, treachery and treason have undermined the will to oppose. For that reason I have not been permitted to lead my people to victory. The General Staff of the Army is not to be compared with the General Staff of the First World War. . . .'

39 Hans Schwarz, *Brennpunkt FHQ. Menschen und Massstäbe im Führerhauptquartier* (Buenos Aires, 1950).

40 Report by Hermann Karnau, quoted from a sound radio recording of the NWDR. In the given context the report says: 'I was commanded by an SS officer to leave my station. . . . I did so and went into the officers' club. After half an hour I returned. The entrance to the Führer's bunker was locked. I went back and tried to get in through the emergency exit, the one which led to the garden of the Reich Chancellery. As I reached the corner between the tall sentry-post bunker and the Führer bunker proper, when I was up there, I suddenly saw what looked like a petrol rag being thrown. In front of me lay Adolf Hitler on his back and Eva Braun on her belly. I definitely established that it was he. I went back and informed my

comrade Hilger Poppen, who however didn't believe me. Half an hour later I returned to the spot. I could no longer recognise him because he was pretty charred. I spoke to Erich Mansfeld, who was at this time on sentry duty in the tower, who also confirmed: There lies Adolf Hitler. He is burning. I left this place ... and by the staircase met Sturmbannführer Schedle, who confirmed that the Chief was burning behind the house in the garden of the Reich Chancellery. At about 13.00 I was at this spot again. ... I saw that Hitler and Eva Braun by now had burnt to the point that the skeletal structure could clearly be seen. Whether during the period from 18.00 to 20.00 petrol was poured over the remains once more, I don't know, but when I was there again at 20.00 cinders were already flying in the wind. ...' On the last phase of the Third Reich, see further H. R. Trevor-Roper, *The Last Days of Hitler*.

41 Heiden, *Adolf Hitler*, Vol. I. In *Ich war dabei. Die Verschwörung der Dämonen*, Martin H. Sommerfeldt suggests that it was no accident that Charlie Chaplin had impersonated Hitler in his famous film.

42 Lüthy, 'Der Führer persönlich,' *Der Monat*, No. 62.

43 Heiden, *Adolf Hitler*, Vol. I; also quoted in slightly different form by Hofmann, *Der Hitlerputsch*.

44 Picker, *Tischgespräche*, entry for July 22, 1942. Hitler drew the same parallel in a speech to the party leaders in Berlin; see *The Goebbels Diaries*, entry for May 8, 1943; also Keitel, *Memoirs*. See further Hitler's speech to the German press on November 10, 1938, which constitutes unique evidence for the overestimation of propaganda methods (reprinted in *VJHfZ*, 1958, No. 2).

45 Hitler on the occasion of a parade of 30,000 SS men in the Berlin Lustgarten on January 30, 1936, quoted by Domarus, *Hitler*, Vol. I. He repeatedly referred, with many similar turns of phrase, to this process of mutual infusion of strength; see *ibid*.

46 Quoted by Görlitz and Quint, *Adolf Hitler*. On Hitler's illness (paralysis agitans), see Bullock, *Hitler*; also Trevor-Roper, *Last Days of Hitler*.

47 Robert Coulondre, *De Staline à Hitler* (Paris, 1950). Hitler's previously cited remark is from Picker, *Tischgespräche*, entry for January 18, 1942.

48 *Mein Kampf*; the definition of politics comes from Hitler's secret address to the officers' class of 1938. It is quoted in Jacobsen and Jochmann, *Ausgewählte Dokumente*.

49 See Dietrich, *Hitler*; also Frank, *Im Angesicht des Galgens*.

50 Picker, *Tischgespräche*, entry for May 14, 1942.

51 See *The Goebbels Diaries*, entry for May 8, 1943: 'The Führer gave expression to his unshakable conviction that the Reich will be the master of all Europe. We shall yet have to engage in many fights, but these will undoubtedly lead to magnificent victories. Thereafter the way to world domination is practically certain. To dominate Europe will be to assume the leadership of the world. In this connection we naturally cannot accept questions of right and wrong even as a basis of discussion. ...'

52 Picker, *Tischgespräche*, entry for May 8, 1942. Frank, *Im Angesicht des Galgens*, notes similarly that Hitler once described the earth to him as 'the challenge trophy of the racial competition'.

53 Hitler in his address to the chief editors of the home press on November 10, 1938; see *VJHfZ*, 1958, No. 2.

54 Karl Dietrich Bracher, 'Das "Phänomen" Adolf Hitler,' *Politische Literatur*, Vol. I, 1952; on the remark cited above that Hitler used to call Germany his 'bride', see Hoffmann, *Hitler Was My Friend*.

55 Quoted by Freund, *Geschichte*, Vol. I.

Part Two

PRACTITIONERS AND TECHNICIANS OF TOTALITARIAN RULE

Hermann Göring – Number Two

1   See Wolfgang Sauer, in Bracher, Sauer and Schulz, *Die nationalsozialistische Machtergreifung*. On Third Reich terminology see Victor Klemperer, *LTI* (*Lingua tertii imperii*), 2nd ed. (Berlin, 1949). The following is a very typical example of the character and style of the philosophy of struggle advocated by Hitler in *Mein Kampf*: 'Nobody can doubt that this world will one day be the scene of dreadful struggles on the part of mankind. In the end the instinct of preservation alone will triumph. Before its consuming fire this so-called humanitarianism, which means no more than a mixture of fatuous timidity and self-conceit, will melt away as under the March sunshine. Man has become great through perpetual struggle. In perpetual peace, his greatness must decline.' In a similar vein, as concise as it is descriptive, Göring notes: 'The history of man is the history of war' (Hermann Göring, *Germany Reborn*). More significantly still, Mussolini announced in 1926: 'In that hard and metallic word "struggle" lay the whole programme of fascism as I dreamed of it, as I wanted it, as I created it' (quoted by Hans Buchheim, *Totalitarian Rule: Its Nature and Characteristics*). On the ideology of National Socialism see Ernst Nolte's significant study, *The Three Faces of Fascism*.

2   Quoted by Douglas M. Kelley, *22 Cells in Nuremberg*. The preceding quotation comes from Baldur von Schirach, *Die Pioniere des Dritten Reiches* (Essen, n.d.).

3   Werner Bross, *Gespräche mit Hermann Göring während des Nürnberger Prozesses*.

4   Trevor-Roper, *Last Days of Hitler*. On Göring's failure and Hitler's criticism, see Dietrich, *Hitler*. Under cross-examination by Robert H. Jackson, the American Chief Prosecutor, Albert Speer recalled a remark by Hitler in April 1945 that he had known for some time that Göring had failed (*IMT*, XVI).

5   Edgar von Schmidt-Pauli, *Die Männer um Hitler* (Berlin, 1932). Martin H. Sommerfeldt speaks of 'Catonic inflexibility' in *Hermann Göring. Ein Lebensbild* (Berlin, 1933).

6   See G. M. Gilbert, *Nuremberg Diary*; also Sommerfeldt, *Ich war dabei*.

7   Sommerfeldt, *Ich war dabei*; Charles Bewley, *Hermann Göring and the Third Reich*; also Schwerin von Krosigk, *Es geschah in Deutschland*. Göring's father had been posted as *Reichskommissar* (governor) to what was later South-West Africa, which he acquired as a German colony.

8   Bross, *Gespräche mit Göring*. Göring's assertion that Streicher's *Stürmer* had always been so repugnant to him that he had forbidden this literature in his department is also credible.

9   Göring, *Germany Reborn*. Also at other points in this chapter on National Socialist ideology, he got around his theoretical embarrassment by formulating very general statements which usually ended with 'Germany'.

10   Lüdecke, *I Knew Hitler*.

11   Göring, *Germany Reborn*.

12   *Ibid*. See also Hermann Göring, *Reden und Aufsätze*.

13   Göring, *Reden und Aufsätze*; also Bewley, *Hermann Goering*.

14   Quoted by Bewley, *Hermann Goering*. Elsewhere Göring said: 'There is something mystical, indescribable, almost inconceivable about this unique man, and he who doesn't feel this will never track it down' (*Germany Reborn*).

15   Hjalmar Schacht, *Account Settled* (London, 1948).

16   Bross, *Gespräche mit Göring*; Schwerin von Krosigk, *Es geschah in Deutschland*,

suggests that Göring only lost his courage when he was designated Hitler's successor and Number Two; the fear that Hitler could annul this appointment robbed him of all power of opposition. This is, however, contradicted by other reports which agree that at a time when the questions of successorship and Number Two were far from decided, Göring was already very dependent on Hitler. Perhaps it is a matter of Göring being less worried for his second-rank position than trembling for fear of losing power as such and all that it meant in terms of personal privilege. 'But one word from the Führer and you are out' – he feared this word and this sentence.

In this connection Rudolf Diels, in *Lucifer ante portas*, makes the illuminating observation: 'Those who saw Göring in the dreadful days after the big shocks with which Hitler brought him down to earth at well-calculated intervals and made him recognise that he was nothing without Hitler, were appalled at how little remained of the magnificent and powerful man. There was nothing left of him when Hitler without warning took away from him the Prussian Ministry of the Interior, the basis of his power, when Hitler ostentatiously stayed away from his Opera Ball, shunned the sumptuous opening of the Prussian Council of State, when he scornfully declined Göring's gift of a hunting lodge in the Schorfheide or deprived him even of the Four-Year Plan. The liquidation of the Prussian ministries through a decree by Hitler in January 1934 literally laid him low. He took to his bed.'

17   Schwerin von Krosigk, *Es geschah in Deutschland*; see also Bross, *Gespräche mit Göring;* Bewley, *Hermann Goering*; Willi Frischauer, *The Rise and Fall of Hermann Goering* (British title: *Goering*).

18   Göring, *Germany Reborn*. See also Göring's remark to Sir Nevile Henderson: 'When a decision has to be taken, none of us count more than the stones on which we are standing. It is the Führer alone who decides' (Sir Nevile Henderson *The Failure of a Mission*).

19   See Goebbels, *My Part in Germany's Fight*.

20   Göring, *Reden und Aufsätze*.

21   *Ibid.* See also Horkenbach, *1933*. The 'bullet quotation' is found in Göring, *Germany Reborn*.

22   Erich Gritzbach, *Hermann Goering: The Man and His Work*. See also Horkenbach, *1933*; also Goebbels, *My Part in Germany's Fight*: 'Goering is cleansing Prussia with zest and courage' (entry for March 2, 1933). The fact alone that of 32 colonels of the municipal police 22 were dismissed gives an idea of the extent of these preventive measures. 'Hundreds of officers and thousands of ordinary policemen followed in the course of the next few months. New forces were drawn on and invariably they came from the great reservoir of the SA and SS,' wrote Göring himself about this in *Germany Reborn*.

23   Speech to a rally of the NSDAP at Frankfurt am Main on March 3, 1933; see Göring, *Reden und Aufsätze*.

24   Quoted by Johannes Hohlfeld, ed., *Deutsche Reichsgeschichte in Dokumenten*, Vol. IV.

25   Carl Jacob Burckhardt, *Meine Danziger Mission 1937–1939*.

26   Goebbels, *My Part in Germany's Fight*, entry for January 29, 1933.

27   Schwerin von Krosigk, *Es geschah in Deutschland*.

28   Reported by Sir Ivone Kirkpatrick, *The Inner Circle*.

29   Frank, *Im Angesicht des Galgens*.

30   Schwerin von Krosigk, *Es geschah in Deutschland*.

31   *Ibid.*; also Sommerfeldt, *Ich war dabei*. In 1943 Göring had himself presented by the city of Berlin with a Van Dyck worth 250,000 reichsmarks; see Rudolf Semmler, *Goebbels – the Man Next to Hitler*. Ulrich von Hassell mentions 'a Sèvres

service of 2,400 pieces, given by three industrialists. Cost: 500,000 reichsmarks. A French hunting lodge, stolen in France and destined to be placed on one of Göring's hunting estates, three medieval statues, valued at 16,000, 17,000 and 18,000 reichsmarks. Gritzbach [adjutant to Göring] had telephoned Schmitt and mentioned the statues in case he was at a loss as to what to give. Schmitt gave them, too, obedient fellow that he is' (*The Von Hassell Diaries, 1938–1944*).

32 Sommerfeldt, *Ich war dabei.*

33 Gritzbach, *Hermann Goering.* Charles Bewley, the former Irish Minister in Berlin, notes in his on the whole well-disposed biography that Göring liked to pile up his jewelry in front of him on the table and let it run through his fingers.

34 Schwerin von Krosigk, *Es geschah in Deutschland.* When Göring visited Italy in 1942, Ciano noted in his diary: 'At the station he wore a great sable coat, something between what motorists wore in 1906 and what a high-grade prostitute wears to the opera' (see Bullock, *Hitler*). Other fantastic outfits are described by E. von Manstein, *Verlorene Siege* (Bonn, 1960), and Heinz Guderian, *Panzer Leader* (New York and London, 1952). Also, collectively, Sommerfeldt, *Ich war dabei.*

35 Burckhardt, *Meine Danziger Mission.* Paul, Prince Regent of Yugoslavia, who as a child had once been to Tsarskoye Selo, exclaimed on seeing the luxury at Karinhall, '*Mais ça n'existait même pas chez les Zsars!*'; see Kordt, *Nicht aus den Akten.*

36 Gerhard Schulz, in Bracher, Sauer and Schulz, *Die nationalsozialistische Machtergreifung.*

37 Hitler's speech to the German industrialists of December 17, 1936, in Berlin, quoted by Domarus, *Hitler*, Vol. I. At the beginning Hitler excused Göring's weaknesses, saying that Göring had been 'a real man' in the First World War and also in the time of struggle; by contrast, he never forgave him later the failure of the Luftwaffe; see Zoller, *Hitler privat.*

38 In fact Göring represented the peace element among Hitler's associates. This did not of course prevent his identifying himself with Hitler's territorial aspirations, though he wanted these to be achieved by 'diplomatic' means, by which he meant dictated terms of settlement. When he recognised that war had become inevitable, he said, 'If we lose this war, then Heaven help us!' (see Paul Schmidt, *Hitler's Interpreter*).

39 Gritzbach, *Hermann Goering*, records the mirror episode. An order of Hitler's was as a matter of fact responsible for the success of the British withdrawal; contrary to the counsel of the troop commanders, he kept Guderian's armoured divisions several miles south of Dunkirk to have them ready for the big final attack on France. But Hitler issued this command only after Göring had insisted that he could annihilate the British by means of the Luftwaffe alone; see B. H. Liddell Hart, *The German Generals Talk* (British title: *The Other Side of the Hill*); Bor, *Gespräche mit Halder*; Guderian, *Panzer Leader.*

40 Bross, *Gespräche mit Göring.* It is not easy now to establish the exact period of the cooling off; the earliest date (Steengracht) says 1938, the latest (General Bodenschatz), 1943. *Cf.* Bewley, *Hermann Goering.*

41 *IMT*, XXXIX, NB–170 USSR. 'In each of the occupied territories,' so it reads, 'I see the people completely satisfied while hunger is rife among our own people. You are, God knows, not sent back to work for the weal and woe of those in your care, but to force them to the limit so that the German people can live. This I expect from your energies. The everlasting worry about the non-Germans must now cease once and for all. I have in front of me statements of what you propose to deliver. It is absolutely nothing when I consider your territories. It makes no difference to me if you say that your people are starving. . . . Formerly the whole thing appeared to me to be commensurately easier. For it was called plunder. It

was the duty of those concerned to take away what they conquered. Now the procedures have become more humane. Nevertheless I mean plunder and even abundantly. . . .'

42 *The Goebbels Diaries*, entry for March 18, 1943.

43 See Diels, *Lucifer ante portas*: 'Göring acted in accordance with a primal vision of life in which he trained himself to throw the spear and shoot with the bow. Down to the minutest technical detail of the air war such ideas of a lost heroic age still lingered on. He obviously would have loved to sail through the air on a wild condor, his overcoat flowing, hurling a spear at the enemy monsters. . . . "My flyers are no projectionists and my fighter craft no cinemas": with these words he once refused to consolidate the supremacy of the long-range bombers by equipping them with navigational instruments, which would have given his Luftwaffe a lead. That ramming was the most dignified form of doing battle he made clear to his nephew K. H. Göring, who contradicted him with bluster and himself crashed a few weeks later over France after an attempt at ramming. Probably his uncle's rebuke "You are all cowards" was still ringing in his ears. The sensible young man had rejoined, "If you are suggesting, uncle, that a war pilot is not supposed to 'think', then we can indeed ram without regard for casualties. We don't lack courage for that." " 'Think, think.' If we had taken the trouble to think, we would not have started the war," were his uncle's concluding words.' See also the view of General Stumpf that Göring prized personal heroism more highly than technical knowhow (Bewley, *Hermann Goering*).

44 *IMT*, XVI. For this see generally Gert Buchheit, *Hitler, der Feldherr*; also by the same author, *Soldatentum und Rebellion. Die Tragödie der deutschen Wehrmacht* (Rastatt, 1961).

Various generals said the same sort of thing, some in devastating terms. General Koller, for example, reproached Göring for 'shirking unpleasant things' (Bross, *Gespräche mit Göring*). Friedrich Hossbach said, 'The leadership of the Luftwaffe . . . has been one of the most momentous failures of the 1939–45 war,' and spoke of a 'literally bloodstained dilettantism' (*Zwischen Wehrmacht und Hitler 1934–1938*). Field Marshal Milch also spoke, as Goebbels confided to his diary, 'in terms of sharpest criticism about the Reich Marshal. He blames him for having let technical research in the German Luftwaffe run down so completely' (*The Goebbels Diaries*, entry for April 9, 1943). For a biting general verdict on Göring's role in the Third Reich there is Raeder's memorandum written in Moscow; see the extract in Gilbert, *Nuremberg Diary*. In complete inversion of the true state of affairs, Hitler on the other hand suspected for a long time that Göring's 'optimistic not to say unrealistic view' of reality was attributable to the fact that he 'was being thoroughly misled by the generals of the Luftwaffe' (*The Goebbels Diaries*, entry for March 9, 1943).

45 Semmler, *Goebbels*. Goebbels noted in his diary the 'unfortunate circumstance' that Göring usually was to be found 'neither in Berlin nor in his GHQ, but up on the Obersalzberg' (entry for March 3, 1943).

46 Semmler, *Goebbels*.

47 *Ibid*. On the other hand, for example, Göring's plea for granting former Ambassador von Hassell, who was involved in the events of July 20, execution by firing squad was refused. See Bewley, *Hermann Goering*; also Bross, *Gespräche mit Göring*.

48 Emmy Göring to Willi Frischauer, *Rise and Fall of Goering*. She expressed herself in almost the same words to G. M. Gilbert (see *Nuremberg Diary*).

49 Frischauer, *Rise and Fall of Goering*.

50 Bross, *Gespräche mit Göring*.

51 Gilbert, *Nuremberg Diary*. Hans Frank mocked Göring's finally gratified ambition: 'Now Göring has finally got his wish – he is speaker No. 1 for the National

Socialist regime, what's left of it!' (*ibid*.) Gilbert's book offers an endless chain of examples of Göring's dictatorial regime among the prisoners. This went so far that finally the prison administration intervened and Göring was rigorously separated from the other prisoners. See also Kelley, *22 Cells*.

In his remarkable though somewhat 'literary' book *Das Gericht vertagt sich*, Carl Haensel, the Nuremberg Defence Counsel, notes: 'Before the recommencement of the trial Göring reclined in his witness chair and examined the other accused from up in front like an officer about to call the roll, and then said thoughtfully to a colleague and me who were standing close by, "Once I had power, complete power. And I enjoyed it. The others over there have had only a half or a third. Or even less. And it will suffice for us all to. . . ." The last word he crumpled like a piece of paper in his hands and threw it under his seat. He made the throwing-away movement convincingly and reflectively. The biographer on whom he currently had his eye told me once – but not in the witness box and not under oath – that Göring had a permanent blacklist of his enemies in his desk and sometimes in the evening when the burgundy was good and he was in a good humour, he refined it. He added one name and rubbed out another; he then wiped away the flecks of the eraser with the same gesture.'

52 Haensel, *Das Gericht vertagt sich*.
53 Bross, *Gespräche mit Göring*. On Göring's hopes of fame after death, see Gilbert, *Nuremberg Diary*. He was also, on his own evidence, 'glad Dönitz got stuck with signing the surrender.' He said, 'I wouldn't want my name attached to that thing in future history' (*Nuremberg Diary*).
54 Kelley, *22 Cells*. References to Göring's hoped-for martyrdom are also found in Gilbert, *Nuremberg Diary*.

Joseph Goebbels: 'Man the Beast'

1 See Werner Stephan, *Joseph Goebbels. Dämon einer Diktatur*. The very real interest that the phenomenon of the Propaganda Minister always aroused is shown by the fact that more accounts have appeared about him than about any other leading figure of the Third Reich except Hitler. Of particular note are: Curt Riess, *Joseph Goebbels: The Devil's Advocate* (New York, 1948; London, 1949); Boris von Borresholm, ed., *Dr Goebbels. Nach Aufzeichnungen aus seiner Umgebung* (Berlin, 1949); Roger Manvell and Heinrich Fraenkel, *Dr Goebbels. His Life and Death* (New York and London, 1960). The value of the last work, however, is strongly impaired by the extreme inaccuracy of the quotations; single remarks especially from Goebbels' diaries are not only garbled but have even had the opposite construction put on them. Helmut Heiber, *Joseph Goebbels*, is the best and most well-founded account of this man. Two contemporary biographies are Willi Krause's *Reichsminister Dr Goebbels* (Berlin, n.d.), and Max Jungnickel's *Goebbels*. Exceedingly illuminating if not to be unhesitatingly recommended are the diaries of two intimate colleagues of the minister: Rudolf Semmler, *Goebbels – the Man next to Hitler*, and Wilfried von Oven, *Mit Goebbels bis zum Ende* (Buenos Aires, 1949–1950).
2 Joseph Goebbels, 'Wenn Hitler spricht,' in *Der Angriff. Aufsätze aus der Kampfzeit* (hereafter cited as *Der Angriff*). The following remarks are characteristic of the pseudo-religious character of the veneration of the Führer by Goebbels: 'What you said there [he is talking to Hitler] is the catechism of a new political belief in the midst of the despair of a collapsing world without gods' (Joseph Goebbels, *Die Zweite Revolution. Briefe an Zeitgenossen*). In his revolutionary diary, *My Part in Germany's Fight*, he wrote of Hitler: 'He alone has never deceived himself.

He has always been right. He has never allowed himself to be blinded or tempted by the propitiousness or otherwise of the moment. Like a servant of God he fulfils the task which was given to him and he does justice in its highest and best sense to his historical mission.' The birthday addresses are especially renowned for their uninhibited idolatry; several are to be found in the collection of miscellaneous essays, *Die Zeit ohne Beispiel. Reden und Aufsätze aus den Jahren 1939/40/41* (Munich, 1941), and in *Das eherne Herz*. Goebbels also published in *Der Angriff* in 1932 a whole series of panegyric articles, which were primarily intended to make Hitler the popular election candidate. One of these articles, which appeared on March 5, 1932, under the title 'Wir wählen Adolf Hitler,' had the following five descriptive headings: 'Hitler, der Grossdeutsche,' 'Hitler, der Führer,' 'Hitler, der Prophet,' 'Hitler, Kämpfer,' 'Hitler, der Reichspräsident'; see Joseph Goebbels, *Wetterleuchten. Aufsätze aus der Kampfzeit* (Vol. II of *Der Angriff*). This also contains the birthday speech of April 20, 1937, parts of which are reminiscent of the dreary practice of glorification in the Stalinist era. A typical example: 'May the Führer remain with us for many years yet, in power, health and strength as the standard-bearer of the people, as the first among many millions of workers, soldiers, peasants and townspeople, as the friend and protector of the young, the defender of the arts, the sponsor of culture and science, the architect of the new unified nation.'

3 Stephan, *Joseph Goebbels*; also Joseph Goebbels, *The Early Goebbels Diaries, 1925–1926*, and Borresholm, *Dr Goebbels*.

4 Birthday speech of April 20, 1942, quoted by Stephan, *Joseph Goebbels*.

5 *The Early Goebbels Diaries*, entries for November 6 and 23, 1925. It seems the more grotesque that Goebbels in *Die Zweite Revolution* declares: 'He [the Führer] does not suffer the base flattery of conceited asses and dreamers. He seeks real men and knows where to find them when he needs to.'

6 Bracher, *Auflösung der Weimarer Republik*. On the destruction of the admittedly modest beginnings of internal democracy see also Goebbels' letter on 'Die Führer-frage' in *Die Zweite Revolution*: 'The great Führer is not chosen. He is there when he is needed. In the pressing stream of time he is drawn upward and stands imperiously challenging before the deeply moved, devout youth.'

7 Hitler's speech in the Sportpalast of October 30, 1936; quoted by Domarus, *Hitler*.

8 *The Early Goebbels Diaries*, entry for January 20, 1926.

9 Joseph Goebbels, *Michael. Ein deutsches Schicksal in Tagebuchblättern*. The published form of the book differs essentially from the original, which however is not yet available. The excessive cult of the Führer and the book's anti-Semitism both spring from subsequent editing.

10 Goebbels, 'Wenn Hitler spricht,' in *Der Angriff*. See also *Die Zweite Revolution*: 'He is one of those who believe in what they say with unshakable certainty and who are therefore so dangerous to the old government and its supporters.'

11 Goebbels, *Michael*. A phrase in a report by Goebbels on the beginning of his political career is also revealing: in *Kampf um Berlin* (Munich, 1933) he quotes approvingly a sentence from Wolfgang Goetz's play *Miedhart von Gneisenau*: 'God give you aims, it doesn't matter which!'

12 The exact profession of his father, Friedrich Goebbels, can evidently no longer be determined. While in earlier accounts he is described as a foreman (i.e. overseer), in the Manvell-Fraenkel biography he figures as office employee, finally on a fairly high level. The two authors base themselves on statements from the family.

13 See Heiden, *Adolf Hitler*, Vol. I.

14 Albert Krebs, *Tendenzen und Gestalten der NSDAP*. The widespread myth that Goebbels was brought up by the Jesuits possibly has its origin here.

15 Goebbels, *Die Zweite Revolution*. According to Goebbels's ideas the élite among

the top leadership had to contribute something more than sentiment; see the article 'Der Generalstab' in *Nationalsozialistischen Briefen*, No. 16, May 15, 1926, in which he expounded: 'By means of breeding and strictness a circle had to be separated of the best, the bravest and most unselfish. Bound to each other with puritanical cruelty, they had to harden their hearts against the day when more would be demanded from us than sentiment: brutality, consistency, sureness of understanding, clarity of vision.'

16 Goebbels, *Die Zweite Revolution* (italics in original).

17 Krebs, *Tendenzen und Gestalten*, describes a revealing episode in the spring of 1931, shortly before the so-called Stennes revolt, which pertinently characterises the Berlin Gauleiter's uncertain position.

18 This complex found its most forcible expression in *Die Zweite Revolution*, in which Goebbels defends himself against being considered a 'bourgeois intellectual'; see also Helmut Heiber's prefatory remarks to *The Early Goebbels Diaries*.

19 Goebbels' sudden vacillations are exemplified in the Bamburger meeting and/or the weeks following it (see below), in the Stennes revolt, in his behaviour during the controversy over the question of government participation in the autumn of 1932, as well as in the Röhm affair.

20 *The Early Goebbels Diaries*, entry for July 15, 1926. On the anti-intellectual quotation, see *Michael*. This work alone contains numerous other examples of Goebbels' hostility to the intellect. In *Kampf um Berlin* he says: 'The intellect is exposed to a thousand temptations while the heart always beats its same measure.'

21 Goebbels, *Michael*; on earlier literary endeavours, see Heiber, *Joseph Goebbels*.

22 Goebbels, *Michael*.

23 Krebs, *Tendenzen und Gestalten*, notes that he himself had 'spread this report for almost two years'; 'finally my good faith was destroyed . . . by Schauwecker's "open letter," which as I recollect appeared in 1927 in one of the many short-lived periodicals of the national revolutionary movement and attacked Goebbels on his "myth of the combat veteran".'

24 *The Early Goebbels Diaries*.

25 *Ibid.*, entry for July 15, 1926.

26 *Ibid.*, entry for July 30, 1926. At that time he openly classified people into radical or 'bourgeois' types. He praised Gregor Strasser, for example, for being apt to go along with 'anything that adds radical content to the idea' (entry for September 30, 1925). As is often true of people with a strong inferiority complex, his imagination was strangely fascinated by anything apocalyptic and it seems as though it expressed more than a contemporary fashion: 'A time of brutality approaches of which we ourselves can have absolutely no conception, indeed we are already in the middle of it . . . a bursting tidal wave with a blood-red crest' (*Die Zweite Revolution*). Several pages later he writes: 'We shall only reach our goal if we have enough courage to destroy, laughingly to shatter what we once held holy, such as tradition, upbringing, friendship and human love.'

27 Goebbels, *Die Zweite Revolution*; in the same context he points out 'that we are anything but a black-white-and-red policeman for bourgeois self-interest and narrowminded quiet and order.'

28 *The Early Goebbels Diaries*, entries for October 23, 1925, and January 31, 1926. In *Die Zweite Revolution* there is another good example of the national Bolshevist tendencies of Goebbels's thinking at that time: 'On this account we look toward Russia, because she sooner than anyone else will accompany us on the path to socialism. Because Russia is the ally given to us by nature against the devilish contamination and corruption of the West. With embittered anguish we must see so-called German statesmen destroy bridge upon bridge to Russia, and this anguish is great, not because we love Bolshevism and the Jewish supporters of Bolshevism,

but because allied with a sincere nationalist and socialist Russia we recognise the beginning of our own nationalist and socialist assertion.'

29 Goebbels, *Die Zweite Revolution*; a statement which could come verbatim from a pamphlet of the radical left: 'We shall and must eternally reproach the German bourgeoisie that has allowed itself to be degraded by the few high financiers, who in reality are the sole cause of the struggle, into slaveowners and bullies of the stock-exchange dictatorship.'

30 *The Early Goebbels Diaries*, entry for September 30, 1925. A certain distrust of him and his radical socialist tendencies remained with the Munich group, among whom in particular were Hess, Rosenberg, Frick and Amann; see Krebs, *Tendenzen und Gestalten*.

31 The statement recorded by Otto Strasser in his book *Hitler and I* is sometimes queried for reasons of some weight; see for example Manvell and Fraenkel, *Goebbels*. Helmut Heiber has given the most intelligible version of the incident in *The Early Goebbels Diaries*, referring to the testimony of Hans Hinkel, a former colleague of the Strasser brothers. According to this, Goebbels no doubt made this remark, though probably not, as Strasser assures us, in a public speech, but in conversation with other people at the meeting.

32 *The Early Goebbels Diaries*, entries for February 15 and April 19, 1926.

33 Goebbels, *Michael*. For the quotation see *The Early Goebbels Diaries*, entry for October 14, 1925.

34 *The Early Goebbels Diaries*, entry for July 24, 1926.

35 Krause, *Reichsminister Dr Goebbels*.

36 Joseph Goebbels, 'Die Strasse,' *Nationalsozialistische Briefe*, No. 17, June 1, 1926. On his appointment to Berlin, see Goebbels, *Kampf um Berlin*. Hitler himself had later emphasised that with this appointment the history of the National Socialist movement 'essentially began, since what had happened earlier was only its pre-history'; see Domarus, *Hitler*, Vol. I.

37 *The Early Goebbels Diaries*, entry for March 27, 1926; for the chapter title mentioned, see Goebbels, *Kampf um Berlin*. An exhaustive explanation of this method of fighting is found in Heiber, *Joseph Goebbels*.

38 Joseph Goebbels, 'Erkenntnis und Propaganda,' in *Signale der neuen Zeit*.

39 Joseph Goebbels, 'Warten können,' in *Der Angriff* (article of February 18, 1929).

40 Quoted by Stephan, *Joseph Goebbels*. Konrad Heiden notes this episode in *Adolf Hitler*, Vol. I.

41 Joseph Goebbels, 'Was wollen wir im Reichstag?' in *Der Angriff* (article of April 30, 1928). The remark that propaganda has absolutely nothing to do with truth is quoted by Oven, *Mit Goebbels bis zum Ende*, Vol. I. The remark about the Young Plan is recorded in the biographies by Stephan, and Manvell and Fraenkel.

42 Joseph Goebbels, 'IdI' and 'Vor der Entscheidung' in *Der Angriff* (articles of May 28 and May 14, 1928).

43 Joseph Goebbels, 'Der Marschall-Präsident'. Characteristically, this article was missing from *Der Angriff* when the collection first appeared in 1935.

44 Jungnickel, *Goebbels*; elsewhere Jungnickel says that the figure of Goebbels lies like 'the shadow of Mephisto' over the rally, that his speech is a mixture of 'hydrochloric acid, copper sulphate and pepper'.

45 Joseph Goebbels, 'Gegen die Reaktion,' in *Der Angriff* (article of May 13, 1929); also *Die Zweite Revolution*.

46 Goebells, 'Warten können'.

47 See Domarus, *Hitler*, Vol. I.

48 Goebbels, *My Part in Germany's Fight*. Once, before a speech in Hamburg, he had himself introduced thus: 'Party member Dr Goebbels, called "the Bandit of Berlin,"

the Bearer of Immunity, can say what he likes' (see *Vossische Zeitung*, February 12, 1931).

49 Quoted by Stephan, *Joseph Goebbels*. In an article on the fortieth birthday of the Propaganda Minister, Alfred Frauenfeld wrote: 'Joseph Goebbels has worn down the nerves of the enemy; he played the register of the propaganda organ, so that they soon thought they were hearing the shrieks of the last trumpet' (quoted in *ibid.*).

50 Horkenbach, *1933*.

51 Shirer, *Rise and Fall of the Third Reich*. Hannah Arendt, *Origins of Totalitarianism*, considers the combination to be not terror and propaganda but organisation and propaganda, which she sees as 'the two sides of the same coin'. But that is a question of means and ends. Organisation, which during the period of growth serves totalitarian movements as a means of attaining power, becomes, after the establishment of that power, an end to which terror and propaganda are subject. See also *The Goebbels Diaries*, entry for September 20, 1943: 'A sharp sword must always stand behind propaganda if it is to be really effective'. In Picker, *Tischgespräche*, entry for July 26, 1942, Hitler says in the same vein: 'If one thinks about the basic rules for conducting the affairs of state . . . one can repeatedly recognise that the laws of the Gestapo alone will not suffice. The masses need an idol.'

52 I. Kirkpatrick, *The Inner Circle*.

53 Heiden, *Adolf Hitler*, Vol. I. *Cf*. the article of Erich Koch already referred to, which under the heading 'Consequences of Interracial Mixing' contains a sharp attack on Goebbels.

54 Stephan, *Joseph Goebbels*. His rather abrupt switch to the anti-Semitic side is documented for the first time in the collection of essays *Die Zweite Revolution*. Perhaps the inner party circle never quite forgave Goebbels for having been one of Friedrich Gundolf's students. Perhaps the fact that his wife, Magda Quandt, had been brought up in a Jewish household after her mother married a Jewish salesman was also held against him. Goebbels himself later boasted that 'once Berlin is free of Jews' one of his 'greatest political achievements' would have been accomplished (*The Goebbels Diaries*, entry for April 18, 1943).

55 See *Das politische Tagebuch Alfred Rosenbergs*, entry for December 3, 1939.

56 See Krebs, *Tendenzen und Gestalten*, who notes that among the Hamburg party adherents many voted for Goebbels as the better speaker, 'which was frequently equivalent to preferring him as the more suitable party leader'. On the other hand Hitler, evidently referring to this rivalry, expressed the following opinion: 'I am conscious that I have no equal in the art of swaying the masses, not even Goebbels. Everything that can be learnt with the intelligence, everything that can be achieved by the aid of clever ideas, Goebbels can do, but real leadership of the masses cannot be learnt' (Rauschning, *Voice of Destruction*); see also Picker, *Tischgespräche*, entry for January 18, 1942. In his study *Hitlers Weg*, Theodor Heuss had remarked similarly in 1932 that Goebbels had 'the liveliest talent for coining felicitous aphorisms and slogans', and in this 'he is more than a match for the long-winded Hitler'.

57 *Mein Kampf*.

58 On this complex see Stephan, *Joseph Goebbels*.

59 See *ibid*.

60 In the *Early Goebbels Diaries* alone this or a similar expression appears four times. See also *Der Angriff*.

61 Rauschning, *Voice of Destruction*.

62 Goebbels, *My Part in Germany's Fight*.

63 Speech at the opening of the Pan-German Art Exhibition on July 4, 1942, in *Das eherne Herz*.

64 *The Early Goebbels Diaries*, entry for June 16, 1926.

65 Birthday speech of April 19, 1945, copy of the recording at the sound archives of the German radio in Frankfurt am Main. 'For us politics is the miracle of the impossible,' he had already written in his book *Die Zweite Revolution*, with Hitler in mind.

66 Goebbels, *Kampf um Berlin*. See also the remark, 'I emphasise, as I have already so often, that I represent no special line in the party. We have after all only one line and that is the one which the Führer decides' (quoted by Domarus, *Hitler*, Vol. I).

67 Hildegard Springer, *Es sprach Hans Fritzsche*. Previously Goebbels had assured his colleagues cynically, 'Why did you work with me! Now you will have your throats cut' (*ibid.*).

68 Speech on 'The Tasks of the German Theatre' at the Hotel Kaiserhof, Berlin, on May 8, 1933, from *Goebbels spricht. Reden aus Kampf und Sieg* (Oldenburg, 1933).

69 Goebbels, *Michael*. See also his article in *Reich*, March 19, 1944: 'We have left our stamp on this century and it will bear our name some day when history will do us honour by its judgment' (quoted by Heiber, *Joseph Goebbels*).

Reinhard Heydrich – The Successor

1 Hitler's remark is recorded by, among others, Walter Schellenberg, *The Labyrinth* (British title: *The Schellenberg Memoirs*). The observation noting the contrast to Himmler comes from Felix Kersten, *The Kersten Memoirs 1940–1945*.

2 Karl Dietrich Bracher, in Bracher, Sauer, and Schulz, *Die nationalsozialistische Machtergreifung*.

3 Hofer, *Der Nationalsozialismus*. See also Heuss, *Hitlers Weg*.

4 See particularly Hedwig Conrad-Martius, *Utopien der Menschenzüchtung*. The investigation makes it frighteningly clear that the whole catalogue of state-controlled breeding measures designed or carried out by the National Socialists, beginning with the so-called studbooks, which defined individual fitness to breed in accordance with certain fixed criteria, and extending to a veto on marriage, liquidation of those considered unfit to live, as well as the establishment of the Lebensborn, the state organisation for the promotion of human propagation, had been anticipated by the spokesmen of various schools of social Darwinism; and even though they had not demanded the extermination of whole nationalities, their ideas were in line with the inhuman projects which showed such a basic contempt for human life.

5 Rauschning, *Voice of Destruction*.

6 Cited by Gerald Reitlinger, *The Final Solution*.

7 Hans F. K. Günther, *Adel und Rasse*, quoted by Hermann Glaser, *Das Dritte Reich. Anspruch und Wirklichkeit*.

8 Richter, *Unsere Führer im Lichte der Rassenfrage und Charakterologie*.

9 Rauschning, *Voice of Destruction*.

10 *Das Schwarze Korps*, memorial article in the issue of June 11, 1942. The observation that Heydrich was sometimes called 'the Blond Beast' by his followers is made by Willi Frischauer in *Himmler the Evil Genius of the Third Reich* (Boston and London, 1953).

11 There is a photocopy of this report at the Institut für Zeitgeschichte (Institute of Contemporary History) in Munich. See also Charles Wighton, *Heydrich, Hitler's Most Evil Henchman*. Particulars of Heydrich's antecedents and more on his attempt to blur the details of his background are to be found in Walter Hagen's (i.e. Wilhelm Höttl's) book *The Secret Front*. Though the facts are sometimes not quite reliable, the book is extremely valuable for Hagen's personal observations.

He was evidently the first not simply to look upon Heydrich as a sadistic monster but to show himself at pains to uncover his complex character.

Hagen further reports that Heydrich removed the gravestone of his grandmother Sarah Heydrich from the Leipzig cemetery and had set in its place a new stone with the more harmless inscription 'S. Heydrich'; the bill for this is said to have been in the Berlin Adjutancy until 1945. This is based of course on the supposition that Heydrich's so-called admixture of Jewish blood came not from his mother's but from his father's side. But this is at variance with Heydrich's family tree. According to it the alleged Sarah Heydrich was actually named Ernestine Wilhelmine, née Lindner. After the early death of her first husband she had married a certain Robert Süss in Meissen. Just as Heydrich's father, as a result of this union, was at times called Bruno Heydrich-Süss, and, since the name had a Jewish ring, was widely known as 'Isidor Süss' among his colleagues, so possibly his mother was called by the name 'Sarah'. In that event this name would of course not have appeared in any circumstances on the gravestone. The author is indebted to the Berlin pianist Helmut Maurer for the information that Bruno Heydrich was called Isidor Süss by his colleagues in Halle. Maurer, who was at that time in Canaris' department as a 'civilian employee of the Wehrmacht High Command,' emphasised in a memorandum that he had obtained copies of incriminating documentary evidence about Heydrich's descent as late as 1940 from the Registry Office for Civil Marriages in Halle. But Maurer also says that if his memory serves him rightly, Heydrich had Jewish blood on his father's side. Maurer's statement further contradicts Hagen's claim that Heydrich had early on got rid of all compromising evidence of his antecedents. This discrepancy will probably never be cleared up. In fact, it is not unreasonable to suppose that Heydrich had tried by the means at his disposal to remove all incriminating documents from church and registry offices. See also the result of the research which Robert M. W. Kempner undertook in Nuremberg and recorded in his book *Eichmann und Komplizen*.

In an inaugural dissertation at the Free University of Berlin in 1967, 'Heydrich und die Anfänge des SD und der Gestapo (1931–1935),' Shlomo Aronson disputes that Heydrich was of Jewish descent at all. The evidence and references he presents are not unpersuasive, though the author is not at the moment in a position to verify them.

The meaning and substance of the foregoing attempt at an interpretation of Heydrich's personality, however, are not affected by the dispute about his origins. It is beyond dispute, reinforced by Aronson's addition of numerous pieces of evidence, that Heydrich attributed Jewish forebears to himself or at least was by no means certain of his antecedents. According to information from Heydrich's sister-in-law, Frau Gertrud Heydrich, he was teased about his alleged Jewish origin even as a schoolboy, constantly felt a strong need for racial compensation, which found expression in belonging to nationalist anti-Semitic circles, and finally, was considered 'more or less a Jew' in the Navy, as one of his Navy comrades later declared. Evidently assuming that his father was a Jew, Heydrich invented as a defence against his comrades the story that his father had been a foundling who was brought to Dresden by gypsies, where, appearing as a musical prodigy, he was subsequently co-opted by the director of the Dresden Conservatory into his family. Even today friends and former comrades of Heydrich are convinced of his Jewish antecedents. For this and other similar information, see Aronson, 'Heydrich'.

Historically it is no doubt important to know whether or not proof exists of Heydrich's alleged Jewish descent. From a psychological standpoint, on the other hand, for the purpose of interpreting his personality, it is of less importance whether Heydrich did in fact have Jewish forebears or whether he and the people around him assumed that he had, i.e., thought it possible. Felix Kersten's *Memoirs* have so far stood up to all checks. They leave no doubt that Himmler considered Heydrich's Jewish descent established fact. Even if this was a misconception, it does not alter any consideration or conclusion stated here.

12 See Hagen, *The Secret Front*. Heydrich had had an affair with the daughter of an influential merchant in Kiel, who had personal contacts with the naval authorities and particularly with Admiral Raeder. According to the popular account of the details which brought about the break, the girl became pregnant and Heydrich refused to marry her since it was not compatible with the honour of a German officer to marry a pregnant woman, even when he himself was responsible. However, this seems to be an invention inspired by caricatures of the German reserve lieutenant, such as Heinrich Mann's *Untertan*. On the other hand Charles Wighton, basing himself on Frau Lina Heydrich, says in his book on Heydrich that by the time it became known that the merchant's daughter was pregnant, Heydrich was already engaged to his future wife and refused to break off this engagement.

13 Kersten, *Memoirs*.

14 *Ibid*.

15 Hagen, *The Secret Front*, cites the outstanding example of Heinrich Müller, the Chief of Department Number IV in the RSHA (Gestapo) and a person noted for his air of secrecy, who until 1933 had even been an outspoken opponent of National Socialism. Frau Heydrich's remark about her husband's lack of political interest in the 1920s is recorded by Charles Wighton, *Heydrich*. It was also Frau Heydrich who, having joined the NSDAP before her husband, awakened Heydrich's interest in politics.

16 Recorded by Carl Jacob Burckhardt, *Meine Danziger Mission*.

17 Kersten, *Memoirs*.

18 This salon went by the name of 'Salon Kitty'; see Schellenberg, *The Labyrinth*.

19 Wighton, *Heydrich*; also Hagen, *Secret Front*, and Schellenberg, *Labyrinth*.

20 See Frischauer's remarks, *Himmler*. Hagen notes in his book that Heydrich 'once developed the theory that the posts of Führer and Reich Chancellor should be separated, by which he meant that the Führer should be relegated to the titular role of a President of the Reich. The Reich Chancellor, on the other hand, would be the man with the real power in his hands, and this was the job he fancied for himself. But Heydrich was no mere dreamer. He did not merely toy with such ideas, but calculatingly chose his objective and worked for it with a systematic planning worthy of the General Staff itself.' See also Schellenberg, *Labyrinth*. Elsewhere Schellenberg describes the cross-examination to which Himmler subjected him a few days after Heydrich's death. The Reichsführer SS asked, 'Did you persuade Heydrich that he was once the only man to be considered as a successor to the Führer? Heydrich himself had given me to understand this, though only fragmentarily.'

21 See Haensel, *Das Gericht vertagt sich*. Ulrich von Hassell noted in *The Von Hassell Diaries*, entry for March 27, 1939, a remark of Frau Göring according to which Heydrich was 'the devil,' Himmler, on the other hand, 'entirely unimportant and basically harmless!' In the same vein see also Schellenberg and Hagen; in a different vein but rather implausible, Edward Crankshaw, *The Gestapo*.

22 Kersten, *Memoirs*.

23 Wighton, *Heydrich*.

24 Hagen, *Secret Front*; Schellenberg, *Labyrinth*.

25 Arendt, *Origins of Totalitarianism*, which analyses the whole scope of the subject of terror and totalitarianism. Hardly anything more emphatically demonstrates the totalitarian character of the National Socialist regime than the observation that the two most astonishing careers (apart from Bormann's, which was due to other factors) were made via the Political Police.

26 See Karl Heinz Abshagen, *Canaris*. According to Maurer's memorandum referred to in note 11 above, Canaris invited Heydrich to his house one evening to let him know 'in all friendliness' that he had managed to come into possession of the incriminating evidence about his antecedents. Heydrich, so Maurer continues, 'smilingly took note of this and from then on his behaviour changed towards us. He got the point and left us alone.' This description agrees with statements made by Wilhelm Stuckart, former State Secretary at the Ministry of the Interior, to Robert M. W. Kempner. Indeed Stuckart says that Canaris, because he possessed these documents, could protect himself 'from Heydrich's clutches'; see Kempner, *Eichmann and Komplizen*. Abshagen has another interpretation which treats this version sceptically, since according to irreproachable witnesses 'from among his acquaintances,' Canaris was always afraid of Heydrich. But this is by no means contradictory. Naturally Heydrich remained an extremely dangerous opponent even after Canaris had secured the evidence.

27 The participation of the German Secret Service in the Tukhachevsky affair, particularly the extent of such participation, is still being disputed. An unsigned study appearing in the periodical *Die Gegenwart*, Vol. 13, arrived at the following carefully balanced conclusion which for the time being must no doubt remain the last word on this affair: 'The probability approaching certainty is that the Tukhachevsky affair was not engineered by the leaders of the Third Reich. On the other hand it can be assumed with the same degree of probability approaching certainty that the rulers of the Third Reich had a finger in the Tukhachevsky affair. It is extremely probable that they sought to contribute to the downfall of Marshal Tukhachevsky. It is almost established fact that they boasted of this. It is possible that Heydrich and his accomplices were the passive and unconscious tools of Stalin.'

28 Walter Hagen, *Unternehmen Bernhard. Ein historischer Tatsachenbericht über die grösste Geldfälschungsaktion aller Zeiten* (Wels and Starnberg, 1955).

29 Hagen, *Secret Front*. Walter Schellenberg, *Labyrinth*, and Rudolf Diels, *Lucifer ante portas*, report an attempt by Heydrich to poison them.

30 *Cf. IMT*, XII (statement by Gisevius). Himmler explained in his memorial speech quoted here from a photocopy of the Institut für Zeitgeschichte in Munich: 'But I know from countless conversations with Heydrich what this man, who was compelled to be outwardly so hard and severe, had inwardly often suffered and had to contend with, and what price he had to pay to make decisions and act according to the law of the SS, which obliges us "to spare neither our own nor the blood of others if the life of the nation demands it".' See also Burckhardt, *Meine Danziger Mission*.

31 See Reitlinger, *Final Solution*; also Hagen, *Secret Front*.

32 Kersten, *Memoirs*. The remark to Schellenberg is recorded by Charles Wighton, *Heydrich*. The essay of Heydrich's referred to was published as a special reprint from the *Schwarze Korps*.

33 Kersten, *Memoirs*; also Schellenberg, *Labyrinth*.

34 Hagen, *Secret Front*. The view that Canaris's fears also played a part is put forward by Maurer in his memorandum. Hitler's statement that Heydrich went to Prague as his 'Duke of Alva' was made by Otto Meissner in *Staatssekretär unter Ebert–Hindenburg–Hitler*. The visit to the Führer's headquarters mentioned in the text below is described by Schellenberg, *Labyrinth*. On the Himmler–Heydrich relationship see *Labyrinth*; also Hagen, *Secret Front*, and Gerald Reitlinger, *The SS, Alibi of a Nation*.

35 Frischauer, *Himmler*; also Wenzel Jaksch, *Europe's Road to Potsdam* (London and New York, 1964), and Wighton, *Heydrich*. See also Hitler's remark noted by Goebbels in his *Diaries* that Heydrich's policy in the Protectorate was 'truly a model one' (entry for January 21, 1942). On such remarks by Hitler, Himmler

commented to his masseur, Felix Kersten: 'Heydrich was one of the few men who knew the right way to treat a foreign nation. If he had trampled on the Czechs with hobnailed boots, the English secret service would have kept a careful watch to see that nothing happened to him' (*Memoirs*). On Heydrich's policy see also *The Goebbels Diaries*, entry for February 15, 1942.

36 Kersten, *Memoirs*.

37 See *Abschlussbericht. Attentat auf den SS-Obergruppenführer Heydrich am 27/5/1942 in Prag*, Appendix D, at the Institut für Zeitgeschichte in Munich, No. 1982/57.

38 See Alexander Mitscherlich and Fred Mielke, *Doctors of Infamy: The Story of the Nazi Medical Crimes* (New York, 1949).

39 Schellenberg, *Labyrinth*.

40 Achim Besgen, *Der stille Befehl. Medizinalrat Kersten, Himmler und das Dritte Reich* (Munich, 1960).

41 See Frischauer, *Himmler*. Schellenberg used to emphasise moreover that Heydrich would not have hesitated to liquidate Hitler himself if he had lived to see the progression towards total disaster. But this assumption is evidently based on an overestimation of the power which Heydrich could have mobilised. On the other hand Aronson (see note 11 above) feels that Heydrich was an insignificant, thoroughly dependent, authority-needing bureaucratic figure; he disputes the idea put forward here of the peculiarly ambivalent relationship between Himmler and Heydrich. Instead he argues Himmler's personal, tactical and administrative superiority. As far as Heydrich is concerned, he gives, I believe, too great weight to the statements of former comrades, particularly those in the Navy; for their remarks on Heydrich's average intelligence, his unremarkableness, and his unimpressive personality were vitiated by the common observation that he had been intolerably taciturn and arrogant. The author's remaining observations are predominantly interpretations of behaviour patterns from which deductions with a different emphasis could also be drawn. Aronson's conclusions are only to be contested to the extent that they seek to deny Heydrich almost any individual significance. There is no question that Heydrich knew himself to be curiously inferior to Himmler and this, in the author's view, is related primarily to Heydrich's unsureness about his origin.

42 Burckhardt, *Meine Danziger Mission*.

43 Rauschning, *Voice of Destruction*.

44 Kersten, *Memoirs*.

Heinrich Himmler – Petty Bourgeois and Grand Inquisitor

1 One of the two death masks appeared in *Time* magazine in the summer of 1945.

2 Heinrich Himmler, *Die Schutzstaffel als antibolschewistische Kampforganisation* (Munich, 1936). *Gnadelos* (merciless) was apparently one of Himmler's favourite words, for it appears in many of his speeches, often several times over.

3 Speer's judgment is reported by Alexander Dallin, *German Rule in Russia 1941–1945*. Walter Schellenberg notes in *The Labyrinth* that Himmler in fact used to give marks. Friedrich Hossbach, *Zwischen Wehrmacht und Hitler*, and Graf Folke Bernadotte, *The Curtain Falls* (British title: *The Fall of the Curtain*; New York and London, 1945) make similar remarks. See also the various assessments collected by Gerald Reitlinger in his book *The SS, Alibi of a Nation*. Actually, one would suspect that a person of stronger susceptibility than Himmler would probably have been incapable of perfecting this type of extermination system. See Conrad–Martius, *Utopien der Menschenzüchtung*.

4 Walter Dornberger, *V2* (London and New York, 1954), quoted by Edward

Crankshaw, *The Gestapo*. The Englishman Stephen H. Roberts described Himmler as 'a man of exquisite courtesy and still interested in the simple things of life. He has none of the pose of those Nazis who act as demigods. . . . No man looks less like his job than this police dictator of Germany . . .' (quoted by Arendt, *Origins of Totalitarianism*).

5 Trevor-Roper, *Last Days of Hitler*.
6 Burckhardt, *Meine Danziger Mission*.
7 Schellenberg, *Labyrinth*. For more details of these conceptual complexes see particularly Felix Kersten, *Memoirs*.
8 *Mein Kampf*.
9 Domarus, Hitler, Vol. I.
10 Trevor-Roper, *Last Days of Hitler*.
11 Himmler's speech to the SS Group Leaders' Conference in Poznan on October 4, 1943; *IMT*, XXIX, 1919–PS.
12 Karl O. Paetel, 'Die SS. Ein Beitrag zur Soziologie des Nationalsozialismus,' *VJHfZ*, 1954, No. 1.
13 *Ibid*.
14 Kersten, *Memoirs*.
15 *Ibid*.
16 Stephen H. Roberts, quoted by Arendt, *Origins of Totalitarianism*.
17 *IMT*, XXIX, 1919–PS. This text is by no means exceptional in character. Many of the themes which appear here, from his conceptions of harshness to his child-kidnapping complex, appear in other speeches too. See Himmler's speech to a conference of commanding officers in Bad Schachen on October 14, 1943, *IMT*, XXXVII, 070–L, or his memorandum of May 1940 on the treatment of racial aliens in the East, reprinted in *VJHfZ*, 1957, No. 2. The reference to Herder's pernicious influence is also found in the speech which Himmler gave to the field headquarters at Hegewald on September 16, 1942; see Jacobson and Jochmann, *Ausgewählte Dokumente*.
18 Kersten, *Memoirs*. See also Schellenberg, *Labyrinth*. Dr Karl Gebhardt, a friend of Himmler's youth and head of Hohenlychen sanatorium, explained at the Nuremberg doctors' trial (Report S.3991): 'Himmler came from Landshut, the same town as myself. . . . If my parents' house was an extraordinarily liberal, free, quiet one, then the Himmler house was that of a strong, orthodox Catholic schoolmaster whose son was brought up very strictly and kept very short of money.' See further George W. F. Hallgarten, 'Mein Mitschüler Heinrich Himmler. Eine Jugenderinnerung,' *Germania–Judaica. Bulletin der Kölner Bibliothek zur Geschichte des deutschen Judentums*, No. 2, 1960/61.
19 Kersten, *Memoirs*.
20 Himmler's speech to the NSDAP Reichsleiters and Gauleiters in Poznan on August 3, 1944, in *VJHfZ*, 1953, No. 4.
21 For the Quedlinburg speech, see *Das Archiv, Nachschlagewerk für Politik, Wirtschaft, Kultur*, July 1936; the other quotation comes from Himmler, *Die Schutzstaffel*.
22 At any rate, according to Joseph Wulf, *Heinrich Himmler. Eine biographische Studie* (Berlin, 1960).
23 See the chapter 'Reinhard Heydrich – The Successor.' The reference to the SS having 52,000 members on January 30, 1933, is found in Gunther d'Alquen, *Die SS. Geschichte, Aufgabe und Organisation der Schutzstaffeln der NSDAP* (Berlin, 1939).
24 See *Dokumente der deutschen Politik*, Vol. IV. Actually June 30, 1934 is one of the most crucial dates in the history of National Socialism, certainly not much less far-reaching than, for example, January 30, 1933; for it not only marked the elimination of all oppositional stirrings, whether within the SA, the Wehrmacht or the bourgeoisie, and swept away the last guarantees of the due process of law

by Hitler's appointment of himself as supreme judge, but also opened to the SS the way to their later power. At the end of the 1930s Himmler was in actual fact the most powerful man of the regime after Hitler. Stalin, at the signing of the Moscow Agreement, proposed in addition to a toast to Hitler a toast to Himmler as the 'guarantor of order in Germany'; see Rosenberg, *Politisches Tagebuch*, entry for October 5, 1959.

25 Paetel, 'Die SS'.
26 From the statutes of the Association, composed by Himmler; see *IMT*, XXVI, 488–PS.
27 See Eugen Kogon, *The Theory and Practice of Hell*. Kogon believes, however, that 'in the quagmire of SS corruption . . . it is very seldom that anyone was destroyed' and points out that here too the candid phrase only concealed the truth. Thus Himmler, in the most famous case of corruption in the history of the SS, had tried for a long time to defend Koch, the commandant of Buchenwald and chief accused, against the charges of SS Obergruppenführer Prinz Waldeck, who finally succeeded, in his capacity as supreme SS and police chief of the regional division to which Buchenwald was attached, in setting proceedings in motion. But this was only after Koch had become 'a public burden on the SS'. See also *IMT*, XLII, Affidavits SS–64 and SS–65.
28 *IMT*, XXIX, 1919–PS.
29 This point was made particularly by Kogon, *Theory and Practice of Hell*, and subsequently by Hannah Arendt as part of her analysis of totalitarianism.
30 Paetal, 'Die SS'. See also the chapter 'Ernst Röhm and the Lost Generation'.
31 *IMT*, XXIX, 1918–PS. From the same speech comes the remark: 'He [the Russian] only counts because of his numbers, and these numbers have to be trampled to death, killed, butchered. To use for once a brutal example, it is as with a pig that is being killed and must gradually bleed to death.'
32 Speech in Bad Schachen, *IMT*, XXXVII, 070–L.
33 Schwerin von Krosigk, *Es geschah in Deutschland*.
34 Himmler in his Poznan speech: 'We have developed according to the law of selection. We have chosen the élite from among a cross-section of our people. . . . We have gone partly by external appearance and then have . . . tested appearance against continually new requirements, continually new tests, physical and mental, of character and of spirit. We have again and again sought out and cast off what doesn't meet these requirements. . . . We are pledged whenever we come together to remind ourselves of our fundamentals, race, selection, hardness' (*IMT*, XXIX, 1919–PS).
35 See *Aufbau*, No. 34 (New York, 1946).
36 Kersten, *Memoirs*.
37 *Ibid.*
38 Kogon, *Theory and Practice of Hell*; *VJHfZ*, 1957, No. 2.
39 Werner T. Angress and Bradley F. Smith, *Diaries of Heinrich Himmler's Early Years*, quoted by Wolfgang Sauer in Bracher, Sauer and Schulz, *Die national-sozialistische Machtergreifung*.
40 Like Dr Kurt Schilling, who sought to develop a malaria serum in Dachau by experimenting on prisoners; see Gilbert, *Nuremberg Diary*. Moreover, this research was part of that far-reaching endeavour to build a 'special SS science'; see Mitscherlich and Mielke, *Doctors of Infamy*. Mention here must also be made of the so-called Freundeskreis Himmler, a gathering of predominantly industrial patrons of the SS. Several members of this circle apparently passed on to Himmler and the quacks who surrounded him a few concrete suggestions in consideration of the fact that human research in the concentration camps presented an unrivalled opportunity to shorten protracted and costly tests; see Mitscherlich and Mielke, *Doctors*; also

the analytically cliché-ridden but factually informative article by Klaus Drobisch, 'Der Freundeskreis Himmler. Ein Beispiel für die Unterordnung der Nazipartei und des faschistischen Staatsapparats durch die Finanzoligarchie,' *Zeitschrift für Geschichtswissenschaft*, No. 2 (East Berlin, 1960).

41 Kersten, *Memoirs;* Himmler also used to enjoy identifying himself with history, which he believed to be 'unsentimental'; see *VJHfZ*, 1953, No. 4.

42 Himmler's statements on the SS State of Burgundy appear in the English but not the German edition of Kersten's *Memoirs*. Here the text mentioned by Paetel in 'Die SS' is taken as a basis. Besgen's book *Der stille Befehl* contains still other material than the German or English edition of Kersten's *Memoirs*. Alsace-Lorraine too played a significant part in the SS concept of the future, particularly as a settlement area; see Paul Kluke, 'Nationalsozialistische Europaideologie,' *VJHfZ*, 1955, No. 3.

43 Kersten, *Memoirs*; on the other hand Himmler was reduced to a state of utmost distress by every critical remark made by Hitler, which, as Kersten notes, to some extent caused violent physical reactions. For him as for most of his leading colleagues, each visit to the Führer's headquarters was like sitting an examination.

44 Schellenberg, *Labyrinth*. Similarly Burckhardt, *Meine Danziger Mission*, notes that Himmler tried at times to transform his gaze 'into a stiff, hypnotic stare in imitation of certain distinguished persons'.

45 Kersten, *Memoirs*.

46 See among others Allen Welsh Dulles, *Germany's Underground*; also Reitlinger, *The SS*. The long vindication passage in the speech Himmler gave to the Reichsleiters and Gauleiters on August 4, 1944 (*VJHfZ* 1953, No. 4) also has a suspect ring.

47 Quoted by Wulf, *Heinrich Himmler*. Masur answered Himmler's greeting: 'There is too much blood between us for that. But I thank you for authorising me to come and I hope that our meeting will save the lives of many men.' In fact Masur succeeded in freeing several thousand prisoners.

48 Walter Lüdde-Neurath, *Regierung Dönitz. Die letzten Tage des Dritten Reiches* (Göttingen, 1953). On the remaining details of Himmler's last weeks see the previously cited works by Schellenberg, Reitlinger, Wulf and Folke Bernadotte and the memoirs and statements of those involved. Possibly Himmler's lack of realism and his indecision at the end were due also to Heydrich's death. That this incident had a lasting effect on him and his position is incontestable, and Göring said that after the death of Heydrich 'anything was possible against Himmler'; see Haensel.

49 Noted by Schellenberg; see Bernadotte, *The Curtain Falls*.

50 Statement by Ohlendorf, quoted by Reitlinger, *Final Solution*. Also, Schwerin von Krosigk sought to make it clear to the Reichsführer of the SS that the only honourable course was for him to declare himself and take responsibility for the SS. But Himmler refused. See Reitlinger, *The SS*. Albert Speer also tried to get Himmler to do this; see *IMT*, Speer–49, W. Baumbach's statement.

51 Kersten, *Memoirs*.

52 Rudolf Höss, *Commandant of Auschwitz*. In fact, in the last phase Himmler completely abandoned his ideological justifications. To Masur he sought to justify the extermination measures with the argument that they had been necessitated by the danger of contagious infection to German troops: 'The Jewish masses were infected with terrible epidemics; in particular, spotted typhus raged. I myself have lost thousands of my best SS men through these epidemics. Moreover the Jews helped the partisans. . . . In order to put a stop to the epidemics we were forced to burn the bodies of incalculable numbers of people who had been destroyed by disease. We were therefore forced to build crematoria, and on this account they are knotting a noose for us' (quoted by Reitlinger, *Final Solution*).

53 *IMT*, XXIX, 1919–PS.

Martin Bormann – The Brown Eminence

1   This term is used by Hannah Arendt, who has devoted a chapter to this topic in *The Origins of Totalitarianism*, to which the author is greatly indebted. She also shows that the characteristic amorphousness as well as the duplication and finally multiplication of authorities and/or institutions is a phenomenon which in greater or lesser degree is common to both Soviet and National Socialist systems of government. This impressive book, however, at times elevates abstraction to principle, particularly in this section. Thus the description of the structure of totalitarian systems sometimes seems like the description of the conditions a totalitarian regime would have to fulfil to be completely totalitarian, while the author's point of departure is that this has already been the National Socialist (or Soviet) reality. She evidently believes the technicians of totalitarianism capable of boundless diabolical ingenuity and often sees design and system in what was in reality only fortuitousness and not infrequently also slovenliness, ignorance, indifference, etc., factors which doubtless play a more important part in the decisions or behaviour of totalitarian systems than is commonly realised.

2   Buchheim, *Totalitarian Rule*, especially the chapter on totalitarian rule and the state. The technique of confusion under discussion was still further perfected through the division of authority along functional lines which cut through the traditional geographical divisions, created new aggregations, overlapped, etc. The territories of the Hitler Youth, for example, had nothing in common with the *Gaue*, which in turn had nothing in common with the geographical structure and position of the SA staff districts, the SS leadership districts, etc., while all of these together ran entirely counter to the division of the *Länder*. See Arendt, *Origins of Totalitarianism*.

3   The concept *Geheime Staatspolizei* (State Secret Police) appears to contradict this position, for it obviously links the Gestapo with the state. However, this is shown to be only another terminological obscurity. Reinhard Höhn has also pointed out in this connection that 'the command of the Secret Police . . . was taken over by a community of men originating and firmly established within the movement. Thus the fact that the word "Staatspolizei" does not really take account of this should be mentioned' (see *Grundfragen der deutschen Polizei*, quoted by Arendt, *Origins*).
    The expression 'the party dictates to the state,' which became familiar in the process of seizing power, described the true situation much more accurately. If it continued to exist alongside the later, also statutorily established, formula of the 'unity of party and state,' this only demonstrated anew the regime's indifference or intent to confuse in the matter of jurisdiction. Though of course the party, or more correctly the movement, had no original right of command; that right lay only with Hitler personally. See in this connection the somewhat artificial system of preponderant powers which Franz Neumann has developed in his book *Behemoth. The Structure and Practice of National Socialism*. Neumann exaggerates the importance of jurisdiction and pays too little attention to the decisive importance of personal relationships in totalitarian systems. Often the authority of a group or institution was dependent on the (still precarious) position which its representative at that time held at Hitler's court. See further on this Hans Buchheim, 'Der Stellvertreter des Führers' in *Gutachten des Instituts für Zeitgeschichte*.

4   Arendt, *Origins*.

5   *The Bormann Letters. The Private Correspondence between Martin Bormann and his Wife from January 1943 to April 1945*, letter of September 10, 1943. The rights to these letters were acquired shortly after the end of the war by François Genoud, the Swiss lawyer who also owns legal rights to other National Socialist source

material and has thus become a sort of literary executor of National Socialism. Bormann's letters have appeared in an English edition, though so far not in a German one.

6　*Hitler's Private Testament*, quoted by Bullock, *Hitler*. Bormann was in all respects Göring's mirror image, his character in photographic negative, so to speak. In fact he pursued Göring right to the end with an extraordinary hate, and the decline in power which Göring experienced was doubtless due in large measure to Bormann's machinations.

7　Rosenberg, *Letzte Aufzeichnungen*.

8　Bormann was labelled 'Hitler's evil spirit' in the report of one of Hitler's secretaries recorded by Albert Zoller. Alfred Rosenberg, *Letzte Aufzeichnungen*, and Hans Frank, *Im Angesicht des Galgens*, have drawn from this the aforementioned conclusion that Bormann had corrupted Hitler, an idea which could only have been dreamt up by naïve National Socialists like Frank and Rosenberg.

9　Frank, *Im Angesicht des Galgens*.

10　Hildegard Springer, *Das Schwert auf der Waage*.

11　Trevor-Roper, *Last Days of Hitler*. See also Göring's remark to G. M. Gilbert, recorded in the latter's *Nuremberg Diary*.

12　Zoller, *Hitler privat*; also Heinrich Hoffmann, *Hitler Was My Friend*, who reports Hitler's passionate defence of Bormann in the course of which he said 'to win this war I need Bormann' and 'Whoever is against Bormann is also against the state.' Hoffmann writes that he had never seen Hitler so excited.

13　See Rosenberg, *Letzte Aufzeichnungen*: 'But Martin Bormann's path could not have been foreseen by the most audacious imagination.'

14　*The Goebbels Diaries*, entry for March 6, 1943.

15　*The Bormann Letters*, letter of November.4, 1944.

16　Bormann was born on June 17, 1900, in Halberstadt, the son of a post office employee and former regimental sergeant-major.

17　For a full account of this affair see Emil Julius Gumbel, *Verräter verfallen der Feme. Opfer, Mörder, Richter 1919–1929* (Berlin, 1929). Bormann, who was jailed for his part in it, later had his biographers spread the version that 'antipathy to the November system' had brought him a year of imprisonment in 1924; see the article 'Profile der Zeit. Reichsleiter Martin Bormann,' *Deutsche Ukrainerzeitung*, September 3, 1942. Also *Münchener Neueste Nachrichten*, June 18, 1940, in an anniversary note in honour of his fortieth birthday.

18　See respectively Schellenberg, *Labyrinth*, and Frank, *Im Angesicht des Galgens*.

19　Frank, *Im Angesicht des Galgens*.

20　Rosenberg, *Letzte Aufzeichnungen*. Also Schwerin von Krosigk, *Es geschah in Deutschland*.

21　In the judicial proceedings at Linz it was established that the whole Obersalzberg complex consisted of 87 buildings valued at about 1.5 million marks. See in this connection the generally not very satisfactory biography by Joseph Wulf, *Martin Bormann. Hitlers Schatten*; also Dietrich, *Hitler*.

22　Semmler, *Goebbels*.

23　On the change of function of the office see Hans Buchheim, 'Stellvertreter des Führers'.

24　Zoller, *Hitler privat*.

25　Semmler, *Goebbels*; Oven, *Mit Goebbels bis zum Ende*, Vol. II.

26　Schellenberg, *Labyrinth*.

27　See Schwerin von Krosigk, *Es geschah in Deutschland*; Frank, *Im Angesicht des Galgens*.

28　Zoller, *Hitler privat*.

29　*The Bormann Letters*, marginal note on a letter of Gerda Bormann of February 4, 1944.

30 H. R. Trevor-Roper, 'Martin Bormann,' *Der Monat*, No. 68, May 1954. On the whole question see also *IMT*, XXIX, 2100–PS. Already by the beginning of 1942 Bormann was able to put through a regulation whereby the participation of the party in all acts of legislation, appointments, promotions, etc. was to take place exclusively in consultation with him.

31 *IMT*, XXXV, 075–D.

32 *Ibid.* Ulrich von Hassell, *Diaries*, has accurately stated: 'Moreover his line of argument shows a lack of education and an idiotic falsification of history that would be hard to beat.' On the whole question of National Socialist religious policy, see Buchheim, *Totalitarian Rule*, and Karl Bracher in Bracher, Sauer and Schulz, *Die nationalsozialistische Machtergreifung*.

33 *The Bormann Letters*. Gerda Bormann was the daughter of Major Walter Buch, president of the Party Tribunal. Bormann had married her in 1929 and had by her ten children, for whom he always seemed extraordinarily solicitous. See Wulf, *Martin Bormann*. As emerges from the correspondence, Bormann not only sent his wife's letters back home to be kept, but also the love letters from M: a bureaucrat through and through, who locked even romance into a filing cabinet.

34 See Buchheim, 'Stellvertreter des Führers'. Frank, *Im Angesicht des Galgens*, maintains that Bormann even had to order the return of already distributed copies of his letter to the Gauleiters when some of this information became public and caused considerable disquiet.

35 Springer, *Das Schwert auf der Waage*.

36 Bormann's note to Rosenberg of July 23, 1942; quoted by Léon Poliakov and Joseph Wulf, *Das Dritte Reich und seine Denker*.

37 See Poliakov and Wulf, *Denker*.

38 See Speer's remark quoted by Trevor-Roper, *Last Days of Hitler*; also Schellenberg, *Labyrinth*.

39 See Semmler, *Goebbels*. Semmler noted on November 20, 1943: 'I noticed for the first time that Goebbels admits to his intimates his weakness in relations with Bormann. He will not allow the slightest ill feeling to arise between himself and the head of the Party Chancellery.

'How inconsequent Goebbels can be. The day before yesterday he elaborated critically on Bormann's modest intellectual capacity. He called him a "primitive GPU type [OGPU]". Today he indicates that he is afraid of him!' And the next day Semmler remarks: 'Goebbels often feels that he has expressed himself too candidly about Bormann. At table he warned us once more not to pass on to anyone what was said there.'

On the Goebbels-Bormann struggle see also Trevor-Roper, 'Martin Bormann'. Incidentally, it was not only towards the end of the war that Bormann attempted to undermine the Propaganda Minister's position. As early as December 1941 Semmler noted: 'Bormann especially does what he can to increase the distance between them [Hitler and Goebbels]' (*Goebbels*, entry for December 12, 1941).

40 *The Bormann Letters*, letter of April 2, 1945.

41 *Ibid.*, letters of January 16 and July 6, 1943.

42 *Ibid.*, letter of October 7, 1944.

43 Affidavit by Else Krüger, *IMT*, XL, Bormann–12.

Ernst Röhm and the Lost Generation

1 The statement is found only in the first edition of Ernst Röhm's autobiography, published in Munich in 1928 under the title *Die Geschichte eines Hochverräters* (hereafter cited as *Hochverräter*); later editions omit it. The book is one of the

most significant sources for the early history of the movement up to 1925.

2 Rauschning, *Voice of Destruction*. Also on this subject, Hitler later remarked: 'He would have his security men at rallies haul out political opponents so roughly that the opposition press – which otherwise would have remained silent about the rallies – ended up reporting the physical injuries at NSDAP rallies and thus drew attention to them' (Picker, *Tischgespräche*). A vivid supplement to this is supplied by the memoirs of Hans Kallenbach, a member of the 'Stosstrupp Adolf Hitler 1923'. It says there of 'the men of the shock troop': 'All false sense of fair play and treading softly were alien to them. They remained faithful to might makes right, the old law of the club, and when hard pressed they were inhibited by no commandment. . . . When Josef Berchthold or his deputy Julius Schreck blew the whistle and the command "Shock troop – to the attack! Left, right, step out, forward, march!" called us to action, the fur started to fly and in minutes the streets and squares were swept clean of opponents. We always played rough when we were let loose, when Berchthold, Schreck and Maurice let go so that the sparks flew.' (Kallenbach, *Mit Adolf Hitler auf der Festung Landsberg*).

3 *Mein Kampf*. Elsewhere Hitler declared: 'We must struggle with ideas, but if necessary also with our fists' (speech in Munich, quoted in *Völkischer Beobachter*, November 22, 1922).

4 The expression 'double party' must of course be used carefully. If it does not describe exactly the unique structure of the movement, to some extent it makes evident something of the essence of this completely new-style creation in the history of political parties. At all events it puts an end to the popular idea that the NSDAP had been in fact the monolithic block that it seemed in retrospect. In addition it should be pointed out that a clear conceptual distinction and demarcation between the SA and the Political Organisation (PO) is hardly possible, since their functions were by no means rigorously separated. The distinction is most easily apprehended, at least in the early stages of the movement, from the divergent organisational structure – the SA following more a military, the PO a regular political party model – as well as from the psychological and sociological characteristics of their members. See further, Wolfgang Sauer in Bracher, Sauer and Schulz, *Die nationalsozialistische Machtergreifung*.

5 Konrad Heiden, *Adolf Hitler*, Vol. I, wrote up short summaries of some of these life histories. A certain divergence is evident at times purely from the fact that not all leading SA men took part in the war; several joined the Freikorps instead in their very early years, often right after school.

6 Edgar J. Jung wrote in *Die Herrschaft der Minderwertigen*: 'A good part of activist youth embraced radicalism. Not because of its ideas or aims, which were mostly non-existent, but in protest against the inactivity and dullness of bourgeois politicians. . . . One should realise that in Germany this is an expression of the characteristic feature of the twentieth century: the activist, prepared to play his part and make sacrifices, replacing the indifferent voter of feeble convictions who constitutes the last remnant of the formally democratic era. Activism versus quietism, liveliness versus dullness, is the battle cry of the new day, which is more stirred by feelings than governed by deliberations.' With all its one-sidedness, this view certainly touches upon one of the basic motives for this generation's alienation from society. On the psychology of the Freikorps see incidentally Ernst von Salomon, *Die Geächteten* (Berlin, 1933).

7 Röhm, *Hochverrater*. The remark originates with Field Marshal Freiherr von Bieberstein, who later likewise joined the SA. See Hofmann, *Der Hitlerputsch*.

8 Röhm, *Hochverräter*.

9 Röhm used the word in a pejorative sense on six different pages, and four times on one single page. A stylistic analysis of his memoirs brings to light character-

istic personality traits. After the word 'prudent', Röhm demonstrates a particular aversion for the word 'compromise', which is mostly used in conjunction with the epithets 'cowardly', 'insipid', etc. Words like 'objective', 'intellectual', 'bourgeois', or 'middle-class' as well as the word 'philistine', for which he has a particular predilection, in this context have for him an entirely negative connotation. In a positive context, particularly apropos of the evaluation of admired comrades, the following words are used: 'fresh', 'untroubled', 'strapping', 'honest', 'daredevil', 'ruthless', and finally, with particular frequency, 'faithful'.

10 Diels, *Lucifer ante portas.*
11 Captain Weiss in *Völkischer Kurier*, May 1, 1925; quoted by Röhm, *Hochverräter.*
12 Viktor Lutze, *Tagebuch*, reprinted in *Frankfurter Rundschau*, May 14, 1957.
13 See Heiden, *Adolf Hitler*, Vol. I.
14 With the addition that he claimed such primacy 'particularly . . . for the more closely defined framework of the National Socialist movement,' this demand still appeared in the 1934 edition of his memoirs, which must have looked to Hitler like a deliberate affront and was presumably meant as such.
15 Sauer, *Machtergreifung*; also Röhm, *Hochverräter*. Röhm developed his ideas fully in a speech which he made on December 7, 1933, to diplomats and representatives of the foreign press at the Adlon Hotel in Berlin; see Horkenbach, *1933.*
16 I. Kirkpatrick, *The Inner Circle*. Also Röhm, *Hochverräter.*
17 Röhm was occasionally called 'the machinegun king of Bavaria'; see Hofmann, *Der Hitlerputsch*. What quantities were involved becomes evident in view of the fact that 'of the material which was required and procured for the enlargement of the Army after Hitler's seizure of power, a third came from the Army stock "saved" by Röhm' (Bor, *Gespräche mit Halder*).
18 See *Mein Kampf*. This certainly did not prevent Hitler's swearing later at the Schweidnitz trial that SA stood for *Schutzabteilung*, 'Self-Defence Section'. On the exaggerations with which National Socialist propaganda, at Hitler's instigation, later embellished this meeting-hall battle, see Heinrich Bennecke, *Hitler und die SA.*
19 Röhm, *Hochverräter.*
20 Sauer, *Machtergreifung.*
21 Heiden, *Adolf Hitler*, Vol. I; see also Röhm, *Hochverräter.*
22 Bennecke, *Hitler und die SA*, Document 3.
23 Order of November 3, 1926, on 'SA and the Public (Propaganda),' quoted by Sauer, *Machtergreifung.*
24 Sauer, *Machtergreifung.*
25 Wilhelm Sauer, *Kriminologie als reine und angewandte Wissenschaft* (Berlin, 1950), quoted by Sauer, *Machtergreifung*. On this whole complex see Martin Broszat, 'Die Anfänge der Berlin NSDAP 1926/27,' *VJHfZ*, 1960, No. 1.
26 Letter of October 3, 1930, from Otto Wagener, interim chief of staff of the SA, to the deputy commander quoted by Sauer, *Machtergreifung.*
27 Quoted by Bennecke, *Hitler und die SA*, Document 13.
28 See Franz-Willing, *Die Hitlerbewegung*; also Sauer, *Machtergreifung*, and Broszat, 'Die Anfänge'.
29 Already in 1928 Röhm, reviewing his efforts in the early 1920s, had written: 'My speculations and aspirations were aimed solely at securing for Hitler dictatorial-political leadership and for Kriebel dictatorial-military leadership in the military groupings' (*Hochverräter*).
30 See Sauer, *Machtergreifung*, for further detailed material on this phase of the 'manhunt'. The four names cited subsequently in the text were also taken from there.
31 SA Sturmbannführer Schäfer, *Konzentrationslager Oranienburg* (Berlin, 1934).

The Berlin SA Commander, Karl Ernst, wrote the foreword to this publication, which was intended as an 'anti-Brown Book'.
32 *Mein Kampf.* Also Horkenbach, *1933.*
33 'Preussens Mission, Rede in der Sitzung der preussischen Landtags vom 18. Mai 1933,' quoted in Göring, *Reden und Aufsätze.*
34 Heiden, *History of National Socialism.* See also Karl O. Paetel, 'Die SS,' *VJHfZ*, 1954, No. 1.
35 I. Kirkpatrick, *The Inner Circle*; also Ernst Röhm, 'SA und deutsche Revolution,' *Nationalsozialistische Monatshefte*, Vol. 4, No. 39.
36 Rauschning, *Voice of Destruction.*
37 See Helmut Krausnick, *Der 30. Juni 1934. Bedeutung, Hintergründe, Verlauf*, supplement to *Das Parlament*, June 30, 1954; also Hermann Mau and Helmut Krausnick, *German History 1933–1945. An Assessment by German Historians* (London, 1959; Chester Springs, Pa., 1961).
38 Heiden, *Adolf Hitler*, Vol. I.
39 Frank, *Im Angesicht des Galgens.*
40 Rauschning, *Voice of Destruction.*
41 Hitler's Reichstag speech of July 13, 1934, quoted by Domarus, *Hitler*, Vol. I.

Part Three

FUNCTIONARIES OF TOTALITARIAN RULE

Franz von Papen and the Conservative Collaboration

1 See Wolfgang Sauer in Bracher, Sauer, and Schulz, *Die nationalsozialistische Machtergreifung.*
2 André François-Poncet, *The Fateful Years.*
3 According to Theodor Eschenburg's character analysis based on Papen's memoirs; see *VJHfZ*, 1953, No. 2. It is appropriate to note here at last that in this chapter the concept 'conservatism' is to be taken purely in its German Nationalist, status-conscious meaning. Neither the radical-intellectual spokesmen of conservatism (Jünger, Niekisch, Tatkreis, etc.) nor the military circles are included in this consideration.
4 See Bracher, *Auflösung der Weimarer Republik*; also for the role of Schleicher as well as that of the German Nationalist and upper agrarian circles in this change of government.
5 Franz von Papen, *Memoirs.* A contemporary National Socialist-inspired pamphlet about Papen reads: 'Much of his policy as a whole is explained by his impetuous urge for movement, change, speedy overriding of opponents; when in difficulty he seeks a tactic of outflanking or new attack, and not of settling in or self-entrenchment. At full gallop some adversities will perhaps be underestimated' (Wendt, *Hitler regiert*).
6 Reported by Hermann Foertsch, to whom Schleicher had made this comment around September 1932, after concluding a telephone conversation with Papen; see Bracher, *Auflösung.*
7 Eschenburg, in *VJHfZ*, 1953, No. 2.
8 On the project of the New State, see the concise and excellent analysis by Bracher, *Auflösung*; also Sontheimer, *Antidemokratisches Denken in der Weimarer Republik.*
9 Sontheimer, *Antidemokratisches Denken.* This feudal political point of view, which

arrogantly denies rights of participation and codetermination to the public, is one of the dominating themes of a publication brought out by Papen under the title *Appell an das deutsche Gewissen. Reden zur nationalen Revolution.* In it he says, for example: 'Once it is claimed that everything wearing a human face already has the right to equality on this earth [!]; it need not be surprising if the collective idea [he means Bolshevism] grows to cover and stifle all of political existence'; and: 'It is nonsense and a misunderstanding of democracy if the exponents of the masses continuously try to have a say in running things. To be a statesman means first of all to be responsible to God, to history, and to one's conscience. Only then does one have to account publicly for one's actions.'

10 W. Schotte, *Der neue Staat* (Berlin, 1932), with a foreword by Papen; *cf.* Bracher, *Auflösung.*

11 Papen, *Memoirs.*

12 *Ibid.* Edgar J. Jung wrote on this: 'The attempt to centre the state's authority around the last great nobleman of Prussian coinage definitely foundered with Papen's cabinet' (*Sinndeutung der deutschen Revolution*).

13 For a brilliant analysis of the Alliance of Cologne, its formation, course and consequences, remorselessly dissecting Papen's attempts at self-justification, see Bracher, *Auflösung.* Out of the chorus of approving Nationalist Socialist voices let just one remark of Göring's be quoted: 'And it turned out that Herr von Papen, against whom we once had to fight on political grounds, had now recognised the importance of the hour. In sincere affection he concluded the alliance with us and became the honest broker between the venerable field marshal and the young lance corporal of the World War' (Göring, *Germany Reborn*).

14 Goebbels, *My Part in Germany's Fight*, entry for August 28, 1932. The affinity between the National Socialist *Weltanschauung* and the ideology of those spiritually at home in the *ancien régime* is especially clearly underlined in the collection of Papen's speeches.

15 Papen, *Memoirs.* For his decisive stance of opposition to the year 1789, see especially Papen, *Appell.*

16 Quoted in *Zwischenspiel Hitler.*

17 'They strut along in top hats and frock coats,' wrote Goebbels in September 1932 in an article entitled 'Politische Erbschleicherei,' 'but in reality they are people hungry for power and looking for prey, and since they are too weak and too cowardly to get it from their own field, they stay behind the fighting front to be able, when the real political army marches forward again, to practise behind the lines the worthy craft of the jackal. . . . That is the most naked, vulgar and indecent political selfishness that has ever existed in Germany' (Goebbels, *Wetterleuchten*).

Engrossed in his illusions of leadership, Papen also welcomed in a speech of February 24, 1933, 'the decisive fact that German youth, in this, is in our [!] camp'; see Papen, *Appell.*

18 See Paul Kluke, 'Der Fall Potempa,' *VJHfZ*, 1957, No. 3. Papen himself had incidentally also seen the difference between conservatism and National Socialism as a matter of tactics. 'It is no accident,' he declared on March 17, 1933, in a speech in Breslau, 'that not only the sensibilities and aims of National Socialism headed in the same direction, but that these conservative trains of thought also played a decisive part in National Socialist circles. The difference between the conservative revolutionary and the Nationalist Socialist movement was clearly one of tactics' (*Appell*).

19 Rauschning, *Revolution of Nihilism.*

20 Jung, *Sinndeutung.* See also Klemens von Klemperer, *Konservative Bewegungen zwischen Kaiserreich und Nationalsozialismus.*

21 Ewald von Kleist-Schmenzin, 'Die letzte Möglichkeit. Zur Ernennung Hitlers zum

Reichskanzler am 30. Januar 1933,' in *Politische Studien*, No. 106.
22 Heiden, *History of National Socialism*.
23 Speech to the Reichstag Party members on April 11, 1933, quoted by Erich Matthais and Rudolf Morsey, *Das Ende der Parteien, 1933* (Düsseldorf, 1960).
24 Karl Bracher, in Bracher, Sauer and Schulz, *Machtergreifung*.
25 See Meissner, *Staatssekretär*.
26 Jung, *Sinndeutung*; also Papen, *Memoirs* and *Appell*.
27 See Gerhard Schulz in Bracher, Sauer and Schulz, *Machtergreifung*: another voice expressing the attitude and expectation of the conservative camp that it was possible to be German in this movement with a clear conscience and without shame for one's character; see Sontheimer, *Antidemokratisches Denken*.
28 Papen, *Memoirs*.
29 For Hitler's speech at the victory Party Congress on September 1, 1933, see Horkenbach, *1933*; on Papen's 'education hopes', see Papen, *Memoirs*.
30 Michael Freund, *Deutsche Geschichte* (Gütersloh, 1960). The dual objective of the events of June 30, 1934 is made convincingly evident in Hitler's remarks as quoted by Rauschning in *Voice of Destruction*.
31 Schwerin von Krosigk, *Es geschah in Deutschland*.
32 Papen, *Memoirs*.
33 Quoted by Bernhard Schwertfeger, *Rätsel um Deutschland* (Heidelberg, 1948).
34 Papen, *Memoirs*. According to G. M. Gilbert, *Nuremberg Diary*, Papen expressed his astonishment at Nuremberg that 'the Allies had allowed Hitler for so long to lead them by the nose'. He also pleaded before the Tribunal the patriotic ideology of service: 'I have served not the Nazi regime but the Fatherland' (*IMT*, XXII).
35 *IMT*, XIX.
36 Rauschning, *Voice of Destruction*.
37 The most important scholarly achievement of this orientation is still Franz Neumann's work *Behemoth*.
38 Jung, *Sinndeutung*. In this formula, Jung continues, 'the apparent contradiction between revolutionary and conservative over which primitive thinkers are continually stumbling is solved'.
39 See *IMT*, XII.
40 Gilbert, *Nuremberg Diary*. When Gilbert asked if, for example, Papen could reconcile the Nuremberg decrees with his religious convictions, Papen replied that he was 'in Austria at the time and really did not pay too much attention to these things'.
41 Papen, *Appell*.
42 'I ask that it be taken into consideration that I am not speaking here for National Socialism. My defence will be that of the other Germany' (*IMT*, XVI).
43 Quoted by Schwertfeger, *Rätsel um Deutschland*.
44 Rauschning, *Voice of Destruction*, and Picker, *Tischgespräche*, entry for May 5, 1942. See also Harry Pross, *Die Zerstörung der deutschen Politik*.
45 See *IMT*, XVI.
46 Thomas Mann, *Germany and the Germans* (Washington, 1945).

Alfred Rosenberg: The Forgotten Disciple

1 Rosenberg, *Letzte Aufzeichnungen*.
2 Rauschning, *Revolution of Nihilism*.
3 Joseph Goebbels, *Wesen und Gestalt des Nationalsozialismus* (Berlin, 1935).
4 Rauschning, *Voice of Destruction*.
5 Frank, *Im Angesicht des Galgens*.

6 Hitler on September 6, 1938, to the cultural session of the Party Rally, quoted by Domarus, *Hitler*, Vol. I.

7 Rosenberg, *Politisches Tagebuch*. The idea is reiterated in something he wrote during his imprisonment at Nuremberg; see Serge Lang and Ernst von Schenck, eds, *Memoirs of Alfred Rosenberg*.

8 See Krebs, *Tendenzen und Gestalten der NSDAP*.

9 Among the more influential men in the early period of the movement, Hess, Rosenberg, Scheubner-Richter, Lüdecke and many other second-rank names, and above all Hitler himself, were not born in the so-called Old Empire. Also Darré, the future Minister of Food and Agriculture, his State Secretary Backe, and Gauleiter Bohle came from the so-called *Auslandsdeutschtum* (persons of German descent born or living beyond the borders of Germany).

10 Richter, *Unsere Führer im Lichte der Rassenfrage und Charakterologie*.

11 Rosenberg, *Letzte Aufzeichnungen*. Elsewhere he says that he had 'unwittingly had a chilling effect on many Southern Germans, who had perceived only irony in many a harmless remark'.

12 Krebs, *Tendenzen und Gestalten*.

13 *Ibid*.

14 Rosenberg, *Letzte Aufzeichnungen*. There he also makes the point that he had come to the Reich 'originally as a person entirely devoted to art, philosophy and history and without so much as a thought of ever dabbling in politics'.

15 The so-called *Protocols of the Elders of Zion* had been launched at the turn of the century by the Tsarist secret police as justification for the anti-Jewish pogroms. They were based on a polemic against Napoleon III which originated with a certain Maurice Joly, who had examined the authoritarian tactics of Machiavellian politics in the form of a *Dialogue in Hell Between Machiavelli and Montesquieu*. After the First World War this long-forgotten tract, in its altered form, enjoyed an unprecedented popularity in many countries. It alleged that an international Jewish conspiracy existed, its aim being world domination by means of infiltration into all the influential key positions in all countries.

16 *Das Werk Alfred Rosenbergs. Eine Bibliographie*, compiled by Karlheinz Rüdiger. Rüdiger also called *The Myth of the Twentieth Century* a 'landmark of . . . eternal Germanhood'. In fact the significance of this book has been very much over-estimated all around, and in a certain sense Rosenberg became a victim of his 'myth' (in both senses of the word) at Nuremberg. To a broad public the title of the book was a synonym for National Socialism. Douglas M. Kelley, the American Army doctor and psychiatrist, reflected this widely held misunderstanding when he wrote in *22 Cells in Nuremberg*: 'This opus was the foundation of his [Rosenberg's] prestige, a basic book of the Nazi Party, and the authority on all racial problems.'

17 Alfred Rosenberg, *Der Mythus des 20. Jahrhunderts*. See also Rosenberg, *Das Wesengefüge des Nationalsozialismus. Grundlagen der deutschen Wiedergeburt* (Munich, 1934).

18 See F. Th. Hart, *Alfred Rosenberg: Der Mann und sein Werk*.

19 Rosenberg, *Mythus*.

20 Rosenberg, *Politisches Tagebuch*. While Rosenberg in the foreword of this book objects to the description 'catechism', this is precisely what this thesis-like recapitulation of National Socialist philosophy is. Moreover, the phrase about the replacement of the rosary by the spade of the worker already appears in a modified form in *Mythus*. There, to be sure, it is the war monuments which replace 'the frightful baroque and rococo crucifixes which display distorted limbs at every street corner'.

21 See Krebs, *Tendenzen und Gestalten*; also Rosenberg, *Letzte Aufzeichnungen*.

22 Picker, *Tischgespräche*. Hitler maintained there too that only opponents of the party were genuinely knowledgeable about the book.

23 See Erich Ebermayer and Hans Roos, *Gefährten des Teufels* (Hamburg, 1952); also Gilbert, *Nuremberg Diary*.

24 See Rosenberg, *Politisches Tagebuch*.

25 'I had at that time the very definite feeling,' Rosenberg wrote later, 'that Hitler saw the dissension within the movement by no means with regret. He . . . fancied it would make his future effectiveness probably easier if he were not to confront a new and firmly established leadership but various splinter groups' (*Letzte Aufzeichnungen*).

26 Krebs, *Tendenzen und Gestalten*. Rosenberg himself was very much addicted to the 'belief in magic' with which he reproached Rome.

27 *Ibid.*

28 See Poliakov and Wulf, *Das Dritte Reich und seine Denker*, letters of August 30, 1934, to Goebbels against Stefan Zweig and Richard Strauss; also Rosenberg, *Politisches Tagebuch*. See also, as symptomatic of Rosenberg's quarrelsomeness, the further examples given by Poliakov and Wulf in regard to Ley, Hess and Bormann.

29 *IMT*, XVIII. On the function of the Foreign Department see Hart, *Alfred Rosenberg*. Rosenberg tried to make contact particularly with Scandinavian but also with Rumanian fascist circles.

30 Remark of Graf Baudissin, quoted by Dietrich Strothmann, *Nationalsozialistische Literaturpolitik*.

31 The unspeakable quotation that celebrates the thunder of cannon at Sédan not only as an expression of artistic value but also as being on a par with *eine Kleine Nachtmusik* comes from the Reich Theatrical Controller Rainer Schlösser, who was incidentally one of the chief lecturers in Rosenberg's Reich Centre for the Advancement of German Literature (referred to below), probably the most important control and censorship authority. On this whole complex see Dietrich Strothmann's excellent work, *Nationalsozialistische Literaturpolitik*, where the quotations are to be found.

32 Bettina Feistel-Rohmeder, who was one of the most merciless spokesmen for the popularly oriented destruction of culture; quoted by Paul Ortwin Rave, *Kunstdiktatur im Dritten Reich* (Hamburg, 1949).

33 Quoted by Rave, *Kunstdiktatur*; the demand was put forward by the *Deutsche Kunstkorrespondenz*, whose leader was Bettina Feistel-Rohmeder.

34 The Reich Centre for the Advancement of German Literature was later designated 'Office for the Encouragement of Literature' and subsequently 'Head Office, Literature.' See Strothmann, *Literaturpolitik*, also for the extension of the lecture staff, censorship measures, prohibited categories, etc.

35 Quoted by Karl Bracher in Bracher, Sauer and Schulz, *Die nationalsozialistische Machtergreifung*.

36 See Rosenberg, *Politisches Tagebuch*.

37 In *Letzte Aufzeichnungen* Rosenberg rapturously notes Hitler's verdict on the draft of a speech which he had put in front of him: 'It agrees to such an extent with my own speech that we might have discussed it previously.'

38 Lang and Schenck, *Rosenberg Memoirs*; on the same theme and with only slight variation, Rosenberg, *Letzte Aufzeichnungen*.

39 Lang and Schenck, *Rosenberg Memoirs*.

40 Rosenberg, *Politisches Tagebuch*.

41 *Ibid.*

42 See notes by Graf Metternich quoted by Poliakov and Wulf, *Das Dritte Reich und seine Denker*.

43 Léon Poliakov and Joseph Wulf, *Das Dritte Reich und die Juden*. The Führer's

edict on Rosenberg's appointment with responsibility for the 'Higher Schools' originated on January 24, 1940; see *IMT*, XXV, 136–PS.

44 *Cf.* Dallin, *German Rule in Russia*. Dallin's study supplies an abundance of insights into the structure of background rivalries.

45 In connection with the maliciously apt 'Cha-ostministerium' tag, Goebbels also criticised Rosenberg for his lack of organisational talent; see *The Goebbels Diaries*, entry for March 21, 1942. Semmler, *Goebbels*, reports the other remark.

46 *IMT*, XLI, Rosenberg–14. Rosenberg himself wrote in *Letzte Aufzeichnungen* of his relations with Hitler: 'In the course of the years a growing estrangement arose between the Führer and me. He brought in as trusted advisers men whose activities instilled in me an increasing measure of worry.'

47 *The Goebbels Diaries*, entry for February 27, 1942.

48 Kelley, *22 Cells*. Being overestimated had apparently always been Rosenberg's fate. Even before 1933 Weigand von Miltenberg cited in his book *Adolf Hitler Wilhelm III* the apparently widespread dictum, 'Hitler commands – what Rosenberg wants.' See *Zwischenspiel Hitler*. See also note 16 above.

49 Rosenberg, *Letzte Aufzeichnungen*.

50 See Arendt, *Origins of Totalitarianism*.

51 Rosenberg, *Letzte Aufzeichnungen*.

Joachim von Ribbentrop and the Degradation of Diplomacy

1 Karl Mannheim, *Mensch und Gesellschaft im Zeitalter des Umbaus* (Leiden, 1935); also Friedrich Meinecke, *The German Catastrophe*.

2 In the light of these hypotheses it becomes understandable for the first time why these rootless, petty bourgeois representatives of the masses gave Hitler's ambitious party its stamp and proved equal so quickly and convincingly to the technical demands of power. During these years were to be found, down to the lowest rungs of the party hierarchy, a profound knowledge of the workings of power that proved surprisingly capable of projecting these men to the top, seeing them successfully through their rivalries, and enabling them to secure and gradually extend their spheres of influence: in short, commanding the whole repertoire of Machiavellian tactics. Such knowledge, however, was accompanied in the majority of cases by extreme professional incompetence in the mastery of the positions thus gained, and only in exceptional cases did the outsiders who forced their way into the key positions of the state and society in 1933 breathe life into the generations-old office routines.

3 Erich Kordt has expressed this opinion in *Wahn und Wirklichkeit*; also Semmler in *Goebbels*.

4 Coulondre, *De Staline à Hitler*. The Spanish Foreign Minister Ramón Serrano Suñer took exception to Ribbentrop's 'arrogance and inflexibility' and said that the political progress of this man was a mystery to him (*Entre les Pyrénées et Gibraltar* [Geneva, 1947]). Georges Bonnet noted 'an affected politeness' in social intercourse in contrast to 'an unrefined and impersonal conduct' as soon as political questions were discussed (*Défense de la paix*).

5 Weizsäcker, *Memoirs*. In connection with his remark that discussions with Ribbentrop were impossible, the former State Secretary wrote: 'According to Bismarck shortsightedness in politics is less serious than farsightedness. But what we had here was no longer farsighted; it wandered off into a world of unrealities. It seemed to me . . . that it would have been better if my brother, Professor of Internal Medicine and Neurology at Heidelberg, had been attached to the minister in my place.' The other verdicts are to be found in Dietrich, *Hitler*; Schwerin von

Krosigk, *Es geschah in Deutschland*. Ribbentrop's tendency to engage in endless monologues was also observed by Burckhardt, *Meine Danziger Mission*.

6   The description of Ribbentrop as a 'second Bismarck' is reported by Dietrich, *Hitler*, and the remark that he was 'a genius' by Burckhardt, *Meine Danziger Mission*. The statement of his secretary, Margarete Blank, is to be found in *IMT*, X.

7   *IMT*, X; also Paul Schmidt, *Hitler's Interpreter*, who remarks that it 'never entered his head to consider him [Ribbentrop] either a statesman or a foreign minister'.

8   Schmidt, *Hitler's Interpreter*; also Ribbentrop, *Memoirs*. The statement variously attributed to Ribbentrop that he had felt in the Kremlin 'as though he were among old party comrades' is denied by him and ascribed to Forster, the Gauleiter of Danzig. But see Rosenberg, *Politisches Tagebuch*; also Weizsäcker, *Memoirs*. It is worth noting that Ribbentrop, in his description of Stalin's merits and important qualities, automatically falls into a vocabulary not unlike that which he employs in his worship of Hitler.

9   Coulondre, *De Staline à Hitler*.

10 See Kordt, *Wahn und Wirklichkeit*; also Frau von Ribbentrop's note in Ribbentrop, *Memoirs*.

11 Paul Schwarz, *This Man Ribbentrop: His Life and Times*, 2nd ed. (New York, 1943).

12 Semmler, *Goebbels*. On the aristocratic side of the Ribbentrop family only one descendant was still living after the First World War, Gertrud von Ribbentrop, by whom the future Foreign Minister was adopted. Until 1918 adoptions of this sort had no legal effect, and in particular the aristocratic title would not have passed on to Ribbentrop. But the Weimar Constitution stipulated that the noble prefix was a component of the name and could accordingly be acquired through adoption. However, the adopted person did not thus become ennobled but merely the bearer of a name encompassing the noble prefix 'von'. Ribbentrop's so-called ennoblement was completely fraudulent, as his letter to Count Maxence de Polignac also proves; in this, according to Paul Schwarz, *This Man Ribbentrop*, he maintained he was raised to the nobility because of personal bravery. It is also reported that Göring had in his possession the particulars of a trial in which an action was brought against Ribbentrop by his adoptive mother to collect payment of the sum which he had promised for the adoption; see Diels, *Lucifer ante portas*. According to report, Ribbentrop's father always dissociated himself from his son's pretentiousness; see Gilbert, *Nuremberg Diary*.

13 See Schwarz, *This Man Ribbentrop*.

14 At Nuremberg Ribbentrop himself incidentally made no secret of his opportunism, possibly because it was linked with his attempt to dissociate himself from National Socialism. Thus he not only made it clear that he had been close to the German People's Party until 1931–32, but also remarked revealingly to G. M. Gilbert, 'You know, I was not an ideological fanatic like Rosenberg or Streicher or Goebbels. I was an international businessman who merely wanted to have industrial problems solved and national wealth properly preserved and used. If Communism could do it – all right. If National Socialism could do it – all right too.' (*Nuremberg Diary*.)

15 Kordt, *Nicht aus den Akten*; also by the same author, *Wahn und Wirklichkeit*. Weizsäcker, *Memoirs*, said: 'He had in fact a special gift for divining Hitler's political intentions, even if those intentions were established, to go along with them and even surpass them.'

16 Ribbentrop, *Memoirs*. But see also Kordt, *Nicht aus den Akten*.

17 Rauschning, *Voice of Destruction*; also Picker, *Tischgespräche*, entry for May 14, 1942. In a remark on July 6, 1942, Hitler emphasised: 'Before Ribbentrop's time

the Foreign Office in Germany had been a real dumping ground for the intelligentsia' (*Tischgespräche*).

18 See Domarus, *Hitler*, Vol. I.

19 Weizsäcker, *Memoirs*. It is true that the Foreign Office was still able to play a certain role in the early years of the Third Reich, though here (as in all attempts at collaboration with the new regime) the question needs to be raised whether this was not just the result of a tactical consideration of Hitler's with which he earned credit that was later repaid in the currency of pure illusion.

20 See Karl Bracher in Bracher, Sauer and Schulz, *Die nationalsozialistische Machtergreifung*.

21 Ribbentrop, *Memoirs*, emphasises that he received the office at his own suggestion. The circumstances, especially the negligence of his administration, unmistakably argue against this version.

22 Paul Seabury, *The Wilhelmstrasse;* also Kordt, *Wahn und Wirklichkeit* and *Nicht aus den Akten*.

23 See Shirer, *Rise and Fall of the Third Reich*. The translation of the passage in the German edition is not only wrong but completely distorting. See also Gilbert, *Nuremberg Diary*.

24 Ribbentrop, *Memoirs*.

25 Dietrich, *Hitler*.

26 See for example Coulondre, *De Staline à Hitler*; Schwerin von Krosigk, *Es geschah in Deutschland*; Seabury, *Wilhelmstrasse*; I. Kirkpatrick, *The Inner Circle*; François-Poncet, quoted by Kordt, *Wahn und Wirklichkeit*; Zoller, *Hitler privat*.

27 Coulondre, *De Staline à Hitler*.

28 Steengracht's statement, *IMT*, X.

29 Weizsäcker, *Memoirs*; see also Kordt, *Nicht aus den Atken*.

30 Goebbels recorded this opinion in *The Goebbels Diaries*, entry for March 2, 1943.

31 Birger Dahlerus, *The Last Attempt* (London, 1948). Weizsäcker, *Memoirs*, made this private note on August 28, 1939: 'There was no room for constructive thought towards a political solution; if it appeared Herr von Ribbentrop tried to nip it in the bud.' Later Weizsäcker conjectured that 'Ribbentrop's advice tipped the scales in the decision to go to war'.

32 See Kordt, *Nicht aus den Akten*. Weizsäcker, *Memoirs*, believes that there was method in sending the heads of mission 'on an enforced holiday' in times of crisis. Hitler kept 'the leading officials of our service away from the focal points out of fear that they might try to resolve the desired crisis along peaceful lines.'

33 Rauschning, *Voice of Destruction*.

34 Weizsäcker, *Memoirs*.

35 Quoted by Bullock, *Hitler*. A colleague of Ribbentrop made this remark to Carl Jacob Burckhardt: 'I am very different from my chief: I like to lie in wait for my game. . . . Ribbentrop on the other hand is always stalking his, running from one boundary of his preserve to the other. If he misses an opportunity in the east he searches for one in the south, ready also to avail himself of the one he encounters halfway' (*Meine Danziger Mission*). This is a fairly precise paraphrasing of what Ribbentrop understood by 'dynamic foreign policy'. Mussolini expressed a similar opinion: 'Ribbentrop belongs to the category of Germans who bring misfortune to Germany. He talks continually of plotting wars left and right without having any definite opponent or aim' (quoted by Kordt, *Nicht aus den Akten*).

36 Quoted in *IMT*, IV. Ribbentrop denied this statement and explained that he had, in line with his instructions, merely clarified the Führer's decision 'to settle the Polish question one way or the other' (Ribbentrop, *Memoirs*). It can undoubtedly be assumed that at least the tone of outrage in which Ciano expressed this opinion was adopted after the fact. According to Weizsäcker, *Memoirs*, Ciano to begin

with had certainly warned against a confrontation with Poland, but in response to Ribbentrop's and Hitler's disagreement had then added, 'Führer, up to now you have been right, and you will be so this time.'

37 Semmler, *Goebbels*. In fact such a chest already existed. Ribbentrop had got it after his return from Moscow from Koch, the Gauleiter of East Prussia. While Ribbentrop kept in it all agreements signed by him at this point, Kordt, *Nicht aus den Akten*, has pointed out that of the 18 agreements in the chest, 17 had already been broken by Ribbentrop, i.e. Hitler.

38 See the report by Schmidt, *Hitler's Interpreter*.

39 Recorded by Dietrich, *Hitler*. Ribbentrop, in his *Memoirs*, mentions a similar remark of Hitler's: 'We don't know what strength we shall find once we have really had to push open the door to the East.'

40 Dietrich, *Hitler*.

41 Ribbentrop, *Memoirs*. For a similar statement by Steengracht, see *IMT*, X. Also Goebbels notes after a conversation with Hitler: 'The Führer believes that in this war diplomacy has not so much of a role to play as in former wars' (*The Goebbels Diaries*, entry for May 9, 1943). On the other hand Goebbels himself apparently was of another opinion, although doubtless his rivalry with the Foreign Minister played a part in this. So he complained frequently that National Socialist foreign policy had become 'completely solidified and sterile' (entry for November 15, 1943).

42 Steengracht's statement, *IMT*, X. The remark about Ribbentrop's loss of influence comes from Weizsäcker, *Memoirs*, who also notes that 'the longer our Office was impugned the better the sport, because Ribbentrop let himself be annoyed so beautifully.'

43 In September 1942, for example, Ribbentrop's State Secretary, Luther, wrote: 'The Herr Reich Foreign Minister today instructed me over the telephone to speed up as much as possible the evacuation of the Jews from the various parts of Europe. . . . After a short presentation on the progress of present evacuation of the Jews from Slovakia, Croatia, Rumania and the occupied territories, the Reich Foreign Minister ordered us to approach the Bulgarian, Hungarian and Danish governments in order to set in train the evacuation of the Jews from these countries' (*IMT*, XIX, 3688–PS). See also *IMT*, XXXV, 736–D.

44 Semmler, *Goebbels*; also Seabury, *Wilhelmstrasse*, and Ribbentrop, *Memoirs*. The number of applications for permission to resign is actually not known. Ribbentrop's secretary remembers only an application in 1941 (*IMT*, X), while Ribbentrop himself spoke of seven attempted resignations. Evidently this number is exaggerated and accords with his efforts to set himself up as a personality independent of Hitler. See Ribbentrop, *Memoirs*.

45 Report by SS Sturmbannführer Eugen Dollmann, who in his capacity as SS Liaison Officer to Mussolini had come to the Führer's headquarters that day together with the Duce; see Dulles, *Germany's Underground*.

46 Bernadotte, *The Curtain Falls*.

47 Schwerin von Krosigk, *Es geschah in Deutschland*.

48 Ribbentrop, *Memoirs*. The remark by Dahlerus is taken from *The Last Attempt*.

49 Ribbentrop, *Memoirs*. He says, for example: 'The reason why the Danzig Corridor dispute, as opposed to the Sudetenland question, could not be settled peacefully was that Britain had decided on war because she did not want Germany to become stronger, and that, on the other hand, Hitler did not shun battle if his reasonable proposals were rejected.' Elsewhere he affirms: 'In this autumn of 1946 . . . I most firmly believe that Adolf Hitler would have respected an alliance with Britain in all circumstances.' Thoughts about the naval agreement which he himself had negotiated obviously did not trouble him at this point. Some time later he said

rashly: 'I am convinced that if an Anglo-German understanding had been reached at that time, Adolf Hitler would have devoted the rest of his life to the peaceful building of a welfare state.' G. M. Gilbert, *Nuremberg Diary*, refers to similarly startling assertions, which were mostly, in view of the astonishment they aroused, dispatched with the remark, 'You know diplomacy is not as simple a matter as it sometimes seems.' In the face of such pronouncements the view expressed by Sir Hartley Shawcross in his speech for the defence that 'never in the history of the world had anyone so degraded diplomacy' is understandable; see *IMT*, XIX.

50 Letter to his wife of October 5, 1946, *Memoirs*.
51 Haensel, *Das Gericht vertagt sich.*
52 Gilbert, *Nuremberg Diary*. Nevertheless Ribbentrop, insecure as he was, had tried at Nuremberg to invent substantial differences with Hitler and to present himself as a passionate fighter for peace, understanding, the saving of the Jews, etc.; see Ribbentrop, *Memoirs*. He assured Gilbert: 'God knows how I fought. It takes less courage to go into ten battles against . . . against atomic bombs or what not, than to argue with the Führer on the Jewish issue'.
53 G. M. Gilbert, *Psychology of Dictatorship.*
54 Haensel, *Das Gericht vertagt sich*. See also Baron Viktor von der Lippe, *Nürnberger Tagebuchnotizen November 1945 bis Oktober 1946* (Frankfurt am Main, 1951), and Gilbert, *Nuremberg Diary*. The co-defendants too had, according to Gilbert, 'scorn and contempt for Ribbentrop and his defence from one end of the dock to the other' (*Nuremberg Diary*). Weizsäcker expressed this opinion in closing: 'If one were to open a clinic for nervous diseases one would find many of this kind. The failure lies in the system in which a type of this sort becomes Minister of Foreign Affairs of a nation of 70 million people and can remain so for seven years' (*Memoirs*).

Rudolf Hess: the Embarrassment of Freedom

1 This thesis has so far been analysed using Communist examples almost exclusively; for example Jules Monnerot, *Sociology and Psychology of Communism* (British title: *Sociology of Communism*; Boston and London, 1953); Raymond Aron, *Opium of the Intellectuals* (New York and London, 1962) and *Ein Gott der Keiner war* (Cologne-Berlin, 1957); Waldemar Gurian, 'Totalitarian Religions,' in *The Review of Politics*, No. 1, January 1952; also, in part, Czeslaw Milosz, *The Captive Mind.*
2 Quoted by Hermann Glaser, *Das Dritte Reich.*
3 Speech of April 8, 1933, to the SA, quoted in W. Gehl, ed., *Die nationalsozialistische Revolution* (Breslau, 1933).
4 The poem in its entirety says:

> Führer, my Führer, by God given to me,
> Defend and protect me as long as may be.
> Thou'st Germany rescued from her deepest need;
> I render thee thanks who dost daily me feed.
> Stay by me forever, or desperate my plight.
> Führer, my Führer, my faith, my light,
> Hail my Führer!

Cf. Franz G. Gross, *Die falschen Götter. Vom Wesen des Nationalsozialismus* (Heidelberg, 1946), quoted by Glaser, *Das Dritte Reich.*
5 *Das Reich*, December 22, 1940.

6   Krebs, *Tendenzen und Gestalten der NSDAP*. Hess's overmodest comportment has been emphasised especially by Hans Frank, *Im Angesicht des Galgens*.

7   J. R. Rees, ed., *The Case of Rudolf Hess*, Similar to the report of Ilse Hess quoted below (see note 15).

8   *IMT*, XXII.

9   Arendt, *Origins of Totalitarianism*.

10   Krebs, *Tendenzen und Gestalten*.

11   *Dokumente der deutschen Politik*, Vol. II.

12   Krebs, *Tendenzen und Gestalten*.

13   Jochen Klepper, *Der Vater. Roman eines Königs* (Stuttgart, 1958).

14   Ilse Hess, *Gefangener des Friedens*. Professor Karl Haushofer has said of his pupil: 'He was one student among others, not particularly gifted, of slow intellectual grasp and dull in his work. He was very dependent on emotions and passionately liked to pursue fantastic ideas. He was only influenced by arguments of no importance at the very limits of human knowledge and superstition; he also believed in the influence of the stars on his personal and political life. . . . I was always disconcerted by the expression of his clear eyes, which had something somnambulistic about it. . . .' (quoted by François Bayle, *Psychologie et éthique du Nationalsocialisme*).

15   Hess, *Gefangener des Friedens*.

16   *Rudolf Hess, der Stellvertreter des Führers* appeared unsigned in the series *Zeitgeschichte* (Berlin, 1933). On the pamphlet affair and Hitler's defence by Hess, see Franz-Willing, *Die Hitlerbewegung*.

17   I. Hess, *Gefangener ds Friedens*.

18   Karl Bracher, in Bracher, Sauer and Schulz, *Die nationalsozialistische Machter-greifung*.

19   *Frankfurter Zeitung*, April 29, 1938. The contemporary publication referred to in note 16 above reports this as follows: 'Over a dozen years he had . . . bound his fate to that of the Führer. And yet only a few knew about the man whom Adolf Hitler in April of this year appointed as his deputy in the party leadership. No one spoke of him. You hardly came across his name. He was seldom seen in pictures. You never heard one of his speeches. Until the Führer himself put him into the public spotlight. Until he stepped out of the background.'

20   See *Hannoverscher Kurier*, January 19, 1941; *Essener National-Zeitung*, April 27, 1941.

21   Krebs, *Tendenzen und Gestalten*.

22   See Rees, *Case of Rudolf Hess;* also Rosenberg, *Politisches Tagebuch*.

23   Rees, *Case of Rudolf Hess*. According to this book, the only other possessions which Hess had on him were some photographs of his son. See I. Kirkpatrick, *The Inner Circle*.

24   *Rudolf Hess, der Stellvertreter des Führers*; see also *Volksdeutsche Zeitung Brünn*, May 3, 1939.

25   Frank, *Im Angesicht des Galgens*.

26   Rosenberg, *Politisches Tagebuch*; also Rees, *Case of Rudolf Hess*.

27   *Das Reich*, December 22, 1940. Strange to say, Alfred Richter too, in his outrageous book *Unsere Führer im Lichte der Rassenfrage und Charakterologie*, emphasises the ability of the Führer's deputy to keep silent: 'In spite of his impulsiveness, he will be very reserved on important questions where it counts, and he knows how to hold his tongue about those things which the public is not yet to know.'

28   More fully, I. Kirkpatrick, *The Inner Circle*. Alan Bullock gives a concise summary in *Hitler*. Apparently Hess had not been informed of the impending attack on Russia; if this is so, it should put an end to certain persistent speculations about

the 'background' of the venture which stubbornly tend to reappear; it should also demonstrate more clearly than anything else how much influence Hess had lost at this point.

29 Picker, *Tischgespräche*, entry for April 19, 1942.

30 Semmler, *Goebbels*. Hans Frank announced at an official assembly of political leaders in the Cracow labour zone on May 19, 1941: 'But I believe I shall never again experience a shock like the one I felt when I came face to face with the Führer on Tuesday. It is a fact that this blow [the flight of Hess] is unique. I have never before seen the Führer so deeply shocked' (*IMT*, *XXIX*, 2233–PS).

31 Quoted by Jacobsen, *1939–1945*. Halder's note of May 15, 1941 (see *ibid*.) also confirms that the flight came as a complete surprise. In the conference with the chiefs of the OKH the following were put forward as motives:
'(a) Hess's internal conflict due to his personal attitude toward England and his sorrow at the Germanic people tearing each other to pieces.
(b) Internal conflict because he was prohibited from going to the front; repeated requests for assignment to the front turned down.
(c) Mystical tendencies ("visions," prophesy aforesaid).
(d) Aeronautical daring. Hence the long-standing ban on flying by the Führer.'
This and various other pieces of evidence have in the meantime made it entirely clear that Hess did this on his own responsibility and not, as J. R. Rees, *Case of Rudolf Hess*, evidently considers possible – basing himself on an unnamed German propaganda expert – with Hitler's knowledge and approval.

32 Quoted by Anders, *Im Nürnberger Irrgarten*.

33 Semmler, *Goebbels*, entry for May 21, 1941.

34 Kelley, *22 Cells in Nuremberg*.

35 *IMT*, XL.

36 Statement by Gauleiter Bohle, quoted by Rees, *Case of Rudolf Hess*.

37 Kelley, *22 Cells*. According to Bayle, *Psychologie et éthique*, astrology had also played its part in the venture. The astrologer Schulte-Strathaus had told Hess in the Autumn of 1940 that his horoscope showed a lucky mission in north-west Europe.

38 Quoted by Rees, *Case of Rudolf Hess*.

39 Note by Dr J. G. Graham, quoted in *ibid*. According to this book there is some suspicion that an aunt on his father's side was mentally unstable and that an uncle on his mother's side committed suicide in obscure circumstances. All psychiatric data cited subsequently in the text without further references are based on the analyses by J. R. Rees.

40 Rees, *Case of Rudof Hess*.

41 On one of the envelopes was written, for example, 'Blotting paper soaked in peach preserve, probably containing *brain poison* and *corrosive acid*' (italics in original). On another wrapper was written: 'Apricots with aperient. Only to be opened in the presence of neutral doctors'; see also the pictures of the facsimiles in G. M. Gilbert, *Psychology of Dictatorship*.

42 Rees, *Case of Rudolf Hess*.

43 *Ibid*.

44 Report by Dr M. K. Johnson, quoted *ibid*.

45 The available accounts of the 'important statement' of February 4, 1945, do not give details but only make reference to the concentration camp guards being hypnotised by Jews. To make clear the absurdity of Hess's hallucinations, a quotation from his notes on his stay in England has been referred to; see Rees, *Case of Rudolf Hess*. On the same page Hess also says that whatever had been asserted about the concentration camps had happened in reality to him and no-one else; for it was 'typical for the Jews to claim that their enemies did what they did

themselves.' Hess also traced back the building of the bridgehead at Remagen, on the Rhine, to the intrigues and hypnotic ingenuity of the Jews, which had influenced those German soldiers who were ordered to blow up the bridge.

46 I. Hess, *Prisoner of Peace*. Of course neither Hess nor his wife was able to demonstrate convincingly why his loss of memory had been feigned. One reason advanced by Hess, that he had wanted to obtain his release to Germany by this means (Rees, *Case of Rudolf Hess*), sounds just as unlikely, even when one allows for the naïvety which one is prepared to concede him, as his other claim, that he had tried to find peace from the annoyances of the doctors. Talking to G. M. Gilbert at Nuremberg, Hess retracted or at least did not maintain the version that it had all been only 'theatre'. On the contrary he stated: 'The first period of memory loss (in England) was really genuine. I suppose it must have been the continual isolation, and disillusionment also played a role. But in the second period (in Nuremberg) I exaggerated somewhat. It wasn't entirely loss of memory' (*Nuremberg Diary*). He said essentially the same thing to J. R. Rees. He recovered his memory instantaneously when he was warned in the so-called second period that he would other vise be pronounced 'incompetent', sent back to his cell, and allowed to take no further part in the trial; see Gilbert, *Psychology of Dictatorship*. When in the middle of January 1946 Gilbert arranged a test with Hess which again showed a degree of amnesia, Hess was very much shocked. He said that nothing was further from his mind than to feign loss of memory again since no one would believe him any more after he had admitted to having fooled the world around him. He said fearfully that he hoped this condition would improve. Nevertheless, so Gilbert explains, his condition deteriorated from week to week and the latest incidents became increasingly obliterated (*Psychology of Dictatorship*). Thus the circumstances are by no means as simple as Ilse Hess's exultant references, intended to satisfy Nazi friends and to construct a Rudolf Hess legend, would suggest.

At this point it is appropriate to point out that the volumes of letters published by Ilse Hess, particularly those parts written by her, are discouragingly offensive examples of the self-righteousness, narrowmindedness, and inferior humanity of certain circles of former leading National Socialists whose self-pity in the face of personal inconveniences (e.g. court proceedings) is in stark contrast to their complete moral apathy toward the millions of their guiltless victims.

47 Rees, *Case of Rudolf Hess*.

48 Anders, *Im Nürnberger Irrgarten*. The consideration that Hess had desperately tried to regain an individuality is supported by various marginal observations. His childlike pleasure at having deceived Hitler over the flight (see Rees, *Case of Rudolf Hess*) suggests this, and so does an extract from a letter to Karl Haushofer of May 20, 1942, where Hess quotes the verse: 'May you crash or may you land/ E'er as your own pilot stand,' and then continues: 'That I crashed is not to be denied; and it is equally certain that I was my own pilot' (I. Hess, *Prisoner of Peace*).

49 *IMT*, XXII.

50 Hitler's final speech at the trial before the Munich People's Court ended: 'Pronounce us guilty a thousand times over: the goddess of the eternal court of history will smile and tear to pieces the Public Prosecutor's submission and the court's verdict; for she acquits us!' See above Part One: 2, note 35.

51 Anders, *Im Nürnberger Irrgarten*. Hess asserted that he had not listened to the sentence of the Tribunal 'in accordance with my refusal, on principle, to recognise the court. . . . As a matter of fact it was quite a long time before I discovered accidentally what the sentence had been' (I. Hess, *Prisoner of Peace*).

52 Ilse Hess, *Gefangener des Friedens*. Hess adds to this the following remark which emphatically proves his unbroken fanaticism: 'To be sure I don't agree entirely [with Hitler's remark]: There was not only one such person, but at least two.

Perhaps if he did not want to know the truth or was not aware of it – his remark speaks for him. In that event I knew him better than he knew himself. This is not modest chatter on my part but my honest opinion.'

53 Opinion of the American psychiatrist Maurice M. Walsch, quoted by Bayle, *Psychologie et éthique*. The text is: 'A l'heure actuelle, Hess ne souffre d'aucun dérangement mental. Nous n'avons relevé aucun symptome de tendance aux hallucinations, aux illusions ou aux désillusions. Au moment de l'examen, le sujet était parfaitement normal. Nous n'avons relevé aucune trace qui permette de le classer dans le type paranoïaque. Bien qu'il estime avoir une mémoire en parfait état, il ne se souvient plus de ses deux crises d'amnésie en Angleterre; ceci renforce l'impression que nous avions, à savoir que ces deux crises sont d'origine hystérique.'

54 Gilbert, *Psychology of Dictatorship*. J. R. Rees's diagnosis is: 'The paranoid features of his personality were clearly seen in his egocentricity, based on a deep feeling of insecurity, a fear of being injured or attacked.... He clearly has no great confidence in the goodness of other people and while withdrawn into himself he is always looking for an idealised person outside himself whom he might love and trust in order to assuage his inner loneliness. In this case the idealised person, by and large, was of course Hitler, but within the narrower pattern of life in his prison camp other men came to embody the opposing qualities. One by one he found them wanting and then identified them with the evil powers who were working against him. In a curious way, the gallant Duke of Hamilton and the chivalrous King of England were playing a role almost identical with Hitler as idealised objects of his veneration. . . .' (*Case of Rudolf Hess*).

55 Quoted by Rees, *Case of Rudolf Hess*.

Albert Speer and the Immorality of the Technicians

1 See the article by Hans Buchheim, 'Struktur der totalitären Herrschaft und Ansätze totalitären Denkens,' *VJHfZ*, 1960, No. 2; also, by the same author, *Totalitarian Rule*. Within a wider framework Max Weber, *Wissenschaft als Beruf*, 2nd ed. (Munich-Leipzig, 1921), also bears on this problem. But see as well Carl Schmitt, *Der Begriff des Politischen mit einer Ansprache über das Zeitalter der Neutralisierungen* (Berlin, 1932). Very illuminating in this context is the reaction of leading nuclear physicists and chemists like Hahn, Bagge, Weizsäcker, Heisenberg *et al.*, interned after the war in a country house in England, to news of the dropping of the first American atom bomb. Although at least some of them, in accordance with their established opposition to the National Socialist regime, 'were happy that we didn't have the bomb', they declared without exception their disappointment at not having been able to count this success as their own. The schism between 'technological' and political man seldom becomes so tangible as in this overheard conversation. See also the book which Leslie Groves, the chief of the American atom bomb project, published under the title *Now It Can Be Told: The Story of the Manhattan Project* (New York, 1962; London, 1963).

2 Zoller, *Hitler Privat*.

3 See Karl Dietrich Bracher, 'Wissenschaft und Widerstand. Das Beispiel der "Weissen Rose",' *Aus Politik und Zeitgeschichte*, supplement to *Das Parlament*, July 17, 1963.

4 *IMT*, XVI; also *IMT*, II, March 4, 1947.

5 See for example *IMT*, XVI.

6 Speer's statement under cross-examination by the American Chief Prosecutor, Robert H. Jackson, through its pros and cons aptly clarifies what is meant here; see *IMT*, XVI.

7 See Springer, *Das Schwert auf der Waage*.

8 Trevor-Roper, *Last Days of Hitler*.

9 Schwerin von Krosigk, *Es geschah in Deutschland*.

10 Stahl, according to his testimony, had come to Speer to nullify his new appointment as liaison officer to the heads of the chief committees of the Technical Department. However, he was so impressed by the minister's personality that he decided to remain; see *IMT*, XLI, Speer–45.

11 Göring to Dönitz and Hess during Speer's examination as the latter emphatically acknowledged the guilt of the regime and his personal responsibility. Speer's confession and the complete incomprehension with which the majority of the accused noted his attitude is conclusive evidence of his otherness; see Gilbert, *Nuremberg Diary*. Gilbert also finds that Speer distinguished 'at the outset between his basic attitudes and those of the military caste,' for he acknowledged 'the validity of the indictment in charging a common responsibility of the Nazi leadership for "such horrible crimes",' and 'the inadmissability of obeying orders as an excuse'.

12 However, the fact that Speer's name was to be found on the conspirators' list of cabinet members was probably also partly due to the decision to assure the new government a certain continuity by minimising the break resulting from a successful assassination and incorporating into it several suitable personalities who had preserved some degree of personal integrity. See also *IMT*, XVI; Jackson's cross-examination is found in the same volume. In their reports the journalists present at Nuremberg also expressed a feeling of respect, whose significance is all the more weighty in view of the very recent end to the war and the dreadful revelations made during the trial. See for example Anders, *Im Nürnberger Irrgarten*: 'At the risk of being misunderstood, I should like to state that I respect Speer alone among the accused, for his clean hands and personal courage.'

13 *IMT* XVI. Speer assured G. M. Gilbert in this connection: 'I must admit that was weakness on my part. I don't want to make myself any prettier than I am. I should have and actually did realise it sooner, but kept playing at this hypocritical game until it was too late. . . . Well, because it was easier. I know, for example, that I could have and should have taken my stand of opposition at least as early as July 20, 1944' (*Nuremberg Diary*).

14 In Beymestrasse Speer established a local headquarters for the Berlin Gau and soon afterwards undertook the rebuilding of the so-called Adolf Hitler House in the Vossstrasse near the house of the Berlin leader of the NSDAP.

15 Hitler's speech of January 30, 1937, quoted by Domarus, *Hitler*, Vol. I.

16 J. Petersen, in *Das Reich*, January 11, 1942. See also Rudolf Wolters' richly illustrated publication *Albert Speer* (Oldenburg, 1943).

17 Quoted by Görlitz and Quint, *Adolf Hitler*.

18 *Mein Kampf*.

19 See Hoffmann *Hitler Was My Friend*. Hoffmann reports that in his Munich apartment Hitler had hung 'The Sin' by Franz von Stuck; also Lenbach's portrait, 'Bismarck in Cuirassier Uniform,' a park landscape by Anselm Feuerbach, many Silesian paintings of scenes from hunting and monastic life by Eduard Grützner ('of whom he was particularly fond'), a work by Heinrich Zügel, and various pictures by Spitzweg. See also Görlitz and Quint, *Adolf Hitler*.

20 See Anders, *Im Nürnberger Irrgarten*.

21 Quoted in *Der Parteitag der Arbeit vom 6. bis 13. September 1937. Offizieller Bericht über den Verlauf des Reichsparteitages mit sämtlichen Kongressreden* (Munich, 1938).

22 Picker, *Tischgespräche*.

23 Adolf Hitler, 'Proklamation zum Reichsparteitag der Arbeit am. 7. September 1937,' see Domarus, *Hitler*, Vol. I. The quotation on the everlasting character of the

city of Nuremberg comes from Hitler's speech of welcome on the preceding day (*ibid.*).

24 See Dietrich, *Hitler*. The measurements and figures given here are provided by Görlitz and Quint, *Adolf Hitler*.

25 Hitler on September 11, 1935, quoted by Domarus, *Hitler*, Vol. I.

26 The idea emanated originally from Speer himself. Speer had developed a theory of the value of ruins (*Ruinenwerttheorie*), as he called it. Stated briefly, this was that the emotional effect of a ruin depended on the material used. Speer says that, to begin with, Hitler's entourage was horrified that the specially favoured architect of National Socialism should occupy himself intellectually with an epoch in which ruins were the only evidence of National Socialism. Rather by chance Hitler learnt of this and to Speer's astonishment was so impressed by the theory that he had sketches prepared showing some of the projected big buildings as ruins. (Verbal communication from Speer to the author.) The remark to Hans Frank is taken from his memoirs, *Im Angesicht des Galgens.*

27 Wolters, *Albert Speer.*

28 Hitler, 'Die Reichskanzlei,' *Völkischer Beobachter*, July 16, 1939.

29 Springer, *Das Schwert auf der Waage: cf. IMT.* XVI. Speer's special position was also shown by the fact that he 'always and at any time had unquestioned access' to Hitler; see Wolters, *Albert Speer.*

30 *IMT*, XXVII, 1435-PS.

31 *The Goebbels Diaries.*

32 Speer's memorandum to Hitler of March 29, 1945, *IMT*, XLI, Speer-24. Schwerin von Krosigk's verdict on Speer's ministerial role: 'Speer's personality played a greater part in his success than his technical knowledge – certainly indisputable in details – or his talent for organisation. His artistic imagination had enabled him to discern the constructive lines more rapidly and to a wider extent than others and to grasp their importance – it also stopped him from giving his ministry a practical plan of organisation. Under him worked, not departments with firmly delineated duties, but men with specific tasks which often overlapped' (*Es geschah in Deutschland*).

33 See Jacobsen, *1939–1945*; also for various other data.

34 *The Goebbels Diaries*. See also Semmler, *Goebbels*. Speer himself maintains that his figures and production data had been correct throughout and that no-one had ever been able to demonstrate that he had made a mistake (verbal information given to the author).

35 Dietrich, *Hitler.*

36 Speer's memorandum to Hitler of March 29, 1945, *IMT*, XLI.

37 See for example Speer's speech in the Berlin Sportpalast on June 5, 1943, printed in *Tatsachen sprechen für den Sieg* (Berlin, n.d.); also Speer's address to the Gauleiters' conference of August 3, 1944, *IfZ*, Munich, 276/52.

38 Speer's memorandum to Hitler of March 29, 1945, *IMT*, XLI.

39 Trevor-Roper, *Last Days of Hitler*. On Speer's remark see *IMT*, XVI.

40 Speer's memorandum to Hitler of March 29, 1945, *IMT*, XLI.

41 *IMT*, XVI.

42 See *The Goebbels Diaries*. Bormann, on the other hand, owing to the mistrust he felt toward Hitler's favourites, had tried for a long time to undermine Speer's position.

43 See Guderian, *Panzer Leader*. Speer himself is convinced that Hitler, contrary to his assertion to Guderian, did in fact read the memorandum. This, he personally assured the author, became clear beyond any doubt in the course of his subsequent discussion with Hitler.

44 Speer's memorandum to Hitler of March 29, 1945, *IMT*, XLI. A quite similar

utterance of Hitler's during the last year of the war is reported by Walter Schellenberg, *Labyrinth*.

45 This refers to the memorandum mentioned in note 44 above.
46 See Speer's testimony in *IMT*, XVI; also sworn deposition of Werner Baumbach, former fighter pilot, *IMT*, XLI, Speer–49. In point of fact, it must be admitted that it was largely as a result of Speer's measures that the leading functionaries' intentions to flee were almost entirely frustrated.
47 Speer's testimony, *IMT*, XVI; also on the assassination plan.
48 *IMT*, XVI.
49 Quoted by Trevor-Roper, *Last Days of Hitler*.
50 *Ibid*. In his speech for the prosecution, Justice Jackson, the American Chief Prosecutor, made a similar point with regard to Speer, but also with regard to Schacht, Neurath, Papen, Jodl *et al*. Without the expert knowledge of this circle of people, Jackson said, Hitler's efforts and those of his close followers could probably not have been realised.
51 *IMT*, XVI. See the same volume on responsibility per se, to which Speer, as mentioned, always returned. Also Gilbert, *Nuremberg Diary*.

Hans Frank: Imitation of a Man of Violence

1 *Im Angesicht des Galgens* is the title of the autobiography which Frank wrote in the Nuremberg prison. In it are found the quotation and the aforementioned formulas.
2 See Gilbert, *Psychology of Dictatorship;* also Daniel Lerner, *The Nazi Elite*.
3 See Frank, *Im Angesicht des Galgens*. The remark with which Frank takes responsibility for his written utterances is reported by Gilbert, *Nuremberg Diary*.
4 Frank's diary, quoted here by Josef Wulf, *Dr Hans Frank, Generalgouverneur im besetzten Polen*, in a supplement to *Das Parlament*, August 2, 1961. In general Wulf's work passes up the opportunity for a fitting character analysis because of its undifferentiating perspective. As in the majority of this author's works, the original texts culled from extensive material are valuable.
5 Hitler to Frank; see Frank, *Im Angesicht des Galgens*.
6 Frank made the first remark at a conference of the *Hauptabteilungsleiter* (chiefs of main departments) and *Reichsgruppenwalter* (Reich group administrators) of the NSRB (Nationalist Socialist Lawyers' Union) in Berlin on November 19, 1941, the other at a government session in Cracow on August 24, 1942; see *IMT*, XXIX, 2233–PS.
7 *Ibid.*, address of December 19, 1940 to the soldiers of his guard battalion, and speech of June 9, 1942, to the Friedrich-Wilhelm University, Berlin.
8 Gilbert, *Nuremberg Diary*. Quite contrarily, Frank for example announced at an address in Cracow on January 14, 1944: 'I am no weakling! I know very well how to recognise my strength. . . . You must have no doubt about this . . .'; see Wulf, *Dr Hans Frank*. On the use of the term 'ice-cold' see *IMT*, XXIX, 22–PS.
9 Gilbert, *Nuremberg Diary*.
10 Quoted in *Dokumente der deutschen Politik*, Vol. I. There are many indications in the speeches Frank made, especially during the early period of the Third Reich, of his creative ambition in the field of law; see *ibid.*, and also Vols II, III and IV.
11 The instrumental function of all law was expressed with singular exactitude when it was publicly asserted that the duty of the People's Courts was 'not to dispense justice but to destroy the opponents of National Socialism'; see Bracher, Sauer and Schulz, *Die nationalsozialistische Machtergreifung*. Occasional references to criminal law as 'combat law' were made by Roland Freisler; see *ibid*.

12 There is ample evidence of Hitler's hatred of lawyers. Frank himself remarked that Hitler considered civil servants to be 'bureaucrats', 'reactionaries', or 'worst of all, lawyers'; see *Im Angesicht des Galgens*. In addition to the celebrated hate speech of April 26, 1942, against the lawyers, impressive examples of this aversion are found especially in his *Tischgespräche*, for example the entries for March 29 and July 22, 1942. Hitler declared that 'in dealing with lawyers he had always been particularly careful. Only three men had been excepted: Pfordten, Pöhner and Frick'; he didn't mention Frank. See Picker, *Tischgespräche*, entry for March 29, 1942.

13 Picker, *Tischgespräche*, entry for July 22, 1942. On Frank's remark see *Dokumente der deutschen Politik*, Vol. IV.

14 Picker, *Tischgespräche*, entry for July 22, 1942. On Frank's remark see *Dokumente der deutschen Politik*, Vol. VI, Pt. 2.

15 Frank, *Im Angesicht des Galgens*.

16 *Ibid*. From a total of 40,000 court proceedings there were prison sentences totalling 14,000 years and fines totalling nearly 1.5 million marks. See Görlitz and Quint, *Adolf Hitler*.

17 Frank, *Im Angesicht des Galgens*.

18 *Ibid*.

19 Hans Frank, 'Die Technik des Staates,' speech on the occasion of the foundation of the Institut für die Technik des Staates in Munich on December 6, 1941. See also the accounts by Gerhard Schulz in Bracher, Sauer and Schulz, *Machtergreifung*.

20 *Dokumente der deutschen Politik*, Vol. IV. The ideas on the 'basic teaching of National Socialist legal thinking and its five great tasks of legal organisation'. In this context the Reich Minister of Justice, Thierack, characterised judges 'as immediate assistants of the State Directorate'; see *Richterbrief*, No. 1, October 1942, quoted by Jacobsen and Jochmann, *Ausgewählte Dokumente*.

21 Frank, *Im Angesicht des Galgens*.

22 *Ibid.*; also on the objections referred to in connection with the Röhm affair.

23 Speech of May 14, 1944, to a conference on the occasion of the meeting of the *Blutorden* holders and holders of NSDAP badges of honour in the Government General; see *IMT*, XXIX, 2233–PS.

24 Frank, *Im Angesicht des Galgens*.

25 Broszat, *Nationalsozialistische Polenpolitik*.

26 *IMT*, XII. Frank made the reference to the 'greatest hour of Germanness' on June 14, 1940, at a conference of department heads; see *IMT*, XXIX, 2233–PS. The 'historical task' was of course more closely defined. On the discussions with Hitler in which the directives on policy in the occupied Polish territories were discussed, see Wulf, *Dr Hans Frank*, and *IMT*, XXIX, 2233–PS.

27 See the instructive study of Broszat already referred to (note 25 above), on which the description in the subsequent text is extensively based.

28 Frank, *Im Angesicht des Galgens*.

29 Frank's statements, in the order cited, are quoted in *IMT*, XXIX, 2233–PS; see further (*ibid.*) the memorandum of August 28, 1942, 'Abschliessende Betrachtung zur Entwicklung des letzten Vierteljahres'. Himmler's remark is reported by SS Obergruppenführer and Waffen SS General Erich von dem Bach-Zelewski; see *IMT*, XL, Frank–8. In the interests of historical accuracy it must be pointed out that the only version of Frank's diaries to be published up to now (*IMT*, XXIX, 2233–PS) gives a one-sided picture, since it reproduces primarily incriminating evidence as a document for the prosecution. His complete diary, on the other hand, contains hints of a conception on Frank's part which was the result of more co-operative impulses but which, in the face of his weakness, his inconstancy and his mania to appear a 'hard man' which kept on breaking through, bore no results. See Frank's own commentary on his diaries, *IMT*, XII.

30 See Frank's statement to the conference of department heads on November 6, 1940, *IMT*, XXIX, 2233–PS. In this connection see also Broszat, *Polenpolitik*, which says that the Government General 'remained from the point of view of constitutional and international law outside the German Reich, a "secondary" German "nation" without formal statehood and with extra-territorial status with respect to the Reich. Its inhabitants were stateless but of Polish nationality. This ad hoc structure was to facilitate the country's rule subject to only the most minimal legal obligations.'

31 *IMT*, XXIX.

32 See Haensel, *Das Gericht vertagt sich.*

33 *The Goebbels Diaries*, entry for March 9, 1943; on the conflict with Krüger see also Broszat, *Polenpolitik*.

34 *IMT*, XXIX, 2233–PS, working session on 'The Security Situation in the Government General' of May 31, 1943.

35 *IMT*, XXIX, 2233–PS, government session of July 22, 1943, in the throne room of Cracow Castle.

36 Memorial oration of October 15, 1944, in Cracow Castle on the 100th anniversary of Nietzsche's birthday; published as part of a series by the Gesellschaft der Wissenschaften des Generalgouvernements. In the same speech Frank also asked whether 'Nietzsche's vision' had not been 'a presentiment of Adolf Hitler' and said finally: 'Today we can declare that the entire German nation has become in Nietzsche's sense the superman!'

    On the final phase of Frank's rule, see *IMT*, XXIX, 2233–PS; also *IfZ*, Munich, Fb50 (Frank's letter to Reich Minister Goebbels in his capacity as deputy for the total war effort), quoted by Broszat, *Polenpolitik*.

37 *IMT*, XII.

38 Frank, *Im Angesicht des Galgens.*

39 *Ibid.*

40 *Ibid.*

41 *Ibid.*

42 See Gilbert, *Nuremberg Diary.*

43 *IMT*, XII.

Baldur von Schirach and the 'Mission of the Younger Generation'

1 B. von Schirach, *Die Hitlerjugend*. The slogan 'Mission of the Younger Generation' (*Sendung der jungen Generation*) is the title of a book published in 1932 by E. Günther Gründel. Gregor Strasser's article is printed in *Kampf um Deutschland* (Munich, 1932). An excellent example of the reaction of outside observers is a leading article in the London *Daily Mail* of July 10, 1933, 'Triumphant Youth'. The article, which described the terror and the transgressions during the process of seizing power as 'isolated deeds of violence, inevitable occurrences for any great nation,' stated: 'It is a question of rather more significance than the institution of a new government. Youth has taken command. A flow of young blood gives new life to the country. . . .'

2 B. von Schirach, *Die Hitlerjugend*; on the importance of the part played by the myth of the 'young nations' in the young conservative ideology, especially in the work of Moeller van den Bruck see the study by Fritz Richard Stern, *The Politics of Cultural Despair: A Study in the Rise of the Germanic Ideology* (Cambridge and Berkeley, Cal., 1961).

3 Quoted by Sontheimer, *Antidemokratisches Denken in der Weimarer Republik.*

4 Erik Reger, 'Naturgeschichte des Nationalsozialismus,' *Vossische Zeitung* August 30,

1931. In the same vein Ludwig Stahl, in an article entitled 'Das Dritte Reich und die Sturmvögel des Nationalsozialismus,' *Hochland*, No. 28, June 1931, wrote: 'With the exception of the National Socialists all German parliamentary parties have a pre-war programme and so they lose the young. For the young perceive that the parties on both left and right would like to confine them within the pre-war social order and that they desire their orientation from bourgeois party principles rather than from the destiny which has already been experienced.'

5 Carlo Mierendorff, 'Was ist Nationalsozialismus?' *Neue Blätter für den Sozialismus*, Vol. II, No. 4. On the radicalisation of the student body, see Bracher, *Auflösung der Weimarer Republik*.

6 Advertisement section in B. von Schirach, *Die Fahne der Verfolgten* (Berlin, n.d.).

7 A comment which illumines this stimulating aspect is found in B. von Schirach, *Die Hitlerjugend*. Looking back to the summer of 1932 when the Hitler Youth was proscribed together with the SA, Schirach writes: 'It was a great time, and it may sound strange, but we have never been so happy as then, when we lived in continual danger. We rode through the Ruhr with pistols in our coat pockets.'

8 As for example Hans Friedrich Blunck in an essay entitled 'Vom Wandervogel zur SA'. 'Not one of the young SA men,' so Blunck thought, 'took part in street marches without being imbued with the spirit and purpose of the so-called *bündisch* movement and thus of the earlier youth movement'; see Will Vesper, ed., *Deutsche Jugend* (Berlin, n.d.).

9 Harry Pross, 'Das Gift der blauen Blume. Eine Kritik der Jugendbewegung,' in *Vor und nach Hitler. Zur deutschen Sozialpathologie* (Olten-Freiburg, 1962).

10 See Robert Minder, *Kultur und Literatur in Deutschland und Frankreich, Fünf Essays* (Frankfurt am Main, 1962).

11 Bracher, *Auflösung*. The following are some of the many writings on the German youth movement which have appeared mostly over the last few years: Walter Z. Laqueur, *Young Germany. A History of the German Youth Movement;* Werner Helwig, *Die blaue Blume des Wandervogels. Vom Aufsteig, Glanz und Sinn einer Jugendbewegung* (Gütersloh, 1960); Karl O. Paetel, *Jugendbewegung und Politik*;

12 Karl O. Paetel, *Das Bild vom Menschen in der deutschen Jugendführung.* quoted by Raabe. *Die Bündische Jugend.*

13 Pross has commented on this aspect in *Die Zerstörung der deutschen Politik.*

14 Helmut Tormin, *Freideutsche Jugend und Politik*, quoted by Paetel.

15 Quoted by Pross, *Zerstörung der deutschen Politik*. In similar vein, a publication quoted by Paetel in *Jugendbewegung und Politik*: 'Youth knows today where it will not be led: into the dirty, muddy and sluggishly flowing canals of the liberal party system. For this reason youth gravitates to the Bünde.'

16 Pross, *Zerstörung der deutschen Politik.*

17 *Der Weisse Ritter*, 6/1921, quoted by Laqueur, *Young Germany.*

18 Initially the Hitler Youth recruited particularly from among sons of workers and, in lesser measure, low-rank white-collar workers in the large towns. According to its own statistics, in 1931–32 the Hitler Youth was composed of 69 per cent young workers and apprentices, 10 per cent commercial tradesmen, and 12 per cent secondary school students. It was then called the 'Greater German Youth Movement' and at the Weimar Party Congress in 1926 its name was changed to 'Hitler Youth. Bund of German Labour Youth,' at the suggestion of Julius Streicher. See further, and on the history and structure of the Hitler Youth generally, Arno Klönne, *Hitlerjugend.*

19 Paetel, *Jugendbewegung und Politik.*

20 B. von Schirach, at the beginning of *Die Hitlerjugend*. The attempt of some Bünde to be absorbed corporately into the Hitler Youth so as to retain a certain independence was unsuccessful. Only the Bund der Artamanen was finally taken into

the Hitler Youth as a unit and formed a nucleus of the Hitler Youth Field Service. Of the others only the Reichsschaft Deutscher Pfadfinder (boy scouts), whose foreign connections appeared important to the regime, and the Catholic youth leagues, which could call attention to the guarantees provided in the Concordat, were exempt from coordination, if only for a limited period. The Protestant youth associations, on the other hand, were incorporated into the Hitler Youth in December 1933 with the help of Reich Bishop Müller.

21 See Klönne, *Hitlerjugend.*
22 On the mobilisation of the student body for National Socialism see the statistics given by Bracher, *Auflösung.*
23 Krebs, *Tendenzen und Gestalten der NSDAP.*
24 Such at any rate was Schirach's own statement at Nuremberg: see *IMT*, XIV.
25 Schirach to Gilbert; see *Nuremberg Diary.* As a student in Munich, Schirach lived in the house of the publisher Bruckmann, who was friendly not only with his parents but also with Hitler.
26 H. von Schirach, *The Price of Glory.*
27 Schirach's testimony, *IMT*, XIV. About Hitler's *Mein Kampf* Schirach said: 'We could not yet justify all our views. We simply believed. And then when Hitler's *Kampf* appeared, it was like a bible to us which we learned almost by heart, so as to be able to answer the questions of doubters and superior [!] critics' (*Die Hitlerjugend*).
28 Rainer Schlösser, 'Über das Wirken der Jugend im Kulturleben,' *Völkischer Beobachter*, January 7, 1937; quoted by Strothmann, *Nationalsozialistische Literaturpolitik.*
29 Hans Helmut Dietze, *Die Rechtsgestalt der HJ* (Berlin, 1939).
30 Speech in Reichenberg on December 2, 1938; recording from the sound archives at Frankfurt am Main, Archive No. C 1326. Hitler spoke on similar lines at the Reich Party Congress in 1935; see Domarus, *Hitler,* Vol. I. Robert Ley put it more crudely: 'He begins as a cub [*Pimpf*], then joins the young people's section [*Jungvolk*], then the Hitler Youth, the Labour Service, and then, if he still has not been softened up, if he should be a hardboiled criminal, he is sent into the Army. If all that does not suffice, he is brought into the SA; if this still does not suffice, he starts as block warden. Believe me, he isn't going to stay a cub. Here you become alert to such a mongrel, to such a traitor. For you know what sort of fellow you have before you . . . this way we watch over everything' (*Dokumente der deutschen Politik*, Vol. V).
31 See Klönne, *Hitlerjugend.*
32 The speeches are printed in B. von Schirach, *Revolution der Erziehung. Reden aus den Jahren des Aufbaus* (Munich, 1938).
33 Werner Klose, 'Hitlerjugend. Die Geschichte einer irregeführten Generation. Nach Quellen und Erlebnissen dargestellt,' *Die Welt am Sonntag*, from February 17, 1963. The quotation given here is from the issue of March 10, 1963. An informative and authentic glance at the motivations that led the broad cross-section of the young to the Hitler Youth is to be found in Melita Maschmann, *Fazit. Kein Rechtfertigungsversuch* (Stuttgart, 1965). See also the collection *Jugend unterm Schicksal. Lebensberichte junger Deutscher 1946–1949* (Hamburg, 1950).
34 B. von Schirach, *Die Hitlerjugend.*
35 See *IMT*, XLI, Schirach-7. Klönne, *Hitlerjugend,* has aptly called the Hitler Youth 'a sort of educational executive' of the National Socialist regime.
36 Quoted by Horkenbach, *1933.*
37 Hellmuth Stellrecht, 'Die Wehrerziehung der deutschen Jugend,' lecture of January 1937 to the Wehrmacht's political education course; printed as 1992–PS in *IMT*, XXIX.

38 Arthur Axmann, *Hitlerjugend 1933–1943*, quoted by Klönne, *Hitlerjugend*.
39 Hitler in Nuremberg on September 1, 1933; see Horkenbach, *1933*. See also Picker, *Tischgespräche*, entries for April 12 and June 8, 1942.
40 On this whole question see Strothmann, *Literaturpolitik*.
41 See Walther A. Berendsohn, *Die humanistische Front. Einführung in die deutsche Emigranten-Literatur* (Zurich, 1946).
42 *Mein Kampf*. The quotation that follows is from Rauschning, *Voice of Destruction*.
43 B. von Schirach on January 15, 1938, on the occasion of laying the foundation stone for nine Adolf Hitler schools; see *Revolution der Erziehung*. On the ideal type of a Hitler Youth see Klönne, *Hitlerjugend*.
44 *IMT*, IX.
45 H. von Schirach, *Price of Glory*. Schirach made detailed statements in Nuremberg about the early history and specific circumstances of the controversy with Hitler; see *IMT*, XIV. However, the conduct of the former Reich Youth Leader was by no means as unequivocal as appears from his own report. Even in the autumn of 1942 he still saw in the evacuation of the Jews 'to the Eastern ghetto,' admittedly begun by his predecessor, 'an active contribution to European culture'; see *IMT*, XXXI, 3048–PS. He later explained that he had no longer known how to justify this remark even to himself and emphasised to G. M. Gilbert that he was ready to die on account of it; see *IMT*, XIV and *Nuremberg Diary*.

General von X: Behaviour and Role of the Officer Corps in the Third Reich

1 For the verdict on Oster see Fabian von Schlabrendorff, *The Secret War Against Hitler*.
2 The psychological situation of younger officers is graphically expressed in a letter that Richard Schering, one of the two condemned Ulm Reichswehr officers, addressed from his cell to the *Völkischer Beobachter*: 'Nothing is known of the tragedy of those five words "twelve years in the second rank". . . . The old should keep quiet. Their lives are behind them, ours are just beginning now. . . . Because of this we have the right to fight with every means for our own and our children's freedom' (*Völkischer Beobachter*, September 6, 1930). See also the letter written by Lieutenant-Colonel Stieff to his wife on October 7, 1930, published by Thilo Vogelsang, *Reichswehr, Staat und NSDAP* (Stuttgart, 1962), Document 8; also Dorothea Groener-Geyer, *General Groener, Soldat und Staatsmann* (Frankfurt am Main, 1955).
3 Major General Oster, in a written explanation of the relationship of the Reichswehr and the Weimar Republic after his arrest in connection with the attempted assassination of July 20, 1944; quoted in a report dated October 24, 1944, by Kaltenbrunner to all higher SS and police chiefs (Appendix: *Der 'unpolitische' Soldat oder 'Nur-Soldat'*, *IfZ*, Munich, MA 146/1–3).
4 Here may be included all Marxist-oriented historical writing and a large part of British and American historical literature from the early postwar period; see for example Gordon A. Craig, *The Politics of the Prussian Army*; also John W. Wheeler-Bennett, *The Nemesis of Power*. On June 1, 1936, Blomberg, the Reich Minister of Defence, had enlarged on this: 'Being apolitical never meant that we approved of the system under earlier governments. It was much more a means for protecting ourselves against too intimate an entanglement.' But to this he added, 'Of course now there will be no more being apolitical' (Blomberg's speech in Bad Wildungen, recorded by General Liebmann and quoted by Jacobsen and Jochmann, *Ausgewählte Dokumente*).
5 See Horkenbach, *1933*. On Hammerstein's *démarche* see Hermann Foertsch,

Schuld und Verhängnis. Hammerstein's threat to Hitler became known through Alfred Rosenberg's Nuremberg notes: 'If you attain power legally, that is all right by me. Otherwise I shall shoot' (Lang and Schenck, *Rosenberg Memoirs*). In comparison, the assertion which comes up all the time that Hammerstein had at the last moment attempted to thwart Hitler's appointment by means of a putsch lacks any foundation, as Foertsch, among others, has pointed out. On the other hand it is also necessary to counter the reproach which is raised again and again against the leaders of the Reichswehr for not attempting this putsch. Apart from the fact that the circumstances of this appointment appeared entirely legal and (ignoring for once the reliability of the Army) stood in the way of all such considerations, as did the very identity of the Reich President, it cannot be the Army's job to prevent political mistakes through the use of armed force unless unforeseeable consequences are to be tolerated.

6 Foertsch, *Schuld und Verhängnis.*

7 Wolfgang Sauer, in Bracher, Sauer and Schulz, *Die nationalsozialistische Machtergreifung.* The quotation following comes from Jacobsen, *1933–1945.*

8 Telford Taylor, *Sword and Swastika* (New York, 1952; London, 1953), quoted here by Sauer, *Machtergreifung.* On the personalities of Blomberg and Reichenau see Sauer, *Machtergreifung*, a sketch as concise as it is striking. Also Foertsch, *Schuld und Verhängnis*; Hossbach, *Zwischen Wehrmacht und Hitler*; Walter Görlitz, *History of the German General Staff, 1657–1945*; testimony by Rundstedt, *IMT*, XXI; *VJHfZ*, 1959, No. 4.

9 See Sauer, *Machtergreifung.* The protesting officer referred to in the following text, whose name deserves to be placed on record, was Lieutenant-Colonel Eugen Ott.

10 Wheeler-Bennett, *Nemesis of Power*, which is almost entirely dated and free neither of contradictions nor of bias. The few generals who energetically undertook the rehabilitation of Schleicher and Bredow were Hammerstein and the old Field Marshal von Mackensen.

11 Quoted by Foertsch, *Schuld und Verhängnis.*

12 Dietrich von Choltitz, *Soldat under Soldaten. Die deutsche Armee in Frieden und Krieg* (Constance-Zurich-Vienna, 1951).

13 This remark, which Hitler made to Halder, began characteristically with the observation, 'Anyone can lead a little operation like that'; see Bor, *Gespräche mit Halder.* Hitler's previously quoted remark in the interview is to be found in Domarus, *Hitler*, Vol. I.

14 Quoted by Foertsch, *Schuld und Verhängnis.*

15 See Sauer, *Machtergreifung*; also Schwerin von Krosigk, *Es geschah in Deutschland.*

16 Hossbach, *Zwischen Wehrmacht und Hitler*; Fritsch's remark is reported by Frank, *Im Angesicht des Galgens.* See also Adolf Heusinger, *Befehl im Widerstreit. Schicksalsstunden der deutschen Armee 1923–1945* (Tübingen-Stuttgart, 1950); Foertsch, *Schuld und Verhängnis*; Craig, *Politics of the Prussian Army*; Rothfels, *German Opposition to Hitler.*

17 See Hossbach, *Zwischen Wehrmacht und Hitler.*

18 Jodl's diary, entry for January 28–29, 1938, quoted by Craig, *Politics of the Prussian Army*; also Keitel, *Memoirs.*

19 See Görlitz and Quint, *Adolf Hitler.*

20 Protocol of February 23, 1938, quoted by Hossbach, *Zwischen Wehrmacht und Hitler;* cf. Foertsch, *Schuld und Verhängnis.*

21 It was Halder who had tried to establish this contact and had prepared an apparently minutely planned coup d'état and whom Fritsch let have this information; see Foertsch, *Schuld und Verhängnis*; also Ulrich von Hassell, *Diaries.*

22 Frank, *Im Angesicht des Galgens.*

23 On the contradictory but on the whole reluctant attitude toward war of the leading

military powers, see Sauer, *Machtergreifung*; also Golo Mann, *Geschichte und Geschichten* (Frankfurt am Main, n.d.).

24 Memorandum to General von Fritsch of January 1937; quoted by Wolfgang Foerster in *Generaloberst Ludwig Beck. Sein Kampf gegen den Krieg. Aus den nachgelassenen Papieren des Generalstabchefs* (Munich, 1953). The book, however, simplifies too much Beck's position for and, even more so, against. Beck had at first welcomed the seizure of power, then changed his mind because of the regime's illegal practices. He was held back time and again by traditional considerations of duty and obedience, and it was a long time before he broke away to pursue a determined and active resistance. See Hossbach, *Zwischen Wehrmacht und Hitler*; H. Krausnick, 'Vorgeschichte und Beginn des militärischen Widerstandes gegen Hitler,' in *Die Vollmacht des Gewissens* (Munich, 1956).

25 Hossbach, *Zwischen Wehrmacht und Hitler*.

26 Bor, *Gespräche mit Halder*. The conspiratorial ineptitude of the German military leaders was attributable not only to inhibitions caused by their upbringing and thought processes but also to a more general lack of adroitness, *savoir-faire* and finesse. Attolico, the Italian ambassador, in this connection, suggested that: 'The Germans are not given to conspiracy. A conspirator needs everything they lack: patience, knowledge of human nature, psychology, tact. . . . To fight conditions like those prevailing here, you ought to be persevering and a good dissembler like Talleyrand and Fouché. Where will you find a Talleyrand between Rosenheim and Eydtkuhnen?' (quoted by Paul Seabury, *Wilhelmstrasse*).

27 Rothfels, *German Opposition to Hitler*. Similarly Tresckow stated: 'The assassination must be attempted at all costs. Even should that fail, the attempt to seize power in the capital must be undertaken. We must prove to the world and to future generations that the men of the German resistance movement dared to take the decisive step and to hazard their lives upon it. Compared with this object, nothing else matters' (*ibid.*).

28 Keitel, *Memoirs*; Keitel expressed these suspicions in respect to Beck. His remarks reflect in unmistakable fashion the categories according to which Keitel's mind apparently worked.

29 See Anders, *Im Nürnberger Irrgarten*, who comes to the same conclusions reached in the text.

30 On Kluge's letter, see Chester Wilmot, *The Struggle for Europe*.

31 Keitel, *Memoirs*.

32 See *IMT*, XXXV, 411–D, as well as Trial XII, NOKW–2523. Also *IMT*, XXIX, 2233–PS.

33 See Ulrich Kayser-Eichberg, *Geist und Ungeist des Militärs*.

34 See Foertsch, *Schuld und Verhängnis*.

35 Halder, *Kriegstagebuch*, Vol. I, entry for January 18, 1940.

36 Schlabrendorff, *Secret War Against Hitler*.

37 *IMT*, XXVIII, 1780–PS; similarly General Schmundt says later, as Goebbels noted in his diary, that on account of their unenthusiastic attitude, the generals deprived themselves 'of the greatest happiness any of our contemporaries can experience – that of serving a genius' (*The Goebbels Diaries*, entry for March 21, 1942).

38 *The Goebbels Diaries*, entry for May 10, 1943.

39 Görlitz, *The German General Staff*. In the face of this evidence, what was said of Seeckt can be applied to the whole General Staff: 'a sphinx without a riddle.'

40 G. Mann, *Geschichte und Geschichten*.

Professor NSDAP: The Intellectuals and National Socialism

('Professor NSDAP' is the caption given to a photograph of a National Socialist college lecturer by the Swiss photographer August Sander)

1 Karl Bracher, in Bracher, Sauer and Schulz, *Die nationalsozialistische Machtergreifung*. The book contains a thorough, extensively documented description of the problem of intellectual 'Gleichschaltung' (standardisation).

2 Letter of June 14, 1935, quoted in *Thomas Mann an Ernst Bertram* (Pfullingen, 1960). Thomas Mann wrote of his correspondent (*ibid.*): 'He saw roses and marble where I saw only asafetida, poison fusel for the people, a native lust for murder, and the certain destruction of Germany and Europe.'

3 These statements hold true especially for the type of intellectual under consideration here and need not be discussed any further. Whenever the concept 'intellectual' is used in this chapter, it is in the most undifferentiated sense possible. This is neither the time nor the place to refine the concept terminologically or confine it by means of one of the many definitions which have been coined, from Karl Mannheim to Josef A. Schumpeter, for we are concerned here all-inclusively with the people belonging to the intellectual professions. See further on this question Paul Noack's concise and instructive *Die Intellektuellen. Wirkung, Versagen, Verdienst* (Munich, 1961).

4 The text reads in context: 'One of the best means of preparation for a new and bolder life is to be found in the annihilation of the values of the free-floating and autocratic spirit, in the destruction of the standards which the bourgeois age has laboured to impart to man. . . . The best answer to the high treason of the spirit against life is high treason of the spirit against the spirit; and to be a part of this blasting operation is one of the great and cruel pleasures of our time' (Ernst Jünger, *Der Arbeiter*, 2nd ed. Hamburg, 1932).

5 Franz L. Neumann aptly called the intellectuals 'perhaps the most important single element within the Fascist élite' (foreword to Lerner, *The Nazi Elite*).

6 Jung, *Sinndeutung der deutschen Revolution*. In an article in the *Deutsche Rundschau* of June 1932, 'Neubelebung von Weimar?' Jung wrote in the same vein: 'The spiritual and intellectual prerequisites for the German revolution were created by forces beyond National Socialism. National Socialism has so to speak taken over the "popular movement department" in this great collective enterprise. It has built it up in grandiose style and has become a proud power. Not only are we pleased about this; we have contributed our part towards this growth. Through unrecountably detailed efforts, especially among the educated classes, we created the prerequisites for that day on which the German people gave the National Socialist candidates their vote.'

7 Thomas Mann, *Die Stellung Freuds in der modernen Geistesgeschichte*, Vol. XI of *Gesammelte Werke* (Frankfurt, 1960).

8 Ludwig Klages, *Der Mensch und das Leben* (Jena, 1937). See also Christian Graf von Krockow, *Die Entscheidung. Eine Untersuchung über Ernst Jünger, Carl Schmitt, Martin Heidegger* (Stuttgart, 1958). From this standpoint Thomas Mann, for example, was judged as follows: 'We acknowledge Thomas Mann's literary art. A great man of letters, but a poet? A great writer but a seer? Delphic laurels elude his grasp. God does not bow to the all too clever . . .' (Wilhelm Stapel in *Deutsches Volkstum*, June 1933, quoted by Kurt Sontheimer, *Thomas Mann und die Deutschen*, Munich, 1961).

9 Max Hildebert Böhm, 'Körperschaft und Gemeinwesen,' *Grundbegriffe der Politik*, No. 1, 1920. It sounds almost an echo when Hitler states: 'We must distrust the intelligence and the conscience, and must place our trust in our instincts. We have

to regain a new simplicity' (Rauschning, *Voice of Destruction*). The alienation of literature in life and in Germany was the theme of Hugo von Hofmannsthal's famous essay 'Das Schrifttum als geistiger Raum der Nation.' See also Robert Mindner's brilliant and instructive essay 'Deutsche und französiche Literatur' in *Kultur und Literatur in Deutschland und Frankreich*. Kayser-Eichberg's study *Geist und Ungeist des Militärs* also contains numerous thoughtful notes on this theme.

10 As symptomatic of the anti-intellectual tendencies of the period M. Scheler listed Bolshevism, fascism, the Youth Movement, the mania for dancing, psychoanalysis, the values newly placed on the child, the passion for primitive mythical mentalities, and others; see Sontheimer, *Antidemokratisches Denken in der Weimarer Republik*. Ernst Robert Curtius' book *Deutscher Geist in Gefahr* (Stuttgart, 1932) is also relevant in this broader context.

11 See Ernst Adolf Dreyer, ed., *Deutsche Kultur im Dritten Reich* (Berlin, 1934).

12 Statements by Bracher, *Machtergreifung*; also Kurt Hirche, 'Nationalsozialistischer Hochschulsommer,' *Die Hilfe*, August 15, 1931. See also Thomas Litt, 'The National-Socialist Use of Moral Tendencies,' printed in International Council for Philosophy and Humanistic Studies, *The Third Reich* (London and New York, 1955), which says in reference to the student body: 'It was from their ranks that the Party drew the most devoted, ingenious and resolute champions.' In his letter to the Dean of the Faculty of Philosophy at Bonn University, Thomas Mann also speaks of 'the heavy share of guilt for all current misfortune which the German universities have burdened themselves with' (see *Gesammelte Werke*, Vol. XII).

13 See Bracher, *Machtergreifung*.

14 Ricarda Huch's letter of April 9, 1933, to Max von Schillings, President of the Prussian Academy of Arts, quoted by Poliakov and Wulf, *Das Dritte Reich und seine Denker*. See also the celebrated letter which Oskar Maria Graf wrote to Goebbels from Vienna, because he felt that he had been falsely spared in the burning of the books: 'Burn me too! . . . ' (quoted by Berendsohn, *Die humanistische Front*).

15 Speech to the Cultural Conference of the NSDAP during the 1933 Reich Party Rally, recorded by Horkenbach, *1933*. The National Socialist historian Walter Frank commented ironically on this opportunism: 'During the rugged years of its struggle the Nationalist Socialist movement enjoyed the unlimited contempt of the little Greeks (i.e. the intellectuals) who lived in Germany. For the little Greeks it was too intellectual. But there was an immediate change as soon as National Socialism triumphed; it was as though an intellectualising power were immanent in victory. From all sides now came the little Greeks, smart, educated, and without character, employing generously "the German greeting" and offering "to establish the intellectual foundation for the National Socialist victory"' (*Kämpfende Wissenschaft*, Hamburg, n.d.).

16 Wilhelm Frick to a rally of the National Socialist Union of Teachers on October 19, 1933, quoted by Horkenbach, *1933*.

17 Speech at the opening of the Reich Chamber of Culture on November 14, 1933, quoted by Horkenbach, *1933*. In one of the first reports on the work of the Reich Chamber of Literature on December 6, 1934, Goebbels explained: 'The first duty of the Reich Chamber of Literature was a mopping-up operation throughout all branches of literature. The Jewish contribution to German literature alone represented no less than 40 per cent. Further, it meant creating a common status of consciousness on the part of the German writers and bringing home to them their great responsibility to the state and the nation. Also, the book trade and lending library system had to be cleansed of elements which possessed perhaps commercial but not cultural qualifications to be employed in these responsible spheres' (*Das*

Archiv, November/December 1934); *cf.* Strothmann, *Nationalsozialistische Literaturpolitik.*

18 Walter von Molo, 'Kritisch waren die Poeten und sie hielten zusammen,' *Die Welt*, June 8, 1957.

19 Rudolf G. Binding, *Antwort eines Deutschen an die Welt* (Frankfurt am Main, 1933). The work was directed against an earlier critical article by Romain Rolland on the situation in Germany. Erwin Guido Kolbenheyer, Wilhelm von Scholz *et al.* used similar arguments against the French writer and defended the book burning as a necessary act of 'cleansing' and 'purification'.

20 See Sontheimer, *Thomas Mann und die Deutschen*; on Börries von Münchhausen's statement see *Neue Literatur*, No. 9, September 1934.

21 Ernst Jünger, *Tagebuch*, entry for September 21, 1929, quoted by Sontheimer, *Antidemokratisches Denken*. See also the comment by Friedrich Georg Jünger, whose critical writings on contemporary thought generally show a tendency to outdistance his brother's radicalism with a special lack of consideration and conscious brutality: 'The great and mighty Germany of the future is willed by him [the National Socialist]. . . . Let thousands, nay millions, die; what meaning have these rivers of blood in comparison with a state, into which flow all the disquiet and longing of the German being!' (F. G. Jünger, *Der Aufmarsch des Nationalismus*, quoted by Sontheimer).

22 Gottfried Benn, *Der neue Staat und die Intellektuellen*, Vol. I of *Gesammelte Werke in vier Bänden* (Wiesbaden, 1958–1960). The quotation referred to comes from an essay, 'Zur Problematik des Dichterischen' (1930), and is taken from the same volume.

23 See Stephan, *Joseph Goebbels*. The self-assured prognoses are from two speeches by Hitler, in particular that to the 1933 Reich Party Cultural Conference, quoted by Horkenbach, *1933*, and the one on the dedication of the House of German Art of July 19, 1937, quoted by Domarus, *Hitler*, Vol. I.

24 These sayings are found in various speeches made on different occasions. Strothmann, *Literaturpolitik*, has made a collection of these and similar expressions, supplemented by several phrases from Rosenberg's vocabulary. What replaced the proscribed 'degenerate art' became popularly known as 'photo-ism'.

25 Minder, *Kultur und Literatur.*

26 See *Goebbels spricht. Reden aus Kampf und Sieg.*

27 Goebbels in his speech at the opening of the Reich Chamber of Culture, quoted by Horkenbach, as well as Gerd Rühle, *Das Dritte Reich* (Berlin, 1934–1939), quoted by Bracher, *Machtergreifung.*

28 The phrase 'soldierliness of the mind' comes from Goebbels, quoted by Dreyer, *Deutsche Kultur*. On poetry as 'fighting power' see Strothmann, *Literaturpolitik*. The scientists were characterised as 'comrades in the nation's service for knowledge' by M. H. Böhm in his Jena inaugural lecture as professor of nationality theory and the sociology of nationality; see Bracher, *Machtergreifung*. Oskar Loerke, in his *Tagebücher 1903–1939*, ed. Hermann Kasack (Heidelberg-Darmstadt, 1955), mentions the 'social evenings of the department of poets'. For other expressions see Strothmann, *Literaturpolitik.*

29 Rainer Schlösser, in *Wille und Macht*, No. 3, 1943.

30 See Eugen Hadamovsky, quoted by Bracher, Sauer and Schulz, *Machtergreifung*. Alfred Rosenberg, in *Blut und Ehre. Ein Kampf für deutsche Wiedergeburt. Reden und Aufsätze von 1919–1933* (Munich, 1934), described Barlach's Magdeburg War Memorial thus: 'A mixed variety of short, undefinable sorts of people wearing semi-idiotic expressions and Soviet helmets are supposed to symbolise German home guards! I believe that every healthy SA man will pass the same judgment here as any conscious artist.' And Göring, in a speech to Prussian theatre managers

on September 12, 1933, quoted by Horkenbach, *1933*: 'Every SA man who has taken part in protests against a *Schwejk* or similar play has more artistic sense than the administrator who brought the piece to the stage.'

31 Wilfried Bade, *Kulturpolitische Aufgaben der deutschen Presse* (Berlin, 1933), quoted by Strothmann, *Literaturpolitik*. Josef Müller-Marein wrote in this connection in the *Völkischer Beobachter:* 'There is certainly no question that it was left almost exclusively to the SA poets to guarantee the poem's continued authority and existence'; see Strothmann, *Literaturpolitik*. Joseph Goebbels went still further when on February 23, 1937, in a speech on 'The Cultural Obligations of the SA,' he praised 'the community of the SA' without hesitation as 'the greatest work of art there is at the present time' (*Das Archiv*, February 1937).

32 See Horkenbach, *1933*. On Ernst Storm's remark see Poliakov and Wulf, *Das Dritte Reich und seine Denker.*

33 See Picker, *Tischgespräche*; also Rauschning, *Voice of Destruction.*

34 *Hans Schemm spricht. Seine Reden und sein Werk*, ed. G. Kahl-Furthmann (Bayreuth, 1935), quoted by Glaser, *Das Dritte Reich*. Hans Schemm was also one of the most ardent spokesmen for 'a German and subjective science'.

35 The aforementioned statements, in the order cited, are found in Rauschning, *Voice of Destruction*; Hermann Schaller, *Die Schule im Staate Adolf Hitlers* (Breslau, 1935); Lenard in *Volk im Werden*, No. 7, 1936, quoted by Poliakov and Wulf, *Das Dritte Reich und seine Denker*; W. Poppelreuther, in *Hitler, der politische Psychologe* (Langensalza, 1934); R. Höhn, in 'Die Volksgemeinschaft als wissenschaftliches Grundprinzip,' *Süddeutsche Monatshefte*, 1934/35. There are many other examples in Bracher, *Machtergreifung.*

36 Thomas Mann, *Leiden an Deutschland. Tagebuchblätter aus den Jahren 1933 und 1934*, Vol. XII of *Gesammelte Werke*. See also the case reported by Konrad Heiden in *Adolf Hitler*, Vol. II, of a celebrated art historian and museum director of a large South German town who, after a reprimand by the party, declared the treatment was perhaps not fair but had been necessary, and looking back over his past said, 'We should have been led'.

37 Bracher, *Machtergreifung.*

38 T. Mann, *Leiden an Deutschland.*

39 The speech is printed in *VJHfZ*, 1958, No. 2. Already in 1935, in a speech referring to the writers, Professor Walter Frank had asked the question 'whether, in times when a Caesar rises and falls, when empires tumble and raise themselves up, when nations clash to decide their existence and nonexistence, power and glory, those who rhyme only for private pleasure are properly worthy of life' (*Zukunft und Nation*, Publications of the Reich Institute for the History of the New Germany, Hamburg, 1935).

40 See Dieter Sauberzweig, 'Die Kapitulation der deutschen Universitäten,' *Die Zeit*, March 17, 1961.

41 Helmut Plessner, *Die verspätete Nation. Uber die politische Verführbarkeit bürgerlichen Geistes* (Stuttgart, 1959).

42 Quoted by Rolf Michaelist, 'Das wandelbare politische Gesicht eines Dichters,' *Der Tagesspiegel*, November 15, 1962. See also the recollections of the writer Ferenc Körmendy on his personal encounter with Gerhart Hauptmann in the summer of 1938, which impressively testify to this ambivalence.

43 Peter de Mendelssohn, *Der Geist in der Despotie* (Berlin, 1953).

44 Hanns Johst in his play *Schlageter.*

45 Quoted by Friedrich Wolters, *Stefan George und die Blätter für die Kunst* (Berlin, 1930); also F. G. Jünger, *Der Aufmarsch des Nationalismus*, quoted by Sontheimer, *Antidemokratisches Denken.*

46 Quoted by Walter Muschg, *Die Zerstörung der deutschen Literatur.*

47 Rauschning, *Voice of Destruction.*
48 Jung, *Sinndeutung.*
49 Carl Schmitt, *Politische Romantik*, 2nd ed. (Munich-Leipzig, 1925).
50 Ernst Barlach, *Als ich von dem Verbot der Berufsausübung bedroht war*, written on July 29/30, 1937, quoted by Barlach in an exhibition catalogue published by the German Academy of Arts, Berlin 1951. In 1941 Karl Schmitt-Rottluff received from Adolf Ziegler, president of the Reich Chamber of Plastic Arts, a letter saying: 'Although . . . you must be aware of the trail-blazing speeches of the Führer at the inauguration of the Great German Art Exhibition in Munich, it is evident on the basis of your recent originals submitted for examination that even today you are still standing apart from the cultural ideas of the National Socialist state. . . . [Therefore] your membership in the Reich Chamber of Plastic Arts is terminated and taking immediate effect you are proscribed from pursuing any professional – and extraprofessional – activity in the field of plastic arts,' (quoted by Hofer, *Der Nationalsozialismus*).
51 See the extracts from the Rosenberg Reports in Poliakov and Wulf, *Das Dritte Reich und seine Denker.*
52 Quoted by Muschg, *Zerstörung der deutschen Literatur.*

German Wife and Mother: The Role of Women in the Third Reich

1 Quoted by Franz-Willing, *Die Hitlerbewegung*; also Rosenberg, *Mythus*. The misogynistic aspect of the movement is expressed especially by Ernst Röhm, *Hochverräter*. According to an official source quoted by Clifford Kirkpatrick in his book *Nazi Germany, Its Women and Family Life* (British title: *Women in Nazi Germany*), only 3 per cent of the party members (evidently he means during the time of struggle) were female.
2 Only Goebbels and Bormann had families fully commensurate with the standards of National Socialist ideology. It must, however, be pointed out here that, strictly speaking, there never was a National Socialist woman or family ideology. There existed, as is altogether characteristic of National Socialist ideology, merely tendencies, which in view of the conscious indifference of National Socialism to systematisation were never brought together and systematically developed, thus guaranteeing great flexibility in the exercise of administrative power. The concept is used here merely for terminological simplification.
3 Wilhelm Frick to the first session of the Advisory Council of Experts on Population and Race Policy on June 28, 1933, quoted in *Dokumente der deutschen Politik*, Vol. I.
4 The exact wording comes from Jung, *Herrschaft der Minderwertigen*. It shows to what degree 'folk' terminology agreed with National Socialist terminology or anticipated it. The accord is shown even more abundantly in the following text. In fact, Wilhelm Hartnacke used the same comparison in an essay, 'Erbgut verpflichtet,' in *Mütter, die uns die Zukunft schenken*.
5 Hitler, at the conference of the National Socialist Women's Organisation within the framework of the 1934 Reich Party Congress; see Domarus, *Hitler*, Vol. I. The classification of 'deserter' for those women who renounced motherhood comes from Ernst Schwabach's book *Die Revolutionierung der Frau* (Leipzig, 1928); see Jung, *Herrschaft der Minderwertigen*.
6 Zoller, *Hitler privat*. Eckart's remark is reported by Heiden, *Adolf Hitler*, Vol. I.
7 So, at all events, Baldur von Schirach to G. M. Gilbert, *Nuremberg Diary*; also Zoller, *Hitler privat*; Strasser, *Hitler and I*. The problem touched on here is discussed to some extent in Part One: 1–3 of this book.

8   Hoffmann, *Hitler Was My Friend*. Hoffmann continues: 'These women were the best propagandists the party had; they persuaded their husbands to join Hitler, they sacrificed their spare time to their political enthusiasms and they devoted themselves utterly and selflessly to the cause of the party's interests.'

9   This remark of course does not burden the women alone with the responsibility for Hitler's rise; it is rather to be understood in the sense of the statement of an English scholar quoted by Simone de Beauvoir in her book *The Second Sex*, that men made the gods but women worshipped them. On Hitler's remark, see Zoller, *Hitler privat*.

10 Lüthy, 'Der Führer personlich,' *Der Monat*, No. 62. The comment of the *Münchener Post* is quoted by Franz-Willing in *Die Hitlerbewegung*; that of Countess Reventlow is to be found in Görlitz and Quint, *Adolf Hitler*.

11 Arendt, *Origins of Totalitarianism*.

12 Kurt Lüdecke notes in his book *I Knew Hitler* that during the early years of the movement he had witnessed how an older woman transferred to the party her whole inheritance, which had just been bequeathed to her. Hitler received further gifts from a Frau von Seidlitz, whose husband died a hostage during the rule of the Soviets. Also, Frau Bechstein declared that her family had repeatedly 'given its support' to Hitler; see Franz-Willing, *Die Hitlerbewegung*.

13 Rauschning, *Voice of Destruction*; also Eva G. Reichmann, *Hostages of Civilisation*, who before 1933 had taken part in an event at the Berlin Sportpalast, mentioned the 'erotic character not only of the words but of the accompanying gestures'.

14 Zoller, *Hitler privat*; also *The Goebbels Diaries*, entry for September 12, 1943.

15 Hitler, in his speech to the National Socialist Women's Organisation at the 1934 Reich Party Congress already referred to; see Domarus, *Hitler*, Vol. I. On the claim of National Socialism to solve the question of women's emancipation, see C. Kirkpatrick, *Women and Family Life*.

16 Quoted by Hanns Kerrl, ed., *Reichstagung in Nürnberg 1935* (Berlin, 1936). The Rosenberg quotation is from *Mythus*.

17 Hitler, in his speech to the 1934 Reich Party Congress; see Domarus, *Hitler*, Vol. I. In the same context Alfred Rosenberg wrote: 'With the doctrine of the erotic "rebirth" the Jew today – aided by doctrines of the emancipation of women – strikes at the roots of our whole existence' (*Mythus*). On the emancipation theory of National Socialism, which sets itself up in total contradiction of all sociological facts and realities, see Heuss, *Hitlers Weg*.

18 Dr Curt Rosten, *Das ABC des Nationalsozialismus*.

19 Thilo von Trotha, 'Volksneubau und Geschlechterfrage,' *Nationalsozialistische Monatshefte*, 1934, quoted by Strothmann, *Nationalsozialistische Literaturpolitik*.

20 See Strothmann, *Literaturpolitik*.

21 Oswald Spengler, quoted by Jung, *Herrschaft der Minderwertigen*.

22 C. Kirkpatrick, *Women and Family Life*.

23 Rosten, *ABC des Nationalsozialismus*. In this book the author also sets himself up as a poet. His unspeakable doggerel would not deserve to be repeated here did it not so strikingly characterise the half-baked, dilettantish tone of the majority of these efforts on 'the rescue of the German woman';

> We want our women tried and true
> Not as decorated toys.
> The German wife and mother too
> Bears riches no foreign woman enjoys.
>
> The German woman is noble wine.
> She loves and enriches the earth.

The German woman is bright sunshine
To home and hearth.

Worthy of respect she must always be seen;
Not of strange races the passion and game.
The people must remain pure and clean:
That is the Führer's high aim.

24 Wilhelm Hartnacke spoke of 'treason toward nature' in his essay 'Erbgut verpflichtet,' in *Mütter, die uns die Zukunft schenken*. See Jung, *Herrschaft der Minderwertigen*, on the 'childbearing strike'.
25 Hanns Johst, 'Rede zur Kundegebung des Deutschen Schrifttums' in *Völkischer Beobachter*, July 24, 1936.
26 *Mein Kampf*. See also R. Walther Darré's writings, particularly *Das Bauerntum als Lebensquell der nordischen Rasse* (Munich, 1929), as well as *Neuadel aus Blut und Boden*, where he swears by the criterion of 'rejecting and fostering' along blood lines exemplified by the Old German legal code.
27 Speech to the German women at the 1937 Reich Party Rally, in *Offizieller Bericht über den Verlauf des Reichsparteitages mit sämtlichen Kongressreden* (Munich, 1938). The preceding quotation is from Rosten, *ABC des Nationalsozialismus*.
28 Rosten, *ABC des Nationalsozialismus*.
29 Quoted by C. Kirkpatrick, *Women and Family Life*. Elsewhere Goebbels enlarges on this: 'It is not because we do not respect women, but because we respect them too highly that we have kept them away from the parliamentary-democratic game of intrigue determined by the policies of the past fourteen years in Germany' ('Deutsches Frauentum,' in *Signale der neuen Zeit*). In fact, it was nothing but a definite contempt for women; the remark by Hitler in his *Tischgespräche*, entry for April 12, 1942, is an example of this.
30 See Domarus, *Hitler*, Vol. I; also Darré, 'The bearing of many children is the mark of a noblewoman,' quoted by Poliakov and Wulf, *Das Dritte Reich und seine Denker*.
31 Hitler to the German women at the 1936 Reich Party Rally, in *Offizieller Bericht über den Verlauf des Reichsparteitages mit sämtlichen Kongressreden* (Munich, 1936). The remark of Hitler's quoted previously comes from his speech at the inauguration of the Ordensburg Sonthofen on November 23, 1937; see Domarus, *Hitler*, Vol. I.
32 State Secretary Reinhardt on the 'early marriage of officials' in an address on June 5, 1937; see *Dokumente der deutschen Politik*, Vol. V. The commentary referred to on the law for the prevention of hereditarily sick offspring comes from Hans F. K. Günther, *Führeradel durch Sippenpflege*. Günther was also one of the most energetic advocates of the conversion of marriage registry offices from 'mere places of registration to consultative and family guidance offices' (*ibid.*). See also Karl Bracher in Bracher, Sauer and Schulz, *Die nationalsozialistische Machtergreifung*. In the same framework also belong attempts at creating an 'advanced breeding bank' for the development of biologically-hereditarily suitable offspring; see Emil Vogt, 'Kinderreichtum als Voraussetzung für den geistigen Hochstand eines Volkes,' in *Mütter, die uns die Zukunft schenken*.
33 See *Dokumente der deutschen Politik*, Vol. VI, Pt 1. There were three degrees of this badge of honour: 'An iron badge of honour for mothers of four children, a silver badge of honour for mothers of six children, and a gold badge of honour for mothers of eight children.'
34 See Hans Retzlaff, *Arbeitsmaiden am Werk*: 'What a present the Führer has given

the young by bringing them together so that they learn to know and love their people through a community of their own!'

35 *Ibid.* In the same text the RAD for the female youth is called 'the great school of a new people's culture'.

36 See Vogt, 'Kinderreichtum'.

37 *Münchener Neueste Nachrichten*, No. 169, quoted by Poliakov and Wulf, *Das Dritte Reich und seine Denker*.

38 *The Bormann Letters.* On the question of editions see the chapter 'Martin Bormann: The Brown Eminence,' note 5. The quotations given here come from Gerda Bormann's letters of January 24 and 27, 1944. Bormann was in the habit of annotating his wife's letters with short marginal notes and incidental remarks.

39 Memorandum of Martin Bormann (*Sicherung der Zukunft des deutschen Volkes*) (The Safeguarding of the Future of the German Nation), January 29, 1944, quoted by Jacobsen and Jochmann, *Ausgewählte Dokumente*.

40 Marie Adelheit Reuss zur Lippe, ed., *80 Merksätze und Leitsprüche über Zucht und Sitte aus Schriften und Reden von R. Walther Darré* (Goslar, 1940), quoted by Poliakov and Wulf, *Denker*.

41 Himmler's speech to the SS Group Leaders' Conference in Poznan on October 4, 1943; see *IMT*, XXIX, 1919–PS.

42 Picker, *Tischgespräche*, entry for January 28, 1942.

43 Memorandum of Martin Bormann of January 29, 1944; see also Picker, *Tischgespräche*, entry for March 1, 1942.

44 Himmler's letter of September 13, 1936, on the foundation of the Lebensborn e.V. had not yet disclosed these purposes but had assigned the institution a fourfold task: (1) aid for racially and biologically hereditarily valuable families; (2) the accommodation of racially and biologically hereditarily valuable mothers in appropriate homes, etc.; (3) care of the children of such families, as well as (4) care of the mothers. In the letter it was at the same time made incumbent on all 'full-time leaders' as a 'duty of honour' to become members of the association; see *IMT*, XXXI, 2825–PS. But Himmler more candidly assured Felix Kersten, his doctor and masseur: 'My first aim in setting up the Lebensborn was to meet a crying need and to give unmarried women who were racially pure the chance to have their children free of cost. Privately I let it be known that any unmarried woman who was alone in the world but longed for a child might turn to the Lebensborn with perfect confidence. The Reichsführung of the SS would sponsor the child and provide for its education. I was well aware that this was a revolutionary step. . . .' Himmler declared that from now on only 'valuable and racially pure men' would be recommended as so-called 'conception assistants' (Kersten, *Memoirs*).

In 1939 the Lebensborn e.V. had homes in Steinhöring, Polzin, Klosterheide (Mark), Hohehörst and in the Vienna woods. Later more hospitals, children's homes, etc. were added from former Jewish properties. So-called 'field offices', or directing offices, were set up in Bromberg as well as in Belgium and Holland; see *IMT*, XXX, 2284–PS; also 4705–NO.

45 Kersten, *Memoirs*.

46 Picker, *Tischgespräche*; Hitler's previously quoted remark that the greatest fighter is entitled to the most beautiful woman is cited by Zoller, *Hitler privat*.

47 Kersten, *Memoirs*.

48 Statement of Bertus Gerdes, *IMT*, XXXII, 3462–PS.

49 Rauschning, *Voice of Destruction*.

50 See Hedwig Conrad-Martius' illuminating book *Utopien der Menschenzüchtung*.

51 Kersten, *Memoirs*; also Conrad-Martius, *Utopien*.

52 On Himmler's Engagement and Marriage Order (*Verlobungs-und Heiratsbefehl*), whose most important clause is the obligation for SS members to obtain permission to marry, see *IMT*, XXXI, 2825–PS. On the Head Office for Race and Settlement a description on the organisational structure and rules of the SS on August 1, 1942, says: 'The SS Central Office for Race and Settlement [RuSHA] is engaged through its offices in the racial selection of SS offspring, guides SS men in their choice of a spouse, and promotes the creation of large biologically hereditarily valuable families. It is made possible for suitable and willing SS settlers to obtain their own farms' (*IMT*, XXXI, 2825–PS). The fact that this was of course only a small part of the function of the RuSHA and that it was described in exceedingly favourable terms needs no special emphasis and is also less important in this context. Himmler ordered the nomination of Munich as the 'capital of the new order and of the family' in a letter to SS Obergruppenführer Pohl on May 8, 1942; see Conrad-Martius, *Utopien*.

53 Kersten, *Memoirs*.

54 Martin Bormann's memorandum of January 29, 1944, on the safeguarding of the future of the German people.

55 See Dietrich, *Hitler*.

Rudolf Höss: The Man from the Crowd

1 Arendt, *Origins of Totalitarianism*, particularly Section III, 'Total Domination,' of Chapter 12, 'Totalitarianism in Power'. Also taken from there is the formula modified – i.e. expanded – here, that at the root of totalitarian beliefs is the conviction that 'everything is possible'. Strictly in this sense, Hitler himself had once declared that he loved it when his party comrades wanted the impossible; see Rauschning, *Voice of Destruction*. On the statements which follow, see also Hans Buchheim's *Totalitarian Rule*.

2 SS Obergruppenführer Heissmayer on April 23, 1941, at the ceremonial opening of a national political educational establishment; see Paetel, 'Die SS,' *VJHfZ*, 1954, No. 1. Similarly Buchheim, *Totalitarian Rule*, summarises the expectations and demands that a totalitarian regime makes on human beings in the formula 'Belief, obedience and efficiency'.

3 Martin Broszat, in his introduction to *Kommandant in Auschwitz. Autobiographische Aufzeichnungen von Rudolf Höss* (the German edition of Rudolf Höss's *Commandant of Auschwitz*). See also Gilbert, *Psychology of Dictatorship*.

4 Höss, *Commandant of Auschwitz*. See also Hannah Arendt, who comments in the same vein on Adolf Eichmann in *Eichmann in Jerusalem* (London and New York, 1963). Their life histories, basic psychological patterns, motivations, and ways of argumentation show a startling resemblance between Eichmann and Höss. In general as in particular, nearly everything is interchangeable with this type – emphatic evidence for the drive toward standardisation inherent in totalitarian training.

5 Höss, *Commandant of Auschwitz*. In *The Theory and Practice of Hell* Eugen Kogon analysed another predominant type, the SS camp functionary. Though some of his conclusions also hold good for Höss, the two types basically vary from each other as much as they in their turn are distinguished from a phenomenon like Josef Kramer, the infamous temporary commandant of Bergen-Belsen.

6 Rauschning, *Voice of Destruction*.

7 Broszat, introduction to Höss, *Kommandant in Auschwitz*. During cross-examination by Counsel for the Defence Dr Kauffmann, Höss assured the Nuremberg Tribunal: 'These so-called ill-treatments and tortures in the concentration camps . . . were

not, as supposed, method, but excesses of individual leaders, deputy leaders and men who laid violent hands on the prisoners' (see *IMT*, XI).

8 Gilbert, *Psychology of Dictatorship*.
9 Arendt, *Origins of Totalitarianism*.
10 Höss, *Commandant of Auschwitz*. The French writer Robert Merle has used Rudolf Höss's autobiographical report as subject for a fictitious portrayal of his life published under the title *La Mort est mon métier*. But the grotesque demonisation of the father, deliberately contrived to make the flesh creep, quite apart from further embellishments which wear out in banality nearly every saleable cliché on 'the' German, banishes the book to the bog of sensational political tabloid literature.
11 Gilbert, *Psychology of Dictatorship*; see also *Nuremberg Diary*.
12 Gilbert, *Nuremberg Diary*. See also Höss, *Commandant of Auschwitz*. This theme re-emerges later when Höss, apropos of his description of the years of his stay in prison, describes the advantages of solitary confinement.
13 Broszat, introduction to Höss, *Commandant of Auschwitz*.
14 Höss, *Commandant of Auschwitz*.
15 *Ibid.*
16 *Ibid.*
17 *Ibid.*
18 *Ibid.* In 1922, while staying in Munich, Höss joined the NSDAP and was given the party number 3240, as Martin Broszat, whose editorial achievement at least deserves a mention at this point, has discovered from the Nuremberg documents.
19 Höss, *Commandant of Auschwitz*.
20 *Ibid.*
21 *Ibid.* To what results a complex about 'weakness' can lead is seen in a conversation which Gunther R. Lys had with Harry Naujocks and recorded in the form of a memorandum which he made available to the author. Naujocks, camp elder of the Sachsenhausen concentration camp from 1936 to 1942, records: 'In midsummer of 1938 I was called to the camp gate one evening after closing time, where Rapportführer Kampe gave me instructions for the following day's work. Casually Kampe added, "And the gardener, Teschner, must go." I assumed the gardener had to be replaced, possibly because he had stolen tomatoes, broken the rules by smoking, or something of the sort. I would not have been able to stand up for a political offender, for Kampe discouraged all favouritism towards protected prisoners. Teschner, however, was a professional criminal. But to my objections, Kampe answered, "Don't you understand German, man? He must go! Adju's orders!" ' According to Naujocks, a direct order for murder was then produced. What was unusual about this was, as he said, (1) the place where the order was passed on, (2) the person who gave it, and (3) the fact that it was given to the camp elder. Generally the SS block leader or fatigue-party leader used the formula 'He must go' for criminals or asocials within the scope of the punishment squad. The adjutant of Sachsenhausen concentration camp at that time was Rudolf Höss. When Kampe dismissed him, Naujocks immediately sought out Teschner, who was already asleep. He asked the gardener whether anything unusual had happened to him during the day. Teschner too thought first of some routine occurrence such as theft or smoking, and denied it. Thereupon Naujocks said, 'Did you have anything to do with Höss?' Then Teschner remembered: that morning Höss, mildly affected by heat or heat plus alcohol, had suffered an attack of weakness in the greenhouse; he, Teschner, had pulled the half-fainting man into the shade and brought some cold water for his forehead and throat. Höss had gone off without thanks. Naujocks says today: 'I understood immediately. His shame that a prisoner should have seen such weakness was Höss's motive for ordering the elimination of this prisoner. I went immediately to Kampe and managed to arrange.

Notes

for Teschner to go to Gross-Rosen with a transport leaving the camp at four o'clock the next morning.' Höss's motive was also clear to Kampe: sensibility, excessive need of virility; he had felt himself 'exposed' by Teschner.

22 Höss, *Commandant of Auschwitz*.
23 Gilbert, *Nuremberg Diary*.
24 Höss, *Commandant of Auschwitz*.
25 *Ibid*.
26 Gilbert, *Nuremberg Diary*.
27 Höss, *Commandant of Auschwitz*; also *IMT*, XXXIII, 3868–PS. 'It was clear to me from the very beginning,' wrote Höss in his life history with the pride of the expert, 'that Auschwitz could be made into a useful camp only through the hard untiring efforts of everyone, from the commandant down to the lowest prisoner.'
28 Höss, *Commandant of Auschwitz*. See also the description of the extermination procedure in Gilbert, *Nuremberg Diary*.
29 Höss, *Commandant of Auschwitz*.
30 *Ibid*.
31 Gilbert, *Nuremberg Diary*.
32 Höss, *Commandant of Auschwitz*.
33 *Ibid*. In his final summing up Höss points out again that he had never approved of the cruelties: 'I myself never maltreated a prisoner, far less killed one.' Precisely from this came his feeling that he had been not only a good SS leader in the sense of Himmler's conception but also a 'decent man'. Only in the two farewell letters which he wrote to his wife and children immediately before his execution does the shock over a life that had miscarried break through and he reaches at least the beginning of a moral appraisal of what he has done. He advises his wife and children to take another name: 'It is best that my name disappear forever with me.' Up to now the two letters have not been published in Germany.

Part Four

THE FACE OF THE THIRD REICH: ATTEMPT AT A SUMMING UP

1 See Rauschning, *Voice of Destruction*.
2 When the five Potempa murderers were sentenced to death in Beuthen in August 1932, an article by Alfred Rosenberg appeared in the *Völkischer Beobachter* entitled 'Mark gleich Mark, Mensch gleich Mensch,' in which he argued that legally also man does not equal man nor deed equal deed; see Hard, *Alfred Rosenberg*. This maxim of National Socialism had been given one of its most impressive statements in 1935 in *Der Untermensch*, a tract published by the SS Head Office. This says: 'Thus as the night rises against the day, as light and shadow are eternally hostile to each other – so is the greatest enemy of man commanding the earth man himself. Subhuman man – that biologically apparently completely identical creation of nature with hands, feet, and a sort of brain, with eyes and mouth – is something quite different, a fearful creature, more than a stone's throw in the direction of man with features resembling a human face – but mentally, spiritually lower than any beast . . . subhuman – nothing more! For all is not equal which bears a human face! Woe to him who forgets this!' (quoted by Poliakov and Wulf, *Das Dritte Reich und die Juden*).
3 Rosenberg, *Mythus*. See also Hans Buchheim's extremely instructive book *Totalitarian Rule*.
4 See Rauschning, *Voice of Destruction*.

5 See Griessmayr, *Das völkische Ideal*. Illuminating in this connection is an article by Ernst Krieck, 'Wandel der Wissenschaftsidee und des Wissenschaftssystems im Bereich der nationalsozialistischen Weltanschauung,' which extols folk political anthropology as 'the essential focal point' in the National Socialist 'Cosmos of Sciences' (quoted by Hofer, *Der Nationalsozialismus*).

6 Quoted by Arendt, *Origins of Totalitarianism*.

7 Rauschning, *Voice of Destruction*. Hitler's speech to the officers' class of 1938 is quoted by Jacobsen and Jochmann, *Ausgewählte Dokumente*, dated January 25, 1939.

8 Rauschning, *Voice of Destruction*.

9 Quoted by Heiden, *Adolf Hitler*, Vol. II. See also Karlheinz Rüdiger's instructive article 'Auslese der Bewegung,' *Wille und Macht. Führerorgan der national-sozialistischen Jugend*, No. 12, June 15, 1936, reprinted in Jacobsen and Jochmann, *Ausgewählte Dokumente*.

10 See Part Three of this book, the chapter 'German Wife and Mother'. How far this conviction of the interdependence of racial and character values went is shown in an episode from *The Kersten Memoirs*. By chance Himmler had got to know a tall, blond young man, and without checking upon him further, and purely on the basis of his well-known racial assumptions, had him transferred to Hitler's body-guard. As he soon learnt, this man was a criminal with several previous convictions, and Himmler was 'dumbfounded. He would never have believed such a thing of a blond man.'

11 Hanns Johst in 'Rede zur Kundgebung des Deutschen Schrifttums,' quoted in the *Völkischer Beobachter* of July 24, 1936.

12 Hitler on September 3, 1933, at the closing of the Party Rally in Nuremberg, quoted by Horkenbach, *1933*. The full text reads: 'This made the method decisive by which we would find such men who, qualified by inheritance, could act as successors to the original creators of our national essence and preserve it. There was only one possibility here: we could not derive capacity from race but had to draw the conclusion that the presence of capacity assured the existence of racial qualifications. Now capacity was determined through the sort of reaction an individual demonstrated to a newly proclaimed idea.'

13 Richter, *Unsere Führer im Lichte der Rassenfrage und Charakterologie*.

14 Quoted by Kelley, *22 Cells in Nuremberg*. The extraordinary importance of the Munich and Bavarian environment for the rise of the NSDAP has been emphasised recently particularly by Hofmann in his able study *Der Hitlerputsch*.

15 *Mein Kampf*. Gregor Strasser's celebrated and apt formula is found in a speech of October 20, 1932, to the NSBO in the Berlin Sportpalast.

16 See Baynes, *Speeches of Adolf Hitler*, Vol. I.

17 Quoted by I. Hess, *Prisoner of Peace*.

18 Rauschning, *Voice of Destruction*. See also Hitler's statement: 'For world history is made by minorities if in this minority is embodied the majority of wills and the power of decision' (*Mein Kampf*).

19 See Wolfgang Sauer in Bracher, Sauer and Schulz, *Die nationalsozialistische Machtergreifung*; also Frank, *Im Angesicht des Galgens*.

20 Neumann, *Behemoth*.

21 *The Goebbels Diaries*, entry for March 21, 1942. This concerns a statement of General Schmundt which Goebbels quotes approvingly.

22 Reported by Henderson, *Failure of a Mission*; quoted in Bullock, *Hitler*.

23 Gilbert, *Nuremberg Diary*.

24 Frank, *Im Angesicht des Galgens*. Hitler's extraordinary suggestive power affected not only his National Socialist followers. Hindenburg, Papen, Blomberg, industrialists and professors came under his spell to a greater or lesser degree of indignity.

In November 1939 General von Brauchitsch simply withdrew from an attempted rebellion by the generals when Hitler shouted at him, and even Hjalmar Schacht, who was firmly protected by his professional arrogance, admitted once that he never left a talk with Hitler 'without feeling uplifted and strengthened' (Rauschning, *Voice of Destruction*). The single exception among the top leadership seems to have been Reinhard Heydrich. This could very well have been because he was not in such close personal contact with Hitler but instead had access to his 'man of straw', Himmler. Röhm's case was quite different. He held himself aloof from the humiliating acts of Byzantinism which were contrary to his soldierly sense of honour, but was evidently no less under Hitler's spell than the other top leaders. This state of affairs, which is easily obscured by the events preceding June 30, 1934, is confirmed by Röhm's conduct during his years in exile and by his precipitate return from Bolivia once he received Hitler's offer to take over the post of Chief of Staff of the SA. Another exception in a certain sense is Albert Speer. But he at least admitted that 'to be in [Hitler's] presence for any length of time made me tired, exhausted and void. The capacity for independent work was paralysed' (Trevor-Roper, *Last Days of Hitler*).

25 Alexandre Koyré, 'The Political Function of the Modern Lie,' *Contemporary Jewish Record*, June 1945, quoted by Arendt, *Origins of Totalitarianism*. See also a statement of Darré's quoted by Rauschning, *Voice of Destruction*: 'It was not until knowledge recovered its character of a secret science, and was no longer universally available, that it would again exercise its normal function, which was to be a means of ruling human, as well as non-human, nature.' In his speech to the officers' class of 1938, Hitler said similarly that he would express ideas 'which perhaps could be openly stated in later decades or centuries [!], whose official expression in past years and also today still could only do damage to the growing approbation which the movement enjoys among some groups of our people'; see Jacobsen and Jochmann, *Ausgewählte Dokumente*.

26 Rauschning, *Voice of Destruction*.

27 See particularly Erwin Faul, *Der moderne Macchiavellismus*, who cited in support of this interpretation the examples of Hitler's 'mystical ideas on the historical hour of Germanhood,' 'the deeply personal conviction of being raised up by decision-making powers, or "Providence", as he called it,' and finally Hitler's 'position on the Jewish question'. Already in 1932 Theodor Heuss had pointed out in his study *Hitlers Weg* that 'in the NSDAP two very different tendencies overlap: one wholly irrational, the other highly rationalistic. Both have their roots in Hitler's personality in the same way that they meet the ambiguity of the German character. One could call it bureaucratic romanticism.'

28 See Rauschning, *Voice of Destruction*.

29 On this whole question see *ibid.*

30 Quoted by Semmler, *Goebbels*.

31 Thus Dietrich, *Hitler*. The dispute between Erich Koch and Alfred Rosenberg during the war over policy in the Eastern territories provides a graphic example of the preference for the tougher type at any time.

32 Oven, *Mit Goebbels bis zum Ende.*

33 Himmler's speech of September 7, 1940 to the Officer Corps of the 'Adolf Hitler' SS Bodyguard, quoted in *IMT*, XXIX, 1918-PS.

34 See Kersten, *Memoirs*.

35 Remark by an SS leader at the Ordensburg Vogelsang in autumn 1937; quoted by Kogon, *Theory and Practice of Hell*. See also Himmler's remarks on the Waffen SS reported by Kersten, *Memoirs*, which also contain numerous general principles and basic rules of selection. On the double function of the SS see also Reinhard Heydrich, *Wandlungen unseres Kampfes* (Munich, 1935).

36 Höss, *Commandant of Auschwitz.*
37 See Rosenberg, *Politisches Tagebuch.*
38 *IMT*, XIX.
39 Bullock, *Hitler.* Goebbels remarked with a similar illustration: 'Just the same in Germany; a few flames burn brightly, the others only reflect their light' (*My Part in Germany's Fight*, entry for January 4, 1932). Almost the same remark emerges apparently exactly a year later, on January 3, 1933, in this same diary.
40 See Hart, *Alfred Rosenberg*; also Kersten, *Memoirs.*
41 Gilbert, *Nuremberg Diary.*
42 Ernst Kaltenbrunner, quoted by Haensel, *Das Gericht vertagt sich.*
43 Johannes Pinsk, *Krisis des Faustischen* (Berlin, 1949). See also the pertinent critique put forward by Helmut Heiber in his book *Joseph Goebbels* regarding the tendencies towards demonisation, which gives the discussion at home and abroad a remarkably similar orientation. Hannah Arendt's ingenious formula of 'the banality of evil' is appropriate not only to Adolf Eichmann and comparable third-rank functionaries; it describes at the same time the type which, with very few exceptions, was prevalent in the innermost circle of the top leadership.
44 Hans Frank to G. M. Gilbert; see *Nuremberg Diary.*
45 Hofmann, *Der Hitlerputsch.*
46 Buchheim, *Totalitarian Rule.*
47 See Ernst Weymar, *Das Selbstverständnis der Deutschen. Ein Bericht über den Geist des Geschichtsunterrichts der höheren Schulen im 19. Jahrhundert* (Stuttgart, 1963), who brings out the responsibility that German educational tradition bears for the susceptibility of broad strata to National Socialism and richly documents his position. At this point the distinguished work of Hans Schwerte, *Faust und das Faustische. Ein Kapitel deutscher Ideologie* (Stuttgart, 1962), also deserves to be pointed out. In the appendix of that book a chapter is devoted to an analysis of the process of ideologisation to which the picture by Dürer, 'The Knight, Death, and the Devil,' mentioned in the text was subjected.
48 Arendt, *Origins of Totalitarianism.*

Bibliography

This bibliography contains all those works that are cited frequently in the text and notes, and also some titles referred to less often but considered of basic importance. Bibliographical information for works not included below is given in the notes.

Anders, Karl, *Im Nürnberger Irrgarten*. Nuremberg, 1948.

Abshagen, Karl Heinz, *Canaris*. London, 1956.

Arendt, Hannah, *The Origins of Totalitarianism*. London, 1950; New York, 1961. Rev. ed. New York, 1966.

Bayle, François, *Psychologie et éthique du Nationalsocialisme. Etude anthropologique des dirigeants SS*. Paris, 1953.

Baynes, Norman H., ed., *The Speeches of Adolf Hitler, April 1922 – August, 1939*. London, 1942; New York, 1943. 2 vols.

Bennecke, Heinrich, *Hitler und die SA*. Munich and Vienna, 1962.

Berndt, A. I., *Der Marsch ins Grossdeutsche Reich*. Munich, 1938.

Bewley, Charles, *Hermann Goering and the Third Reich*. New York, 1962.

Bor, Peter, *Gespräche mit Halder*. Wiesbaden, 1950.

Borch, Herbert von, *Obrigkeit und Widerstand. Zur politischen Soziologie des Beamtentums*. Tübingen, 1954.

Bonnet, Georges, *Défense de la paix*. Geneva, 1946–1948. 2 vols.

Bormann, Martin, *The Bormann Letters. The Private Correspondence Between Martin Bormann and his Wife from January 1943 to April 1945*. London, 1954.

Bracher, Karl Dietrich, *Die Auflösung der Weimarer Republik. Eine Studie zum Problem des Machtverfalls in der Demokratie*. Stuttgart and Düsseldorf, 1955.

———, 'Das Anfangsstadium der Hitlerschen Aussenpolitik,' *VJHfZ*, 1957, No. 1.

———, 'Zusammenbruch des Versailler Systems und zweiter Weltkrieg,' *Propyläen-Weltgeschichte*, Vol. 9, Berlin, 1960.

———, Wolfgang Sauer and Gerhard Schulz, *Die nationalsozialistische Machtergreifung. Studien zur Errichtung des totalitären Herrschaftssystems in Deutschland 1933/34*. Cologne and Opladen, 1960.

Brecht, Arnold, *Prelude to Silence. The End of the German Republic*. New York, 1944; London, 1945

Bross, Werner, *Gespräche mit Hermann Göring während des Nürnberger Prozesses*. Flensburg and Hamburg, 1950.

Broszat, Martin, *German National Socialism, 1919–1945*. Santa Barbara, Cal., 1966.

———, *Nationalsozialistische Polenpolitik 1939–1945*. Stuttgart, 1961.

Buchheim, Hans, *Totalitarian Rule. Its Nature and Characteristics*. Middletown, Conn., 1968.

Buchheit, Gert, *Hitler, der Feldherr. Die Zerstörung einer Legende*. Rastatt, 1958.

Bullock, Alan, *Hitler. A Study in Tyranny*, rev. ed. New York and London, 1960.

Burckhardt, Carl Jacob, *Meine Danziger Mission 1937–1939*. Zürich and Munich, 1960.

Conrad-Martius, Hedwig, *Utopien der Menschenzüchtung. Der Sozialdarwinismus und seine Folgen*. Munich, 1955.

Craig, Gordon A., *The Politics of the Prussian Army, 1640–1945*. New York, 1964; London, 1967.

Crankshaw, Edward, *The Gestapo. Instrument of Tyranny*. New York and London, 1956.

Daim, Wilfried, *Der Mann, der Hitler die Ideen gab*. Munich, 1958.

Dallin, Alexander, *German Rule in Russia 1941–1945*. London and New York, 1957.

Darré, Walther R., *Neuadel aus Blut und Boden*. Munich, 1935.

Diels, Rudolf, *Lucifer ante portas . . . es spricht der erste Chef der Gestapo. . . .* Stuttgart, 1950.

Dietrich, Otto, *Hitler*. Chicago, 1955; London, 1957. (British title: *The Hitler I Knew*.)

Dokumente der Deutschen Politik, ed. Paul Meier-Benneckenstein. Berlin, 1935–1943. 7 vols.

Domarus, Max, *Hitler. Reden und Proklamationen 1932–1945. Kommentiert von einem deutschen Zeitgenossen*. Vol. I, *Triumph (1932–1938)*. Würzburg, 1962.

Dulles, Allen Welsh, *Germany's Underground*. New York and London, 1947.

Erfurth, Waldemar, *Die Geschichte des deutschen Generalstabes von 1918 bis 1945*. Göttingen-Berlin-Frankfurt, 1957.

Faul, Erwin, *Der moderne Macchiavellismus*. Cologne and Berlin, 1951.

Foertsch, Hermann, *Schuld und Verhängnis. Die Fritschkrise im Frühjahr 1938 als Wendepunkt in der Geschichte der nationalsozialistischen Zeit*. Stuttgart, 1951.

François-Poncet, André, *The Fateful Years. Memoirs of a French Ambassador in Berlin*. London, 1948; New York, 1949.

Frank, Hans, *Im Angesicht des Galgens. Deutung Hitlers und seiner Zeit auf Grund eigener Erlebnisse und Erkenntnisse*, 2nd ed. Neuhaus, 1955.

Franz-Willing, Georg, *Die Hitlerbewegung. Der Ursprung 1919–1922*. Hamburg and Berlin, 1962.

Freund, Michael, *Geschichte des Zweiten Weltkrieges in Dokumenten*. Gütersloh, 1962. 3 vols.

Friedensburg, Ferdinand, *Die Weimarer Republik*. Hanover and Frankfurt am Main, 1957.

Frischauer, Willi, *The Rise and Fall of Hermann Goering*. Boston and London, 1951. (British title: *Goering*.)

Gilbert, G. M., *Nuremberg Diary*. New York, 1947; London, 1948.

———, *The Psychology of Dictatorship*. New York, 1950.

Glaser, Hermann, *Das Dritte Reich. Anspruch und Wirklichkeit*. Freiburg, 1961.

Goebbels, Joseph, *Der Angriff. Aufsätze aus der Kampfzeit*. Munich, 1935.

———, *The Early Goebbels Diaries*, ed. Alan Bullock and Helmut Heiber. London, 1962; New York, 1963.

———, *Das eherne Herz. Reden und Aufsätze aus den Jahren 1941–42*. Munich, 1943.

———, *The Goebbels Diaries*, ed. Louis P. Lochner. New York and London, 1948.

———, *Michael. Ein deutsches Schicksal in Tagebuchblättern*, 3rd ed. Munich, 1933.

———, *My Part in Germany's Fight*. London, 1935; Toronto, 1938.

———, *Signale der neuen Zeit. 25 augsgewählte Reden von Dr Joseph Goebbels*. Munich, 1934.

———, *Wetterleuchten. Aufsätze aus der Kampfzeit* (Vol. II of *Der Angriff*). Munich, 1938.

———, *Die Zweite Revolution. Briefe an Zeitgenossen*. Zwickau, n.d.

Göring, Hermann, *Germany Reborn*. London, 1934.

———, *Reden und Aufsätze*, ed. Erich Gritzbach. Munich, 1942.

Görlitz, Walter, *History of the German General Staff 1657–1945*. New York and London, 1953. (British title: *The German General Staff. Its History and Structure*.)

———, and Herbert A. Quint, *Adolf Hitler. Eine Biographie*. Stuttgart, 1952.

Grebing, Helga, *Der Nationalsozialismus. Ursprung und Wesen*. Munich, 1959.

Gritzbach, Erich, *Hermann Goering. The Man and His Work*. London, 1939.

Günther, Hans, F. K., *Führeradel durch Sippenpflege*. Munich, 1936.

Gutachten des Instituts für Zeitgeschichte. Munich, 1958.

Haensel, Carl, *Das Gericht vertagt sich. Aus dem Tagebuch eines Nürnberger Verteidigers*. Hamburg, 1950.

Bibliography

Hagen, Walter (Wilhelm Höttl), *The Secret Front.* London, 1953; New York, 1954.

Halder, Franz, *Kriegstagebuch. Tägliche Aufzeichnungen des Chefs des Generalstabes des Heeres, 1939–1942.* Stuttgart, 1962–1964. 3 vols.

Hart, F. Th., *Alfred Rosenberg. Der Mann und sein Werk*, 3rd ed. Munich, 1937.

Hartnacke, Wilhelm, *Mütter, die uns die Zukunft schenken.* Königsberg, 1936.

Hassell, Ulrich von, *The Von Hassell Diaries, 1938–1944.* New York, 1947; London, 1948.

Heiber, Helmut, *Adolf Hitler.* Chester Springs, Pa., and London, 1961.

———, *Joseph Goebbels.* Berlin, 1962.

Heiden, Konrad, *Adolf Hitler. Das Zeitalter der Verantwortungslosigkeit. Eine Biographie.* Zurich, 1936–1937. 2 vols. (A translation of the first volume, *Hitler. A Biography*, was published in New York and London, 1936.)

———, *Der Führer. Hitler's Rise to Power.* New York and London, 1944. Reprinted London, 1967.

———, *A History of National Socialism.* London, 1934; New York, 1935.

Henderson, Sir Nevile, *The Failure of a Mission, Berlin 1937–1939.* New York and London, 1940.

Hess, Ilse, *Gefangener des Friedens. Neue Briefe aus Spandau.* Leoni, 1955.

———, *Prisoner of Peace.* London, 1954. (*Translation of England–Nürnberg–Spandau. Ein Schicksal in Briefen.*)

Heuss, Theodor, *Hitlers Weg. Eine historisch-politische Studie über den Nationalsozialismus*, 7th ed. Stuttgart–Berlin–Leipzig, 1932.

Hitler, Adolf, *Hitler's Secret Book.* New York, 1962.

———, *Mein Kampf*, trans. James Murphy. London, 1939. (A translation by Ralph Manheim was published in Boston in 1943.)

Der Hitler-Prozess. Bericht über die Verhandlungen des Volksgerichtshofs in München 1924. Munich, 1924.

Hofer, Walther, *Der Nationalsozialismus. Dokumente 1933–1945.* Frankfurt and Hamburg, 1957.

———, *Die Diktatur Hitlers bis zum Beginn des zweiten Weltkrieges.* Constance, 1960.

Höss, Rudolf, *Commandant of Auschwitz.* London, 1959. New York, 1960. (German edition: *Kommandant in Auschwitz. Autobiographische Aufzeichnungen von Rudolf Höss* [Stuttgart, 1958].)

Hoffmann, Heinrich, *Hitler Was My Friend.* London, 1955.

Hofmann, Hanns Hubert, *Der Hitlerputsch. Krisenjahre deutscher Geschichte 1920 bis 1924.* Munich, 1961.

Hohlfeld, Johannes, ed., *Deutsche Reichsgeschichte in Dokumenten. Urkunden und Aktenstücke zur inneren und äusseren Politik des Deutschen Reiches*, Vol. IV, *Die nationalsozialistische Revolution, 1931–1934.* 2nd ed. Berlin, 1934.

Horkenbach, Cuno, *Das Deutsche Reich von 1918 bis Heute. Das Jahr 1933.* Berlin, 1935.

Hossbach, Friedrich, *Zwischen Wehrmacht und Hitler 1934–1938.* Wolfenbüttel and Hanover, 1949.

Jacobsen, Hans-Adolf, *1939–1945. Der Zweite Weltkrieg in Chronik und Dokumenten*, 5th ed. Darmstadt, 1961.

———, and Werner Jochmann, *Ausgewählte Dokumente zur Geschichte des Nationalsozialismus 1933–1945.* Bielefeld, 1961.

Jetzinger, Franz, *Hitler's Youth.* London, 1958.

Jung, Edgar J., *Die Herrschaft der Minderwertigen–ihr Zerfall und ihre Ablösung durch ein neues Reich.* Berlin, 1930.

———, *Sinndeutungd er deutschen Revolution.* Oldenburg, 1933.

Jungnickel, Max, *Goebbels.* Leipzig, 1933.

Kallenbach, Hans, *Mit Adolf Hitler auf der Festung Landsberg*, 4th ed. Munich, 1943.

Kayser-Eichberg, Ulrich, *Geist und Ungeist des Militärs. Versuch über ein Missverständnis.* Stuttgart, 1958.

Keitel, Wilhelm, *The Memoirs of Field-Marshal Keitel, Chief of the German High Command, 1938–1945,* ed. Walter Görlitz. London, 1965. New York, 1966.

Kelley, Douglas M., *22 Cells in Nuremberg.* New York and London, 1947.

Kempner, Robert M. W., *Eichmann und Komplizen.* Zurich–Stuttgart–Vienna, 1961.

Kersten, Felix, *The Kersten Memoirs 1940–1945.* London, 1956; New York, 1957.

Kirkpatrick, Clifford, *Nazi Germany, Its Women and Family Life.* New York, 1938; London, 1939. (British title: *Women in Nazi Germany.*)

Kirkpatrick, Sir Ivone, *The Inner Circle.* London, 1959.

Klemperer, Klemens von, *Konservative Bewegungen zwischen Kaiserreich und Nationalsozialismus.* Munich and Vienna, 1962.

Klönne, Arno, *Hitlerjugend. Die Jugend und ihre Organisation im Dritten Reich.* Hanover and Frankfurt am Main, 1960.

Kogon, Eugen, *The Theory and Practice of Hell. The German Concentration Camps and the System Behind Them.* New York and London, 1950.

Kordt, Erich, *Nicht aus den Akten. Die Wilhelmstrasse in Frieden und Krieg. Erlebnisse, Begegnungen und Eindrücke 1928–1945.* Stuttgart, 1950.

———, *Wahn und Wirklichkeit. Die Aussenpolitik des Dritten Reiches. Versuch einer Darstellung.* Stuttgart, 1948.

Krebs, Albert, *Tendenzen und Gestalten der NSDAP. Erinnerungen an die Frühzeit der Partei.* Stuttgart, 1959.

Kubizek, August, *The Young Hitler I Knew.* London, 1954; Boston, 1955. (British title: *Young Hitler. The Story of our Friendship.*)

Lang, Serge, and Ernst von Schenck, *Memoirs of Alfred Rosenberg.* New York, 1949.

Laqueur, Walter Z., *Young Germany, a History of the German Youth Movement.* New York and London, 1962.

Lerner, Daniel, *The Nazi Elite.* Stanford, Cal., and London, 1951.

Liddell Hart, B. H., *The German Generals Talk.* New York and London, 1956. (British title: *The Other Side of the Hill.*)

Lüdecke, Kurt, *I Knew Hitler.* New York, 1937; London, 1938.

Meinck, Gerhard, *Hitler und die deutsche Aufrüstung 1933–1937.* Wiesbaden, 1959.

Meinecke, Friedrich, *The German Catastrophe. Reflections and Recollections.* Cambridge, Mass., and London, 1950. Reprinted Boston, 1964.

Meissner, Otto, *Staatssekretär unter Ebert–Hindenburg–Hitler. Der Schicksalsweg des deutschen Volkes von 1918–1945, wie ich ihn erlebte,* 3rd ed. Hamburg, 1950.

Milosz, Czeslaw, *The Captive Mind.* New York and London, 1953.

Miltenberg, Weigand von, *Adolf Hitler Wilhelm III.* Berlin, 1931.

Mohler, Armin, *Die konservative Revolution in Deutschland 1918–1932. Grundriss ihrer Weltanschauungen.* Stuttgart, 1950.

Muschg, Walter, *Die Zerstörung der deutschen Literatur.* Munich, n.d.

Neumann, Franz Leopold, *Behemoth. The Structure and Practice of National Socialism.* New York and London, 1942. Rev. ed. New York, 1944.

Niekisch, Ernst, *Das Reich der niederen Dämonen.* Hamburg, 1953.

Nolte, Ernst, *The Three Faces of Fascism. Action française, Italian Fascism, National Socialism.* London, 1965; New York, 1966.

Olden, Rudolf, *Hitler.* New York and London, 1936. (British title: *Hitler the Pawn.*)

Paetel, Karl O., *Jugendbewegung und Politik. Randbemerkungen.* Bad Godesberg, 1961.

Papen, Franz von, *Appell an das deutsche Gewissen. Reden zur nationalen Revolution.* Oldenburg, 1933.

———, *Memoirs.* New York and London, 1953.

Picker, Henry, *Hitlers Tischgespräche in Führerhauptquartier 1941–1942.* Bonn, 1951.

Bibliography

Poliakov, Léon, and Joseph Wulf, *Das Dritte Reich und die Juden. Dokumente und Aufsätze.* Berlin, 1955.

——, *Das Dritte Reich und seine Denker. Weltanschauung–Philosophie–Naturwissenschaften–Geschichte.* Berlin, 1956.

Pross, Harry, *Die Zerstörung der deutschen Politik. Dokumente 1871–1933.* Frankfurt am Main, 1959.

Rauschning, Hermann, *The Revolution of Nihilism.* New York and London, 1939. (British title: *Germany's Revolution of Destruction.*)

——, *Voice of Destruction.* London, 1939; New York, 1940. (British title: *Hitler Speaks.*)

Rees, John Rawlings, ed., *The Case of Rudolf Hess. A Problem in Diagnosis and Forensic Psychiatry.* London, 1947; New York, 1948.

Reichmann, Eva G., *Hostages of Civilization. The Social Sources of National Socialist Anti-Semitism.* London, 1950; New York, 1951.

Reitlinger, Gerald. *The Final Solution. The Attempt to Exterminate the Jews of Europe, 1939–1945,* New York and London, 1953.

——, *The SS, Alibi of a Nation, 1922–1945.* London, 1956; New York, 1957.

Retzlaff, Hans, *Arbeitsmaiden am Werk.* Leipzig, 1940.

Ribbentrop, Joachim von, *The Ribbentrop Memoirs.* London, 1954.

Richter, Alfred, *Unsere Führer im Lichte der Rassenfrage und Charakterologie. Eine rassenmässige und charakterologische Beurteilung von Männern des Dritten Reiches.* Leipzig, 1933.

Röhm, Ernst, *Die Geschichte eines Hochverräters,* 5th ed. Munich, 1934.

Rosenberg, Alfred, *Letzte Aufzeichnungen.* Göttingen, 1955.

——, *Der Mythus des 20. Jährhunderts. Eine Wertung der seelischgeistigen Gestaltungskämpfe unserer Zeit,* 12th ed. Munich, 1943.

——, *Das politische Tagebuch Alfred Rosenbergs aus den Jahren 1934/35 und 1939/40,* ed. Hans-Günther Seraphim. Göttingen, 1956.

(See also Lang, Serge, and Ernst von Schenck.)

Rosten, Curt, *Das ABC des Nationalsozialismus,* 5th ed. Berlin, 1933.

Rothfels, Hans, *The German Opposition to Hitler. An Appraisal.* Chicago, 1948.

Rüdiger, Karlheinz, *Das Werk Alfred Rosenbergs. Eine Bibliographie.* Munich, c. 1941.

Sauer, Wolfgang, 'Die Reichswehr,' in Karl Dietrich Bracher, *Die Auflösung der Weimarer Republik.* Stuttgart and Düsseldorf, 1955.

Schellenberg, Walter, *The Labyrinth.* New York, 1956; London, 1961. (British title: *The Schellenberg Memoirs.*)

Schirach, Baldur von, *Die Hitlerjugend, Idee und Gestalt.* Berlin, 1934.

Schirach, Henriette von, *The Price of Glory.* London and Toronto, 1960.

Schlabrendorff, Fabian von, *The Secret War Against Hitler.* New York, 1965; London, 1966.

Schmidt, Paul, *Hitler's Interpreter.* New York and London, 1951.

Schwarz, Paul, *This Man Ribbentrop. His Life and Times,* 2nd ed. New York, 1943.

Schwerin von Krosigk, Lutz Graf, *Es geschah in Deutschland. Menschenbilder unseres Jahrhunderts.* Tübingen and Stuttgart, 1951.

Seabury, Paul, *The Wilhelmstrasse. A Study of German Diplomats under the Nazi Regime.* Berkeley, Cal., and Cambridge, 1954.

Semmler, Rudolf, *Goebbels – the Man Next to Hitler.* London, 1947.

Shirer, William L., *The Rise and Fall of the Third Reich.* New York and London, 1960.

Sommerfeldt, Martin H., *Ich war dabei. Die Verschwörung der Dämonen.* Darmstadt, 1949.

Sontheimer, Kurt, *Antidemokratisches Denken in der Weimarer Republik. Die politischen Ideen des deutschen Nationalismus zwischen 1918 und 1933.* Munich, 1962.

Springer, Hildegard, *Es sprach Hans Fritzsche*. Stuttgart, 1949.

———, *Das Schwert auf der Waage. Hans Fritzsche über Nürnberg*. Heidelberg, 1933.

Stephan, Werner, *Joseph Goebbels, Dämon einer Diktatur*. Stuttgart, 1949.

Strasser, Otto. *Hitler and I*. Boston and London, 1940.

Strothmann, Dietrich, *Nationalsozialistische Literaturpolitik. Ein Beitrag zur Publizistik im Dritten Reich*. Bonn, 1960.

Trevor-Roper, H. R., *Blitzkrieg to Defeat. Hitler's War Directives, 1939–1945*. London, 1964; New York, 1965. (British title: *Hitler's War Directives, 1939–1945*.)

———, *The Last Days of Hitler*. New York and London, 1947.

Trial of the Major War Criminals Before the International Military Tribunal. Nuremberg, 1947–1949. 42 vols. (Cited throughout as *IMT*.)

Weizsäcker, Ernst von, *The Memoirs of Ernst von Weizsäcker*. Chicago and London, 1951.

Wendt, Hans, *Hitler regiert*. Berlin, 1933.

Wheeler-Bennett, John W., *The Nemesis of Power. The German Army in Politics, 1918–1945*, 2nd ed. New York and London, 1964.

Wighton, Charles, *Heydrich, Hitler's Most Evil Henchman*. Philadelphia and London, 1962.

Wilmot, Chester, *The Struggle for Europe*. New York and London, 1952.

Wulf, Joseph, *Martin Bormann. Hitlers Schatten*. Gütersloh, 1962.

———, *Dr. Hans Frank. Generalgouverneur im besetzten Polen*. Supplement to *Das Parlament*, August 2, 1961.

Zoller, Albert, *Hitler privat*. Düsseldorf, 1949.

Zwischenspiel Hitler. Ziele und Wirklichkeit des Nationalsozialismus, 2nd ed. Vienna and Leipzig, 1932.

Index